KW-550-979

Contents

Page

Introduction

The introduction pages contain lots of valuable advice and information. They include tips on studying for and passing the exam, also the content of the syllabus and what has been examined.

Contents

ACCA

Paper 3.2

ADVANCED TAXATION
(FINANCE ACT 2006)

For the exam in June 2007

Study Text

In this August 2006 new edition

- A new **user-friendly format** for easy navigation
- **Exam-centred topic coverage**, directly linked to ACCA's syllabus and study guide
- **Exam focus points** showing you what the examiner will want you to do
- Regular **fast forward** summaries emphasising the key points in each chapter
- **Questions** and **quick quizzes** to test your understanding
- **Exam question bank** containing exam standard questions with answers
- **A full index**

BPP's **i-Pass** product supports this paper.

FOR THE EXAM IN JUNE 2007

BPP PROFESSIONAL EDUCATION

First edition 2001
Sixth edition August 2006

ISBN 0 7517 2715 6 (Previous edition 0 7517 2356 8)

British Library Cataloguing-in-Publication Data
A catalogue record for this book
is available from the British Library

Published by

BPP Professional Education
Aldine House, Aldine Place
London W12 8AW

www.bpp.com

Printed in Great Britain by W M Print
Frederick Street,
Walsall,
West Midlands WS2 9NE.

All our rights reserved. No part of this publication may be reproduced, stored in a retrieval system or transmitted, in any form or by any means, electronic, mechanical, photocopying, recording or otherwise, without the prior written permission of BPP Professional Education.

We are grateful to the Association of Chartered Certified Accountants for permission to reproduce past examination questions. The suggested solutions in the exam answer bank have been prepared by BPP Professional Education.

©
BPP Professional Education
2006

Computer-based learning products from BPP

For **self-testing**, try **i-Pass,** which offers a large number of **objective test questions**.

Learn Online

Learn Online uses BPP's wealth of teaching experience to produce a fully **interactive** e-learning resource **delivered via the Internet**. The site offers comprehensive **tutor support** and features areas such as **study**, **practice**, **email service**, **revision** and **useful resources**.

Visit our website www.bpp.com/acca/learnonline to sample aspects of Learn Online free of charge.

Learning to Learn Accountancy

BPP's ground-breaking **Learning to Learn Accountancy** book is designed to be used both at the outset of your ACCA studies and throughout the process of learning accountancy. It challenges you to consider how you study and gives you helpful hints about how to approach the various types of paper which you will encounter. It can help you **focus your studies on the subject and exam**, enabling you to **acquire knowledge**, **practise and revise efficiently and effectively**.

The BPP Effective Study Package

Recommended period of use	The BPP Effective Study Package
From the outset and throughout	**Learning to Learn Accountancy** Read this invaluable book as you begin your studies and refer to it as you work through the various elements of the BPP Effective Study Package. It will help you to acquire knowledge, practise and revise, efficiently and effectively.
Three to twelve months before the exam	**Study Text** Use the Study Text to acquire knowledge, understanding, skills and the ability to apply techniques.
Throughout	**Learn Online** Study, practise, revise and take advantage of other useful resources with BPP's fully interactive e-learning site with comprehensive tutor support.
Throughout	**i-Pass** **i-Pass**, our computer-based testing package, provides objective test questions in a variety of formats and is ideal for self-assessment.
One to six months before the exam	**Practice & Revision Kit** Try the numerous examination-format questions, for which there are realistic suggested solutions prepared by BPP's own authors. Then attempt the two mock exams.
From three months before the exam until the last minute	**Passcards** Work through these short, memorable notes which are focused on what is most likely to come up in the exam you will be sitting.
One to six months before the exam	**Success CDs** The CDs cover the vital elements of your syllabus in less than 90 minutes per subject. They also contain exam hints to help you fine tune your strategy.

How the BPP Study Text can help you pass

It provides you with the knowledge and understanding, skills and application techniques that you need to be successful in your exams

This Study Text has been targeted at the **Advanced Taxation** syllabus.

- It is **comprehensive**. It covers the syllabus content. No more, no less.
- It is written at the **right level**. Each chapter is written with ACCA's syllabus and study guide in mind.
- It is aimed at the **exam**. We have taken account of recent exams, guidance the examiner has given and the assessment methodology.
- It is fully up to date for FA2006. This will be examined in June 2007.

It allows you to study in the way that best suits your learning style and the time you have available, by following your personal Study Plan (see page (ix))

You may be studying at home on your own or you may be attending a full-time course. You may like to read every word, or you may prefer to skim-read and practise questions the rest of the time. However you study, you will find the BPP Study Text meets your needs in designing and following your personal Study Plan.

It ties in with the other components of the BPP Effective Study Package to ensure you have the best possible chance of passing the exam (see page (vi))

Help yourself study for your ACCA exams

Exams for professional bodies such as ACCA are very different from those you have taken at college or university. You will be under **greater time pressure before** the exam – as you may be combining your study with work. Here are some hints and tips.

The right approach

1 **Develop the right attitude**

Believe in yourself	Yes, there is a lot to learn. But thousands have succeeded before and you can too.
Remember why you're doing it	You are studying for a good reason: to advance your career.

2 **Focus on the exam**

Read through the Syllabus and Study Guide	These tell you what you are expected to know and are supplemented by **Exam focus points** in the text.
Study the Exam paper section	Past papers are likely to be good guides to what you should expect in the exam.

3 **The right method**

See the whole picture	Keeping in mind how all the detail you need to know fits into the whole picture will help you understand it better. • The **Introduction** of each chapter puts the material in context. • The **Syllabus content, Study guide** and **Exam focus points** show you what you need to **grasp**.
Use your own words	To absorb the information (and to practise your written communication skills), you need to **put it into your own words**. • **Take notes.** • Answer the **questions** in each chapter. • Draw **mindmaps**. We have an example for the whole syllabus. • Try **'teaching' a subject** to a colleague or friend.
Give yourself cues to jog your memory	The BPP Study Text uses **bold** to **highlight key points**. • Try **colour coding** with a highlighter pen. • Write **key points** on cards.

4 **The right recap**

Review, review, review	Regularly reviewing a topic in summary form can **fix it in your memory**. The BPP Study Text helps you review in many ways. • **Chapter roundups** summarise the 'Fast forward' key points in each chapter. Use them to recap each study session. • The **Quick quiz** actively tests your grasp of the essentials. • Go through the **Examples** in each chapter a second or third time.

Developing your personal Study Plan

BPP's **Learning to Learn Accountancy** book emphasises the need to use a study plan. Planning and sticking to the plan are key elements of learning successfully.
There are five steps you should work through.

Step 1 **How do you learn?**

First you need to be aware of your style of learning. BPP's **Learning to Learn Accountancy** book commits a chapter to this **self-discovery**. What types of intelligence do you display when learning? You might be advised to brush up on certain study skills before launching into this Study Text.

BPP's **Learning to Learn Accountancy** book helps you to identify what intelligences you show more strongly and then details how you can tailor your study process to your preferences. It also includes handy hints on how to develop intelligences you exhibit less strongly, but which might be needed as you study accountancy.

Step 2 **What do you prefer to do first?**

If you prefer to get to grips with a theory before seeing how it is applied, we suggest you concentrate first on the explanations we give in each chapter before looking at the examples and case studies. If you prefer to see first how things work in practice, skim through the detail in each chapter, and concentrate on the examples and case studies, before supplementing your understanding by reading the detail.

Step 3 **How much time do you have?**

Work out the time you have available per week, given the following.

- The standard you have set yourself
- The time you need to set aside later for work on the Practice & Revision Kit and Passcards
- The other exam(s) you are sitting
- Practical matters such as work, travel, exercise, sleep and social life

		Hours
Note your time available in box A.	A	

Step 4 **Allocate your time**

• Take the time you have available per week for this Study Text shown in box A, multiply it by the number of weeks available and insert the result in box B.	B	
• Divide the figure in box B by the number of chapters in this text and insert the result in box C.	C	

Remember that this is only a rough guide. Some of the chapters in this book are longer and more complicated than others, and you will find some subjects easier to understand than others.

Step 5 **Implement**

Set about studying each chapter in the time shown in box C, following the key study steps in the order suggested by your particular learning style.

This is your personal **Study Plan**. You should try to combine it with the study sequence outlined below. You may want to modify the sequence to adapt it to your **personal style**.

BPP's **Learning to Learn Accountancy** gives further guidance on developing a study plan, and deciding where and when to study.

Tackling your studies

The best way to approach this Study Text is to tackle the chapters in order. Taking into account your individual learning style, you could follow this sequence for each chapter.

Key study steps	Activity
Step 1 **Topic list**	This topic list helps you navigate each chapter; each numbered topic is a numbered section in the chapter.
Step 2 **Introduction**	This sets your objectives for study by giving you the big picture in terms of the context of the chapter. The content is referenced to the Study Guide, and Exam guidance shows how the topic is likely to be examined. The Introduction tells you **why** the topics covered in the chapter need to be studied.
Step 3 **Knowledge brought forward boxes**	N/a in this text.
Step 4 **Fast forward**	Fast forward boxes give you a quick summary of the content of each of the main chapter sections. They are listed together in the roundup at the end of each chapter to help you review each chapter quickly.
Step 5 **Explanations**	Proceed methodically through each chapter, particularly focussing on areas highlighted as significant in the chapter introduction, or areas that are frequently examined.
Step 6 **Key terms and Exam focus points**	• Key terms can often earn you **easy marks** if you state them clearly and correctly in an exam answer. They are highlighted in the index at the back of this text. • Exam focus points state how the topic has been or may be examined, difficulties that can occur in questions about the topic, and examiner feedback on common weaknesses in answers.
Step 7 **Note taking**	Take brief notes, if you wish. Don't copy out too much. Remember that being able to record something yourself is a sign of being able to understand it. Your notes can be in whatever format you find most helpful; lists, diagrams, mindmaps.
Step 8 **Examples**	Work through the examples very carefully as they illustrate key knowledge and techniques.
Step 9 **Case studies**	N/a in this text.
Step 10 **Questions**	Attempt each one, as they will illustrate how well you've understood what you've read.

Step 11 **Answers**	Check yours against ours, and make sure you understand any discrepancies.
Step 12 **Chapter roundup**	Review it carefully, to make sure you have grasped the significance of all the important points in the chapter.
Step 13 **Quick quiz**	Use the Quick quiz to check how much you have remembered of the topics covered and to practise questions in a variety of formats.
Step 14 **Question practice**	Attempt the Question(s) suggested at the very end of the chapter. You can find these in the Exam Question Bank at the end of the Study Text, along with the answers so you can see how you did. If you have bought i-Pass, use this too.

Short of time: Skim study technique?

You may find you simply do not have the time available to follow all the key study steps for each chapter, however you adapt them for your particular learning style. If this is the case, follow the **skim study** technique below.

Read the **topic list and chapter introduction.**

↓

Skim through the **explanations**, focusing on the points highlighted as important in the **fast forward boxes**.

↓

Read the **key terms** and **exam focus points** carefully.

↓

Go through the **examples** and **case studies**.

↓

Prepare outline **answers** to the **questions**.

↓

Revisit the fast forwards in the **chapter roundups**.

↓

Answer the **quick quiz** and look back at any areas where you got questions wrong.

↓

Do a plan for the **question(s) in the exam question bank** and review our answers carefully.

↓

Brief notes may help you skim study, although you may simply rely on the **passcards** for notes you can use for revision.

Moving on...

When you are ready to start revising, you should still refer back to this Study Text.

- As a source of **reference** (you should find the index particularly helpful for this)
- As a way to **review** (the Fast forwards, Exam focus points, Chapter roundups and Quick quizzes help you here)

Remember to keep careful hold of this Study Text – you will find it invaluable in your work.

More advice on Study Skills can be found in BPP's **Learning to Learn Accountancy** book.

Syllabus

STOP PRESS

At the time of printing this study text, the ACCA had not issued a syllabus or study guide for the 2007 exams. However, the ACCA informed BPP Professional Education that there will be no substantial changes to the syllabus and study guide printed on the following pages. As soon as the updated syllabus and study guide are available they will be available on the ACCA's website (www.accaglobal.com). We recommend that you check this before you take your exam.

Aim

To ensure candidates can apply judgement and technique in the provision of a range of taxation services. In particular to equip candidates with the ability to resolve problems involving the computation of tax liabilities, basic tax and financial planning and which draw upon the interaction of a wide range of taxes. The primary focus of the paper will be based around taxation issues.

Objectives

On completion of this paper candidates should be able to:

- prepare computations for and advise clients on issues relating to the tax liabilities of individuals arising from income receipts, capital disposals and transfers of value
- prepare computations for and advise clients on issues relating to the tax liabilities of corporations arising from income generation and capital disposals
- provide advice on minimising or deferring tax liabilities for individuals or corporations by using exemptions and/or reliefs
- evaluate a corporation's and individual's financial position with particular regard to the importance of taxation in decision making and to recommend appropriate personal financial plans and
- demonstrate the skills expected in Part 3.

Position of the paper in the overall syllabus

This is the final tax paper and builds upon the knowledge acquired in Paper 2.3 Business Taxation concerning the taxation of businesses and employees. A thorough understanding of the Paper 2.3 syllabus is therefore considered requisite for Paper 3.2.

Candidates also need to understand formats of accounts used for sole traders, partnerships and companies from Paper 1.1 and also the need to have an understanding of some of the financial reporting standards from Paper 2.5. There is no substantial integration with other papers in Part 3.

Syllabus content

1 Taxation of individuals

(a) Principles of income tax
(b) Income tax on income from land and buildings
(c) Income tax on income from Investment
(d) Income tax on income from employment
(e) Income tax on income from self-employment

(f) Capital gains tax
(g) Trusts
(h) Administration of income tax and CGT
(i) Inheritance tax
(j) Overseas aspects of income tax, capital gains tax, inheritance tax and value added tax
(k) Value added tax
(l) National insurance contributions
(m) Stamp duty and stamp duty reserve tax.

2 Taxation of corporate businesses

(a) Corporation tax on income and chargeable gains of single companies and groups of companies and consortia trading in the UK and overseas

(b) Value added tax

(c) National insurance contributions

(d) Stamp duty and stamp duty reserve tax.

3 Financial planning

(a) Sources of finance
(b) Personal financial planning
(c) Financial services products
(d) The regulatory framework.

Excluded topics

Note that the labelling of excluded topics relates to the relevant section of the syllabus

1 Taxation of individuals

(c) Income tax on income from investments

(i) detailed knowledge of anti-avoidance procedures

(d) Income tax on income from employment

(i) PAYE system
(ii) an employee share ownership plan (ESOP) will not be examined in its own right

(e) Income tax on income from selfemployment

(i) averaging of farmers profits

(ii) averaging of profits for authors and creative artists

(iii) the allocation of notional profits and losses for a partnership

(iv) research and development expenditure

(v) capital allowances for agricultural buildings, patents, flats above shops, scientific research and know-how

(vi) in respect of industrial buildings allowance: enterprise zones, initial allowances and the sale of an industrial building at less than original cost following a period of non industrial use (note that sales for more than original cost are examinable)

(vii) detailed anti-avoidance legislation.

(f) Capital gains tax

(i) assets held at 31 March 1982
(ii) the grant of a lease or sub-lease out of either a freehold, long lease or short lease
(iii) a detailed knowledge of the statements of practice on partnership capital gains
(iv) retirement relief
(v) relief for losses on loans made to traders.

(g) Trusts

(i) overseas aspects

(i) Inheritance Tax

(i) double grossing up on death

(ii) pre 18 March 1986 lifetime transfers

(iii) woodlands relief

(iv) conditional exemption for heritage property

(v) relief on relevant business property and agricultural property given as exempt legacies

(vi) valuation of an annuity or an interest in possession where the trust interest is subject to an annuity

(v) detailed knowledge of the double charges legislation

(vi) an accumulation and maintenance trust ceasing to qualify

(vii) double taxation relief calculation involving the formula $\frac{A}{A+B} \times C$

(viii) IHT aspects of discretionary trusts prior to 27 March 1974.

(k) Value added tax

(i) capital goods scheme
(ii) in respect of property and land leases and do it yourself builders
(iii) flat rate scheme for farmers
(iv) special schemes for retailers.

(l) National insurance contributions

(i) detailed calculation of director's NIC on a month by month basis – a knowledge of the annual earnings period rules (including where a person becomes a director part way through a tax year is, however, required)

(ii) offset of trading losses against non-trading income (for Class 4 purposes).

2 Taxation of corporate businesses

(a) Corporation tax on income and chargeable gains of single companies and groups of companies and consortia trading in the UK and overseas

(i) a detailed knowledge of antiavoidance provisions (with the exception of those detailed in the Study Guide)

(ii) corporation tax rates on companies in the process of winding up

(iii) 51% groups and group income elections

(iv) quarterly accounting for income tax

(v) anti-avoidance provisions where arrangements exist for a company to leave a group

(vi) detailed knowledge of double taxation agreements

(vii) migration of a UK resident company

(viii) mixer companies

(ix) expense relief in respect of overseas tax

(x) detailed computational questions on the carry back and carry forward of unrelieved foreign tax

(xi) an awareness of these provisions is required

(xii) detailed computational questions on the 'onshore pooling' provisions

(xiii) again an awareness of these provisions is all that is required.

(b) Value added tax

(i) as for individuals.

(c) National insurance contributions

(i) detailed calculations of director's NIC on a month by month basis – a knowledge of the annual earnings period rules (including where a person becomes a director part way through a tax year is, however, required.)

3 Financial planning

(a) Sources of finance

(i) the mortgage code.

(c) Financial services products

(i) detailed knowledge of the conditions which must be met to obtain HMRC approval for an occupational pension scheme

(ii) personal pension rules applicable prior to 6 April 2001

(iii) knowledge of the different maximum benefit regimes in occupational schemes

(iv) calculation of maximum or actual benefits available on early or late retirement

(v) calculation of a pension cash equivalent transfer value.

Key areas of the syllabus

All areas of the syllabus may be regarded as important.

Study sessions

Items in italics refer to syllabus areas that can be examined within Section A.

1 Taxation of individuals

(a) Principles of income tax

(i) *paper 2.3 syllabus section 2a plus*
(ii) *schedular system*
(iii) *concept of independent taxation and jointly held assets*
(iv) *personal allowances and reliefs*
(v) *non business charges on income and Gift Aid*

(b) Income tax on income from land and buildings

(i) *income liable*
(ii) *basis of assessment and computation of assessable profits and losses*
(iii) *reverse premiums*
(iv) *premiums received on the grant of a short lease*
(v) *furnished holiday lettings and implications*
(vi) *rent a room relief*

(c) Income tax on income from investments

- (i) *tax free investments*
- (ii) *schedule D case III*
- (iii) *taxation of savings income and dividends*
- (iv) *accrued income scheme*
- (v) *schedule D case vi*
- (vi) *double taxation relief*

(d) Income tax on income from employment

- (i) *paper 2.3 syllabus sections 3a(i),*
- (ii) *and (iv) plus*
- (ii) *share and share option incentive schemes (approved and unapproved schemes)*
- (iii) *lump sum receipts*
- (iv) *exempt benefits*
- (v) *personal service companies*

(e) Income tax on income from self-employment

- (i) paper 2.3 syllabus sections 2c(i) – (vii)
- (ii) losses on shares in qualifying companies (section 574 ICTA 1988)

(f) Capital gains tax

- (i) *paper 2.3 section 2d (have scope now for both business and non business assets including shares and securities) plus*
- (ii) *exempt assets and disposals (particularly on disposals arising at death)*
- (iii) *concept of independent taxation and transfers between spouses*
- (iv) *timing of disposal (particularly in the context of conditional contracts)*
- (v) *losses in the year of death*
- (vi) *variations/disclaimers arising on death*
- (vii) *connected persons*
- (viii) *payment of tax by instalments*
- (ix) *part disposals*
- (x) *principal private residence relief*
- (xi) *matching rules for shares and securities*
- (xii) *basic reorganisations and takeovers (particularly s135 TGGA 1992, the conditions, including for bona fide commercial purposes, and the advance clearance procedure)*
- (xiii) *leases, chattels and wasting assets*
- (xiv) *compensation and insurance receipts*
- (xv) *EIS/VCT reinvestment relief*
- (xvi) *appropriations to and from trading stock*
- (xvii) *gift relief where there is an immediate charge to IHT (s260 CGTA 1992)*

(g) Trusts

(i) *define a trust*

(ii) *distinguish between interest in possession trusts and discretionary trusts*

(iii) *explain how income tax applies to:*

- *interest in possession trusts*
- *discretionary trusts*

(iv) *explain how inheritance tax applies to*

- *transfers of property into trusts*
- *transfers of property out of an interest in possession trust upon the termination of the life tenant's interest – discretionary trusts – ten year charges and exit charge*

(v) *define accumulation and maintenance trusts and explain their advantages*

(vi) *explain how capital gains tax applies to:*

- *transfers of property into trust*
- *disposals made by trustees of settled property within trusts to third properties*
- *disposals made by trustees of settled property within trusts to beneficiaries*

(vii) *explain how trusts can be used in tax and financial planning.*

(h) Administration of income tax and capital gains tax

(i) *paper 2.3 syllabus Section 2b*

(i) Inheritance tax

(i) *basic principles – explain the terms transfer of value, chargeable transfer, potentially exempt transfer, excluded property and persons chargeable – loss of donor principle*

(ii) *principle chargeable occasions for IHT – chargeable lifetime transfers – potentially exempt transfers becoming chargeable – death*

(iii) *seven year cumulation principle*

(iv) *concept of grossing up*

(v) *how IHT is calculated on chargeable lifetime transfers, potentially exempt transfers becoming chargeable and upon death*

(vi) *exemptions available covering lifetime gifts*

(vii) *concept of independent taxation particularly in the context of transfers between spouses*

(viii) *other exempt transfers (gifts to charities, political parties, for national purposes and to housing associations)*

(ix) *tax treatment of transfers of value by close companies*

(x) *principles of valuation:*

- *general open market valuation rule*
- *specific rules*
- *related party rules*

(xi) *business property and agricultural property relief and the relevant conditions applying*

(xii) *quick succession relief*

(xiii) *tapering relief*

(xiv) *determine the value of an individual's estate at death including the liabilities and other deductions that may be taken into account*

(xv) *relief available for the fall in value of assets the subject of a chargeable lifetime transfer*

(xvi) *adjustments to the value of the death state in respect of the sale Advanced Taxation (United Kingdom) (Continued) of assets following death and the effect of reinvestment*

(xvii) *allocation of the estate at death where:*

- *the entire estate is chargeable and specific gifts of UK property are made*
- *there are exempt specific gifts with a chargeable residue and vice versa*

(xviii) *explain how wills can be varied after death and the conditions applying*

(xix) *explain the rules governing gifts with reservation of benefit*

(xx) *explain the rules relating to associated operations*

(xxi) *administration of inheritance tax*

- *who is responsible for payment?*
- *instalment option – property*
- *due dates*

(j) Overseas aspects of income tax, capital gains tax, inheritance tax and value added tax

(i) *explain the concepts of residence, ordinary residence and domicile*

(ii) *application of the rules at (i) above to income tax*

(iii) *detailed rules in circumstances where an individual comes to the UK or leaves the UK*

(iv) *schedule D case iv and v – basis of assessment arising or remittance*

(v) *overseas trades travelling expenses*

(vi) *employment income – overseas aspects*

(vii) *employees travelling and subsistence expenses*

(viii) *double taxation relief*

(ix) *application of the rules at (i) above to CGT*

(x) *temporary absence rules*

(xi) *overseas aspects of inheritance tax:*

- *extended definition of domicile for inheritance tax purposes*
- *rules governing location of assets*
- *calculate double taxation relief*

(xii) explain how VAT is applied to imports and exports and to acquisitions within the EU

(k) Value added tax

(i) paper 2.3 syllabus section 1j and 2e plus

(ii) explain the application of the disaggregation rules

(iii) group registration and divisional registration

(iv) second hand goods

(v) explain the consequences for being partially exempt and calculate the input tax recovery for a partially exempt trader

(vi) explain in broad terms the principal rules governing the supply of land and buildings in the UK

(l) National insurance contributions

(i) *paper 2.3 syllabus section 2f and 3c*

(m) Stamp duty and stamp duty reserve tax

(i) *basic principles – concept of tax on documents*

(ii) *chargeable occasions*

- *shares and securities*
- *other assets*
- *leases*

(iii) *exemptions*

- *gifts*
- *goodwill*
- *group transactions (basic transactions involving transfers between associated companies and share transfers where there is no real change of ownership)*

(iv) *fixed duty.*

2 Taxation of Corporate Businesses

(a) Corporation tax on income and chargeable gains of single companies and groups of companies and consortia trading in the UK and overseas

(i) paper 2.3 syllabus sections 2.3 1a – i plus

(ii) determination of accounting periods when a company is being wound up

(iii) explain the treatment of returns of capital to shareholders after a company has commenced winding up

(iv) treatment of a company's non trading deficits on loan relationships

(v) restrictions on the use of trading loss reliefs (particularly upon a change in ownership of an entity)

(vi) corporate venturing scheme

(vii) Rules governing the transfer of a company's trade and assets within a group situation

(viii) exemption for disposal of substantial shareholdings

(ix) explain how intangible assets and goodwill are treated within a corporation tax environment including the reinvestment relief introduced by FA2002

(x) explain the rules governing the treatment of controlled foreign companies, including reporting requirements

(xi) explain the terms consortium owned company and consortium member; operation of consortium relief

(xii) explain the concept of permanent establishment

(xiii) explain how profits chargeable to corporation tax are determined for an investment company

(xiv) explain the consequences of being a close company and close investment holding company

(xv) explain the taxation consequences from a company purchasing its own shares and the conditions applying to satisfy treatment as a capital distribution

(b) Value added tax

(i) as for individuals

(c) National insurance contributions

(i) paper 2.3 syllabus section 3c

(d) Stamp duty and stamp duty reserve tax

(i) as for individuals.

3 Financial Planning

(a) Sources of finance

(i) describe the sources of finance available to:

- individuals
- companies

(ii) distinguish between the tax implications of raising equity finance and of raising loan finance

(iii) explain the tax implications involved in the decision whether to lease, use hire purchase or to purchase outright

(iv) evaluation of the impact of taxation on a business' cash flows

(v) describe the mortgage products available to individuals involved in purchasing their own home

(vi) identify circumstances in which it is appropriate to repay/replace borrowings

(b) Personal financial planning

(i) evaluating an individual's financial position

- calculating an individual's net worth having regard to future capital taxation liabilities
- *calculating an individual's net of tax disposable income*
- identify potential disaster scenarios for both individuals and businesses
- determining sensible strategies to protect wealth and income levels

(c) Financial services products

(i) protection products awareness of the basic structure, types, risk that is being covered, the form in which proceeds are paid upon a valid claim being made and the tax treatment of the premiums and proceeds of the following classes of product:

- life assurance
- health insurance
- provision for long-term care
- redundancy insurance

(ii) investment products awareness of the basic structure, types and *tax treatment* of the following investments

- deposit based investments (including cash mini ISAs)
- fixed interest securities
- packaged investments
- collective investments (including ISAs)
- equities
- enterprise investment scheme
- venture capital trusts
- property

Note for section A purposes only the tax treatment of the above is examinable

(iii) constructing investment portfolios having regard to such factors as risk, accessibility, liquidity, marketability, flexibility and volatility

(iv) pension products awareness of the main features and *tax treatment* of premiums payable (where applicable – by both individuals and employers) and eventual benefits in making provision for retirement through the following:

- *occupational pension schemes*
  - explain the difference between defined benefits and defined contribution schemes
  - explain the difference between approved and unapproved schemes
  - explain the operation of self-administered occupational schemes
  - describe the options upon changing employment
  - personal pension (including stakeholder) schemes
  - explain the operation of self-invested personal pensions
  - describe the options available on reaching retirement
- state pension schemes

Note for Section A only the tax treatment of the items in italics is examinable

(v) explain the options available as regards pension rights on divorce

(d) The regulatory framework

(i) describe the regulatory framework in place

(ii) explain the meaning of investment and investment business

(iii) explain the regulations and 'best practice' affecting investment advice laid down by the FSA and ACCA

(iv) explain the compensation and redress available.

Examiner guidance for June 2007

The examiner has provided the following guidance for students sitting the June 2007 exam.

Comments for students in respect of 2007 exams.

1. **Non-corporate distributions**

   Knowledge of non-corporate distributions will not be required.

2. **Pensions**

   Only those rules applicable for 2006/07 onwards will be examined.

   (i) The following areas will not be examined.

   - Unauthorised member payments
   - Unauthorised employer payments
   - The possibilities available on leaving an occupational scheme including transfer values.

   (ii) The following areas will be examined but not in detail. Students will require outline knowledge of these issues but would not be expected to write about them in depth or to perform calculations.

   - Spreading provisions for large contributions
   - Computation of pension inputs
   - Detailed examples of benefit crystallisation events
   - Benefits from the pension fund in lifetime and on death
   - Prohibited assets
   - The lifetime allowance charge
   - Build up of memory purchase schemes
   - Choices available in respect of AVCs
   - Pensions and divorce
   - The choices available to an individual on retirement in respect of different types of annuity and income drawdown.

3. **Inheritance tax and trusts**

   Students will be expected to know that there have been changes to the rules regarding trusts and IHT. In particular, they need to be aware of the IHT implications of transferring assets into trust both pre and post 22 March 2006.

   In recognition of the complexity of the developments in the Finance Bill, detailed planning questions involving the use of trusts and detailed questions on the taxation of the trusts themselves will not be set in 2007.

The exam paper

Approach to examining the syllabus

The examination is a three hour paper divided into two sections.

Section A: Two compulsory scenario based questions worth a total of 50 marks set in the following areas:

- Non business income tax (although including employment income)
- Capital gains tax
- Inheritance tax
- Overseas aspects of income tax, inheritance tax and capital gains tax
- Taxation of trusts

The detailed syllabus areas that will feature are those set out in italics within the Study Guide. It is to be noted that these are primarily the syllabus areas new to 3.2.

Section B: Four 25 marks scenario based questions from which candidates will be required to select and answer two. One of these questions, at least, will focus upon business taxation. One of the questions in Section B will have as its main focus personal financial planning. The other question will be set on other areas of the syllabus.

The following further guidance should be noted.

Section A

- To assist in the transition from paper 2.3 to paper 3.2 the compulsory questions, whilst being set within a scenario involving some elements of planning and tax interaction, the emphasis will be on computation (as an approximate guide around 50%). A mainly discursive question is therefore unlikely in Section A.
- Questions involving mainly financial planning will not feature in Section A. Note, however, that questions may involve the taxation elements of, for example, investment or pension products (for example calculating an individual's maximum permissible pension contributions).
- As a general guide Section A questions will primarily focus upon (non business) income tax, inheritance tax and capital gains tax (both business and non business aspects).
- Whilst no detailed questions will be set involving income tax aspects of businesses this will not preclude the inclusion within questions of, for example, a trading profit figure (or possibly even series of figures). Candidates will, however, not be required to calculate those figures as part of Section A questions.
- A question will not be set that exclusively examines the taxation of trusts, stamp duty or overseas taxation although these may feature as part of a question.

Section B

- The 25 mark format adopted in Section B will allow more developed optional questions.
- Questions can be set in any area of the syllabus but within the broad overall guidelines mentioned above.

- The question focusing upon financial planning is likely to be scenario based, including some taxation elements, with candidates required to analyse a particular set of circumstances and make sensible financial planning recommendations going forward. As a guide it is likely that the pure financial planning elements of this question will not exceed 60-70%.
- As a general rule it is likely that Section B questions will examine letter or report-writing skills to a greater extent than Section A. Two marks will always be allocated within one of the Section B questions covering these skills.

In summary:

		Number of Marks
Section A:	2 compulsory questions	50
Section B:	Choice of 2 from 4 (25 marks each)	50
		100

Tax rates, allowances and relevant benefits will be given in the examination paper.

Additional information

The ACCA applies a six month rule in that questions requiring an understanding of new legislation will not be set until at least six calendar months after the last day of the month in which the legislation received the Royal Assent. The same rule applies to the effective date of the provisions of an Act introduced by statutory instrument. It would however be considered inappropriate to examine legislation it is proposed to repeal or substantially alter.

Knowledge of section numbers will not be needed to understand questions in this paper, not will students be expected to use them in their answers. If students wish to refer to section number they may do so and will not be penalised if old, or even incorrect, section numbers are used.

Names of cases or a detailed knowledge of the judgement are not required but knowledge of the principles decided in leading cases is required.

Analysis of past papers

June 2006

Section A

1 Income Tax and IHT computations in year of death. CGT and IHT planning. (25 marks)

2 Incorporation of a business. Share options. CGT and IT issues on creating a trust. (25 marks)

Section B (25 marks each)

3 IT and NIC on low emission vehicles. Tax residence status. Holding company – CGT, VAT, CT and Stamp Duty issues.

4 Profit extraction from a company. Sale of company. Purchase of own shares.

5 Group relief. Intellectual property. Purchase of shares versus assets. VAT compliance (default surcharge).

6 CGT on asset disposals. Pension schemes. EIS relief.

December 2005

Section A

1 CGT on PPR. Investment advice. IHT planning. (25 marks)
2 CGT, IT and IHT implications of various asset disposals. (25 marks)

Section B (25 marks each)

3 Group of companies loss relief and restructuring. CT and VAT on overseas operation.

4 IT and CGT for individuals including residence status. VAT on business start up. IT and NIC payments – amounts and due dates.

5 IT, NIC and CT on alternative business structures including tax and cash flow impact of dividend versus salary. CGT on asset disposal. IT loss relief.

6 Extracting cash from a company. Investment advice IHT and CGT on asset purchased as investment.

June 2005

Section A

1 IHT on death. Lifetime IHT planning. (25 marks)

2 Income tax for employee. Investment income. Overseas aspects. Accommodation benefit. CGT takeover. Qualifying Corporate Bond. (25 marks)

Section B (25 marks each)

3 Corporation tax payable. Due date and filing requirements. VAT returns.

4 Badges of trade. Loss reliefs.

5 Capital gain by company. Rollover relief. Group and consortium relief. VAT group.

6 Shares given to employee. Share options in unapproved and approved schemes. Personal financial planning protection products.

December 2004

Section A

1 IT, CGT and IHT for UK resident but not UK domiciled individual. Deferral of capital gains. Gift with reservation of benefit. IHT planning. (25 marks)

2 Furnished holiday letting. Taxable income. CGT liability. Gift of shareholdings. CGT reliefs. (25 marks)

Section B (25 marks each)

3 VAT registration. Flat rate scheme. Car use by employee.
4 Group and consortium relief. CT, VAT, SD/SDLT on sale of shares/sale of assets.
5 Employing spouse v forming partnership with spouse. Self assessment. Partnership loss reliefs.
6 Choice of business medium. Equity and loan finance. Pension provision.

June 2004

Section A

1 Income tax with age allowance. Income tax declaration for jointly held asset. IHT and CGT on transfers in life and on death. (28 marks)

2 CGT principal private residence relief. Income tax on letting. (22 marks)

Section B (25 marks each)

3 Use of own car or company car. Sale of shares or repurchase of shares by company.
4 Employment versus self employment. Status issues.
5 Residence for companies. Loss reliefs.
6 Pension contributions by employer and employee.

December 2003

Section A

1 Income tax in year of death. IHT on lifetime gifts and death estate. Variation of death estate. (25 marks)

2 CGT on shareholding. Incorporation relief. Stamp duty. (25 marks)

Section B (25 marks each)

3 CT calculation and use of losses. Group structure and restructuring for tax efficiency.
4 Adjustment of profits. NIC for self employed. Interest and penalties. Other administrative matters.
5 Salary versus dividend. Pension payment versus loan. Gift of shares.
6 Redundancy package. Financial planning – redemption of mortgage; investments.

June 2003

Section A

1 Gift aid scheme. Income tax and NIC liabilities. IHT on lifetime gifts. (28 marks)
2 Schedule A. Computation of chargeable gains on the sale of property. (22 marks)

Section B (25 marks each)

3 Calculation of and payment dates for Corporation Tax. Purchasing a new company.
4 Acquisition of a vehicle either personally or through a limited company.
5 Tax implications of setting up an overseas operation.
6 Computation of income tax and NIC liabilities. Sources of finance.

Oxford Brookes BSc (Hons) in Applied Accounting

The standard required of candidates completing Part 2 is that required in the final year of a UK degree. Students completing Parts 1 and 2 will have satisfied the examination requirement for an honours degree in Applied Accounting, awarded by Oxford Brookes University.

To achieve the degree, you must also submit two pieces of work based on a **Research and Analysis Project.**

- A 5,000 word **Report** on your chosen topic, which demonstrates that you have acquired the necessary research, analytical and IT skills.
- A 1,500 word **Key Skills Statement**, indicating how you have developed your interpersonal and communication skills.

BPP was selected by the ACCA and Oxford Brookes University to produce the official text *Success in your Research and Analysis Project* to support students in this task. The book pays particular attention to key skills not covered in the professional examinations.

BPP also offers courses and mentoring services.

For further information, please see BPP's website: www.bpp.com/bsc

ACCA professional development requirements

Soon, you will possess a professional qualification. You know its value by the effort you have put in. To uphold the prestige of the qualification, ACCA, with the other professional bodies that form the International Federation of Accountants (IFAC), requires its members to undertake continuous professional development (CPD). This requirement applies to all members, not just those with a practising certificate. Happily, BPP Professional Education is here to support you in your professional development with materials, courses and qualifications.

For further information, please see ACCA's website: www.accaglobal.com

Professional development with BPP

You do not have to do exams for professional development (PD) – but you need relevant technical updating and you may also benefit from other work-related training. BPP can provide you with both. Visit our professional development website, www.bpp.com/pd for details of our PD courses in accounting, law, general business skills and other important areas. Offering defined hours of structured CPD, and delivered by top professionals throughout the year and in many locations, our courses are designed to fit around your busy work schedule. Our unique PD passport will give you access to these PD services at an attractive discount.

For further information, please see BPP's website: www.bpp.com/pd

Master of Business Administration (MBA)

ACCA and Oxford Brookes University, a leading UK university, have worked together on an MBA programme. The MBA, accredited by AMBA (the Association of MBAs), lasts 21 months for ACCA members, and is taught by distance learning with online seminars delivered to a global student base over the Internet. BPP provides the user-friendly materials. As an ACCA member, you will receive credits towards this MBA and you can begin your studies when you have completed your ACCA professional exams. Flexibility, global reach and value for money underpin a high quality learning experience.

The qualification features an introductory module (*Foundations of Management*). Other modules include *Global Business Strategy, Managing Self Development*, and *Organisational Change and Transformation.*

Research Methods are also taught, as they underpin the **research dissertation**.

For further information, please visit: www.accaglobal.com, www. brookes.ac.uk or www.bpp.com/mba

Diploma in International Financial Reporting

The ACCA's Diploma in International Financial Reporting is designed for those whose country-specific accounting knowledge needs to be supplemented by knowledge of international accounting standards. BPP offers books and courses in this useful qualification – it also earns you valuable CPD points.

For further information, please see ACCA's website: www.accaglobal.com and BPP's website: www.bpp.com/dipifr

Tax and financial services

If you are interested in tax, BPP offers courses for the ATT (tax technician) and CTA (Chartered Tax Adviser, formerly ATII) qualifications. You can also buy our user-friendly CTA texts to keep up-to-date with tax practice.

For further information, please see BPP's website: www.bpp.com/att and www.bpp.com/cta

If your role involves selling financial services products, such as pensions, or offering investment advice, BPP provides learning materials and training for relevant qualifications. BPP also offers training for specialist financial markets qualifications (eg CFA®) and insolvency.

For further information, please see BPP's website: www.bpp.com/financialadvisers

Other business qualifications

BPP supports many business disciplines, such as market research, marketing, human resources management and law. We are the official provider of distance learning programmes for the Market Research Society. We train for the Chartered Institute of Personnel and Development qualification, with a number of other supporting qualifications in training and personnel management. BPP's law school is an industry leader.

Visit www.bpp.com for further details of all that we can offer you. BPP's personalised online information service, My BPP, will help you keep track of the details you submit to BPP.

Tax rates and allowances

A INCOME TAX

1 *Rates*

	2006/07	
	£	%
Starting rate	1 – 2,150	10
Basic rate	2,151 – 33,300	22
Higher rate	33,301 and above	40

2 *Personal allowance*

	2006/07
	£
Personal allowance	5,035
Personal allowance (65 – 74)	7,280
Personal allowance (75 and over)	7,420
Married couple's allowance – minimum amount	2,350
Married couple's allowance – (65 – 74)	6,065
Married couple's allowance (75 and over)	6,135
Income limit for age-related allowances	20,100
Blind person's allowance	1,660

3 *Cars – 2006/07*

Base level of CO_2 emissions – 140g/km

4 *Car fuel base level – 2006/07*

Base figure £14,400

5 *Personal pension contribution limits*

	Annual Allowance	*Lifetime Allowance*
2006/07	£215,000	£1,500,000

Maximum contribution without evidence of earnings, £3,600.

6 *Authorised mileage*

All cars:	
Up to 10,000 miles	40p
Over 10,000 miles	25p

6 *Capital allowances*

	%
Plant and machinery	
Writing down allowance*	25
First year allowance**	40
First year allowance (information and communication technology equipment until 31.3.04, low emission cars (CO_2 emissions of less than 120 g/km))	100
Industrial buildings allowance	
Writing down allowance	4

* 6% reducing balance for certain long life assets

** 50% for small enterprises between 1.4.06 – 31.3.07 (6.4.06 – 5.4.07 for unincorporated businesses) and also between 1.4.04 – 31.3.05 (6.4.04 – 5.4.05 for unincorporated businesses).

B CORPORATION TAX

1 *Rates*

Financial year	*2004*	*2005*	*2006*
Starting rate	Nil	Nil	–
Small companies rate	19%	19%	19%
Full rate	30%	30%	30%
	£	£	
Starting rate lower limit	10,000	10,000	–
Starting rate upper limit	50,000	50,000	–
Small companies rate lower limit	300,000	300,000	300,000
Small companies rate upper limit	1,500,000	1,500,000	1,500,000
Taper relief fraction			
Starting rate	19/400	19/400	–
Small companies rate	11/400	11/400	11/400

2 *Marginal relief*

$(M - P) \times I/P \times$ Marginal relief fraction

C VALUE ADDED TAX

Registration and deregistration limits

Registration limit	£61,000
Deregistration limit	£59,000

VAT on private fuel – quarterly scale charges		*Petrol* £	*Diesel* £
CC of car:	1400cc or less	273	260
	Over 1400cc up to 2000cc	346	260
	Over 2000cc	508	331

D INHERITANCE TAX

6.4.06 onwards	*Rate*
£1 - £285,000	Nil
Excess	40%

E RATES OF INTEREST

Official rate of interest: 5% (assumed)
Rate of interest on unpaid tax: 7.5% (assumed)
Rate of interest on overpaid tax: 3.5% (assumed)

F CAPITAL GAINS TAX

1 *Lease percentage table*

Years	*Percentage*	*Years*	*Percentage*	*Years*	*Percentage*
50 or more	100.000	33	90.280	16	64.116
49	99.657	32	89.354	15	61.617
48	99.289	31	88.371	14	58.971
47	98.902	30	87.330	13	56.167
46	98.490	29	86.226	12	53.191
45	98.059	28	85.053	11	50.038
44	97.595	27	83.816	10	46.695
43	97.107	26	82.496	9	43.154
42	96.593	25	81.100	8	39.399
41	96.041	24	79.622	7	35.414
40	95.457	23	78.055	6	31.195
39	94.842	22	76.399	5	26.722
38	94.189	21	74.635	4	21.983
37	93.497	20	72.770	3	16.959
36	92.761	19	70.791	2	11.629
35	91.981	18	68.697	1	5.983
34	91.156	17	66.470	0	0.000

2 *Annual exemption*

2006/07	£8,800
Individuals	
Trusts (divided by number of qualifying settlements created by the same settlor on the same day to a minimum of one fifth)	£4,400

3 *Taper relief*

Complete years after 5.4.98 for which asset held	*Gains on business assets*	*Gains on non business assets*
1	50	100
2	25	100
3	25	95
4	25	90
5	25	85
6	25	80
7	25	75
8	25	70
9	25	65
10	25	60

G NATIONAL INSURANCE (NOT CONTRACTED OUT RATES) 2006/07

Class 1 contributions

		%
Class 1 Employee	£1–£5,035 per year	Nil
	£5,036–£33,540 per year	11.0
	£33,541 and above per year	1.0
Class 1 Employer	£1–£5,035 per year	Nil
	£5,036 and above per year	12.8

Class 2 contributions

Rate £2.10 pw

Class 4 contributions

	%
£1–£5,035 per year	Nil
£5,036–£33,540 per year	8.0
£33,541 and above per year	1.0

H STAMP DUTY LAND TAX

Transfers of property (consideration paid)

Rate (%)	All land in the UK		Land in disadvantaged areas	
	Residential	**Non-residential**	**Residential**	**Non-residential**
Zero	£0 - £125,000	£0 - £150,000	£0 - £150,000	£0 - £150,000
1	Over £125,000 - £250,000	Over £150,000 - £250,000	Over £150,000 - £250,000	Over £150,000 - £250,000
3	Over £250,000 - £500,000	Over £250,000 - £500,000	Over £250,000 - £500,000	Over £250,000 - £500,000
4	Over £500,000	Over £500,000	Over £500,000	Over £500,000

New leases

Duty on rent

Rate (%)	Net present value (NPV) of rent	
	Residential	**Non-residential**
Zero	£0 - £125,000	£0 - £150,000
1%	Over £125,000	Over £150,000

Stamp duty on shares and securities

0.5%

Syllabus mindmap

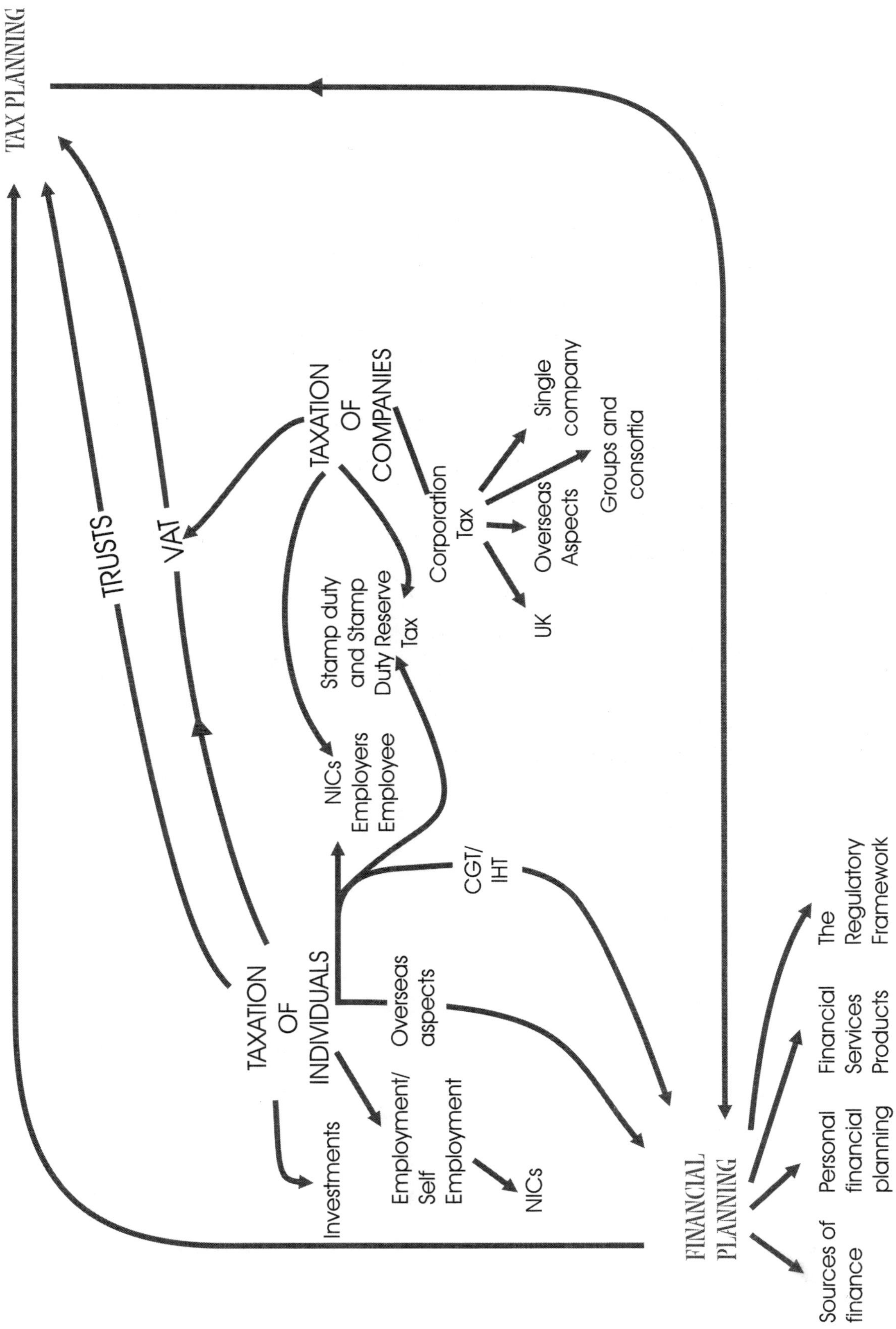

Part A
Taxation of individuals

1

Principles of income tax

Introduction

We start our study of taxation with an introduction to the UK tax system.

We then look in detail at income tax, which is a tax on what individuals make from their jobs, their businesses and their savings. We see how to collect together all of an individual's income in a personal tax computation, and then work out the tax on that income.

In later chapters, we look at particular types of income in more detail.

Topic list	Syllabus references
1 Taxes in the UK	1, 2, 3
2 The aggregation of income	1(a)
3 Various types of income	1(a)
4 Charges on income	1(a)
5 Allowances deducted from STI	1(a)
6 Charitable donations	1(a)
7 Tax reducers	1(a)
8 The personal tax computation	1(a)
9 Families	1(a)

1 Taxes in the UK

FAST FORWARD

UK tax law is contained in statute. This is interpreted and amplified by case law.

Central government raises revenue through a wide range of taxes. Tax law is made by **statute** and statute is interpreted and amplified by **case law**. HM Revenue and Customs also issue:

(a) **Statements of practice**, setting out how they intend to apply the law

(b) **Extra-statutory concessions**, setting out circumstances in which they will not apply the strict letter of the law

(c) A wide range of **explanatory leaflets**

(d) **Business economic notes**. These are notes on particular types of business, which are used as background information by HMRC and are also published

(e) The **Tax Bulletin**. This is a newsletter giving HMRC's view on specific points.

(f) The **Internal Guidance**, a series of manuals used by HMRC staff

A great deal of information and HMRC publications can be found on the HM Revenue and Custom's Internet site (www.hmrc.gov.uk). None of the HMRC publications has the force of law.

The main taxes, their incidence and their sources, are set out in the table below.

Tax	Suffered by	Source
Income tax	**Individuals** **Partnerships** **Trusts**	Income and Corporation Taxes Act 1988 (ICTA 1988) and subsequent Finance Acts; Capital Allowances Act 2001 (CAA 2001); Income Tax (Earnings and Pensions) Act 2003 (ITEPA 2003), Income Tax (Trading and Other Income) Act 2005 (ITTOIA 2005)
Corporation tax	**Companies**	ICTA 1988, Finance Acts and CAA 2001 as above
Capital gains tax	**Individuals** **Partnerships** **Trusts** **Companies** (which pay tax on capital gains in the form of corporation tax)	Taxation of Chargeable Gains Act 1992 (TCGA 1992) and subsequent Finance Acts
Value added tax	**Businesses**, both incorporated and unincorporated	Value Added Tax Act 1994 (VATA 1994) and subsequent Finance Acts
Inheritance tax	**Individuals** **Partnerships** **Trusts**	Inheritance Tax Act 1984 (IHTA 1984) and subsequent Finance Acts

In addition, you will meet stamp duty, stamp duty land tax and national insurance at Paper 3.2. **Stamp duty is payable on the execution of certain documents relating to shares. Stamp duty land tax is a land transaction tax. National insurance is payable by employers, employees and the self employed.**

Key term

The **tax year**, or **fiscal year**, or **year of assessment** runs from 6 April to 5 April. For example, the tax year 2006/07 runs from 6 April 2006 to 5 April 2007.

Finance Acts are passed each year, incorporating proposals set out in the **Budget**. They make changes which apply mainly to the tax year ahead. **This Study Text includes the provisions of the Finance Act 2006.** This is examinable in June 2007.

As a general rule, income tax is charged on receipts which might be expected to recur (such as weekly wages or profits from running a business) **whereas capital gains tax is charged on one-off gains** (for example from selling a painting owned for 20 years).

2 The aggregation of income

FAST FORWARD

In a personal income tax computation, bring together income from all sources, splitting the sources into non-savings, savings (excl. dividend) and dividend income.

An individual's income from all sources is brought together in a personal tax computation. Three columns are needed. Here is an example. All items are explained later in this text.

RICHARD: INCOME TAX COMPUTATION 2006/07

	Non-savings income	*Savings (excl dividend) income*	*Dividend income*	*Total*
	£	£	£	£
Income from employment	41,000			
Building society interest		1,000		
National savings bank interest		360		
UK dividends			1,000	
	41,000	1,360	1,000	
Less charges on income	(2,000)			
Statutory total income (STI)	39,000	1,360	1,000	41,360
Less personal allowance	(5,035)			
Taxable income	33,965	1,360	1,000	36,325

	£	£
Income tax on non savings income		
£2,150 × 10%		215
£31,150 × 22%		6,853
£665 × 40%		266
Tax on savings (excl. dividend) income		
£1,360 × 40%		544
Tax on dividend income		
£1,000 × 32.5%		325
		8,203
Less tax reduction		
Investment under the EIS £10,000 × 20%		(2,000)
Add basic rate tax withheld on charges		
paid net £2,000 × 22%		440
Tax liability		6,643
Less tax suffered		
PAYE tax on salary (say)	5,650	
Tax on building society interest	200	
Tax credit on dividend income	100	
		(5,950)
Tax payable		693

Key term

The **tax liability** is the amount which must be accounted for to HMRC. **Tax payable** is the balance of the liability still to be settled in cash. **Statutory total income** (STI) is all income before deducting the personal allowance or the blind person's allowance.

Income tax is charged on **'taxable income'**. Non-savings income is dealt with first, then savings (excl. dividend) income and then dividend income.

For non-savings income, the first £2,150 (the starting rate band) is taxed at the starting rate (10%), the next £31,150 (the basic rate band) is taxed at the basic rate (22%) and the rest at the higher rate (40%). We will look at the taxation of the other types of income later in this chapter.

The remainder of this chapter gives more details of the income tax computation.

3 Various types of income

FAST FORWARD

Don't forget to gross up dividends by 100/90 and interest by 100/80.

3.1 Classification of income

All income received must be classified according to the nature of the income. This is because different computational rules apply to different types of income. The main types of income are:

- Income from employment, pensions and some social security benefits
- Profits of trades, professions and vocations
- Profits of property businesses
- Savings and investment income, including interest and dividends
- Miscellaneous income.

These classes of income have replaced the old classification system under which the different types of income were known as Schedules, some of which were divided into cases. These old rules still apply for corporation tax, for example trading profits are called Schedule D Case I income and the profits of a property business are called Schedule A income (see the corporation tax chapters later in this text).

Although the names have changed, the rules for the computation of the taxable income have not changed.

3.2 Savings income received net of 20% tax

The following savings income is received net of 20% tax. **This is called income taxed at source.**

(a) Bank and building society interest paid to individuals (but not National Savings Bank interest)

(b) Interest paid to individuals by unlisted UK companies on debentures and loan stocks

(c) The income portion of a purchased annuity

(d) Savings income (excluding dividends) from non discretionary trusts

The amount received is grossed up by multiplying by 100/80 and is included gross in the income tax computation. The tax deducted at source is deducted in computing tax payable and may be repaid.

Exam focus point

In examinations you may be given either the net or the gross amount of such income: read the question carefully. If you are given the net amount (the amount received or credited), you should gross up the figure at the rate of 20%. For example, net building society interest of £160 is equivalent to gross income of £160 × 100/80 = £200 on which tax of £40 (20% of £200) has been suffered.

Although bank and building society interest paid to individuals is generally paid net of 20% tax, if a recipient is not liable to tax, he can recover the tax suffered, or he can certify in advance that he is a non-taxpayer and receive the interest gross.

3.3 Dividends on UK shares

Dividends on UK shares are received net of a 10% tax credit. This means a dividend of £90 has a £10 tax credit, giving gross income of £100 to include in the income tax computation. The tax credit can be deducted in computing tax payable but it cannot be repaid.

3.4 Exempt income

Some income is exempt from income tax. Several of these exemptions are mentioned at places in this text where the types of income are described in detail, but you should note the following types of exempt income now.

(a) Scholarships (exempt as income of the scholar. If paid by a parent's employer, a scholarship may be taxable income of the parent)

(b) Betting and gaming winnings, including **premium bond prizes**

(c) Interest or terminal bonus on **National Savings Certificates**

(d) Certain social security benefits

(e) Gifts

(f) Damages and payments for personal injury. The exemption applies to lump sum and periodical payments, including payments made via trusts and payments made by buying annuities. Payments under annuities are made gross (unlike most annuities)

(g) Certain payments under insurance policies to compensate for loss of income on illness or disability (permanent health insurance) or while out of work (eg policies to pay interest on mortgages). (See later in this text.)

(h) The amount by which a pension awarded on a retirement due to a disability caused at work, by a work related illness or by war wounds exceeds the pension that would have been payable if the retirement had been on ordinary ill health grounds. This exemption only applies to pensions paid under non-approved pension schemes.

(i) Interest on amounts repaid to borrowers under the income contingent student loans scheme

(j) Payments made under the 'new deal 50 plus' scheme and payments made under the employment zones programme.

(k) Income on investments made through **individual savings accounts (ISAs).**

Exam focus point

Learn the different types of exempt income. They are popular items in the exam. Always state on your exam script that such income is exempt (do not ignore it) to gain an easy half mark.

4 Charges on income

FAST FORWARD

Charges on income are deducted to arrive at Statutory Total Income (STI).

4.1 Charges on income are deducted in computing taxable income

Key term

A **charge on income** is a payment by the taxpayer which income tax law allows as a deduction.

Examples of charges on income are:

(a) Eligible interest
(b) Patent royalties
(c) Copyright royalties

Charges on income paid in money fall into two categories: those from which basic rate (22%) income tax is first deducted by the payer (charges paid net) and those which are paid gross (without any tax deduction). Always deduct the gross figure in the payer's tax computation.

Patent royalties are an example of a charge on income which individuals pay net. Eligible interest and copyright royalties are paid gross.

In the personal tax computation of someone who *receives* a charge, you should:

(a) Include the **gross** amount under non-savings income. If the charge is paid gross, the gross amount is the amount received. If it is paid net, the gross amount is the amount received × 100/78.

(b) If the charge was received net, then under the heading 'less tax suffered' (between tax liability and tax payable) include the tax deducted. This is the gross amount × 22%.

4.2 Eligible interest

Interest qualifies for tax relief as a charge if the loan concerned is used for a qualifying purpose:

(a) **The purchase of an interest in a partnership, or contribution to the partnership of capital or a loan**. The borrower must be a partner (other than a limited partner), and relief ceases when he ceases to be one.

(b) **The purchase of ordinary shares in, or the loan of money to, a close trading company.** When the interest is paid the individual must either have (with any associates) a material (more than 5%) interest in the company, or he must hold (ignoring associates) **some** ordinary share capital and work full time as a manager or director of the company. A close company is (broadly) a company controlled by its shareholder-directors or by five or fewer shareholders. Relief for interest paid is not available if relief for the investment is claimed under the enterprise investment scheme (see later in this Text).

(c) **Investment in a co-operative**. This applies to investment in shares/loans to the co-operative. The borrower must work for the greater part of his time in the co-operative.

(d) **The purchase of shares in an employee-controlled company** which must be an unquoted trading company resident in the UK with at least 50% of the voting shares held by employees.

(e) **The payment of inheritance tax by personal representatives** before a grant of representation. Interest is allowed for 12 months only.

(f) **The purchase by a partner of plant or machinery used in the business**. Interest is allowed for three years from the end of the tax year in which the loan was taken out. If the plant is used partly for private purposes, then the allowable interest is apportioned.

(g) **The purchase by an employee of plant or machinery used by him in the performance of his duties**. The interest is allowable for three years from the end of the tax year in which the loan was taken out.

(h) The replacement of other loans qualifying under (a) to (g) above.

Interest on a loan within (a) to (d) above continues to be allowable if a partnership is succeeded by a new partnership or is incorporated into a close company, a co-operative or an employee controlled company, or if shares in a company of one of these kinds are exchanged for shares in a company of another of these kinds, provided that interest on a new loan (to make the loan to or buy the shares in the new entity) would have qualified.

Interest is never allowed if it is payable under a scheme or arrangement of which the expected sole or main benefit was tax relief on the interest. Interest on an overdraft or on a credit card debt does not qualify. Relief under (a) to (d) above is reduced or withdrawn if capital is withdrawn from the business.

4.3 Business interest

A taxpayer paying interest wholly and exclusively for business purposes can deduct such interest in computing his trading profit, instead of as a charge. The interest need not fall into any of the categories outlined above, and it may be on an overdraft or a credit card debt.

If interest is allowable as a trading expense, the amount payable (on an accruals basis) is deducted. Only interest paid in the tax year may be set against total income as a charge.

4.4 Charges in personal tax computations

The gross amount of any charge is deducted from total income to arrive at STI. Deduct charges from non-savings income, then from savings (excl dividend) income and lastly from dividend income.

If a charge has been paid net, the basic rate income tax deducted (22% of the gross charge) is added to any tax liability. The taxpayer obtained tax relief because the charge reduced his income: he cannot keep the basic rate tax as well, but must pay it to HMRC.

If charges paid net exceed total income (ignoring charges paid net) **minus allowances deductible from STI, the payer of the charge must, under s 350 ICTA 1988, pay HMRC the tax withheld when the excess charge was paid**. In other words, HMRC ensure that you do not get tax relief for charges if you are not a payer of tax.

4.5 Example

Three taxpayers have the following trading income and allowances for 2006/07. Taxpayers A and B pay a patent royalty of £176 (net). Taxpayer C pays a patent royalty of £1,248 (net).

	A	*B*	*C*
	£	£	£
Trading Income	6,000	4,000	40,795
Less: charge on income (× 100/78)	(226)	(226)	(1,600)
	5,774	3,774	39,195
Less: personal allowance	(5,035)	(5,035)	(5,035)
Taxable income	739	–	34,160
Income tax			
10% on £739–/£2,150	74	–	215
22% on –/–/£31,150			6,853
40% on –/–/£860			344
	74	–	7,412
Add: 22% tax retained on charge	50	50	352
Tax payable	124	50	7,764

5 Allowances deducted from STI

FAST FORWARD

Deduct the personal allowance and the blind person's allowance. Remember that there are increased allowances for the over 65s.

5.1 Introduction

Once taxable income from all sources has been aggregated and any charges on income deducted, the remainder is the taxpayer's statutory total income (STI). Two allowances, the personal allowance and the blind person's allowance, are deducted from STI. Like charges, they come off non savings income first, then off savings (excl. dividend) income and lastly off dividend income. The amounts given in the following paragraphs are for 2006/07.

5.2 PA: personal allowance

All persons (including children) are entitled to the personal allowance of £5,035.

A person aged 65 or over (at any time in the tax year) gets an age allowance of £7,280 instead of the ordinary PA of £5,035.

Where statutory total income exceeds £20,100, cut the age allowance by £1 for every £2 of income over £20,100 until it comes down to £5,035.

Question — **Calculation of age allowance**

Jonah is 69 and single. In 2006/07 he has pension income totalling £18,000 plus bank interest received of £4,000. What is Jonah's taxable income?

Answer

	Non savings	*Savings*	*Total*
2006/07	£	£	£
Pension income	18,000		
Interest 4,000 × 100/80		5,000	
	18,000	5,000	23,000
Less: PAA (W1)	(5,830)		
Taxable income	12,170	5,000	17,170

W1

PAA 65+	7,280
Less: income restriction (23,000 – 20,100) × ½	(1,450)
	5,830

PAA of £5,830 exceeds basic allowance of £5,035.

Individuals aged 75 or over (at any time in the tax year) get a slightly more generous age allowance of £7,420. In all respects, the higher age allowance works in the same way as the basic age allowance, with the same income limit of £20,100.

Someone who dies in the tax year in which they would have had their 65th or 75th birthday gets the age allowance (for 65 year olds or 75 year olds) for that year.

When a taxpayer has made a donation under the gift aid scheme (see below) the STI that is compared with the income limit must be reduced by the gross amount of the gift aid donation.

5.3 BPA: blind person's allowance

A taxpayer who is registered with a local authority as a blind person gets an allowance of £1,660. The allowance is also given for the year before registration, if the taxpayer had obtained the proof of blindness needed for registration before the end of that earlier year.

Question — **Calculation of taxable income**

Susan has an annual salary of £40,000. She has a loan of £7,000 at 10% interest to buy shares in her employee-controlled company, and another loan of £5,000 at 12% interest to buy double glazing for her house. She receives building society interest of £2,000 a year. What is her taxable income for 2006/07?

Answer

	Non-savings	*Savings (excl dividend)*	*Total*
	£	£	£
Salary	40,000		
Building society interest £2,000 × 100/80		2,500	
	40,000	2,500	
Less charge £7,000 × 10%	(700)		
STI	39,300	2,500	41,800
Less personal allowance	(5,035)		
Taxable income	34,265	2,500	36,765

Note. Susan's STI is £41,800, so even if she is aged 65 or more she will not get any age allowance. The loan to purchase double glazing is not a qualifying loan.

6 Charitable donations

FAST FORWARD: Extend the basic rate band by the gross amount of any gift aid payment.

6.1 Gift aid donations

Key term

One-off and regular charitable gifts of money, including donations made under a legally enforceable deed of covenant, qualify for tax relief under the **gift aid scheme** provided the donor gives the charity a gift aid declaration.

Gift aid declarations can be made in writing, electronically through the internet or orally over the phone. A declaration can cover a one-off gift or any number of gifts for the future or retrospectively.

The gift must not be subject to any condition for repayment, and the total benefits received by the donor and any persons connected with him from the charity must not be worth more than:

Aggregate donations In the tax year	*Aggregate value of benefits in the tax year*
£0 – £100	25% of the donations
£101 – £1,000	£25
£1,001 – £10,000	2.5% of the donations
£10,000 +	£250

Charitable donations are often used as a means of paying subscriptions to charities that offer free or reduced rate admission (as with the National Trust). Where this benefit is offered to the donor and members of his family, it does not infringe the gift aid rules, so long as the right of admission applies for at least one year or the visitor pays at least 10% more than the normal admission charge. This exemption applies to any charity that grants the public the right to pay to view property preserved, maintained, kept or created by a charity in relation to its charitable work.

Gift aid relief is also given for donations to Community Amateur Sports Clubs.

A gift aid donation is treated as though it was paid net of basic rate tax (22%, 2006/07). Additional tax relief is given in the personal tax computation by increasing the donor's basic rate band by the gross amount of the gift. To arrive at the gross amount of the gift you must multiply the amount paid by 100/78.

Question

Tax relief for gift aid donation

James earns a salary of £59,040 but has no other income. In 2006/07 he paid £7,800 (net) under the gift aid scheme. No claims (see below) were made in respect of the gift aid donation.

Compute James' income tax liability for 2006/07.

Answer

		Non-savings
		£
Salary		59,040
Less: personal allowance		(5,035)
Taxable income		54,005
Income tax	£	£
Starting rate band	2,150 × 10%	215
Basic rate band	31,150 × 22%	6,853
Basic rate band (extended)	10,000 × 22%	2,200
Higher rate band	10,705 × 40%	4,282
	54,005	13,550

The basic rate band is extended by the gross amount of the gift (£7,800 × 100/78).

When comparing statutory total income (STI) with the income limit for age allowance purposes, you must reduce the STI by the gross amount of any gift aid payment. This reduction is made as a working in computing age allowances only: the gift aid payment is not deducted in arriving at taxable income.

The gift aid declaration must include a confirmation by the donee that an appropriate amount of tax has been paid. For example, if an individual gives £78, the gross value is £100 (£78 × 100/78) and £22 of tax is recoverable by the charity. For a donor who pays insufficient tax it may be necessary to restrict his personal allowance or raise an assessment to ensure that the tax recovered by the charity has been paid by the individual.

Higher rate taxpayers are allowed to carry back their additional tax relief (ie relief above the relief at the basic rate) on gift aid donations for one year.

Question **Carrying back tax relief on gift aid donations**

Zoë earns £22,000 in 2006/07 and £46,000 in 2005/06. She had no other income. In 2006/07, she paid £7,800 under the gift aid scheme. Zoë made a claim to have additional tax relief on the gift aid donation in 2005/06. Show Zoë's tax liability in both years assuming that tax rates and allowances were the same in 2005/06 as in 2006/07.

Answer

	2005/06	*2006/07*
	£	£
Salary	46,000	22,000
Less: personal allowance	(5,035)	(5,035)
Taxable income	40,965	16,965
Tax		
£2,150 × 10%	215	215
£31,150/£14,815 × 22%	6,853	3,259
£7,665 × 22%	1,686	
	8,754	3,474

Income is below the higher rate threshold in 2006/07, so even if no claim were made no additional relief would be given on the gift aid donation in 2006/07. The claim allows £7,665 of income in 2005/06 to be taxed at 22% rather than 40%, saving tax of £1,380. The basic rate band could be extended by up to £10,000 in 2005/06.

A claim for carry back has to be made no later than the date on which the taxpayer files his return for the earlier year of assessment, and in any event no later than the statutory filing date for that year. A claim to carry back relief from 2006/07 to 2005/06 will therefore have to be made by 31 January 2007.

Where an individual overpays tax, he is able (by ticking a box on his annual tax return) to instruct HMRC to send the repayment to the charity of his choice. The donation cannot be carried back to a previous tax year.

6.2 Donations of shares and securities

An income tax deduction is available if the whole of any beneficial interest in qualifying shares or securities is given, or sold at an undervalue, to a charity. The amount that an individual can deduct in calculating his total income is:

(a) The market value of the share or securities at the date of disposal, plus

(b) Any incidental costs of disposing of the shares (broker's fees, etc), less

(c) Any consideration given in return for disposing of the shares, and less

(d) The value of any other benefits received by the donor, or a person connected with the donor, in consequence of disposing of the shares.

The following are qualifying shares and securities for the purpose of the above paragraph:

(a) Shares or securities listed on a recognised stock exchange (UK or otherwise)

(b) Shares or securities dealt with on a recognised stock exchange (UK or otherwise) (this definition appears to include Alternative Investment Market shares)

(c) Units in an authorised unit trust

(d) Shares in an open-ended investment company

(e) Holdings in certain foreign collective investment schemes.

6.3 Donations of land or buildings to charity

Individuals can claim an **income tax deduction equal to the market value of any freehold or leasehold land or buildings given to charity**. Where land is sold at an undervalue, relief is given for the difference between market value and the price paid by the charity.

7 Tax reducers

FAST FORWARD Tax reducers reduce tax on income at a set rate of relief.

7.1 Introduction

Tax reducers do not affect income; they reduce tax on income. The tax reducers are:

(a) Investments in venture capital trusts and under the enterprise investment scheme
(b) The married couple's age allowance
(c) Maintenance payments following the breakdown of a marriage

7.2 Venture capital trusts (VCTs) and the enterprise investment scheme (EIS)

Investments in the above companies may qualify for a tax reduction of up to the lower of:

(a) A percentage of the amount subscribed for qualifying investments, and
(b) The individual's tax liability.

For investments in VCTs, the percentage is 30% for 2006/07 (it was 40% for 2005/06). For investments under the EIS, the percentage is 20%. Further details are given later in this text.

7.3 MCAA: married couple's age allowance

A married man whose wife is living with him gets a married couples age allowance (MCAA) of £6,065 if he or his wife was 65 before 6 April 2000 (in other words born before 6 April 1935). The tax reduction is 10% of the allowance.

There is a minimum amount of MCAA of £2,350. The wife can unilaterally elect, by the start of the relevant tax year, to have half of the tax reduction from the minimum amount of MCAA set against her tax instead of her husband's. Alternatively, the couple can jointly elect, by the start of the relevant tax year, to transfer half or all of this tax reduction to the wife. An election remains in force until revoked, and any revocation only applies from the following 6 April. For the year of marriage, an election may be made during the year.

Any MCAA which turns out to be wasted (because the husband or wife has insufficient tax to reduce) may be passed to the other spouse. The spouse who gives away the MCAA must notify HMRC within 5 years from 31 January next following the end of the relevant tax year.

A married man, if he **or his wife** is 75 or over (at any time in the tax year), gets an age allowance of £6,135 instead of the ordinary MCAA of £6,065. Half or all of the tax reduction from the minimum amount may be transferred to the wife, exactly as for ordinary MCAA.

When statutory total income exceeds £20,100, cut the personal age allowance by half of the excess to a minimum of £5,035. Once £5,035 has been reached, cut the married couple's age allowance by any remaining excess, but not to below the minimum amount of £2,350. The reduction in the married couple's age allowance has historically depended on the **husband's** STI. STI for this purpose must be reduced by the gross amount of any gift aid donation.

Same sex partners registered under the Civil Partnerships Act 2004 (CPA 2004) will be entitled to the MCAA if either partner was born before 6 April 2000. The reduction in the MCAA will be based on the STI of the member of the partnership who has the highest STI. The CPA 2004 came into force on 5 December 2005. From that date, civil partners and married couples, married on or after that date, are treated in the same way. As a consequence, if a couple marry once the CPA 2004 is in force (ie from 5 December 2005 onwards), the reduction in their MCAA will also be based on the highest STI. For marriages before then the reduction will continue to be based on the husband's STI.

If one of the couple dies in the tax year in which they would have had their 75th birthday the couple is still entitled to the higher age-related MCAA for that year.

In the year of marriage (or registration under the CPA 2004) the MCAA is reduced by 1/12 for each complete tax month (from the 6th of one month to the 5th of the next) which has passed before the marriage or registration.

Question — **Computation of MCAA**

A married man aged 79 has STI of £26,500 for 2006/07. He did not make any gift aid payments. His wife has no income. What personal allowance and MCAA is he entitled to?

Answer

As STI exceeds £20,100, the age allowances are reduced. The personal allowance is initially reduced to £5,035. Any further reduction is taken from the MCAA.

Reduction: £(26,500 – 20,100) × 0.5 = £3,200

Personal allowance = £(7,420 – 2,385) = £5,035

Married couple's allowance = £(6,135 – 815) = £5,320

7.4 Maintenance payments

All maintenance payments are made gross. A tax reduction of 10% of qualifying maintenance payments is available if at least one party to the marriage was aged 65 or over on 5 April 2000 (again born before 6 April 1935). **Qualifying payments** are certain legally required payments made under written agreements.

Provided that the payment is made for the benefit of the former or separated spouse or of a child of the family and is made to the spouse (but not directly to a child or to an agent such as a school), **the payer can claim a tax reduction of 10% of the lower of**:

(a) **The payments due in the tax year**, and
(b) **£2,350** (for 2006/07).

There is no tax reduction for payments made after the recipient remarries.

The recipient is not liable to income tax on maintenance payments made, however large.

These rules also apply to civil partnerships

7.5 Giving tax reductions

Tax reducers are deducted in computing an individual's income tax liability. The full tax reduction can only be given if the individual has enough tax to reduce. If, for example, the tax before the reduction is £50 and the reduction is £200, the tax liability is only reduced to zero. The individual **cannot** claim a repayment of £(50 – 200) = £150.

The tax which can be reduced is the tax on taxable income. It does not include tax retained on charges paid net.

An individual may be entitled to several different tax reducers. In such cases they must be applied in a set order, and we must stop when the tax is reduced to zero.

The order is as follows.

(a) Investments in venture capital trusts
(b) Investments under the enterprise investment scheme
(c) Maintenance payments
(d) The married couple's age allowance

Question — Tax reducers

Peter, a married man aged 72, makes qualifying investments of £2,000 a year under the enterprise investment scheme. His wife has no income. Show his tax position for 2006/07 if his income consists of:

(a) trading profits of £40,000;
(b) trading profits of £8,385.

Answer

	(a): High income Non-savings	*(b): Low income Non-savings*
	£	£
Trading profits	40,000	8,385
Less personal allowance/age allowance	(5,035)	(7,280)
Taxable income	34,965	1,105
Non savings income		
£2,150/£1,105 × 10%	215	111
£31,150 × 22%	6,853	
£1,665 × 40%	666	
	7,734	111
Tax reducers		
EIS £2,000 × 20%	(400)	(111)
	7,334	0
MCAA £2,350 × 10% (minimum amount)	(235)	–
Tax liability	7,099	0

The tax reducers cannot lead to repayments of tax, so in (b) the MCAA and some of the EIS relief is wasted.

In (a) Peter is not entitled to the personal age allowance because his STI is too high. The MCAA is reduced to the minimum amount.

8 The personal tax computation

FAST FORWARD

Work out income tax on the taxable income in three stages, then, take account of tax reducers, tax retained on charges and tax already suffered.

8.1 Steps in the personal tax computation

Step 1 **The first step in preparing a personal tax computation is to set up three columns**. One column for non-savings income, one for savings (excl. dividend) income and one for dividend income.

Step 2 **Deal with non-savings income first**. Income of up to £2,150 is taxed at 10%. Next any income in the basic rate band is taxed at 22%, and finally income above the basic rate threshold is taxed at 40%.

Step 3 **Now deal with savings (excl dividend) income.** If any of the starting or basic rate bands remain **after taxing non savings income**, they can be used here. Savings (excl) dividend income is taxed at 10% in the starting rate band and in the basic rate band at 20% (not 22%). Once income is above the higher rate threshold, it is taxed at 40%.

Step 4 **Lastly, tax dividend income.** If dividend income falls within the starting or basic rate bands, it is taxed at 10% (never 20% or 22%). If the dividend income exceeds the basic rate threshold of £33,300, it is taxable at 32.5%.

Step 5 Once tax has been computed, deduct any available tax reducers (eg the MCAA).

Step 6 Next, deduct the tax credit on dividends. Although deductible this tax credit cannot be repaid if it exceeds the tax liability calculated so far.

Step 7 Finally deduct the tax deducted at source from savings (excluding dividend) income and any PAYE. These amounts can be repaid to the extent that they exceed the income tax liability.

In each of the following examples, the taxpayer is aged under 65. We have shown the STI, but you would only need this where age allowance might be available.

8.2 Examples: personal tax computations

(a) Kathe has a business profit of £10,000 and receives dividends of £4,500. She invested £2,000 under the Enterprise Investment Scheme.

	Non-savings	*Dividends*	*Total*
	£	£	£
Business profits	10,000		
Dividends £4,500 × 100/90		5,000	
STI	10,000	5,000	15,000
Less personal allowance	(5,035)		
Taxable income	4,965	5,000	9,965

	£
Non savings income	
£2,150 × 10%	215
£2,815 × 22%	619
Dividend income	
£5,000 × 10%	500
Less: tax reducers	
EIS (£2,000 × 20%)	(400)
Tax liability	934
Less tax credit on dividend	(500)
Tax payable	434

The dividend income falls within the basic rate band so it is taxed at 10% (*not* 22%).

(b) Jules has a business profit of £50,000, net dividends of £6,750 and building society interest of £3,000 net. He pays gross charges of £2,000 and makes a gift aid donation of £780 (net).

	Non-savings	*Savings (excl dividend)*	*Dividend*	*Total*
	£	£	£	£
Business profits	50,000			
Dividends £6,750 × 100/90			7,500	
Building society interest £3,000 × 100/80	-	3,750	-	
	50,000	3,750	7,500	
Less charges	(2,000)			
STI	48,000	3,750	7,500	59,250
Less personal allowance	(5,035)			
Taxable income	42,965	3,750	7,500	54,215

	£
Non savings income	
£2,150 × 10%	215
£31,150 × 22%	6,853
£1,000 (£780 × $\frac{100}{78}$) × 22%	220
£8,665 × 40%	3,466
	10,754
Savings (excl. dividend) income	
£3,750 × 40%	1,500
Dividend income	
£7,500 × 32.5%	2,434
Less tax credit on dividend income	(750)
Less tax suffered on building society interest	(750)
Tax payable	13,188

Savings (excl. dividend) income and dividend income fall above the basic rate threshold so they are taxed at 40% and 32.5% respectively. The basic rate band is extended by the gross amount of the gift aid donation.

(c) Jim does not work. He receives net bank interest of £38,000. He pays gross charges of £2,000.

	Savings (excl dividend)	*Total*
	£	£
Bank interest × 100/80	47,500	
Less charges	(2,000)	
STI	45,500	45,500
Less personal allowance	(5,035)	
	40,465	40,465

	£
Savings (excluding dividend) income	
£2,150 × 10%	215
£31,150 × 20%	6,230
£7,165 × 40%	2,866
Tax liability	9,311
Less tax suffered	(9,500)
Tax repayable	(189)

Savings (excl. dividend) income within the basic rate band is taxed at 20% (*not* 22%).

Two types of income come above dividend income, so that dividend income is not always the top slice of income:

(a) Chargeable gains on life assurance policies (see later in this text).
(b) The taxable portions of partly exempt payments on the termination of employment.

Thus someone with wages of £15,000, dividend income of £20,000 and a £100,000 termination payment will still have some dividend income taxed at 10%.

8.3 What is savings income?

'Savings income' does not include everything you might expect it to. Here are lists of savings and non-savings income.

8.3.1 Savings income

(a) **Interest** (includes interest from banks, buildings societies, gilts and debentures and under the accrued income scheme)

(b) **Dividends**

(c) **The income part of a purchased life annuity**. This is an annuity which lasts for a period depending on someone's lifespan, and which is bought for a lump sum. Part of each payment is treated as income and is paid net of 20% tax, while the rest is treated as a return of capital and is tax-free (see later in this text).

(d) Chargeable gains on life assurance policies

8.3.2 Non-savings income

Income from a job
Income from running a business (alone or as a partner)
Rental income
Charges **received** (other than interest)

Interest and dividends from abroad are savings income unless the taxpayer is only taxed on money he brings to the UK (the remittance basis). In that case, they are non-savings income (see later in this text).

8.4 The complete proforma

Here is a complete proforma computation. It is probably too much for you to absorb at this stage, but refer back to it as you work through this text.

	Non-savings	*Savings (excl dividend)*	*Dividend*	*Total*
	£	£	£	£
Business profits	X			
Less losses set against business profits	(X)			
	X			
Wages less occupational pension contributions	X			
Other non-savings (as many lines as necessary)	X			
Building society interest (gross)		X		
Other savings (excl. dividends) (gross)		X		
(as many lines as necessary)				
Dividends (gross)			X	
	X	X	X	
Less charges (gross)	(X)	(X)	(X)	
	X	X	X	
Less losses set against general income	(X)	(X)	(X)	
STI	X	X	X	X
Less personal allowance	(X)	(X)	(X)	
Taxable income	X	X	X	X

9 Families

FAST FORWARD

Husbands, wives and children are all separate taxpayers. There are special rules to prevent parents from exploiting a child's personal allowance. Civil partners are taxed as if they were a married couple.

9.1 Spouses and civil partners

Husband and wife are taxed as two separate people. The general position on allowances (PA and MCAA) has been set out above.

Same sex couples can register as a civil partnership. This is treated in the same way as a marriage for income tax purposes, and dissolution of a partnership is the same as a divorce. The following paragraphs apply to civil partnerships, with the terms husband, wife, spouse etc also applying to civil partners.

9.2 Joint property

When spouses jointly own income-generating property, it is assumed that they are entitled to equal shares of the income. (This does not apply to income from shares held in close companies – see later in this text).

If, in fact, the spouses are not entitled to equal shares in the income-generating property (other than shares in close companies), they may make a joint declaration to HMRC, specifying the proportion to which each is entitled. These proportions are used to tax each of them separately, in respect of income arising on or after the date of the declaration.

If one spouse's marginal tax rate (the rate on the highest part of his or her income) is higher than the other spouse's marginal rate, it is sensible to transfer income-yielding assets to the spouse with the lower rate.

9.3 The year of marriage

The husband may receive part of the married couple's age allowance (MCAA). **He receives the full amount less 1/12 for each complete tax month during which the couple were unmarried**. A tax month runs from the 6th of one month to the 5th of the next month.

In any year, one half or all of the minimum amount of MCAA (£2,350, 2006/07) may be transferred to the wife by election. The maximum amount that may be transferred in the year of marriage is the minimum amount reduced by 1/12 for each complete tax month before the wedding.

9.4 The year of death

If a wife dies during a tax year her widower receives the personal allowance (PA) and a full MCAA (if appropriate) for that year. The wife will have a full PA to cover income to the date of death.

When a husband dies, his tax affairs up to the date of his death are dealt with on the basis of his receiving the full PA and MCAA (if appropriate). The widow obtains her PA for the year.

9.5 Divorce and separation

Divorce is usually preceded by separation. Where a couple become separated under a court order or separation deed, or in circumstances such that the separation is likely to be permanent, they are then taxed as single people from the date of separation.

In the tax year in which the separation takes place, however, the husband receives the PA plus a full MCAA (if appropriate). As usual, half or all of the £2,350 minimum MCAA may be transferred to the wife.

9.6 Minor children

There is legislation to prevent the parent of a minor child transferring income to the child in order to use the child's personal allowance and starting and basic rate tax bands. **Income which is directly transferred by the parent, or is derived from capital so transferred, remains income of the parent for tax purposes.** This applies only to parents, however, and tax saving is therefore possible by other relatives. Even where a parent is involved, the child's income is not treated as the parent's if it does not exceed £100 a year.

This legislation is concerned with gifts from a parent to a child. It may therefore be possible to use the child's personal allowance and starting and basic rate bands if the child is employed in the parent's trade.

The legislation does not apply to income from a Child Trust Fund (CTF). CTFs are dealt with later in this text.

9.7 Social security benefits and tax credits

There are various social security benefits and tax credits that can be claimed by family members in a variety of circumstances. The examinability of these is limited:

Exam focus point

Questions will not be set requiring a detailed knowledge of the UK welfare system and state benefits (including benefits which are effectively administered through the UK tax system). Such benefits may be included as a small part of a question but candidates will be told the amount of the benefit and its taxation status within a question. There will be no need to calculate benefit entitlements.

9.8 Child tax credit (CTC) and Working tax credit (WTC)

The CTC is paid to the main carer of a **qualifying child**. A child is a qualifying child until 1 September following their 16th birthday or until they are 19 if they are in full time education.

WTC is paid in addition to the CTC to help top up earnings of certain working people.

The availability and amount of both credits depends on income (or if part of a couple, combined income).

The tax credits are paid directly to the claimant and do not feature in the income tax computation.

Chapter roundup

- In a personal income tax computation, bring together income from all sources, splitting the sources into non-savings, savings (excl. dividend) and dividend income. Don't forget to gross up dividends by 100/90 and interest by 100/80.
- Deduct charges, and then the personal allowance and the blind person's allowance. Remember that there are increased allowances for the over 65s.
- Patent royalties are paid net of 22% tax but must be deducted gross. Eligible interest and copyright royalties are paid gross.
- Work out income tax on the taxable income in three stages, then, take account of tax reducers, tax retained on charges and tax already suffered.
- Extend the basic rate band by the gross amount of any gift aid payment.
- Husbands, wives and children are all separate taxpayers. There are special rules to prevent parents from exploiting a child's personal allowance. Civil partners are taxed as if they were a married couple.

Quick quiz

1 At what rates is income tax charged on non-savings income?

2 Is UK rental income savings income?

3 List three types of savings income that is received by individuals net of 20% tax.

4 Give an example of a charge on income paid net.

5 How is tax relief given for a gift aid donation?

6 At what rate does the MCAA reduce tax?

7 How is dividend income taxed?

8 What is the de-minimis threshold below which a child's income deriving from a parental disposition is not taxed as the parents?

Answers to quick quiz

1 Income tax on non-savings income is charged at 10% in the starting rate band, at 22% in the basic rate band and at 40% in the higher rate band.

2 No.

3 Interest paid by unquoted UK companies on UK debentures and loan stock, bank and building society interest (but not National Savings Bank interest), the income portion of a purchased annuity.

4 Patent royalties

5 Basic rate tax relief is given by treating a gift aid donation as though it were paid of net of basic rate tax. Additional tax relief is given in the personal tax computation by increasing the donor's basic rate band by the gross amount of the gift.

6 10%

7 Dividend income in the starting and basic rate band is taxed at 10%. Dividend income in excess of the higher rate threshold is taxed at 32.5%

8 £100

Now try the question below from the Exam Question Bank

Number	Level	Marks	Time
Q1	Examination	25	45 mins

2

Income from investments

Introduction

This chapter is concerned mainly with the taxation of income arising from the letting of property in the UK. It looks at the basis of assessment of such income and at the computation of assessable profits and losses. The chapter also looks at the taxation of income from other investments.

Topic list	Syllabus references
1 UK property businesses	1(b)
2 Furnished holiday lettings	1(b)
3 Rent a room relief	1(b)
4 Interest income	1(c)
5 Accrued income scheme	1(c)
6 Dividend income	1(c)
7 Miscellaneous income	1(c)
8 Pre-owned assets	1(c)
9 Trust income	1(c)

1 UK property businesses

1.1 Profits of UK property business

FAST FORWARD

Income from a UK property business is computed for tax years on an accruals basis.

Income from land and buildings in the UK, including caravans and houseboats which are not moved, is taxed as non-savings income.

(a) **A taxpayer (or a partnership) with UK rental income is treated as running a business, his 'UK property business'. All the rents and expenses for all properties are pooled, to give a single profit or loss. Profits and losses are computed in the same way as trading profits are computed for tax purposes**, on an accruals basis.

Expenses will often include rent payable where a landlord is himself renting the land which he in turn lets to others. For individuals, interest on loans to buy or improve properties is treated as an expense (on an accruals basis). The rules on post-cessation receipts and expenses apply to UK property businesses in the same way that they apply to trades.

Relief is available for irrecoverable rent as an impaired debt.

(b) **Capital allowances are given on plant and machinery used in the UK property business and on industrial buildings, in the same way as they are given for a trading business** with an accounting date of 5 April. Capital allowances are not normally available on plant or machinery used in a dwelling. As someone who lets property furnished cannot claim capital allowances on the furniture he can choose instead between the **renewals basis** and the **10% wear and tear allowance**.

(i) Under the *renewals* basis, there is no deduction for the cost of the first furniture provided, but the cost of replacement furniture is treated as a revenue expense. However, the part of the cost attributable to improvement, as opposed to simple replacement, is not deductible.

(ii) Under the *10% wear and tear* basis, the actual cost of furniture is ignored. Instead, an annual deduction is given of 10% of rents. The rents are first reduced by amounts which are paid by the landlord but are normally a tenant's burden. These amounts include any **water rates** and **council tax** paid by the landlord.

If plant and machinery is used partly in a dwelling house and partly for other purposes a just and reasonable apportionment of the expenditure can be made.

(c) **No deduction is usually allowed for capital expenditure**. However, for expenditure incurred before 5 April 2009, there is **an allowable deduction of up to £1,500** for installation of **loft, cavity and solid wall insulation, draught proofing and insulation of hot water systems** in a let dwelling house. This deduction **only applies for income tax purposes**; it does not apply for corporation tax (see later in this text).

(d) Rent for furniture supplied with premises is taxed as part of the rent for the premises, unless there is a separate trade of renting furniture.

(e) The profits of the UK property business are computed for tax years. Each tax year's profit is taxed in that year.

1.2 Losses of UK property business

FAST FORWARD

A loss on a UK property business is carried forward to set against future profits from the UK property business.

A loss from a UK property business is carried forward to set against the first future profits from the UK property business. It may be carried forward until the UK property business ends, but it must be used as soon as possible.

Certain types of loss from a UK property business may alternatively be set against the taxpayer's total income (after charges but before allowances) for the tax year of loss and/or the next tax year. The loss goes against non-savings income before savings income. The types of loss are:

(a) Losses due to capital allowances up to the lower of:

 (i) The excess of capital allowances over balancing charges. Balancing allowances are included in capital allowances.

 (ii) The total loss in the UK property business.

(b) Losses due to agricultural expenses up to the lower of:

 (i) The total agricultural expenses. These are expenses on the maintenance, repair, insurance or management of an agricultural estate, excluding any loan interest. Expenses on parts of the land not used for husbandry are excluded.

 (ii) The total loss in the UK property business.

The claim must be for the full amount of the loss, up to the available income, even if this leads to a wasted personal allowance. Losses from a UK property business brought forward from earlier years are set against the UK property business profit for the year in which relief is claimed before the available income is computed. The taxpayer may claim relief in the year of loss, and then relief for any remaining loss in the next year, or vice-versa, or he may claim for just one year. However, he cannot decide how to split the loss between the two years (for example half for each year). If relief is claimed in a year both for the previous year's loss and for the current year's loss, the previous year's loss must be relieved first.

The time limit for claiming this relief is the 31 January which is nearly two years after the end of the tax year (so 31 January 2009 for relief against 2006/07 income).

Any loss not relieved against total income (because the relief was not claimed or there was less income than loss) is carried forward against future profits from the UK property business.

1.3 Premiums on leases

FAST FORWARD

Part of the premium received on the grant of a short lease is taxed as rent. In addition any premiums paid to a tenant to induce him to take out a lease is also taxable as income from a UK property business, or as trading income if the tenant is in business.

When a premium or similar consideration is received on the grant (that is, by a landlord to a tenant) **of a short lease (50 years or less), part of the premium is treated as rent received in the year of grant.** A lease is considered to end on the date when it is most likely to terminate.

The premium taxed as rent is the whole premium, less 2% of the premium for each complete year of the lease, except the first year.

This rule does not apply on the *assignment* of a lease (one tenant selling his entire interest in the property to another).

1.4 Premiums paid by traders

Where a trader pays a premium for a lease he may deduct an amount from his taxable trading profits in each year of the lease. The amount deductible is the figure treated as rent received by the landlord divided by the number of years of the lease. For example, suppose that B, a trader, pays A a premium of £30,000 for a ten year lease. A is treated as receiving £30,000 – (£30,000 × (10 – 1) × 2%) = £24,600. B can therefore deduct £24,600/10 = £2,460 in each of the ten years. He starts with the accounts year in which the lease starts and apportions the relief to the nearest month.

Question

UK property income

Pete over the last few years has purchased several properties in Manchester as "buy to let" investments.

5 Whitby Ave is let out furnished at £500 per month. A tenant moved in on 1 March 2005 but left unexpectedly on 1 May 2007 having paid rent only up to 31 December 2006. The tenant left no forwarding address.

17 Bolton Rd has been let furnished to the same tenant for a number of years at £800 per month.

A recent purchase, 27 Turner Close has been let unfurnished since 1 August 2006 at £750 per month having been empty whilst Pete redecorated it after its purchase in March 2006.

Pete's expenses during 2006/07 are:

	No 5	*No 17*	*No 27*
	£	£	£
Insurance	250	250	200
Letting agency fees	–	–	100
Repairs	300	40	–
Redecoration	–	–	500

No 27 was in a fit state to let when Pete bought it but he wanted to redecorate the property as he felt this would allow him to achieve a better rental income.

Water rates and council tax are paid by the tenants. Pete made a UK property business loss in 2005/06 of £300.

What is Pete's taxable property income for 2006/07?

Answer

	No 15	*No 17*	*No 27*
2006/07	£	£	£
Accrued income			
12 × £500	6,000		
12 × £800		9,600	
8 × £750			6,000
Less:			
Insurance	(250)	(250)	(200)
Letting agency fees			(100)
Impairment (irrecoverable rent)			
3 × £500	(1,500)		
Repairs	(300)	(40)	(500)
Wear and Tear Allowance			
£(6,000 – 1,500) × 10%	(450)		
£9,600 × 10%		(960)	
Property Income	3,500	8,350	5,200

	£
Total property income	17,050
Less: loss b/fwd	(300)
Taxable property income for 2006/07	16,750

1.5 Premiums for granting subleases

A tenant may decide to sublet property and to charge a premium on the grant of a lease to the subtenant. This premium is treated as rent received in the normal way (because this is a grant and not an assignment, the original tenant retaining an interest in the property). **Where the tenant originally paid a premium for his own head lease, this deemed rent is reduced by:**

$$\text{Rent part of premium for head lease} \times \frac{\text{duration of sub-lease}}{\text{duration of head lease}}$$

If the relief exceeds the part of the premium for the sub-lease treated as rent (including cases where there is a sub-lease with no premium), the balance of the relief is treated as rent payable by the head tenant, spread evenly over the period of the sub-lease. This rent payable is an expense, reducing the overall profit from the UK property business.

Question — **Taxable premium received**

C granted a lease to D on 1 March 1996 for a period of 40 years. D paid a premium of £16,000. On 1 June 2006 D granted a sublease to E for a period of ten years. E paid a premium of £30,000. Calculate the amount treated as rent out of the premium received by D.

Answer

	£
Premium received by D	30,000
Less £30,000 × 2% × (10-1)	(5,400)
	24,600
Less allowance for premium paid	
(£16,000 - (£16,000 × 39 × 2%)) × 10/40	(880)
Premium treated as rent	23,720

1.6 Reverse premiums

Lump sum payments are sometimes paid by a landlord to induce potential tenants to take out a lease. These payments are often called '**reverse premiums**'.

Reverse premiums are taxable on the recipient.

The timing of the tax charge (to income tax or corporation tax as appropriate) follows accepted accountancy practice and thus will be spread over the period in which the reverse premium is recognised in the accounts.

Where the person receiving the premium is a trader occupying the building for the purposes of his trade then the reverse premium received will be treated as income of the trade. In most other cases, such as a receipt by an intermediate landlord for a lease which will be sublet, the sum received will be taxed as income of the UK property business.

It should be noted that where receipts are taken into account to reduce the amount which qualifies for capital allowances the same amount will not also be charged to tax as a reverse premium.

1.7 Real Estate Investment Trusts (REITs)

From 1 January 2007 property companies will be able to operate as Real Estate Investment Trusts (REITs). They will be exempt from corporation tax on their property income and gains, but distributions paid to shareholders will be taxed as property income, not as company dividends.

Basic rate tax (22%) will be deducted at source from the distribution paid.

Distributions by REITs out of other income (ie not property income or gains) are taxed as dividends in the normal way.

Question — Income and REITs

Sue has a holding of shares in The Property Business which is a REIT. During 2006/07 she received a dividend from her investment of £6,240. She also has a salary of £30,000 and interest income (gross) of £1,000 in the year.

Calculate Sue's tax liability for 2006/07.

Answer

2006/07	*Non-savings Income*	*Savings Income*	*Total*
	£	£	£
Salary	30,000		
Dividend from REIT – Property income £6,240 × 100/78	8,000		
Interest		1,000	
STI	38,000	1,000	39,000
PA	(5,035)		
	32,965	1,000	33,965
Non-savings income			
£2,150 @ 10%			215
£30,815 @ 22%			6,779
Savings income			
335 @ 20%			67
665 @ 40%			266
Tax liability			7,327

Note. Dividends from REITs are taxed as property income not as company dividends. Basic rate tax (22%) is deducted at source from such distributions.

2 Furnished holiday lettings

FAST FORWARD

There are special rules for furnished holiday accommodation let on a commercial basis with a view to realisation of profit.

There are special rules for furnished holiday lettings. The letting is treated as if it were a trade. This means that, although the income is taxed as income from a UK property business, the provisions which apply to actual trades also apply to furnished holiday lettings, as follows.

(a) Relief for losses is available as if they were trading losses, including the facility to set losses against other income. The usual UK property business loss reliefs do not apply.

(b) Capital allowances are available on furniture: the renewals basis and the 10% wear and tear basis do not apply if capital allowances are claimed.

(c) The income qualifies as relevant UK earnings for pension relief (see later in this text).

(d) Capital gains tax rollover relief, business asset taper relief and relief for gifts of business assets are available (see later in this text).

Note, however, that the basis period rules for trades do not apply, and the profits or losses must be computed for tax years.

The letting must be of furnished accommodation made on a **commercial basis with a view to the realisation of profit**. The property must also satisfy the following three conditions.

(a) **The availability condition** – during the **relevant period**, the accommodation is available for **commercial let** as **holiday accommodation** to the **public** generally, for **at least 140 days**.

(b) **The letting condition** – during the **relevant period**, the accommodation is **commercially let** as holiday accommodation to members of the public **for at least 70 days**. If the **landlord has more than one FHL**, at least one of which satisfies the 40 day rule ('qualifying holiday accommodation') and at least one of which does not, ('the underused accommodation'), he may elect to **average the occupation of the qualifying holiday accommodation and any or all of the underused accommodation**. If the average of occupation is at least 70 days, the under-used accommodation will be treated as qualifying holiday accommodation.

(c) **The pattern of occupation condition** - during the **relevant period, not more that 155 days fall during periods of longer term occupation**. Longer term occupation is defined as **a continuous period of more than 31 days during which the accommodation is in the same occupation** unless there are abnormal circumstances.

The relevant period is normally the tax year. Where the FHL starts or ceases in a tax year, the relevant period is the 12 months beginning or ending with the first or last days of letting as appropriate.

If someone has furnished holiday lettings and other lettings, **draw up two profit and loss accounts as if they had two separate UK property businesses**. This is so that the profits and losses treated as trade profits and losses can be identified.

3 Rent a room relief

FAST FORWARD

The first £4,250 of rent received from letting a room or rooms in a main residence is tax free.

If an individual lets a room or rooms, furnished, in his or her main residence as living accommodation, then a special exemption may apply.

The limit on the exemption is gross rents (before any expenses or capital allowances) of £4,250 a year. This limit is halved if any other person (including the first person's spouse/civil partner) also received income from renting accommodation in the property while the property was the first person's main residence.

If gross rents (plus balancing charges arising because of capital allowances in earlier years) **are not more than the limit, the rents** (and balancing charges) **are wholly exempt from income tax** and expenses and capital allowances are ignored. However, the taxpayer may claim to ignore the exemption, for example to generate a loss by taking into account both rent and expenses.

If gross rents exceed the limit, the taxpayer will be taxed in the ordinary way, ignoring the rent a room scheme, unless he elects for the 'alternative basis'. If he so elects, he will be taxable on gross receipts plus balancing charges less £4,250 (or £2,125 if the limit is halved), with no deductions for expenses or capital allowances.

An election to ignore the exemption or an election for the alternative basis must be made by the 31 January which is 22 months from the end of the tax year concerned. An election to ignore the exemption applies only for the tax year for which it is made, but an election for the alternative basis remains in force until it is withdrawn or until a year in which gross rents do not exceed the limit.

Question

Rent a Room Relief

Sylvia owns a house near the sea in Norfolk. She has a spare bedroom and during 2006/07 this was let to a chef working at a nearby restaurant for £85 per week which includes the cost of heating, lighting etc.

Sylvia estimates that her lodger costs her an extra:

£50 on gas
£25 on electricity
£50 on insurance

each year.

How much property income must Sylvia pay tax on?

Answer

Sylvia has a choice;

(1) Total rental income of £85 × 52 = £4,420 exceeds £4,250 limit so taxable income is £170 (ie 4,420 – 4,250) if rent a room relief claimed.

(2) Alternatively she can be taxed on her actual profit;

	£
Rental income	4,420
Less: expenses (50 + 25 + 50)	(125)
	4,295

Sylvia would be advised to elect for option 1.

4 Interest income

FAST FORWARD Interest may be received with or without deduction of tax. It is taxed as savings income.

4.1 Interest received without deduction of tax

Interest is taxed as savings income. Some interest, such as bank and building society interest, is taxed at source. This has been discussed earlier in this text. Other interest is received without deduction of tax at source. Examples are interest on:

- Loans between individuals
- Government stocks (although the individual can opt to have the income paid net of tax if they prefer)
- Debentures and loan stocks of UK companies which are listed on a recognised Stock Exchange
- National Savings Bank accounts. (Eg Investment account, Easy Access Savings (EASA) account)

The amount of income taxable for a tax year is the amount arising in that year. Income arises when it is paid or credited: accrued income not yet paid or credited is ignored.

The rules for companies are different. These are covered later in this text.

4.2 Deeply discounted securities

Some securities are issued at a discount, that is the issue price is less than the redemption price. This is a way of giving investors an extra return in addition to interest. Small discounts are ignored for tax purposes, but if the discount is more than a certain percentage of the redemption price, it is taken into account. This percentage is the lower of 15% and the years from issue to redemption × 0.5%.

When an individual holding such a security sells or redeems it, the profit (selling price – purchase price) is taxed as savings income. We simply tax the profit, and do not give an indexation allowance or taper relief as we would for a capital gain.

These rules do not apply to companies because they take into account all profits and losses on securities, whether they arise from discounts or from some other cause. The rules for companies are covered later in this text.

5 Accrued income scheme

FAST FORWARD

The accrued income scheme taxes interest that arose up to the date that a security was sold cum interest and gives relief for interest arising between the sale and next interest payment date for sales ex interest.

If the owner of securities sells them before a certain date, he will not be entitled to the next interest payment on them. The new owner will receive it. This is called selling **cum interest.** However, the sale proceeds will include interest accrued to the date of sale.

If securities are sold after a certain date, they are sold **ex interest** and the original owner is entitled to the whole of the next interest payment despite the fact that he has sold the securities to a new owner. This time, the sale proceeds will exclude interest accruing after the date of sale.

Under the **accrued income scheme**, where securities are transferred the accrued interest reflected in the value of securities is taxed separately as savings income. The seller is treated as entitled to the proportion of interest which has accrued since the last interest payment. The buyer is entitled to relief against the interest he receives. This relief is equal to the amount assessable on the seller.

Conversely, where the transfer is ex interest, the seller will receive the whole of the next interest payment. He will be entitled to relief for the amount of interest assessed on the purchaser. The purchaser is treated as entitled to the proportion of the interest accrued between the sale and the next payment date and it is taxed as savings income.

The accrued income scheme does not apply where the seller:

- carries on a trade and the sale is taken into account in computing trading profits
- did not hold securities with a nominal value exceeding £5,000 during the tax year in which the interest period ends
- was neither resident nor ordinarily resident in the UK during any part of the period in question
- is taxed on the interest under the manufactured payment rules (not examinable)

Question — **Accrued income scheme**

Nigel bought £10,000 5% Loan Stock many years ago. Interest is payable on 30 June and 31 December each year. Nigel sells the loan stock to Evie on 30 November 2006 cum interest.

What are the amounts assessable for Nigel and Evie in respect of the loan stock for 2006/07?

Answer

Nigel

	£
Interest paid 30.6.06	
£10,000 x 5% x 6/12	250
Accrued interest deemed received 31.12.06	
£10,000 x 5% x 5/12	208
Total assessable	458

Evie

	£
Interest paid 31.12.06	
£10,000 x 5% x 6/12	250
Less: relief for accrued interest	
£10,000 x 5% x 5/12	(208)
Total assessable (ie 1 month's interest)	42

6 Dividend income

Cash dividends and stock dividends are treated as being received net of a 10% tax credit.

6.1 Introduction

We have already seen that **dividends from UK companies are received net of a 10% tax credit and are taxed at special rates**. This also applies to **distributions from authorised unit trusts and open ended investments companies (OEICs)**, other than distributions which are specifically designated as interest distributions.

6.2 Stock dividends

Sometimes a company will offer shares in lieu of a cash dividend. A shareholder who takes the shares receives a stock dividend. The amount of the stock dividend is:

(a) The cash alternative, if that equals the market value of the shares offered plus or minus 15%.

(b) The market value of the shares offered, if that differs from the cash alternative by more than 15% or if there is no cash alternative.

The shareholder is treated as receiving a gross dividend of the stock dividend × 100/90, with a tax credit of 10% of the gross dividend.

7 Miscellaneous income

FAST FORWARD

Some income is taxable as miscellaneous income if it does not fall in any other category.

Miscellaneous income includes:

- Income from royalties and other income from intellectual property
- Sales of patents and know how

- Income from settlements which is taxed as the Settlor's income
- Income from estates in administration
- Any other income which is not taxed any other provision (unless it is specifically exempt, for example casual earnings).

The income arising in a tax year is taxed in that year.

8 Pre-owned assets

FAST FORWARD

There is an income tax charge on the use of pre-owned assets such as land and chattels.

There is an income tax charge on the annual benefit of using or enjoying certain assets that were once owned by the user. The charge does not apply if the asset was sold to an unconnected person, or if it was sold at market value to a connected person either before 7 March 2005 or if the proceeds were not money or readily convertible assets.

There is no charge if the user pays a full market rent for the use of the asset. However, if less than a full rent is paid, any amount paid does not reduce the charge.

The charge applies to:

- **Land (the taxable amount is the annual rental value of the land)**
- **Chattels, such as works of art (the taxable amount is the value of the chattel multiplied by the official rate of interest), and**
- **Intangible property, such as cash and insurance policies, held in a trust where the settlor can benefit (the taxable amount is the value of the property multiplied by the official rate of interest, less any income or capital gains tax paid by the settlor in respect of that property).**

The property is valued at 6 April 2005, or, if later, the date the asset falls within the scope of the legislation. However land and chattels need only be valued every 5 years, as at the start of the tax year in which the relevant anniversary falls. Thus if a chattel first comes within the charge on 17 May 2006 it must be valued at that date and then on 6 April 2011.

There is no charge if the taxable amount is £5,000 or less. If this de minimus limit is exceeded the full amount is taxable.

There is no charge if the asset was disposed of before 18 March 1986 or if the disposition falls within the "gifts with reservation" rules so that the asset is treated as part of the taxpayer's estate for IHT purposes (see later in this text). **A taxpayer can choose to disapply the income tax charge by electing that the disposition should be treated as a gift with reservation**. The election must be made by 31 January following the first year in which the charge arises, ie by 31 January 2007 for all assets which were caught in 2005/06 (the first year the charge applied), or by 31 January 2008 for assets first caught in 2006/07.

There are various other exemptions including gifts between spouses and deeds of variation.

9 Trust income

FAST FORWARD

Income from trusts must be grossed up by either 100/60 (discretionary and accumulation & maintenance) or by 100/78, 100/80 or 100/90 (life tenant trusts).

A trust is a vehicle in which assets are legally owned by the trustees but for the benefit of the beneficiaries. There are two sorts of trust for income tax purposes:

(i) A life tenant trust (sometimes known as a life interest or interest in possession trust)
(ii) A discretionary or accumulating trust

Income from discretionary and accumulating trusts is received net of 40% tax. Gross it up in the income tax computation by multiplying by 100/60 and give credit for the tax already suffered when working out the final amount of tax payable. Such income is always treated as non-savings income.

If income from a life tenant trust is paid out of the trust's non-savings income, it will be received by the beneficiary net of 22% tax and must, therefore, be grossed up by multiplying by 100/78. If income from a life tenant trust has been paid out of the trust's savings (excl dividend) income then it is received net of 20% tax and must be grossed up by multiplying by 100/80. If it is paid out of dividend income it must be grossed up by multiplying by 100/90. This tax credit cannot be repaid. Each type of income is then taxed on the beneficiary under the normal rules.

Question — Income from trusts

Victoria, aged 6, received the following income in 2006/07.

	£
Building society interest (received net)	5,000
Dividends	2,250
Income from accumulation and maintenance trust	6,000
Income from life interest trust	780

The income from the life interest trust was paid out of the trust's rental income.

What income tax is payable by/repayable to Victoria?

Answer

	Non savings	*Savings*	*Dividends*	
	£	£	£	£
Building society interest (× 100/80)		6,250		
Dividends (× 100/90)			2,500	
Income from accumulation and maintenance trust (× 100/60)	10,000			
Income from life interest trust (× 100/78)	1,000			
	11,000	6,250	2,500	19,750
Less: PA	(5,035)			
	5,965	6,250	2,500	14,715

		£
Tax on non savings income	£2,150 × 10%	215
	£3,815 × 22%	839
Tax on savings (excl dividend) income	£6,250 × 20%	1,250
Tax on dividend income	£2,500 × 10%	250
		2,554
Less: Dividend tax credits		(250)
Tax on building society interest		(1,250)
A & M Trust		(4,000)
Life interest trust		(220)
Income tax repayable		(3,166)

Chapter roundup

- Income from a UK property business is computed for tax years on an accruals basis.
- A loss on a UK property business is carried forward to set against future profits from the UK property business.
- Part of the premium received on the grant of a short lease is taxed as rent. In addition any premiums paid to a tenant to induce him to take out a lease is also taxable as income from a UK property business, or as trading income if the tenant is in business.
- There are special rules for furnished holiday accommodation let on a commercial basis with a view to realisation of profit.
- The first £4,250 of rent received from letting a room or rooms in a main residence is tax free.
- The accrued income scheme taxes interest that arose up to the date that a security was sold cum interest and gives relief for interest arising between the sale and next interest payment date for sales ex interest.
- There is an income tax charge on the use of pre-owned assets such as land and chattels.
- Income from trusts must be grossed up by either 100/60 (discretionary and accumulating trusts) or by 100/78, 100/80 or 100/90 (life tenant trusts).

Quick quiz

1. Describe the renewals basis and the 10% wear and tear basis.
2. What relief is given when a lessee who paid a premium on the grant of a lease grants a sublease for a premium?
3. What are the conditions for a letting to be a furnished holiday letting?
4. A discretionary beneficiary receives £450 income from a trust. How much does the beneficiary enter as the gross amount in his tax return? Is it savings or non-savings income?

Answers to quick quiz

1. Renewals basis – no deduction for first furniture costs
   – replacement furniture is revenue expense

   10% wear and tear – cost of furniture ignored
   – annual deduction of 10% of rents (less water rates and council tax)

2. Deemed rent reduced by:

   $$\text{Rent part of premium for head lease} \times \frac{\text{duration of sub-lease}}{\text{duration of head lease}}$$

3. FHL is – available for letting at least 140 days per tax year
   – actually let at least 70 days per tax year
   – not in longer term occupation (more than 31 days) for not more than 155 days

4. $£450 \times \dfrac{100}{60}$ = £750 gross. Non savings income.

Now try the question below from the Exam Question Bank

Number	Level	Marks	Time
Q2	Examination	25	45 mins

3

Employment income

Introduction

Most people have jobs, which pay them wages or salaries. They may also get other benefits from their employers and/or they may pay expenses connected with their employment. In this chapter, we see how to work out the basic employment income they must pay tax on.

Topic list	Syllabus references
1 Employment income	1(d)
2 Taxable benefits	1(d)
3 Exempt benefits	1(d)
4 Allowable deductions	1(d)
5 Personal service companies	1(d)

1 Employment income

1.1 Outline of the charge

Employment income includes income arising from an employment under a contract of service (see below) and the income of office holders, such as directors. The term 'employee' is used in this text to mean anyone who receives employment income (ie both employees and directors).

There are two types of employment income:

- **General earnings**, and
- **Specific employment income**.

General earnings are an employees' earnings (see key term below) plus the 'cash equivalent' of any taxable non-monetary benefits.

Key term

'Earnings' means any salary, wage or fee, any gratuity or other profit or incidental benefit obtained by the employee if it is money or money's worth (something of direct monetary value or convertible into direct monetary value) or anything else which constitutes an emolument of the employment.

'Specific employment income' includes payments on termination of employment and share related income. This type of income is covered in the next chapter of this Study Text.

The residence and domicile status of an employee determines whether earnings are taxable. If an employee is resident, ordinarily resident and domiciled in the UK, **taxable earnings from an employment in a tax year are the general earnings received in that tax year**. The rules relating to other employees are dealt with later in this Study Text.

1.2 When are earnings received?

FAST FORWARD

General earnings are taxed in the year of receipt. Money earnings are generally received on the earlier of the time payment is made and the time entitlement to payment arises. Non-money earnings are generally received when provided.

General earnings consisting of money are treated as received at the earlier of:

- **The time when payment is made**
- **The time when a person becomes entitled to payment of the earnings.**

If the employee is a director of a company, earnings from the company are received on the earliest of:

- The earlier of the two alternatives given in the general rule (above)
- The time when the amount is credited in the company's accounting records
- The end of the company's period of account (if the amount was determined by then)
- The time the amount is determined (if after the end of the company's period of account).

Taxable benefits are generally treated as received when they are provided to the employee.

The receipts basis does not apply to pension income or taxable social security benefits. Both of these sources of income are taxed on the amount accruing in the tax year, whether or not it has actually been received in that year.

Question

When earnings received

John is a director of X Corp Ltd. His earnings for 2006/07 are;

Salary	£60,000
Taxable Benefits	£5,000

For the year ended 31 December 2006 the Board of Directors decide to pay John a bonus of £40,000. This is decided on 1 March 2007 at a board meeting and credited in the company accounts 7 days later. However John only received the bonus in his April pay on 30 April 2007.

What is John's taxable income from employment for 2006/07?

Answer

Salary	£60,000
Taxable benefits	5,000
Bonus (1.3.06) 1.03.07	40,000
Taxable employment Income	105,000

The salary and benefits were paid/made available during 2006/07 and hence taxed in 2006/07. The bonus was paid/made available on 30 April 2007 (2007/08) **but** was determined after the Company year end (31.12.06) by the board meeting on 1 March 2007 (2006/07) – hence taxed in 2006/07.

1.3 Net taxable earnings

Total taxable earnings less total allowable deductions (see below) **are net taxable earnings of a tax year. Deductions cannot usually create a loss: they can only reduce the net taxable earnings to nil.** If there is more than one employment in the tax year, separate calculations are required for each employment.

1.4 Person liable for tax on employment income

The person liable to tax on employment income is generally the **person to whose employment the earnings relate**. However, if the tax relates to general earnings received after the death of the person to whose employment the earnings relate, the person's personal representatives are liable for the tax. The tax is a liability of the estate.

1.5 Employment and self employment

FAST FORWARD

Employment involves a contract of service whereas self employment involves a contract for services.

The distinction between employment (receipts taxable as earnings) and self employment (receipts taxable as trading income) is a fine one. Employment involves a contract of service, whereas self employment involves a contract for services. Taxpayers tend to prefer self employment, because the rules on deductions for expenses are more generous.

Factors which may be of importance include:

- The degree of control exercised over the person doing the work
- Whether he must accept further work
- Whether the other party must provide further work
- Whether he provides his own equipment
- Whether he hires his own helpers

- What degree of financial risk he takes
- What degree of responsibility for investment and management he has
- Whether he can profit from sound management
- Whether he can work when he chooses
- The wording used in any agreement between the parties.

Relevant cases include:

(a) *Edwards v Clinch 1981*
A civil engineer acted occasionally as an inspector on temporary ad hoc appointments.

Held: there was no ongoing office which could be vacated by one person and held by another so the fees received were from self employment not employment.

(b) *Hall v Lorimer 1994*
A vision mixer was engaged under a series of short-term contracts.

Held: the vision mixer was self employed, not because of any one detail of the case but because the overall picture was one of self-employment.

(c) *Carmichael and Anor v National Power plc 1999*
Individuals engaged as visitor guides on a casual 'as required' basis were not employees. An exchange of correspondence between the company and the individuals was not a contract of employment as there was no provision as to the frequency of work and there was flexibility to accept work or turn it down as it arose. Sickness, holiday and pension arrangements did not apply and neither did grievance and disciplinary procedures.

A worker's status also affects national insurance contributions. The self-employed generally pay less than employees.

2 Taxable benefits

2.1 Introduction

FAST FORWARD

Most employees are taxed on benefits under the benefits code. 'Excluded employees' (lower paid/non-directors) are only subject to part of the provisions of the code.

The Income Tax (Earnings and Pensions) Act 2003 (ITEPA 2003) provides comprehensive legislation covering the taxation of benefits.

The legislation generally applies to all employees. However, only certain parts of it apply to 'excluded employees'.

(a) **An excluded employee is an employee in lower paid employment who is either not a director of a company or is a director but has no material interest in the company** ('material' means control of more than 5% of the ordinary share capital) and either:

  (i) **He is full time working director**, or
  (ii) **The company is non-profit-making or is established for charitable purposes only.**

(b) **The term 'director' refers to any person who acts as a director or any person in accordance with whose instructions the directors are accustomed to act** (other than a professional advisor).

(c) **Lower paid employment is one where the earnings rate for the tax year is less than £8,500**. To decide whether this applies, add together the **total earnings and benefits that would be taxable, if the employee were *not* an excluded employee**.

(d) A number of **specific deductions** must be taken into account to determine lower paid employment. These include **contributions to authorised pension schemes and payroll**

giving. However, general deductions from employment income (see later in this cha are not taken into account.

(e) Where a car is provided but the employee could have chosen an alternative benefit, an extra amount is added to the lower paid employment calculation. This amount is the higher of:

(i) the cash equivalents of the car benefit and of any fuel benefit, and
(ii) the amount which might be chargeable to tax as earnings.

Question

Excluded employee?

Tim earns £6,500 per annum working full time as a sales representative at Chap Co Ltd. The company provides the following staff benefits to Tim:

Private health insurance	£300
Company car	£1,500
Expense allowance	£2,000

Time used £1,900 of the expense allowance on business mileage petrol and on entertaining clients.

Is Tim an excluded employee?

Answer

No. Although Tim's taxable income is less than £8,500 this is only after his expense claim. The figure to consider and compare to £8,500 is the £10,300 as shown below.

Salary	6,500
Benefits: health insurance	300
car	1,500
expense allowance	2,000
Earnings to consider if Tim is lower paid	10,300
Less: claim for expenses paid out	(1,900)
Taxable income	8,400

2.2 General business expenses

If business expenses on such items as travel or hotel stays, are reimbursed by an employer, the reimbursed amount is a taxable benefit for employees other than excluded employees. To avoid being taxed on this amount, **an employee must then make a claim to deduct it as an expense** under the rules set out below. **In practice**, however, **many such expense payments are not reported to HMRC and can be ignored because it is agreed in advance that a claim to deduct them would be possible (a P11D dispensation**).

When an individual has to spend one or more nights away from home, his employer may reimburse expenses on items incidental to his absence (for example meals and private telephone calls). **Such incidental expenses are exempt** if:

(a) The expenses of travelling to each place where the individual stays overnight, throughout the trip, are incurred necessarily in the performance of the duties of the employment (or would have been, if there had been any expenses).

(b) The total (for the whole trip) of incidental expenses not deductible under the usual rules is no more than £5 for each night spent wholly in the UK and £10 for each other night. If this limit is exceeded, all of the expenses are taxable, not just the excess. The expenses include any VAT.

This incidental expenses exemption applies to expenses reimbursed, and to benefits obtained using credit tokens and non-cash vouchers.

2.3 Vouchers

If any employee (including an excluded employee):

(a) receives cash vouchers (vouchers exchangeable for cash)
(b) uses a credit token (such as a credit card) to obtain money, goods or services, or
(c) receives exchangeable vouchers (such as book tokens), also called non-cash vouchers

he is taxed on the cost of providing the benefit, less any amount made good.

However, the first 15p per working day of meal vouchers (eg luncheon vouchers) is not taxed. In addition, the first £55 per week of child care vouchers is exempt.

2.4 Accommodation

FAST FORWARD

The benefit in respect of accommodation is its annual value. There is an additional benefit if the property cost the employer over £75,000.

The taxable value of accommodation provided to an employee (including an excluded employee) is the rent that would have been payable if the premises had been let at their annual value (taken to be their **rateable value**). **If the premises are rented** rather than owned by the employer, then **the taxable benefit is the higher of the rent actually paid and the annual value**. If property does not have a rateable value HMRC estimate a value.

If a property cost the employer more than £75,000, an additional amount is chargeable:

(Cost of providing the accommodation - £75,000) × the official rate of interest at the start of the tax year.

Thus with an official rate of 5%, the total benefit for accommodation costing £90,000 and with an annual value of £2,000 would be £2,000 + £(90,000 – 75,000) × 5% = £2,750.

The 'cost of providing' the living accommodation is the aggregate of the cost of purchase and the cost of any improvements made before the start of the tax year for which the benefit is being computed. It is therefore not possible to avoid the charge by buying an inexpensive property requiring substantial repairs and improving it.

If a property was acquired more than six years before first being provided to the employee, the market value when first provided plus the cost of subsequent improvements is used as the cost of providing the accommodation. However, unless the actual cost plus improvements to the start of the tax year in question exceeds £75,000, the additional charge cannot be imposed, however high the market value. In addition, the additional charge can only be imposed if the employer owns (rather than rents) the property concerned.

Exam focus point

The 'official rate' of interest will be given to you in the exam.

There is no taxable benefit in respect of job related accommodation. Accommodation is job related if:

(a) Residence in the accommodation **is necessary for the proper performance of the employee's duties** (as with a caretaker), or

(b) The accommodation is provided **for the better performance of the employee's duties** and the employment is of a kind in which it is **customary for accommodation to be provided** (as with a policeman), or

(c) The **accommodation is provided as part of arrangements in force because of a special threat to the employee's security**.

Directors can only claim exemptions (a) or (b) if:

(i) They have no **material interest** ('material' means over 5%) in the company, and

(ii) Either they are **full time working directors** or the company is **non-profit making or is a charity**.

Any contribution paid by the employee is deducted from the annual value of the property and then from the additional benefit.

If the employee is given a cash alternative to living accommodation, the benefits code still applies in priority to treating the cash alternative as earnings. If the cash alternative is greater than the taxable benefit, the excess is treated as earnings.

2.5 Expenses connected with living accommodation

In addition to the benefit of living accommodation itself, **employees, other than excluded employees, are taxed on related expenses paid by the employer**, such as:

(a) **Heating, lighting or cleaning the premises**
(b) **Repairing, maintaining or decorating the premises**
(c) **The provision of furniture (the annual value is 20% of the cost)**

Unless the accommodation qualifies as 'job related' (as defined above) **the full cost of ancillary services** (excluding structural repairs) **is taxable. If the accommodation is 'job related'**, however, **taxable ancillary services are restricted to a maximum of 10% of the employee's 'net earnings'**. For this purpose, net earnings are all earnings from the employment (excluding the ancillary benefits (a) - (c) above) less any allowable expenses, statutory mileage allowances, contributions to approved occupational pension schemes and retirement annuity schemes (but not personal pension plans), and capital allowances. If there are ancillary benefits other than those falling within (a) - (c) above (such as a telephone) they are taxable in full.

Question — Expenses connected with living accommodation

Mr Quinton has a gross salary in 2006/07 of £28,850. He normally lives and works in London, but he is required to live in a company house in Scotland which cost £70,000 three years ago, so that he can carry out a two year review of his company's operations in Scotland. The annual value of the house is £650. In 2006/07 the company pays an electricity bill of £550, a gas bill of £400, a gardener's bill of £750 and redecoration costs of £1,800. Mr Quinton makes a monthly contribution of £50 for his accommodation. He also pays £1,450 occupational pension contributions.

Calculate Mr Quinton's taxable employment income for 2006/07.

Answer

	£	£
Salary		28,850
Less occupational pension scheme contributions		(1,450)
Net earnings		27,400
Accommodation benefits		
Annual value: exempt (job related)		
Ancillary services		
Electricity	550	
Gas	400	
Gardener	750	
Redecorations	1,800	
	3,500	
Restricted to 10% of £27,400	2,740	
Less employee's contribution	(600)	
		2,140
Employment income		29,540

Council tax and water or sewage charges paid by the employer are taxable in full as a benefit unless the accommodation is 'job-related'.

2.6 Cars

FAST FORWARD

Employees who have a company car are taxed on a % of the car's list price which depends on the level of the car's CO_2 emissions. The same % multiplied by £14,400 determines the benefit where private fuel is also provided. Authorised mileage allowances can be paid tax free to employees who use their own vehicle for business journeys.

A car provided by reason of the employment to an employee or member of his family or household for private use gives rise to a taxable benefit. This does not apply to excluded employees. **'Private use' includes home to work travel.**

(a) A tax charge arises whether the car is provided by the employer or by some other person. The benefit is computed as shown below, even if the car is taken as an alternative to another benefit of a different value.

(b) The starting point for calculating a car benefit is the list price of the car (plus accessories). **The percentage of the list price that is taxable depends on the car's CO_2 emissions.**

(c) The price of the car is the sum of the following items.

  (i) The list price of the car for a single retail sale at the time of first registration, including charges for delivery and standard accessories. The manufacturer's, importer's or distributor's list price must be used, even if the retailer offered a discount. A notional list price is estimated if no list price was published.

  (ii) The price (including fitting) of all optional accessories provided when the car was first provided to the employee, excluding mobile telephones and equipment needed by a disabled employee. The extra cost of adapting or manufacturing a car to run on road fuel gases is not included.

  (iii) The price (including fitting) of all optional accessories fitted later and costing at least £100 each, excluding mobile telephones and equipment needed by a disabled employee. Such accessories affect the taxable benefit from and including the tax year in which they are fitted. However, accessories which are merely replacing existing accessories and are not superior to the ones replaced are ignored. Replacement accessories which *are* superior are taken into account, but the cost of the old accessory is then ignored.

(d) There is a special rule for classic cars. If the car is at least 15 years old (from the time of first registration) at the end of the tax year, and its market value at the end of the year (or, if earlier, when it ceased to be available to the employee) is over £15,000 and greater than the price found under (c), that market value is used instead of the price. The market value takes account of all accessories (except mobile telephones and equipment needed by a disabled employee).

(e) Capital contributions are payments by the employee in respect of the price of the car or accessories. In any tax year, we take account of capital contributions made in that year and previous years (for the same car). The maximum deductible capital contributions is £5,000: contributions beyond that total are ignored.

(f) If the price or value found under (c) or (d) exceeds £80,000, then £80,000 is used instead of the price or value. This £80,000 is after capital contributions (see (e) above) have been taken into account.

(g) For cars that emit **CO_2 of 140g/km (2006/07) or less, the taxable benefit is 15% of the car's list price. This percentage increases by 1% for every 5g/km (rounded down to the nearest multiple of 5) by which CO_2 emissions exceed 140g/km up to a maximum of 35%.**

Exam focus point

> The CO_2 baseline figure will be given to you in the tax rates and allowances section of the exam paper.

(h) Diesel cars have a supplement of 3% of the car's list price added to the taxable benefit. However, the benefit is discounted for cars that are particularly environmentally friendly. The maximum percentage, however, remains 35% of the list price.

(i) Cars which do not have an approved CO_2 emissions figure are taxed according to engine size.

(j) **The benefit is reduced on a time basis where a car is first made available or ceases to be made available during the tax year** or is incapable of being used for a continuous period of not less than 30 days (for example because it is being repaired).

(k) **The benefit is reduced by any payment the user must make for the private use of the car** (as distinct from a capital contribution to the cost of the car). Payments for insuring the car do not count *(IRC v Quigley 1995)*. The benefit cannot become negative to create a deduction from the employee's income.

(l) Pool cars are exempt. A car is a pool car if **all** the following conditions are satisfied.

- It is used by more than one employee and is not ordinarily used by any one of them to the exclusion of the others.
- Any private use is merely incidental to business use.
- It is not normally kept overnight at or near the residence of an employee.

There are many ancillary benefits associated with the provision of cars, such as insurance, repairs, vehicle licences and a parking space at or near work. No extra taxable benefit arises as a result of these, with the exception of the cost of providing a driver.

2.7 Fuel for cars

Where fuel is provided there is a further benefit in addition to the car benefit.

No taxable benefit arises where either

(a) **All the fuel provided was made available only for business travel**, or

(b) **The employee is required to make good, and has made good, the whole of the cost of any fuel provided for his private use**.

Unlike most benefits, a reimbursement of only part of the cost of the fuel available for private use does not reduce the benefit.

The taxable benefit is a percentage of a base figure. The base figure for 2006/07 is £14,400. The percentage is the same percentage as is used to calculate the car benefit (see above).

Exam focus point

> The fuel base figure will be given to you in the tax rates and allowances section of the exam paper.

The fuel benefit is reduced in the same way as the car benefit **if the car is not available for 30 days or more**.

The fuel benefit is also reduced if private fuel is not available for part of a tax year. However, if private fuel later becomes available in the same tax year, the reduction is not made. If, for example, fuel is provided from 6 April 2006 to 30 June 2006, then the fuel benefit for 2006/07 will be restricted to just three months. This is because the provision of fuel has permanently ceased. However, if fuel is provided from 6 April 2006 to 30 June 2006, and then again from 1 September 2006 to 5 April 2007, then the fuel benefit will not be reduced since the cessation was only temporary.

Question — Car and fuel benefit

An employee was provided with a new car (2,500 cc) costing £15,000. The car emits 191g/km of CO_2. During 2006/07 the employer spent £900 on insurance, repairs and a vehicle licence. The firm paid for all petrol, costing £1,500, without reimbursement. The employee paid the firm £270 for the private use of the car. Calculate the taxable benefit.

Answer

Round CO_2 emissions figure down to the nearest 5, ie 190 g/km.

Amount by which CO_2 emissions exceed the baseline:

(190 – 140) = 50 g/km

Divide by 5 = 10

Taxable percentage = 15% + 10% = 25%

	£
Car benefit £15,000 × 25%	3,750
Fuel benefit £14,400 × 25%	3,600
	7,350
Less contribution towards use of car	(270)
	7,080

If the contribution of £270 had been towards the petrol the benefit would have been £7,350.

2.8 Vans and heavier commercial vehicles

If a van (of normal maximum laden weight up to 3,500 kg) **is made available for an employee's private use, there is an annual scale charge of £500, or £350 if the van is at least four years old at the end of the tax year**. The scale charge covers ancillary benefits such as insurance and servicing. Paragraphs 2.6 (j) and (k) above apply to vans as they do to cars.

There is , however, **no taxable benefit where an employee takes a van home** (ie uses the van for home to work travel) but is not allowed any other private use.

From 6 April 2007, the **discount for older vans** will be removed and the **scale charge will rise to £3,000** for unrestricted private use. In addition, if the employer provides **fuel for unrestricted private use**, an additional **fuel charge of £500** will apply.

If a commercial vehicle of normal maximum laden weight over 3,500 kg is made available for an employee's private use, but the employee's use of the vehicle is not wholly or mainly private, no taxable benefit arises except in respect of the provision of a driver.

2.9 Statutory mileage allowances

A single authorised mileage allowance for business journeys in an employee's own vehicle applies to all cars and vans. There is no income tax on payments up to this allowance and employers do not have to report mileage allowances up to this amount. The allowance for 2006/07 is 40p per mile on the first 10,000 miles in the tax year with each additional mile over 10,000 miles at 25p per mile. The authorised mileage allowance for employees using their own motor cycle is 24p per mile. For employees using their own pedal cycle it is 20p per mile.

If employers pay less than the statutory allowance, employees can claim tax relief up to that level.

The statutory allowance does not prevent employers from paying higher rates, but any excess will be subject to income tax. There is a similar (but slightly different) system for NICs, covered later in this text.

Employers can make income tax and NIC free payments of up to 5p per mile for each fellow employee making the same business trip who is carried as a passenger. If the employer does not pay the employee for carrying business passengers, the employee cannot claim any tax relief.

Question — **Mileage allowance**

Sophie uses her own car for business travel. During 2006/07, Sophie drove 15,400 miles in the performance of her duties. Sophie's employer paid her 35p a mile. How is the mileage allowance received by Sophie treated for tax purposes?

Answer

	£
Mileage allowance received (15,400 × 35p)	5,390
Less: tax free [(10,000 × 40p) + (5,400 × 25p)]	(5,350)
Taxable benefit	40

£5,350 is tax free and the excess amount received of £40 is a taxable benefit.

2.10 Beneficial loans

FAST FORWARD

Taxable cheap loans are charged to tax on the difference between the official rate of interest and any interest paid by the employee.

2.10.1 Introduction

Employment related loans to employees (other than excluded employees) and their relatives give rise to a benefit equal to:

(a) **Any amounts written off** (unless the employee has died), and

(b) **The excess of the interest based on an official rate prescribed by the Treasury, over any interest actually charged ('taxable cheap loan')**. Interest payable during the tax year but paid after the end of the tax year is taken into account, but if the benefit is determined before such interest is paid a claim must be made to take it into account.

The following loans are normally not treated as taxable cheap loans for calculation of the interest benefits (but not for the purposes of the charge on loans written off).

(a) A loan on normal commercial terms made in the ordinary course of the employer's money-lending business.

(b) A loan made by an individual in the ordinary course of the lender's domestic, family or personal arrangements.

2.10.2 Calculating the interest benefit

There are two alternative methods of calculating the taxable benefit. The simpler **'average' method** automatically applies unless the taxpayer or HMRC elect for the alternative **'strict' method**. (HMRC normally only make the election where it appears that the 'average' method is being deliberately exploited.) In both methods, the benefit is the interest at the official rate minus the interest payable.

The 'average' method averages the balances at the beginning and end of the tax year (or the dates on which the loan was made and discharged if it was not in existence throughout the tax year) and applies the official rate of interest to this average. If the loan was not in existence throughout the tax year only the number of complete tax months (from the 6th of the month) for which it existed are taken into account.

The 'strict' method is to compute interest at the official rate on the actual amount outstanding on a daily basis.

Question — **Loan benefit**

At 6 April 2006 a taxable cheap loan of £30,000 was outstanding to an employee earning £12,000 a year, who repaid £20,000 on 7 December 2006. The remaining balance of £10,000 was outstanding at 5 April 2007. Interest paid during the year was £250. What was the benefit under both methods for 2006/07, assuming that the official rate of interest was 5%?

Answer

Average method

	£
$5\% \times \frac{30,000+10,000}{2}$	1,000
Less interest paid	(250)
Benefit	750

Alternative method (strict method)

	£
$£30,000 \times \frac{245}{365}$ (6 April - 6 December) $\times 5\%$	1,007
$£10,000 \times \frac{120}{365}$ (7 December - 5 April) $\times 5\%$	164
	1,171
Less interest paid	(250)
Benefit	921

HMRC might opt for the alternative method.

2.10.3 The de minimis test

The benefit is not taxable if:

(a) The **total of all taxable cheap loans to the employee did not exceed £5,000** at any time in the tax year, or

(b) **The loan is not a qualifying loan and the total of all non-qualifying loans to the employee did not exceed £5,000** at any time in the tax year.

A qualifying loan is one on which all or part of any interest paid would qualify as a charge.

When the £5,000 threshold is exceeded, a benefit arises on interest on the whole loan, not just on the excess of the loan over £5,000.

When a loan is written off and a benefit arises, there is no £5,000 threshold: writing off a loan of £1 gives rise to a £1 benefit.

2.10.4 Qualifying loans

If the whole of the interest payable on a qualifying loan is eligible for tax relief, then no taxable benefit arises. If the interest is only partly eligible for tax relief, then the employee is treated as receiving earnings because the actual rate of interest is below the official rate. He is also treated as paying interest equal to those earnings. This **deemed interest paid may qualify as a business expense or as a charge in addition to any interest actually paid.**

Question

Beneficial loans

Anna, who is single, has an annual salary of £30,000, and two loans from her employer.

(a) A season ticket loan of £2,300 at no interest

(b) A loan, 90% of which was used to buy shares in her employee-controlled company, of £54,000 at 3% interest

The official rate of interest is to be taken as 5%.

What is Anna's tax liability for 2006/07?

Answer

	£
Salary	30,000
Season ticket loan: not over £5,000	0
Loan to buy shares £54,000 × (5 –3 = 2%)	1,080
Earnings	31,080
Less: charge on income (£54,000 × 5%× 90%)	(2,430)
	28,650
Less personal allowance	(5,035)
Taxable income	23,615
Income tax	
£2,150 × 10%	215
£21,465 × 22%	4,722
Tax liability	4,937

2.11 Other assets made available for private use

FAST FORWARD

20% of the value of assets made available for private use is taxable.

When assets are made available to employees or members of their family or household, the taxable benefit is the higher of 20% of the market value when first provided as a benefit to any employee, or on the rent paid by the employer if higher. The 20% charge is time-apportioned when the asset is provided for only part of the year. The charge after any time apportionment is reduced by any contribution made by the employee.

Certain assets, such as bicycles provided for journeys to work, are exempt. These are described later in this chapter.

There is an exemption for computers made available by employers for private use prior to 6 April 2006 for the first £500 worth of benefit.

For example on 6 April 2005 Jane is provided with a new laptop costing £2,800 by her employer. The taxable benefit for 2005/06 is £60 as follows:

£2,800 × 20%	£560
Less exemption	(500)
Taxable benefit	60

The £60 taxable benefit will also be the amount taxed in 2006/07 on Jane. However if the computer had been provided new on 6 April 2006 Jane's 2006/07 benefit would be £560.

If an asset made available is subsequently acquired by the employee, **the taxable benefit on the acquisition is the *greater* of:**

- The **current market value minus the price paid by the employee**.
- The **market value when first provided minus any amounts already taxed (ignoring contributions by the employee) minus the price paid by the employee**.

This rule prevents tax free benefits arising on rapidly depreciating items through the employee purchasing them at their low second-hand value.

There is an exception to this rule for bicycles which have previously been provided as exempt benefits. The taxable benefit on acquisition is restricted to current market value, minus the price paid by the employee. This also applies to computers which were first provided before 6 April 2006.

2.12 Example: assets made available for private use

A suit costing £400 is purchased by an employer for use by an employee on 6 April 2005. On 6 April 2006 the suit is purchased by the employee for £30, its market value then being £50.

The benefit in 2005/06 is £400 × 20%	£80

The benefit in 2006/07 is £290, being the *greater* of:

		£
(a)	Market value at acquisition by employee	50
	Less price paid	(30)
		20
(b)	Original market value	400
	Less taxed in respect of use	(80)
		320
	Less price paid	(30)
		290

Question — **Bicycles**

Rupert is provided with a new bicycle by his employer on 6 April 2006. The bicycle is available for private use as well as commuting to work. It cost the employer £1,500 when new. On 6 October 2006 the employer transfers ownership of the bicycle to Rupert when it is worth £800. Rupert does not pay anything for the bicycle.

What is the total taxable benefit on Rupert for 2006/07 in respect of the bicycle?

Answer

	£
Use benefit	*Exempt*
Transfer benefit (use MV at acquisition by employee only)	
MV at transfer	800

2.13 Scholarships

If scholarships are given to members an employee's family, the **employee is taxable on the cost** unless the scholarship fund's or scheme's payments by reason of people's employments are not more than 25% of its total payments.

2.14 Residual charge

FAST FORWARD: There is a residual charge for other benefits, usually equal to the cost of the benefits.

We have seen above how certain specific benefits are taxed. **A 'residual charge' is made on the taxable value of other benefits. In general, the taxable value of a benefit is the cost of the benefit less any part of that cost made good by the employee to the persons providing the benefit.**

The residual charge applies to any benefit provided for an employee or a member of his family or household, by reason of the employment. There is an exception where the employer is an individual and the provision of the benefit is made in the normal course of the employer's domestic, family or personal relationships.

This rule does not apply to taxable benefits provided to excluded employees. **These employees are taxed only on the second hand value of any benefit that could be converted into money**.

3 Exempt benefits

FAST FORWARD: Some benefits are exempt from tax such as removal expenses and childcare (subject to certain limits).

Various benefits are exempt from tax. These include:

(a) **Entertainment provided to employees by genuine third parties** (eg seats at sporting/cultural events), even if it is provided by giving the employee a voucher.

(b) **Gifts of goods** (or vouchers exchangeable for goods) from third parties (ie not provided by the employer or a person connected to the employer) if the total cost (incl. VAT) of all gifts by the same donor to the same employee in the tax year is £250 or less. If the £250 limit is exceeded, the full amount is taxable, not just the excess.

(c) **Non-cash awards for long service** if the period of service was at least 20 years, no similar award was made to the employee in the past 10 years and the cost is not more than £50 per year of service.

(d) **Awards under staff suggestion schemes if**:

- (i) There is a formal scheme, open to all employees on equal terms.
- (ii) The suggestion is outside the scope of the employee's normal duties.
- (iii) Either the award is not more than £25, or the award is only made after a decision is taken to implement the suggestion.
- (iv) Awards over £25 reflect the financial importance of the suggestion to the business, and either do not exceed 50% of the expected net financial benefit during the first year of implementation or do not exceed 10% of the expected net financial benefit over a period of up to five years.
- (v) Awards of over £25 are shared on a reasonable basis between two or more employees putting forward the same suggestion.

If an award exceeds £5,000, the excess is always taxable.

(e) **The first £8,000 of removal expenses if:**

- (i) The employee does not already live within a reasonable daily travelling distance of his new place of employment, but will do so after moving.
- (ii) The expenses are incurred or the benefits provided by the end of the tax year following the tax year of the start of employment at the new location.

(f) The cost of running a **workplace nursery or play scheme (without limit). Otherwise up to £55 a week of childcare is tax free** if the employer contracts with an approved childcare or provides childcare vouchers to pay an approved childcare. The childcare must be available to all employees and the childcare must either be registered or approved home-childcare.

(g) **Sporting or recreational facilities available to employees generally and not to the general public**, unless they are provided on domestic premises, or they consist in an interest in or the use of any mechanically propelled vehicle or any overnight accommodation. Vouchers only exchangeable for such facilities are also exempt, but membership fees for sports clubs are taxable.

(h) **Assets or services used in performing the duties of employment** provided any private use of the item concerned is insignificant. This exempts, for example, the benefit arising on the private use of employer-provided tools.

(i) **Welfare counselling** and similar minor benefits if the benefit concerned is available to employees generally.

(j) **Bicycles or cycling safety equipment provided to enable employees to get to and from work or to travel between one workplace and another**. The equipment must be available to the employer's employees generally. Also, it must be used mainly for the aforementioned journeys.

(k) **Workplace parking**

(l) **Up to £7,000 a year paid to an employee who is on a full-time course lasting at least a year**, with average full-time attendance of at least 20 weeks a year. If the £7,000 limit is exceeded, the whole amount is taxable.

(m) **Work related training and related costs. This includes the costs of** training material and assets either made during training or incorporated into something so made.

(n) **Air miles or car fuel coupons** obtained as a result of business expenditure but used for private purposes.

(o) **The cost of work buses and minibuses or subsidies to public bus services.**

A works bus must have a seating capacity of 12 or more and a works minibus a seating capacity of 9 or more but not more than 12 and be available generally to employees of the employer concerned. The bus or minibus must mainly be used by employees for journeys to and from work and for journeys between workplaces.

(p) Transport/overnight costs where public transport is disrupted by industrial action, late night taxis and travel costs incurred where car sharing arrangements unavoidably breakdown.

(q) The private use of one **mobile phone**. Top up vouchers for exempt mobile phones are also tax free. If more than one mobile phone is provided to an employee for private use only the second or subsequent phone is a taxable benefit valued using "cost of provision to the employer".

(r) **Employer provided uniforms** which employees must wear as part of their duties.

(s) The cost of **staff parties** which are open to staff generally provided that the **cost per staff member per year (including VAT) is £150 or less**. The £150 limit may be split between several parties. If exceeded, the full amount is taxable, not just the excess over £150.

(t) **Private medical insurance premiums paid to cover treatment when the employee is outside the UK in the performance of his duties**. Other medical insurance premiums are taxable as is the cost of medical diagnosis and treatment except for routine check ups. Eye tests and glasses for employees using VDUs are exempt.

(u) **The first 15p per day of meal vouchers (eg luncheon vouchers).**

(v) Cheap loans **that do not exceed £5,000** at any time in the tax year (see earlier).

(w) **Job related accommodation.**

(x) **Employer contributions towards additional household costs incurred by an employee who works wholly or partly at home**. Payments up to £2 pw (£104 pa) may be made without supporting evidence. Payments in excess of that amount require supporting evidence that the payment is wholly in respect of additional household expenses.

(y) **Meals or refreshments for cyclists** provided as part of official 'cycle to work' days.

(z) Computers provided to employees prior to 6 April 2006 – first £500 of benefit is exempt (see earlier in this text)

Where a voucher is provided for a benefit which is exempt from income tax the provision of the voucher itself is also exempt.

4 Allowable deductions

FAST FORWARD

To be deductible, expenses must be for qualifying travel or wholly, exclusively and necessarily incurred.

4.1 General principles

Certain expenditure is specifically deductible in computing net taxable earnings:

(a) **Contributions** (within certain limits) **to approved occupational pension schemes**.

(b) **Subscriptions to professional bodies** on the list of bodies issued by HMRC (which includes most UK professional bodies), if relevant to the duties of the employment

(c) Payments for certain **liabilities relating to the employment** and for insurance against them (see below)

(d) **Payments to charity made under the payroll deduction scheme** operated by an employer

(e) **Mileage allowance** relief (see above)

Otherwise, **allowable deductions are notoriously hard to obtain. They are limited to**:

- **Qualifying travel expenses** (see below)
- **Other expenses the employee is obliged to incur and pay as holder of the employment which are incurred wholly, exclusively and necessarily in the performance of the duties of the employment**
- **Capital allowances on plant and machinery (other than cars or other vehicles) necessarily provided for use in the performance of those duties.**

4.2 Liabilities and insurance

If a director or employee incurs a liability related to his employment or pays for insurance against such a liability, the cost is a deductible expense. If the employer pays such amounts, there is no taxable benefit.

A liability relating to employment is one which is imposed in respect of the employee's acts or omissions as employee. Thus, for example, liability for negligence would be covered. Related costs, for example the costs of legal proceedings, are included.

For insurance premiums to qualify, the insurance policy must:

(a) Cover only liabilities relating to employment, vicarious liability in respect of liabilities of another person's employment, related costs and payments to the employee's own employees in respect of their employment liabilities relating to employment and related costs, and

(b) It must not last for more than two years (although it may be renewed for up to two years at a time), and the insured person must not be not required to renew it.

4.3 Travel expenses

Tax relief is not available for an employee's normal commuting costs. This means relief is not available for any costs an employee incurs in getting from home to his normal place of work. However **employees are entitled to relief for travel expenses which basically are the full costs that they are obliged to incur and pay as holder of the employment in travelling in the performance of their duties or travelling to or from a place which they have to attend in the performance of their duties (other than a permanent workplace).**

4.4 Example: travel in the performance of duties

Judi is an accountant. She often travels to meetings at the firm's offices in the North of England returning to her office in Leeds after the meetings. Relief is available for the full cost of these journeys as the travel is undertaken in the performance of her duties.

Question

Relief for travelling costs

Zoe lives in Wycombe and normally works in Chiswick. Occasionally she visits a client in Wimbledon and travels direct from home. Distances are shown in the diagram below:

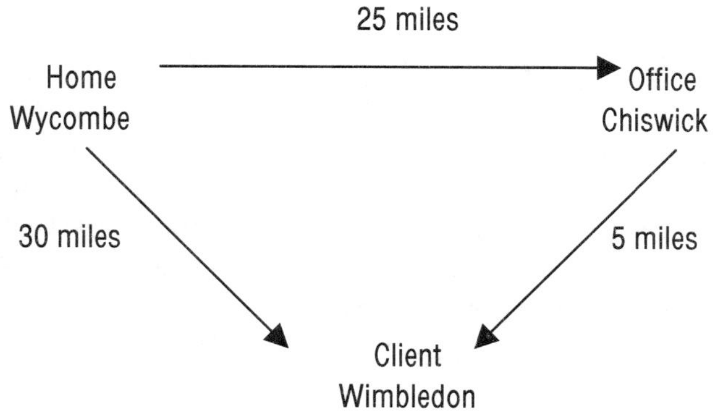

What tax relief is available for Zoe's travel costs?

Answer

Zoe is not entitled to tax relief for the costs incurred in travelling between Wycombe and Chiswick since these are normal commuting costs. However, relief is available for all costs that Zoe incurs when she travels from Wycombe to Wimbledon to visit her client.

To prevent manipulation of the basic rule normal commuting will not become a business journey just because the employee stops en-route to perform a business task (eg make a 'phone call'). Nor will relief be available if the journey is essentially the same as the employee's normal journey to work.

4.5 Example: normal commuting

Judi is based at her office in Leeds City Centre. One day she is required to attend a 9.00 am meeting with a client whose premises are around the corner from her Leeds office. Judi travels from home directly to the meeting. As the journey is substantially the same as her ordinary journey to work relief is not available.

Site based employees (eg construction workers, management consultants etc) who do not have a permanent workplace, are entitled to relief for the costs of all journeys made from home to wherever they are working. This is because these employees do not have an ordinary commuting journey or any normal commuting costs. However there is a caveat that the employee does not spend more than 24 months of continuous work at any one site.

Tax relief is available for travel, accommodation and subsistence expenses incurred by an employee who is working at a temporary workplace on a secondment expected to last up to 24 months. If a secondment is initially expected not to exceed 24 months, but it is extended, relief ceases to be due from the date the employee becomes aware of the change. When looking at how long a secondment is expected to last, HMRC will consider not only the terms of the written contract but also any verbal agreement by the employer and other factors such as whether the employee buys a house etc.

Question **Temporary workplace**

Philip works for Vastbank at its Newcastle City Centre branch. Philip is sent to work full-time at another branch in Morpeth for 20 months at the end of which he will return to the Newcastle branch. Morpeth is about 20 miles north of Newcastle.

What travel costs is Philip entitled to claim as a deduction?

Answer

Although Philip is spending all of his time at the Morpeth branch it will not be treated as his normal work place because his period of attendance will be less than 24 months. Thus Philip can claim relief in full for the costs of travel from his home to the Morpeth branch.

There is also tax relief for certain travel expenses relating to overseas employment. These are dealt with later in this text.

4.6 Other expenses

The word 'exclusively' strictly implies that the expenditure must give no private benefit at all. If it does, none of it is deductible. In practice inspectors may ignore a small element of private benefit or make an apportionment between business and private use.

Whether an expense is 'necessary' is not determined by what the employer requires. The test is whether the duties of the employment could not be performed without the outlay.

- *Sanderson v Durbridge 1955*
  The cost of evening meals taken when attending late meetings was not deductible because it was not incurred in the performance of the duties.
- *Blackwell v Mills 1945*
  As a condition of his employment, an employee was required to attend evening classes. The cost of his textbooks and travel was not deductible because it was not incurred in the performance of the duties.
- *Lupton v Potts 1969*
  Examination fees incurred by a solicitor's articled clerk were not deductible because they were incurred neither wholly nor exclusively in the performance of the duties, but in furthering the clerk's ambition to become a solicitor.
- *Brown v Bullock 1961*
  The expense of joining a club that was virtually a requisite of an employment was not deductible because it would have been possible to carry on the employment without the club membership, so the expense was not necessary.
- *Elwood v Utitz 1965*
  A managing director's subscriptions to two residential London clubs were claimed by him as an expense on the grounds that they were cheaper than hotels.

  The expenditure was deductible as it was necessary in that it would be impossible for the employee to carry out his London duties without being provided with first class accommodation. The residential facilities (which were cheaper than hotel accommodation) were given to club members only.

- *Lucas v Cattell 1972*
  The cost of business telephone calls on a private telephone is deductible, but **no part of the line or** telephone **rental charges is deductible**.
- *Fitzpatrick v IRC 1994; Smith v Abbott 1994*
  Journalists cannot claim a deduction for the cost of buying newspapers which they read to keep themselves informed, since they are merely preparing themselves to perform their duties.

The cost of clothes for work is not deductible, except that for certain trades requiring protective clothing there are annual deductions on a set scale.

An employee required to work at home may be able to claim a deduction for an appropriate proportion of his or her expenditure on lighting, heating and (if a room is used exclusively for work purposes) **the council tax.** Employers can pay up to £2 per week without the need for supporting evidence of the costs incurred by the employee. Payments above the £2 limit require evidence of the employee's actual costs.

5 Personal service companies

FAST FORWARD

The IR35 provisions prevent avoidance of tax by providing services through a company.

5.1 Application and outline of computation

We looked at the distinction between employment and self employment earlier in this chapter. Taxpayers normally prefer to avoid being classified as employees. Consequently, there are anti-avoidance rules which prevent workers avoiding tax and National Insurance contributions by offering their services through an intermediary, such as a personal service company. **These provisions are commonly known as the IR35 provisions**.

Broadly, the IR35 provisions provide that

(a) if an individual ('the worker') performs, or has an obligation to perform, services for 'a client'; and

(b) the performance of those services is referable to arrangements involving a third party (eg the personal service company), rather than referable to a contract between the client and the worker; and

(c) if the services were to be performed by the worker under a contract between himself and the client, he would be regarded as employed by the client

then **a salary payment may be deemed to have been made to the worker at the end of the tax year**. This deemed payment is subject to PAYE and NICs.

The following steps should be followed to compute the amount of the deemed payment.

Step 1 **Take 95% of all payments and benefits received in respect of the relevant engagements by the third party**.

Step 2 **Add amounts received in respect of the relevant engagements by the worker otherwise than from the third party**, if they are not chargeable as employment income, but would have been so chargeable if the worker had been employed by the client.

Step 3 **Deduct expenses met by the third party** if those expenses would have been deductible had they been paid out of the taxable earnings of the employment by the worker. This also includes expenses paid by the worker and reimbursed by the third party. Mileage allowances up to the statutory amounts are also deductible where a vehicle is provided by the third party.

Step 4 **Deduct capital allowances on expenditure incurred by the third party** if the worker would have been able to deduct them had he incurred the expenditure and had he been employed by the client.

Step 5 **Deduct any 'approved' pension contributions and employer's NICs paid by the third party** in respect of the worker.

Step 6 **Deduct amounts received by the worker from the third party** that are chargeable as employment income but were not deducted under Step 3.

Step 7 Find the amount that together with employer's NIC (see later in this text) on it, is equal to the amount resulting from Step 6 above. This means that you should multiply the amount in Step 6 by 12.8/112.8 and deduct this amount from the amount in Step 6.

Step 8 The result is the amount of the deemed employment income.

5.2 Example

Alison offers technical writing services through a company. During 2006/07 the company received income of £40,000 in respect of relevant engagements performed by Alison. The company paid Alison a salary of £20,000 plus employer's NIC of £1,916. The company also pays £3,000 into an occupational pension scheme in respect of Alison. Alison incurred travelling expenses of £400 in respect of the relevant engagements.

The deemed employment income taxed on Alison is

	£
Income (£40,000 × 95%)	38,000
Less: travel	(400)
pension	(3,000)
employer NIC	(1,916)
Salary	(20,000)
	12,684
Less: employer's NIC	
$\frac{12.8}{112.8} \times$ £12,684	(1,439)
Deemed employment income	11,245

Chapter roundup

- General earnings are taxed in the year of receipt. Money earnings are generally received on the earlier of the time payment is made and the time entitlement to payment arises. Non-money earnings are generally received when provided.
- Employment involves a contract of service whereas self employment involves a contract for services.
- Most employees are taxed on benefits under the benefits code. 'Excluded employees' (lower paid/non-directors) are only subject to part of the provisions of the code.
- The benefit in respect of accommodation is its annual value. There is an additional benefit if the property cost over £75,000.
- Employees who have a company car are taxed on a % of the car's list price which depends on the level of the car's CO_2 emissions. The same % multiplied by £14,400 determines the benefit where private fuel is also provided. Authorised mileage allowances can be paid tax free to employees who use their own vehicle for business journeys.
- Taxable cheap loans are charged to tax on the difference between the official rate of interest and any interest paid by the employee.
- 20% of the value of assets made available for private use is taxable.
- There is a residual charge for other benefits, usually equal to the cost of the benefits.
- To be deductible, expenses must be for qualifying travel or wholly, exclusively and necessarily incurred.
- The IR35 provisions prevent avoidance of tax by providing services through a company.

Quick quiz

1. Ben is paid £14,000 per annum. For the Company year ended 31 December 2006 he is paid a £5,000 bonus on 1 May 2007. He was paid a similar bonus of £3,000 on 1 May 2006 based on the year ended 31 December 2005 results. How much is Ben's taxable income for 2006/07? Ben is not a director.
2. What accommodation does not give rise to a taxable benefit?
3. Josh was provided with a company car on 1 July 2006. It cost £25,000 and has a CO_2 emission of 160g/km. Josh uses the car 60% for business use as a sales representative. The company pays for Josh's private diesel for use in the car. What is Josh's benefit(s) in respect of the car?
4. When may an employee who is provided with a fuel by his employer avoid a fuel scale charge?
5. To what extent are removal expenses paid for by an employer taxable?
6. When may travel expenses be deducted from the taxable earnings of an employee?
7. Lucy is provided with a mobile phone by her employer costing £350 per annum. What is taxable on Lucy?
8. What are the IR35 provisions designed to prevent?

Answers to quick quiz

1 £17,000 (14,000 + 3,000 bonus paid in 2006/07)

2 Job related accommodation

3 £5,779 (3,667 + 2,112)

$$\text{Car}: \ £25{,}000 \times \left(\left[\frac{160-140}{5}\right] + 15\% + 3\%\right) \text{ (diesel car)}$$

£25,000 × 22%

£5,500 for 12m

£5,500 × 8/12

Car: £3,667

Fuel: £14,400 × 22% × 8/12 = £2,112

4 There is no fuel scale charge if:

(a) All the fuel provided was made available only for business travel, or
(b) the full cost of any fuel provided for private use was completely reimbursed by the employee

5 The first £8,000 of removal expenses are exempt. Any excess is taxable.

6 An employee can deduct travel costs incurred in travelling in the performance of his duties or in travelling to a place which he has to attend in the performance of his duties (other than the normal place of work).

7 Nothing. The provision of one mobile phone for private use is an exempt benefit.

8 The provisions are designed to prevent workers avoiding tax and NIC by offering their services through an intermediary.

Now try the question below from the Exam Question Bank

Number	Level	Marks	Time
Q3	Examination	8	15 mins

4

Employment income: additional aspects

Introduction

In this chapter we look at some tax efficient means by which employees may be remunerated.

1 Payments on the termination of employment

FAST FORWARD

Payments made on the termination of employment may be fully taxable, partially exempt or exempt. The first £30,000 of a genuinely ex gratia termination payment is normally exempt.

1.1 Charge to tax

Termination payments may be entirely exempt, partly exempt or entirely chargeable.

The following payments on the termination of employment are exempt.

- Payments on account of injury, disability or accidental death
- Lump sum payments from approved pension schemes
- Legal costs recovered by the employee from the employer following legal action to recover compensation for loss of employment, where the costs are ordered by the court or (for out-of-court settlements) are paid directly to the employee's solicitor as part of the settlement.

Payments to which the employee is contractually entitled are, in general, taxable in full as general earnings *(Thorn EMI Electronics Ltd v Coldicott 1999).* Payments for work done (terminal bonuses), for doing extra work during a period of notice, payments in lieu of notice where stated in the original contract, or for extending a period of notice are therefore taxable in full. A payment by one employer to induce an employee to take up employment with another employer is also taxable in full (*Shilton v Wilmshurst 1991*).

Other payments on termination (such as compensation for loss of office and including statutory redundancy pay), which are not taxable under the general earnings rules because they are not in return for services, are nevertheless brought in as amounts which count as employment income. Such payments **are partly exempt: the first £30,000 is exempt; any excess is taxable as specific employment income**.

Payments and other benefits provided in connection with termination of employment (or a change in terms of employment) **are taxable in the year in which they are received**. 'Received' in this case means when it is paid or the recipient becomes entitled to it (for cash payments) or when it is used or enjoyed (non-cash benefits).

Employers have an obligation to report termination settlements which include benefits to HMRC by 6 July following the tax year end. No report is required if the package consists wholly of cash. Employers must also notify HMRC by this date of settlements which (over their lifetime) may exceed £30,000.

HMRC regard payments notionally made as compensation for loss of office but which are made on retirement or death (other than accidental death) as lump sum payments under unapproved pension schemes, and therefore taxable in full. It may be possible to obtain approval for such a deemed pension scheme so as to make the whole payment tax exempt, provided that the employee is not already a member of an approved pension scheme and the payment is within the statutory limits on lump sum payments from approved schemes (see later in this text). Also, payments in circumstances which amount to unfair dismissal are treated as eligible for the £30,000 exemption.

The provision of counselling for unemployment or to help an employee leaving to find new employment or self-employment is not a taxable benefit, nor is the reimbursement of the cost of such counselling taxable. There are a number of other excluded benefits such as continued use of one mobile telephone and work related.

An employee may, either on leaving an employment or at some other time, accept a limitation on his future conduct or activities in return for a payment. Such payments are taxable as general earnings. However, a payment accepted in full and final settlement of any claims the employee may have against the employer is not automatically taxable under this rule.

A payment to an employee as compensation for the loss of rights under a redundancy scheme has been held not to be taxable (*Mairs v Haughey 1993*). A payment to compensate for loss of rights under a share option scheme, following a management buyout of the subsidiary which the employee worked for, has also been held not to be taxable *(Wilcock v Eve 1994).*

All payments to an employee on termination, both cash and non-cash, should be considered. Non-cash benefits are taxed by reference to their cash equivalent (using the normal benefits rules). Thus if a company car continues to be made available to an ex-employee say for a further year after redundancy he will be taxed on the same benefit value as if he had remained in employment.

If the termination package is a partially exempt one and exceeds £30,000 then the £30,000 exempt limit is allocated to earlier benefits and payments. In any particular year the exemption is allocated to cash payments before non-cash benefits.

1.2 Example: redundancy package

Jonah is made redundant on 31 December 2006. He receives (not under a contractual obligation) the following redundancy package:

- cash in total of £40,000 payable as £20,000 in January 2007 and £20,000 in January 2008
- use of company car for period to 5 April 2008 (benefit value per annum £5,000)

In 2006/07 Jonah receives as redundancy:

	£
Cash	20,000
Car (£5,000 × $^{3}/_{12}$)	1,250
	21,250

Wholly exempt (allocate £21,250 of £30,000 exemption to cash first then benefit).

In 2007/08 Jonah receives:

	£
Cash	20,000
Car	5,000
	25,000
Exemption (remaining)	(8,750)
Taxable	16,250

Thus of the cash payment £11,250 (£20,000 less £8,750) is taxable.

2 Shares and share options

2.1 Shares

The ownership of shares in an employing company may lead to a tax charge:

(a) **If a director or an employee is given shares, or is sold shares for less than their market value, there is a charge on the difference between the market value and the amount (if any) which the director or employee pays for the shares.**

(b) If, while the director or employee still has a beneficial interest in the shares, a 'chargeable event' occurs, there is a charge on the increase in the value of the interest caused by the chargeable event as specific employment income.

A chargeable event is a change of rights or restrictions attaching to either the shares in question or to other shares which leads to the value of the shares in question increasing, and which takes place while the person concerned is a director or employee (of the company or of an associated company) or within seven years of his ceasing to be one. However, where the change applies to all shares of the same class there is not in general a chargeable event.

(c) If an employee, having obtained shares by reason of his being a director or employee, receives any special benefit because of his owning the shares, he is taxable under on the benefit as specific employment income unless:

   (i) The benefit is available to at least 90% of persons holding shares of the same class, and

   (ii) • The majority of the shares of the same class are not held by directors or employees, or

   • The company is employee-controlled by virtue of holdings of the same class of shares.

(d) If an employee or director receives shares which may later be forfeited, there is no income tax charge when the shares are acquired. There is an income tax charge when the risk of forfeiture is lifted or when the shares are sold, if sooner. The amount of specific employment income will be the difference between the market value of the shares less the cost of the shares.

(e) If shares received as a result of employment are subsequently converted to shares of another class, there is an income tax charge on conversion on the difference between the market value and cost of the shares.

In the above situations when the base cost of the shares is being calculated for capital gains tax purposes (see later in this text) any amount charged to income tax is added to the acquisition cost of the shares.

2.2 Share options

(a) **If a director or an employee is granted an option to acquire shares, then, in general, there is no income tax charge on the grant of the option**. However, for options granted up to 1 September 2003, if the option could be exercised more than ten years after grant, there was a specific employment income charge at the time of grant. The charge was on the market value of the shares that could be acquired at the time of the grant minus the sum of what the director or employee paid for the option and what he would have to pay for the shares (taking the lowest price at which he could acquire the shares). Any amount taxable under this rule is deducted from the amount taxable on any later specific employment income charge in relation to the same option (see below).

(b) On the exercise of the option **there is a charge as specific employment income on the market value of the shares after date of exercise minus the sum of what (if anything) was paid for the option and what was paid for the shares**. If he assigns or releases the option for money, or agrees (for money) not to exercise it or to grant someone else a right to acquire the shares, he is likewise taxable on the amount he gets minus the amount he paid for the option.

Question — **Pre September 2003 option**

Mr Wilkes was granted an option to buy 10,000 shares in his employer company in June 1993. The option could be exercised between June 1993 and June 2007. The cost of the option was £1 per share. The value of the shares was £2.50 in June 1993. The price at which the option could be exercised was £1.25.

Mr Wilkes exercised his option in August 2006, when the shares had a market value of £8.

What is the amount of specific employment income taxable in 2006/07?

Answer

Amount taxed on grant of option (could be exercised more than 10 years after grant).

	£
Market value at grant 10,000 × £2.50	25,000
Less cost of option 10,000 × £1	(10,000)
cost of exercise 10,000 × £1.25	(12,500)
Amount charged	2,500

Amount taxed on exercise

	£
Market value at exercise 10,000 × £8	80,000
Less price paid for option	(10,000)
price paid for shares	(12,500)
amount charged on grant	(2,500)
Chargeable on exercise	55,000

Note that total amount charged £(1,500 + 55,000) is the difference between the market value of shares at exercise and the amount payable by Mr Wilkes for the option and the shares.

National insurance contributions (NICs) (see later in this text) are payable by both an employee and employer when gains are realised on the exercise of an unapproved share option and where the shares are readily convertible into cash. The employer and employee may agrees that the employee should bear the employer's NICs, as well as his own. In this case the amount of employer NIC paid by the employee can be deducted from the taxable gain arising on the exercise of the option.

2.3 Special schemes

FAST FORWARD

There are a range of tax efficient schemes under which an employer may be able to give employees a stake in the business.

Successive governments have recognised the need to encourage schemes that broaden share ownership among employees or reward personnel. A number of tax efficient schemes exist. These are detailed in sections 2.4 to 2.8 below.

2.4 Employee share ownership trusts (ESOTs)

Exam focus point

ESOTs may also be called employee share ownership plans (ESOPs). The examiner has stated that this area will not be examined in its own right.

Under ESOTs shares may be distributed to employees through a specially established trust. Shares must be distributed to employees within a maximum of 20 years of their acquisition by the trust. Broadly, all employees (except part-time directors, who must be excluded) must be eligible on similar terms.

The trust established by the ESOT can receive funds to buy shares from a number of sources, principally from the company establishing the ESOT (the founding company), from subsidiaries of the founding company and by borrowing.

The shares can be transferred to employees exercising options under savings-related share option schemes (see below). The shares can also be transferred by the trustees to a share incentive plan (see below) without a chargeable event occurring.

2.5 SAYE option schemes

An employer can set up a scheme, under which employees can choose to make regular monthly investments in special bank or building society accounts called sharesave accounts.

(a) **Employees can save a fixed monthly amount of between £5 and £250.**

(b) **The investments are made for three or five years, and a tax-free bonus is then added to the account by way of interest.** The employee may either withdraw the money or leave it for another two years. If he leaves it in the account, another tax-free bonus is added.

(c) **At the withdrawal date, the employee may take the money in cash.**

(d) **Alternatively, he may use it to buy ordinary shares in his employer company or its holding company. The price of these shares is fixed when the employee starts to save in the account, by granting the employee options to buy shares.**

(e) The option price must be at least 80% of the market value at the date the options are granted.

(f) **The only tax charge is to capital gains tax, on the gain on the shares when they are finally sold.** This gain is computed as if the employee bought the shares for the price he actually paid for them.

(g) A scheme must be open to all employees and full-time directors, and on similar terms. Part-time directors may be included, but can be excluded. However, a minimum qualifying period of employment (of up to five years) may be imposed, and there may be differences based on remuneration or length of service.

(h) Anyone who has within the preceding 12 months held over 25% of the shares of a close company which is the company whose shares may be acquired under the scheme, or which controls that company either alone or as part of a consortium, must be excluded from the scheme.

2.6 Company share option plans (CSOP)

(a) **An employee can be granted options on shares under a CSOP. There is no income tax on the grant of an option, on the profit arising from the exercise of an option between three and ten years after the grant or on the disposal of the shares. Capital gains tax will, however, arise on the gain made when an employee eventually sells his shares.**

(b) **To obtain HMRC approval schemes must satisfy** the following **conditions**.

   (i) The shares must be fully paid ordinary shares.

   (ii) The price of the shares must not be less than their market value at the time of the grant of the option.

   (iii) Participation in the scheme must be limited to employees and full-time directors. Options must not be transferable. However, ex-employees and the personal representatives of deceased employees may exercise options; personal representatives must do so within one year after the death. The scheme need not be open to all employees and full-time directors.

   (iv) No options may be granted which take the total market value of shares for which an employee holds options above £30,000. Shares are valued as at the times when the options on them are granted.

   (v) If the issuing company has more than one class of shares, the majority of shares in the class for which the scheme operates must be held other than by:
   - Persons acquiring them through their positions as directors or employees (unless the company is an employee controlled company)
   - A holding company (unless the scheme shares are quoted)

   (vi) Anyone who has within the preceding 12 months held over 25% of the shares of a close company which is the company whose shares may be acquired under the scheme, or which controls that company either alone or as part of a consortium, must be excluded from the scheme.

(c) The tax exemption is lost in respect of an option if it is exercised earlier than three years or later than ten years after grant. However, this three year waiting period does not need to be observed when personal representatives exercise the options of a deceased employee (but the ten year rule still applies). In addition, if the options are exercised before three years after the grant they will remain tax exempt if the exercise (and exit from the scheme) arises from the injury, disability, redundancy or retirement of the employee.

(d) Schemes may be altered so that in the event of the company concerned being taken over, employees may exchange their existing options for equivalent options over shares in the acquiring company.

(e) The costs of setting up approved share option schemes (both savings related and company share option plans) are deductible provided they are paid within nine months of the end of the accounting period.

2.7 Enterprise Management Incentives (EMI)

FAST FORWARD

No income tax or NIC is chargeable on either the grant or exercise of options under the enterprise management incentive scheme provided the exercise takes place within 10 years of the grant and the exercise price is the market value of the shares at the date of the grant.

2.7.1 Introduction

This scheme is intended to encourage experienced people to 'take the plunge' and leave established careers in large companies for riskier jobs in smaller, start-up or developing firms.

(a) **A qualifying company can grant each of its employees options over shares worth up to £100,000 at the time of grant, subject to a maximum of £3m in total**.

(b) **No income tax or national insurance is chargeable on either the grant or exercise of the options provided the exercise takes place within 10 years of the grant and the exercise price is the market value of the shares at the date of the grant**. If options are granted at a discount, the discount is taxed at the date of exercise as normal.

(c) An employing company may set a target to be achieved before an option can be exercised. The target must clearly be defined at the time the option is granted.

(d) **When the shares are sold, the gain is subject to CGT**.

2.7.2 Qualifying company

The company, which can be quoted or unquoted, must meet certain conditions when the options are granted. In particular, **the company's gross assets must not exceed £30m. The company must not be under the control of any other company.**

The company must carry out one of a number of qualifying trades.

2.7.3 Eligible employees

Employees must be employed by the company or group for at least 25 hours a week, or, if less, for at least 75% of their working time (including self-employment). **Employees who own 30% or more of the ordinary shares in the company** (disregarding unexercised options shares) **are excluded**.

2.7.4 Qualifying shares

The share must be **fully paid up irredeemable ordinary shares**. The rules permit restrictions on sale, forfeiture conditions and performance conditions.

2.7.5 Limit

At any one time, an employee may hold EMI options over shares with a value of up to £100,000 at the date of grant. Restrictions and conditions attaching to the shares may not be taken into account when valuing shares. Where options are granted above the £100,000 limit, relief is given on options up to the limit. Once the employee has reached the limit, no more EMI options may be granted for 3 years ie the employee may not immediately top up with new options following the exercise of old options. Any options granted under a **CSOP reduce the £100,000 limit**, but savings related share options can be ignored.

2.7.6 Disqualifying events

There are a number of disqualifying events including an employee ceasing to spend at least 75% of his working time with the company. EMI relief is available up to the date of the event.

2.7.7 Capital gains tax

The shares are a 'business asset' for taper relief purposes. The taper relief period runs from the date the option is granted. Where a disqualifying event takes place after the shares have been acquired, business assets taper relief ceases from that time onwards.

2.7.8 Relief for costs

The costs of setting up a scheme and on-going administration are deductible in computing profits.

2.7.9 Approval

It is not necessary to submit schemes to HMRC for approval. Instead, HMRC must be notified of the grant of options within 92 days. HMRC then has 12 months to check whether the grants satisfy the EMI rules.

A company may submit details in writing to the Small Company Enterprise Centre before the options are granted. The Inspector will then confirm in writing whether he is satisfied that the company will be a qualifying company on the basis of information supplied. The details to be submitted include:

(a) a copy of the latest accounts for the company and its subsidiaries

(b) a company of the memorandum and articles of association and details of any proposed changes, and

(c) details of trading and other activities carried on, or to be carried on, by the company or its subsidiaries.

Advance approval is not possible in respect of any other aspect of EMI such as whether an employee is an eligible employee.

2.8 Share Incentive Plans (SIPs)

FAST FORWARD

Employees may be given £3,000 of 'free' shares a year under the share incentive plan. In addition they can purchase up to £1,500 worth of 'partnership' shares a year and employers can provide up to £3,000 worth of matching shares. Once the shares have been held for five years there is no income tax or NIC.

(a) **Employers can give up to £3,000 of 'free shares' a year to employees with no tax or NICs**.

(b) Employees can purchase '**partnership shares**' at any time in the year. These shares are funded through deductions of **up to £1,500 in any tax year**.

(c) Employers can award 'matching shares' free to employees who purchase partnership shares at a maximum ratio of 2:1.

(d) Employers offering free shares must offer a minimum amount to each employee on 'similar terms'. Between the minimum and the maximum of £3,000, the employer can offer shares in different amounts and on different bases to different employees. This means that employers can reward either individual or team performance. Employers can set performance targets subject to the overriding requirement that a plan must not contain any features that concentrate rewards on directors and more highly paid employees.

(e) **Free and matching shares must normally be held in a plan for at least three years. If shares are withdrawn within three years** (because the employee leaves) **there is a charge to income tax (as specific employment income) and NIC on the market value of the shares at the time of withdrawal. If shares are taken out of the plan after three years but before five years, there is charge to income tax and NIC based on the lower of the initial value of the shares** - and their value at the date of withdrawal so any increase in value is free of income tax and NIC. If one of the specified reasons applies, eg redundancy or retirement, there is no tax or NIC charge. **Once the shares have been held for five years there is no income tax or NIC.**

(f) **Partnership shares can be taken out at any time. If the shares are held for less than three years, there is a charge to income tax and NIC on the market value at the time the shares are removed. If the share are removed after three years but before five years, the charge to income tax and NIC is based on the lesser of salary used to buy the shares and the market value at the date of removal. Once the shares have been held for five years there is no income tax or NICs.**

(g) **Dividends of up to £1,500 on shares in the plan are tax-free provided the dividends are used to acquire additional shares in the company, which are then held in the plan for three years. These 'dividend' shares do not affect entitlement to partnership or matching shares.**

(h) A plan may provide for free and matching shares to be forfeited if the employee leaves within three years, unless the employee leaves for specified reasons such as retirement or redundancy. All shares have to come out of a plan if an employee leaves his job.

(i) Provided they were held in the plan for at least 3 years, there is no charge to CGT on shares taken out of a plan and sold immediately. A charge to CGT will arise on sale to the extent that the shares increase in value after they are withdrawn from the plan.

(j) The plan must be operated through a UK resident trust. The trustees acquire the shares from the company or – if the plan incorporates partnership shares – from the employees. The existence of arrangements to enable employees to sell shares held in a new plan trust will not of itself make those shares readily convertible into cash and require employers, for example, to operate national insurance.

(k) Stamp duty is not payable when an employee purchases shares from a SIP trust. The trust must pay stamp duty when it acquires the shares. No taxable benefit arises on an employee as a result of a SIP trust or an employer paying either stamp duty or the incidental costs of operating the plan.

(l) A deduction in computing profits is given for:

- The costs of setting up and administering the plan.
- The gross salary allocated by employees to buy partnership shares.
- The costs of providing shares to the extent that the costs exceed the employees contributions.
- The market value of free and matching shares when they are acquired by the trustees.
- Interest paid by the trustees on borrowing to acquire shares where the company meets the trustees' costs.

(m) Shares in the plan must be fully paid irredeemable ordinary shares in a company either:-

(i) Listed on a recognised stock exchange (or in its subsidiary), or
(ii) Not controlled by another company.

(n) A plan established by a company that controls other companies, may be extended to any or all of these other companies. Such a plan is called a group plan.

(o) A plan need not include all the components – it is possible to have a plan with only free shares.

(p) Companies must offer all full and part-time employees the opportunity to participate in the plan. A minimum qualifying period of employment of up to 18 months my be specified. Any minimum period specified can be satisfied by working for any company within a group.

Chapter roundup

- Payments made on the termination of employment may be fully taxable, partially exempt or exempt.
- The first £30,000 of a genuinely ex gratia termination payment is normally exempt.
- There are a range of tax efficient schemes under which an employer may be able to give employees a stake in the business.
- No income tax or NIC is chargeable on either the grant or exercise of options under the enterprise management incentive scheme provided the exercise takes place within 10 years of the grant and the exercise price is the market value of the shares at the date of the grant.
- Employees may be given £3,000 of 'free' shares a year under the share incentive plan. In addition they can purchase up to £1,500 worth of 'partnership' shares a year and employers can provide up to £3,000 worth of matching shares. Once the shares have been held for five years there is no income tax or NIC.

Quick quiz

1 Which termination payments are partly exempt?

2 Thomas was made redundant on 4 January 2007. His severance package was;

Statutory redundancy pay	£12,000
Golden Goodbye	£40,000

The "Golden Goodbye" was a payment made by the company to "soften the blow" of redundancy to Thomas. It was not paid as part of his contract of employment.

How much of the above is taxable?

3 What is the maximum amount of enterprise management incentive scheme options that an employee can hold?

4 How may 'free shares' can an employee receive under a share incentive plan?

5 How many matching shares can be given in respect of each partnership share purchased?

6 On what value is income tax charged if shares held within a share incentive plan are disposed of within three years?

Answers to quick quiz

1 The first £30,000 of genuinely ex-gratia termination payments

2 £22,000.

Golden Goodbye	40,000
Partial exemption (30,000 – 12,000)	(18,000)
	22,000

Statutory redundancy of £12,000 exempt but the £30,000 exemption for ex-gratia amounts is reduced by this amount.

3 At any one time an employee may hold options over shares worth up to £100,000 at the date of grant.

4 Up to £3,000 worth of free shares

5 Up to two.

6 Tax is charged on the market value of the shares on the date of withdrawal.

Now try the question below from the Exam Question Bank

Number	Level	Marks	Time
Q36	Examination	25	45 mins

This question has been analysed to show you how to approach such questions in the exam.

5

Trading income

Introduction

We are now going to look at the taxation of unincorporated businesses. We work out a business's profit as if it were a separate entity (the separate entity concept familiar to you from basic bookkeeping) but as an unincorporated business has no legal existence apart from its proprietor, we cannot tax it separately. We have to feed its profit into the proprietor's personal tax computation.

In this chapter, we look at the computation and taxation of profits. Standard rules on the computation of profits are used instead of individual traders' accounting policies, so as to ensure fairness. We also need special rules, the basis period rules, to link the profits of periods of account to the personal computations of tax years.

In the next chapter we study the allowances available for capital expenditure.

Before the tax rules for trading income for unincorporated businesses were rewritten in the Income Tax (Trading and Other Income) Act 2005 (ITTOIA 2005), most of the tax rules for such businesses applied equally to companies (with the exception of the basis period rules). As the rewrite project is not intended to change the tax rules, merely rewrite them in a more useable form, this is still true. However the detailed rules are now contained in two separate parts of the legislation (see the chapters on corporation tax).

Topic list	Syllabus references
1 The badges of trade	1(e)
2 The computation of trade profits	1(e)
3 Basis periods	1(e)
4 Change of accounting date	1(e)

1 The badges of trade

FAST FORWARD

The badges of trade can be used to decide whether or not a trade exists.

1.1 Introduction

Before a tax charge can be imposed it is necessary to establish the existence of a trade.

Key term

A trade is defined in the legislation only in an unhelpful manner as including every trade, manufacture, adventure or concern in the nature of a trade. It has therefore been left to the courts to provide guidance. This guidance is often summarised in a collection of principles known as the **'badges of trade'**. These are set out below.

1.2 The subject matter

Whether a person is trading or not may sometimes be decided by examining the subject matter of the transaction. Some assets are commonly held as investments for their intrinsic value: an individual buying some shares or a painting may do so in order to enjoy the income from the shares or to enjoy the work of art. A subsequent disposal may produce a gain of a capital nature rather than a trading profit. But **where the subject matter of a transaction is such as would not be held as an investment** (for example 34,000,000 yards of aircraft linen (*Martin v Lowry 1927*) or 1,000,000 rolls of toilet paper (*Rutledge v CIR 1929*)), **it is presumed that any profit on resale is a trading profit.**

1.3 The frequency of transactions

Transactions which may, in isolation, be of a capital nature will be interpreted as trading transactions where their **frequency indicates the carrying on of a trade**. It was decided that whereas normally the purchase of a mill-owning company and the subsequent stripping of its assets might be a capital transaction, where the taxpayer was embarking on the same exercise for the fourth time he must be carrying on a trade (*Pickford v Quirke 1927*).

1.4 The length of ownership

The courts may infer adventures in the nature of **trade where items purchased are sold soon afterwards.**

1.5 Supplementary work and marketing

When work is done to make an asset more marketable, or steps are taken to find purchasers, the courts will be more ready to ascribe a trading motive. When a group of accountants bought, blended and recasked a quantity of brandy they were held to be taxable on a trading profit when the brandy was later sold (*Cape Brandy Syndicate v CIR 1921*).

1.6 A profit motive

The absence of a profit motive will not necessarily preclude a tax charge as trading income, but its presence is a strong indication that a person is trading. The purchase and resale of £20,000 worth of silver bullion by the comedian Norman Wisdom, as a hedge against devaluation, was held to be a trading transaction (*Wisdom v Chamberlain 1969*).

1.7 The way in which the asset sold was acquired

If goods are acquired deliberately, trading may be indicated. If goods are acquired unintentionally, for example by gift or inheritance, their later sale is unlikely to be trading.

1.8 The taxpayer's intentions

Where a transaction is clearly trading on objective criteria, **the taxpayer's intentions are irrelevant**. If, however, a transaction has (objectively) a dual purpose, the taxpayer's intentions may be taken into account. An example of a transaction with a dual purpose is the acquisition of a site partly as premises from which to conduct another trade, and partly with a view to the possible development and resale of the site.

This test is not one of the traditional badges of trade, but it may be just as important.

Exam focus point

> If on applying the badges of trade HMRC do not conclude that income is 'trading income' then they can potentially treat it as other income or a capital gain.

Profits from professions and vocations are taxed in the same way as profits from a trade.

2 The computation of trade profits

FAST FORWARD

> The accounts profits need to be adjusted in order to establish the taxable trade profits.

2.1 The adjustment of profits

Although the net profit before taxation shown in the accounts is the starting point in computing the taxable trade profits, many adjustments may be required to calculate the taxable amount.

Here is an illustrative adjustment.

		£	£
Net profit per accounts			140,000
Add:	expenditure charged in the accounts which is not deductible for tax purposes	50,000	
	income taxable as trade profits which has not been included in the accounts	30,000	
			0,000
			220,000
Less:	profits included in the accounts but which are not taxable as trade profits	40,000	
	expenditure which is deductible for tax purposes but has not been charged in the accounts	20,000	
			60,000
Trade profits as adjusted for tax purposes			160,000

You may refer to deductible and non-deductible expenditure as allowable and disallowable expenditure respectively. The two sets of terms are interchangeable.

2.2 Accounting policies

The fundamental concept is that the profits of the business must be calculated in accordance with generally accepted accounting practice. These profits are subject to any adjustment specifically required for income tax purposes.

2.3 Capital allowances

Under the Capital Allowances Act 2001 (CAA 2001) **capital allowances are treated as trade expenses and balancing charges are treated as trade receipts**.

2.4 Non-deductible expenditure

Certain expenses are specifically disallowed by the legislation. These are covered in paragraphs 2.4.1 – 2.4.11. If however a deduction is specifically permitted this overrides the disallowance.

2.4.1 Capital expenditure

Income tax is a tax solely on income and so capital expenditure is not deductible. This denies a deduction for depreciation or amortisation (although there are special rules for companies in relation to intangible assets – see later in this text)**. The most contentious items of expenditure will often be repairs** (revenue expenditure) **and improvements** (capital expenditure).

- The cost of restoration of an asset by, for instance, replacing a subsidiary part of the asset is revenue expenditure. Expenditure on a new factory chimney replacement was allowable since the chimney was a subsidiary part of the factory (*Samuel Jones & Co (Devondale) Ltd v CIR 1951*). However, in another case a football club demolished a spectators' stand and replaced it with a modern equivalent. This was held not to be repair, since repair is the restoration by renewal or replacement of subsidiary parts of a larger entity, and the stand formed a distinct and *separate* part of the club (*Brown v Burnley Football and Athletic Co Ltd 1980*).
- The cost of initial repairs to improve an asset recently acquired to make it fit to earn profits is disallowable capital expenditure. In *Law Shipping Co Ltd v CIR 1923* the taxpayer failed to obtain relief for expenditure on making a newly bought ship seaworthy prior to using it.
- The cost of initial repairs to remedy normal wear and tear of recently acquired assets is allowable. *Odeon Associated Theatres Ltd v Jones 1971* can be contrasted with the *Law Shipping* judgement. Odeon were allowed to charge expenditure incurred on improving the state of recently acquired cinemas.

Other examples to note include:

- A one-off payment made by a hotel owner to terminate an agreement for the management of a hotel was held to be revenue rather than capital expenditure in *Croydon Hotel & Leisure Co v Bowen 1996.* The payment did not affect the whole structure of the taxpayer's business; it merely enabled it to be run more efficiently.
- A one-off payment to remove a threat to the taxpayer's business was also held to be revenue rather than capital expenditure in *Lawson v Johnson Matthey plc 1992.*
- An initial payment for a franchise (as opposed to regular fees) is capital and not deductible.

2.4.2 Expenditure not wholly and exclusively for the purposes of the trade

Expenditure is not deductible if it is not for trade purposes (the remoteness test), or if it reflects more than one purpose (the duality test). The private proportion of payments for motoring expenses, rent, heat and light and telephone expenses of a proprietor is not deductible. If an exact apportionment is possible relief is given on the business element. Where the payments are to or on behalf of employees, the full amounts are deductible but the employees are taxed under the benefits code.

The remoteness test is illustrated by the following cases.

- *Strong & Co of Romsey Ltd v Woodifield 1906*
  A customer injured by a falling chimney when sleeping in an inn owned by a brewery claimed compensation from the company. The compensation was not deductible: 'the loss sustained by the appellant was not really incidental to their trade as innkeepers and fell upon them in their character not of innkeepers but of householders'.

- *Bamford v ATA Advertising Ltd 1972*
  A director misappropriated £15,000. The loss was not allowable: 'the loss is not, as in the case of a dishonest shop assistant, an incident of the company's trading activities. It arises altogether outside such activities'.
- Expenditure which is wholly and exclusively to benefit the trades of several companies (for example in a group) but is not wholly and exclusively to benefit the trade of one specific company is not deductible *(Vodafone Cellular Ltd and others v Shaw 1995).*
- *McKnight (HMIT) v Sheppard (1999)* concerned expenses incurred by a stockbroker in defending allegations of infringements of Stock Exchange regulations. It was found that the expenditure was incurred to prevent the destruction of the taxpayer's business and that as the expenditure was incurred for business purposes it was deductible. It was also found that although the expenditure had the effect of preserving the taxpayer's reputation, that was not its purpose, so there was no duality of purpose.

The **duality test** is illustrated by the following cases.

- *Caillebotte v Quinn 1975*
  A self-employed carpenter spent an average of 40p per day when obliged to buy lunch away from home but just 10p when he lunched at home. He claimed the excess 30p. It was decided that the payment had a dual purpose and was not deductible: a taxpayer 'must eat to live not eat to work'.
- *Mallalieu v Drummond 1983*
  Expenditure by a lady barrister on black clothing to be worn in court (and on its cleaning and repair) was not deductible. The expenditure was for the dual purpose of enabling the barrister to be warmly and properly clad as well as meeting her professional requirements.
- *McLaren v Mumford 1996*
  A publican, traded from a public house which had residential accommodation above it. He was obliged to live at the public house but he also had another house which he visited regularly. It was held that the private element of the expenditure incurred at the public house on electricity, rent, gas, etc was not incurred for the purpose of earning profits, but for serving the non-business purpose of satisfying the publican's ordinary human needs. The expenditure, therefore had a dual purpose and was disallowed.

However, the cost of overnight accommodation when on a business trip may be deductible and reasonable expenditure on an evening meal and breakfast in conjunction with such accommodation is then also deductible.

2.4.3 Impaired trade receivables (bad debts)

Only impairment debts incurred wholly and exclusively for the purposes of the trade are deductible for taxation purposes. Thus loans to employees written off are not deductible unless the business is that of making loans, or it can be shown that the writing-off of the loan was earnings paid out for the benefit of the trade. If a trade debt is released as part of a voluntary arrangement under the Insolvency Act 1986, or a compromise or arrangement under s 425 Companies Act 1985, the amount released is deductible as an impaired debt.

Under FRS 26 Financial Instruments: measurement, a review of all trade receivables should be carried out to assess their fair value at the balance sheet date, and any impairment debts written off. As a specific provision, no adjustment to the accounts profit is needed for impairment review.

2.4.4 Unpaid remuneration and employee benefit contributions

If earnings for employees are charged in the accounts but are not paid within nine months of the end of the period of account, the cost is only deductible for the period of account in which the earnings are paid. When a tax computation is made within the nine month period, it is initially assumed that unpaid earnings will not be paid within that period. The computation is adjusted if they are so paid.

Earnings are treated as paid at the same time as they are treated as received for employment income purposes.

Similar rules apply to employee benefit contributions.

2.4.5 Entertaining and gifts

The general rule is that expenditure on entertaining and gifts is non-deductible. This applies to amounts reimbursed to employees for specific entertaining expenses and gifts, and to round sum allowances which are exclusively for meeting such expenses.

There are specific exceptions to the general rule:

- **Entertaining for and gifts to employees are normally deductible** although where gifts are made, or the entertainment is excessive, a charge to tax may arise on the employee under the benefits legislation.
- **Gifts to customers not costing more than £50 per donee per year are allowed if they carry a conspicuous advertisement for the business and are not food, drink, tobacco or vouchers exchangeable for goods.**
- Gifts to charities may also be allowed although many will fall foul of the 'wholly and exclusively' rule above. If a gift aid declaration is made in respect of a gift, tax relief will be given under the gift aid scheme, not as a trading expense.

2.4.6 Lease charges for expensive cars

Although leasing costs will normally be an allowable expense, there is a restriction for costs relating to expensive cars. **If the retail price of the car when new exceeds £12,000 the deductible part of any leasing charge is reduced by multiplying it by the fraction (£12,000 + RP) / 2RP, where RP is the retail price of the car.**

Thus for a car with a retail price of £20,000 and an annual leasing charge of £5,000 the allowable deduction is £5,000 x [(12,000 + 20,000) / 2 x 20,000] = £4,000, so £1,000 of the charge is added back.

This restriction does not apply to low emission cars, ie those with carbon dioxide emissions not exceeding 120 g/km and electrically propelled cars.

2.4.7 Patent royalties

Patent royalties are charges and are dealt with in the personal tax computation. They are not also deducted in computing trading profits.

2.4.8 Interest payments

Interest which is allowed as a charge on income (see earlier in this text) is not also allowed as a trading expense.

2.4.9 National insurance contributions

No deduction is allowed for any national insurance contributions **except for employer's contributions**. These are Class 1 secondary contributions, Class 1A contributions and Class 1B contributions. National insurance contributions are dealt with later in this text.

2.4.10 Penalties and interest on tax

Penalties and interest on late paid tax are not allowed as a trading expense. Tax includes income tax, capital gains tax, VAT and stamp duty land tax.

2.4.11 Crime related payments

A payment is not deductible if making it constitutes an offence by the payer. This covers protection money paid to terrorists, bribes and similar payments made overseas which would be criminal payments if they were made in the UK. Statute also prevents any deduction for payments made in response to blackmail or extortion.

2.5 Deductible expenditure

Most expenses will be deductible under the general rule that expenses incurred wholly and exclusively for the purpose of the trade are not disallowed. Some expenses which might otherwise be disallowed under the "wholly or exclusively" rule, or under one or other of the specific rules discussed above are, however, specifically allowed by the legislation. These are covered in paragraphs 2.5.1 – 2.5.12.

2.5.1 Pre-trading expenditure

Expenditure incurred before the commencement of trade is deductible, if it is incurred within seven years of the start of trade and it is of a type that would have been deductible had the trade already started. **It is treated as a trading expense incurred on the first day of trading**.

2.5.2 Incidental costs of obtaining finance

Incidental costs of obtaining loan finance, or of attempting to obtain or redeeming it, are deductible other than a discount on issue or a premium on redemption (which are really alternatives to paying interest). This deduction for incidental costs does not apply to companies because they get a deduction for the costs of borrowing in a different way. We will look at companies later in this text.

2.5.3 Short leases

A trader may deduct an annual sum in respect of the amount liable to income tax on a lease premium which he paid to his landlord (see chapter 2). Normally, the amortisation of the lease will have been deducted in the accounts (and must be added back as capital expenditure).

2.5.4 Renewals

Where a tool is replaced or altered then the cost of the renewal or alteration may be deducted as an expense in certain instances. These are that:

- A deduction would only be prohibited because the expenditure is capital expenditure, and
- No deduction can be given under any other provisions, such as under the capital allowances legislation.

2.5.5 Restrictive covenants

When an employee leaves his employment he may accept a limitation on his future activities in return for a payment. **Provided the employee is taxed on the payment as employment income** (see earlier in the text) **the payment is a deductible trading expense.**

2.5.6 Secondments

The **costs of seconding employees to charities or educational establishments are deductible.**

2.5.7 Contributions to agent's expenses

Many employers run payroll giving schemes for their employees. **Any payments made to the agent who administers the scheme towards running expenses are deductible.**

2.5.8 Counselling and retraining expenses

Expenditure on providing counselling and retraining for leaving employees is allowable.

2.5.9 Redundancy

Redundancy payments made when a trade ends are deductible on the earlier of the day of payment and the last day of trading. If the trade does not end, they can be deducted as soon as they are provided for, so long as the redundancy was decided on within the period of account, the provision is accurately calculated and the payments are made within nine months of the end of the period of account. **The deduction extends to additional payments of up to three times the amount of the redundancy pay on cessation of trade.**

2.5.10 Personal security expenses

If there is a particular security threat to the trader because of the nature of the trade, **expenditure on his personal security is allowable.**

2.5.11 Contributions to local enterprise organisations or urban regeneration companies

This allows a deduction for donations made to a local enterprise agency, a training and enterprise council, a Scottish local enterprise company, a business link organisation or an urban regeneration company. If any benefit is received by the trade from the donation, this must be deducted from the allowable amount.

2.5.12 Patents and trade marks

The costs of **registering patents and trade marks** are deductible for trades only (not professions or vocations).

2.6 Trading income

There are also statutory rules governing whether certain receipts are taxable or not. These are discussed in 2.6.1 to 2.6.6.

2.6.1 Capital receipts

As may be expected, capital receipts are not included in trading income. They may, of course, be taken into account in the capital allowances computation, or as a capital gain.

However, compensation received in one lump sum for the loss of income is likely to be treated as income (*Donald Fisher (Ealing) Ltd v Spencer 1989*).

In some trades, (eg petrol stations and public houses), a wholesaler may pay a lump sum to a retailer in return for the retailer's only supplying that wholesaler's products for several years (an **exclusivity agreement**). If the payment must be used for a specific capital purpose, it is a capital receipt. If that is not the case, it is an income receipt. If the sum is repayable to the wholesaler but the requirement to repay is waived in tranches over the term of the agreement, each tranche is a separate income receipt when the requirement is waived.

2.6.2 Debts released

If the trader incurs a deductible expense but does not settle the amount due to the supplier, then if the creditor releases the debt other than under a statutory arrangement, the amount released must be brought into account as trading income.

2.6.3 Takeover of trade

If a trader takes over a trade from a previous owner, then if he receives any amounts from that trade which related to a period before the takeover they must be brought into account unless the previous owner has already done so.

2.6.4 Reverse premiums

If a trader receives a reverse premium in respect of his trade it must be included in trading income. (The rules for reverse premiums have been discussed earlier in this text for UK property businesses.)

2.6.5 Insurance receipts

Insurance receipts which are revenue in nature, such as for loss of profits, are trading receipts. Otherwise the receipt must be brought in as trading income if, and to the extent that, any deduction has been claimed for the expense that the receipt is intended to cover.

2.6.6 Gifts of trading stock to educational establishments or schools

When a business makes a gift of equipment manufactured, sold or used in the course of its trade to an educational establishment or for a charitable purpose, nothing need be brought into account as a trading receipt or (if capital allowances had been obtained on the asset) as disposal proceeds, so full relief is obtained for the cost.

2.7 Excluded income

2.7.1 Income taxed in another way

Although the accounts may include other income, such as interest, such income may not be trading income. It will instead be taxed under the specific rules for that type of income, such as the rules for savings income.

Certain types of income are specifically exempt from tax, and should be excluded from trade profits.

2.8 Application of general rules

These general rules can be applied to particular types of expenditure and income that you are likely to come across.

2.8.1 Appropriations

Salary or interest on capital paid to a proprietor, and general provisions are not deductible.

2.8.2 Subscriptions and donations

The general 'wholly and exclusively' rule determines the deductibility of expenses. Subscriptions and donations are not deductible unless the expenditure is for the benefit of the trade. The following are the main types of subscriptions and donations you may meet and their correct treatments.

(a) Trade subscriptions (such as to a professional or trade association) are generally deductible.

(b) Charitable donations are deductible only if they are small and to local charities. Tax relief may be available for donations under the gift aid scheme. In the latter case they are not a deductible trading expense.

(c) Political subscriptions and donations are generally not deductible. However, if it can be shown that political expenditure is incurred for the survival of the trade then it may be deducted. This follows a case in which it was held that expenditure incurred in resisting nationalisation was allowable on the grounds that it affected the survival of the business (*Morgan v Tate and Lyle Ltd 1954*).

(d) Where a donation represents the most effective commercial way of disposing of stock (for example, where it would not be commercially effective to sell surplus perishable food), the donation can be treated as for the benefit of the trade and the disposal proceeds taken as £Nil. In other cases, the amount credited to the accounts in respect of a donation of stock should be its market value.

2.8.3 Legal and professional charges

Legal and professional charges relating to capital or non-trading items are not deductible. These include charges incurred in acquiring new capital assets or legal rights, issuing shares, drawing up partnership agreements and litigating disputes over the terms of a partnership agreement.

Charges are deductible if they relate directly to trading. Deductible items include:

- Legal and professional charges incurred defending the taxpayer's title to fixed assets
- Charges connected with an action for breach of contract
- Expenses of the **renewal** (not the original grant) of a lease for less than 50 years
- Charges for trade debt collection
- Normal charges for preparing accounts/assisting with the self assessment of tax liabilities

Accountancy expenses arising out of an enquiry into the accounts information in a particular year's return are not allowed where the enquiry reveals discrepancies and additional liabilities for the year of enquiry, or any earlier year, which arise as a result of negligent or fraudulent conduct.

Where, however, the enquiry results in no addition to profits, or an adjustment to the profits for the year of enquiry only and that assessment does not arise as a result of negligent or fraudulent conduct, the additional accountancy expenses are allowable.

2.8.4 Goods for own use

The usual example is when a proprietor takes goods for his own use. In such circumstances the normal selling price of the goods is added to the accounting profit. In other words, the proprietor is treated for tax purposes as having made a sale to himself (*Sharkey v Wernher 1955*). This rule does not apply to supplies of services, which are treated as sold for the amount (if any) actually paid (but the cost of services to the trader or his household is not deductible).

2.8.5 Other items

Here is a list of various other items that you may meet.

Item	Treatment	Comment
Educational courses for staff	Allow	
Educational courses for proprietor	Allow	If to update existing knowledge or skills, not if to acquire new knowledge or skills
Removal expenses (to new business premises)	Allow	Only if not an expansionary move
Travelling expenses to the trader's place of business	Disallow	*Ricketts v Colquhoun 1925*: unless an itinerant trader (*Horton v Young 1971*)
Compensation for loss of office and ex gratia payments	Allow	If for benefit of trade: *Mitchell v B W Noble Ltd 1927*

Item	Treatment	Comment
Pension contributions (to schemes for employees and company directors)	Allow	Special contributions may be spread over the year of payment and future years
Parking fines	Allow	For employees using their employer's cars on business.
	Disallow	For proprietors/directors
Damages paid	Allow	If not too remote from trade: *Strong and Co v Woodifield 1906*
Preparation and restoration of waste disposal sites	Allow	Spread preparation expenditure over period of use of site. Pre-trading expenditure is treated as incurred on the first day of trading. Allow restoration expenditure in period of expenditure
Dividends on trade investments	Deduct	Taxed as savings income
Rental income from letting part of premises	Deduct	Taxed as income of a UK property business unless it is the letting of surplus business accommodation.

Exam focus point

In the exam you could be given a profit and loss account and asked to calculate 'taxable trade profits'. You must look at every expense in the accounts to decide if it is (or isn't) 'tax deductible'. This means that you must become familiar with the many expenses you may see and the correct tax treatment. Look at the above paragraphs again noting what expenses are (and are not) allowable for tax purposes. Similarly you must decide whether income included in the accounts should be included in the taxable trade profits, or whether it should be excluded.

Question

Calculation of taxable trade profits

Here is the profit and loss account of S Pring, a trader.

	£	£
Gross operating profit		30,000
Taxed interest received		860
		30,860
Wages and salaries	7,000	
Rent and rates	2,000	
Depreciation	1,500	
Impairment of trade receivables	150	
Entertainment expenses	750	
Patent royalties	1,200	
Bank interest	300	
Legal expenses on acquisition of new factory	250	
		(13,150)
Net profit		17,710

(a) Salaries include £500 paid to Mrs Pring who works full time in the business.

(b) No staff were entertained.

(c) Taxed interest and patent royalties were received and paid net but have been shown gross.

Compute the taxable trade profits.

Answer

	£	£
Profit per accounts		17,710
Add: Depreciation	1,500	
Entertainment expenses	750	
Patent royalties paid (to treat as a charge)	1,200	
Legal expenses	250	
		3,700
		21,410
Less interest received (to tax as savings income)		(860)
Taxable trade profits		20,550

2.9 Rounding

Where an individual, a partnership or a single company (not a group of companies) has an annual turnover of at least £5,000,000, and prepares its accounts with figures rounded to at least the nearest £1,000, figures in computations of adjusted profits (including, for companies, non-trading profits but excluding capital gains) may generally be rounded to the nearest £1,000.

2.10 The cessation of trades

2.10.1 Post cessation receipts and expenses

Post-cessation receipts (including any releases of debts incurred by the trader) **are chargeable to income tax as miscellaneous income**. If they are received in the tax year of cessation or the next six tax years, the trader can elect that they be treated as received on the day of cessation. The time limit for electing is the 31 January which is 22 months after the end of the tax year of receipt.

An individual trader or a partner (not a company) can claim **post-cessation expenses in respect of payments made within seven years of a discontinuance** which are incurred wholly and exclusively:

(a) in remedying defective work done, goods supplied or services rendered;

(b) in paying legal or other professional costs and expenses relating to a claim that the work done, etc was defective;

(c) in insuring against liabilities arising out of any such claim or against such costs and expenses; and

(d) for the purpose of collecting debts taken into account in computing the profits or the former trade etc.

Relief is also allowed for trade receivables owed to the former business which were taken into account in computing the profits of the trade prior to discontinuance but which have subsequently proved to be impaired.

Relief for allowable post-cessation expenses is given against income and gains in the year in which each allowable payment is made, or in which a trade receivable is proved to be impaired. The relief must be claimed by 31 January following the year of assessment concerned.

If there is insufficient income and gains to cover allowable expenditure in a given year, the unrelieved expenditure for that year cannot be carried forward except against any future post cessation receipts.

If relief was given and at a later date a related amount is received under an insurance policy or a trade receivables is recovered, this will be treated as a taxable post cessation receipt.

2.10.2 Valuing trading stock on cessation

When a trade ceases, the closing stock must be valued. The higher the value, the higher the profit for the final period of trading will be.

If the stock is sold to a UK trader who will deduct its cost in computing his taxable profits, it is valued under the following rules.

(a) If the seller and the buyer are unconnected, take the actual price.

(b) If the seller and the buyer are connected, take what would have been the price in an arm's length sale.

(c) However, if the seller and the buyer are connected, the arm's length price exceeds both the original cost of the stock and the actual transfer price, and both the seller and the buyer make an election, then take the greater of the original cost of the stock and the transfer price. The time limit for election for unincorporated business is the 31 January which is 22 months after the end of the tax year of cessation (for companies, it is two years after the end of the accounting period of cessation).

In all cases covered above, the value used for the seller's computation of profit is also used as the buyer's cost.

Key term

An individual is **connected** (connected person) with his spouse (or civil partner), with the relatives (brothers, sisters, ancestors and lineal descendants) of himself and his spouse (or civil partner), and with the spouses (or civil partners) of those relatives. He is also connected with his partners (except in relation to bona fide commercial arrangements for the disposal of partnership assets), and with their spouses (or civil partners) and relatives. Partners are connected with their partnerships, two partnerships are connected if they have any member in common, and partnerships are connected with companies under common control.

If the stock is not transferred to a UK trader who will be able to deduct its cost in computing his profits, then it is valued at its open market value as at the cessation of trade.

3 Basis periods

FAST FORWARD

Basis periods are used to link periods of account to tax years.

3.1 Introduction

A tax year runs from 6 April to 5 April, but most businesses do not have periods of account ending on 5 April. **Thus there must be a link between a period of account of a business and a tax year.** The procedure is to **find a period to act as the basis period for a tax year. The profits for a basis period are taxed in the corresponding tax year**. If a basis period is not identical to a period of account, the profits of periods of account are time-apportioned as required on the assumption that profits accrue evenly over a period of account. We will apportion to the nearest month for exam purposes.

We will now look at the basis period rules that apply in the opening, continuing and closing years of a business when there is no change of accounting date. Special rules are needed when the trader changes his accounting date. We will look at these rules in the next section.

The first tax year is the year during which the trade commences. For example, if a trade commences on 1 June 2006 the first tax year is 2006/07.

3.2 The first tax year

FAST FORWARD

In opening and closing years, special rules are applied so that a new trader can start to be taxed quickly, and a retiring trader need not be taxed long after his retirement.

The **basis period for the first tax year runs from the date the trade starts to the next 5 April** (or to the date of cessation if the trade does not last until the end of the tax year).

So continuing the above example a trader commencing in business on 1 June 2006 will be taxed on profits arising form 1 June 2006 to 5 April 2007 in 2006/07, their first tax year.

3.3 The second tax year

(a) **If the accounting date falling in the second tax year is at least 12 months after the start of trading, the basis period is the 12 months down to that accounting date**.

(b) **If the accounting date falling in the second tax year is less than 12 months after the start of trading, the basis period is the first 12 months of trading**.

(c) **If there is no accounting date falling in the second tax year**, because the first period of account is a very long one which does not end until a date in the third tax year, **the basis period for the second tax year is the year itself (from 6 April to 5 April).**

The following flowchart may help you determine the basis period for the second tax year.

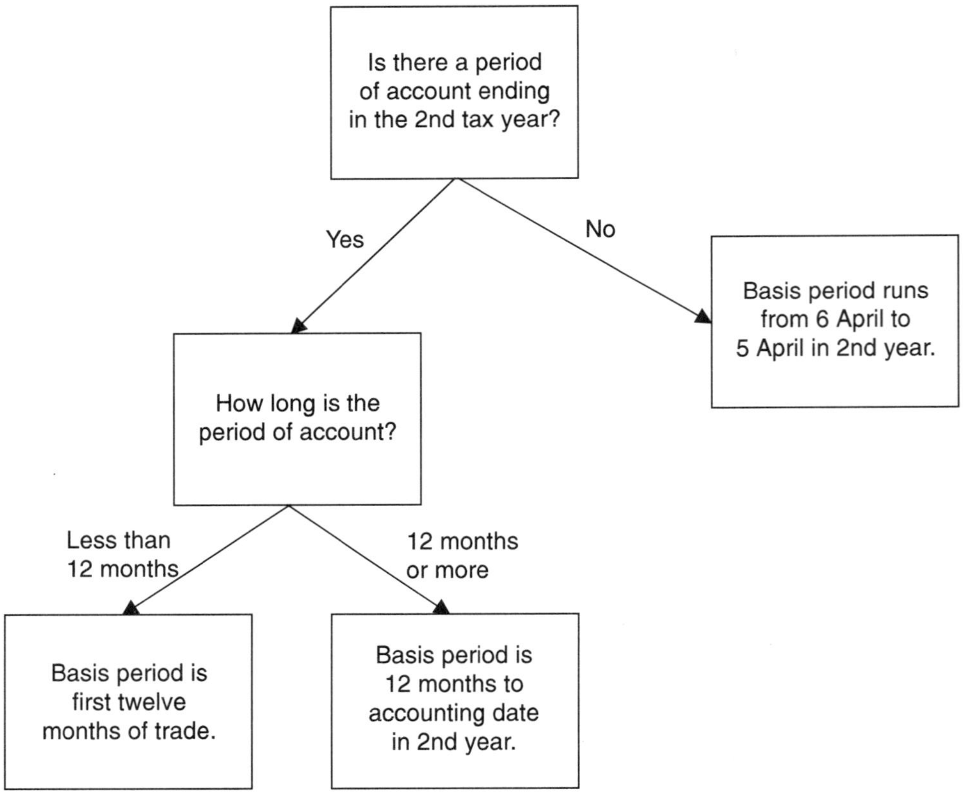

3.4 Examples: the first and second tax year

(a) John starts to trade on 1 January 2007 making up accounts to 31 December 2007.

1st tax year: 2006/07 – tax profits 1.1.07 – 5.4.07

2nd tax year: 2007/08

- Is there a period of account ending in 2007/08?

  Yes – Y.E. 31.12.07 ends 31.12.07.

- How long is the period of account?

  12 months or more ie 12m (exactly) to 31.12.07.

- So in 2007/08 tax profits of 12m to 31.12.07.

(b) Janet starts to trade on 1 January 2006 making up accounts as follows;

6m to 30 June 2007
12m to 30 June 2008.

1st tax year: 2006/07 – tax profits 1.1.07 – 5.4..07

2nd tax year: 2007/08.

- Is there a period of account ending in 2007/08?

  Yes – p.e. 30.6.07 ends 30.6.07

- How long is the period of account?

  Less than 12m ie 6m long.

- So in 2007/08 tax profits of first 12m of trade ie 1.1.07 – 31.2.07, ie

  p.e. 30.6.07 profits

  plus

  6/12 of y.e 30.6.08 profits

(c) Jodie starts to trade on 1 March 2007 making up a 14 month set of accounts to 30 April 2008.

1st tax year: 2006/07 – tax profits 1.3.07 – 5.4.07

2nd tax year: 2007/08

- Is there a period of account ending in 2007/08?

  No (p.e. 30.4.08 ends in 2008/09)

- So in 2007/08 tax profits of 6.4.07 – 5.4.08.

3.5 The third tax year

(a) **If there is an accounting date falling in the second tax year, the basis period for the third tax year is the period of account ending in the third tax year.**

(b) If there is no accounting date falling in the second tax year, the basis period for the third tax year is the 12 months down to the accounting date falling in the third tax year.

3.6 Later tax years

For later tax years, except the year in which the trade ceases, **the basis period is the period of account ending in the tax year**. This is known as the **current year basis of assessment**.

3.7 The final year

(a) If a trade starts and ceases in the same tax year, the basis period for that year is the whole lifespan of the trade.

(b) If the final year is the second year, the basis period runs from 6 April at the start of the second year to the date of cessation. This rule overrides the rules that normally apply for the second year.

(c) If the final year is the third year or a later year, **the basis period runs from the end of the basis period for the previous year to the date of cessation**. This rule overrides the rules that normally apply in the third and later years.

3.8 Overlap profits

Key term

> Profits which have been taxed more than once are called **overlap profits**.

When a business starts, some profits may be taxed twice because the basis period for the second year includes some or all of the period of trading in the first year or because the basis period for the third year overlaps with that for the second year.

Overlap profits may be deducted on a change of accounting date (see below). Any overlap profits unrelieved when the trade ceases are deducted from the final year's taxable profits. Any deduction of overlap profits may create or increase a loss. The usual loss reliefs (covered later in this text) are then available.

3.9 Example: accounting date in 2nd year at least 12 months

Jenny trades from 1 July 2001 to 31 December 2006, with the following results.

Period	*Profit*
	£
1.7.01 – 31.8.02	7,000
1.9.02 – 31.8.03	12,000
1.9.03 – 31.8.04	15,000
1.9.04 – 31.8.05	21,000
1.9.05 – 31.8.06	18,000
1.9.06 – 31.12.06	5,600
	78,600

The profits to be taxed in each tax year from 2001/02 to 2006/07, and the total of these taxable profits are calculated as follows.

Year	*Basis period*	*Working*	*Taxable profit*
			£
2001/02	1.7.01 – 5.4.02	£7,000 × 9/14	4,500
2002/03	1.9.01 – 31.8.02	£7,000 × 12/14	6,000
2003/04	1.9.02 – 31.8.03		12,000
2004/05	1.9.03 – 31.8.04		15,000
2005/06	1.9.04 – 31.8.05		21,000
2006/07	1.9.05 – 31.12.06	£(18,000 + 5,600 – 3,500)	20,100
			78,600

The overlap profits are those in the period 1 September 2001 to 5 April 2002, a period of seven months. They are £7,000 × 7/14 = £3,500. Overlap profits are either relieved on a change of accounting date (see below) or are deducted from the final year's taxable profit when the business ceases. In this case the overlap profits are deducted when the business ceases. Over the life of the business, the total taxable profits equal the total actual profits.

Question — **Calculation of taxable profits for six tax years**

Peter trades from 1 September 2001 to 30 June 2006, with the following results.

Period	*Profit*
	£
1.9.01 – 30.4.02	8,000
1.5.02 – 30.4.03	15,000
1.5.03 – 30.4.04	9,000
1.5.04 – 30.4.05	10,500
1.5.05 – 30.4.06	16,000
1.5.06 – 30.6.06	950
	59,450

Show the profits to be taxed in each year from 2001/02 to 2006/07, the total of these taxable profits and the overlap profits.

Answer

Year	*Basis period*	*Working*	*Taxable profits*
			£
2001/02	1.9.01 – 5.4.02	£8,000 × 7/8	7,000
2002/03	1.9.01 – 31.8.02	£8,000 + (£15,000 × 4/12)	13,000
2003/04	1.5.02 – 30.4.03		15,000
2004/05	1.5.03 – 30.4.04		9,000
2005/06	1.5.04 – 30.4.05		10,500
2006/07	1.5.05 – 30.6.06	£(16,000 + 950 − 12,000)	4,950
			59,450

The overlap profits are the profits from 1 September 2001 to 5 April 2002 (taxed in 2001/02 and in 2002/03) and those from 1 May 2002 to 31 August 2002 (taxed in 2002/03 and 2003/04).

	£
1.9.01 – 5.4.02 £8,000 × 7/8	7,000
1.5.02 – 31.8.02 £15,000 × 4/12	5,000
Total overlap profits	12,000

3.10 Example: no accounting date in the second year

Thelma starts to trade on 1 March 2005. Her first accounts, covering the 16 months to 30 June 2006, show a profit of £36,000. The taxable profits for the first three tax years and the overlap profits are as follows.

Year	*Basis period*	*Working*	*Taxable profits*
			£
2004/05	1.3.05 – 5.4.05	£36,000 × 1/16	2,250
2005/06	6.4.05 – 5.4.06	£36,000 × 12/16	27,000
2006/07	1.7.05 – 30.6.06	£36,000 × 12/16	27,000

The overlap profits are the profits from 1 July 2005 to 5 April 2006: £36,000 × 9/16 = £20,250.

3.11 The choice of an accounting date

A new trader should consider which accounting date would be best. There are **three factors to consider** from the point of view of taxation.

- **If profits are expected to rise, a date early in the tax year** (such as 30 April) will delay the time when rising accounts profits feed through into rising taxable profits, whereas a date late in the tax year (such as 31 March) will accelerate the taxation of rising profits. This is because with an accounting date of 30 April, the taxable profits for each tax year are mainly the profits earned in the previous tax year. With an accounting date of 31 March the taxable profits are almost entirely profits earned in the current year.
- If the accounting date in the second tax year is less than 12 months after the start of trading, the taxable profits for that year will be the profits earned in the first 12 months. If the accounting date is at least 12 months from the start of trading, they will be the profits earned in the 12 months to that date. **Different profits may thus be taxed twice (the overlap profits)**, and if profits are fluctuating this can make a considerable difference to the taxable profits in the first few years. **It may be many years before relief for the overlap profits is obtained.**
- **The choice of an accounting date affects the profits shown in each set of accounts**, and this may affect the taxable profits.

Question — The choice of an accounting date

Christine starts to trade on 1 December 2004. Her monthly profits are £1,000 for the first seven months, and £2,000 thereafter. Show the taxable profits for the first three tax years with each of the following accounting dates (in all cases starting with a period of account of less than 12 months).

(a) 31 March
(b) 30 April
(c) 31 December

Answer

(a) *31 March*

Period of account	*Working*	*Profits*
		£
1.12.04 – 31.3.05	£1000 × 4	4,000
1.4.05 – 31.3.06	£1,000 × 3 + £2,000 × 9	21,000
1.4.06 – 31.3.07	£2,000 × 12	24,000

Year	*Basis period*	*Taxable profits*
		£
2004/05	1.12.04 – 5.4.05	4,000
2005/06	1.4.05 – 31.3.06	21,000
2006/07	1.4.06 – 31.3.07	24,000

(b) *30 April*

Period of account	*Working*	*Profits*
		£
1.12.04 – 30.4.05	£1,000 × 5	5,000
1.5.05 – 30.4.06	£1,000 × 2 + £2,000 ×10	22,000

Year	Basis period	Working	Taxable profits
			£
2004/05	1.12.04 – 5.4.05	£5,000 × 4/5	4,000
2005/06	1.12.04 – 30.11.05	£5,000 + £22,000 × 7/12	17,833
2006/07	1.5.05 – 30.4.06		22,000

(c) *31 December*

Period of account	Working	Profits
		£
1.12.04 – 31.12.04	£1,000 × 1	1,000
1.1.05 – 31.12.05	£1,000 × 6 + £2,000 × 6	18,000
1.1.06 – 31.12.06	£2,000 × 12	24,000

Year	Basis period	Working	Taxable profits
			£
2004/05	1.12.04 – 5.4.05	£1,000 + £18,000 × 3/12	5,500
2005/06	1.1.05 – 31.12.05		18,000
2006/07	1.1.06 – 31.12.06		24,000

4 Change of accounting date

FAST FORWARD

On a change of accounting date, special rules may apply for fixing basis periods.

4.1 Introduction

A trader may change the date to which he prepares his annual accounts for a variety of reasons. For example, he may wish to move to a calendar year end or to fit in with seasonal variations of his trade. Special rules normally apply for fixing basis periods when a trader changes his accounting date.

On a change of accounting date there may be

- One set of accounts covering a period of less than twelve months, or
- One set of accounts covering a period of more than twelve months, or
- No accounts, or
- Two sets of accounts

ending in a tax year. In each case, the basis period for the year relates to the new accounting date. We will look at each of the cases in turn.

4.2 One short period of account

When a change of accounting date results in one short period of account ending in a tax year, the basis period for that year is always the 12 months to the new accounting date.

4.3 Example

Sue prepares accounts to 31 December each year until she changes her accounting date to 30 June by preparing accounts for the six months to 30 June 2006.

There is one short period of account ending during 2006/07. This means the basis period for 2006/07 is the twelve months to 30 June 2006.

Sue's basis period for 2005/06 was the twelve months to 31 December 2005. This means the profits of the six months to 31 December 2005 are overlap profits that have been taxed twice. These overlap profits must be added to any overlap profits that arose when the business began. The total is either relieved when the business ceases or it is relieved on a subsequent change of accounting date (see paragraphs 4.3 and 4.7).

4.4 One long period of account

When a change of accounting date results in one long period of account ending in a tax year, the basis period for that year ends on the new accounting date. It begins immediately after the basis period for the previous year ends. This means the basis period will exceed 12 months.

No overlap profits arise in this situation. However, more than twelve months worth of profits are taxed in one income tax year and to compensate for this, relief is available for brought forward overlap profits. The overlap relief cannot reduce the number of months worth of profits taxed in the year to below twelve. So, if you have a fourteen month basis period you can give relief for up to two months worth of overlap profits.

4.5 Example

Zoe started trading on 1 October 2003 and prepared accounts to 30 September until she changed her accounting date by preparing accounts for the fifteen months to 31 December 2006. Her results were as follows

Year to 30 September 2004	£24,000
Year to 30 September 2005	£48,000
Fifteen months to 31 December 2006	£75,000

Profits for the first three tax years of the business are:

2003/04 (1.10.03 – 5.4.04)	
6/12 × £24,000	£12,000
2004/05 (1.10.03 – 30.9.04)	£24,000
2005/06 (1.10.04 – 30.9.05)	£48,000

Overlap profits are £12,000. These arose in the six months to 5.4.04.

The change in accounting date results in one long period of account ending during 2006/07 which means the basis period for 2006/07 is the fifteen months to 31 December 2006. Three months worth of the brought forward overlap profits can be relieved.

	£
2006/07 (1.10.05 – 31.12.06)	75,000
Less: Overlap profits 3/6 × £12,000	(6,000)
	69,000

The unrelieved overlap profits of £6,000 (£12,000 – £6,000) are carried forward for relief either when the business ceases or on a further change of accounting date.

4.6 No accounting date ending in the year

If a change of accounting date results in there being no period of account ending in a tax year there is a potential problem because basis periods usually end on an accounting date. To get round this problem **you must manufacture a basis period by taking the new accounting date and deducting one year. The basis period is then the twelve months to this date.**

4.7 Example

Anne had always prepared accounts to 31 March. She then changed her accounting date by preparing accounts for the thirteen months to 30 April 2007.

There is no period of account ending during 2006/07 so the basis period for this year is the manufactured basis period of the twelve months to 30 April 2006.

You've probably spotted that this produces an overlap with the previous basis period. The overlap period is 1 May 2005 to 31 March 2006. The overlap profits arising in this period are added to any other unrelieved overlap profits and are carried forward for future relief.

4.8 Two Accounting Dates Ending in the Year

When two periods of account end in a tax year, the basis period for the year ends on the new accounting date. It begins immediately following the previous basis period. This means that the basis period will exceed 12 months and overlap relief can be allowed to ensure that only twelve months worth of profits are assessed in the tax year.

4.9 Example

Elizabeth prepared accounts to 30 September until 2007 when she changed her accounting date by preparing accounts for the six months to 31 March 2007.

The new accounting date is 31 March 2007. This is the end of the basis period for 2006/07. The basis period for 2005/06 ended on 30 September 2005. The 2006/07 basis period is therefore the eighteen month period 1 October 2005 to 31 March 2007. Six months worth of overlap profits can be relieved in this year.

4.10 Conditions

The above changes in basis period automatically occur if the trader changes his accounting date during the first three tax years of his business.

In other cases **the following conditions must be met before a change in basis periods can occur**:

- The trader must notify HMRC of the change by the 31 January, following the tax year in which the change is made. (By 31 January 2008 for a change made during 2006/07.)
- The period of account resulting from the change must not exceed 18 months.
- In general, there must have been no previous change of accounting date in the last 5 tax years. However, a second change can be made within this period if the later change is for genuine commercial reasons. If HMRC do not respond to a notification of a change of accounting date within 60 days of receiving it, the trader can assume that they are satisfied that the reasons for making the change are genuine commercial ones.

If the above conditions are not satisfied because the first period of account ending on the new date exceeds 18 months or the change of accounting date was not notified in time, but the 'five year gap or commercial reasons' condition is satisfied, then the basis period for the year of change is the 12 months to the *old* accounting date in the year of change. The basis period for the next year is then found using rules above as if it were the year of change.

If the 'five year gap or commercial reasons' test is not satisfied, the old accounting date remains in force for tax purposes (with the profits of accounts made up to the new date being time-apportioned as necessary) until there have been five consecutive tax years which were not years of change. The sixth tax year is then treated as the year of change to the new accounting date, and the rules above apply.

Chapter roundup

- The badges of trade can be used to decide whether or not a trade exists. If one does exist, the accounts profits need to be adjusted in order to establish the taxable trade profits.
- Basis periods are used to link periods of account to tax years.
- In opening and closing years, special rules are applied so that a new trader can start to be taxed quickly, and a retiring trader need not be taxed long after his retirement.
- On a change of accounting date, special rules may apply for fixing basis periods.

Quick quiz

1 List the six traditional badges of trade.

2 What are the remoteness test and the duality test?

3 What pre-trading expenditure is deductible?

4 In which period of account are earnings paid 12 months after the end of the period for which they are charged deductible?

5 What is the maximum allowable amount of redundancy pay on the cessation of a trade?

6 What is the basis period for the tax year in which a trade commenced?

7 On what two occasions may overlap profits potentially be relieved?

Answers to quick quiz

1 The subject matter
The frequency of transactions
The length of ownership
Supplementary work and marketing
A profit motive
The way in which goods were acquired

2 Expenditure is not deductible if it is not for trade purposes (the remoteness test), or if it reflects more than one purpose (the duality test)

3 Pre-trading expenditure is deductible if it is incurred within seven years of the start of the trade and is of a type that would have been deductible if the trade had already started.

4 In the period in which they are paid

5 3 × statutory amount

6 Date of commencement to 5 April in that year

7 On a change of accounting date where a basis period resulting from the change exceeds 12 months or on the cessation of a business

Now try the question below from the Exam Question Bank

Number	Level	Marks	Time
Q4	Introductory	10	18 mins

6

Capital allowances

Introduction

Depreciation cannot be deducted in computing taxable trade profits. Instead, capital allowances are given. In this chapter, we look at capital allowances, starting with plant and machinery.

Our study of plant and machinery falls into three parts. Firstly, we look at what qualifies for allowances: many business assets get no allowances at all. Secondly, we see how to compute the allowances and lastly, we look at special rules for assets with short lives, for assets which the taxpayer does not buy outright and for transfers of whole businesses.

We then look at industrial buildings. Again, we start off by looking at what qualifies for the allowances and then how to compute the allowances.

1 Capital allowances in general

FAST FORWARD

Capital allowances are available on plant and machinery and industrial buildings.

Capital expenditure may not be deducted in computing taxable trade profits, but it *may* attract capital allowances. Capital allowances are treated as a trading expense and are deducted in arriving at taxable trade profits. Balancing charges, effectively negative allowances, are added in arriving at those profits.

Capital expenditure on plant and machinery qualifies for capital allowances. Expenditure on industrial buildings may also qualify for allowances.

Both incorporated businesses and companies are entitled to capital allowances. For completeness, in this chapter we will look at the rules for companies alongside those for unincorporated businesses. We will look at companies in more detail later in this text.

For unincorporated businesses, capital allowances are calculated for periods of account. These are simply the periods for which the trader chooses to make up accounts. For companies, capital allowances are calculated for accounting periods. (See later in this text.)

For capital allowances purposes, expenditure is generally deemed to be incurred when the obligation to pay becomes unconditional. This will often be the date of a contract, but if for example payment is due a month after delivery of a machine, it would be the date of delivery. However, amounts due more than four months after the obligation becomes unconditional are deemed to be incurred when they fall due.

2 Plant and machinery – qualifying expenditure

2.1 Introduction

Capital expenditure on plant and machinery qualifies for capital allowances if the plant or machinery is used for a qualifying activity, such as a trade. "Plant" is not defined by the legislation, although some specific exclusions and inclusions are given. The word "machinery" may be taken to have its normal everyday meaning.

2.2 The statutory exclusions

FAST FORWARD

Statutory rules generally exclude specified items from treatment as plant, rather than include specified items as plant.

2.2.1 Buildings

Expenditure on a building and on any asset which is incorporated in a building or is of a kind normally incorporated into buildings does not qualify as expenditure on plant, but see below for exceptions.

In addition to complete buildings, **the following assets count as 'buildings', and are therefore not plant**.

- Walls, floors, ceilings, doors, gates, shutters, windows and stairs
- Mains services, and systems, of water, electricity and gas
- Waste disposal, sewerage and drainage systems
- Shafts or other structures for lifts etc.

2.2.2 Structures

Expenditure on structures and on works involving the alteration of land **does not qualify as expenditure on plant**, but see below for exceptions.

A 'structure' is a fixed structure of any kind, other than a building.

2.2.3 Exceptions

Over the years a large body of case law has been built up under which plant and machinery allowances have been given on certain types of expenditure which might be thought to be expenditure on a building or structure. Statute therefore gives a list of various assets which *may* still be plant. These are:

- Any machinery not within any other item in this list
- Electrical (including lighting), cold water, gas and sewerage systems:
  - (i) Provided mainly to meet the particular requirements of the trade, or
  - (ii) Provided mainly to serve particular machinery or plant used for the purposes of the trade
- Space or water heating systems and powered systems of ventilation
- Manufacturing and display equipment
- Cookers, washing machines, refrigeration or cooling equipment, sanitary ware and furniture and furnishings
- Lifts etc
- Sound insulation provided mainly to meet the particular requirements of the trade
- Computer, telecommunication and surveillance systems
- Sprinkler equipment, fire alarm and burglar alarm systems
- Strong rooms in bank or building society premises; safes
- Partition walls, where movable and intended to be moved
- Decorative assets provided for the enjoyment of the public in the hotel, restaurant or similar trades; advertising hoardings
- Glasshouses which have, as an integral part of their structure, devices which control the plant growing environment automatically
- Swimming pools (including diving boards, slides) and structures for rides at amusement parks.
- Caravans provided mainly for holiday lettings
- Movable buildings intended to be moved in the course of the trade
- Expenditure on altering land for the purpose only of installing machinery or plant
- Dry docks and jetties
- Pipelines, and also underground ducts or tunnels with a primary purpose of carrying utility conduits
- Silos provided for temporary storage and storage tanks, slurry pits and silage clamps
- Fish tanks, fish ponds and fixed zoo cages
- A railway or tramway

Items falling within the above list of exclusions will only qualify as plant if they fall within the meaning of plant as established by case law. This is discussed below.

2.2.4 Land

Land or an interest in land does not qualify as plant and machinery. For this purpose 'land' excludes buildings, structures and assets which are installed or fixed to land in such a way as to become part of the land for general legal purposes.

2.3 The statutory inclusions

Certain expenditure is specifically deemed to be expenditure on plant and machinery.

The following are deemed to be on plant and machinery.

- Expenditure incurred by a trader in complying with fire regulations for a building which he occupies
- Expenditure by a trader on thermal insulation of an industrial building
- Expenditure by a trader in meeting statutory safety requirements for sports ground
- Expenditure (by an individual or a partnership, not by a company) on *security assets* provided to meet a special threat to an individual's security that arises wholly or mainly due to the particular trade concerned. Cars, ships, aircraft and dwellings are specifically excluded from the definition of a security asset

On disposal, the sale proceeds for the above are deemed to be zero, so no balancing charge (see below) can arise.

Capital expenditure on computer software (both programs and data) **qualifies as expenditure on plant and machinery**:

(a) Regardless of whether the software is supplied in a tangible form (such as a disk) or transmitted electronically, and

(b) Regardless of whether the purchaser acquires the software or only a licence to use it.

Disposal proceeds are brought into account in the normal way, except that if the fee for the grant of a licence is taxed as income of the licensor, no disposal proceeds are taken into account in computing the licensee's capital allowances.

Where someone has incurred expenditure qualifying for capital allowances on computer software (or the right to use software), and receives a capital sum in exchange for allowing someone else to use the software, that sum is brought into account as disposal proceeds. However, the cumulative total of disposal proceeds is not allowed to exceed the original cost of the software, and any proceeds above this limit are ignored for capital allowances purposes (although they may lead to chargeable gains).

If software is expected to have a useful economic life of less than two years, its cost may be treated as revenue expenditure.

For companies the rules for computer software are overridden by the rules for intangible fixed assets unless the company elects otherwise.

2.4 Case law

FAST FORWARD

There are several cases on the definition of plant. To help you to absorb them, try to see the function/setting theme running through them.

The original case law **definition of plant** (applied in this case to a horse) is **'whatever apparatus is used by a businessman for carrying on his business: not his stock in trade which he buys or makes for sale; but all goods and chattels, fixed or movable, live or dead, which he keeps for permanent employment in the business'** (*Yarmouth v France 1887*).

Subsequent cases have refined the original definition and have largely been concerned with the **distinction between plant actively used in the business (qualifying) and the setting in which the business is carried on (non-qualifying). This is the 'functional' test**. Some of the decisions have now been enacted as part of statute law, but they are still relevant as examples of the principles involved.

The whole cost of excavating and installing a swimming pool was allowed to the owners of a caravan park. *CIR v Barclay Curle & Co 1969* was followed: the pool performed **the function** of giving 'buoyancy and enjoyment' to the persons using the pool (*Cooke v Beach Station Caravans Ltd 1974*) (actual item now covered by statute).

A barrister succeeded in his claim for his law library: 'Plant includes a man's tools of his trade. It extends to what he uses day by day in the course of his profession. It is not confined to physical things like the dentist's chair or the architect's table' (*Munby v Furlong 1977*).

Office partitioning was allowed. Because it was movable it was not regarded as part of the setting in which the business was carried on (*Jarrold v John Good and Sons Ltd 1963*) (actual item now covered by statute).

A ship used as a floating restaurant was regarded as a 'structure in which the business was carried on rather than apparatus employed ... ' (Buckley LJ). No capital allowances could be obtained *(Benson v Yard Arm Club 1978)*. The same decision was made in relation to a football club's spectator stand. The stand performed no function in the actual carrying out of the club's trade (*Brown v Burnley Football and Athletic Co Ltd 1980*).

At a motorway service station, false ceilings contained conduits, ducts and lighting apparatus. **They did not qualify because they did not perform a function in the business. They were merely part of the setting in which the business was conducted** (*Hampton v Fortes Autogrill Ltd 1979*).

Light fittings, decor and murals can be plant. A company carried on business as hoteliers and operators of licensed premises. The function of the items was the creation of an atmosphere conducive to the comfort and well being of its customers (*CIR v Scottish and Newcastle Breweries Ltd 1982*) (decorative assets used in hotels etc, now covered by statute).

On the other hand, it has been held that when an attractive floor is provided in a restaurant, the fact that the floor performs the function of making the restaurant attractive to customers is not enough to make it plant. It functions as premises, and the cost therefore does not qualify for capital allowances (*Wimpy International Ltd v Warland 1988*).

General lighting in a department store is not plant, as it is merely setting. Special display lighting, however, can be plant (*Cole Brothers Ltd v Phillips 1982*).

Free-standing decorative screens installed in the windows of a branch of a building society qualified as plant. Their function was not to act a part of the setting in which the society's business was carried on; it was to attract local custom, and accordingly the screens formed part of the apparatus with which the society carried on its business (*Leeds Permanent Building Society v Proctor 1982*).

In *Bradley v London Electricity plc 1996* an electricity substation was held not to be plant because it functioned as premises in which London Electricity carried on a trading activity rather than apparatus with which the activity was carried out.

3 Allowances on plant and machinery

FAST FORWARD

With capital allowances computations, the main thing is to get the layout right. Having done that, you will find that the figures tend to drop into place.

3.1 Pooling expenditure

Most expenditure on plant and machinery is put into a pool of expenditure on which capital allowances may be claimed. An addition increases the pool whilst a disposal decreases it.

Exceptionally the following items are not pooled.

(i) cars costing more than £12,000
(ii) assets with private use by the proprietor
(iii) short life assets where an election has been made.

Each of these items is dealt with in further detail below.

3.2 Writing down allowances

FAST FORWARD

Most expenditure on plant and machinery qualifies for a WDA at 25% every 12 months.

Key term

A **writing down allowance (WDA)** is given on pooled expenditure **at the rate of 25% a year** (on a reducing balance basis). The WDA is calculated on the written down value (WDV) of pooled plant, after adding the current period's additions and taking out the current period's disposals.

When plant is sold, proceeds (but **limited to a maximum of the original cost**) are taken out of the pool. Provided that the trade is still being carried on, the pool balance remaining is written down in the future by WDAs, even if there are no assets left.

3.3 Example

Elizabeth has a balance of unrelieved expenditure on her general pool of plant and machinery of £16,000 on 1.4.06. In the year to 31.3.07 she bought a car for £8,000 and she disposed of plant which originally cost £4,000 for £6,000.

Calculate the capital allowances available for the year.

	£
Pool value b/f	16,000
Addition	8,000
Less: Disposal (limited to cost)	(4,000)
	20,000
WDA @ 25%	(5,000)
TWDV c/f	15,000

WDAs are 25% × months/12:

(a) For unincorporated businesses where the period of account is longer or shorter than 12 months

(b) For companies where the accounting period is shorter than 12 months (a company's accounting period for tax purposes is never longer than 12 months), or where the trade concerned started in the accounting period and was therefore carried on for fewer than 12 months. Remember that we will be studying companies in detail later in this text.

Expenditure on plant and machinery by a person about to begin a trade is treated as incurred on the first day of trading. Assets previously owned by a trader and then brought into the trade (at the start of trading or later) are treated as bought for their market values at the times when they are brought in.

Allowances are claimed in the tax return.

Exam focus point

Note that from a tax planning point of view any business can claim less than the full allowances. **Adjusting capital allowances may be advantageous, if, for example, a trader wants to avoid making such a large loss claim as to lose the benefit of the personal allowance (see later in this text).** Higher capital allowances will then be available in later years because the WDV carried forward will be higher.

3.4 First year allowances

FAST FORWARD

First year allowances (FYA) may be available for certain expenditure. FYAs are never pro-rated in short or long periods of account.

3.4.1 Spending by medium sized enterprises

Expenditure incurred on plant and machinery (other than leased assets, cars, sea going ships, railway assets or long life assets) by **medium sized enterprises qualifies for a first year allowance (FYA) of 40%.**

Exam focus point

The rates of FYAs will be given to you on the exam paper.

Key term

A **medium sized enterprise**, is an individual, partnership or company that either satisfies at least two of the following conditions in the chargeable period/financial year in which the expenditure is incurred.

(a) **Turnover not more than £22.8 million**
(b) **Assets not more than £11.4 million**
(c) **Not more than 250 employees**

or which was medium sized in the previous year. A company must not be a member of a large group when the expenditure is incurred.

3.4.2 Spending by small sized enterprises

Expenditure incurred on plant and machinery by small sized enterprises **qualifies for a FYA** in the same way as for medium sized enterprises, but a higher rate of FYA may be available. The rate are:

Before 6 April 2004 (1 April 2004 for companies)	40%
6 April 2004 to 5 April 2005 (1 April 2004 to 31 March 2005 for companies)	50%
6 April 2005 to 5 April 2006 (1 April 2005 to 31 March 2006 for companies)	40%
6 April 2006 to 5 April 2007 (1 April 2006 to 31 March 2007 for companies)	50%
6 April 2007 (1 April 2007 onwards for companies)	40%

Key term

A **small enterprise** is an individual, partnership or company, which satisfies at least two of the following conditions in the chargeable period/financial year in which the expenditure is incurred:

(a) **Turnover not more than £5.6 million**
(b) **Assets not more than £2.8 million**
(c) **Not more than 50 employees**

or which was small in the previous year. If a company is a member of a group, the group must also be small when the expenditure is incurred.

3.4.3 100% FYAs

A 100% FYA is available to all businesses for expenditure incurred on designated energy saving technologies and on plant and equipment meeting strict water saving or efficiency criteria (eg water meters, flow controllers, efficient toilets!). The equipment must be used in the person's business.

A car registered between 17 April 2002 and 31 March 2008 qualifies for 100% FYAs if it either:

- **emits not more than 120 gm/km CO_2 ; or**
- **it is electrically propelled**

In addition, the special rules for expensive cars (see below), which restrict the availability of capital allowances and the deductibility of lease rental payments, do not apply to low emission cars.

A 100% FYA is available to all businesses in respect of expenditure incurred on plant to refuel vehicles with compressed natural gas or hydrogen, between 17 April 2002 and 31 March 2008.

Equipment acquired for leasing does not normally qualify for the 100% FYA. Exceptionally, leased low emission and electric cars, natural gas/hydrogen refuelling equipment and certain energy and water saving equipment all do qualify for FYAs.

Exam focus point

In exam questions you should only treat motor cars as low emission cars if they are specifically described as such. You are not expected to know the 120g/km limit.

3.4.4 Calculation

For FYA purposes, the provisions which treat capital expenditure incurred prior to the commencement of trading as incurred on the first day of trading do not apply except insofar as they require the FYAs to be given in the first period of account (or accounting period for companies).

First year allowances are given in the place of writing down allowances. For subsequent years a WDA is given on the balance of expenditure at the normal rate. You should therefore transfer the balance of the expenditure to the pool at the end of the first period.

FYAs are given for incurring expenditure. It is irrelevant whether the basis period of expenditure is twelve months or not. FYAs are not scaled up or down by reference to the length of the period.

Question — **Calculation of taxable profits**

Walton starts a trade on 1 March 2003, and has the following results (before capital allowances).

Period of account	*Profits*
	£
1.3.03 – 31.7.04	42,500
1.8.04 – 31.7.05	36,800
1.8.05 – 31.7.06	32,000

Plant (none of which is eligible for 100% FYAs) is bought as follows.

Date	*Cost*
	£
1.3.03	13,000
1.6.03	9,603
1.5.05	5,000
1.6.06	1,600

On 1 May 2005, plant which cost £7,000 is sold for £4,000.

Walton's business is a small enterprise for FYA purposes.

Show the taxable trade profits arising in the above periods of account.

Answer

The capital allowances are as follows.

	FYA	Pool	Allowances
	£	£	£
FYA			
1.3.03 – 31.7.03			
Additions (1.3.03 and 1.6.03)	22,603		
FYA 40%	(9,041)		9,041
		13,562	
1.8.04 – 31.7.05			
Disposals (1.5.05)		(4,000)	
		9,562	
WDA 25%		(2,391)	2,391
		7,171	
Addition (1.5.05)	5,000		
FYA 40%	(2,000)		2,000
		3,000	4,391
		10,171	
b/f		10,171	
1.8.05 – 31.7.06			
WDA 25%		(2,543)	2,543
		7,628	
Addition (1.6.06)	1,600		
FYA 50%	(800)		800
		800	
TWDV c/f		8,428	
			3,343

Note: First year allowances are not pro-rated in a long period of account.

The profits of the first three periods of account are as follows.

Period of account	*Working*	*Profits*
		£
1.3.03 – 31.7.04	£(42,500 – 9,041)	33,459
1.8.04 – 31.7.05	£(36,800 – 4,391)	32,409
1.8.05 – 31.7.06	£(32,000 – 3,343)	28,657

Exam focus point

Note the tax planning opportunities available. It may be important to buy plant just before an accounting date, so that allowances become available as soon as possible. On the other hand, it may be worthwhile to claim less than the maximum allowances so as to even out the annual assessments and avoid higher rate tax.

3.5 The disposal value of assets

The most common disposal value at which assets are entered in a capital allowances computation is the sale proceeds. But there are a number of less common situations.

Where the asset is sold at below market value (or is given away) the market value is used instead of the actual sale proceeds. This general rule has two exceptions. The actual proceeds of sale are used:

(a) Where the buyer will be able to claim capital allowances on the expenditure

(b) Where an employee acquires an asset from his employer at undervalue (or as a gift) and so faces a charge under the employment income benefit rules

If the asset is demolished, destroyed or otherwise lost, the disposal value is taken to be the actual sale proceeds from any resulting scrap, plus any insurance or other compensation moneys.

With all these rules, there is an overriding rule that the capital allowances **disposal value cannot exceed the original purchase price.**

When a building is sold, the vendor and purchaser can make a joint election to determine how the sale proceeds are apportioned between the building and its fixtures. There are anti-avoidance provisions that ensure capital allowances given overall on a fixture do not exceed the original cost of the fixture.

3.6 Balancing charges and allowances

Balancing charges occur when the disposal value deducted exceeds the balance remaining in the pool. The charge equals the excess and is effectively a negative capital allowance, increasing profits. Most commonly this happens when the trade ceases and the remaining assets are sold. It may also occur, however, whilst the trade is still in progress.

Balancing allowances on the capital allowance pools of expenditure arise only when the trade ceases. The balancing allowance is equal to the remaining unrelieved expenditure after deducting the disposal value of all the assets. Balancing allowances also arise on items which are not pooled (see below) whenever those items are disposed of.

3.7 Long life assets

Key term

Long life assets are assets with an expected working life of 25 years or more.

The writing down allowance available on such assets is 6% per annum on a reducing balance basis. Expenditure on such assets must be kept in a pool that is separate from the general pool.

The following are not **treated as long life assets** (and therefore (with the exception of expensive cars: see below) still qualify for writing down allowances of 25% per annum):

(a) **Plant and machinery in dwelling houses, retail shops, showrooms, hotels and offices**
(b) **Motor cars**
(c) **Ships and railways assets** bought before 1 January 2011
(d) **Second-hand machinery in respect of which the vendor obtained allowances at 25%**

The **long life asset rules do not apply to companies whose total expenditure on long life assets in a chargeable period is £100,000**, or less. If the expenditure exceeds £100,000, the whole of the expenditure qualifies for allowances at 6% per annum only. For this purpose all expenditure incurred under a contract is treated as incurred in the first chargeable period to which that contract relates.

Individuals and partnerships spending less than £100,000 a year are also excluded from the long life asset rules provided the individual, or at least half the partners, works full time in the business.

The £100,000 limit is reduced or increased proportionately in the case of a chargeable period of less or more than 12 months. In the case of groups of companies, the limit must be divided between the number of associated companies in the group (see later in this text).

The £100,000 exclusion is not available in respect of leased assets, second-hand assets where the vendor was only able to claim allowances of 6%, or assets where the trader has only bought a share.

3.8 Assets which are not pooled

FAST FORWARD

Private use assets by sole traders and partners have restricted capital allowances.

A separate record of allowances and WDV must be kept for each asset which is not pooled and when it is sold a balancing allowance or charge emerges.

Motor cars costing more than £12,000 are not pooled. The maximum WDA is £3,000 a year. The limit is £3,000 × months/12:

(a) For short or long periods of account of unincorporated businesses
(b) For short accounting periods of companies

FYAs are not available on cars (except for certain low emission or electric cars – see above).

An asset (for example, a car) which is used partly for private purposes by a sole trader or a partner is not pooled. Make all calculations on the full cost but claim only the business use proportion of the allowances. An asset with some private use by an employee (not a proprietor), however, suffers no such restriction. The employee may be taxed under the benefits code so the business gets capital allowances on the full cost of the asset.

Question

Capital allowances on a car

A trader started to trade on 1 July 2003, making up accounts to 31 December 2003 and each 31 December thereafter. On 1 August 2003 he bought a car for £15,500. The private use proportion is 10%. The car was sold in July 2006 for £4,000. What are the capital allowances?

Answer

	Car	*Allowances*
		90%
	£	£
1.7.03 – 31.12.03		
Purchase price	15,500	
WDA 25% × 6/12 of £15,500 = £1,938, Limited to £3,000 × 6/12 = £1,500	(1,500)	1,350
	14,000	
1.1.04 – 31.12.04		
WDA 25% of £14,000 = £3,500, Limited to £3,000	(3,000)	2,700
	11,000	
1.1.05 – 31.12.05		
WDA 25% of £11,000	(2,750)	2,475
	8,250	
1.1.06 – 31.12.06		
Proceeds	(4,000)	
Balancing allowance	4,250	3,825

Short life assets are not pooled (see below).

3.9 The cessation of a trade

When a business ceases to trade no FYAs or WDAs are given in the final period of account (unincorporated businesses) or accounting period (companies – see later in this text). Each asset is deemed to be disposed of on the date the trade ceased (usually at the then market value). Additions in the relevant period are brought in and then the disposal proceeds (limited to cost) are deducted from the balance of qualifying expenditure. If the proceeds exceed the balance then a balancing charge arises. If the balance of qualifying expenditure exceeds the proceeds then a balancing allowance is given.

4 Short-life assets

FAST FORWARD

Short life asset elections can bring forward the allowances due on an asset.

A trader can elect that specific items of plant be kept separately from the general pool. The election is irrevocable. For an unincorporated business, the time limit for electing is the 31 January which is 22 months after the end of the tax year in which the period of account of the expenditure ends. (For a company, it is two years after the end of the accounting period of the expenditure.) **Any asset subject to this election is known as a 'short-life asset', and the election is known as a 'de-pooling election'.**

Key term

Provided that the asset is disposed of within four years of the end of the period of account or accounting period in which it was bought, it is a **short life asset** and a balancing charge or allowance is made on its disposal.

The receipt of a capital sum in return for the right to use computer software does not count as a disposal for this purpose. If the asset is not disposed of in the correct time period, its tax written down value is added to the general pool at the end of that time.

The election should be made for assets likely to be sold within four years for less than their tax written down values. It should not be made for assets likely to be sold within four years for more than their tax written down values. (These are, of course, only general guidelines based on the assumption that a trader will want to obtain allowances as quickly as possible. There may be other considerations, such as a desire to even out annual taxable profits.)

Question — Short life assets

Caithlin bought an asset on 1 May 2002 for £12,000 and elected for de-pooling. His accounting year end is 30 April. Calculate the capital allowances due if:

(a) The asset is scrapped for £300 in August 2006.
(b) The asset is scrapped for £200 in August 2007.

Answer

(a)

Year to 30.4.03	£
Cost	12,000
WDA 25%	(3,000)
	9,000
Year to 30.4.04	
WDA 25%	(2,250)
	6,750
Year to 30.4.05	
WDA 25%	(1,688)
	5,062
Year to 30.4.06	
WDA 25%	(1,266)
	3,796
Year to 30.4.07	
Disposal proceeds	(300)
Balancing allowance	3,496

(b) If the asset is still in use at 30 April 2007, a WDA of 25% × £3,796 = £949 would be claimable in the year to 30 April 2007. The tax written down value of £3,796 – £949 = £2,847 would be added to the general pool at the beginning of the next period of account. The disposal proceeds of £200 would be deducted from the general pool in that period's capital allowances computation.

Short-life asset treatment cannot be claimed for:

- Motor cars
- Plant used partly for non-trade purposes
- Plant brought into use for the trade following non-business use
- Plant received by way of gift
- Plant in respect of which a subsidy is received
- Long life assets

Where a short-life asset is disposed of within the four year period to a connected person (see below):

(a) The original owner receives a balancing allowance calculated as normal and the new owner receives WDAs on the cost to him, but

(b) **If both parties so elect, the asset is treated as being sold for its tax written down value at the start of the chargeable period in which the transfer takes place, so there is no balancing charge or allowance for the vendor.**

In both situations, the acquiring party will continue to 'de-pool' the asset up to the same date as the original owner would have done.

5 Hire purchase and leasing

FAST FORWARD

Capital allowances are available on assets acquired by hire purchase or lease.

5.1 Assets on hire purchase or long term leases

Any asset (including a car) bought on hire purchase (HP) is treated as if purchased outright for the cash price. Therefore:

(a) The buyer normally obtains **capital allowances on the cash price** when the agreement begins.

(b) He may write off the **finance charge as a trade expense** over the term of the HP contract.

Long term leases, (those with a term of 5 or more years), are treated in the same way as HP transactions.

5.2 Assets on long term leases

Under a long term lease, the lessee merely hires the asset over a period. The hire charge can normally be deducted in computing trade profits. If an expensive car (one costing over £12,000) is leased, the maximum allowable deduction from trading profits for lease rentals is limited as described earlier in this text.

A long term lessor of plant normally obtains the benefit of capital allowances although there are anti-avoidance provisions which deny or restrict capital allowances on certain finance leases. Leasing is thus an activity which attracts tax allowances and which can be used to defer tax liabilities where the capital allowances given exceed the rental income. For individuals, any losses arising from leasing are available for offset against other income only if the individual devotes substantially all of his time to the conduct of a leasing business.

6 Successions

FAST FORWARD

Balancing adjustments are needed when a business ceases. If the business is transferred to a connected person, the written down value can be transferred instead.

Balancing adjustments arise on the cessation of a business. No writing down allowances are given, but the final proceeds (limited to cost) on sales of plant are compared with the tax WDV to calculate balancing allowances or charges.

Balancing charges may be avoided where the trade passes from one connected person to another. If a succession occurs both parties must elect if the avoidance of the balancing adjustments is required. **An election will result in the plant being transferred at its tax written down value for capital allowances purposes**. The predecessor can write down the plant for the period prior to cessation and the successor can write it down from the date of commencement. The election must be made within two years of the date of the succession.

If no election is made on a transfer of business to a connected person, assets are deemed to be sold at their market values.

An individual is connected with his spouse, his, or his spouse's brothers, sisters, ancestors and lineal descendants, with their spouses, and with a company he controls. 'Spouses' includes civil partners.

Where a person succeeds to a business under a will or on intestacy, then even if he was not connected with the deceased he may elect to take over the assets at the lower of their market value and their tax written down value.

For both connected persons transfers and transfers on death, where the elections are made, the limit on proceeds to be brought into account on a later sale of an asset is the original cost of the asset, not the deemed transfer price.

7 Industrial buildings – types

FAST FORWARD

The computations for industrial buildings are a little more complicated than those for plant and machinery, but there is less case law to learn. Basically allowances equal to the fall in value of the building whilst it was being used industrially are available to the trader.

7.1 Introduction

A special type of capital allowance (an **industrial buildings allowance** or IBA) is available in respect of **expenditure on industrial buildings**.

The allowance is available to:

- Traders
- Landlords who let qualifying buildings to traders.

Traders can choose whether to segregate expenditure on long life assets in buildings and claim plant and machinery allowances (see above) or whether to claim industrial buildings allowances on the expenditure.

Key term

Industrial buildings include:

(a) All factories and ancillary premises used in:

(i) A manufacturing business
(ii) A trade in which goods and materials are subject to any process
(iii) A trade in which goods or raw materials are stored

(b) Staff welfare buildings (such as workplace nurseries and canteens, but not directors' restaurants) where the trade is qualifying

(c) Sports pavilions in any trade

(d) Buildings in use for a transport undertaking, agricultural contracting, mining or fishing

(e) Roads operated under highway concessions. The operation of such roads is treated as a trade for capital allowances purposes. The operator is treated as occupying the roads.

The key term in (a) (ii) above is 'the subjection of goods to any process'.

- The unpacking, repacking and relabelling of goods in a wholesale cash and carry supermarket did not amount to a 'process' but was a mere preliminary to sale (*Bestway Holdings Ltd v Luff 1998*).

- The mechanical processing of cheques and other banking documents was a process but pieces of paper carrying information were not 'goods' and thus the building housing the machinery did not qualify (*Girobank plc v Clarke 1998*).

Estate roads on industrial estates qualify, provided that the estate buildings are used wholly or mainly for a qualifying purpose.

Dwelling houses, retail shops, showrooms and offices are not industrial buildings.

Warehouses used for storage often cause problems in practice. A warehouse used for storage which is merely a transitory and necessary incident of the conduct of the business is not an industrial building. Storage is only a qualifying purpose if it is an end in itself.

Any building is an industrial building if it is constructed for the welfare of employees of a trader whose trade is a qualifying one (that is, the premises in which the trade is carried on are industrial buildings).

Sports pavilions provided for the welfare of employees qualify as industrial buildings. In this case, it does not matter whether the taxpayer is carrying on a trade in a qualifying building or not. Thus a retailer's sports pavilion would qualify for IBAs.

Drawing offices which serve an industrial building are regarded as industrial buildings themselves (*CIR v Lambhill Ironworks Ltd 1950*).

7.2 Hotels

Allowances on hotels are given as though they were industrial buildings.

Key term

For a building to qualify as a '**hotel**' for industrial buildings allowance purposes:

(a) It must have at least ten letting bedrooms

(b) It must have letting bedrooms as the whole or main part of the sleeping accommodation

(c) It must offer ancillary services including at least:

- (i) Breakfast
- (ii) Evening meals
- (iii) The cleaning of rooms
- (iv) The making of beds

(d) It must be open for at least four months during the April to October season.

7.3 Eligible expenditure

Capital allowances are computed on the amount of eligible expenditure incurred on qualifying buildings. The eligible expenditure is:

- The original cost of a building if built by the trader, or
- The purchase price if the building was acquired from a person trading as a builder.

If the building was acquired other than from a person trading as a builder, the eligible expenditure is the lower of the purchase price and the original cost incurred by the person incurring the construction expenditure.

If a building is sold more than once before being brought into use, the last buyer before the building is brought into use obtains the allowances. If, in such cases, the building was first sold by someone trading as a builder, the eligible expenditure is the lower of the price paid by the first buyer and the price paid by the last buyer.

In all cases where a building is sold before use and artificial arrangements have increased the purchase price, it is reduced to what it would have been without those arrangements.

Where part of a building qualifies as an industrial building and part does not, the whole cost qualifies for IBAs, provided that the cost of the non-qualifying part is not more than 25% of the total expenditure. If the non-qualifying part of the building does cost more than 25% of the total, its cost must be excluded from the capital allowances computation.

Difficulties arise where non-qualifying buildings (particularly offices and administration blocks) are joined to manufacturing areas. In *Abbott Laboratories Ltd v Carmody 1968* a covered walkway linking manufacturing and administrative areas was not regarded as creating a single building. The administrative area was treated as a separate, non-qualifying building.

The cost of land is disallowed but expenditure incurred in preparing land for building does qualify. The cost of items which would not be included in a normal commercial lease (such as rental guarantees) also does not qualify.

Professional fees, for example architects' fees, incurred in connection with the construction of an industrial building qualify. The cost of repairs to industrial buildings also qualifies, provided that the expenditure is not deductible as a trading expense.

8 Allowances on industrial buildings

FAST FORWARD

An allowance, normally at the rate of 4% per annum, is given if a building is in industrial use on the last day of the period of account concerned. If the building is in non industrial use a notional allowance may be given.

8.1 Writing down allowances

A writing down allowance (WDA) is given to the person holding the 'relevant interest'. Broadly, the relevant interest is the interest of the first acquirer of the industrial building and may be a freehold or leasehold interest.

Where a long lease (more than 50 years) has been granted on an industrial building, the grant may be treated as a sale so that allowances may be claimed by the lessee rather than the lessor. A claim must be made by the lessor and lessee jointly, within two years of the start of the lease. The election allows allowances to be claimed on industrial buildings where the lessor is not subject to tax (as with local authorities).

The WDA is given for a period provided that the industrial building was in use as such on the last day of the period concerned.

If the building was not in use as an industrial building at the end of the relevant period it may have been:

- **Unused** for any purpose, or
- **Used for a non-industrial purpose.**

The distinction is important in ascertaining whether WDAs are due to the taxpayer. **If any disuse is temporary and previously the building had been in industrial use, WDAs may be claimed in exactly the same way as if the building were in industrial use.** The legislation does not define 'temporary' but in practice, any subsequent qualifying use of the building will usually enable the period of disuse to be regarded as temporary.

Non-industrial use has different consequences. If this occurs a notional WDA is deducted from the balance of unrelieved expenditure but no WDA may be claimed by the taxpayer.

The WDA is 4% of the eligible expenditure incurred by the taxpayer. For expenditure before 6 November 1962, the rate is 2%.

The allowance is calculated on a straight line basis (in contrast to WDAs on plant and machinery which are calculated on the reducing balance), starting when the building is brought into use.

The WDA is 4% (or 2%) × **months/12 if the period concerned is not 12 months long.**

Buildings always have a **separate computation for each building**. They are never pooled.

8.2 Balancing adjustments on sale

8.2.1 The tax life

The 'tax life' of an industrial building is 25 years after it is first used, or 50 years if constructed before 6 November 1962. Balancing adjustments apply *only* if a building is sold within its tax life.

On a sale between connected persons, the parties may jointly elect that the transfer price for IBAs purposes should be the lower of the market value and the residue of unallowed expenditure before the sale. This avoids a balancing charge unless there has been non-industrial use.

8.2.2 Sales without non-industrial use

The seller's calculation is quite straightforward providing the building has not been put to non-industrial use at any time during his ownership. It takes the following form.

	£
Cost	X
Less allowances previously given	(X)
Residue before sale	X
Less proceeds (limited to cost)	(X)
Balancing (charge)/allowance	(X)

The buyer obtains annual straight line WDAs for the remainder of the building's tax life (25 years if constructed after 5 November 1962). This life is calculated to the nearest month. The allowances are granted on the residue after sale which is computed thus.

	£
Residue before sale	X
Plus balancing charge or less balancing allowance	X
Residue after sale	X

This means that **the second owner will write off the lower of his cost or the original cost**.

Question — Calculation of IBAs

Frankie, who started to trade in 2001 preparing accounts to 31 December, bought an industrial building for £100,000 (excluding land) on 1 October 2002. He brought it into use as a factory immediately. On 1 September 2006 he sells it for £120,000 to Holly, whose accounting date is 30 September and who brought the building into industrial use immediately. Show the IBAs available to Frankie and to Holly.

Answer

	£
Frankie	
Cost 1.10.02	100,000
Y/e 31.12.02 to y/e 31.12.05 WDA 4 × 4%	(16,000)
Residue before sale	84,000
Y/e 31.12.06 Proceeds (limited to cost)	(100,000)
Balancing charge	(16,000)
Holly	
Residue before sale	84,000
Balancing charge	16,000
Residue after sale	100,000

The tax life of the building ends on 1.10.02 + 25 years = 30.9.2027

The date of Holly's purchase is 1.9.06. The unexpired life is therefore 21 years 1 month

	£
Y/e 30.9.06 WDA £100,000/21.083333	4,743
Next 20 accounting periods at £4,743 a year	94,860
Y/e 30.9.27 (balance)	397
	100,000

Exam focus point

HMRC allow IBAs equal to the fall in value of a building over the trader's use of that building. As a general rule if an industrial building is sold for more than its original cost a balancing charge equal to the allowances given to date will arise. This is because there was no fall in value so no allowances are actually due.

If it is sold for less than original cost we could calculate the fall in value of the building and that would equal the allowances available for this building. If we compare this to the allowances already given, the difference would be the balancing adjustment due on the sale.

In the above question if Frankie sold the building Holly for £90,000:

	£
Fall in value (£100,000 – £90,000) = allowances due	10,000
Less: allowances already given to Frankie	16,000
Balancing adjustment = Balancing charge	6,000

Over the use of the building by Frankie £16,000 of IBAs were claimed. On the sale of the building the fall in value is calculated as £10,000. Thus Frankie should only have received £10,000 of allowances not £16,000. So £6,000 is paid back as a balancing charge.

Businesses are denied a balancing allowance where disposal proceeds are less than they would have been as a result of a tax avoidance scheme.

8.3 Sales after non-industrial use

If at the end of a period, an industrial building was in non-industrial use, then the owner will not have been able to claim WDAs, but the building will have been written down by notional WDAs.

If, following a period of non-industrial use, an industrial building is sold for more than its original cost, the balancing charge is the actual allowances given. The residue after sale is the original cost minus the notional allowances.

Exam focus point

Sales for less than original cost after a period of non industrial use will not be examined.

Question — Non-industrial use

The facts are as in the above question except that on 1 October 2003 Frankie ceases manufacturing in the building, letting it out as a theatrical rehearsal studio. On 1 June 2005 he recommences manufacturing in the building and, as before, sells it to Holly for £120,000 on 1 September 2006. Show the IBAs available to Frankie and to Holly.

Answer

	£
Frankie	
Cost 1.10.02	100,000
Y/e 31.12.02 WDA 4%	(4,000)
	96,000
Y/e 31.12.03 and y/e 31.12.04 No WDA since not in industrial use at the ends of the accounting periods, but deduct notional allowances 2 × 4%	(8,000)
	88,000
Y/e 31.12.05 WDA 4%	(4,000)
Residue before sale	84,000
Balancing charge for y/e 31.12.06: real (not notional) allowances £(4,000 + 4,000)	£(8,000)

	£
Holly	
Residue before sale	84,000
Add: balancing charge	8,000
Residue after sale	92,000

	£
Y/e 30.9.06 WDA £92,000/21.083333	4,364
Next 20 account periods at £4,364 a year	87,280
Y/e 30.9.27 (balance)	356
	92,000

Chapter roundup

- Statutory rules generally exclude specified items from treatment as plant, rather than include specified items as plant.
- There are several cases on the definition of plant. To help you to absorb them, try to see the function/setting theme running through them.
- With capital allowances computations, the main thing is to get the layout right. Having done that, you will find that the figures tend to drop into place.
- Most expenditure on plant and machinery qualifies for a WDA at 25% every 12 months.
- First year allowances (FYA) may be available for certain expenditure. FYAs are never pro-rated in short or long periods of account.
- Private use assets by sole traders and partners have restricted capital allowances.
- Short life asset elections can bring forward the allowances due on an asset.
- The computations for industrial buildings are a little more complicated than those for plant and machinery, but there is less case law to learn. Basically allowances equal to the fall in value of the building whilst it was being used industrially are available to the trader.
- An allowance, normally at the rate of 4% per annum, is given if a building is in industrial use on the last day of the period of account concerned. If the building is in non industrial use a notional allowance may be given.

Quick quiz

1 For what periods are capital allowances for unincorporated businesses calculated?
2 Are writing down allowances pro-rated in a six month period of account?
3 Are first year allowances pro-rated in a six month period of account?
4 When may balancing allowances arise?
5 Within what period must an asset be disposed of if it is to be treated as a short life asset?
6 List four types of building which do not usually qualify for industrial buildings allowance.
7 When are drawing offices industrial buildings?
8 What are the conditions for a hotel to qualify for allowances?
9 When must a 'notional allowance' be deducted from the qualifying cost of an industrial building?
10 What is the amount of the balancing charge on a sale where there been non-industrial use?

Answers to quick quiz

1 Periods of account

2 Yes. In a six month period, writing down allowance are pro-rated by multiplying by 6/12.

3 No. First year allowances are given in full in a short period of account.

4 Balancing allowances may arise in respect of pooled expenditure only when the trade ceases. Balancing allowances may arise on non-pooled items whenever those items are disposed of.

5 Within four years of the end of the period of account (or accounting period) in which it was bought

6 Dwelling houses, retail shops, showrooms and offices

7 Drawing offices which serve an industrial building are industrial buildings

8 (a) It must have ten letting bedrooms

(b) It must have letting bedrooms as the whole or main part of the sleeping accommodation

(c) It must offer ancillary services including at least

(i) Breakfast
(ii) Evening meals
(iii) The cleaning of rooms
(iv) The making of beds

(d) It must be open for at least four months during the April to October letting season.

9 A notional allowance will be given if a building was in non-industrial use at the end of the period of account (accounting period) concerned

10 The balancing charge is equal to the industrial buildings allowances actually given

Now try the question below from the Exam Question Bank

Number	Level	Marks	Time
Q5	Introductory	20	36 mins

7

Trading losses

Introduction

Traders sometimes make losses rather than profits. In this chapter we consider the reliefs available for losses. A loss does not in itself lead to getting tax back from HMRC. Relief is obtained by setting a loss against trading profits, against other income or against capital gains, so that tax need not be paid on them. An important consideration is the choice between different reliefs. The aim is to use a loss to save as much tax as possible, as quickly as possible.

Topic list	Syllabus references
1 Losses	1(e)
2 Relief for trading losses by carry forward: s 385 ICTA 1988	1(e)
3 Setting trading losses against total income: s 380 ICTA 1988	1(e)
4 Businesses transferred to companies: s 386 ICTA 1988	1(e)
5 Trade charges: s 387 ICTA 1988	1(e)
6 Losses in the early years of a trade: s 381 ICTA 1988	1(b)
7 Losses on the cessation of a trade: s 388 ICTA 1988	1(e)
8 Losses on unquoted shares: s 574 ICTA 1988	1(e)

1 Losses

FAST FORWARD

Trade losses may be relieved against future profits of the same trade, against total income and against capital gains.

This chapter considers how losses are calculated and how a loss-suffering taxpayer can use a loss to reduce his tax liability. Most of the chapter concerns the trade losses in respect of trades, professions and vocations.

The rules in this chapter apply only to individuals, trading alone or in partnership. Loss reliefs for companies are completely different and are covered later in this text.

Losses incurred in foreign trades are computed and relieved in a similar manner to those of UK trades and are discussed later in this text. Losses from a UK property business have been discussed earlier, and losses on an overseas property business are relieved similarly. If a loss arises on a transaction which, if profitable, would give rise to taxable miscellaneous income (see earlier in this text), it can be set against any other similar income in the same year, and any excess carried forward for relief against miscellaneous income in future years.

Losses of one spouse or civil partner cannot be relieved against income of the other spouse or civil partner.

When computing taxable trade profits, profits may turn out to be negative, that is a loss has been made in the basis period. **A loss is computed in exactly the same way as a profit**, making the same adjustments to the accounts profit or loss.

If there is a loss in a basis period, the taxable trade profits for the tax year based on that basis period are nil.

2 Relief for trading losses by carry forward: s 385 ICTA 1988

FAST FORWARD

A trade loss carried forward must be set against the first available trade profits of the same trade.

A trade loss not relieved in any other way may be **carried forward to set against the first available trade profits of the same trade**. Losses may be carried forward for any number of years.

2.1 Example: carrying forward losses

B has the following results.

Year ending	£
31 December 2004	(6,000)
31 December 2005	5,000
31 December 2006	11,000

B's taxable profits, assuming that he claims loss relief only under s 385 are:

	2004/05		*2005/06*		*2006/07*
	£		£		£
Trade profits	0		5,000		11,000
Less s 385 relief	(0)	(i)	(5,000)	(ii)	(1,000)
Profits	0		0		10,000

Loss memorandum		£
Trading loss, y/e 31.12.04		6,000
Less: claim in y/e 31.12.05	(i)	(5,000)
claim in y/e 31.12.06 (balance of loss)	(ii)	(1,000)
		0

3 Setting trading losses against total income: s 380 ICTA 1988

FAST FORWARD

It is important for a trader to choose the right loss relief, so as to save tax at the highest possible rate and so as to obtain relief reasonably quickly.

3.1 Introduction

Instead of carrying a trade loss forward against future trade profits, it may be relieved against current income of all types.

3.2 The computation of the loss

The trade loss for a tax year is the trade loss in the basis period for that tax year. However, **if basis periods overlap then a loss in the overlap period is a trade loss for the earlier tax year only**.

3.3 Example

Here is an example of a trader who starts to trade on 1 July 2006 and makes losses in opening years.

Period of account	*Loss*
	£
1.7.06 – 31.12.06	9,000
1.1.07 – 31.12.07	24,000

Tax year	*Basis period*	*Working*	*Trade loss for the tax year*
			£
2006/07	1.7.06 – 5.4.07	£9,000 + (£24,000 × 3/12)	15,000
2007/08	1.1.07 – 31.12.07	£24,000 – (£24,000 × 3/12)	18,000

3.4 Example

The same rule against using losses twice applies when losses are netted off against profits in the same basis period. Here is an example, again with a commencement on 1 July 2006 but with a different accounting date.

Period of account	*(Loss)/profit*
	£
1.7.06 – 30.4.07	(10,000)
1.5.07 – 30.4.08	24,000

Tax year	*Basis period*	*Working*	*Trade (Loss)/Profit*
			£
2006/07	1.7.06 – 5.4.07	£(10,000) × 9/10	(9,000)
2007/08	1.7.06 – 30.6.07	£24,000 × 2/12 + £(10,000) × 1/10	3,000

3.5 Relieving the loss

Relief under s 380 **is against the income of the tax year in which the loss arose**. **In addition or instead,** relief may be claimed **against the income of the preceding year**.

If there are losses in two successive years, and relief is claimed against the first year's income both for the first year's loss and for the second year's loss, relief is given for the first year's loss before the second year's loss.

A claim for a loss must be made by the 31 January which is 22 months after the end of the tax year of the loss: thus by 31 January 2009 for a loss in 2006/07.

The taxpayer cannot choose the amount of loss to relieve: thus the loss may have to be set against income part of which would have been covered by the personal allowance. However, the taxpayer can choose whether to claim full relief in the current year and then relief in the preceding year for any remaining loss, or the other way round.

Set the loss against non-savings income then against savings (excluding dividend) income and finally against dividend income.

Relief is available by carry forward under s 385 for any loss not relieved under s 380.

Question

s 380 relief

Janet has a loss in her period of account ending 31 December 2006 of £25,000. Her other income is £18,000 rental income a year, and she wishes to claim loss relief for the year of loss and then for the preceding year. Show her taxable income for each year, and comment on the effectiveness of the loss relief. Assume that tax rates and allowances for 2006/07 have always applied.

Answer

The loss-making period ends in 2006/07, so the year of the loss is 2006/07.

	2005/06	*2006/07*
	£	£
Income	18,000	18,000
Less s 380 relief	(7,000)	(18,000)
STI	11,000	0
Less personal allowance	(5,035)	(5,035)
Taxable income	5,965	0

In 2006/07, £5,035 of the loss has been wasted because that amount of income would have been covered by the personal allowance. If Janet claims s 380 relief, there is nothing she can do about this waste of loss relief.

3.6 Capital allowances

The trader may adjust the size of the total s 380 claim by not claiming all the capital allowances he is entitled to: a reduced claim will increase the balance carried forward to the next year's capital allowances computation. This may be a useful **tax planning point where the effective rate of relief for capital allowances in future periods will be greater than the rate of tax relief for the s 380 loss**.

3.7 Trading losses relieved against capital gains

Where relief is claimed against total income of a given year, the taxpayer may include **a further claim to set the loss against his chargeable gains for the year** less any allowable capital losses for the same year or for previous years. This amount of net gains is computed ignoring taper relief and the annual exempt amount (see later in this text).

The trading loss is first set against total income of the year of the claim, and only any excess of loss is set against capital gains. The taxpayer cannot specify the amount to be set against capital gains, so the annual exempt amount may be wasted. We include an example here for completeness. You will study chargeable gains later in this text and we suggest that you come back to this example at that point.

Question — Loss relief against income and gains

Sibyl had the following results for 2006/07.

	£
Loss available for relief under s 380	27,000
Income	19,500
Capital gains less current year capital losses	10,000
Annual exemption for capital gains tax purposes	8,800
Capital losses brought forward	4,000

Assume no taper relief is due.

Show how the loss would be relieved against income and gains.

Answer

	£
Income	19,500
Less loss relief	(19,500)
STI	0
Capital gains	10,000
Less loss relief: lower of £(27,000 – 19,500) = £7,500 (note 1) and £(10,000 – 4,000) = £6,000 (note 2)	(6,000)
	4,000
Less annual exemption (restricted)	(4,000)
	0

Note 1 This equals the loss left after the S380 claim

Note 2 This equals the gains left after losses b/fwd but ignoring taper relief and the annual exemption.

A trading loss of £(7,500 – 6,000) = £1,500 is carried forward. Sibyl's personal allowance and £(8,800 – 4,000) = £4,800 of her capital gains tax annual exemption are wasted. Her capital losses brought forward of £4,000 are carried forward to 2007/08. Although we deducted this £4,000 in working out how much trading loss we were allowed to use in the claim, we do not actually use any of the £4,000 unless there are gains remaining after the annual exemption.

3.8 Restrictions on s 380 relief

Relief cannot be claimed under s 380 unless a business is conducted on a commercial basis with a view to the realisation of profits; this condition applies to all types of business.

3.9 The choice between loss reliefs

When a trader has a choice between loss reliefs, he should aim to obtain relief both quickly and at the highest possible tax rate. However, do consider that losses relieved against income which would otherwise be covered by the personal allowance are wasted.

Another consideration is that a trading loss cannot be set against the capital gains of a year unless relief is first claimed under s 380 against income of the same year. It may be worth making the claim against income and wasting the personal allowance in order to avoid a CGT liability.

Question — The choice between loss reliefs

Felicity's trading results are as follows.

Year ended 30 September	*Trading profit/(loss)*
	£
2004	1,900
2005	(21,000)
2006	13,000

Her other income (all non-savings income) is as follows.

	£
2004/05	2,200
2005/06	26,500
2006/07	15,000

Show the most efficient use of Felicity's trading loss. Assume that the personal allowance has been £5,035 throughout.

Answer

Relief could be claimed under s 380 for 2004/05 and/or 2005/06, with any unused loss being carried forward under s 385. Relief in 2004/05 would be against total income of £(1,900 + 2,200) = £4,100, all of which would be covered by the personal allowance anyway, so this claim should not be made. A s 380 claim should be made for 2005/06 as this saves tax quicker than a s 385 claim in 2006/07 would. The final results will be as follows:

	2004/05	*2005/06*	*2006/07*
	£	£	£
Trading income	1,900	0	13,000
Less s 385 relief	(0)	(0)	(0)
	1,900	0	13,000
Other income	2,200	26,500	15,000
	4,100	26,500	28,000
Less s 380 relief	(0)	(21,000)	(0)
STI	4,100	5,500	28,000
Less personal allowance	(5,035)	(5,035)	(5,035)
Taxable income	0	465	22,965

Exam focus point

Before recommending s 380 loss relief consider whether it will result in the waste of the personal allowance and any tax reducers. Such waste is to be avoided if at all possible.

4 Businesses transferred to companies: s 386 ICTA 1988

FAST FORWARD

If a business is transferred to a company, a loss of the unincorporated business can be set against income received from the company.

Although the set-off under s 385 is restricted to future profits of the same business, this is extended to cover income received from a company to which the business is sold under s 386.

The amount carried forward is the total unrelieved trading losses of the business. The set-off must be made against the first available income from the company. The order of set-off is:

(a) Against **salary** derived from the company by the former proprietor of the business; **then**
(b) Against **interest and dividends** from the company

The consideration for the sale must be wholly or mainly shares, which must be retained by the vendor throughout any tax year in which the loss is relieved; HMRC treat this condition as being satisfied if 80% or more of the consideration consists of shares.

5 Trade charges: s 387 ICTA 1988

FAST FORWARD

Excess trade charges can be used in the same way as losses under s 385.

5.1 Introduction

Annual charges such as patent royalties, although they may be paid out wholly and exclusively for business purposes, are nevertheless not deducted in arriving at the adjusted trade profits or losses.

But it is possible to suffer a 'loss' if STI is reduced to zero by such a charge because HMRC will collect the tax withheld from the charge under s 350 ICTA 1988. **Excess trade charges can be carried forward against future profits from the same trade** in the same way as losses under s 385. Non-trade charges, however cannot be relieved in this way.

5.2 Example: excess trade charges

A taxpayer has the following results for 2006/07.

	£
Trading profit	4,000
Other income	1,000
	5,000
Less patent royalty	(7,000)
STI	0

Basic rate tax would be due on the unrelieved £2,000, so that the taxpayer accounted for 22% × £2,000 = £440, but the taxpayer could then carry forward the £2,000 against future profits from the trade.

6 Losses in the early years of a trade: s 381 ICTA 1988

FAST FORWARD

In opening years, a special relief involving the carry back of losses against total income is available. Losses arising in the first four tax years of a trade may be set against total income in the three years preceding the loss making year, taking the earliest year first.

S 381 relief is available for **trading losses incurred in the first four tax years of a trade**.

Relief is obtained by **setting the allowable loss against total income in the three years preceding the year of loss**, applying the loss to the earliest year first. Thus a loss arising in 2006/07 may be set off against income in 2003/04, 2004/05 and 2005/06 in that order.

A claim under s 381 applies to all three years automatically, provided that the loss is large enough. The taxpayer cannot choose to relieve the loss against just one or two of the years, or to relieve only part of the loss. However, the taxpayer could reduce the size of the loss by not claiming the full capital allowances available to him. This will result in higher capital allowances in future years.

Do not double-count a loss. If basis periods overlap, a loss in the overlap period is treated as a loss for the earlier tax year only. This is the same rule as applies for s 380 purposes.

Claims for the relief must be made by the 31 January which is 22 months after the end of the tax year in which the loss is incurred.

The 'commercial basis' test is stricter for loss relief under s 381 than under s 380. The trade must be carried on in such a way that profits could reasonably have been expected to be realised in the period of the loss or within a reasonable time thereafter.

Question — s 381 loss relief

Mr A is employed as a dustman until 1 January 2005. On that date he starts up his own business as a scrap metal merchant, making up his accounts to 30 June each year. His earnings as a dustman are:

	£
2001/02	5,000
2002/03	6,000
2003/04	7,000
2004/05 (nine months)	6,000

His trading results as a scrap metal merchant are:

	Profit/(Loss) £
Six months to 30 June 2005	(3,000)
Year to 30 June 2006	(1,500)
Year to 30 June 2007	(1,200)
Year to 30 June 2008	0

Assuming that loss relief is claimed as early as possible, show the final taxable income before personal allowances for each of the years 2001/02 to 2007/08 inclusive.

Answer

Since reliefs are to be claimed as early as possible, s 381 ICTA 1988 is applied. The losses available for relief are as follows.

	£	£	*Years against which relief is available*
2004/05 (basis period 1.1.05 – 5.4.05)			
3 months to 5.4.05 £(3,000) × 3/6		(1,500)	2001/02 to 2003/04
2005/06 (basis period 1.1.05 – 31.12.05)			
3 months to 30.6.05			
(omit 1.1.05 – 5.4.05: overlap) £(3,000) × 3/6	(1,500)		
6 months to 31.12.05 £(1,500) × 6/12	(750)		
		(2,250)	2002/03 to 2004/05
2006/07 (basis period 1.7.05 – 30.6.06)			
6 months to 30.6.06			
(omit 1.7.05 – 31.12.05: overlap) £(1,500) × 6/12		(750)	2003/04 to 2005/06
2007/08 (basis period 1.7.06 – 30.6.07)			
12 months to 30.6.07		(1,200)	2004/05 to 2006/07

The revised taxable income before personal allowances is as follows.

	£	£
2001/02		
Original	5,000	
Less 2004/05 loss	(1,500)	
		3,500
2002/03		
Original	6,000	
Less 2005/06 loss	(2,250)	
		3,750
2003/04		
Original	7,000	
Less 2006/07 loss	(750)	
		6,250
2004/05		
Original	6,000	
Less 2007/08 loss	(1,200)	
		4,800

The taxable trade profits for 2004/05 to 2007/08 are zero. There were losses in the basis periods.

7 Losses on the cessation of a trade: s 388 ICTA 1988

FAST FORWARD

On the cessation of trade, a loss arising in the last 12 months of trading may be set against trade profits of the tax year of cessation and the previous 3 years, taking the last year first.

S 380 relief will often be insufficient on its own to deal with a loss incurred in the last months of trading. For this reason there is a special relief, **terminal loss relief, which allows a loss on cessation to be carried back for relief in previous years.**

7.1 Computing the terminal loss

A terminal loss under s 388 is **the loss of the last 12 months of trading**.

It is built up as follows.

		£
(a)	The actual trade loss for the tax year of cessation (calculated from 6 April to the date of cessation)	X
(b)	The actual trade loss for the period from 12 months before cessation until the end of the penultimate tax year	X
(c)	Any excess trade charges for the tax year of cessation	X
(d)	A proportion of any excess trade charges for the penultimate tax year	X
Total terminal loss		X

If either (a) or (b) above yields a profit as opposed to a loss, the profit is regarded as zero for this purpose.

The terminal loss cannot include any amounts for which relief has already been given. Make sure that computations exclude any amounts claimed under s 380 and also any losses which have been set off in computing the taxable profits for the final tax year.

The proportion mentioned in (d) above is needed to ensure that only trade charges of the last 12 months are included. The figure included in the terminal loss is limited to the total trade charges multiplied by:

$$\frac{\text{number of months in item (b) in the computation}}{12}$$

Any unrelieved overlap profits may be deducted in the tax year of cessation and should, therefore, be included within (a) above.

7.2 Relieving the terminal loss

The income against which the terminal loss can be set in any one year is computed as follows.

	£
Taxable trade profits	X
Less the excess of the gross amount of charges paid net of tax over other income *	(X)
Available for s 388 relief	X

* This amount also comes off the terminal loss available for relief in earlier years to the extent that it is charges which are non-trade *and* do not give rise to a s 350 charge.

Relief is given in the tax year of cessation and the three preceding years, later years first.

Question — Terminal loss relief

Set out below are the results of a business up to its cessation on 30 September 2006.

	Profit/(loss) £
Year to 31 December 2003	2,000
Year to 31 December 2004	400
Year to 31 December 2005	300
Nine months to 30 September 2006	(1,950)

Overlap profits on commencement were £450. These were all unrelieved on cessation.

Show the available terminal loss relief, and suggest an alternative claim if the trader had had other non-savings income of £10,000 in each of 2005/06 and 2006/07. Assume that 2006/07 tax rates and allowances apply to all years.

Answer

The terminal loss comes in the last 12 months, the period 1 October 2005 to 30 September 2006. This period is split as follows.

2005/06	Six months to 5 April 2006
2006/07	Six months to 30 September 2006

The terminal loss is made up as follows.

		£	£
Unrelieved trading losses			
2005/06			
3 months to 31.12.05	£300 × 3/12	75	
3 months to 5.4.06	£(1,950) × 3/9	(650)	
			(575)
2006/07			
6 months to 30.9.06	£(1,950) × 6/9		(1,300)
Overlap relief	£(450)		(450)
			(2,325)

Taxable trade profits will be as follows.

Year	*Basis period*	*Profits*	*Terminal loss relief*	*Final taxable profits*
		£	£	£
2003/04	Y/e 31.12.03	2,000	1,625	375
2004/05	Y/e 31.12.04	400	400	0
2005/06	Y/e 31.12.05	300	300	0
2006/07	1.1.06 – 30.9.06	0	0	0
			2,325	

If the trader had had £10,000 of other income in 2005/06 and 2006/07, we would have had to consider s 380 claims for these two years, using the loss of £(1,950 + 450) = £2,400 for 2006/07.

The final results would be as follows. (We could alternatively claim loss relief in 2005/06.)

	2003/04	*2004/05*	*2005/06*	*2006/07*
	£	£	£	£
Trade profits	2,000	400	300	0
Other income	0	0	10,000	10,000
	2,000	400	10,300	10,000
Less s 380 claims	0	0	0	(2,400)
STI	2,000	400	10,300	7,600

8 Losses on unquoted shares: s 574 ICTA 1988

FAST FORWARD

Capital losses arising on certain unquoted shares can be set against total income of the year of the loss and then against total income of the preceding year.

Relief is available for capital losses on unquoted shares (originally **subscribed for**) against total income of the taxpayer for the year **in which the loss arose and/or the preceding year** (ie the operation of the relief mirrors s 380).

In summary, the relief is available only if the shares satisfy the conditions of the Enterprise Investment Scheme (see later in this text).

A claim must be made by 31 January 22 months after the end of the year of the loss. Relief is given against income of the year of the loss and if there is an unused balance, against income of the preceding year.

Chapter roundup

- Trade losses may be relieved against future profits of the same trade, against total income and against capital gains.
- In opening years, a special relief involving the carry back of losses against total income is available. Losses arising in the first four tax years of a trade may be set against total income in the three years preceding the loss making year, taking the earliest year first.
- On the cessation of trade, a loss arising in the last 12 months of trading may be set against trade profits of the tax year of cessation and the previous 3 years, taking the last year first.
- It is important for a trader to choose the right loss relief, so as to save tax at the highest possible rate and so as to obtain relief reasonably quickly.
- Capital losses arising on certain unquoted shares can be set against total income of the year of the loss and then against total income of the preceding year.

Quick quiz

1 Against what income trade losses carried forward be set off?

2 When a loss is to be relieved against total income, how are losses linked to particular tax years?

3 Against which years' total income may a loss be relieved under s 380 ICTA 1988?

4 For which losses is s 381 relief available?

5 In which years may relief for a terminal loss be given?

Answers to quick quiz

1 Against trade profits from the same trade.

2 The loss for a tax year is the loss in the basis period for that tax year. However, if basis periods overlap, a loss in the overlap period is a loss of the earlier tax year only.

3 The year in which the loss arose and/or the preceding year.

4 Losses incurred in the first four years of a trade.

5 In the year of cessation and then in the three preceding years, later years first.

Now try the question below from the Exam Question Bank

Number	Level	Marks	Time
Q6	Examination	25	45 mins

8

Partnerships

Introduction

We now see how the income tax rules for traders are adapted to deal with business partnerships. On the one hand, a partnership is a single trading entity, making profits as a whole. On the other hand, each partner has a personal tax computation, so the profits must be apportioned to the partners. The general approach is to work out the profits of the partnership, then tax each partner as if he were a sole trader running a business equal to his slice of the partnership (for example 25% of the partnership).

1 Partnerships

FAST FORWARD

A partnership is simply treated as a source of profits and losses for trades being carried on by the individual partners. Divide profits or losses between the partners according to the profit sharing ratio in the period of account concerned. If any of the partners are entitled to a salary or interest on capital, apportion this first, not forgetting to pro-rate in periods of less than 12 months.

1.1 Introduction

A business partnership is treated like a sole trader for the purposes of computing its profits. (As usual, 'trade' in this chapter includes professions and vocations.) Partners' salaries interest on capital are not deductible expenses and must be added back in computing profits, because they are a form of drawings.

Once the partnership's profits for a period of account have been computed, they are shared between the partners according to the profit sharing arrangements for that period of account.

1.2 The tax positions of individual partners

Each partner is taxed like a sole trader who runs a business which:

- Starts when he joins the partnership
- Finishes when he leaves the partnership
- Has the same periods of account as the partnership (except that a partner who joins or leaves during a period will have a period which starts or ends part way through the partnership's period)
- Makes profits or losses equal to the partner's share of the partnership's profits or losses

A partnership may have non-trading income, such as interest on the partnership's bank deposit account or dividends on shares, or non-trading losses. **Such items are kept separate from trading income, but they** (and any associated tax credits) **are shared between the partners in a similar way to trading income.** That is, the following steps are applied.

(a) Find out which period of account the income arose in.

(b) Share the income between the partners using the profit sharing arrangements for that period. If partners have already been given their salaries and interest on capital in sharing out trading income, do not give them those items again in sharing out non-trading income.

(c) For income not taxed at source attribute each partner's share of the income to tax years using the same basis periods as are used to attribute his share of trading profits to tax years. When working out the basis periods for *untaxed* income (which excludes income taxed at source and dividends) or for non-trading losses, we always have a commencement when the partner joins the partnership and a cessation when he leaves, even if he carried on the trade as a sole trader before joining or after leaving. If the relief for overlap untaxed income on leaving the firm exceeds the partner's share of untaxed income for the tax year of leaving, the excess is deducted from his total income for that year.

(d) For income taxed at source assume that income accrued evenly over the accounting period and time apportion on an actual basis into tax years (6 April to 5 April).

1.3 Changes in membership

FAST FORWARD

Commencement and cessation rules apply to partners individually when they join or leave.

When a trade continues but partners join or leave (including cases when a sole trader takes in partners or a partnership breaks up leaving only one partner as a sole trader), **the special rules for basis periods in opening and closing years do not apply to the people who were carrying on the trade both before and after the change. They carry on using the period of account ending in each tax year as the basis period for the tax year. The commencement rules only affect joiners, and the cessation rules only affect leavers.**

However, when no-one carries on the trade both before and after the change, as when a partnership transfers its trade to a completely new owner or set of owners, the cessation rules apply to the old owners and the commencement rules apply to the new owners.

1.4 Loss reliefs

FAST FORWARD

There are restrictions on loss reliefs for non-active partners in the first four years of trading.

Partners are entitled to the same loss reliefs as sole traders. A partner is entitled to s 381 relief for losses in the four tax years starting with the year in which he is treated as starting to trade and he is entitled to terminal loss relief when he is treated as ceasing to trade. This is so even if the partnership trades for many years before the partner joins or after he leaves. Loss relief under s 380 and s 385 is also available to partners. Different partners may claim loss reliefs in different ways.

There is a restriction for loss relief for a partner who does not spend a significant amount of time (less than 10 hours a week) in running the trade of the partnership. Such a partner can only use loss relief under s 380 and s 381 ICTA 1988 or against capital gains **up to an amount equal to the amount that he contributes to the partnership.** These rules apply in any of the first four years in which the partner carries on a trade.

1.5 Example: loss relief restriction

Laura, Mark and Norman form a partnership and each contribute £10,000. Laura and Mark run the trade full time. Norman is employed elsewhere and plays little part in running the trade. Profits and losses are to be shared 45: 35: 20 to L:M:N. The partnership makes a loss of £60,000 of which £12,000 is allocated to Norman.

Norman may only use £10,000 of loss under s 380 (plus against capital gains) or s 381. £2,000 is carried forward, for example to be relieved against future profits under s 385.

When a partnership business is transferred to a company, each partner can carry forward his share of any unrelieved losses against income from the company under s 386 ICTA 1988.

1.6 Assets owned individually

Where the partners own assets (such as their cars) individually, a capital allowances computation must be prepared for each partner in respect of the assets he owns (not forgetting any adjustment for private use). **The capital allowances must go into the partnership's tax computation.**

1.7 Example: a partnership

Alice and Bertrand start a partnership on 1 July 2003, making up accounts to 31 December each year. On 1 May 2005, Charles joins the partnership. On 1 November 2006, Charles leaves. On 1 January 2007, Deborah joins. The profit sharing arrangements are as follows.

	Alice	*Bertrand*	*Charles*	*Deborah*
1.7.03 – 31.1.04				
Salaries (per annum)	£3,000	£4,500		
Balance	3/5	2/5		
1.2.04 – 30.4.05				
Salaries (per annum)	£3,000	£6,000		
Balance	4/5	1/5		
1.5.05 – 31.10.06				
Salaries (per annum)	£2,400	£3,600	£1,800	
Balance	2/5	2/5	1/5	
1.11.06 – 31.12.06				
Salaries (per annum)	£1,500	£2,700		
Balance	3/5	2/5		
1.1.07 onwards				
Salaries (per annum)	£1,500	£2,700		£600
Balance	3/5	1/5		1/5

Profits and losses as adjusted for tax purposes are as follows.

Period	*Profit(loss)*
	£
1.7.03 – 31.12.03	22,000
1.1.04 – 31.12.04	51,000
1.1.05 – 31.12.05	39,000
1.1.06 – 31.12.06	15,000
1.1.07 – 31.12.07	(18,000)

Show the taxable trade profits for each partner for 2003/04 to 2006/07, and outline the loss reliefs available to the partners in respect of the loss in the year ending 31 December 2007. All the partners work full time in the partnership. Assume that the partnership will continue to trade with the same partners until 2018.

Solution

We must first share the trade profits and losses for the periods of account between the partners, remembering to adjust the salaries for periods of less than a year.

	Total	*Alice*	*Bertrand*	*Charles*	*Deborah*
	£	£	£	£	£
1.7.03 – 31.12.03					
Salaries	3,750	1,500	2,250		
Balance	18,250	10,950	7,300		
Total (P/e 31.12.03)	22,000	12,450	9,550		
1.1.04 – 31.12.04					
January					
Salaries	625	250	375		
Balance	3,625	2,175	1,450		
Total	4,250	2,425	1,825		

	Total	Alice	Bertrand	Charles	Deborah
	£	£	£	£	£
February to December					
Salaries	8,250	2,750	5,500		
Balance	38,500	30,800	7,700		
Total	46,750	33,550	13,200		
Total for y/e 31.12.04	51,000	35,975	15,025		
1.1.05 – 31.12.05					
January to April					
Salaries	3,000	1,000	2,000		
Balance	10,000	8,000	2,000		
Total	13,000	9,000	4,000		
May to December					
Salaries	5,200	1,600	2,400	1,200	
Balance	20,800	8,320	8,320	4,160	
Total	26,000	9,920	10,720	5,360	
Total for y/e 31.12.05	39,000	18,920	14,720	5,360	
1.1.06 – 31.12.06					
January to October					
Salaries	6,500	2,000	3,000	1,500	
Balance	6,000	2,400	2,400	1,200	
Total	12,500	4,400	5,400	2,700	
November and December					
Salaries	700	250	450		
Balance	1,800	1,080	720		
Total	2,500	1,330	1,170		
Total for y/e 31.12.06	15,000	5,730	6,570	2,700	
1.1.07 – 31.12.07					
Salaries	4,800	1,500	2,700		600
Balance	(22,800)	(13,680)	(4,560)		(4,560)
Total loss for y/e 31.12.07	(18,000)	(12,180)	(1,860)		(3,960)

The next stage is to work out the basis periods and hence the taxable trade profits for the partners. All of them are treated as making up accounts to 31 December, but Alice and Bertrand are treated as starting to trade on 1 July 2003, Charles as trading only from 1 May 2005 to 31 October 2006 and Deborah as starting to trade on 1 January 2007. Applying the usual rules gives the following basis periods and taxable profits.

Alice

Year	*Basis period*	*Working*	*Taxable profits*
			£
2003/04	1.7.03 – 5.4.04	£12,450 + (£35,975 × 3/12)	21,444
2004/05	1.1.04 – 31.12.04		35,975
2005/06	1.1.05 – 31.12.05		18,920
2006/07	1.1.06 – 31.12.06		5,730

Note that for 2003/04 we take Alice's total for the year ended 2004 and apportion that, because the partnership's period of account runs from 1 January to 31 December 2004. Alice's profits for 2003/04 are *not* £12,450 + £2,425 + (£33,550 × 2/11) = £20,975.

Alice will have overlap profits for the period 1 January to 5 April 2004 (£35,975 × 3/12 = £8,994) to deduct when she ceases to trade.

Bertrand

Year	*Basis period*	*Working*	*Taxable profits*
			£
2003/04	1.7.03 – 5.4.04	£9,550 + (£15,025 × 3/12)	13,306
2004/05	1.1.04 – 31.12.04		15,025
2005/06	1.1.05 – 31.12.05		14,720
2006/07	1.1.06 – 31.12.06		6,570

Bertrand's overlap profits are £15,025 × 3/12 = £3,756.

Charles

Year	*Basis period*	*Working*	*Taxable profits*
			£
2005/06	1.5.05 – 5.4.06	£5,360 + (£2,700 × 3/10)	6,170
2006/07	6.4.06 – 31.10.06	£2,700 × 7/10	1,890

Because Charles ceased to trade in his second tax year of trading, his basis period for the second year starts on 6 April and he has no overlap profits.

Deborah

Year	*Basis period*	*Working*	*Taxable profits*
			£
2006/07	1.1.07 – 5.4.07	A loss arises	0

Finally, we must look at the loss reliefs available to Alice, Bertrand and Deborah. Charles is not entitled to any loss relief, because he left the firm before any loss arose.

Alice and Bertrand

For 2007/08, Alice has a loss of £12,180 and Bertrand has a loss of £1,860. They may claim relief under s 380 or under s 385.

Deborah

Deborah's losses are as follows, remembering that a loss which falls in the basis periods for two tax years is only taken into account in the earlier year.

Year	*Basis period*	*Working*	*Loss*
			£
2006/07	1.1.07 – 5.4.07	£3,960 × 3/12	990
2007/08	1.1.07 – 31.12.07	£3,960 – £990 (used in 2006/07)	2,970

Deborah may claim relief for these losses under s 380, s 381 (because she has just started to trade) or s 385.

Exam focus point

Partners are effectively taxed in the same way as sole traders with just one difference. Before you tax the partner you need to take each set of accounts (as adjusted for tax purposes) and divide the trade profit (or loss) between each partner.

Then carry on as normal for a sole trader – each partner is that sole trader in respect of his trade profits for each accounting period.

2 Limited liability partnerships

FAST FORWARD

Limited liability partnerships are taxed on virtually the same basis as normal partnerships but loss relief is restricted for all partners.

It is possible to form a limited liability partnership. The difference between a limited liability partnership (LLP) and a normal partnership is that **in a LLP the liability of the partners is limited to the capital they contributed.**

The partners of a LLP are taxed on virtually the same basis as the partners of a normal partnership (see above). However, the amount of loss relief that a partner can claim under s 380 and s 381 ICTA 1988 when the claim is against non-partnership income is restricted to the capital he contributed. This rule is not restricted to the first four years of trading and the rules apply to all partners whether or not involved in the running of the trade.

Chapter roundup

- A partnership is simply treated as a source of profits and losses for trades being carried on by the individual partners. Divide profits or losses between the partners according to the profit sharing ratio in the period of account concerned. If any of the partners are entitled to a salary or interest on capital, apportion this first, not forgetting to pro-rate in periods of less than 12 months.
- Commencement and cessation rules apply to partners individually when they join or leave.
- There are restrictions on loss reliefs for non-active partners in the first four years of trading.
- Limited liability partnerships are taxed on virtually the same basis as normal partnerships but loss relief is restricted for all partners.

Quick quiz

1. How are partnership trading profits divided between the individual partners?
2. What loss reliefs are partners entitled to?
3. Janet and John are partners sharing profits 60:40. For the years ended 30 June 2006 and 2007 the partnership made profits of £100,000 and £150,000 respectively. What are John's taxable trading profits in 2006/07?
4. Yolanda and Yan are in partnership sharing profits 80:20. For the year ended 31 December 2006 the business makes a loss of £40,000. If Yan decides to use his share of the loss under S.380 what loss relief(s) can Yolanda claim?
5. Pete and Doug have been joint partners for many years. On 1 January Dave joins the partnership and it is agreed to share profits 40:40:20. For the year ended 30 June 2006 profits are £100,000.

   What is Doug's share of these profits?

Answers to quick quiz

1 Profits are divided in accordance with the profit sharing ratio that existed during the period of account in which the profits arose.

2 Partners are entitled to the same loss reliefs as sole traders. This means that partners may claim relief for their share or a loss under s 380, s 381, s 385, s 388 or s 386 as appropriate.

3 £40,000.

2006/07: ye 30 June 2006

£100,000 × 40% = £40,000.

4 Yolanda has a choice of loss reliefs:

s.380 or s.385

Her loss relief claim is unaffected by Yan's.

5 £45,000

	Pete	*Doug*	*Dave*
Ye 30 June 2006	£	£	£
1.7.05 – 31.12.05			
6m × 100,000			
£50,000 50:50	25,000	25,000	
1.1.06 – 30.6.06			
6m × £100,000			
£50,000 40:40:20	20,000	20,000	10,000
	45,000	45,000	10,000

Now try the question below from the Exam Question Bank

Number	Level	Marks	Time
Q7	Introductory	15	27 mins

9

Chargeable gains: an outline

Introduction

Taxpayers can have both income and capital gains. If, for example, you buy a picture for £10,000, hang it on your wall for 20 years and then sell it for £200,000, you will have a capital gain.

In this chapter we see what gains are taxed and how to work out the tax on an individual's taxable gains. We also see how married couples are treated. In the next chapter, we will see how to compute gains.

Topic list	Syllabus references
1 History of taxing chargeable gains	1(f)
2 Chargeable and exempt persons, disposals and assets	1(f)
3 CGT payable by individuals	1(f)
4 Married couples and civil partners	1(f)

1 History of taxing chargeable gains

FAST FORWARD

The rules of taxing chargeable gains have changed over the years.

Since its introduction by the Finance Act 1965, the taxation of chargeable gains has undergone significant amendment. As some knowledge of the history of taxing gains may help you understand the present rules, we summarise the main changes below:

1965	The taxation of chargeable gains was introduced.
1982	An indexation allowance was introduced to give some relief in respect of gains due to inflation.
1985	There were major amendments to the calculation of the indexation allowance.
1988	The base date for taxing gains was generally moved from 1965 to 1982, the tax charge being confined to gains accruing from 31 March 1982. **You will not have to deal with gains or losses on assets acquired before 31 March 1982.**
1992	Legislation concerning the taxation of gains was consolidated into the Taxation of Chargeable Gains Act 1992 (TCGA 1992).
1993	The use of the indexation allowance to create or increase a loss ended.
1998	For individuals and trustees, indexation allowance was abolished after April 1998 and taper relief introduced.

2 Chargeable and exempt persons, disposals and assets

FAST FORWARD

For CGT to apply, there needs to be a chargeable person, a chargeable disposal and a chargeable asset.

Exam focus point

For a chargeable gain to arise there must be:

- A chargeable person; and
- A chargeable disposal; and
- A chargeable asset

otherwise no charge to tax occurs.

2.1 Chargeable persons

The following are chargeable persons.

- Individuals
- Companies
- Partnerships
- Trustees

We will look at the taxation of chargeable gains on companies later in this text.

The following are exempt persons.

- Charities using gains for charitable purposes
- Approved superannuation funds
- Local authorities
- Registered friendly societies
- Approved scientific research associations
- Authorised unit trusts and investment trusts
- Diplomatic representatives
- Persons who are neither resident nor ordinarily resident in the UK

2.2 Chargeable disposals

FAST FORWARD

A chargeable disposal occurs on the date of the contract or when a conditional contract becomes unconditional.

The following are chargeable disposals.

- Sales of assets or parts of assets
- Gifts of assets or parts of assets
- Receipts of capital sums following the surrender of rights to assets
- The loss or destruction of assets
- The appropriation of assets as trading stock

A chargeable disposal occurs on the date of the contract (where there is one, whether written or oral), or the date of a conditional contract becoming unconditional. This may differ from the date of transfer of the asset. However, when a capital sum is received on a surrender of rights or the loss or destruction of an asset, the disposal takes place on the day the sum is received.

The timing of a disposal should be carefully considered, bearing in mind these rules. For example, an individual may wish to accelerate a gain into an earlier tax year to obtain earlier loss relief or to delay a gain until a later tax year when a lower rate of tax may be applicable.

Where a disposal involves an acquisition by someone else, the date of acquisition is the same as the date of disposal.

The following are exempt disposals.

- **Transfers of assets on death** (the heirs inherit assets as if they bought them at death for their then market values, but there is no capital gain or allowable loss on death). It is possible to vary or disclaim inherited assets. The CGT effect of such a variation or disclaimer is dealt with later in this text.
- Transfers of assets as security for a loan or mortgage
- Gifts to charities and national heritage bodies

Chargeable gains do not arise in respect of betting winnings or cashbacks, for example on new mortgages or cars.

2.3 Transfers to and from trading stock

When a taxpayer acquires an asset other than as trading stock and then uses it as trading stock, the appropriation to trading stock normally leads to an immediate chargeable gain or allowable loss, based on the asset's market value at the date of appropriation. The asset's cost for income tax purposes is that market value.

Alternatively, the trader can elect to have no chargeable gain or allowable loss: if he does so, the cost for income tax purposes is reduced by the gain or increased by the loss.

When an asset which is trading stock is appropriated to other purposes, the trade profits are calculated as if the trader had sold it for its market value, and for capital gains tax purposes as if he had bought it at the time of the appropriation for the same value.

2.4 Chargeable assets

All forms of property, wherever in the world they are situated, are chargeable assets unless they are specifically designated as exempt.

The following are exempt assets (thus gains are not taxable and losses on their disposal are not in general allowable losses: the few exceptions are explained in this text).

- Motor vehicles suitable for private use
- National savings certificates and premium bonds
- Foreign currency for private use
- Decorations for valour unless acquired by purchase
- Damages for personal or professional injury
- Life assurance policies (only exempt in the hands of the original beneficial owner)
- Works of art, scientific collections and so on given for national purposes
- Gilt-edged securities
- Qualifying corporate bonds (QCBs) (although any gain deferred when a security changed status to a QCB remains taxable)
- Certain chattels
- Debts (except debts on a security)
- Pension rights and annuity rights
- Investments held in individual savings accounts

There are also exemptions for enterprise investment scheme (EIS) shares and venture capital trust (VCT) shares (see later in this text).

3 CGT payable by individuals

Individuals pay CGT on their taxable gains. Gains are taxed as an extra slice of savings (excl dividend) income. Individuals are entitled to taper relief and an annual exemption.

3.1 Introduction

Individuals are liable to CGT on the disposal of assets situated anywhere in the world if for any part of the tax year of disposal they are resident or ordinarily resident in the UK. 'Residence' and 'ordinary residence' have the same meaning as for income tax purposes (see later in this text). Trustees also pay CGT on their gains.

An individual pays CGT on any taxable gains arising in the tax year. **Taxable gains are the net chargeable gains (gains minus losses) of the tax year reduced by unrelieved losses brought forward from previous years, a taper relief and the annual exemption.**

There is an annual exemption for each tax year. For 2006/07 it is £8,800. It is the last deduction to be made in the calculation of taxable gains.

3.2 Calculating CGT

Taxable gains are chargeable to capital gains tax as if the gains were an extra slice of savings (excl dividend) income for the year of assessment concerned. This means that CGT may be due at 10%, 20% or 40%.

The rate bands are used first to cover income and then gains. If a gift aid payment and/or a personal pension contribution is made, the basic rate can be extended, as for income tax calculations (see Chapter 1).

Question

Rates of CGT

In 2006/07, Carol, a single woman, has the following income, gains and losses. Find the CGT payable.

	£
Salary	36,050
Chargeable gains (not eligible for taper relief – see later)	26,700
Allowable capital losses	7,700

Answer

(a) Carol's taxable income is as follows.

	£
Salary	36,050
Less personal allowance	(5,035)
Taxable income	31,015

(b) The gains to be taxed are as follows.

	£
Gains	26,700
Less losses	(7,700)
	19,000
Less annual exemption	(8,800)
Taxable gains	10,200

(c) The tax bands are allocated as follows.

	Total	*Income*	*Gains*
Starting rate	2,150	2,150	0
Basic rate	31,150	28,865	2,285
Higher rate	7,915	0	7,915
		31,015	10,200

(d) The CGT payable is as follows.

	£
£2,285 × 20%	457
£7,915 × 40%	3,166
Total CGT payable	3,623

3.3 Allowable losses

Deduct allowable capital losses from chargeable gains in the tax year in which they arise. Any loss which cannot be set off is carried forward to set against future chargeable gains. Losses must be used as soon as possible (subject to the following paragraph). Losses may not normally be set against income.

Allowable losses brought forward are only set off to reduce current year chargeable gains less current year allowable losses to the annual exempt amount. No set-off is made if net chargeable gains for the current year do not exceed the annual exempt amount.

3.4 Example: the use of losses

(a) George has chargeable gains for 2006/07 of £10,000 and allowable losses of £6,000. As the losses are *current year losses* they must be fully relieved against the £10,000 of gains to produce net gains of £4,000, despite the fact that net gains are below the annual exemption.

(b) Bob has gains of £12,700 for 2006/07 and allowable losses brought forward of £6,000. Bob restricts his loss relief to £3,900 so as to leave net gains of £(12,700 – 3,900) = £8,800, which will be exactly covered by his annual exemption for 2006/07. The remaining £2,100 of losses will be carried forward to 2007/08.

(c) Tom has chargeable gains of £5,000 for 2006/07 and losses brought forward from 2005/06 of £4,000. He will leapfrog 2006/07 and carry forward all of his losses to 2007/08. His gains of £5,000 are covered by his annual exemption for 2006/07.

3.5 Losses in the year of death

The only facility to carry back capital losses arises on the death of an individual. **Losses arising in the tax year in which an individual dies can be carried back to the previous three tax years, later years first, and used so as to reduce gains for each of the years to an amount covered by the appropriate annual exemption.** Only losses in excess of gains in the year of death can be carried back.

Question — Loss in year of death

Joe dies on 1 January 2007. His chargeable gains (no taper relief available – see later) and allowable loss have been as follows.

	Gain/(loss)	*Annual exemption*
	£	£
2006/07	2,000	8,800
	(12,000)	
2005/06	8,700	8,500
2004/05	4,000	8,200
2003/04	28,000	7,900

How will the loss be set off?

Answer

The £10,000 net loss which arises in 2006/07 will be carried back. We must set off the loss against the 2006/07 gains first even though the gains are more than covered by the 2006/07 annual exemption.

£200 of the loss will be used in 2005/06. None of the loss will be used in 2004/05 (because the gains for that year are covered by the annual exemption), and so the remaining £9,800 will be used in 2003/04. Repayments of CGT will follow.

3.6 Taper relief

FAST FORWARD

Taper relief is more generous for business assets than non-business assets.

Taper relief may be available to reduce gains realised after 5 April 1998 by individuals and trustees.

Taper relief reduces the percentage of the gain chargeable according to how many complete years the asset had been held since acquisition or 6 April 1998 if later. Taper relief is more generous for business assets than for non-business assets.

The percentages of gains which remain chargeable after taper relief are set out below.

Number of complete years after 5.4.98 for which asset held	*Gain on business assets % of gain chargeable*	*Gain on non business assets % of gain chargeable*
0	100	100
1	50	100
2	25	100
3	25	95
4	25	90
5	25	85
6	25	80
7	25	75
8	25	70

Exam focus point

You will be given the above percentages in your exam.

Non-business assets acquired before 17 March 1998 qualify for an addition of 1 year (a 'bonus year') to the period for which they are actually held after 5 April 1998.

3.7 Example: complete years held for taper relief

Peter buys a non business asset on 1 January 1998 and sells it on 1 July 2006. For the purposes of the taper Peter is treated as if he had held the asset for 9 complete years (eight complete years after 5 April 1998 plus one additional year).

If the asset had been a business asset, Peter holds the asset for eight years only but in any case has maximum taper relief after two years ownership.

3.8 Application of taper relief

FAST FORWARD

Losses are set off before taper relief against gains of the same year or of future years.

3.9 Example: use of losses and taper relief

Ruby sold a business asset in July 2006 which she had purchased in January 2005. She realised a chargeable gain (before taper relief) of £18,000. She also sold a painting in 2006/07 realising a capital loss of £6,000. She has a capital loss brought forward from 2005/06 of £10,000.

Losses are dealt with **before** taper relief. However losses brought forward are only deducted from net current gains to the extent that the gains exceed the CGT annual exemption:

	£
Gain	18,000
Loss	(6,000)
Current net gains	12,000
Less: brought forward loss	(3,200)
Gains before taper relief	8,800
Gains after taper relief (1 year ownership) £8,800 × 50%	4,400
Less: annual exemption	(8,800)
Taxable gains	Nil

Note that the benefit of the taper relief is effectively wasted since the brought forward loss reduces the gain down to the annual exemption amount but the taper is then applied to that amount reducing it further.

The loss carried forward is £6,800 (£10,000 – £3,200).

Allocate losses to gains in the way that produces the lowest tax charge. Losses should therefore be deducted from the gains attracting the lowest rate of taper (ie where the highest percentage of the gain remains chargeable).

3.10 Example: allocation of losses to gains

Alastair made the following capital losses and gains in 2006/07:

	£
Loss	10,000
Gains (before taper relief)	
Asset A (non-business asset)	25,000
Asset B (business asset)	18,000

Asset A was purchased in December 1997 and sold in January 2007. Taper relief reduces the gain to 65% of the original gain (9 years including additional year; non-business asset). Asset B was purchased on 5 November 2003 and sold on 17 December 2006. Taper relief reduces the gain to 25% of the original gain (3 years; business asset).

The best use of the loss is to offset it against the gain on the non-business asset:

	£	£
Gain – Asset A	25,000	
Less loss	(10,000)	
Net gain before taper relief	15,000	
Gain after taper relief (£15,000 × 65%)		9,750
Gain – Asset B	18,000	
Gain after taper relief £18,000 × 25%		4,500
Gains after taper relief		14,250
Less annual exemption		(8,800)
Taxable gains		5,450

There are certain special situations which will affect the operation of taper relief:

(a) Where there has been a transfer of assets between spouses or civil partners (a no loss/no gain transfer; see below) the taper on a subsequent disposal will be based on the combined period of holding by the spouses or civil partners.

(b) Where gains have been relieved under a provision which reduces the cost of the asset in the hands of a new owner (such as gift relief, see later in this text) the taper will operate by reference to the holding period of the new owner.

3.11 Shares and securities

Special rules apply to shares and securities. We cover these later in this text.

3.12 Business assets

A business asset is:

- An asset **used for the purposes of a trade** carried on by any individual, partnership, trustee or PR (whether or not the owner of the asset is involved in carrying on the trade concerned) or by a qualifying company.
- An asset **held for the purposes of any office or employment** held by the individual owner with a person carrying on a trade.
- **Shares in a qualifying company** held by an individual.

A qualifying company is a **trading company** (or holding company of a trading group) where:

(a) The company is **not listed** on a recognised stock exchange nor is a 51% subsidiary of a listed company (companies listed on the Alternative Investment Market (AIM) are unlisted for this purpose), or

(b) The individual is an **officer or employee** of the company or of a company with a **relevant connection**, or

(c) The individual holds at least **5% of the voting rights** in the company.

A company is also a qualifying company if it is a **non-trading company** (or holding company of a non-trading group) where:

(a) The individual is an **officer or employee** of the company or a company with a relevant connection, and

(b) The individual did not have a **material interest** in the company or in any other company which at that time had control of the company.

A **material interest** is defined as possession or the ability to control more than 10% of the issued shares in the company, or more than 10% of the voting rights in the company, or an entitlement to more than 10% of the income of the company or more than 10% of the assets of the company available for distribution. For this purpose, an individual is treated as having a material interest if he, together with one or more connected persons (see next chapter) has a material interest. For example, if A holds 5% of the voting rights in the company and his brother B (a connected person) has 15% of the voting rights, A will have a material interest in the company as between them A and B hold more than 10% of the voting rights.

A company has a **relevant connection** with another company if:

(a) The companies are both members of a 51% group, or

(b) The companies are under common control and they carry on a complementary business which can reasonably be regarded as one composite undertaking, or

(c) One company (X Ltd) is a joint enterprise company in which 75% or more of the ordinary shares capital is held by five or fewer persons and the other company (Y Ltd) holds 10% or more of the ordinary share capital in X Ltd.

The rules for business assets apply in a similar way to assets held by trustees.

If an asset qualifies as a business asset for part of the time of ownership, and part not, the business part and the non-business part are treated as separate assets calculated by time apportionment over the period of ownership of the asset (not just complete years). Taper relief applies to each gain separately but the period of ownership for calculating the taper relief percentage is taken to be the *whole* number of years of ownership of the asset.

Question — Mixed asset

Robert bought a warehouse on 5 August 2000. He used the whole of the building for his trade until 4 April 2004. The building was then let out to a quoted company until it was sold on 4 December 2006. The gain on sale was £140,000.

Show Robert's gain after taper relief.

Answer

	Business use	*Non business use*
Period between 5.8.00 – 4.4.04	44 months	
Period between 5.4.04 – 4.12.06		32 months

Number of complete years ownership is 5.8.00 – 4.8.06 = 6 years

Gain on business asset after taper relief is:

£140,000 × 44/76 × 25% (6 years) = £20,263

Gain on non-business asset after taper relief is:

£140,000 × 32/76 × 80% (6 years) = £47,158

Total gain 20,263 + 47,158 = £67,421

If the asset was acquired before 6 April 1998, only use on or after that date is taken into account. If the asset is owned for more than ten years after 5 April 1998, only the use in the **last ten years** of ownership is taken into account.

4 Married couples and civil partners

FAST FORWARD

Spouses are treated as separate people. Transfers of assets between spouses give rise to neither a gain nor a loss. Civil partners are treated as spouses.

Spouses are taxed as two separate people. Each has an annual exemption, and losses of one spouse cannot be set against gains of the other. Civil partners are taxed in the same way as spouses.

Disposals between spouses who are living together give rise to no gain and no loss, whatever actual price (if any) **was charged by the person transferring the asset** to their spouse. Details of the calculation are dealt with later in this text. A couple are treated as living together unless they are separated under a court order or separation deed, or are in fact separated in circumstances which make permanent separation likely.

Where an asset is jointly owned, the beneficial interests of the spouses will determine the treatment of any gain on disposal. If, for example, there is evidence that the wife's share in an asset was 60%, then 60% of any gain or loss on disposal would be attributed to her. If there is no evidence of the relative interests, HMRC will normally accept that the asset is held in equal shares. Where a declaration of how income from the asset is to be shared for income tax purposes has been made, there is a presumption that the same shares will apply for CGT purposes.

If a spouse whose marginal tax rate is 40% wishes to dispose of an asset at a gain and the other spouse would only be taxed on the gain at a lower rate, the asset should first be transferred to the spouse with the lower tax rate. Similarly, assets or parts of assets should be transferred between spouses to use both CGT annual exemptions.

Chapter roundup

- For CGT to apply, there needs to be a chargeable person, a chargeable disposal and a chargeable asset.
- A chargeable disposal occurs on the date of the contract or when a conditional contract becomes unconditional.
- Individuals pay CGT on their taxable gains.
- Individuals are entitled to taper relief and an annual exemption.
- Taper relief is more generous for business assets than non-business assets.
- Losses are set off before taper relief against gains of the same year or of future years.
- Spouses/civil partners are treated as separate people. Transfers of assets between spouses/civil partners give rise to neither a gain nor a loss. Civil partners are treated as spouses.

Quick quiz

1 Give some examples of chargeable disposals.

2 Are the following assets chargeable to CGT or exempt?

(a) Shares (not held in ISA)
(b) Car
(c) Land
(d) Victoria Cross awarded to owner
(e) National Savings Certificates

3 At what rate or rates do individuals pay CGT?

4 To what extent must allowable losses be set against chargeable gains?

5 What is a qualifying company for business asset taper relief?

Answers to quick quiz

1 Sales of assets or parts of assets
Gifts of assets or parts of assets
Receipts of capital sums following the surrender of rights to assets
Loss or destruction of assets
Appropriation of assets as trading stock

2 (a) Shares – Chargeable
(b) Car – Exempt as motor vehicle suitable for private use
(c) Land – Chargeable
(d) Victoria Cross – Exempt as medal for valour not acquired by purchase
(e) National Savings Certificates – Exempt

3 10%, 20% and 40%

4 Current year losses must be set off against gains in full, even if this reduces gains below annual exemption
Losses brought forward or carried back from year of death, are set off to bring down untapered gains to level of annual exemption.

5 A trading company (or holding company of trading group) which is unlisted or of which the individual is an officer or employee or of which the individual holds at least 5% voting rights.

A non-trading company (or holding company of a non-trading group) of which the individual is an officer or employee and in which the individual does not have a material interest.

Now try the question below from the Exam Question Bank

Number	Level	Marks	Time
Q8	Introductory	20	36 mins

10 The computation of gains and losses

Introduction

We now see how to compute a chargeable gain. The basic computation is to take the proceeds minus the cost. In certain cases we then deduct an allowance for inflation (the indexation allowance). We also look at some special cases, where the rules are modified because of the relationship between the disposer and the acquirer of an asset: without such rules, people could do deals with their relatives to avoid tax.

We also look briefly at how chargeable gains on partnership assets are dealt with.

1 The basic computation

FAST FORWARD

A chargeable gain is computed by taking the proceeds and deducting both the costs and the indexation allowance. For individuals and trustees indexation is not given after April 1998 but a taper relief may be available.

1.1 Introduction

A chargeable gain (or an allowable loss) is generally calculated as follows.

	£
Disposal consideration (or market value)	45,000
Less incidental costs of disposal	(400)
Net proceeds	44,600
Less allowable costs	(21,000)
Unindexed gain	23,600
Less indexation allowance (if available)	(8,800)
Indexed gain	14,800

For individuals, taper relief may then apply (see the previous chapter).

Incidental costs of disposal may include:

- Valuation fees (but not the cost of an appeal against HMRC's valuation)
- Estate agency fees
- Advertising costs
- Legal costs

These costs should be deducted separately from any other allowable costs (because they do not qualify for any indexation allowance if it was available on that disposal).

Allowable costs include:

- The original cost of acquisition
- Incidental costs of acquisition
- Capital expenditure incurred in enhancing the asset

Incidental costs of acquisition may include the types of cost listed above as incidental costs of disposal, but acquisition costs do qualify for indexation allowance (from the month of acquisition) if it is available on the disposal.

Enhancement expenditure is capital expenditure which enhances the value of the asset and is reflected in the state or nature of the asset at the time of disposal, or expenditure incurred in establishing, preserving or defending title to, or a right over, the asset. Excluded from this category are:

- Costs of repairs and maintenance
- Costs of insurance
- Any expenditure deductible for income tax purposes
- Any expenditure met by public funds (for example council grants)

Enhancement expenditure may qualify for indexation allowance from the month in which it becomes due and payable.

1.2 The consideration for a disposal

Usually the disposal consideration is the proceeds of sale of the asset, but a disposal is deemed to take place at market value:

(a) Where the disposal is **not a bargain at arm's length**
(b) Where the disposal is made for a **consideration which cannot be valued**
(c) Where the disposal is by way of a **gift**

Sometimes an asset is sold for a fixed sum plus a possible addition depending on some contingency. For example, land might be sold without planning permission, and with an extra payment to be made to the vendor if planning permission is obtained. In such cases, **the contingent right to additional proceeds must be valued, and that value must be added to the known proceeds.**

If additional proceeds are in fact received, that receipt is treated as proceeds of the disposal of the contingent right. A chargeable gain or allowable loss will then arise: the allowable cost is the value of the right brought into account in the initial computation of the capital gain (*Marren v Ingles 1980*).

Taxpayers (other than companies) can carry back a loss on the disposal of the contingent right to the tax year in which the gain on the main disposal arose. This does not apply where the right to the deferred consideration was acquired second-hand.

2 The indexation allowance

FAST FORWARD

Indexation allowance removes the inflationary element of a capital gain. It is restricted for individuals and traders.

2.1 Introduction

The purpose of having an indexation allowance is to remove the inflationary element of a gain from taxation.

Individuals and trustees are entitled to an indexation allowance from the date of acquisition of an asset until April 1998.

Companies are entitled to an indexation allowance from the date of acquisition until the date of disposal of an asset, even if this is after April 1998. We look at companies in more detail later in this text.

2.2 Example: indexation allowance

John bought a painting on 2 January 1987 and sold it on 19 November 2006.

Indexation allowance is available from January 1987 until April 1998.

Exam formula

The indexation factor is:

$$\frac{\text{RPI for month of disposal (or April 1998)} - \text{RPI for month of acquisition}}{\text{RPI for month of acquisition}}$$

The calculation is expressed as a decimal and is rounded to three decimal places.

The indexation factor is multiplied by the cost of the asset to calculate the indexation allowance. If the RPI has fallen, the indexation allowance is zero: it is not negative.

RPI values are given in questions where required. If necessary estimated values have been given for January 2006 onwards.

Question — The indexation allowance

An asset is acquired by an individual on 15 February 1983 (RPI = 83.0) at a cost of £5,000. Enhancement expenditure of £2,000 is incurred on 10 April 1984 (RPI = 88.6). The asset is sold for £20,500 on 20 December 2006. Incidental costs of sale are £500. Calculate the chargeable gain before taper relief.

Answer

The indexation allowance is available until April 1998 (RPI = 162.6) and is computed as follows.

	£
$\frac{162.6 - 83.0}{83.0} = 0.959 \times £5,000$	4,795
$\frac{162.6 - 88.6}{88.6} = 0.835 \times £2,000$	1,670
	6,465

The computation of the chargeable gain is as follows.

	£
Proceeds	20,500
Less incidental costs of sale	(500)
Net proceeds	20,000
Less allowable costs £(5,000 + 2,000)	(7,000)
Unindexed gain	13,000
Less indexation allowance (see above)	(6,465)
Chargeable gain before taper relief	6,535

2.3 Indexation and losses

The indexation allowance cannot create or increase an allowable loss. If there is a gain before the indexation allowance, the allowance can reduce that gain to zero, but no further. If there is a loss before the indexation allowance, there is no indexation allowance.

3 Valuing assets

FAST FORWARD

Market value must be used in certain capital gains computations. There are special rules for shares and securities.

3.1 General rules

Where market value is used in a chargeable gains computation (see Section 1 above), **the value to be used is the price which the assets in question might reasonably be expected to fetch on a sale in the open market.**

3.2 Shares and securities

Quoted shares and securities are valued using prices in The Stock Exchange Daily Official List, taking the lower of:

(a) Lower quoted price + $^{1}/_{4}$ × (higher quoted price - lower quoted price) ('quarter up' rule).

(b) The average of the highest and lowest marked bargains (ignoring bargains marked at special prices).

Question

Calculation of CGT value

Shares in A plc are quoted at 100-110p. The highest and lowest marked bargains were 99p and 110p. What would be the market value for CGT purposes?

Answer

The value will be the lower of:

(a) $100 + \frac{1}{4} \times (110 - 100) = 102.5$

(b) $\frac{110+99}{2} = 104.5$

The market value for CGT purposes will therefore be 102.5p per share.

Unquoted shares are harder to value than quoted shares. HMRC have a special office, the Shares Valuation Division, to deal with the valuation of unquoted shares.

3.3 Negligible value claims

If a chargeable asset's value becomes negligible a claim may be made to treat the asset as though it were sold, and then immediately reacquired at its current market value. This will probably give rise to an allowable loss.

The sale and reacquisition are treated as taking place when the claim is made, or at a specified earlier time. The earlier time can be any time up to two years before the start of the tax year in which the claim is made. (For companies, it can be as far back as the start of the earliest accounting period which ends within two years of the date of claim.) The asset must have been of negligible value at the specified earlier time.

On a subsequent actual disposal, any gain is computed using the negligible value as the acquisition cost.

4 Connected persons

FAST FORWARD

Disposals between connected persons are deemed to take place for a consideration equal to market value. Any loss arising on a disposal to a connected person can be set only against a gain arising on a disposal to the same connected person.

4.1 Definition and effect

A transaction between 'connected persons' is treated as one between parties to a transaction otherwise than by way of a bargain made at arm's length. This means that the acquisition and disposal are deemed to take place for a consideration equal to the market value of the asset, rather than the actual price paid. In addition, if a loss results, it can be set only against gains arising in the same or future years from disposals to the same connected person and the loss can only be set off if he or she is still connected with the person sustaining the loss.

Key term

Connected person. An individual is connected with:

- His spouse (the term 'spouse' includes civil partners)
- His relatives (brothers, sisters, ancestors and lineal descendants)
- The relatives of his spouse
- The spouses of his and his spouse's relatives

4.2 Assets disposed of in a series of transactions

A taxpayer might attempt to avoid tax by disposing of his property piecemeal to persons connected with him. For example, a majority holding of shares might be broken up into several minority holdings, each with a much lower value per share, and each of the shareholder's children could be given a minority holding.

To prevent the avoidance of tax in this way, **where a person disposes of assets to one or more persons, with whom he is connected, in a series of linked transactions, the disposal proceeds for each disposal will be a proportion of the value of the assets taken together**. Thus in the example of the shareholding, the value of the majority holding would be apportioned between the minority holdings. Transactions are linked if they occur within six years of each other.

5 Intraspouse transfers of assets

FAST FORWARD

Disposals between spouses and civil partners take place on a no gain/no loss basis.

Disposals between spouses/civil partners do not give rise to chargeable gains or allowable losses. References to husband, wife and spouse should be taken as applying equally to civil partners.

Special rules apply to the indexation allowance and taper relief on no gain/no loss disposals. To illustrate the rules, we assume that a husband (H) buys an asset and later transfers it to his wife (W). The wife sells the asset to an outsider. The rules are exactly the same if the roles of H and W are reversed.

H buys an asset and transfers it to W. W is deemed to have bought the asset at the time when H transferred it to her. Her cost is H's cost plus indexation allowance up to the time of the transfer (or 6 April 1998 if earlier). When she sells the asset, she computes indexation allowance from the time of the transfer. If the transfer was after 5 April 1998, no further indexation allowance is given.

For taper relief purposes, the ownership period of W will be treated as the combined ownership period of H and W. For assets other than shares, business use by one spouse is treated as business ownership by the other spouse.

6 Business partnerships

FAST FORWARD

The CGT position of partnerships recognises the fact that individual partners have (potentially variable) stakes in partnership assets.

When a business partnership disposes of an asset, any chargeable gain or allowable loss is apportioned to the partners in their capital profit sharing ratio.

Partners may decide to change their shares in the firm, for example when a new partner joins the firm or a partner retires. Each partner is treated as acquiring or disposing of an appropriate share in the partnership assets. Thus a partner whose share rises from 20% to 50% acquires a 30% share.

On these deemed disposals, the assets of the firm are treated as sold for their current balance sheet values plus the indexation allowance which would apply on an actual disposal. If assets have not been revalued in the balance sheet, the consequence is that the partners reducing their shares have chargeable gains of zero. If assets have been revalued, each such partner will have gains equal to the revaluations × the percentage fall in his share. A corresponding allowable loss arises if assets have been revalued downwards.

When one partner pays another and the payment does not go through the accounts, each partner receiving money has a chargeable gain equal to the amount he receives, in addition to any gain under the paragraph above.

A partner whose share is increased (including a new partner) has a deemed acquisition cost equal to the deemed disposal proceeds of the share he is acquiring from the other partners. If he makes a payment outside the accounts, it is generally treated as being for goodwill.

When assets are revalued with no changes in shares in the firm, there is no chargeable gain or allowable loss at that time.

7 Part disposals

FAST FORWARD

On a part disposal, the cost must be apportioned between the part disposed of and the part retained.

7.1 Basic rule

The disposal of part of a chargeable asset is a chargeable event. The chargeable gain (or allowable loss) is computed by deducting from the disposal value a fraction of the original cost of the whole asset.

Exam formula

The fraction is:

$$\frac{A}{A+B} = \frac{\text{value of the part disposed of}}{\text{value of the part disposed of} + \text{market value of the remainder}}$$

In this fraction, A is the proceeds (for arm's length disposals) *before* deducting incidental costs of disposal.

The part disposal fraction should not be applied indiscriminately. Any expenditure incurred wholly in respect of a particular part of an asset should be treated as an allowable deduction in full for that part and not apportioned. An example of this is incidental selling expenses, which are wholly attributable to the part disposed of.

Question — Part disposals

Mr Heal owns a painting which originally cost him £27,000 in March 1984 (RPI = 87.5). He sold a quarter interest in the painting in July 2006 for £18,000. The market value of the three-quarter share remaining is estimated to be £36,000. What is the chargeable gain after taper relief? RPI April 1998 = 162.6

Answer

The amount of the original cost attributable to the part sold is

$$\frac{18{,}000}{18{,}000+36{,}000} \times £27{,}000 = £9{,}000$$

	£
Proceeds	18,000
Less cost (see above)	(9,000)
Unindexed gain	9,000
Less indexation allowance (March 1984 to April 1998)	
$\frac{162.6-87.5}{87.5}$ = 0.858 × £9,000	(7,722)
Gain before taper relief	1,278
Gain after taper relief (6.4.98 – 5.4.06 = 8 years plus additional year = 9 years)	
65% × £1,278	£831

7.2 Land: small disposal proceeds

Where the **consideration** for a part disposal of land **does not exceed 20% of the market value of the entire holding** of land prior to the part disposal, a chargeable disposal does not take place. The taxpayer must make a **claim** by the first anniversary of 31 January following the end of the tax year. The net disposal proceeds are deducted from allowable expenditure when computing a gain on a later disposal of the remaining land.

Question — **Small part disposals of land**

Bertha buys 10 acres of land in January 2000 for £20,000. She sells $1\frac{1}{2}$ acres for £5,000 in June 2006 and disposal costs amount to £50. Market value of the land immediately prior to the disposal is £30,000.

You are required to show Bertha's CGT position.

Answer

The consideration (£5,000) is less than 20% of market value (20% of £30,000 = £6,000). Bertha may therefore claim for the relief to apply. As a result, no chargeable disposal takes place in June 2006.

Allowable cost of the land retained is:

	£
Cost of 10 acres	20,000
Deduct: net proceeds of part disposal (£5,000 – £50)	(4,950)
Allowable expenditure of land retained	15,050

There are two further conditions to meet before this relief can apply:

- proceeds from the part disposal do not exceed £20,000; and
- aggregate proceeds from the part disposal and any other disposals of land (including buildings) in the same tax year do not exceed £20,000.

7.3 Example: proceeds exceed £20,000

If, in the previous example, Bertha had made another disposal of land for £15,750 in 2006/07, the relief could not apply since proceeds for the tax year (ie. £15,750 + £5,000 = £20,750) would exceed £20,000. The normal part disposal rules would apply.

Where the capital sum received is not treated as a disposal, but is instead deducted from allowable expenditure as above, any indexation calculation on a later disposal is calculated in two stages:

(a) the indexed rise on the original expenditure is calculated and deducted normally from date of purchase, to date of sale or April 1998 if earlier; then

(b) the indexed rise on a notional item of expenditure equal to the amount of the capital sum received, from date of receipt to date of sale or April 1998 if earlier, is added back. This is effectively 'negative indexation'.

Taper relief applies to the whole gain from the later of the acquisition and 6 April 1998.

Chapter roundup

- A chargeable gain is computed by taking the proceeds and deducting both the costs and the indexation allowance. For individuals and trustees indexation is not given after April 1998 but a taper relief may be available.
- Disposals between connected persons are deemed to take place for a consideration equal to market value. Any loss arising on a disposal to a connected person can be set only against a gain arising on a disposal to the same connected person.
- Disposals between spouses and civil partners take place on a no gain/no loss basis.
- The CGT position of partnerships recognises the fact that individual partners have (potentially variable) stakes in partnership assets.
- On a part disposal, the cost must be apportioned between the part disposed of and the part retained.

Quick quiz

1 Jed buys a house. He repairs the roof, installs central heating and builds an extension. The extension is blown down in a storm and not replaced. Which of these improvements is allowable as enhancement expenditure on a subsequent sale?

2 Shares in A plc are quoted at 410 – 414, with bargains at 408, 410 and 416. What is the value for CGT?

3 With whom is an individual connected?

4 What is the CGT effect of a change in partnership profit sharing ratios without any revaluation of assets or payment between business partners?

5 10 acres of land are sold for £15,000 out of 25 acres. Original cost in 1990 £9,000. Costs of sale £2,000. Rest of land valued at £30,000. What is the allowable expenditure?

Answers to quick quiz

1 Repairs to roof – not allowable as enhancement expenditure because not capital in nature
Central heating – allowable as enhancement expenditure
Extension – not allowable as not reflected in state of asset at time of disposal.

2 Lower of:

$410 + \frac{1}{4}(414 - 410) = 411$

$\frac{416+408}{2} = 412$

ie 411

3 An individual is connected with:

- his spouse ('spouse' includes civil partners)
- his relatives (brothers, sisters, ancestors and lineal descendants)
- the relatives of his spouse
- the spouses of his and his spouse's relatives

4 The assets of the firm are treated as sold at current balance sheet values plus indexation. Where there has been no revaluation, the disposing partner will have a nil gain. The acquiring partner will have a base cost equal to the deemed sale proceeds.

5 $\frac{15{,}000}{15{,}000+30{,}000} \times £9{,}000 = £3{,}000 + £2{,}000 \text{ (costs of disposal)} = £5{,}000$

Now try the question below from the Exam Question Bank

Number	Level	Marks	Time
Q9	Examination	25	45 mins

11

Shares and securities

Introduction

In this chapter, we look at shares and securities held by individuals. Shares and securities need a special treatment because an investor may hold several shares or securities in the same company, bought at different times for different prices but otherwise identical.

The rules for shares and securities held by companies are different and are dealt with later in this text.

Topic list	Syllabus references
1 The matching rules for individuals	1(f)
2 The FA 1985 pool	1(f)
3 Post April 1998 acquisitions and disposals	1(f)
4 Alterations of share capital	1(f)
5 Gilts and qualifying corporate bonds	1(f)

1 The matching rules for individuals

FAST FORWARD

There are different share matching rules for individuals from those for companies.

Quoted and unquoted shares and securities and units in a unit trust present special problems when attempting to compute gains or losses on disposal. For instance, suppose that an individual buys some quoted shares in X plc as follows.

Date	*Number of shares*	*Cost*
		£
5 May 1983	100	150
17 January 1999	100	375

On 15 June 2006, he sells 120 of the shares for £1,450. To determine the chargeable gain, we need to be able to work out which shares out of the two original holdings were actually sold.

We therefore need **matching rules**. These **allow us to decide which shares have been sold and so work out what the allowable cost on disposal should be.**

At any one time, we will only be concerned with shares or securities of the same class in the same company. If an individual owns both ordinary shares and preference shares in X plc, we will deal with the two classes of share entirely separately, because they are distinguishable.

In what follows, we will use 'shares' to refer to both shares and securities.

For individuals, share disposals are matched with acquisitions in the following order.

(a) Same day acquisitions.

(b) Acquisitions within the following 30 days (known as the 'bed and breakfast rule').

(c) Previous acquisitions after 5 April 1998 identifying the most recent acquisition first (a LIFO basis).

(d) Any shares in the FA 1985 pool at 5 April 1998 (see below).

The 'bed and breakfast' rule stops shares being sold to crystallise a capital gain or loss and then being repurchased a day or so later. Without the rule a gain or loss would arise on the sale since it would be 'matched' to the original acquisition.

Exam focus point

Learn the 'matching rules' because a crucial first step to getting a shares question right is to correctly match the shares sold to the original shares purchased.

2 The FA 1985 pool

FAST FORWARD

When dealing with shares held by individuals we need to construct a FA 1985 pool running (with indexation allowance) to 5 April 1998 and then a list of shares acquired from 6 April 1998 onwards.

2.1 Composition of pool

We treat shares as a 'pool' which grows as new shares are acquired and shrinks as they are sold. **The FA 1985 pool** (so called because it was introduced by rules in the Finance Act 1985) **comprises the following shares of the same class in the same company.**

- **Shares held by an individual on 5 April 1985 and acquired by that individual on or after 6 April 1982.**
- **Shares acquired by that individual on or after 6 April 1985, but before 6 April 1998.**

In making computations which use the FA 1985 pool, we must keep track of:

(a) The **number** of shares
(b) The **cost** of the shares ignoring indexation
(c) The **indexed cost** of the shares

Each FA 1985 **pool is started by aggregating the cost and number of shares acquired between 6 April 1982 and 6 April 1985** inclusive. In order to calculate the indexed cost of these shares, an indexation allowance, computed from the relevant date of acquisition of the shares to April 1985, is added to the cost.

2.2 Example: the FA 1985 pool

Oliver bought 1,000 shares in Judith plc for £2,750 in August 1984 (RPI = 89.9) and another 1,000 for £3,250 in December 1984 (RPI = 90.9). The FA 1985 pool at 6 April 1985 (RPI = 94.8) is as follows.

Solution

	No of shares	*Cost* £	*Indexed cost* £
August 1984 (a)	1,000	2,750	2,750
December 1984 (b)	1,000	3,250	3,250
	2,000	6,000	6,000
Indexation allowance			
$\frac{94.8-89.9}{89.9} = 0.055 \times £2,750$			151
$\frac{94.8-90.9}{90.9} = 0.043 \times £3,250$			140
Indexed cost of the pool at 6 April 1985			6,291

Disposals and acquisitions of shares which affect the indexed value of the FA 1985 pool are termed **'operative events'**. **Prior to reflecting each such operative event within the FA 1985 share pool, a further indexation allowance (described as an indexed rise) must be computed up to the date of the operative event concerned from the date of the last such operative event** (or from the later of the first acquisition and April 1985 if the operative event in question is the first one).

Indexation calculations within the FA 1985 pool (after its April 1985 value has been calculated) **are not rounded to three decimal places**. This is because rounding errors would accumulate and have a serious effect after several operative events.

If there are several operative events between 6 April 1985 and the date of a disposal, the indexation procedure described above will have to be performed several times over.

Question — **Value of FA 1985 pool**

Following on from the above example, assume that Oliver acquired 2,000 more shares on 10 July 1986 (RPI = 97.5) at a cost of £4,000. Recalculate the value of the FA 1985 pool on 10 July 1986 following the acquisition.

Answer

	No of shares	Cost	Indexed cost
		£	£
Value at 6.4.85	2,000	6,000	6,291
Indexed rise			
$\frac{97.5 - 94.8}{94.8} \times £6,291$			179
	2,000	6,000	6,470
Acquisition	2,000	4,000	4,000
Value at 10.7.86	4,000	10,000	10,470

In the case of a disposal, following the calculation of the indexed rise to the date of disposal, the cost and the indexed cost attributable to the shares disposed of are deducted from the amounts within the FA 1985 pool. The proportions of the cost and indexed cost to take out of the pool should be computed using the A/(A + B) fraction that is used for any other part disposal. However, we are not usually given the value of the remaining shares (B in the fraction). We then just use numbers of shares.

The indexation allowance is the indexed cost taken out of the pool minus the cost taken out. As usual, the indexation allowance cannot create or increase a loss.

For all FA 1985 pools held by an individual at 5 April 1998 indexation allowance to April 1998 is calculated for the first disposal after 5 April 1998. No further indexation then applies.

Question

The FA 1985 pool

Continuing the above exercise, suppose that Oliver sold 3,000 shares on 10 July 2006 for £17,000. Compute the gain before taper relief, and the value of the FA 1985 pool following the disposal. RPI April 1998 = 162.6

Answer

	No of shares	Cost	Indexed cost
		£	£
Value at 10.7.86	4,000	10,000	10,470
Indexed rise to April 1998			
$\frac{162.6 - 97.5}{97.5} \times £10,470$			6,991
	4,000	10,000	17,461
Disposal	(3,000)		
Cost and indexed cost $\frac{3,000}{4,000} \times$ £10,000 and £17,461		(7,500)	(13,096)
	1,000	2,500	4,365

The gain is computed as follows:

	£
Proceeds	17,000
Less cost	(7,500)
	9,500
Less indexation allowance £(13,096 – 7,500)	(5,596)
Chargeable gain before taper relief	3,904

Taper relief will then apply.

	Cost
	£
Proceeds	7,200
Less: cost less £350	(2,650)
Unindexed gain	4,550
Less indexation allowance (March 1987 to April 1998)	
$\frac{162.6 - 100.6}{100.6} \times$ £3,000 (before distribution)	(1,849)
	2,701

The chargeable gain before taper relief on the November 2006 distribution is £2,701.

Gain after taper relief (6 April 1998 – 5 April 2006 = 8 years plus additional year = 9 years)

65% × £2,701	£1,756

4.3 Bonus issues (scrip issues)

When a company issues bonus shares all that happens is that the size of the original holding is increased. Since bonus shares are issued at no cost there is no need to adjust the original cost. Instead the numbers purchased at particular times are increased by the bonus. The normal matching rules will then be applied.

4.4 Example: bonus issues

The following transactions in the ordinary shares of X plc would be matched as shown below

6.4.83	Purchase of 1,000 shares
6.10.86	Bonus issue of one for four
6.5.06	Sale of 1,250 shares

(a) *The FA 1985 pool*

	No of shares
6.4.83	1,000
6.10.86 Bonus issue one for four	250
	1,250
Disposal 6.5.06	(1,250)

4.5 Rights issues

The difference between a bonus issue and a rights issue is that in a rights issue the new shares are paid for and this results in an adjustment to the original cost. For the purposes of calculating the indexation allowance, expenditure on a rights issue is taken as being incurred on the date of the issue and not on the date of acquisition of the original holding.

As with bonus issues, rights shares derived from shares in the 1985 pool go into that pool and, for individuals, those derived from post 5.4.98 holdings attach to those holdings.

In an **open offer**, shareholders have a right to subscribe for a minimum number of shares based on their existing holdings and may buy additional shares. Subscriptions up to the minimum entitlement are treated as a rights issue. Additional subscriptions are treated as new purchases of shares.

Question — Rights issues on or before 5 April 1998

Julia had the following transactions in the shares of T plc.

July 1985	Purchased 1,000 shares for £3,000 (RPI = 95.2)
May 1986	Took up one for four rights issue at £4.20 per share (RPI = 97.8)
October 2006	Sold 1,250 shares for £10,000

The shares are not business assets for taper relief.

Compute the chargeable gain or allowable loss arising on the sale in October 2006. RPI April 1998 = 162.6, July 1985 = 95.2, May 1986 = 97.8.

Answer

(a) *The FA 1985 pool*

	No of shares	*Cost*	*Indexed cost*
		£	£
July 1985	1,000	3,000	3,000
Indexed rise to May 1986			
$\frac{97.8-95.2}{95.2} \times £3,000$			82
May 1986 one for four rights	250	1,050	1,050
	1,250	4,050	4,132
Indexed rise to April 1998			
$\frac{162.6-97.8}{97.8} \times £4,132$			2,738
Balance at 5 April 1998	1,250	4,050	6,870
Disposal in October 2006	(1,250)	(4,050)	(6,870)

(b) *The chargeable gain*

FA 1985 pool shares

	£
Proceeds	10,000
Less cost	(4,050)
	5,950
Less indexation allowance £(6,870 – 4,050)	(2,820)
Chargeable gain before taper relief	3,130

(c) Gains after taper relief (6 April 1998 – 5 April 2006 = 8 years plus additional year = 9 years)

65% × £3,130 — £2,035

Question — Rights issues after 5 April 1998

Simon had the following transactions in S Ltd.

1.10.95	Bought 10,000 shares (10%) holding for £15,000 (RPI = 149.8)
11.9.05	Bought 2,000 shares for £5,000
1.2.06	Took up rights issue 1 for 2 at £2.75 per share
14.10.06	Sold 5,000 shares for £15,000

Compute the gain arising in October 2006, after taper relief (if applicable). The shares have always been a business asset for taper relief purposes. RPI April 1998 = 162.6, October 1995 = 149.8

Answer

(a) *Post 5.4.98 holding*

	Number	*Cost*
		£
Shares acquired 11.9.05	2,000	5,000
Shares acquired 1.2.06 (rights) 1:2 @ £2.75	1,000	2,750
	3,000	7,750

Gain

	£
Proceeds $\frac{3,000}{5,000} \times £15,000$	9,000
Less: cost	(7,750)
Gain	1,250
Taper relief (based on ownership of original holding 11.9.05 – 10.9.06)	
50% (One year: business asset) × £1,250	£625

(b) *FA 1985 pool*

	Number	*Cost*	*Indexed cost*
		£	£
1.10.95	10,000	15,000	15,000
IA to 4.98 $\frac{162.6-149.8}{149.8} \times £15,000$			1,282
Pool at 5.4.98	10,000	15,000	16,282
Rights issues 1.2.06	5,000	13,750	13,750
	15,000	28,750	30,032
14.10.06 Sale	(2,000)	(3,833)	(4,004)
c/F	13,000	24,917	26,028

Gain

	£
Proceeds $\frac{2,000}{5,000} \times £15,000$	6,000
Less: cost	(3,833)
Unindexed gain	2,167
Less: indexation £(4,004 – 3,833)	(171)
Indexed gain	1,996
Taper relief (based on original holding 6.4.98 – 5.4.06)	
25% (Eight years: business asset) × £1,996	£499

(c) Total gains (after taper relief)

£(625 + 499)	£1,124

4.6 Sales of rights nil paid

Where the shareholder does not take up his rights but sells them to a third party without paying the company for the rights shares, the proceeds are treated as a capital distribution (see above) **and will be dealt with either under the part disposal rules or, if not more than the higher of £3,000 and 5% of the value of the shareholding giving rise to the disposal, as a reduction of original cost** (unless the taxpayer wants a part disposal).

4.7 Stock dividends

A stock dividend is the receipt of a dividend by the issue of additional shares rather than cash. For shareholders which are companies, **a stock dividend is treated as a rights issue taken up** (see later in this text for details of the treatment of shares held by companies). For individuals such shares are treated as free-standing acquisitions and any gain on their disposal is tapered by reference to the period from that acquisition to the disposal of the shares. In both cases, the shares are treated as bought for the value of the (net) stock dividend as calculated for income or corporation tax purposes.

4.8 Reorganisations

A reorganisation takes place where new shares or a mixture of new shares and debentures are issued in exchange for the original shareholdings. The new shares take the place of the old shares. The problem is how to apportion the original cost between the different types of capital issued on the reorganisation.

If the new shares and securities are quoted, then the cost is apportioned by reference to the market values of the new types of capital on the first day of quotation after the reorganisation.

Question — Reorganisations

An original quoted shareholding is made up of ordinary shares purchased as follows.

1985	3,000 shares costing £13,250
2001	2,000 shares costing £9,000

In 2006 there is a reorganisation whereby each ordinary share is exchanged for two 'A' ordinary shares (quoted at £2 each) and one preference share (quoted at £1 each). Show how the original costs will be apportioned.

Answer

The new holding will be as follows.

	Value
	£
10,000 ordinary shares at £2	20,000
5,000 preference shares at £1	5,000
	25,000

The costs will be apportioned between the new 'A' ordinary shares and the preference shares in the ratio of 20,000:5,000 = 4:1 as follows.

FA 1985 pools	£
6,000 ($^{3}/_{5}$ x 10,000) new 'A' ordinary shares, deemed acquired in 1985 ($^{4}/_{5}$ x £13,250)	10,600
3,000 ($^{3}/_{5}$ x 5,000) preference shares, deemed acquired in 1985 ($^{1}/_{5}$ x £13,250)	2,650
	13,250

2001 holding	£
4,000 ($^{2}/_{5}$ x 10,000) new 'A' ordinary shares, deemed acquired in 2001 ($^{4}/_{5}$ x £9,000)	7,200
2,000 ($^{2}/_{5}$ x 5,000) preference shares, deemed acquired in 2001 ($^{1}/_{5}$ x £9,000)	1,800
	9,000

Where a reorganisation takes place and the new shares and securities are unquoted, the cost of the original holding is apportioned using the values of the new shares and securities when they come to be disposed of.

For both quoted and unquoted shares and securities, any incidental costs (such as professional fees) are treated as additional consideration for the new shares and securities.

4.9 Takeovers

FAST FORWARD

The special rules on takeovers only apply if the exchange is for bona fide commercial reasons and not for the avoidance of tax.

A chargeable gain does not arise on a 'paper for paper' takeover. The cost of the original holding is passed on to the new holding which takes the place of the original holding. **If part of the takeover consideration is cash then a gain must be computed**: the normal part disposal rules will apply. If the cash received is not more than the higher of 5% of the total value on the takeover, and £3,000, then the small distribution rules apply and the cash received will be deducted from cost for the purpose of further disposals.

The takeover rules apply where the company issuing the new shares ends up with more than 25% of the ordinary share capital of the old company or the majority of the voting power in the old company, or the company issuing the new shares makes a general offer to shareholders in the other company which is initially made subject to a condition which, if satisfied, would give the first company control of the second company.

The exchange must take place for bona fide commercial reasons and does not have as its main purpose, or one of its main purposes, the avoidance of CGT or corporation tax.

Provision is made for the acquiring company to obtain advance clearance from HMRC that the above condition has been met. HMRC must, within 30 days of receiving the application, either ask for further information or give notice of its decision. If further information is given, HMRC must give its decision within 30 days of the receipt of information. There is an appeal, against an HMRC decision that the condition has not been satisfied, to the Special Commissioners.

Question — Takeovers

Mr Le Bon held 20,000 £1 shares out of a total number of issued shares of one million bought for £2 each in Duran plc. In 2006 the board of Duran plc agreed to a takeover bid by Spandau plc under which shareholders in Duran received three Spandau shares plus 90p cash for every four shares held in Duran plc. Immediately following the takeover, the shares in Spandau plc were quoted at £5 each. What gain (before taper relief) has Mr Le Bon made? The RPI rose by 18% from the acquisition date to April 1998.

Answer

The total value due to Le Bon on the takeover is as follows.

		£
Shares	20,000 × 3/4 × £5	75,000
Cash	20,000 × 1/4 × 90p	4,500
		79,500

Since the cash (£4,500) exceeds both £3,000 and 5% of £79,500 it cannot be rolled over by deducting it from the acquisition cost. There is a part disposal.

		£
Disposal proceeds		4,500
Apportioned cost:		
$\frac{\text{Value of disposal}}{\text{Value of disposal} + \text{value of part retained}} \times \text{cost}$		
$\frac{£4{,}500}{£4{,}500 + £75{,}000} \times 20{,}000 \times £2$		(2,264)
		2,236
Less indexation allowance £2,264 × 0.180		(408)
Indexed gain before taper relief		1,828

Part of the takeover consideration may include the right to receive deferred consideration in the form of shares or debentures in the new company. The amount of the deferred consideration may be unascertainable at the date of the takeover, perhaps because it is dependent on the future profits of the company whose shares are acquired. The right is valued and treated as a security. This means the takeover rules apply and there is no need to calculate a gain in respect of the right. The issue of shares or debentures as a result of the right is treated as a conversion of the right and, again, no gain arises.

5 Gilts and qualifying corporate bonds

FAST FORWARD

Gilts and QCBs held by individuals and trusts are exempt from CGT.

5.1 Definitions and treatment

Key term

Gilts are British Government and Government guaranteed securities as shown on Treasury list. Gilt strips (capital or interest entitlements sold separately) are also gilts. You may assume that the list of gilts includes all issues of Treasury Loan, Treasury Stock, Exchequer Loan, Exchequer Stock and War Loan.

Disposals of gilt edged securities (gilts) and qualifying corporate bonds by individuals and trusts are exempt from CGT. The rules for companies are different, and are explained later in this text.

Key term

A **qualifying corporate bond (QCB)** is a security (whether or not secured on assets) which:

(a) Represents a **'normal commercial loan'**. This excludes any bonds which are convertible into shares (although bonds convertible into other bonds which would be QCBs are not excluded), or which carry the right to excessive interest or interest which depends on the results of the issuer's business

(b) Is **expressed in sterling** and for which no provision is made for conversion into or redemption in another currency

(c) Was **acquired** by the person now disposing of it **after 13 March 1984**, and

(d) Does not have a redemption value which depends on a published index of share prices on a stock exchange.

Permanent interest bearing shares issued by building societies which meet condition (b) above are also QCBs.

5.2 Reorganisations involving QCBs

Special rules apply when a reorganisation involves qualifying corporate bonds, either as the security in issue before the reorganisation (the 'old asset') or as a security issued on the reorganisation (a 'new asset').

Where QCBs are the old asset, the newly issued shares are treated as acquired at the time of the reorganisation, for the then market value of the old asset. This market value is reduced by any money paid to the security-holders, or increased by any money paid by them. If a company holds the QCBs, then the QCBs are treated as sold at the same time for their market value, so as to find the company's profit or loss.

Where QCBs are a new asset, the chargeable gain which would have accrued if the old asset had been sold at its market value at the time of the reorganisation must be computed, and apportioned between the new assets issued. When the QCBs are disposed of, the part of that gain apportioned to them becomes chargeable. However, if that disposal is a no gain/no loss disposal to a spouse, the gain does not become chargeable until a disposal outside the marriage. Furthermore, if the reorganisation is followed by the owner's death while he still owns the QCBs, the gain never becomes chargeable.

Chapter roundup

- When dealing with shares held by individuals we need to construct a FA 1985 pool running (with indexation allowance) to 5 April 1998 and then a list of shares acquired from 6 April 1998 onwards. Shares acquired after 6.4.98 are deemed to be disposed of first on a LIFO basis.
- On an alteration of share capital, the general principle is only to tax gains immediately if cash is paid to the investors.
- The special rules on takeovers only apply if the exchange is for bona fide commercial reasons and not for the avoidance of tax.
- Gilts and QCBs held by individuals and trusts are exempt from CGT.

Quick quiz

1. In what order are acquisitions of shares acquired since 6 April 1982 matched with disposals for individuals?
2. An individual acquired 1,000 shares on each of 15 January 1990, 15 January 2004 and 15 January 2007 in X plc. He sells 2,500 shares on 10 January 2007. How are the shares matched on sale?
3. Sharon acquired 10,000 share in Z plc in 1986. She takes up a 1 for 2 rights offer in 2006. How are the rights issue shares dealt with?
4. What is a qualifying corporate bond?

Answers to quick quiz

1 (a) Same day acquisitions
(b) Acquisitions in following 30 days
(c) Previous acquisitions after 5 April 1998 on LIFO basis
(d) Shares in FA 1985 pool

2 January 2007 1,000 shares (following 30 days)
January 2004 1,000 shares (after 5 April 1998)
January 1990 (FA 1985 pool) 500 shares

3 The rights issue shares are added to the FA 1985 pool holding (1986 acquisition).

4 A qualifying corporate bond is a security which:

- represents a normal commercial loan
- is expressed in sterling
- was acquired after 13 March 1984
- is not redeemable in relation to share prices on a stock exchange

Now try the question below from the Exam Question Bank

Number	Level	Marks	Time
Q10	Examination	25	45 mins

12

Deferral reliefs

Introduction

In certain circumstances it may be possible to defer a gain – that is to remove it from an immediate charge to CGT. However, it is important to realise the gain has not been exempted and it may become charged in the future.

Deferral reliefs operate in two ways. First, the gain may be deducted from the base cost of an asset (for example, 'roll over' relief for reinvestment in non-depreciating business assets, incorporation relief, gift relief, compensation). Second, the gain may be held in suspense until a certain event occurs (deferral relief for reinvestment into depreciating business assets, EIS deferral relief).

Topic list	Syllabus references
1 The replacement of business assets (rollover relief)	1(f)
2 Gift relief ('holdover' relief)	1(f)
3 The transfer of a business to a company (incorporation relief)	1(f)
4 EIS deferral relief	1(f)
5 Compensation and insurance proceeds	1(f)

1 The replacement of business assets (rollover relief)

1.1 Conditions

FAST FORWARD

When assets falling within certain classes are sold and other such assets are bought, it is possible to defer gains on the assets sold.

A gain may be 'rolled over' (deferred) where it arises on the disposal of a business asset which is replaced. This is **rollover relief**. A claim cannot specify that only part of a gain is to be rolled over.

All the following conditions must be met.

(a) **The old asset sold and the new asset bought are both used only in the trade** or trades carried on **by the person claiming rollover relief**. Where part of a building is in non-trade use for all or a substantial part of the period of ownership, the building (and the land on which it stands) can be treated as two separate assets, the trade part (qualifying) and the non-trade part (non-qualifying). This split cannot be made for other assets.

(b) **The old asset and the new asset both fall within one** (but not necessarily the same one) **of the following classes.**

   (i) Land and buildings (including parts of buildings) occupied as well as used only for the purpose of the trade

   (ii) Fixed (that is, immovable) plant and machinery

   (iii) Ships, aircraft and hovercraft

   (iv) Goodwill

   (v) Satellites, space stations and spacecraft

   (vi) Milk quotas, potato quotas and ewe and suckler cow premium quotas

   (vii) Fish quota

(c) **Reinvestment of the proceeds of the old asset takes place in a period beginning one year before and ending three years after the date of the disposal.**

(d) **The new asset is brought into use in the trade on its acquisition** (not necessarily immediately, but not after any significant and unnecessary delay).

Goodwill and the various quotas are not qualifying assets for the purposes of corporation tax (ie for companies). Companies are covered later in this text.

The new asset can be for use in a different trade from the old asset.

A rollover claim is not allowed when a taxpayer buys premises, sells part of the premises at a profit and then claims to roll over the gain into the part retained. However, a rollover claim is allowed (by concession) when the proceeds of the old asset are spent on improving a qualifying asset which the taxpayer already owns. The improved asset must already be in use for a trade, or be brought into trade use immediately the improvement work is finished.

1.2 Operation of relief

FAST FORWARD

If an amount less than the proceeds of the old asset is invested in the new assets, a gain equal to the difference will be chargeable, if this is less than the actual gain.

Deferral is obtained by deducting the chargeable gain from the cost of the new asset. For full relief, the whole of the consideration for the disposal must be reinvested. Where only part is reinvested, a

part of the gain equal to the lower of the full gain and the amount not reinvested will be liable to tax immediately.

The new asset will have a base 'cost' for chargeable gains purposes, of its purchase price less the gain rolled over into its acquisition.

If a trader expects to buy new assets, he can make a provisional rollover claim on the tax return which includes the gain on the old asset. The gain is reduced accordingly. If new assets are not actually acquired, HMRC collect the tax saved by the provisional claim.

Question

Rollover relief

A freehold factory was purchased by Zoë for business use in August 1997. It was sold in December 2006 for £70,000, giving rise to an indexed gain of £17,950. A replacement factory was purchased in June 2007 for £60,000. Compute the base cost of the replacement factory, taking into account any possible rollover of the gain from the disposal in December 2006. Ignore taper relief.

Answer

	£
Total gain	17,950
Less: amount not reinvested, immediately chargeable £(70,000 – 60,000)	(10,000)
Rollover gain	7,950
Cost of new factory	60,000
Less rolled over gain	(7,950)
Base cost of new factory	52,050

Rollover relief applies to the untapered gain. Any gain left in charge will then be eligible for taper relief. When the replacement asset is sold taper relief on that sale will only be given by reference to the holding period for that asset (assuming further rollover relief is not claimed on this disposal). **Effectively, taper relief on the rolled over gain, for the period of ownership of the original asset, is lost.**

Question

Rollover relief and taper relief interaction

Karen is a sole trader who bought a business asset for £170,625 on 5 November 1991 (RPI = 135.6) and sold it on 31 December 2006 for £491,400. A replacement business asset was acquired on 1 November 2006 at a cost of £546,000. The new asset was sold on 3 September 2008 for £914,550. Karen made a claim for rollover relief on the first asset sale but not on the second asset sale.

Calculate the taxable gains for each asset disposal. RPI April 1998 = 162.6.

Answer

31 December 2006 disposal

	£
Sale proceeds	491,400
Cost (5.11.1991)	(170,625)
	320,775
Less: indexation allowance to April 1998	
$\frac{162.6-135.6}{135.6}$ = 0.199 x £170,625	(33,954)
Chargeable gain before taper relief	286,821

Since the asset was sold for £491,400 and within the required time period a replacement asset was purchased for £546,000 there was a full reinvestment of the sale proceeds. Thus the full gain before taper relief of £286,821 is rolled over against the cost of the new asset.

3 September 2008 disposal

	£	£
Sale proceeds		914,550
Cost (1 November 2006)	546,000	
Less: rollover relief	(286,821)	
		(259,179)
Gain		655,371
Ownership period is 1 November 2006 to 3 September 2008		
= 1 complete year of ownership		
Gain after taper relief		
Taxable gain (50%) for Karen		£327,686

Where an old asset has not been used in the trade for a fraction of its period of ownership, the amount of the gain that can be rolled over is reduced by the same fraction. If the proceeds are not fully reinvested the restriction on rollover by the amount not reinvested is also calculated by considering only the proportion of proceeds relating to the part of the asset used in the trade or the proportion relating to the period of trade use.

Question — Assets with non-business use

John bought a factory for £150,000 on 11 November 2001, for use in his business. From 11 November 2002, he let the factory out to a quoted company, for a period of two years. He then used the factory for his own business again, until he sold it on 10 May 2006 for £225,000. On 13 December 2006, he purchased another factory for use in his business. This second factory cost £100,000.

Calculate the chargeable gain on the sale of the first factory and the base cost of the second factory.

Answer

Gain on first factory

	£
Proceeds of sale	225,000
Less: cost	(150,000)
Gain (no indexation allowance)	75,000

Attributable to non business use:

$$\frac{11.11.02-10.11.04}{11.11.01-10.5.06}=\frac{24\text{ months}}{54\text{ months}}\times £75{,}000 \qquad £33{,}333$$

Attributable to business use (remainder ie 30 months): £41,667

The proceeds of the business element of the factory are:

$$\frac{30}{54}\times £225{,}000 \qquad £125{,}000$$

Proceeds of business element not invested in second factory:

	£
Proceeds of business element	125,000
Less: cost of new factory	(100,000)
Not reinvested	25,000

Therefore of the business gain only £(41,667 - 25,000) = £16,667 is available for rollover relief.

The chargeable gain on the first factory is:

	£
Non business element (4 years taper relief)	
£33,333 x 90%	30,000
Business element (4 years taper relief)	
£25,000 x 25%	6,250
Total chargeable gain	36,250

Base cost of second factory

	£
Cost	100,000
Less rolled over	(16,667)
Base cost	83,333

1.3 Depreciating assets

Where the replacement asset is a depreciating asset, the gain is not rolled over by reducing the cost of the replacement asset. Rather it is deferred until it crystallises on the earliest of:

(a) The disposal of the replacement asset.

(b) Ten years after the acquisition of the replacement asset.

(c) The date the replacement asset ceases to be used in the trade (but the gain does not crystallise on the taxpayer's death).

Key term

An asset is a **depreciating asset** if it is, or within the next ten years will become, a wasting asset. Thus, any asset with an expected life of 60 years or less is covered by this definition. Plant and machinery (including ships, aircraft, hovercraft, satellites, space stations and spacecraft) is always treated as depreciating unless it becomes part of a building: in that case, it will only be depreciating if the building is held on a lease with 60 years or less to run.

Taper relief is applied to the original gain *before* it is deferred, in relation to the ownership of the original asset. No further relief is given for the time that the gain is deferred. Taper relief applies on the depreciating asset from the date of purchase in the normal way.

Question — Deferred gain on investment into depreciating asset

Norma bought a freehold shop for use in her business in June 2005 for £125,000. She sold it for £140,000 on 1 August 2006. On 10 July 2006, Norma bought some fixed plant and machinery to use in her business, costing £150,000. She then sells the plant and machinery for £167,000 on 19 November 2008. Show Norma's CGT position.

Answer

Gain deferred

	£
Proceeds of shop	140,000
Less cost	(125,000)
Gain	15,000

Gain after taper relief (1 year)

50% x £15,000	£7,500

This gain is deferred in relation to the purchase of the plant and machinery.

Sale of plant and machinery

	£
Proceeds	167,000
Less cost	(150,000)
Gain	17,000

Gain on plant and machinery after taper relief (2 years)

£17,000 × 25%	£4,250

Total gain chargeable on sale (gain on plant and machinery plus deferred gain)

£(4,250 + 7,500)	£11,750

Where a gain on disposal is deferred against a replacement depreciating asset it is possible to transfer the deferred gain to a non-depreciating asset provided the non-depreciating asset is bought before the deferred gain has crystallised.

Question — **Transfer of deferred gain into non-depreciating asset**

In July 1996, Julia sold a warehouse used in her trade, realising a gain of £30,000. Julia invested the whole of the proceeds of sale of £95,000 into fixed plant and machinery in January 1997 and made a claim to defer the gain on the warehouse.

In August 2006, Julia bought a freehold shop for use in her business costing £100,000. Julia has not bought any other assets for use in her business and wishes to minimise chargeable gains arising in 2006/07. What advice would you give Julia? Ignore taper relief.

Answer

Julia should claim to transfer the deferred gain of £30,000 to the purchase of the shop. If she does not do so, the deferred gain will be chargeable in January 2007, at the latest (10 years after the acquisition of the plant and machinery). The effect of the claim will be to reduce the base cost of the shop to £(100,000 - 30,000) = £70,000.

Both types of relief can also be claimed by an individual on assets owned by him but used in the trade of his 'personal company' (defined as for gift relief below).

1.4 The choice of assets for claims

Sometimes more than one eligible asset will be sold, but acquisitions will not allow all the gains to be rolled over or deferred. A choice must then be made, and the choice may affect the total gains rolled over or deferred and thus the total immediately chargeable.

Question **The choice of assets**

Asset A was bought for £98 and is sold for £108, giving a gain of £10.

Asset B was bought for £45 and is sold for £50, giving a gain of £5.

Asset C is bought for £100, and gains on assets A and B could be rolled over against this purchase. Compute the gains chargeable immediately under the possible claims.

Answer

If a claim is made for asset A, the gains chargeable immediately will be £8 (proceeds not reinvested) + £5 (asset B) = £13.

If a claim is made for asset B, the gain chargeable immediately will be £10 (asset A). Note that an additional claim for asset A would have no effect, because the balance of cost of asset C after claiming for asset B would be £(100 – 50) = £50, and the proceeds of asset A not reinvested would be £(108 – 50) = £58, which exceeds the gain on asset A.

If there are plenty of acquisitions, but not enough disposals to make full use of the capacity to rollover or defer gains consider the following points:

(a) Rollover claims against non-depreciating assets allow gains to be deferred indefinitely, whereas gains deferred against depreciating assets will crystallise within ten years (unless rollover claims are substituted).

(b) If two alternative rollover claims or two alternative deferral claims are possible, it is probably better to choose the new assets which are likely to be retained for longer, so as to maximise the period before the gains become chargeable.

(c) If an asset is likely to be retained until the trader's death, it is good tax planning to use it for rollover claims, because the gain on its disposal (as increased by the effect of the rollover claim) may escape tax altogether.

2 Gift relief ('holdover' relief)

2.1 The relief

If an individual gives away a qualifying asset, the transferor and the transferee can jointly elect, or where a trust is the transferee, the transferor alone can elect, by the 31 January which is nearly six years after the end of the tax year of the transfer, **that the transferor's gain be reduced to nil. The transferee is then deemed to acquire the asset for market value at the date of transfer less the transferor's deferred gain** (no taper relief given). The transferee will qualify for further indexation allowance (if available) on that reduced base cost from the date of the transfer. The transferee will start a new period for taper relief from the date of his acquisition.

If a disposal involves actual consideration rather than being a pure gift but is still not a bargain made at arm's length (so that the proceeds are deemed to be the market value of the asset), **then any excess of actual consideration over allowable costs** (excluding indexation allowance) **is chargeable immediately and only the balance of the gain is deferred**. Of course, the amount chargeable immediately is limited to the full gain after indexation allowance.

2.2 Qualifying assets

FAST FORWARD

Gift relief is available on both gifts and sales at an undervalue of business assets. Gift relief is also available on gifts which are immediately chargeable to inheritance tax.

Gift relief can be claimed on gifts or sales at undervalue as follows.

(a) Transfers of **business assets**

(i) Trade assets
(ii) Agricultural property
(iii) Shares and securities (except where the transferee is a company)

(b) Transfers subject to an **immediate inheritance tax charge**

Transfers of business assets are transfers of assets

(a) **Used in a trade, profession or vocation** carried on:

(1) By the donor

(2) If the donor is an individual, by a trading company which is his 'personal company' or a member of a trading group of which the holding company is his 'personal company' (a personal company is one in which the individual can exercise at least 5% of the voting rights).

(3) If the donor is a trustee, by the trustee or by a beneficiary who has an interest in possession in the settled property

If the asset was used for the purposes of the trade, profession or vocation for only part of its period of ownership, the gain to be held over is the gain otherwise eligible × period of such use/total period of ownership.

If the asset was a building or structure only partly used for trade, professional or vocational purposes, only the **part of the gain attributable to the part so used is eligible for gift relief**

(b) **Agricultural property** which would attract inheritance tax agricultural property relief. The restrictions for periods of non-trade use and for partial trade use mentioned above do not apply.

(c) **Shares and securities in trading companies**, or holding companies of trading groups, where:

(1) The shares or securities are **not listed on a recognised stock exchange** (but they may be on the AIM), or

(2) If the donor is an individual, the company concerned is his **personal company** (defined as above), or

(3) If the donor is a trustee, the trustee can exercise 25% or more of the voting rights.

If the company has chargeable non-business assets at the time of the gift, and either (2) or (3) applied at any time in the last 12 months, **the gain to be held over is the gain otherwise chargeable × the value of the chargeable business assets/the value of the chargeable assets**

If relief is claimed on a transfer of business assets, and that transfer is (or later becomes) chargeable to inheritance tax, then when the transferee disposes of the assets his gain is reduced by the inheritance tax finally payable (but not so as to create a loss).

Transfers subject to an immediate inheritance tax charge include most gifts to trusts. A transfer will be regarded as chargeable to inheritance tax even if it falls within the nil rate band of that tax or is covered by the inheritance tax annual exemption. Gifts to settlor interested trusts, however, do not qualify for gift relief.

If a transfer of business assets could also be subject to an immediate charge to inheritance tax, the rules relating to the latter category apply and the restrictions related to period of use and to chargeable business assets therefore do not apply.

Question — Gift relief

On 6 December 2006 Angelo sold to his son Michael a freehold shop valued at £200,000 for £50,000, and claimed gift relief. Angelo had originally purchased the shop from which he had run his business in July 2002 for £30,000. Michael continued to run a business from the shop premises but decided to sell the shop in May 2008 for £195,000. Compute any chargeable gains arising. Assume the rules of CGT in 2006/07 continue to apply in May 2008.

Answer

(a) *Angelo's CGT position (2006/07)*

	£
Proceeds	200,000
Less cost	(30,000)
Gain	170,000
Less gain deferred £170,000 – £(50,000 – 30,000)	(150,000)
Gain left in charge	20,000
Gain after taper relief (note)	£5,000

(b) *Michael's CGT position (2007/08)*

	£
Proceeds	195,000
Less cost £(200,000 – 150,000)	(50,000)
Gain	145,000
Chargeable gain after taper relief (50%)	£72,500

Note. Taper relief is available for Angelo since the asset disposed of in December 2006 is a 'business asset'. The period of ownership is four complete years. Thus only 25% of the gain will be taxable.

Michael acquired the asset on 6 December 2006 and sold it in May 2008. He therefore owned the asset for one complete year. 50% of the gain is taxable.

2.3 Restriction of hold over relief

It is not possible to claim gift relief on transfers to a settlor-interested trust. This is a trust from which the settlor, or his spouse, civil partner or minor child (who is neither married nor in a civil partnership) can benefit.

Gift relief may be claimed on a transfer to a trust which is not at that time settlor-interested. However, if the **trust becomes settlor interested within six tax years of the end of the tax year in which the disposal was made there is a claw back of the gift relief.**

The gain that was deferred using gift relief will be treated as becoming taxable on the settlor when the trust becomes settlor interested. The trustees' allowable cost will be increased by the amount of the gain taxable on the settlor. If the trustees have already disposed of the gifted asset before the gain becomes clawed back, the trustees' gain or loss will be recomputed as if the gift relief had never been claimed and the tax payable or repayable is adjusted accordingly.

2.4 Instalments

FAST FORWARD

CGT can be paid by instalments on transfer of certain assets where gift relief is not available.

Any **CGT payable** on transfers of certain assets **where no gift relief is available** (and any CGT payable because part of a gain cannot be deferred) **can be paid by annual instalments over ten years**. These assets are:

(a) Land

(b) A controlling holding of shares or securities in a company

(c) Minority holdings of shares or securities in a company which is not listed on a stock exchange (but it may be on the AIM)

Note that gift relief must be *unavailable*, not merely not elected for.

Interest is chargeable on the outstanding balance from the normal due date.

The first instalment is due on the normal due date. If for example land is given away on 30 June 2006 and the instalment option is claimed, the first instalment will be due for payment on 31 January 2008.

If the transfer is to a connected person and the asset is subsequently sold within the ten year instalment period, any outstanding tax and accrued interest will become payable immediately.

If the taxpayer wishes, the balance with interest to date may be paid at any time.

2.5 Anti-avoidance rules

Gift relief is not available if the transferee is neither resident nor ordinarily resident in the UK at the time of the gift. If the transferee is an individual who becomes neither resident nor ordinarily resident in the UK in any of the six tax years following the year of the transfer and before disposing of the asset transferred, then the gain held over is chargeable on him as if it arose immediately before he becomes neither resident nor ordinarily resident in the UK.

3 The transfer of a business to a company (incorporation relief)

FAST FORWARD

When an individual incorporates his business, the gain arising will be deducted from the cost of the shares received, unless the individual elects otherwise.

If a person transfers his business to a company then he makes a disposal of the business assets for CGT purposes and realises net chargeable gains (chargeable gains less allowable losses) on those assets. (Note that the individual assets are disposed of. Contrast this with a sale of shares, when shares are disposed of but business assets remain the property of the company which issued the shares, and are not disposed of.) It is, however, clearly undesirable to discourage entrepreneurs from incorporating their businesses and so a relief is available.

The relief (sometimes called Incorporation Relief) is automatic (so no claim need be made). **All or some of the gains are held over if all the following conditions are met.**

(a) The **business is transferred as a going concern.**

(b) **All its assets** (or all its assets other than cash) **are transferred** (but see below for a claim to disapply the relief).

(c) **The consideration is wholly or partly in shares.**

The amount held over is found by applying the fraction:

$$\frac{\text{Value of shares received from the company}}{\text{Total value of consideration from the company}}$$

to the indexed gain. This amount is then deducted from the base cost of the shares received. The company is deemed to acquire assets transferred at their market values.

Incorporation relief applies to the chargeable gain calculated before taper relief.

Question — Incorporation relief

Mr P transferred his business to a company in May 2006, realising a gain after indexation allowance but before taper relief of £24,000 on the only business asset transferred (a factory). The consideration comprised cash of £15,000 and shares at a market value of £75,000.

(a) What is the gain on the transfer before taper relief?
(b) What is the base cost of the shares for any future disposal?

Answer

(a)

	£
Gain	24,000
Less held over $\frac{75,000}{15,000+75,000} \times £24,000$	(20,000)
Chargeable gain before taper relief	4,000

(b)

	£
Market value	75,000
Less gain held over	(20,000)
Base cost of shares	55,000

An individual can elect not to receive incorporation relief. He might do this, for example, to keep his entitlement to taper relief on the gain arising on incorporation. The election must in general be made by 31 January, 34 months after the end of the tax year of disposal. This long time limit is to allow shareholders to see whether they want to elect to disapply incorporation relief depending on whether they have built up two years (the maximum) taper relief on shares between incorporation and disposal. For example if a business was incorporated on 1 April 2007 (2006/07) the shares will need to be held at least to 1 April 2009 (tax year 2008/09) to see whether they have got full taper relief. In this case an election need not be made until 31 January 2010.

4 EIS deferral relief

FAST FORWARD Gains can be deferred if an individual invests in shares in a EIS company.

4.1 Introduction

An individual may defer a gain arising on the disposal of any type of asset if he invests in qualifying Enterprise Investment Scheme (EIS) shares (see later in this text). This is a deferral relief because the deferred gain will become chargeable, for example when the shares are disposed of (subject to a further claim for the relief being made).

It is not necessary for the shares acquired to be subject to the EIS income tax relief which is discussed later in this text.

4.2 Calculation of relief

The amount of the gain (before taper relief) that can be deferred is the lower of:

(a) The amount subscribed by the investor for his shares, which has not previously been matched under this relief, and

(b) The amount specified by the investor in the claim. This can take into account the availability of losses, taper relief and the annual exemption.

Taper relief is then applied to any remaining gain in the usual way.

Question — **Deferral of gain**

Robert made a gain of £196,000 (before taper relief) on the disposal of a property in 2005/06. The property qualifies for one year taper relief as a business asset. He subscribed for some shares in a company which qualified under the EIS rules. What will the gain to defer be if:

(a) The shares cost £200,000 and Robert wants to take the maximum deferral relief possible.

(b) The shares cost £170,000 and Robert wants to take the maximum deferral relief possible.

(c) The shares cost £200,000 and Robert, who has no other chargeable assets, wishes to utilise his annual exemption.

Answer

(a) £196,000. The qualifying expenditure on the shares exceeds the gain, so the whole gain can be deferred. See further in this section for the taper relief position when the gain becomes chargeable eg when the shares are sold.

(b) £170,000. The gain deferred is restricted to the qualifying expenditure. The remainder of the gain of £26,000 will remain in charge (subject to relief for any further investment). If no such investment is made and there are no losses to take into account, the gain after taper relief left in charge will be £26,000 × 50% = £13,000.

(c) A claim can be made to defer £178,400. This is calculated as follows:

	£
Gain before relief	196,000
Less EIS reinvestment relief (balancing figure)	(178,400)
Gain before taper relief	17,600
Gain after taper relief (50%)	8,800
Less annual exemption	(8,800)
Taxable	nil

4.3 Conditions for the relief

4.3.1 The gain to be deferred

The gain must either arise due to the disposal of an asset or on a gain coming back into charge under this relief.

4.3.2 The investor

The investor must either be an individual or trustees of trusts for individuals. The investor must be UK resident or ordinarily resident at the time the gain to be deferred was made and at the time the investment was made in the shares.

4.3.3 The company

The company must be a qualifying company under the EIS rules (see later in this Text).

4.3.4 The shares

The shares (other than any bonus shares) must be subscribed for wholly in cash by the investor. The shares (other than bonus shares) must be new ordinary shares, fully paid up. The shares must not be redeemable broadly within three years of their issue, nor must they have preferential rights to dividends or assets on a winding up within that period.

The shares must be subscribed and issued for bona fide commercial purposes (not for the avoidance of tax) and for the purpose of raising money for a qualifying business activity. At least 80% of the money raised by the issue of EIS shares must be used for this purpose within twelve months of the issue of the shares (or within twelve months of the commencement of the trade). All of the money must be used for this purpose within twelve months of the end of the first twelve month period (ie within twenty-four months). If this condition is not satisfied the shares cease to be eligible shares (see below).

4.3.5 Time for investment

The shares must be issued to the investor within the period of one year before and three years after the gain to be deferred accrues (or such longer period as HMRC may allow). If the gain accrues after the issue of the shares, the shares must still be held by the investor at the time that the gain arises.

4.3.6 The claim

The claim to be made is broadly similar to that for the EIS income tax relief. The latest date for a claim to be made is 31 January nearly six years after the end of the tax year in which the gain to be deferred arose.

4.4 Gain coming back into charge

The gain deferred will come back into charge on the following events:

(a) The investor disposing of the shares except by an inter-spouse disposal.

(b) The spouse of an investor disposing of the shares, if the spouse acquired the shares from the investor.

(c) The investor becoming non resident, broadly within three years of the issue of the shares (except if employed full time abroad for up to three years and retaining the shares until his return to the UK).

(d) The spouse of an investor becoming non resident, broadly within three years of the issue of the shares (except if employed full time abroad for up to three years and retaining the shares until his return to the UK), if the spouse acquired the shares from the investor.

(e) The shares ceasing to be eligible shares, eg the company ceases to be a qualifying company, the money subscribed not being used for a qualifying business activity. However, relief is not withdrawn if the company becomes a quoted company. This is provided that there were no arrangements in existence at the time of the issue of the shares for the company to cease to be unquoted.

Remember that 'spouse' includes civil partners.

Note that the gain becomes chargeable in the year of the event, not the year when the original gain was made (if different). It will be charged on the holder of the shares at the date of the event, eg on the investor if he/she still holds the shares or the spouse if the shares have been passed to her/him.

Taper relief generally applies to the deferred gain with reference to the original asset which gave rise to the deferred gain. No further taper relief can be given to the deferred gain. However, separate taper relief will apply to the holding of the shares.

Question **Gain coming back into charge**

In 2006/07, Victor made a gain of £160,000 on the disposal of a business asset, qualifying for one year's taper relief. He invested £180,000 in eligible EIS shares on 13 August 2007. The shares were business assets for the purposes of taper relief. Victor sold the shares on 15 October 2009 for £240,000. Show the gains chargeable as a result of the sale.

Answer

	£
Proceeds	240,000
Less : cost	(180,000)
Gain	60,000
Gain after taper relief (2 years business) (25%)	15,000
Gain deferred recharged after taper relief (1 year business) (50%)	80,000
Total gains arising on sale	95,000

There is special taper relief treatment for investors who defer a gain on EIS shares into further EIS shares. In this case the taper relief given on the disposal of the second investment of shares is cumulative (ie. includes the ownership of the first and second investment of shares on the disposal of the second investment of shares). This rule only applies to the gain on the original EIS shares, not a gain on any other asset which was originally deferred into the EIS shares.

4.5 Reorganisations and amalgamations

There are rules relating to reorganisations and amalgamations which are similar to the rules for EIS income tax relief (see later in this text). In general, their purpose is to enable the identification of the original EIS shares (and any associated relief) with replacement shares and to stop the dilution of the relief into rights issue shares. In certain circumstances a reorganisation or amalgamation may result in a chargeable event, for example, if the replacement shares are not new ordinary shares or on a takeover if the new company does not satisfy the rules for EIS qualifying companies.

4.6 Anti-avoidance

There are a number of provisions designed to prevent abuse of the relief. Relief is usually not given if any of these provisions apply before the investment is made or is withdrawn if the rule is broken. The provisions include:

(a) Shares disposed of in a company and investment made in the same company or member of the same group of companies

(b) There is a pre-arranged exit from the investment

(c) The shares are subject to options to buy or sell

(d) Value is received from the company by the investor or other persons (subject to similar rules as for income tax eg to ignore receipts of insignificant value (see later in this text))

(e) There is an investment-linked loan

5 Compensation and insurance proceeds

FAST FORWARD

The gain which would otherwise arise on the receipt of insurance proceeds may, subject to certain conditions, be deferred.

5.1 Damaged assets

If an asset is damaged and compensation or insurance money is received as a result, then this will normally be treated as a part disposal. By election, however, the taxpayer can avoid a part disposal computation. A capital sum received can be deducted from the cost of the asset rather than being treated as a part disposal if:

(a) Any amount not spent in restoring the asset is small, or
(b) The capital sum is small.

HMRC accept a sum as 'small' if it is either less than 5% of the value of the asset or is less than £3,000. There are special restrictions if the asset is wasting (that is, it has a remaining useful life of 50 years or less).

(a) The *whole* capital sum must be spent on restoration.

(b) The capital sum can only be deducted from what would have been the allowable expenditure on a sale immediately after its application. This will be less than the full cost of the asset, because the cost of a wasting asset is run down over its life (see later in this text).

If the amount not used in restoring the asset is not small, then the taxpayer can elect for the amount used in restoration to be deducted from the cost; the balance will continue to be treated as a part disposal.

Question — **Damaged assets**

Mr J bought an office block for renting out which cost £18,000 on 15 August 1983. On 10 September 2006 it was damaged in a fire and, as a result, £27,000 insurance proceeds were received in December 2006. £20,000 was spent to restore the building in October 2006; the market value of the building immediately after restoration was £62,000. What gain arose and what will be the base cost of the building in future computations? Assume that Mr J elects for the amount used in restoration to be deducted from the base cost of the building. Assume an indexation factor of August 1993 to April 1998 = 0.897.

Answer

The part disposal in December 2006

	£	£
Capital sum not used for restoration		
£(27,000 - 20,000)		7,000
Less: part of original cost (incurred August 1983)		
$£18,000 \times \dfrac{7,000}{7,000+62,000}$	1,826	
part of restoration cost (incurred October 2006)		
$£20,000 \times \dfrac{7,000}{7,000+62,000}$	2,029	
		(3,855)
Unindexed gain		3,145
Less indexation allowance (August 1983 to April 1998)		
0.897 × £1,826		(1,638)
Indexed gain		1,507
Gain after taper relief £1,507 × 65%		980

The base cost of the restored building

	£	£
Original cost		18,000
Restoration expenditure		20,000
		38,000
Less: costs used in part disposal	3,855	
restoration expenditure rolled over	20,000	
		(23,855)
Base cost		14,145

The date of the part disposal is the date of receipt of the insurance monies (December 2006). Mr J purchased the asset in August 1983 and also spent £20,000 in restoring the building in October 2006. There is an indexation allowance from August 1983 to April 1998 on the part of the original cost but on the part of the restoration cost there is no indexation allowance since this cost was incurred post April 1998 (the date on which indexation allowance was abolished). Taper relief is due for 9 years as the asset is not a business asset. There are 8 years ownership post 6 April 1998 plus the additional year.

5.2 Destroyed assets

If an asset is destroyed (as opposed to merely being damaged) any compensation or insurance monies received will normally be brought into an ordinary CGT disposal computation as proceeds. But if all the proceeds from a non-wasting asset are applied for the replacement of the asset within 12 months, any gain can be deducted from the cost of the replacement asset. If only part of the proceeds are used, the gain immediately chargeable can be limited to the amount not used. The rest of the gain is then deducted from the cost of the replacement.

Question — Destroyed assets

Fiona bought a non-business asset for £25,000 in June 2006. It was destroyed three years and one month later. Insurance proceeds were £34,000, and Fiona spent £32,500 on a replacement asset. Compute the chargeable gain and the base cost of the new asset.

Answer

	£
Proceeds	34,000
Less cost	(25,000)
	9,000
Gain immediately chargeable £(34,000 – 32,500)	(1,500)
Deduction from base cost	7,500

The base cost of the new asset is £(32,500 – 7,500) = £25,000.

The gain chargeable of £1,500 qualifies for taper relief (3 complete years of ownership of a non-business asset). 95% of the gain is charged to tax which equals £1,425.

5.3 The compulsory purchase of land

If land is sold to an authority exercising or having powers of compulsory purchase and the proceeds are applied to buy other land, the gain on the land disposed of may, if the landowner claims, be deducted from the base cost of the land bought (instead of being chargeable). If only part of the proceeds are reinvested, the balance (up to the amount of the gain) is chargeable.

The replacement land must be acquired within the period from one year before to three years after the disposal of the land compulsorily purchased.

Relief is not available if, at any time in the six years after acquisition, the replacement land is the buyer's principal private residence for CGT purposes.

If the replacement land is a depreciating asset (a lease with 60 years or less to run), the gain on the land compulsorily purchased is not deducted from the cost of the replacement land, but is deferred from the date of acquisition of the replacement land until the earlier of its disposal and ten years later; but if non-depreciating land is acquired before the gain becomes chargeable, the gain can be deducted from the cost of that non-depreciating land and therefore deferred indefinitely.

If a taxpayer expects to acquire new land, he can make a provisional claim on the tax return which includes the gain on the old land to reduce the gain accordingly. If he does not actually acquire new land, HMRC collect the tax saved by the provisional claim.

5.4 Replacement leases

If a lessee surrenders a lease (before its expiry) and takes a new lease for a longer term, the disposal of the old lease is ignored if all of the following conditions are met.

(a) The parties are unconnected and bargain at arm's length.

(b) The transaction is not part of, or connected with, a larger scheme or a series of transactions.

(c) The lessee does not receive a capital sum.

(d) The new lease covers exactly the same property as the old lease.

(e) The only differences between the terms of the leases are the duration and the rent payable.

Chapter roundup

- When assets falling within certain classes are sold and other such assets are bought, it is possible to defer gains on the assets sold.
- If an amount less than the proceeds of the old asset is invested in the new assets, a gain equal to the difference will be chargeable, if this is less than the actual gain.
- Gift relief is available on both gifts and sales at an undervalue of business assets.
- Gift relief is also available on gifts which are immediately chargeable to inheritance tax.
- CGT can be paid by instalments on transfer of certain assets where gift relief is not available.
- When an individual incorporates his business, the gain arising will be deducted from the cost of the shares received, unless the individual elects otherwise.
- Gains can be deferred if an individual invests in shares in a EIS company.
- The gain which would otherwise arise on the receipt of insurance proceeds may, subject to certain conditions, be deferred.

Quick quiz

1 What assets are eligible for rollover relief on the replacement of business assets?

2 What deferral of a gain is available when a business asset is replaced with a depreciating business asset?

3 Which disposals of shares qualify for gift relief?

4 When may CGT be paid by ten annual instalments?

5 What are the conditions for deferring gains on the incorporation of a business?

6 When is EIS reinvestment relief available?

7 When will a gain come back into charge under EIS reinvestment relief?

8 When may a part disposal computation be avoided on the receipt of insurance proceeds?

9 Emma drops and destroys a vase. She receives compensation of £2,000 from her insurance company. How can she avoid a charge to CGT arising?

Answers to quick quiz

1 Assets eligible for rollover relief are:

- land and buildings
- fixed plant and machinery
- ships, aircraft and hovercraft
- goodwill
- satellites, space stations and spacecraft
- milk quota, potato quota, ewe and suckler cow premium quota
- fish quota

2 Where a depreciating asset is acquired, the gain is deferred until it crystallises on the earliest of the replacement of the replacement asset, ten years after the acquisition of the replacement asset and the date the replacement asset ceases to be used in the trade.

3 Shares which qualify for gift relief are those in trading companies which

- are not listed on a recognised stock exchange, or
- where the donor is an individual, which are in that individual's personal company, or
- where the donor is a trustee, where the trustee can exercise 25% or more of the voting rights in the company

4 The instalment option is available on transfers of:

- land, or
- controlling holdings of share or securities in a company, or
- minority holdings of shares or securities in an unlisted company

provided the transfer concerned is not eligible for gift relief.

5 The conditions for incorporation relief are:

- the business is transferred as a going concern,
- all of its assets (or all assets other than cash) are transferred,
- the consideration is wholly or partly in shares

6 EIS reinvestment relief is available where an individual makes a gain (on any type of asset) and invests in EIS shares.

7 A gain will come back into charge under EIS reinvestment relief where:

- investor disposes of the shares (except inter-spouse/civil partner)
- investor's civil partner/spouse disposes of shares (if acquired from investor)
- investor (or investor's spouse/civil partner who acquires shares from investor) becomes non-resident within 3 years of issue of shares, unless employed full-time abroad for up to 3 years
- shares cease to be eligible shares (does not generally include becoming quoted)

8 No part disposal on receipt of compensation if:

- any amount not spent in restoring the asset is small, or
- the capital sum received is small

9 Emma can avoid a charge to CGT on receipt of the compensation by investing at least £2,000 in a replacement asset within 12 months.

Now try the question below from the Exam Question Bank

Number	Level	Marks	Time
Q11	Examination	25	45 mins

13 Chargeable gains – additional aspects

Introduction

Some gains are too small, and arise too often, to be worth taxing. These are gains on movable physical property (such as furniture) which is sold for £6,000 or less. These gains are exempt.

Other movable physical assets, such as computers, tend to fall in value over their lives, so that losses are more likely than gains. These assets are generally exempt and losses are not allowable. HMRC are happy to miss out on a few gains in exchange for ruling out a lot of losses.

Leases of land also fall in value over their lives: a lease with ten years left to run is worth less than one with thirty years left to run. Rather than making a lease exempt, HMRC run down its cost so that the cost falls as the value falls. This makes losses unlikely.

Because gains and capital allowances can arise on the same assets, we need rules to cater their interaction. We cover these rules in Section 2.

Gains people make on their homes are exempt. This means there is no capital gains tax charge when people move home. However it also means that there is no relief if their house is sold at a loss.

Topic list	Syllabus references
1 Chattels	1(f)
2 Chargeable gains and capital allowances	1(f)
3 Wasting assets	1(f)
4 Leases	1(f)
5 Private residences	1(f)

1 Chattels

FAST FORWARD

When a chattel is sold for up to £6,000, any gain is exempt and any loss is restricted. Gains on most wasting chattels sold for any amount are exempt, and losses on them are not allowable.

1.1 Gains

Key term

A **chattel** is tangible movable property.

A **wasting asset** is an asset with an estimated remaining useful life of 50 years or less.

Plant and machinery, whose predictable useful life is always deemed to be less than 50 years, is an example of a wasting chattel (unless it is immovable, in which case it will be wasting but not a chattel). Machinery includes, in addition to its ordinary meaning, motor vehicles (unless exempt as cars), railway and traction engines, engine-powered boats and clocks.

Wasting chattels are exempt (so that there are no chargeable gains and no allowable losses). There is one exception to this: assets used for the purpose of a trade, profession or vocation in respect of which capital allowances have been or could have been claimed. This means that items of plant and machinery used in a trade are not exempt merely on the ground that they are wasting. (However, cars are always exempt.)

If a chattel is not exempt under the wasting chattels rule, any gain arising on its disposal will still be exempt if the asset is sold for gross proceeds of £6,000 or less, even if capital allowances were claimed on it.

If sale proceeds exceed £6,000, any gain is limited to a maximum of 5/3 × (gross proceeds – £6,000).

Question

Gains on chattels

Adam purchased a Chippendale chair on 1 June 1984 for £800. On 10 October 2006 he sold the chair at auction for £6,300 (which was net of the auctioneer's 10% commission). What was the chargeable gain? Assume the indexation factor for June 1984 to April 1998 is 0.823.

Answer

	£
Proceeds	7,000
Less incidental costs of sale	(700)
Net proceeds	6,300
Less cost	(800)
Unindexed gain	5,500
Less indexation allowance (June 1984 to April 1998)	
0.823 × £800	(658)
Indexed gain	4,842

The maximum gain is 5/3 × £(7,000 – 6,000) = £1,667

The chargeable gain before taper relief is the lower of £4,842 and £1,667, so it is £1,667.

Gain after taper relief £1,667 × 65% £1,084

Note. Taper relief is available to reduce this gain on a non-business asset with eight years post 5.4.98 ownership (including the additional year).

1.2 Losses

Where a chattel, not exempt under the wasting chattels rule is sold for less than £6,000 and a loss arises, the allowable loss is restricted by assuming that the chattel was sold for £6,000. This rule cannot turn a loss into a gain, only reduce the loss, perhaps to zero.

Question — Computaiton of gain or loss

Eve purchased a rare first edition on 1 July 1998 for £8,000 which she sold in October 2006 at auction for £2,700 (which was net of 10% commission). Compute the gain or loss.

Answer

	£
Proceeds (assumed)	6,000
Less incidental costs of disposal (£2,700 x 10/90)	(300)
	5,700
Less cost	(8,000)
Allowable loss	(2,300)

1.3 Sets

The £6,000 chattel exemption cannot be exploited by selling separately each of a number of items which make up a set, unless the purchasers are unconnected with each other. **If two or more assets which have formed part of a set all owned by the same person** (for example a set of Chippendale chairs) **are disposed of separately to the same person or to persons either acting in concert or connected with one another, then the separate disposals are treated as a single transaction**. Gains will only be wholly exempt if the aggregate proceeds do not exceed £6,000. Otherwise the maximum total gain on all the disposals will be 5/3 × (total proceeds – £6,000).

Where losses arise and total proceeds are less than £6,000, deemed total proceeds of £6,000 are compared with the total of all actual costs and indexation allowances to determine the maximum total loss.

1.4 A part disposal by way of disposal of a right or interest

Where there is a disposal of a right or interest in or over tangible movable property, the chattel exemption is applied only if the sum of the consideration and the value of what remains undisposed of does not exceed £6,000. Where the aggregate value exceeds £6,000, the limit on the gain is

$$5/3 \times (\text{aggregate value} - £6{,}000) \times \frac{\text{consideration}}{\text{aggregate value}}$$

If a loss arises, it is restricted (but cannot be either increased or turned into a gain) by using deemed proceeds of $£6{,}000 \times \dfrac{\text{consideration}}{\text{aggregate value}}$

2 Chargeable gains and capital allowances

FAST FORWARD

The CGT rules are modified for assets eligible for capital allowances.

The wasting chattels exemption does not apply to chattels on which capital allowances have been claimed or could have been claimed. The chattels rules based on £6,000 do apply.

Where capital allowances have been obtained on any asset, and a loss would arise before indexation allowance, the allowable cost for chargeable gains purposes must be reduced by the lower of the unindexed loss and the net amount of allowances (taking into account any balancing allowances or charges, but not any notional allowances during periods of non-industrial use of buildings). For plant and machinery, and for industrial buildings which have always been in industrial use, the result is no gain and no loss.

Question — CGT and capital allowances

David buys a machine for £100,000 in June 2000 and sells it for £70,000 in June 2006. Show the capital gains consequences.

Answer

The capital allowances after any balancing adjustment, are £(100,000 – 70,000) = £30,000.

	£
Proceeds	70,000
Less reduced cost £(100,000 – 30,000)	(70,000)
No gain and no loss	0

If there is a gain before indexation allowance, the cost is not adjusted for capital allowances. As usual, the indexation allowance may only reduce the gain to zero.

3 Wasting assets

FAST FORWARD

Other wasting assets generally have their cost written down over time.

3.1 Introduction

As we have seen, a wasting asset is one which has an estimated remaining useful life of 50 years or less and whose original value will depreciate over time. **Freehold land is never a wasting asset**, and there are special rules for leases of land, given below.

Wasting chattels are exempt except for those on which capital allowances have been (or could have been) **claimed**. This is dealt with later in this text.

3.2 Options

An option (for example an option to buy shares) **is a wasting asset**, because after a certain time it can no longer be exercised.

We must distinguish between traded options (or 'quoted' options) with dealings on an exchange and other options.

3.3 Traded options

If a traded option is exercised, the grantor's position varies, depending on whether it is a put option (the grantee's right to sell the underlying asset) **or a call option** (the grantee's right to buy the underlying asset). In the case of a call option, the grantor must add the consideration received for the sale of the option to the sale proceeds of the assets covered by the option. In the case of a put option, the grantor must deduct the consideration received from the acquisition cost of the assets covered. The grantee's position is the same in either case: he increases his allowable cost by the cost of the option. The cost of the option is not written down over time, either here or on abandonment or sale of an option.

When a traded option is abandoned, the abandonment is regarded as a disposal for CGT purposes and so an allowable loss will arise.

When a traded option is sold, there is a normal CGT computation. Where it is designed to be settled and is in fact settled by a cash payment by the grantor to the grantee, the grantor has a chargeable gain (or allowable loss) of the amount received for the option – the amount paid to the grantee; the grantee has a normal CGT computation based on proceeds of the receipt from the grantor, a cost of the option's cost and indexation from grant to settlement (or April 1998 if earlier, for an individual).

When a person sells (grants) a traded option and then effectively cancels his obligations under it by buying an identical option, the cost of the purchase is treated as an incidental expense of the original sale.

3.4 Other options

Other options can also be exercised or abandoned. If a non-traded option is exercised, the position is the same as with traded options, but the cost is progressively written down over the life of the option (as described below). If a non-traded option is abandoned, no deemed disposal arises and so there is no allowable loss.

Options on both gilts and qualifying corporate bonds are exempt assets for individuals and trusts.

3.5 Other wasting assets

The cost is written down on a straight line basis before calculating the indexation allowance. Thus, if a taxpayer acquires such an asset with a remaining life of 40 years and disposes of it after 15 years (with 25 years remaining) only 25/40 of the cost is deducted from the disposal consideration. Indexation allowance is computed on the written down cost rather than the full original cost.

Examples of such assets are copyrights (with 50 years or less to run) and registered designs.

Where the asset has an estimated residual value at the end of its predictable life, it is the cost less residual value which is written off on a straight line basis over the asset's life. Where additional expenditure is incurred on a wasting asset the additional cost is written off over the life remaining when it was incurred.

Assets eligible for capital allowances and used throughout the period of ownership in a trade, profession or vocation do not have their allowable expenditure written down.

4 Leases

FAST FORWARD

An ordinary disposal computation is made on the disposal of a lease with 50 years or more to run. For leases of land with less than 50 years to run, a special table of percentages is used.

4.1 Types of disposal

The gain that arises on the disposal of a lease will be chargeable according to the terms of the lease disposed of. We must consider:

(a) The assignment of a lease or sub-lease with 50 years or more to run.
(b) The assignment of a lease or sub-lease with less than 50 years to run.

There is an assignment when a lessee sells the whole of his interest. There is a grant when a new lease or sub-lease is created out of a freehold or existing leasehold, the grantor retaining an interest. The rules on the grant of leases will not be examined.

The duration of the lease will normally be determined by the contract terms. The expiry date, however, will be taken as the first date on which the landlord has an option to terminate the lease or the date beyond which the lease is unlikely to continue because of, for example, the likelihood that the rent will be substantially increased at that date.

4.2 The assignment of a lease with 50 years or more to run

An **ordinary disposal computation** is made and the whole of any gain on disposal will be chargeable to CGT (subject to any private residence exemption, see below).

4.3 The assignment of a lease with less than 50 years less to run

In calculating the gain on the disposal of a lease with less than 50 years to run only a certain proportion of the original expenditure counts as an allowable deduction. This is because a lease is losing value anyway as its life runs out: only the cost related to the tail end of the lease being sold is deductible. The proportion is determined by a table of percentages, which is reproduced in the Rates and Allowances Tables in this text.

The allowable cost is given by original cost × X/Y, where X is the percentage for the number of years left for the lease to run at the date of the assignment, and Y is the percentage for the number of years the lease had to run when first acquired by the seller.

The table only provides percentages for exact numbers of years. Where the duration is not an exact number of years the relevant percentage should be found by adding 1/12 of the difference between the two years on either side of the actual duration for each extra month. Fourteen or more odd days count as a month.

Question — The assignment of a short lease

Mr A acquired a 20 year lease on a block of flats which he rents out on 1 August 2000 for £15,000. He assigned it on 2 August 2006 for £19,000. Compute the chargeable gain arising.

Answer

	£
Proceeds	19,000
Less cost £15,000 × $\frac{58.971}{72.770}$	(12,156)
Gain	6,844

58.971 = percentage for 14 years (life from 1.8.06)
72.770 = percentage for 20 years (life from 1.8.00)

Gain after taper relief (6 years) 80% × £6,844	£5,475

5 Private residences

5.1 General principles

FAST FORWARD

There is an exemption for gains on principal private residences, but the exemption may be restricted because of periods of non-occupation or because of business use.

A gain arising on the sale of an individual's only or main private residence (his principal private residence or PPR) is exempt from CGT. The exemption also covers grounds of up to half a hectare. The grounds can exceed half a hectare if the house is large enough to warrant it, but if not, only the gain on the excess grounds is taxable. If the grounds do not adjoin the house (for example when a road separates the two), they *may* still qualify but they may not: each case must be argued on its merits.

For the exemption to be available the taxpayer must have occupied the property as a residence rather than just as temporary accommodation. In the case of *Goodwin v Curtis 1998* the Court held that a considerable degree of permanence and continuity is required in order to turn a simple occupation into a residence. This meant the taxpayer was not entitled to the exemption in respect of one of three properties which he had consecutively acquired and disposed of between April and December 1985 because he had only occupied the property concerned for a short time during which the property was up for sale.

The gain is wholly exempt where the owner has occupied the whole of the residence throughout his period of ownership. Where occupation has been for only part of the period, the proportion of the gain exempted is

$$\textbf{Total gain} \times \frac{\textbf{Period of occupation}}{\textbf{Total period of ownership}}$$

A further proportionate restriction is made where only part of the property has been occupied as the owner's residence.

The **last 36 months of ownership are always** treated as **a period of occupation**, if at some time the residence has been the taxpayer's main residence, even if within those last 36 months the taxpayer also has another house which is his principal private residence.

Where a loss arises but all or a proportion of any gain would have been exempt, all or the same proportion of the loss is not allowable.

The **period of occupation is also deemed to include certain periods of absence, provided the individual had no other exempt residence at the time and the period of absence was at some time both preceded by and followed by a period of actual occupation.** Deemed but non-actual occupation during the last 36 months of ownership does not count for this purpose.

These periods of **deemed occupation** are:

(a) Any period (or periods taken together) of absence, for any reason, **up to three years,** and

(b) **Any periods** during which the owner was **required by his employment (ie employed taxpayer) to live abroad**, and

(c) Any period (or periods taken together) **up to four years** during which the owner was **required to live elsewhere due to his work** (ie both employed and self employed taxpayer) so that he could not occupy his private residence.

It does not matter if the residence is let during the absence.

Exempt periods of absence must normally be preceded and followed by periods of actual occupation. An extra-statutory concession relaxes this where an individual who has been required to work abroad or elsewhere (ie the latter two categories mentioned above) is unable to resume residence in his home because the terms of his employment require him to work elsewhere.

Where a taxpayer buys land and builds a house on it, or buys a house but delays moving in because he has work done on it or he is still disposing of his old house, the period from purchase to actual moving in counts as a period of residence if it is immediately followed by actual residence, and does not exceed one year. The one year period may be increased by up to a further year if there are good reasons.

Question

Principal private residences

Mr A purchased a house on 31 March 1983 for £50,000. He lived in the house until 30 June 1983. He then worked abroad for two years before returning to the UK to live in the house again on 1 July 1985. He stayed in the house until 31 December 1999 before retiring and moving out to live with friends in Spain until the house was sold on 28 December 2006 for £150,000.

Calculate any chargeable gain arising. Assume an indexation factor March 1983 to April 1998 = 0.956

Answer

(a) *Exempt and chargeable periods*

Period		*Exempt months*	*Chargeable months*
(ii)	April 1983 – June 1983 (occupied)	3	0
(iii)	July 1983 – June 1985 (working abroad)	24	0
(iv)	July 1985 – December 1999 (occupied)	174	0
(v)	January 2000 – December 2003 (see below)	0	48
(vi)	January 2004 – December 2006 (last 36 months)	36	0
		237	48

No part of the period from January 2000 to December 2003 can be covered by the exemption for three years of absence for any reason because it is not followed at any time by actual occupation.

(b) *The chargeable gain*

	£
Proceeds	150,000
Less cost	(50,000)
Unindexed gain	100,000
Less indexation allowance (March 1983 to April 1998)	
0.956 × £50,000	(47,800)
Indexed gain	52,200
Less exempt under PPR provisions	
$\frac{237}{285} \times £52,200$	(43,408)
Chargeable gain	8,792
Gain after taper relief (9 years including additional year) 65% × £8,792	£5,715

Exam focus point

To help you to answer questions such as that above it is useful to draw up a table showing period of ownership, exempt months (real/deemed occupation) and chargeable months (non-occupation). The number of months in the first column should equal the sum of months in columns two and three.

Case law has introduced a restriction of the exemption. In *Varty v Lynes 1976*, the dwelling house and part of the garden were sold, leaving the rest of the garden to be sold separately (for development purposes) at a later date. When this later sale took place, the PPR exemption was not available since the garden was no longer part of the individual's PPR, the house having been sold some time previously.

In *Batey v Wakefield 1981*, the taxpayer had built a bungalow for the use of a caretaker who occupied it rent-free. Since the bungalow was within the grounds of the main dwelling house it formed part of the taxpayer's principal private residence. However, a gardener's cottage 175m from the main house was held not to be part of the same residence in *Lewis v Rook 1992*. Several flats close together in different buildings in a single London square and used by members of one family for various domestic purposes, have been held not to constitute a single private residence: *Honour v Norris 1992*. In *Green v CIR 1982* it was held that the unoccupied wings of a mansion house partly occupied by the taxpayer were not necessarily a part of his main residence. A caravan connected to mains water and electricity has been held to be a qualifying dwelling for the purposes of principal private residence relief: *Makins v Elson 1977*.

5.2 Relocations

When an employee is required to move by his employer, and sells his house to the employer or to a relocation company for a guaranteed value plus a share in any profit made by the employer or relocation company when it sells the house, the profit share is exempt to the same extent as the initial gain on selling the house. Thus if only 60% of that gain was exempt, 60% of the profit share will also be exempt. This is an extra-statutory concession.

5.3 More than one residence

5.3.1 The election for a residence to be treated as the main residence

Where a person has more than one residence (owned or rented), he may elect for one to be regarded as his main residence by notice to the Inspector of Taxes within two years of commencing occupation of the second residence. An election can have effect for any period beginning not more than two years prior to the date of election until it is varied by giving further notice. (The further notice may itself be backdated by up to two years.)

In order for the election to be made, the individual must actually reside in both residences.

Any period of ownership of a residence not nominated as the main residence will be a chargeable period for that residence.

Where there are two residences and the second one is being treated as a residence under the 'delay in moving in' rule (see above), the election is not needed and both may count as principal private residences simultaneously.

5.3.2 Job-related accommodation

The rule limiting people to only one main residence is relaxed for individuals living in job-related accommodation.

Such individuals will be treated as occupying any second dwelling house which they own if they intend in due course to occupy the dwelling house as their only or main residence. Thus it is not necessary to establish any actual residence in such cases. This rule extends to self-employed persons required to live in job-related accommodation (for example tenants of public houses).

Key term

A person lives in **job-related accommodation** where:

(a) It is necessary for the **proper performance of his duties**, or

(b) It is provided for the **better performance of his duties** and his is one of the kinds of employment in which it is **customary** for employers to provide accommodation, or

(c) There is a **special threat to the employee's security** and use of the accommodation is part of security arrangements.

5.4 Husbands and wives

Where a husband and wife live together only one residence may qualify as the main residence for relief. If each owned one property before marriage, a new two year period for electing for which is to be treated as the main residence starts on marriage.

Where a marriage has broken down and one spouse owning or having an interest in the matrimonial home has ceased to occupy the house, by concession the departing spouse will continue to be treated as resident for capital gains tax purposes provided that the other spouse has continued to reside in the home and the departing spouse has not elected that some other house should be treated as his or her main residence for this period. This only applies where one spouse disposes of his interest to the other spouse.

Where a house passes from one spouse to the other (for example on death), the new owner also inherits the old owner's periods of ownership and occupation for PPR relief purposes.

Same sex couples registered under the CPA 2004 are treated the same way as married couples. In particular they may only have one main residence, and if they each owned a property prior to registration a new two year period for electing which property should be treated as the main residence starts from the date of registration.

5.5 Lettings

FAST FORWARD

There is also a relief for letting out a principal private residence if the gain arising during the letting would not be covered by the main relief.

The principal private residence exemption is extended to any gain accruing while the property is let, up to a certain limit. The two main circumstances in which the letting exemption applies are:

(a) When the owner is absent and lets the property, where the absence is not a deemed period of occupation.

(b) When the owner lets part of the property while still occupying the rest of it. The absence from the let part cannot be a deemed period of occupation, because the owner has another residence (the rest of the property). However, the let part will qualify for the last 36 months exemption *if* the let part has *at some time* been part of the only or main residence.

In both cases the letting must be for residential use. **The extra exemption is restricted to the lowest of:**

(a) The gain accruing during the letting period (the **letting part of the gain**)

(b) **£40,000**

(c) The amount of the total **gain** which is already **exempt under the PPR provisions** (including the last 36 months exemption)

The letting exemption cannot convert a gain into an allowable loss.

If a lodger lives as a member of the owner's family, sharing their living accommodation and eating with them, the whole property is regarded as the owner's main residence.

Question — The letting exemption

Miss Coe purchased a house on 31 March 1993 for £90,000. She sold it on 31 August 2006 for £340,000. In 1995 the house was redecorated and Miss Coe began to live on the top floor renting out the balance of the house (constituting 60% of the total house) to tenants between 1 January 1996 and 31 December 2005. On 2 January 2006 Miss Coe put the whole house on the market but continued to live only on the top floor until the house was sold. What was the chargeable gain? Assume an indexation factor March 1993 to April 1998 = 0.167.

Answer

		£	£
Proceeds			340,000
Less: cost			(90,000)
Unindexed gain			250,000
Less indexation allowance (March 1993 to April 1998)			
0.167 × £90,000			(15,030)
Indexed gain			234,970
Less PPR exemption			
$£234,970 \times \frac{33(1.4.93-31.12.95)+36(1.9.03-31.8.06)}{161(1.4.93-31.8.06)}$		100,701	
$£234,970 \times \frac{92(1.1.96-31.8.03)}{161(1.4.93-31.8.06)} \times 40\%$		53,707	
			(154,408)
	c/f		80,562
	c/f		80,562
Less letting exemption			
Lowest of:			
(a) gain attributable to letting $£234,970 \times \frac{92}{161} \times 60\% = £80,561$			
(b) £40,000			(40,000)
(c) gain exempt under PPR rules			
Gain left in charge			40,562
Gain after taper relief (9 years including additional year)			
65% × £40,562			£26,365

Working

Period	*Ownership months*	*Notes*
1.4.93 – 31.12.95	33	100% of house occupied
1.1.96 – 31.8.03	92	40% of house occupied 60% of house let
1.9.03 – 31.8.06	36	Last 36 months treated as 100% of house occupied
	161	

Note. The gain on the 40% of the house always occupied by Miss Coe is fully covered by PPR relief. The other 60% of the house has not always been occupied by Miss Coe and thus any gain on this part of the house is taxable where it relates to periods of time when Miss Coe was not actually (or deemed to be) living in it.

As a further point if Miss Coe had reoccupied the lower floors (60% part) of the house prior to the sale then 3 years worth of the non-occupation period between 1.1.96 and 31.8.03 could have been treated as deemed occupation under the special 3 years absence for any reason rule.

5.6 Business use

Where part of a residence is used exclusively for business purposes throughout the period of ownership, the gain attributable to use of that part is taxable. The 'last 36 months always exempt' rule does not apply to that part.

Question

Calculation of gain on property

Mr Smail purchased a property for £35,000 on 31 May 2001 and began operating a dental practice from that date in one quarter of the house. On 31 December 2004 he purchased a second house and submitted an election to treat this second house as his main residence from the date of purchase. He closed the dental practice on 31 December 2006, selling the old house on that date for £130,000.

Compute the chargeable gain, if any, arising before taper relief.

Answer

	£
Proceeds	130,000
Less: cost	(35,000)
Gain	95,000
Less PPR exemption 0.75 × £95,000	(71,250)
Chargeable gain before taper relief	23,750

Exemption is lost on one quarter throughout the period of ownership (including the last 36 months) because of the use of that fraction for business purposes. The last 36 months are exempt (for the non-business part), despite the acquisition of a second house which is treated as the PPR.

If part of a house was used for business purposes for part of the period of ownership, the gain is apportioned between chargeable and exempt parts in a just and reasonable manner. If the business part was *at some time* used as part of the only or main residence, the gain apportioned to that part *will* qualify for the last 36 months exemption.

5.7 Tax planning points

Where a second residence is acquired, careful consideration should be given as to which residence is to be treated as the main residence. One should generally choose the residence on which the greatest gain is likely to arise.

When considering what proportion of relief can be claimed for household expenses where part of the residence is used for business, a taxpayer should take care not to jeopardise any PPR exemption.

There are no exemptions on properties acquired wholly or partly to make a gain. HMRC normally only apply this rule when a residence appears to have been bought with the primary purpose of an early disposal. More commonly, gains attributed to the extra expenditure incurred wholly or partly to make a gain are denied the exemption. An example is the conversion of a house into flats.

Chapter roundup

- When a chattel is sold for up to £6,000, any gain is exempt and any loss is restricted. Gains on most wasting chattels sold for any amount are exempt, and losses on them are not allowable.
- The CGT rules are modified for assets eligible for capital allowances.
- Other wasting assets generally have their cost written down over time. For leases of land with less than 50 years to run, a special table of percentages is used.
- An ordinary disposal computation is made on the disposal of a lease with 50 years or more to run.
- There is an exemption for gains on principal private residences, but the exemption may be restricted because of periods of non-occupation or because of business use.
- There is also a relief for letting out a principal private residence if the gain arising during the letting would not be covered by the main relief.

Quick quiz

1. How are gains on non-wasting chattels sold for more than £6,000 restricted?
2. How are losses on non-wasting chattels sold for less than £6,000 restricted?
3. What is the general treatment of intangible wasting assets (eg a copyright)?
4. Distinguish between the grant and the assignment of a lease.
5. When a lease with less than 50 years to run is assigned, what proportion of the cost is allowable?
6. For what periods may an individual be deemed to occupy his principal private residence?
7. What is the maximum letting exemption?

Answers to quick quiz

1. Gain restricted to 5/3 × (gross proceeds – £6,000)
2. Allowable loss restricted by deeming proceeds to be £6,000
3. The cost is written down on a straight line basis
4. Grant of lease – creating of new lease or sub-lease
   Assignment of lease – disposal of existing lease
5. Allowable cost is original cost × X/Y where X is the % for the years left of the lease to run at assignment and Y is the % for the years the lease had to run when first acquired by the seller.
6. Periods of deemed occupation are:
   - last 36 months of ownership, and
   - any period of absence up to three years, and
   - any period during which the owner was required by his employment to work abroad, and
   - any period up to four years during which the owner was required to live elsewhere due to his work (employed or self-employed) so that he could not occupy his private residence.
7. £40,000

Now try the questions below from the Exam Question Bank

Number	Level	Marks	Time
Q12	Examination	25	45 mins
Q13	Introductory	20	36 mins

BPP PROFESSIONAL EDUCATION

14

Overseas aspects of personal taxation

Introduction

In this chapter, we look at the overseas aspects of income taxation and CGT.

We start this chapter by looking at where taxpayers live and at how that affects their tax positions. We then consider the special rules which apply to people working away from their home countries. We then look at the rules for foreign investment income of people in the UK. Finally, we look at the help which can be given when income is taxed both abroad and in the UK, and at the CGT rules when either the asset or the owner is abroad.

Topic list	Syllabus references
1 Residence, ordinary residence and domicile	1(j)
2 Employment abroad and non-residents employed in the UK	1(j)
3 Overseas trades	1(j)
4 Overseas investment income	1(j)
5 Double taxation relief (DTR)	1(j)
6 Overseas aspects of CGT	1(j)

1 Residence, ordinary residence and domicile

FAST FORWARD

An individual may be any or all of resident, ordinarily resident and domiciled in the UK, and his liability to UK tax will be determined accordingly. Overseas source income is charged on a remittance basis for persons non-domiciled in the UK and British subjects not ordinarily resident in the UK.

1.1 Introduction

A taxpayer's **residence**, **ordinary residence** and **domicile** have important consequences in establishing the treatment of his UK and overseas income.

1.2 Residence and ordinary residence

1.2.1 General principles

An individual is resident in the UK for a given tax year if, in that tax year, he satisfies either of the following criteria.

(a) **He is present in the UK for 183 days or more** (days of arrival and departure are excluded).

(b) **He makes substantial annual visits to the UK**. Visits averaging 91 days or more a year for each of four or more consecutive years will make the person resident for each of these tax years (for someone emigrating from the UK, the four years are reduced to three).

If days are spent in the UK because of exceptional circumstances beyond the individual's control (such as illness), those days are ignored for the purposes of the 91 day rule (but not for the 183 day rule above).

A person who is resident in the UK will be ordinarily resident where his residence is of a habitual nature. Ordinary residence implies a greater degree of permanence than residence. A person deemed by HMRC to be ordinarily resident may appeal to the Special Commissioners within three months of the inspector's decision. The significance of ordinary residence is principally in connection with the basis of assessment for overseas income (see below), and exemption for interest on some government securities and bank deposit interest. A person who is ordinarily resident in the UK and who goes abroad for a period which does not include a complete tax year, is regarded as remaining resident and ordinarily resident throughout.

Strictly, each tax year must be looked at as a whole. A person is resident and/or ordinarily resident either for no part of, or for all of, the tax year. It is the practice for income tax purposes by concession, however, to split the tax year if the person:

(a) Is a new permanent resident or comes to stay in the UK for at least two years, provided he has not been ordinarily resident

(b) Has left the UK for permanent residence abroad provided that he becomes not ordinarily resident in the UK, or

(c) Is going abroad to take up employment for at least a whole tax year (see below).

A spouse's residence and ordinary residence is not governed by the other spouse's status but is determined independently. If for example, one spouse is employed abroad full-time, and the other one also goes abroad but later returns to the UK without having been away for a complete tax year, then the latter spouse is regarded as remaining resident and ordinarily resident in the UK although the former spouse may be not resident and not ordinarily resident. 'Spouse' includes civil partners under CPA 2004.

1.2.2 Coming to the UK

A person whose home has previously been abroad and who comes to the UK to take up permanent residence, or with the intention of staying for at least three years, is regarded as resident and ordinarily resident from the date of his arrival.

A person who comes to the UK to work for a period of at least two years is treated as resident for the whole period from arrival to departure.

A person who comes to the UK and does not intend to stay for at least three years is treated as ordinarily resident in the UK from 6 April following the third anniversary of his arrival in the UK. However, once an intention to stay for at least three years is shown (for example by acquiring accommodation on a lease of three years or more), he is treated as ordinarily resident from the start of the tax year in which the intention is shown.

Someone who comes to the UK only for temporary purposes (such as a brief spell of employment) is not UK resident for a tax year unless he spends 183 days or more in the UK in that year. Someone who expects to spend fewer than 91 days a year in the UK for a limited period (for example a five year term of duty) will be treated as in the UK for temporary purposes.

1.2.3 Leaving the UK

A person who has been resident or ordinarily resident here is treated as remaining resident if he goes abroad only for occasional residence (periods of less than one complete tax year).

If a person claims that he has ceased to be resident and ordinarily resident in the UK and can produce some evidence for this, such as selling his UK home and setting up a permanent home abroad, then his claim is normally provisionally admitted from the day of his departure. If no such evidence can be produced the decision will be postponed for three years and then retrospective adjustments will be made.

If a person goes abroad for full-time service under a contract of employment such that:

(a) **his absence from the UK is for a period which includes a complete tax year, and**

(b) **interim visits to the UK do not amount to six months or more in any one tax year or three months or more per tax year on average,**

he is normally regarded as not resident and not ordinarily resident for the whole period of the contract.

If the employee's spouse accompanies him, and the spouse also satisfies conditions (a) and (b), the spouse is also regarded as not resident and not ordinarily resident for the whole period of the contract. 'Spouse' includes a civil partner under CPA 2004.

1.3 Domicile

A person is domiciled in the country in which he has his permanent home. Domicile is distinct from nationality or residence. A person may be resident in more than one country, but he can be domiciled in only one country at a time. **A person acquires a domicile of origin at birth**; this is normally the domicile of his father (or that of his mother if his father died before he was born or his parents were unmarried at his birth) and therefore not necessarily the country where he was born. **A person retains this domicile until he acquires a different domicile of dependency (if, while he is under 16, his father's domicile changes) or domicile of choice. A domicile of choice can be acquired only by individuals aged 16 or over.**

To acquire a domicile of choice a person must sever his ties with the country of his former domicile and settle in another country with the clear intention of making his permanent home there. Long residence in another country is not in itself enough to prove that a person has acquired a domicile of choice: there has to be evidence that he firmly intends to live there permanently.

1.4 Applications of the rules

1.4.1 General principle

Generally, a UK resident is liable to UK income tax on his UK and overseas income whereas a non-resident is liable to UK income tax only on income arising in the UK.

1.4.2 Allowances

In general, non-residents are not entitled to allowances. However, the following people are entitled to allowances despite being non-resident:

- Citizens of European Economic Area and Commonwealth countries
- Individuals resident in the Isle of Man and the Channel Islands
- Current or former Crown servants and their widows or widowers
- Former residents who have left the country for health reasons
- Missionaries

These rules for non-residents apply both to allowances deducted from STI (the PA and the BPA) and to allowances which reduce tax (the MCAA).

There is a special limit on the income tax borne by someone who is, for a complete tax year, not resident in the UK. (The limit does not apply to a year which is split under the concessionary rule described above.) The tax cannot exceed the sum of:

(a) The tax which would be borne if they were taxed on all their income apart from their excluded income, and they had no allowances.

(b) The tax deducted at source from excluded income (including tax credits on dividends).

Excluded income is income which is not from the trade, profession or vocation of a UK branch or agency, nor derived from property or rights used or held by a UK branch or agency, and which falls within one of the following categories.

- UK interest, deeply discounted securities, purchased life annuities
- UK dividends
- Profits on dealing in deposits
- Taxable social security benefits
- Pensions from retirement annuity contracts
- Other investment income arising from transactions carried out through a broker or investment manager

1.4.3 The remittance basis

A UK resident who is not domiciled in the UK is liable to UK tax on overseas income on a remittance basis only, that is only income brought to the UK is taxable. There are special rules for earnings deal with later in this chapter.

The remittance basis for overseas income also applies to British subjects resident but not ordinarily resident in the UK.

1.4.4 Savings income and charges received

Interest payable on all gilt-edged securities (UK government securities) is exempt from UK income tax if the recipient is not ordinarily resident in the UK.

Income tax must be deducted at source from the following payments to non-UK residents.

- Proceeds of the sale of UK patent rights: tax at 22%
- Copyright royalties and public lending right payments: tax at 22%
- Interest: tax at 20%

However, banks and building societies pay interest gross to persons who have certified that they are not ordinarily resident in the UK.

2 Employment abroad and non-residents employed in the UK

FAST FORWARD

Individuals working abroad may claim certain deductions for travel expenses.

2.1 Chargeability of employment income

2.1.1 Introduction

The residence, ordinary residence and domicile status of an employee (and, in some cases, whether he carries out his duties in the UK or outside it) determine the tax treatment of his earnings.

2.1.2 Individual resident and ordinarily resident and domiciled in the UK

A resident, ordinarily resident and domiciled individual is taxed on his general earnings on a receipts basis (see Chapter 3) whether the duties of the employment are carried out in the UK or outside it.

2.1.3 Individual resident and ordinarily resident, but not domiciled in the UK

A **resident and ordinarily resident, but not domiciled individual**, is usually taxed on all general earnings on the receipts basis, wherever the duties of his employment are carried out. However, only any **'overseas earnings' remitted to the UK are chargeable in the UK**. Overseas earnings arise where the employer is a foreign employer and the duties of the employment are performed ***wholly*** **outside the UK**.

2.1.4 Individual resident, but not ordinarily resident in the UK

A resident, but not ordinarily resident, individual is subject to tax on his earnings in two ways. First, he is taxable on his general earnings in respect of duties performed in the UK on the normal receipts basis. Second, he is taxable on his 'foreign earnings' (those relating to non-UK duties) remitted to the UK. In this circumstance, the residence status of the employer is not relevant.

2.1.5 Individual not resident in the UK

A non resident is taxed on his general earnings in respect of UK duties on the receipts basis but there is no UK income tax on foreign earnings (those in respect of non-UK duties).

If the person is absent for a complete tax year as described in Section 1 above then he becomes non-resident for the period of the contract of employment. There will be no UK tax on the foreign earnings.

2.2 Travel and subsistence expenses for employment abroad

2.2.1 Travel expenses incurred by the employee

Travel expenses relating to employment duties abroad (whether or not reimbursed by the employer) may be deducted from earnings in certain circumstances.

(a) **A deduction is allowed for starting and finishing travel expenses.** Starting travel expenses are those incurred by the employee in travelling from the UK to take up employment abroad and finishing travel expenses are those incurred by the employee in travelling to the UK on the termination of the employment. **Three conditions need to be met:**

- **The duties of the employment are performed wholly outside the UK (incidental UK duties are ignored)**
- **The employee is resident and ordinarily resident in the UK**
- **If the employer is a foreign employer, the employee is domiciled in the UK**

If the travel is only partly attributable to the taking up or termination of the employment, the deduction applies only to the part of the expenses properly so attributable.

(b) **There is also a deduction from earnings from an employment for travel expenses where an employee has two or more employments and the duties of at least one of them are performed abroad**. The following conditions must be met:

- **The travel is for the purpose of performing duties of the employment at the destination**
- **The employee has performed duties of another employment at the place of departure**
- **The place of departure or the destination or both are outside the UK**
- **The duties of one or both of the employments are performed wholly or partly outside the UK**
- **The employee is resident and ordinarily resident in the UK**
- **If the employer is a foreign employer, the employee is domiciled in the UK**

2.2.2 Travel expenses borne by employer

There are a number of deductions which may be made from a person's earnings where an amount has been included in those earnings **in respect of provision of (or reimbursement of expenses relating to) travel abroad. The allowable deduction is generally equal to the amount included in the earnings. Note that these deductions do not apply where the employee incurs such costs but does not receive reimbursement.**

(a) **The first deduction relates to the provision of travel facilities for a journey made by the employee**. This deduction applies in two circumstances:

- **The employee is absent from the UK wholly and exclusively for the purpose of performing the duties of one or more employments, the duties can only be performed outside the UK and the journey is from a place outside the UK to the UK or a return journey following such a journey**
- **The duties of the employment are performed partly outside the UK, the journey is between the UK and the place the non-UK duties are performed, the non-UK duties can only be performed there and the journey is made wholly and exclusively for the purpose of performing the duties or returning after performing them**

The deduction only applies from earnings which are chargeable because the individual is UK resident and ordinarily resident but not from 'overseas earnings' (foreign employer/non-domiciled employee/ non-UK duties). This is because the overseas earnings are taxed on the remittance basis.

(b) **There is also a deduction for the provision of travel facilities for a journey made by the employee's spouse or child** (aged under 18 at the beginning of the outward journey) **or the reimbursement of expenses incurred by the employee on such a journey**. The following conditions need to be met:

- **The employee is absent from the UK for a continuous period of at least 60 days for the purpose of performing the duties of the employment**
- **The journey is between the UK and the place outside the UK that the duties are performed**
- **The employee's spouse/child is either accompanying the employee at the beginning of the period of absence or visiting the employee during that period or is returning to the UK after accompanying or visiting the employee**

A deduction is not allowed for more than two outward and two return journeys by the same person in a tax year.

Again, the deduction only applies from earnings which are chargeable because the individual is UK resident and ordinarily resident, but not from 'overseas earnings' taxed on the remittance basis.

(c) **There are also rules which apply to non-domiciled employee's travel costs and expenses where duties are performed in the UK. The deduction is only from earnings for duties performed in the UK.**

The first deduction applies to the provision of travel facilities for a journey made by the employee or the reimbursement of expenses incurred by the employee for such a journey. The conditions that must be met are:

- **The journey ends on or during the period of 5 years beginning with a qualifying arrival date** (see below)
- **The journey is made from the country outside the UK where the employee normally lives to the UK in order to perform the duties of the employment or to that country from the UK after performing such duties**

If the journey is only partly for such a purpose, the deduction is equal to so much of the included journey as is properly attributable to that purpose.

A 'qualifying arrival date' is a date on which the person arrives in the UK to perform UK duties where either:

- The person has not been in the UK for any purpose during the two tax years before the tax year in which the date falls, or
- The person was not UK resident in either of the two tax years before the tax year in which the date falls.

2.2.3 Foreign accommodation and subsistence costs and expenses

A deduction from earnings from an employment is allowed if:

- **The duties of the employment are performed wholly outside the UK (incidental UK duties ignored)**
- **The employee is resident and ordinarily resident in the UK**
- **If the employer is a foreign employer, the employee is domiciled in the UK**
- **The earnings include an amount in respect of the provision of accommodation or subsistence outside the UK to enable the employee to perform the duties of the employment or the reimbursement of such expenses incurred by the employee.**

The deduction is equal to the amount included in the earnings.

2.3 Tax planning when employed abroad

2.3.1 General considerations

The following points highlight the pitfalls and planning possibilities to be considered when going to work abroad.

(a) Timing is vital. Leaving just before the end of a tax year may enable the taxpayer to spend a complete year outside the UK so qualifying for non-resident status.

(b) Insurance policies are available to cover the risk of extra tax liabilities should an early return to the UK be necessary.

(c) If the employer bears the cost of board and lodging abroad this will represent a tax-free benefit. The employee may visit home as many times as he likes without the costs being taxed as benefits. Likewise, for absences of 60 days or more, travelling expenses for a spouse and minor children are also tax-free if paid or reimbursed by the employer. Up to two return visits per person per tax year are allowed.

(d) Where the remittance basis applies it may be advisable to keep funds abroad separate so that it can be proved that sums remitted to the UK are capital (not subject to income tax) or income from a specific source.

(e) Having established non-residence in the UK, any UK investments should be reviewed to ensure they are still tax effective. Bank and building society interest, otherwise paid net, may be paid gross where the deposit-taker is given a written declaration that the recipient is not ordinarily resident in the UK.

(f) Consider carefully the tax system in the foreign country concerned and the terms of any double taxation agreement. The UK has such agreements with most countries: they contain rules on where income and gains are to be taxed, and on other matters.

2.3.2 The OECD model agreement

Most double taxation agreements follow fairly closely the Organisation for Economic Co-operation and Development (OECD) Model Double Taxation Agreement. Under that Model, someone who is resident in country R but is employed in country E will normally be taxed on the earnings in country E. He may only be taxed on the earnings in country R if:

- He is in country E for less than 184 days in total in any 12 month period starting or ending in the year,
- The employer is not resident in country E, and
- The earnings are not borne by a permanent establishment or fixed base which the employer has in country E.

If an individual resident in country R is a director of a company resident in country D, his director's fees may be taxed in country D.

2.4 Foreign pensions

For persons taxed on the arising basis (but not those on the remittance basis), only 90% of the amount of a foreign pension is taxed.

3 Overseas trades

FAST FORWARD

Profits of an overseas trade are computed as for UK trades. However, the remittance basis applies for non-UK domiciled individuals.

3.1 General principles

If a UK resident trader has a business which is conducted wholly or mainly overseas, the trade profits are chargeable to income tax. The trade profits are calculated in the same way as are UK trade profits, and the basis periods are determined in the same way also.

If, however, the trader:

- **is not domiciled in the UK or**
- **is a British subject not ordinarily resident in the UK,**

then the trader may claim that the trade profits should be assessed on the remittance basis.

A person who is not UK resident is only taxable in the UK on UK income. The profits of trades carried on abroad by non-residents are therefore not liable to UK income tax. Where a person who carries on a trade wholly or partly abroad becomes or ceases to be UK resident, the profits of the trade carried on abroad will become or cease to be liable to UK income tax respectively. To ensure that only the foreign profits which arise whilst the trader is UK resident are taxed there is a deemed cessation and recommencement of the trade. This rule also applies to a partner who changes residence if the partnership is carrying on a trade wholly or partly abroad.

This deemed cessation and recommencement does not prevent any losses which was being carried forward from before the change from being set off under s 385 ICTA 1988 against profits arising after the change.

Under the OECD Model Agreement, a resident of country R trading in country T is taxable in country T on his profits only if he has a permanent establishment there (see later in this text). A resident of country R carrying on a profession in country P is taxable in country P on his profits only if he has a fixed base regularly available to him in country P.

The general rule for overseas traders doing business with UK customers is that they are trading in the UK (and therefore liable to UK tax on their profits) if contracts are concluded in the UK.

3.2 Travel expenses

A deduction is available against trade profits income for travel expenses incurred by UK domiciled individuals who carry on a trade wholly outside the UK and who travel to and from the UK. So long as the taxpayer's absence abroad is wholly and exclusively for the purposes of his trade then any travel expenses to and from the UK together with the cost of board and lodging at the overseas location are deductible. If the taxpayer's absence is for a continuous period of 60 days or more, the cost of up to two visits in any tax year by his spouse and/or children under 18 is also deductible.

No deduction is however given for these travel expenses where the trade profits are taxed on a remittance basis. Instead the trader should arrange and pay for the travel whilst abroad, thus avoiding the need to remit that amount to the UK.

3.3 Overseas losses

A loss sustained in a trade (or profession or vocation) carried on abroad can be relieved in the same manner as UK trade losses: s 380, s 381, s 385 and s 388 all apply.

However, if relief is sought under ss 380 and 381 for a loss in a trade which is wholly carried on abroad, the income which the loss can be set against is restricted to:

- Overseas trade profits
- Overseas pensions
- Overseas earnings

4 Overseas investment income

FAST FORWARD

Income from overseas sources is taxed on a similar basis to UK income.

4.1 Introduction

UK residents are taxable on their overseas investment income. Non-residents are not taxable in the UK on overseas investment income, although they are taxable on their UK investment income.

Foreign income is identified and taxed in broadly the same way as UK income, but the points set out below should be noted.

4.2 Overseas property business

An individual who receives rents and other income from property abroad is treated as carrying on an overseas property business. The income from the overseas property business is liable to income tax in the same way as income from a UK property business, and is calculated in the same way. If an individual has both a UK and an overseas property business, the profits must be however calculated separately.

If a loss arises in an overseas property business, it may be carried forward and set against future income from the overseas property business, as soon as it arises.

The special treatment of furnished holiday lettings does not apply to overseas properties.

4.3 Foreign dividends

Foreign dividends are dividends from non-UK companies. The income is taxable in the year it arises, as it is taxed in the same way as UK dividend income, ie at 10% if it falls within the starting and basic rate bands and at 32.5% if it falls within the higher rate band. Foreign dividends do not, however, have the notional 10% tax credit that UK dividends do.

4.4 Other savings income

Other foreign savings income, such as interest, purchased life annuities etc are taxed in the same way as UK savings income, ie at 10% in the starting rate band, 20% in the basic rate band, and at 40% in the higher rate band.

4.5 Remittance basis

A claim for the remittance basis (under which only income brought to the UK is taxed) to apply may be made by:

- **Persons not domiciled in the UK, and**
- **British subjects not ordinarily resident in the UK.**

Where the remittance basis applies, all income from the relevant source counts as non-savings income, even if it is interest or dividends. It is taxed in the same way as other non-savings income.

5 Double taxation relief (DTR)

FAST FORWARD

Double taxation relief may be available to reduce the burden of taxation. It is generally given by reducing the UK tax charged by the foreign tax suffered.

5.1 Introduction

As we have seen, **UK tax applies to the worldwide income of UK residents and the UK income of non-residents.**

When other countries adopt the same approach it is clear that some income may be taxed twice:

- Firstly in the country where it arises
- Secondly in the country where the taxpayer resides

Double taxation relief (DTR) as a result of international agreements may avoid the problem, or at least diminish its impact.

5.2 Double taxation agreements

Typical provisions of double taxation agreements based on the OECD Model are:

(a) Total exemption from tax is given in the country where income arises in the hands of, for example visiting diplomats and teachers on exchange programmes.

(b) Preferential rates of withholding tax are applied to, for example, payments of rent, interest and dividends. The usual rate is frequently replaced by 15% or less.

(c) DTR is given to taxpayers in their country of residence by way of a credit for tax suffered in the country where income arises. This may be in the form of relief for withholding tax only or, given a holding of specified size in a foreign company, for the underlying tax on the profits out of which dividends are paid.

(d) There are exchange of information clauses so that tax evaders can be chased internationally.

(e) There are rules to determine a person's residence and to prevent dual residence (tie-breaker clauses).

(f) There are clauses which render certain profits taxable in only one rather than both of the contracting states.

(g) There is a non-discrimination clause so that a country does not tax foreigners more heavily than its own nationals.

5.3 Unilateral relief

If no relief is available under a double taxation agreement, UK legislation provides for unilateral relief. However, unilateral relief is not available if relief is specifically excluded under the terms of a double tax agreement.

Foreign income must be included gross of any foreign tax in the UK tax computation. The foreign tax is deducted from the UK tax liability (this is credit relief) but the relief cannot exceed the UK tax on the foreign income so the taxpayer bears the higher of:

- The UK tax
- The foreign tax

The UK tax on the foreign income is the difference between:

(a) The UK tax before DTR on all income including the foreign income
(b) The UK tax on all income except the foreign income

In both (a) and (b), we take account of tax reducers.

Question — Double tax relief

A single person has the following income for 2006/07.

	£
UK salary	30,212
Interest on foreign debenture (net of foreign tax at 5%)	4,750
Foreign rents (net of foreign tax at 60%)	1,500

Assuming that maximum DTR is claimed, show the UK tax liability.

Answer

	Non-savings £	Savings (excl dividends) £	Total £
Salary	30,212		
Foreign interest £4,750 × 100/95		5,000	
Overseas property business £1,500 × 100/40	3,750		
STI	33,962	5,000	38,962
Less personal allowance	(5,035)		
Taxable income	28,927	5,000	33,927

		£
Non-savings income		
£2,150 × 10%		215
£26,777 × 22%		5,891
Savings (excl dividend) income		
£4,373 × 20%		875
£627 × 40%		251
		7,232
Less double taxation relief		
Interest	250	
Rents (see below)	951	
		(1,201)
UK tax liability		6,031

Since the rents are taxed more highly overseas, these should be regarded as the top slice of UK taxable income. Taxable income excluding the rents is £30,177 and the UK tax on this is:

	£
Non-savings income	
£2,150 × 10%	215
£23,027 × 22%	5,066
Savings (excl. dividend) income	
£5,000 × 20%	1,000
	6,281

The UK tax on the rents is £951 (£7,232 – 6,281). Since foreign tax of £2,250 (60% of £3,750) is greater, the DTR is the smaller figure of £951. Foreign interest was taxed abroad at the rate of 5% (£250). Since the UK rate is clearly higher the DTR given is £250.

Where there is no point in claiming credit relief as above, perhaps because loss relief has eliminated any liability to UK tax, the taxpayer may elect for expense relief instead. No credit is given for foreign tax suffered, but only the income after foreign taxes is brought into the tax computation.

If foreign taxes are not relieved in the year in which the income is taxable in the UK, no relief can be obtained in any earlier or later year.

Credit relief, whether under a treaty or unilateral, is ignored when working out the tax which remains to be reduced by tax reducers.

Taxpayers who have claimed relief against their UK tax bill for taxes paid abroad must notify HMRC in writing of any changes to the foreign liabilities if these changes result in the DTR claimed becoming excessive. This rule applies to all taxes not just income tax.

6 Overseas aspects of CGT

FAST FORWARD

CGT applies primarily to persons resident or ordinarily resident in the UK and persons only temporarily abroad.

6.1 General principles

Individuals are liable to CGT on the disposal of assets situated anywhere in the world if for any part of the tax year in which the disposal occurs they are resident or ordinarily resident in the UK. By concession, when a person first becomes resident in the UK, he is normally charged to CGT only on those gains which arise after his arrival provided he has not been resident or ordinarily resident in the UK for four out of the last seven years.

If a person is not domiciled in the UK but is resident or ordinarily resident in the UK, gains on the disposal of assets situated overseas are taxable only to the extent that the proceeds of the sale are remitted to the UK. No account is given for overseas capital losses for this person even if all of the proceeds are remitted.

Some of the rules about where assets are situated are contained in legislation. Some of them are a matter of general law. Most of the rules are obvious, for example, land is situated where it actually is, chattels are situated where they are physically present. There are special rules relating to intangible assets, the most important of which are shares and securities in a company. **All shares and securities of a UK incorporated company are treated as situated in the UK, regardless of where the share certificate is kept.**

If a gain made on the disposal of an overseas asset suffers overseas taxation, relief will be available in the UK against any CGT on the same disposal.

If an asset is bought and/or sold for amounts in a foreign currency, each such amount is first translated into sterling (using the rate at the time of purchase or sale), and the gain or loss is computed using these sterling amounts.

Tax on gains accruing on assets situated outside the UK may be deferred if:

- The taxpayer makes a claim
- The gain could not be remitted to the UK because of the laws of the country where it arose, because of executive action of its government or because it was impossible to obtain foreign currency, and
- This was not because of any lack of reasonable endeavours on the taxpayer's part.

The time limit for this claim, for individuals, is the 31 January which is nearly 6 years after the end of the tax year of disposal. For companies, it is six years after the end of the accounting period of disposal.

However, the gain deferred is taxable if it becomes remittable, as if it were a gain accruing in the year in which it ceases to be non-remittable.

6.2 Non-UK residents

Normally a disposal of assets situated in the UK is not a chargeable event if the vendor is neither resident nor ordinarily resident in the UK at the time of disposal. However, a liability to CGT may arise if the person is carrying on a trade, profession or vocation in the UK through a branch or agency and an asset which has been used for the purpose of the branch or agency is either disposed of or removed from the UK.

A charge will also arise if the UK trade, profession or vocation ceases. In this case, and in the case of removal of assets from the UK, there is a deemed disposal of assets at their market value.

6.3 Temporary non-residence

Temporary non residents may be taxable on gains realised whilst they are abroad if:

(a) They are outside the UK for less than five years between the year of departure and the year of return.

(b) They were UK resident or ordinarily resident for the four out of the seven years immediately preceding the year of departure.

Net gains realised in the year of departure are taxed in that year (this applies whether the absence is temporary or permanent under general principles). Subsequent gains/ losses are chargeable/allowable in the year of return as if they were gains/losses of that year. Taper relief apples to the time of actual disposals, not until the time the gain becomes chargeable.

Gains on assets acquired in the non-resident period are not included in the above charge nor are gains which are already chargeable because they arise on branch or agency assets (see above).

Question — **Temporary non residence**

Sue was resident in the UK until January 2006. She then left the UK and was not resident or ordinarily resident in the UK until she returned in 2010/11. In July 2006 Sue sold a business asset for £150,000 that she had acquired in May 2005 for £87,000. In June 2008 she sold an investment asset for £80,000 that she had bought in May 2004 for £100,000. Sue makes no other disposals. Show the amount of Sue's net chargeable gains in 2010/11. Assume 2006/07 tax rates and allowances continue to apply.

Answer

Sale 2006

	£
Proceeds	150,000
Less: cost	(87,000)
Gain	63,000

This business asset has been held for 1 year. Taper relief is given after the loss arising in June 2008 is relieved because both the gain and the loss are treated as arising in the year of return, 2010/11:

Loss 2008

	£
Proceeds	80,000
Cost	(100,000)
Loss	(20,000)

Net gain chargeable 2010/11

	£
Gain	63,000
Loss	(20,000)
	43,000
Gain after taper relief (50%)	21,500
Less: annual exemption	(8,800)
	12,700

6.4 The OECD model agreement

Where a double tax agreement follows the OECD model, a person resident in country R disposing of an asset in country A may be taxed in country A on any gain only if the asset is:

- Immovable property in country A, or
- A permanent establishment (see later in this text) used for a business carried on in country A, a fixed base used for carrying on a profession in country A or movable property pertaining to such an establishment or base.

Otherwise, a gain may be taxed only in country R.

Chapter roundup

- An individual may be any or all of resident, ordinarily resident and domiciled in the UK, and his liability to UK tax will be determined accordingly.
- Individuals working abroad may claim certain deductions for travel expenses.
- Income from overseas sources is taxed on a similar basis to UK income.
- Overseas source income is charged on a remittance basis for persons non-domiciled in the UK and British subjects not ordinarily resident in the UK.
- Double taxation relief may be available to reduce the burden of taxation. It is generally given by reducing the UK tax charged by the foreign tax suffered.
- CGT applies primarily to persons resident or ordinarily resident in the UK and persons only temporarily abroad.

Quick quiz

1 When will an individual be resident in the UK?

2 On what basis is a UK resident who is not domiciled in the UK taxed on overseas income?

3 What earnings are taxed on a remittance basis?

4 How many return journeys by John's family can an employer pay for tax free for John if he is working overseas for 100 days?

5 How will a foreign dividend be taxed on a higher rate taxpayer if he is:

(a) domiciled in the UK
(b) not domiciled in the UK?

6 What is the maximum amount of credit relief that can be given for overseas tax on overseas income?

Answers to quick quiz

1 An individual is resident in the UK if he is here for 183 days or more, or he makes visits to the UK averaging 91 days or more a year for each of four consecutive years.

2 On the remittance basis

3 (a) Individual resident and ordinarily resident in UK, but not UK domiciled, working for a foreign employer, duties performed wholly outside UK ('overseas earnings')

(b) Individual resident but not ordinarily resident in UK relating to duties performed outside UK ('foreign earnings')

4 Two

5 (a) On an arising basis as dividend income liable to tax at 32.5%.
(b) On a remittance basis as non-savings income liable to tax at 40%.

6 The lower of:

(i) UK tax on the overseas income, and
(ii) The overseas tax on the overseas income

Now try the question below from the Exam Question Bank

Number	Level	Marks	Time
Q14	Introductory	10	18 mins

15

Self assessment for individuals, trustees and partnerships

Introduction

In this chapter we look at the overall system for the administration of tax. We then see how individuals, trustees and partnerships must 'self assess' their liability to income tax and capital gains tax. We deal with self assessment for companies later in this text.

1 The administration of taxation

FAST FORWARD

Direct taxes are administered by Her Majesty's Revenue and Customs.

The **Treasury** formally imposes and collects taxation. The management of the Treasury is the responsibility of the Chancellor of the Exchequer. **The administrative function for the collection of tax is undertaken by Her Majesty's Revenue and Customs (HMRC).** Previously there were two separate bodies called the Inland Revenue (responsible for direct taxes such as income tax and corporation tax) and HM Customs and Excise (responsible for indirect taxes such as VAT). Rules on these administrative matters are contained in the **Taxes Management Act 1970 (TMA 1970)**.

HMRC consists of the commissioners for Her Majesty's Revenue and Customs and staff known **as Officers of Revenue and Customs.**

The UK has historically been divided into **tax districts**. These are being merged into larger **areas**, with the separate offices in each area being responsible for different aspects of HMRC's work. For example, one office may be designated to deal with taxpayer's queries, another to deal with the PAYE procedures for joiners and leavers, whilst end of year PAYE returns may be dealt with by a third office. Some offices also act as **enquiry offices**, where taxpayers can visit the office and see a member of HMRC staff in person without an appointment.

Each area is headed by an area director. The HMRC staff were historically described as **'Inspectors'** and '**Collectors'**. The legislation now refers to an **'Officer of the Revenue and Customs'** when setting out HMRC's powers. They are responsible for supervising the self-assessment system and agreeing tax liabilities. Collectors may be referred to as **receivable management officers**, and are local officers who are responsible for following up amounts of unpaid tax referred to them by the **HMRC Accounts Office.**

The structure of offices is also being changed. **Taxpayer service offices** are being set up to do routine checking, computation *and* collection work, while **Taxpayer district offices** investigate selected accounts, deal with corporation tax and enforce the payment of tax when it is not paid willingly. **Taxpayer assistance offices** handle enquiries and arrange specialist help for taxpayers.

The **General Commissioners** (not to be confused with the Commissioners for HMRC) are appointed (at the moment) by the Lord Chancellor to hear **appeals** against HMRC decisions. They are part-time and unpaid. They are appointed for a local area (a **division**). They appoint a clerk who is often a lawyer or accountant and who is paid for his services.

The **Special Commissioners** are also appointed by the Lord Chancellor. They are full-time paid professionals. They generally hear the more complex appeals.

Many taxpayers arrange for their accountants to prepare and submit their tax returns. The taxpayer is still the person responsible for submitting the return and for paying whatever tax becomes due: the accountant is only acting as the taxpayer's agent.

2 Notification of liability to income tax and CGT

FAST FORWARD

Individuals who do not receive a tax return must notify their chargeability to income tax or CGT.

Individuals and trustees who are chargeable to income tax or CGT for any tax year and who have not received a notice to file a return are required to give notice of chargeability to an Officer of the Revenue and Customs within six months from the end of the year ie by 5 October 2007 for 2006/07.

A person who has no chargeable gains and who is not liable to higher rate tax does not have to give notice of chargeability if all his income:

(a) Is taken into account under PAYE
(b) Is from a source of income not subject to tax under a self-assessment
(c) Has had (or is treated as having had) income tax deducted at source, or
(d) Is a UK dividend.

The maximum mitigable penalty where notice of chargeability is not given is 100% of the tax assessed which is not paid on or before 31 January following the tax year.

3 Tax returns and keeping records

FAST FORWARD

Tax returns must be filed within certain time limits. There are penalties for late submission.

3.1 Tax returns

The tax return comprises a Tax Form, together with supplementary pages for particular sources of income. Taxpayers are sent a Tax Form and a number of supplementary pages depending on their known sources of income, together with a Tax Return Guide and various notes relating to the supplementary pages. Taxpayers with new sources of income may have to ask the orderline for further supplementary pages.

If a return for the previous year was filed electronically, or a computer generated substitute form used, the taxpayer may be sent a notice to file a return, rather than the official HMRC form.

Taxpayers with simple tax affairs may be asked to complete a Short four page Tax Return. Short Tax Returns may be sent to employees (not directors) with taxable benefits, sole traders with three line accounts (see later in this text) and pensioners who have pensions and simple investment income. HMRC process these returns using an automated data capture facility. Taxpayers can also choose to file the return online.

Notice to make a trust tax return may be given to any one relevant trustee, or to all the relevant trustees, or to some of the relevant trustees, as the officer of the Board thinks fit.

Partnerships must file a separate return which includes 'a partnership statement' showing the firm's profits, losses, proceeds from the sale of assets, tax suffered, tax credits, charges on income and the division of all these amounts between partners. The partnership return must normally be made by the senior partner (or whoever else may be nominated by the partnership), but HMRC have power to require any, all, or some of the partners (or their nominated successors) to submit the return.

A partnership return must include a declaration of the name, residence and tax reference of each partner, as well as the usual declaration that the return is correct and complete to the best of the signatory's knowledge.

Each partner must then include his share of partnership profits on his personal tax return.

3.2 Time limit for submission of tax returns

Key term

The **filing due date for filing a tax return is the later of:**

- **31 January following the end of the tax year which the return covers.**
- **Three months after the notice to file the return was issued.**

If an individual or trustees wish HMRC to prepare the self-assessment on their behalf, earlier deadlines apply. The filing date is then the later of:

- **30 September following the tax year; eg for 2006/07, by 30 September 2007.**
- **Two months after notice to file the return was issued.**

Since a partnership return does not include a self-assessment these revised deadlines do not apply to partnership returns. This may, of course, create problems if one of the partners wishes HMRC to complete his personal self-assessment.

The filing due dates are to be advanced for 2007/08 onwards as part of the move towards online filing. The deadline for paper returns will be 30 September following the tax year, and that for online returns will be 30 November following the tax year.

3.3 Penalties for late filing

3.3.1 Individual and trustees returns

The maximum penalties for delivering a tax return after the filing due date are:

(a)	**Return up to 6 months late:**	**£100**
(b)	**Return more than 6 months but not more than 12 months late:**	**£200**
(c)	**Return more than 12 months late:**	**£200 + 100% of the tax liability**

In addition, the General or Special Commissioners can direct that a maximum penalty of £60 per day be imposed where failure to deliver a tax return continues after notice of the direction has been given to the taxpayer. In this case the additional £100 penalty, imposed under (b) if the return is more than six months late, is not charged.

The fixed penalties of £100/£200 can be set aside by the Commissioners if they are satisfied that the taxpayer had a reasonable excuse for not delivering the return. If the tax liability shown on the return is less than the fixed penalties, the fixed penalty is reduced to the amount of the tax liability. The tax geared penalty is mitigable by HMRC or the Commissioners.

3.3.2 Partnership returns

The maximum penalties for late delivery of a partnership tax return are as shown above, save that there is no tax-geared penalty if the return is more than 12 months late. The penalties apply separately to each partner.

3.3.3 Reasonable excuse

A taxpayer only has a reasonable excuse for a late filing if a default occurred because of a factor outside his control. This might be non-receipt of the return by the taxpayer, an industrial dispute in the post office after the return was posted, serious illness of the taxpayer or a close relative, or destruction of records through fire and flood. Illness etc is only accepted as a reasonable excuse if the taxpayer was taking timeous steps to complete the return, and if the return is filed as soon as possible after the illness etc.

3.3.4 Returns rejected as incomplete

If a return, filed before the filing date, is rejected by HMRC as incomplete later than 14 days before the filing deadline of 31 January, a late filing penalty will not be charged if the return is completed and returned within 14 days of the rejection. This only applies if the omission from the return was a genuine error. It does not apply if a return was deliberately filed as incomplete in the hope of extending the time limit.

3.4 Electronic lodgement of tax returns

The electronic lodgement of tax returns and other documents is possible if:

(a) The information is transferred by persons approved by HMRC.

(b) The information is transmitted using approved hardware and software.

(c) A hard copy of the information (signed by the taxpayer etc) was made before the information is transmitted electronically and the fact that this has been done is signified as part of the transmission.

(d) The information is accepted by HMRC's computer.

Where a return is filed electronically, supporting documents may be sent separately (eg. by post). Provided they are submitted within one month of the return and have been referred to in the return HMRC accept that they 'accompany' the return.

3.5 Standard accounting information

'Three line' accounts (ie income less expenses equals profit) only need be included on the tax return of businesses with a turnover (or gross rents from property) of less than £15,000 pa. This is not as helpful as it might appear, as underlying records must still be kept for tax purposes (disallowable items etc) when producing three line accounts.

Large businesses with a turnover of at least £5 million which have used figures rounded to the nearest £1,000 in producing their published accounts can compute their profits to the nearest £1,000 for tax purposes.

The tax return requires trading results to be presented in a standard format. Although there is no requirement to submit accounts with the return, accounts may be filed. If accounts accompany the return, HMRC's power to raise a discovery assessment (see below) is restricted.

3.6 Keeping of records

All taxpayers must keep and retain all records required to enable them to make and deliver a correct tax return.

Records must be retained until the later of:

(a) (i) **5 years after the 31 January following the tax year where the taxpayer is in business** (as a sole trader or partner or letting property), or

(ii) **1 year after the 31 January following the tax year otherwise, or**

(b) Provided notice to deliver a return is given before the date in (a):

(i) **The time after which enquiries by HMRC into the return can no longer be commenced**, or

(ii) **The date any such enquiries have been completed.**

Where a person receives a notice to deliver a tax return after the normal record keeping period has expired, he must keep all records in his possession at that time until no enquiries can be raised in respect of the return or until such enquiries have been completed.

The maximum (mitigable) penalty for each failure to keep and retain records is £3,000 per tax year/accounting period.

The duty to preserve records can generally be satisfied by retaining copies of original documents except that for documents which show domestic or foreign tax deducted or creditable, the originals (eg. dividend certificates) must be kept.

Record keeping failures are taken into account in considering the mitigation of other penalties. Where the record keeping failure is taken into account in this way, a penalty will normally only be sought in serious and exceptional cases where, for example, records have been destroyed deliberately to obstruct an enquiry or there has been a history of serious record keeping failures.

4 Self-assessment and claims

FAST FORWARD

Although taxpayers must normally self assess their income tax, Class 4 NIC and CGT liabilities HMRC will calculate the tax on their behalf if they file their tax return by 30 September following the end of the tax year.

4.1 Self assessment

Every full personal and trust tax return must be accompanied by a self-assessment.

Key term

A self-assessment is a calculation of the amount of taxable income and gains after deducting reliefs and allowances, and a calculation of the income tax and CGT payable after taking into account tax deducted at source and tax credits.

Although Tax Calculation Working Sheets are provided with the tax return there is no requirement for the taxpayer to use these in computing his self-assessment. It is sufficient to enter the appropriate figures on the tax return.

The self-assessment calculation may either be made by the taxpayer or HMRC. If a return is filed within certain time limits (normally, 30 September following the tax year to which it relates, see above) an Officer of Revenue and Customs must make a self-assessment on the taxpayer's behalf on the basis of the information contained in the return. He must send a copy of the assessment to the taxpayer. These assessments, even though raised by HMRC, are treated as self-assessments.

If the taxpayer files a return after the above deadline but without completing the self-assessment, HMRC will not normally reject the return as incomplete. However HMRC are not then bound to complete the self-assessment in time to notify the taxpayer of the tax falling due on the normal due date (generally the following 31 January), and it is the taxpayer's responsibility to estimate and pay his tax on time.

Within nine months of receiving a tax return, HMRC can amend a taxpayer's self-assessment to correct any obvious errors or mistakes; whether errors of principle, arithmetical mistakes or otherwise. The taxpayer does have the right to reject any corrections of obvious errors made by HMRC.

Within 12 months of the due filing date (*not* the actual filing date), the taxpayer can give notice to an officer to amend his tax return and self-assessment. Such amendments by taxpayers are not confined to the correction of obvious errors. An amendment may be made whilst HMRC are making enquiries into the return, but will not take effect until the end of the enquiry.

The same rules apply to corrections and amendments of partnership statements and stand alone claims (see below).

The Short Tax Return form does not have the facility for the taxpayer to complete a self-assessment although if needed there is a two-page simple calculation to give people a rough idea of their tax liability. HMRC calculate the tax for such returns. Therefore HMRC encourage taxpayers to file the return by 30 September following the tax year. However, the latest date for filing is 31 January.

4.2 Claims

4.2.1 Introduction

All claims and elections which can be made in a tax return must be made in this manner if a return has been issued. A claim for any relief, allowance or repayment of tax must be quantified at the time it is made. These rules do not apply to claims involving two or more years.

Certain claims have a time limit that is longer than the time limit for filing or amending a tax return. A claim may therefore be made after the time limit for amending the tax return has expired. Claims not made on the tax return are referred to as **'stand alone' claims**.

Claims made on a tax return are subject to the administrative rules governing returns, for the making of corrections, enquiries etc.

4.2.2 Stand alone claims

Claims and elections not made in a tax return are governed by provisions which are similar to the rules governing the treatment of tax returns. The rules cover:

(a) Keeping supporting records. Records must be kept until enquiries may no longer be made into the claim, or until any enquiries which are made have been completed

(b) Amending the claim. HMRC's nine month time limit is unchanged, but the taxpayer has twelve months from the date the claim was made (see below)

(c) Giving effect to the claim (ie repaying the tax)

(d) Enquiring into the claim and making any necessary amendments (see below)

4.2.3 Claims involving more than one year

Self-assessment is intended to avoid the need to reopen earlier years, so relief should be given for the year of the claim. This rule can best be explained by considering a claim to carry back a trade loss to an earlier year of assessment:

(a) The claim for relief is treated as made in relation to the year in which the loss was actually incurred

(b) The amount of any tax repayment due is calculated in terms of tax of the earlier year to which the loss is being carried back, and

(c) Any tax repayment etc is treated as relating to the later year in which the loss was actually incurred. A repayment supplement may accrue from the later year.

These rules apply not only to trading losses, but also to the carry back of post cessation receipts.

4.2.4 Time limits

The time limit for making a claim is 5 years from 31 January following the tax year, unless a different limit is specifically set for the claim. Many reliefs have a shorter time limit specifically set – of one year from the 31 January following the end of the tax year. These time limits are mentioned, where relevant, throughout this text.

Since a taxpayer needs to be able to calculate his tax liability under self-assessment a certain amount of formality in the claims procedure is needed. For example, capital losses are only allowable if notified to an officer of the Board and such notification is treated as a claim for relief for the year in which the loss accrues. Therefore, notification of such losses has to be made within 5 years from 31 January following the tax year in which they accrue.

A taxpayer may normally make a claim if the conditions for relief are fulfilled. A claim for enterprise investment scheme deferral relief, however, may not be made until the relevant certificates have been received from the EIS company. It may be necessary to submit the tax return before the certificate is available, and to claim the relief subsequently.

4.2.5 Error or mistake claims

An error or mistake claim may be made for errors in a return or partnership statement where tax would otherwise be overcharged. The claim may not be made where the tax liability was computed in accordance with practice prevailing at the time the return or statement was made.

An error or mistake claim may not be made in respect of a claim. If a taxpayer makes an error or mistake in a claim, he may make a supplementary claim within the time limits allowed for the original claim.

The taxpayer may appeal to the Special Commissioners against any refusal of an error or mistake claim.

5 Payment of income tax and capital gains tax

FAST FORWARD

Two payments on account and a final balancing payment of income tax and Class 4 NICs are due. All capital gains tax is due on 31 January following the end of the tax year.

5.1 Payment dates

The self-assessment system may result in the taxpayer making three payments of income tax and Class 4 NICs.

Date	Payment
31 January in the tax year	1st payment on account
31 July after the tax year	2nd payment on account
31 January after the tax	Final payment to settle the remaining liability

HMRC issue payslips/demand notes in a credit card type 'Statement of Account' format, but there is no statutory obligation for it to do so and **the onus is on the taxpayer to pay the correct amount of tax on the due date.**

Key term

Payments on account are usually required where the income tax and Class 4 NICs due in the previous year exceeded the amount of income tax deducted at source; this excess is known as **'the relevant amount'**. Income tax deducted at source includes tax suffered, PAYE deductions and tax credits on dividends.

The payments on account are each equal to 50% of the relevant amount for the previous year.

Question — Payments on account

Sue is a self employed writer who paid tax for 2006/07 as follows:

		£
Total amount of income tax charged		9,200
This included:	Tax deducted on savings income	3,200
She also paid:	Class 4 NIC	1,900
	Class 2 NIC	109
	Capital gains tax	4,800

How much are the payments on account for 2007/08?

Answer

	£
Income tax:	
Total income tax charged for 2006/07	9,200
Less: tax deducted for 2006/07	(3,200)
	6,000
Class 4 NIC	1,900
'Relevant amount'	7,900
Payments on account for 2007/08:	
31 January 2008 £7,900 × ½	3,950
31 July 2008 As before	3,950

There is no requirement to make payments on account of capital gains tax nor Class 2 NIC.

Payments on account are not required if the relevant amount falls below a de minimis limit of £500. Also, payments on account are not required from taxpayers who paid 80% or more of their tax liability for the previous year through PAYE or other deduction at source arrangements.

If the previous year's liability increases following an amendment to a self-assessment, or the raising of a discovery assessment, an adjustment is made to the payments on account due.

Payments on account are normally fixed by reference to the previous year's tax liability but if a taxpayer expects his liability to be lower than this **he may claim to reduce his payments on account to:**

(a) **A stated amount**, or

(b) **Nil**.

The claim must state the reason why he believes his tax liability will be lower, or nil.

If the taxpayer's eventual liability is higher than he estimated he will have reduced the payments on account too far. Although the payments on account will not be adjusted, the taxpayer will suffer an interest charge on late payment.

A penalty of the difference between the reduced payment on account and the correct payment on account may be levied if the reduction was claimed fraudulently or negligently.

The balance of any income tax and Class 4 NICs together with all CGT due for a year, is normally payable on or before the 31 January following the year.

Question

Payments of tax

Giles made payments on account for 2006/07 of £6,500 each on 31 January 2007 and 31 July 2007, based on his 2005/06 liability. He then calculates his total income tax and Class 4 NIC liability for 2006/07 at £18,000 of which £2,750 was deducted at source. In addition he calculated that his CGT liability for disposals in 2006/07 is £5,120.

What is the final payment due for 2006/07?

Answer

Income tax and Class 4 NIC: £18,000 – £2,750 – £6,500 – £6,500 = £2,250. CGT = £5,120.

Final payment due on 31 January 2008 for 2006/2007 £2,250 + £5,120 = £7,370

In one case the due date for the final payment is later than 31 January following the end of the year. **If a taxpayer has notified chargeability by 5 October but the notice to file a tax return is not issued before 31 October, then the due date for the payment is three months after the issue of the notice.**

Tax charged in an amended self-assessment is usually payable on the later of:

(a) The normal due date, generally 31 January following the end of the tax year, and
(b) The day following 30 days after the making of the revised self-assessment.

Tax charged on a discovery assessment is due thirty days after the issue of the assessment.

5.2 Surcharges

FAST FORWARD

Self assessment is enforced through a system of automatic surcharges, penalties and interest.

Key term

Surcharges are normally imposed in respect of amounts paid late:

	Paid	*Surcharge*
(a)	Within 28 days of due date:	none
(b)	More than 28 days but not more than six months after the due date:	5%
(c)	More than six months after the due date:	10%

Surcharges apply to:

(a) Balancing payments of income tax and Class 4 NICs and any CGT under self-assessment or a determination

(b) Tax due on the amendment of a self-assessment

(c) Tax due on a discovery assessment

The surcharge rules do not apply to late payments on account.

No surcharge will be applied where the late paid tax liability has attracted a tax-geared penalty on the failure to notify chargeability to tax, or the failure to submit a return, or on the making of an incorrect return (including a partnership return).

5.3 Interest

Interest is chargeable on late payment of both payments on account and balancing payments. In both cases interest runs from the due date until the day before the actual date of payment.

Interest is charged from 31 January following the tax year (or the normal due date for the balancing payment, in the rare event that this is later), even if this is before the due date for payment on:

(a) Tax payable following an amendment to a self-assessment
(b) Tax payable in a discovery assessment, and
(c) Tax postponed under an appeal which becomes payable.

Since a determination (see below) is treated as if it were a self-assessment, interest runs from 31 January following the tax year.

If a taxpayer claims to reduce his payments on account and there is still a final payment to be made, interest is normally charged on the payments on account as if each of those payments had been the lower of:

(a) the reduced amount, plus 50% of the final income tax liability; and
(b) the amount which would have been payable had no claim for reduction been made.

Question

Interest

Herbert's payments on account for 2006/07 based on his income tax liability for 2005/06 were £4,500 each. However when he submitted his 2005/06 income tax return in January 2006 he made a claim to reduce the payments on account for 2006/07 to £3,500 each. The first payment on account was made on 29 January 2007, and the second on 12 August 2007.

Herbert filed his 2006/07 tax return in December 2007. The return showed that his tax liabilities for 2006/07 (before deducting payments on account) were income tax and Class 4 NIC: £10,000, capital gains tax: £2,500. Herbert paid the balance of tax due of £5,500 on 19 February 2008.

For what periods and in respect of what amounts will Herbert be charged interest?

Answer

Herbert made an excessive claim to reduce his payments on account, and will therefore be charged interest on the reduction. The payments on account should have been £4,500 each based on the 2005/06 liability (not £5,000 each based on the 2006/07 liability). Interest will be charged as follows:

(a) First payment on account

  (i) On £3,500 – nil – paid on time
  (ii) On £1,000 from due date of 31 January 2007 to day before payment, 18 February 2008

(b) Second payment on account

  (i) On £3,500 from due date of 31 July 2007 to day before payment, 11 August 2007
  (ii) On £1,000 from due date of 31 July 2007 to day before payment, 18 February 2008

(c) Balancing payment

  (i) On £3,500 from due date of 31 January 2008 to day before payment, 18 February 2008

Where interest has been charged on late payments on account but the final balancing settlement for the year produces a repayment, all or part of the original interest is remitted.

If a taxpayer provided HMRC in good time with the information needed to calculate the payment on account due on 31 January but did not receive a Statement of Account in time to make the correct payment by 31 January, it is HMRC practice to treat the due date for interest purposes as 30 days after the issue of the Statement.

5.4 Repayment of tax and repayment supplement

Tax is repaid when claimed unless a greater payment of tax is due in the following 30 days, in which case it is set-off against that payment.

Interest is paid on overpayments of:

(a) Payments on account

(b) Final payments of income tax and Class 4 NICs and CGT, including tax deducted at source or tax credits on dividends, and

(c) Penalties and surcharges.

Repayment supplement runs from the original date of payment (even if this was prior to the due date), until the day before the date the repayment is made. Income tax deducted at source and tax credits are treated as if they were paid on the 31 January following the tax year concerned.

Tax repaid is identified with tax payments in the following order:

(a) Final balancing payment
(b) Equally to the payments on account
(c) Income tax deducted at source/tax credits
(d) If it is attributable to tax paid in instalments, to a later instalment before an earlier one.

5.5 Payment of CGT by instalments

Where the consideration for a disposal of an asset is receivable in instalments over a period exceeding 18 months, the taxpayer has the option to pay the CGT arising in instalments. HMRC then allow payment of CGT to be spread over the shorter of:

(a) The period of instalment, and
(b) Eight years.

6 Enquiries, determinations and discovery assessments

FAST FORWARD

The Revenue can enquire into tax returns but strict procedural rules govern enquiries.

6.1 Enquiries into returns

An officer of the Revenue and Customs has a limited period within which to commence enquiries into a return or amendment. The officer must give written notice of his intention by:

(a) The **first anniversary of the due filing date (not the actual filing date)**, or

(b) **If the return is filed after the due filing date, the quarter day following the first anniversary of the actual filing date. The quarter days are 31 January, 30 April, 31 July and 31 October.**

If the taxpayer amended the return after the due filing date, the enquiry 'window' extends to the quarter day following the first anniversary of the date the amendment was filed. Where the enquiry was not raised within the limit which would have applied had no amendment been filed, the enquiry is restricted to matters contained in the amendment.

Enquiries may be made into partnership returns (or amendments) upon which a partnership statement is based within the same time limits. A notice to enquire into a partnership return is deemed to incorporate a notice, to enquire into each individual partner's return.

Enquiries may also be made into stand alone claims, provided notice is given by the Officer of Revenue and Customs by the later of:

(a) The quarter day following the first anniversary of the making or amending of the claim

(b) 31 January next but one following the tax year, if the claim relates to a tax year, or

(c) The first anniversary of the end of the period to which a claim relates if it relates to a period other than a tax year.

The procedures for enquiries into claims mirror those for enquiries into returns.

The officer does not have to have, or give, any reason for raising an enquiry. In particular the taxpayer will not be advised whether he has been selected at random for an audit. Enquiries may be full enquiries, or may be limited to 'aspect' enquiries.

In the course of his enquiries **the officer may require the taxpayer to produce documents, accounts or any other information required. The taxpayer can appeal to the Commissioners.**

During the course of his enquiries an officer may amend a self-assessment if it appears that insufficient tax has been charged and an immediate amendment is necessary to prevent a loss to the Crown. This might apply if, for example, there is a possibility that the taxpayer will emigrate.

If a return is under enquiry HMRC may postpone any repayment due as shown in the return until the enquiry is complete. HMRC have discretion to make a provisional repayment but there is no facility to appeal if the repayment is withheld.

At any time during the course of an enquiry, the taxpayer may apply to the Commissioners to require the officer to notify the taxpayer within a specified period that the enquiries are complete, unless the officer can demonstrate that he has reasonable grounds for continuing the enquiry.

If both sides agree, disputes concerning a point of law can be resolved through litigation without having to wait until the whole enquiry is complete.

An officer must issue a notice that the enquiries are complete, and a statement of the amount of tax that he considers should be included in the tax return, or the amounts which should be contained in the partnership statement, or the amount of the claim. The taxpayer then has thirty days to amend his self-assessment, partnership statement or claim to give effect to the officer's conclusions. He may also make any other amendments that he could have made had the enquiry not been commenced (amendments may not be made whilst enquiries are in progress).

If the officer is not satisfied with the taxpayer's amendment he has thirty days in which to amend the self-assessment, partnership statement or claim. Also if a claim has been disallowed, but does not affect the self-assessment, he must advise the taxpayer of the extent to which it has been disallowed.

If the taxpayer is not satisfied with the officer's amendment he may, within 30 days, appeal to the Commissioners.

Once an enquiry is complete the officer cannot make further enquiries. HMRC may, in limited circumstances, raise a discovery assessment if they believe that there has been a loss of tax (see below).

6.2 Determinations

HMRC may only raise enquiries if a return has been submitted.

If notice has been served on a taxpayer to submit a return but the return is not submitted by the due filing date, an officer of Revenue and Customs may make a determination of the amounts liable to income tax and CGT tax and of the tax due. Such a determination must be made to the best of the officer's information and belief, and is then treated as if it were a self-assessment. This enables the officer to seek payment of tax, including payments on account for the following year and to charge interest.

The determination must be made within the period ending 5 years after 31 January following the tax year. It may be superseded by a self-assessment made within the same period or, if later, within 12 months of the date of the determination.

6.3 Discovery assessments

If an officer of Revenue and Customs discovers that profits have been omitted from assessment, that any assessment has become insufficient, or that any relief given is, or has become excessive, an assessment may be raised to recover the tax lost.

If the tax lost results from an error in the taxpayer's return but the return was made in accordance with prevailing practice at the time, no discovery assessment may be made.

A discovery assessment may only be raised where a return has been made if:

(a) There has been fraudulent or negligent conduct by the taxpayer or his agent, or

(b) At the time that enquiries into the return were completed, or could no longer be made, the officer did not have information to make him aware of the loss of tax.

Information is treated as available to an officer if:

(a) It is contained in the taxpayer's return for the period (or for either of the two preceding periods) or in any accompanying documents.

(b) It is contained in a claim made in respect of that period or in any accompanying documents;

(c) It is contained in any documents, produced in connection with an enquiry into a return (or claim) for the period or either of the two preceding periods;

(d) It is information, the existence and relevance of which, could reasonably be expected to be inferred by an officer from the information described above, or which was notified in writing by or on behalf of the taxpayer to an officer. The information supplied must be sufficiently detailed to draw HMRC's attention to contentious matters, such as the use of a valuation or estimate.

These rules do not prevent HMRC from raising assessments in cases of genuine discoveries, but prevent assessments from being raised due to HMRC's failure to make timely use of information or to a change of opinion on information made available.

6.4 Appeals and postponement of payment of tax

A taxpayer may appeal against an amendment to a self-assessment or partnership statement, or an amendment to or disallowance of a claim, following an enquiry, or against an assessment which is not a self-assessment, such as a discovery assessment.

The appeal must normally be made within 30 days of the amendment or self-assessment.

The notice of appeal must state the **grounds** of appeal. These may be stated in general terms. At the hearing the Commissioners may allow the appellant to put forward grounds not stated in his notice if they are satisfied that his omission was not wilful or unreasonable.

In some cases it may be possible to agree the point at issue by negotiation with HMRC, in which case the appeal may be settled by agreement. If the appeal cannot be agreed, it will be heard by the General or Special Commissioners.

An appeal does not relieve the taxpayer of liability to pay tax on the normal due date unless he obtains a 'determination' of the Commissioners or agreement of the Inspector that payment of all or some of the tax may be postponed pending determination of the appeal. The amount not postponed is due 30 days after the determination or agreement is issued, if that is later than the normal due date.

If any part of the postponed tax becomes due a notice of the amount payable is issued and the amount is payable 30 days after the issue of the notice. Interest, however, is still payable from the normal due date.

6.5 Income tax fraud

There is a statutory offence of evading income tax. The penalty may be up to seven years in prison or an unlimited fine, or both.

Chapter roundup

- Individuals who do not receive a tax return must notify their chargeability to income tax or CGT.
- Although taxpayers must normally self assess their income tax, Class 4 NIC and CGT liabilities they can opt out of self assessment if they file their tax return by 30 September following the end of the tax year.
- Two payments on account and a final balancing payment of income tax and Class 4 NICs are due.
- All capital gains tax is due on 31 January following the end of the tax year.
- Self assessment is enforced through a system of automatic surcharges, penalties and interest.
- HMRC can enquire into tax returns but strict procedural rules govern enquiries.

Quick quiz

1. By when must a taxpayer who has not received a tax return give notice of his chargeability to capital gains tax due in 2006/07?
2. By when must a taxpayer, who intends to calculate his own tax, file a tax return for 2006/07?
3. What are the normal payment dates for income tax?
4. What surcharges are due in respect of income tax payments on account that are paid two months after the due date?

Answers to quick quiz

1. Within six months of the end of the year, ie by 5 October 2007.
2. By 31 January 2008 or, if later, 3 months after a notice to file the return was issued.
3. Two payments on account of income tax are due on 31 January in the tax year and on the 31 July following. A final balancing payment is due on 31 January following the tax year.
4. None. Surcharges do not apply to late payment of payment on account.

Now try the question below from the Exam Question Bank

Number	Level	Marks	Time
Q15	Introductory	15	27 mins

16

Inheritance tax: basic principles, lifetime transfers and exemptions

Introduction

In this chapter we introduce a new tax, inheritance tax (IHT). IHT is primarily a tax on wealth left on death. It also applies to gifts within seven years of death and to certain lifetime transfers of wealth.

The tax is different from income tax and CGT, where the basic question is: how much has the taxpayer made? With IHT, the basic question is, how much has he given away? We tax the amount which the taxpayer has transferred - the amount by which he is worse off. If the taxpayer pays IHT on a lifetime gift, he is worse off by the amount of the gift plus the tax, and we have to take that into account. Some transfers are however exempt from IHT.

We will see that the first £285,000 of transfers is taxed at 0% (the 'nil rate band'), and is therefore effectively tax-free. To stop people from avoiding IHT by, for example, giving away £1,425,000 in five lots of £285,000, we need to look back seven years every time a transfer is made to decide how much of the nil rate band is available to set against the current transfer.

We end this chapter by looking at IHT on transfers of value by close companies.

1 Basic principles

1.1 Introduction

FAST FORWARD

IHT applies to transfers on death, to transfers within the seven years before death and to transfers to discretionary trusts.

IHT is a tax on gifts or '**transfers of value**'. There are two main chargeable occasions:

(a) gifts made in the lifetime of the donor (**lifetime transfers**), and
(b) gifts made on death, for example when property is left in a will (**death estate**).

We will look in detail at lifetime transfers later in this chapter and at the death estate in the next chapter.

First, however, we start our study of IHT by looking at some general principles which apply to both chargeable occasions.

1.2 Transfers of value and chargeable transfers

Inheritance tax cannot arise unless there is a transfer of value. This is any gratuitous disposition made by a person which results in his being worse off, that is, he suffers a diminution in the value of his estate.

The measure of a gift is always the loss to the transferor (the diminution in value of his estate), not the amount gained by the transferee.

The term 'disposition' is not given any particular technical meaning. It covers any act whereby a person divests himself of the beneficial ownership of his property.

Inheritance tax arises on any chargeable transfer. This is any transfer of value not covered by an exemption.

1.3 Diminution in value

In many cases the diminution in value of the transferor's estate will be the same as the increase in the value of the transferee's estate. However, sometimes the two will not be the same.

1.4 Example: diminution in value

A holds 5,100 of the shares in an unquoted company which has an issued share capital of 10,000 shares. Currently A's majority holding is valued at £15 per share.

A wishes to give 200 shares to his son, B. However, to B the shares are worth only £2.50 each, since B will have only a small minority holding in the company. After the gift A will hold 4,900 shares and these will be worth £10 each. The value per share to A will thus fall from £15 to £10 per share since he will lose control of the company.

The diminution in value of A's estate is £27,500, as follows.

	£
Before the gift: 5,100 shares × £15	76,500
After the gift: 4,900 shares × £10	(49,000)
Diminution in value	27,500

B has only been given shares worth 200 × £2.50 = £500. This value will be used in any capital gains tax computation, but IHT uses the principle of diminution in value which can, as in this case, give a much greater value than the value of the asset transferred.

1.5 Chargeable persons

Individuals and trustees of settled property are chargeable persons for IHT purposes.

Companies are not chargeable persons. However, an IHT liability can arise on the participators in a close company (see later in this chapter) where such a company makes a transfer of value.

1.6 Exceptions to the IHT charge

(a) **IHT is charged only where there is gratuitous intent**. Therefore, a transfer of value will not be taxed if there was no intention to confer gratuitous benefit on anyone, and either the transfer was a transaction made at arm's length between unconnected persons or it was such as might be expected to be made at arm's length between unconnected persons.

(b) **No IHT liability will arise on transfers made in the course of a trade**: for example Christmas gifts to employees.

(c) Expenditure on family maintenance is not within the scope of IHT. An example of this would be school fees paid for a child.

(d) Waivers of remuneration are not chargeable.

(e) Waivers of dividends are not chargeable provided the waiver is made within the 12 months before the dividend is declared.

(f) The value of any **excluded property** (see below) which is transferred is ignored.

(g) Any transfer covered by a specific exemption is not chargeable (see further below).

1.7 The scope of the charge

All transfers of assets (worldwide) made by persons domiciled in the UK (see later in this text) **whether during lifetime or on death are within the charge to IHT.**

For individuals not domiciled in the UK, only transfers of UK assets are within the charge to IHT.

Transfers of settled property made by trustees are also within the charge to IHT.

1.8 Excluded property

In computing the diminution in value of a transferor's estate, no account is taken of the value of any excluded property which ceases to be part of the transferor's estate. So if excluded property is given away, there will be no IHT consequence unless the value of other property retained by the transferor is affected.

The following are excluded property.

(a) A reversionary interest in settled property. A reversionary interest is a future interest as opposed to a present interest, an example being the remainderman's interest in trust property that will pass to him on the life tenant's death. A reversionary interest will not, however, be treated as excluded property if it is:

  (i) An interest which has at any time been acquired for a consideration in money or money's worth

  (ii) An interest to which either the settlor or his spouse is or has been beneficially entitled at any time, or

  (iii) An interest expectant on the termination of a lease treated as a settlement (such as a lease which will end on a person's death).

(b) Pensions and gratuities due from governments of certain former colonies.

(c) Emoluments and tangible movable property of members of overseas forces posted to the UK.

(d) Decorations awarded for valour or gallant conduct which have never been transferred for consideration in money or money's worth.

In addition, some assets owned by non-UK domiciled persons are excluded property (see later in this text).

The following assets are also ignored on a person's death.

(a) Assets of a member of the armed forces passing on his or her death if the death resulted from wounds, accident or disease while on active service.

(b) Cash options which could have been taken under approved personal pension schemes instead of an annuity for a dependant.

(c) By concession, the amount of certain wartime compensation payments.

1.9 Husbands and wives

FAST FORWARD

Spouses and civil partners are taxable separately. There is an exemption for transfers between spouses and between civil partners.

Husbands and wives are taxed separately. On the death of one spouse it is necessary to value his or her estate. That estate includes only the property (or share of property) actually belonging to the deceased. Each spouse has the benefit of the nil rate band (the £285,000 band on which IHT is at 0%), exemptions and reliefs independently of the other spouse.

Transfers between spouses (whether or not living together) **are exempt**. Two simple planning points follow from the exemption for inter-spouse transfers.

(a) A married couple may avoid IHT, at least in the short term, if each spouse makes a will leaving most of his or her property to the other spouse.

(b) A couple should consider making lifetime transfers between themselves so as to achieve, as far as possible, estates of equal value. If they should die together the combined estate will then enjoy the full benefit of two nil rate bands.

Same sex couples registered under the CPA 2004 are treated in the same way as married couples, and references to spouses include civil partners.

1.10 Trusts

Historically trusts have been used by wealthy families for estate planning, and favourable IHT rules have applied to certain types of trust. The rules have been radically revised from 22 March 2006 so that most trusts are subject to the same IHT regime. This will be discussed later in this text, but the basic rules from 22 March 2006 are:

(a) **Lifetime transfers to trusts are chargeable at the time they are made.**
(b) **A principal charge is applied every ten years to the capital in the trust.**
(c) **When property leaves the trust, it is subject to an exit charge.**

There are exceptions for three types of trust if set up on death.

(a) **Trusts for bereaved minors (TBM)**. These are trusts set up on the will or intestacy of a parent for a beneficiary who is still a minor. The beneficiary must be entitled to take the trust assets absolutely at age 18 (or less). Income may be paid to or applied for the benefit of the beneficiary whilst still a minor, but not to any other person. There will be no principal charge, nor will there be an exit charge when the beneficiary becomes entitled to the trust assets.

(b) **Age 18-25 Trusts**. These are trusts set up on the will or intestacy of a parent for a beneficiary who is under 25. The beneficiary must be entitled to take the trust assets absolutely at age 25 (or less). Income may be paid to or applied for the benefit of the beneficiary whilst under 25, but not to any other person. There will be no principal charge, but there will be an exit charge when the beneficiary becomes entitled to the trust assets, dependent on his age at that time. A TBM is not an age 18-25 trust.

(c) **Immediate post-death interest trusts (IPDI)**. These are interest in possession trusts arising under a will or on an intestacy where the beneficiary takes an interest in possession immediately on the death of the settlor. An interest in possession trust (sometimes called a life interest trust) is one in which the beneficiary (sometime called the life tenant) is entitled to the income of the trust as it arises. The capital is destined for a remainderman when the interest in possession ends, or may then be held on other trusts. TBM and trusts for disabled persons are not IPDI trusts.

The initial life tenant is treated as if he actually owned that portion of the capital whose income he enjoyed. Thus the capital value of the trust property is added to the deceased life tenant's own property at death in order to calculate the total tax. The trust property is referred to as settled property, and the life tenant's own property as his free estate. The proportion of the total tax applicable to the trust property is payable by the trustees out of the trust capital. If the interest in possession terminates before the life tenant's death then this is a transfer by the life tenant. (It is a potentially exempt transfer (PET) if the trust capital is advanced to another beneficiary is held on a TBM or on trusts for a disabled person – this will be discussed in more detail beyond).

There is also an exception from the general IHT rules for **trusts for disabled persons**. Transfers to such trusts are treated as PETs, and the disabled person is treated as if he actually owned the trust assets.

Other terminology that you may come across includes **"discretionary trusts"** and **"accumulation and maintenance trusts"**. A discretionary trust is one where the trustees have discretion as to how the income and capital should be allocated between beneficiaries. They may include the power to accumulate income. An accumulation and maintenance trust is a particular type of discretionary trust used where the beneficiaries are initially under the age of 25. The income may be accumulated for the beneficiary or used for his maintenance at the trustees' discretion. The beneficiary will obtain either an interest in possession or the capital outright at or under the age of 25. Accumulation and maintenance trust were particularly popular before 22 March 2006 as they were entitled to special IHT reliefs.

Prior to 22 March 2006 transfers to Interest in Possession trusts and to Accumulation and Maintenance trusts were treated as PETs; from 22 March 2006 such transfers are chargeable lifetime transfers (CLTs).

Trusts are discussed in more detail later in this text.

2 Exemptions

FAST FORWARD

Exemptions may apply to make transfers or parts of transfers non chargeable. Some exemptions only apply on lifetime transfers (annual, normal expenditure out of income, marriage), whilst some apply on both life and death transfers (spouses, charities, political parties, national purposes, housing associations).

2.1 Introduction

There are various exemptions available to eliminate or reduce the chargeable amount of a lifetime transfer or property passing on an individual's death. Some exemptions apply to both lifetime transfers and property passing on death, whilst others apply only to lifetime transfers.

Some lifetime transfers are always chargeable to IHT (Chargeable lifetime transfers – CLTs) whilst others are only chargeable if the donor dies within seven years (potentially exempt transfers – PETs). These will be discussed later, but you should note that the exemptions apply to PETs as well as to CLTs.

2.2 Exemptions applying to lifetime transfers only (including PETs)

2.2.1 The small gifts exemptions

Outright gifts to individuals totalling £250 or less per donee in any one tax year are exempt. If gifts total more than £250 the whole amount is chargeable. A donor can give up to £250 each year to each of as many donees as he wishes. The small gifts exemption cannot apply to gifts into trusts.

2.2.2 The annual exemption (AE)

The first £3,000 of value transferred in a tax year is exempt from IHT. The annual exemption is used only after all other exemptions (such as for transfers to spouses or charities). If several gifts are made in a year, the £3,000 exemption is applied to earlier gifts before later gifts. The annual exemption is used up by PETs as well as CLTs, even though the PETs might never become chargeable.

Any unused portion of the annual exemption is carried forward for one year only. Only use it the following year after that year's own annual exemption has been used.

Question — **Annual exemptions**

F has no unused annual exemption brought forward at 6 April 2005.

On 1 August 2005 he makes a transfer of £600 to P.
On 1 September 2005 he makes a transfer of £2,000 to Q.
On 1 July 2006 he makes a transfer of £3,300 to a discretionary trust.
On 1 June 2007 he makes a transfer of £5,000 to R.

Show the application of the annual exemptions.

Answer

	£
2005/06	
1.8.05 Gift to P	600
Less AE 2005/06	(600)
	0

	£
1.9.05 Gift to Q	2,000
Less AE 2005/06	(2,000)
	0

The unused annual exemption carried forward is £3,000 – £600 – £2,000 = £400.

	£	£
2006/07		
1.7.06 Gift to a discretionary trust		3,300
Less: AE 2006/07	3,000	
AE 2005/06 b/f	300	
		(3,300)
		0

The unused annual exemption carried forward is zero because the 2006/07 exemption must be used before the 2005/06 exemption brought forward. The balance of £100 of the 2005/06 exemption is lost, because it cannot be carried forward for more than one year.

	£
2007/08	
1.6.07 Gift to R	5,000
Less AE 2007/08	(3,000)
	2,000

2.2.3 Normal expenditure out of income

Inheritance tax is a tax on transfers of capital, not on dispositions of income. A transfer of value is exempt if:

(a) It is made as part of the normal expenditure of the transferor
(b) Taking one year with another, it was made out of income, and
(c) It leaves the transferor with sufficient income to maintain his usual standard of living.

As well as covering such things as regular presents **this exemption can cover regular payments out of income under deeds of covenant, and the payment of life assurance premiums on a policy for someone else.** In general there should be evidence of a prior commitment or a settled pattern of expenditure: *Bennett v IRC 1995.*

2.2.4 Gifts in consideration of marriage

Gifts in consideration of marriage are exempt up to:

(a) **£5,000 if from a parent of a party to the marriage;**
(b) **£2,500 if from a remoter ancestor or from one of the parties to the marriage;**
(c) **£1,000 if from any other person.**

The limits apply to gifts from any one donor for any one marriage.

The gift must either be an outright gift to a party to the marriage or, if it is made into a marriage settlement, the beneficiaries must be limited to:

(a) the parties to the marriage, the children of the marriage and their spouses;

(b) any subsequent spouse of a party to the marriage, any children of this subsequent marriage and spouses of those children.

The exemption is available only if the marriage actually takes place.

The same exemptions apply to gifts in consideration of the registration of a civil partnership.

2.3 Exemptions applying to both lifetime transfers and transfers on death

2.3.1 Gifts between husband and wife

Any transfers of value between husband and wife are exempt provided the transferee is domiciled in the UK at the time of transfer. The exemption covers gifts between them, property passing under a will or on intestacy, and outright transfers of settled property where the transferor spouse has an immediate post-death interest.

If the transferor spouse is domiciled in the UK but the transferee spouse is not domiciled in the UK the exemption is limited to a cumulative total of £55,000, but any gift in excess of the £55,000 cumulative total can qualify as a PET. If neither spouse is domiciled in the UK there is no limit on the exemption.

The same exemptions apply to members of civil partnerships registered under the CPA 2004 since they are treated in the same way as married couples, the terms spouse, husband and wife referring equally to civil partners.

A further exemption relating to husband and wife is available, known as the **surviving spouse exemption**. Where one spouse died before 13 November 1974 and passed property to the surviving spouse not absolutely but with an interest in possession, there would have been a charge to estate duty. Consequently, since such a transfer would now be exempted under IHT rules, where the surviving spouse dies with an interest in possession in such property, or transfers such an interest during his lifetime, the property is left out of account for IHT purposes. In addition, any income earned before the transfer but not yet received by the trustees on such property is deemed to be part of the settled fund so that this also avoids a charge to IHT.

2.3.2 Other exempt transfers

Transfers (whether outright or by settlement) **to charities** which are established in the UK **are wholly exempt** from inheritance tax.

Gifts to a qualifying political party are exempt. A political party qualifies if, at the general election preceding the transfer of value, either:

(a) At least two members were elected to the House of Commons, or
(b) One member was elected and the party polled at least 150,000 votes.

Gifts for national purposes are exempt. Eligible recipients, include:

(a) Museums
(b) Art galleries
(c) The National Trust
(d) Universities
(e) Local authorities
(f) Government departments

Maintenance settlements can be made free of inheritance tax if they are for the upkeep of historic property.

Gifts of land to housing associations are exempt.

Question

Exemptions

D made a gift of £141,000 to her son on 17 October 2002 on the son's marriage. D gave £100,000 to her spouse on 1 January 2006. D gave £70,000 to her daughter on 11 May 2006. The only other gifts D made were birthday and Christmas presents of £100 each to her grandchildren.

Show what exemptions are available assuming:

(a) D's spouse is domiciled in the UK
(b) D's spouse is not domiciled in the UK

Answer

(a) *17 October 2002*

	£
Gift to D's son	141,000
Less: ME	(5,000)
AE 2002/03	(3,000)
AE 2001/02 b/f	(3,000)
	130,000

1 January 2006

	£
Gift to D's spouse	100,000
Less spouse exemption	(100,000)
	0

11 May 2006

	£
Gift to D's daughter	70,000
Less AE 2006/07	(3,000)
AE 2005/06 b/f	(3,000)
	64,000

The gifts to the grandchildren are covered by the small gifts exemption.

(b) *17 October 2002*

As in part (a)

1 January 2006

		£
Gift to D's spouse		100,000
Less spouse exemption (restricted)		(55,000)
Less	AE 2005/06	(3,000)
	AE 2004/05 b/f	(3,000)
		39,000

Note that the annual exemption is available to set against the gift remaining after deducting the spouse exemption.

11 May 2006

	£
Gift to D's daughter	70,000
Less AE 2006/07	(3,000)
	67,000

A transfer of value attributable to a disposal of shares in a company by an individual to an employee trust is an exempt transfer.

There are three main conditions to be satisfied.

(a) The shares must be held on trust for the benefit of all or most of the employees.

(b) At the date of the transfer or within one year thereafter, the trustees must hold more than half of the ordinary shares in the company and must have voting control on most questions affecting the company as a whole.

(c) No part of the settled property can be applied for the benefit of a person who is entitled to 5% or more of any class of shares in the company or to 5% or more of its assets on a winding up.

3 Calculation of tax on lifetime transfers

3.1 Basic principles

FAST FORWARD

In order to make the tax effective, transfers are cumulated for seven years so that the nil rate band is not available in full on each of a series of transfers in rapid succession.

There are two aspects of the calculation of tax on lifetime transfers:

(a) **lifetime tax on chargeable lifetime transfers (CLTs),** and

(b) **additional death tax on CLTs and on potentially exempt transfers (PETs) where the transferor dies within seven years of making the transfer.**

Note here that in any question you should calculate the lifetime tax on any CLTs first, then move on to calculate the death tax on all CLTs and PETs made within seven years of death.

Do not worry about the definitions of what is a CLT and what is a PET at this stage. We will consider that later in this chapter. It is sufficient at this stage that you know that a lifetime transfer of value by an individual to a discretionary trust is a CLT.

3.2 Lifetime tax

FAST FORWARD

Tax is charged on what a donor loses. In some cases grossing up is required, to take account of the fact that the donor loses both the asset given away and the money with which he paid the tax due on it.

When a CLT is made and the transferee (ie the trustees in the case of a transfer to a trust) pays the lifetime tax, follow these steps to work out the lifetime IHT on it:

Step 1 Look back seven years from the date of the transfer to see if any other CLTs have been made. If so, these transfers use up the nil rate band available for the current transfer. Work out the value of any nil rate band still available.

Step 2 Compute the gross value of the CLT. You may be given this in the question or you may have to work out the diminution of value, deduct reliefs (such as business property relief as described later in the text) or exemptions (such as the annual exemption described earlier in this chapter).

Step 3 Any part of the CLT covered by the nil rate band is taxed at 0%. Any part of the CLT not covered by the nil rate band is charged at 20%.

Question — Lifetime tax on CLTs – transferee pays the tax

Eric makes a chargeable lifetime transfer of £296,000 to a discretionary trust on 10 July 2006. The trustees agree to pay the tax due.

Calculate the lifetime tax payable by the trustees if Eric has made:

(a) a lifetime chargeable transfer of value of £100,000 in August 1998,
(b) a lifetime chargeable transfer of value of £100,000 in August 1999,
(c) a lifetime chargeable transfer of value of £300,000 in August 1999.

Answer

(a) **Step 1** No lifetime transfers in seven years before 10 July 2006. Nil rate band of £285,000 available.

Step 2

		£
Gift		296,000
Less	AE 2006/07	(3,000)
	AE 2005/06 b/f	(3,000)
		290,000

Step 3

	IHT
	£
£285,000 × 0%	0
£ 5,000 × 20%	1,000
£290,000	1,000

(b) **Step 1** Lifetime transfer of value of £100,000 in seven years before 10 July 2006 (transfers after 10 July 1999). Nil rate band of £(285,000 – 100,000) = £185,000 available.

Step 2 Value of CLT is £290,000 (as before).

Step 3

	IHT
	£
£185,000 × 0%	0
£105,000 × 20%	21,000
£290,000	21,000

(c) **Step 1** Lifetime transfer of value of £300,000 in seven years before 10 July 2006 (transfers after 10 July 1999). No nil rate band available as all covered by previous transfer.

Step 2 Value of CLT is £290,000 (as before)

Step 3

	IHT
	£
£290,000 @ 20%	58,000

Where IHT is payable on a CLT, the **primary liability to pay tax is on the transferor,** although the transferor may agree with the transferee (as in the above example) that the transferee is to pay the tax instead.

If the transferor pays the lifetime IHT due on a CLT, the total diminution of value of his estate is the transfer of value plus the IHT due on it. The transfer is therefore a net transfer and must be grossed up in order to find the gross value of the transfer. **We do this by working out the tax on that part of the transfer not covered by the nil rate band as 20 (rate of tax) divided by 80 (100 minus the rate of tax).**

When a CLT is made and the transferor pays the lifetime tax, follow these steps to work out the lifetime IHT on it:

Step 1 Look back seven years from the date of the transfer to see if any other CLTs have been made. If so, these transfers use up the nil rate band available for the current transfer. Work out the value of any nil rate band still available.

Step 2 Compute the net value of the CLT. You may be given this in the question or may have to work out the diminution of value, deduct reliefs (such as business property relief as described later in the text) or exemptions (such as the annual exemption discussed earlier in this chapter).

Step 3 Any part of the CLT covered by the nil rate band is taxed at 0%. Any part of the CLT not covered by the nil rate band is taxed at 20/80.

Step 4 Work out the gross transfer by adding the net transfer and the tax together. You can check your figure by working out the tax on the gross transfer.

Question — Lifetime tax on CLTs – transferor pays the tax

James makes a chargeable lifetime transfer of £296,000 to a discretionary trust on 10 July 2006. James will pay the tax due.

Calculate the lifetime tax payable, if James has made:

(a) a lifetime chargeable transfer of value of £100,000 in August 1998,
(b) a lifetime chargeable transfer of value of £100,000 in August 1999,
(c) a lifetime chargeable transfer of value of £300,000 in August 1999.

Ignore any reliefs and exemptions.

Answer

(a) **Step 1** No lifetime transfers in seven years before 10 July 2006. Nil rate band of £285,000 available.

Step 2

		£
Gift		296,000
Less	AE 2006/07	(3,000)
	AE 2005/06 b/f	(3,000)
Net CLT		290,000

Step 3

	IHT £
£285,000 × 0%	0
£ 5,000 × 20/80	1,250
£290,000	1,250

Step 4 Gross transfer is £(290,000 + 1,250) = £291,250. *Check:* Tax on the gross transfer would be:

	IHT £
£285,000 × 0%	0
£ 6,250 × 20%	1,250
£291,250	1,250

(b) **Step 1** Lifetime transfer of value of £100,000 in seven years before 10 July 2006 (transfers after 10 July 1999). Nil rate band of £(285,000 – 100,000) = £185,000 available.

Step 2 Net value of CLT is £290,000 (as before).

Step 3

	IHT £
£185,000 × 0%	0
£105,000 × 20/80	26,250
£290,000	26,250

Step 4 Gross transfer is £(290,000 + 26,250) = £316,250. *Check:* Tax on the gross transfer would be:

	IHT £
£185,000 × 0%	0
£131,250 × 20%	26,250
£316,250	26,250

(c) **Step 1** Lifetime transfer of value of £300,000 in seven years before 10 July 2006 (transfers after 10 July 1999). No nil rate band available as all covered by previous transfer.

Step 2 Net value of CLT is £290,000 (as before).

Step 3

	IHT £
£290,000 × 20/80	72,500

Step 4 Gross transfer is £(290,000 + 72,500) = £362,500. Tax on the gross transfer would be:

	IHT £
£362,500 × 20%	72,500

3.3 Death tax

There may be additional tax to pay if the transferor dies within seven years of making a CLT. The longer the transferor survives after making the transfer, the lower the death tax. This is because a taper relief applies to lower the amount of death tax payable as follows:

Years between transfer and death	*% reduction in death tax*
3 years or less	0
More than 3 but less than 4	20
More than 4 but less than 5	40
More than 5 but less than 6	60
More than 6 but less than 7	80

Death tax on a lifetime transfer is payable by the transferee, so grossing up is not relevant.

Follow these steps to work out the death IHT on a CLT:

Step 1 Look back seven years from the *date of the transfer* to see if any other chargeable transfers were made. If so, these transfers use up the nil rate band available for the current transfer. Work out the value of any nil rate band remaining.

Step 2 Compute the value of the CLT. This is the gross value of the transfer that you worked out for computing lifetime tax.

Step 3 Any part of the CLT covered by the nil rate band is taxed at 0%. Any part of the CLT not covered by the nil rate band is charged at 40%.

Step 4 Reduce the death tax by taper relief (if applicable).

Step 5 Deduct any lifetime tax paid. The death tax may be reduced to nil, but there is no repayment of lifetime tax.

Question — Lifetime tax and death tax on CLTs

Trevor makes a gross chargeable transfer of value of £181,000 in December 1999. He then makes a gift to a discretionary trust of £198,000 on 15 November 2006 and the trustees pay the lifetime tax due.

Trevor dies in February 2010.

Compute:

(a) the lifetime tax payable by the trustees on the lifetime transfer in November 2006; and

(b) the death tax payable on the lifetime transfer in November 2006 assuming the nil rate band in February 2010 remains £285,000.

Answer

Lifetime tax

Step 1 Lifetime transfer of value of £181,000 in seven years before 15 November 2006 (transfers after 15 November 1999). Nil rate band of £(285,000 – 181,000) = £104,000 available.

Step 2

		£
Gift		198,000
Less	AE 2006/07	(3,000)
	AE 2005/06 b/f	(3,000)
		192,000

Step 3

	IHT
	£
£104,000 × 0%	0
£ 88,000 × 20%	17,600
£192,000	17,600

Death tax

Step 1 Lifetime transfer of value of £181,000 *in seven years before 15 November 2006* (transfers after 15 November 1999). Nil rate band of £(285,000 – 181,000) = £104,000 available.

Step 2 Value of CLT is £192,000 as before

Step 3

	IHT
	£
£ 104,000 × 0%	0
£ 88,000 × 40%	35,200
£192,000	35,200

Step 4 Death more than 3 years but less than 4 years after transfer

	£
Death tax	35,200
Taper relief @ 20%	(7,040)
Death tax left in charge (80%)	28,160

Step 5 Tax due £(28,160 – 17,600) 10,560

3.4 Potentially exempt transfers

Certain lifetime transfers of value which are not exempt will not incur a lifetime liability to IHT. Such transfers are called potentially exempt transfers (PETs).

Key term

A **PET** is a lifetime transfer made by an individual to:

(a) Another individual
(b) A trust for the disabled

If a transfer by an individual does not fall within the definition of a PET, it is a CLT (eg a transfer to any trust other than a trust for the disabled).

Prior to 22 March 2006 the following gifts by an individual were also treated as PETs;

(c) to an accumulation and maintenance trust
(d) to an interest in possession trust

You will still see these PETs when looking back 7 years.

If an individual who has a life interest in an IPDI trust assigns his life interest so that the assets pass to another individual outright, the life tenant is deemed to make a PET of the corresponding trust assets. He is also deemed to make a PET if the assets become held in a TBM or on trusts for a disabled person. If the assets become held on any other sort of trust (discretionary, age 18-25, accumulation and maintenance or interest in possession), then the life tenant is deemed to make a CLT.

Prior to 22 March 2006, however, if a life tenant assigned his interest so that it was held on trust for another life tenant or on accumulation and maintenance trust, the transfer was a PET.

A PET is treated as being exempt from IHT when made, and will remain so if the transferor survives for at least seven years from making the gift. If the transferor dies within seven years of making the gift, it will become chargeable to death IHT in the same way as a CLT. Of course, there will be no lifetime tax paid, so Step 5 above will not apply.

Question — IHT treatment of gifts

Classify the following transfers by Susan as PETs, CLTs or exempt.

(a) £300,000 to her husband

(b) £30,000 to a trust which will pay the income received by the trust to her son for his life

(c) £100,000 to a trust which may pay the trust income to or withhold it from various beneficiaries aged over 25

Answer

(a) Exempt (transfer to spouse)
(b) CLT (interest in possession trust) if on or after 22 March 2006, PET if before 22 March 2006.
(c) CLT (discretionary trust)

The exemptions which apply to lifetime transfers only, such as the annual exemption and the marriage exemption, are available to set against PETs. You must apply them in chronological order, so that if a PET is made before a CLT in the same tax year, the exemption is set against the PET. This may waste the exemption unless the donor dies within seven years, and is disadvantageous in cash flow terms since lifetime tax is paid on CLTs but not on PETs.

We will now work through an example in which there is both a PET and a CLT. In such cases you should always calculate lifetime tax on any CLT first. Next you should calculate any death tax due, working through the PETs and CLTs in chronological order. Remember that on death PETs become chargeable so they must be taken into account in calculating the death tax on later CLTs.

Question — Lifetime tax and death tax on CLTs and PETs

Louise gave £299,000 to her son on 1 February 2003. This was the first transfer she had made for IHT.

On 10 October 2006, Louise gave £344,000 to a discretionary trust. The trustees paid the lifetime IHT due.

On 11 January 2007, Louise died.

Compute:

(a) the lifetime tax payable by the trustees on the lifetime transfer made in 2006,
(b) the death tax payable on the lifetime transfer made in 2003, and
(c) the death tax payable on the lifetime transfer made in 2006.

Ignore any exemptions and reliefs.

Answer

(a) *Lifetime tax – 2006 CLT*

Step 1 There are no lifetime transfers in the seven years before 10 October 2006. This is because the transfer made in 2003 is a PET and therefore treated as exempt whilst Louise is alive. Nil rate band of £285,000 available.

Step 2

		£
Gift		344,000
Less	AE 2006/07	(3,000)
	AE 2005/06 b/f	(3,000)
CLT		338,000

Step 3

	IHT £
£285,000 × 0%	0
£ 53,000 × 20%	10,600
£338,000	10,600

(b) *Death tax – 2003 PET*

Step 1 No lifetime transfers of value in seven years before 1 February 2003 (transfers after 1 February 1996). Nil rate band of £285,000 available.

Step 2

		£
Gift		299,000
Less	AE 2002/03	(3,000)
	AE 2001/02 b/f	(3,000)
CLT		293,000

Step 3

	IHT £
£285,000 × 0%	0
£ 8,000 × 40%	3,200
£293,000	3,200

Step 4 Death more than 3 years but less than 4 years after transfer

	£
Death tax	3,200
Taper relief @ 20%	(640)
Death tax left in charge (80%)	2,560

(c) *Death tax – 2006 CLT*

Step 1 Lifetime transfer of value of £293,000 in seven years before 10 October 2006 (transfers after 10 October 1999). Note that as the PET becomes chargeable on death, its value is now included in calculating the death tax on the CLT. No nil rate band available.

Step 2 Value of CLT is £338,000 as before

Step 3

	IHT £
£338,000 @ 40%	135,200

Step 4 Death within 3 years of transfer so no taper relief.

Step 5 Tax due £(135,200 – 10,600) 124,600

4 Relief for the fall in value of lifetime gifts

FAST FORWARD

If an asset falls in value between a lifetime gift and death, there is a relief reducing the death tax payable. The relief affects the tax on the transfer concerned. It does not reduce the value of the gross chargeable transfer for the purpose or computing later IHT (see the next chapter).

Relief may be claimed where a lifetime gift becomes chargeable to IHT on death (whether that gift was a PET or a CLT) **and the value of the gift has fallen between the date of the gift and the death of the transferor** (or the sale of the property if this precedes death). **Relief is available only if the transferee** (or his spouse) **still holds the property at the date of death, or it has been sold in an arm's length transaction** which was not to a connected person.

Relief is not available for tangible movable property which was a wasting asset at the time of the transfer (that is, had a predictable useful life of 50 years or less). Plant and machinery is always treated as wasting.

When the relief applies, it affects the tax on the transfer concerned. However, the value of the gross chargeable transfer is not reduced by that relief when considering how much of the £Nil band remains to set against later chargeable transfers (including the death estate – see next chapter).

Question — The fall in value of lifetime gifts

H transferred a house worth £307,000 to his son on 1 June 2003. H then gave £205,000 cash to his daughter on 20 August 2005. Shortly before H's death his son sold the house on the open market for £242,000. H died on 14 July 2006. Calculate the IHT liabilities arising.

Answer

1 June 2003

There is no IHT liability when the gift is made because it is a PET.

	£
Gift	307,000
Less AE 2003/04	(3,000)
Less AE 2002/03 b/f	(3,000)
PET	301,000

The PET becomes chargeable as a result of death within seven years. The value of the chargeable transfer is reduced by the fall in value of the house:

	Chargeable transfer £
PET	301,000
Less: relief for fall in value (307,000 – 242,000)	(65,000)
	236,000

This is within the £Nil band so the IHT payable by the son is £Nil

20 August 2005

There is no IHT liability when the gift is made because it is a PET.

	£
Gift	205,000
Less AE 2005/06	(3,000)
Less AE 2004/05 b/f	(3,000)
PET	199,000

Gross chargeable transfers in the seven years prior to the gift total £301,000 (not *£236,000*), so none of the £Nil band remains available to use when calculating IHT on the PET to the daughter. The IHT payable by her is, therefore, £199,000 × 40% = £79,600. No taper relief applies as gift was within three years of death.

5 Close companies

FAST FORWARD

Transfers by a close company may be attributed to its participators.

A close company is a company controlled by five or fewer participators (broadly, shareholders) or by any number of participators who are directors. A transfer of value by a close company is (unless exempted) apportioned amongst its participators according to their respective rights and interests (normally given by their shareholdings) in the company immediately before the transfer, and any amount so apportioned to another close company is further apportioned among its participators, and so on. **Each individual to whom an amount is apportioned is treated as having made a net chargeable transfer of value of the apportioned amount which must be grossed up at his appropriate tax rates** (but see below for participators with holdings of 5% or less).

If the value of the individual's estate has also been increased as a result of the company's transfer (but ignoring his rights and interests in the company), then this increase is deducted from the net transfer of value apportioned to the individual before grossing up.

The persons liable for the tax chargeable are:

(a) The company; and, so far as tax remains unpaid after it ought to have been paid,

(b) The participators and any individual (whether a participator or not) the value of whose estate increased as a result of the company's transfer. However, a person to whom not more than 5% of the value transferred is apportioned is not liable for any of the tax, and such a person's cumulative total is not increased.

The £250 small gifts exemption, the normal expenditure out of income exemption and the marriage exemption are not available for participators to whom an amount is apportioned by reason of a transfer by a close company. However, the exemptions for gifts to charities, political parties and housing associations and gifts for national purposes are available. A participator can set his annual exemption against any amount apportioned to him.

Alterations in a close company's unquoted share or loan capital or in the rights of its unquoted shares or debentures are treated as dispositions by the participators.

Chapter roundup

- IHT applies to transfers on death, to transfers within the seven years before death and to transfers to trusts.
- Spouses/civil partners are taxable separately. There is an exemption for transfers between spouses/civil partners.
- Exemptions may apply to make transfers or parts of transfers non chargeable.
- Some exemptions only apply on lifetime transfers (annual, normal expenditure out of income, marriage), whilst some apply on both life and death transfers (spouses, charities, political parties, national purposes, housing associations).
- In order to make the tax effective, transfers are cumulated for seven years so that the nil rate band is not available in full on each of a series of transfers in rapid succession.
- Tax is charged on what a donor loses. In some cases grossing up is required, to take account of the fact that the donor loses both the asset given away and the money with which he paid the tax due on it.
- If an asset falls in value between a lifetime gift and death, there is a relief reducing the death tax payable. The relief affects the tax on the transfer concerned. It does not reduce the value of the gross chargeable transfer for the purpose or computing later IHT (see the next chapter).

Quick quiz

1. What is a transfer of value?
2. Who is chargeable to inheritance tax?
3. What is the effect of property being excluded property?
4. What are the inheritance tax consequences of having an immediate post-death interest in a trust?
5. To what extent may unused annual exemption be carried forward?
6. Don gives some money to his daughter on her marriage. What marriage exemption is applicable?
7. What types of transfer during 2006/07 by an individual are defined as potentially exempt transfers?
8. Which lifetime transfers may lead to tax being charged on death of the transferor?
9. Why must some lifetime transfers be grossed up?
10. What is taper relief?

Answers to quick quiz

1. A transfer of value is any gratuitous disposition by a person resulting in a diminution of the value of his estate.
2. Individuals and trustees.
3. Excluded property is not taken into account in computing the diminution of a transferor's estate.
4. The life tenant is treated as owning the capital whose income he enjoys under the terms of the immediate post-death interest in a trust for IHT purposes.
5. An unused annual exemption can be carried forward one tax year.
6. The marriage exemption for a gift to the transferor's child is £5,000.
7. A potentially exempt transfer is a lifetime transfer made by an individual to:
   - another individual
   - a trust for the disabled
8. An IHT charge on death arises on:
   - lifetime transfers which were PETs made within seven years of death of the transferor
   - chargeable lifetime transfers made within seven years of death of the transferor
9. A transfer must be grossed up where the donor pays the lifetime tax due, so as to compute the diminution in value of the transfer's estate on which the tax is due.
10. Taper relief is a reduction in death tax where a transfer is made between three and seven years before death.

Now try the question below from the Exam Question Bank

Number	Level	Marks	Time
Q16	Introductory	12	22 mins

17

Inheritance tax: valuation, reliefs and death estate

Introduction

This chapter opens with a section on how assets are valued. Pay particular attention to the related property rules, which prevent one way of avoiding IHT.

Two of the reliefs described in this chapter, business property relief and agricultural property relief, are very generous. If the conditions are satisfied, assets can be exempted from IHT without any limit on the value of the assets. These reliefs are meant to ensure that a family business or farm does not have to be sold when an owner dies, but they also extend to non-family businesses and farms.

Finally, we will see how to bring together all of a deceased person's assets at death, and compute the tax on the estate. There are some adjustments which may be made after death, because, for example, property is sold at a loss.

1 The valuation of assets for IHT purposes

FAST FORWARD

There are special rules for valuing particular kinds of assets, such as quoted shares and securities. The related property rules prevent artificial reductions in values.

1.1 The general principle

The value of any property for the purposes of IHT is the price which the property might reasonably be expected to fetch if sold in the open market at the time of the transfer.

We do not reduce the market price on the grounds that the whole property is placed on the market at one time. However, two or more assets can be valued jointly if disposal as one unit is the course that a prudent hypothetical vendor would have adopted in order to obtain the most favourable price: *Gray v IRC 1994.*

1.2 Quoted shares and securities

The valuation of quoted shares and securities is easy: the Stock Exchange daily official list gives the closing bid and offer prices of all quoted securities. **Inheritance tax valuations are done on the basis of the 'quarter up rule', taking the bid price plus a quarter of the difference between it and the offer price. Thus if the closing price for a particular day is 300 – 304p the inheritance tax valuation is 300 + (304 – 300)/4 = 301p.**

An alternative to the quarter up rule is available. Each day certain bargains on the Stock Exchange will be 'marked' and the alternative is to take the average of the highest and lowest marked bargains, ignoring bargains marked at special prices.

The rule for valuation of quoted securities is therefore to take the lower of:

(a) **The value on the quarter up basis.**

(b) **The average of the highest and lowest marked bargains** for the day, ignoring those marked at special prices.

The transfer may take place on a day on which the Stock Exchange is closed, in which case the valuation is done on the basis of the prices or bargains marked on the last previous day of business or the first following day of business. The lowest of, in this case, the four alternatives will be taken.

Valuations for transfers on death must be cum dividend or cum interest, including the value of the right to the next dividend or interest payment. If a question just gives a closing price you may assume that it is the cum dividend or cum interest price.

However, if the question gives an ex dividend or an ex interest price and the transfer is on death then the valuation is done on the basis of adding the whole of the impending net dividend, or the whole of the impending interest payment net of 20% tax. For lifetime transfers, the Stock Exchange list prices are used without adjustment, whether they are cum or ex dividend or interest.

1.3 Example: securities quoted ex interest

If someone owned £10,000 12% Government stock (interest payable half yearly) quoted at 94-95 ex interest, the valuation would be as follows.

	£	£
£10,000 at 94.25		9,425
Add ½ × 12% × £10,000	600	
Less income tax at 20%	(120)	
		480
		9,905

1.4 Unquoted shares and securities

There is no easily identifiable open market value for shares in an unquoted company. The Shares Valuation Division of HMRC is the body with which the taxpayer must negotiate. If agreement cannot be reached, appeal lies to the Special Commissioners and then to the courts.

1.5 Unit trusts

Units in authorised unit trusts are valued at the managers' bid price (**the lower of the two published prices**).

1.6 Life assurance policies

Where a person's estate includes a life policy which matures on his death, the proceeds payable to his personal representatives must be included in his estate for IHT purposes. But where a person's estate includes a life policy which matures on the death of someone else, the open market value must be included in his estate.

If an individual takes out a policy on his own life, pays some premiums and then decides to give the policy to someone else by assignment, he makes a PET.

The value transferred is the greater of:

(a) The premiums or other consideration paid before the transfer of the policy.
(b) The open market value of the policy at the date of transfer.

If an individual writes a policy in trust, or assigns a policy, or makes a subsequent declaration of trust, the policy proceeds will not be paid to his estate but to the assignee or to the trustees for the trust beneficiaries. The proceeds will, therefore, not be included as part of his free estate at death. It is common to write policies in trust for the benefit of dependants to avoid IHT. In many cases these transfers will be exempted as normal expenditure out of income.

1.7 Overseas property

The basis of valuation is the same as for UK property. The value is converted into sterling at the exchange rate (the 'buy' or 'sell' rate) which will give the lower sterling equivalent. Overseas debts are deductible. **If the property passes on death, the costs of administering and realising overseas property are deductible up to a maximum of 5% of the gross value of the property**, so far as those expenses are attributable to the property's location overseas. **Capital taxes paid overseas which are the foreign equivalent of IHT may give rise to double taxation relief** (see later in this Text). Such taxes are given as a credit against the IHT payable: they do not reduce the value of the asset.

1.8 Related property

Key term

Property is related to that in a person's estate (**related property**) if:

(a) It is included in the estate of his spouse or civil partner (including property held in an immediate post-death interest trust in which either has the initial interest in possession), or

(b) It has been given to a charity, political party, national public body or housing association as an exempt transfer by either spouse or civil partner and still is, or within the preceding five years has been, the property of the body it was thus given to.

To reduce the value transferred individuals might fragment an asset into several parts which are collectively worth less than the whole. This way of reducing the value of an asset or set of assets is normally prevented using the diminution in value principle. However, this application of the principle could be thwarted by use of exempt inter-spouse transfers. To deter this method of avoiding IHT, there are provisions under which related property is taken into account.

Property which is related to other property must be valued as a proportion of the value of the whole of the related property but only if, by so doing, a higher value is produced. For example, where a husband and wife each hold 40% of the issued shares of a company, the husband's holding will normally be valued as a proportion (one half) of the price which an 80% shareholding would fetch, as an 80% interest would normally be more valuable than two 40% interests.

1.9 Example: related property

Lofty has a leasehold interest in a property. The value of his interest is £25,000. His wife Michelle holds the freehold reversion of the property, which has a market value of £40,000. The value of the freehold not subject to the lease (that is the value of the freehold reversion plus the lease) is £80,000. If Lofty wishes to transfer his interest to their daughter Vicky the value transferred will be the greater of:

(a) The value of the interest by itself, £25,000, and

(b) The value of his part of the total related property, which is

$$\frac{\text{The value of the property transferred at its } \textit{unrelated} \text{ value}}{\text{The value of the property transferred at its } \textit{unrelated} \text{ value} + \text{The value of any related property at its } \textit{unrelated} \text{ value}} \times \text{The value of the whole property}$$

$$\frac{25{,}000}{25{,}000 + 40{,}000} \times £80{,}000 = £30{,}769.$$

The greater of £25,000 and £30,769 is £30,769. This is therefore the value transferred by Lofty.

If the property in question is shares, then in arriving at the fraction set out above, the numbers of shares held are used instead of unrelated values.

Question — Valuation of shares

Shares in an unquoted company are held as follows.

	Number of shares
Husband (H)	4,000
Wife (W)	2,000
Son (S)	750
Shares given by H to a charity by an exempt transfer eight years ago (and still owned by the charity)	3,250
	10,000

Estimated values for different sizes of shareholding are as follows.

Number of shares	*Pence per share*	£
750	60	450
2,000	90	1,800
4,000	130	5,200
7,250	200	14,500
9,250	250	23,125

What is the value of H's holding, taking into account related property?

Answer

There are three related holdings.

	Shares
H	4,000
W	2,000
Charity	3,250
	9,250

The value of H's 4,000 shares is $\frac{4{,}000}{9{,}250} \times$ £23,125 = £10,000 (ie 250 pence × 4,000 shares).

If in the above exercise H gives away half of his holding to his son, the transfer of value is as follows.

	£
Holding before transfer (as above)	10,000
Less holding after transfer	
$\frac{2{,}000}{7{,}250} \times$ £14,500	(4,000)
Transfer of value	6,000

If H transferred all his shares the value transferred would be £10,000 (no holding after, so no value in the calculation performed above).

Note that if a transferor owns some shares in a company, and other shares in the same company are held in an immediate post-death trust in which he has the initial interest in possession, the transferor's percentage holding for valuation purposes includes the shares in the trust. This is not under the related property rules, but because the life tenant of such a trust is treated as owning the property in the trust.

2 Business property relief (BPR)

FAST FORWARD

BPR can reduce the values of assets by 100% or 50%. However, there are strict conditions, which are largely intended to prevent people near death from obtaining the reliefs by investing substantial sums in businesses.

2.1 Business property

BPR is applied to the value of relevant business property transferred, to prevent large tax liabilities arising on transfers of businesses.

Relevant business property is:

(a) Property consisting of a **business or an interest in a business** (such as a partnership share)

(b) **Securities of a company which are unquoted and which** (alone or with other securities or unquoted shares) **gave the transferor control of the company** immediately before the transfer (control may be achieved by taking into account related property)

(c) **Any unquoted shares** (not securities) **in a company**

(d) **Shares in or securities of a company which are quoted and which** (alone or with other such shares or securities) **gave the transferor control of the company** immediately before the transfer (control may be achieved by taking into account related property)

(e) **Any land or building, machinery or plant which**, immediately before the transfer, **was used wholly or mainly for the purposes of a business carried on by a company of which the transferor then had control, or by a partnership of which he was then a partner**

(f) As in (e) where the asset was used in a business carried on by the transferor and was settled property in which he was then beneficially entitled to an interest in possession.

Shares or securities on the AIM count as unquoted.

The reliefs available are percentage reductions in the value transferred: 100% for assets within Paragraph (a), (b) or (c) above, and 50% for assets within Paragraph (d), (e) or (f) above.

2.2 Conditions for BPR

BPR is only available if the relevant business property:

(a) was owned by the transferor for at least the two years preceding the transfer, or

(b) replaced other relevant business property (which includes agricultural property used in a farming business) where the combined period of ownership of both sets of property was at least two out of the last five years. In this situation relief is given on the lower of the values of the two sets of property.

If the property was inherited, it is deemed to have been owned from the date of the death. If it was inherited (on death) from the transferor's spouse or civil partner, the transferor is deemed also to have owned it for the period the spouse or civil partner owned it.

BPR is still available even if the transferor cannot fulfil either of the two year ownership criteria if when he acquired the property it was eligible for BPR and either the previous or the current transfer was made on death.

2.3 Additional conditions for BPR on lifetime transfers

If BPR is claimed either:

(a) where there is a PET made during an individual's lifetime which becomes chargeable following the donor's death in the next seven years, or

(b) where additional inheritance tax is payable following death within seven years of a chargeable lifetime transfer,

then two further conditions must be fulfilled.

(a) The original property must be owned by the donee from the date of its receipt from the donor to the date of the donor's death, or the donee's death if earlier. This condition is fulfilled if the donee disposed of the property but reinvested all of the disposal proceeds in replacement property within three years of the disposal.

(b) The (original or replacement) property must comprise relevant business property (ignoring the two year rule and including agricultural property used in a farming business) at the date of the donor's death, or the donee's death if earlier. However, this condition does not apply if there has been no replacement and the asset transferred was shares or securities quoted at the time of the transfer.

2.4 Non-qualifying businesses

BPR is not available if the business consists wholly or mainly of:

(a) Dealing in securities, stocks and shares (except for discount houses and market makers on the Stock Exchange or on LIFFE)

(b) Dealing in land or buildings

(c) Making or holding investments (including land which is let)

Shares in holding companies, where the subsidiaries have activities which would qualify shares in them for BPR, are eligible for relief.

2.5 Excepted assets

Relevant business property excludes assets which were neither used wholly or mainly for the purposes of the business in the two years preceding the transfer nor required at the time of the transfer for future use in the business.

For shares or securities in a company, the value which we compute BPR on (at 100% or 50%) is the total value × the company's relevant business property/the company's total assets before deducting liabilities.

2.6 Contracts for sale

BPR is not available if at the date of transfer there is a binding contract for the sale of a business or an interest in a business, unless the sale is to a company which will continue the business and the consideration is wholly or mainly shares or securities in the company.

BPR is not available if at the date of the transfer there is a binding contract for the sale of shares or securities of a company unless the sale is for the purpose of reconstruction or amalgamation.

If any other relevant business property is subject to a binding contract for sale, BPR is not available on it at all.

Partnership agreements often contain a buy/sell clause under which surviving partners must buy a deceased partner's share in the partnership. HMRC regard such a clause as a binding contract for sale which disentitles the deceased partner to BPR. However, neither an accruer clause whereby the deceased partner's share accrues to the surviving partners, nor an option for the surviving partners to buy the deceased partner's share is regarded as binding contract for sale. This means that from a tax planning point of view the later types of arrangement should be used.

Question — BPR

On 31 July 2006 relevant business property valued at £16,800 is transferred in a CLT. Assuming that the 2005/06 and 2006/07 annual exemptions have not been used what will the chargeable transfer be if:

(a) The property consists of unquoted shares?
(b) The property consists of land used by a company in which the transferor has a controlling interest?
(c) The property consists of quoted shares which formed part of a 20% interest before the transfer?

Answer

		(a)	(b)	(c)
		£	£	£
Value transferred		16,800	16,800	16,800
Less BPR		(16,800)	(8,400)	0
		0	8,400	16,800
Less AE:	2006/07		(3,000)	(3,000)
	2005/06 b/f		(3,000)	(3,000)
Chargeable transfer		0	2,400	10,800

Question

BPR and related property

J had shares in a quoted trading company, J plc. The shares in the company were held as follows.

	%
J	40
J's wife	30
Other unconnected persons	30
	100

The shareholdings have been unchanged since 1987. On 1 May 2006 J gave a 30% holding to his son. The values of the shares in May 2006 were agreed as follows.

	£
70% holding	1,600,000
40% holding	900,000
30% holding	840,000
10% holding	200,000

J, who had made a previous chargeable lifetime transfer of £300,000 in 2000, died in January 2007.

Calculate the IHT arising on the gift of the shares, if

(i) J's son still holds the shares in January 2007

(ii) J's son sells the shares in June 2006 and retains the cash proceeds.

Answer

No IHT arises when the gift was made, because it was a PET. It becomes chargeable as a result of J's death within seven years as follows.

PET – May 2006

(i) If J's son still holds the shares, BPR at 50% is available to reduce the chargeable transfer:

		£
Before:	$\frac{40\%}{40\%+30\%} \times £1,600,000$	914,286
After:	$\frac{10\%}{10\%+30\%} \times £900,000$	(225,000)
		689,286
Less	BPR at 50% (quoted company)	(344,643)
		344,643
Less:	AE 2006/07	(3,000)
	AE 2005/06 b/f	(3,000)
Chargeable transfer		338,643

Gross chargeable transfers in the seven years before May 2006 amount to £300,000. This means none of the £Nil band remains and IHT payable on death amounts to:

IHT at 40% = £135,457

(ii) If J's son does not hold the shares on J's death, BPR is not available to reduce the value of the chargeable transfer:

		£
Transfer (see above)		689,286
Less:	Annual exemption (2006/07)	(3,000)
	Annual exemption (2005/06)	(3,000)
Chargeable transfer		683,286

IHT @ 40% = £273,314

3 Agricultural property relief (APR)

FAST FORWARD

APR usually reduces a transfer by 100% of agricultural value of agricultural property.

3.1 Agricultural property

APR is available on the agricultural value of agricultural property.

Agricultural property is agricultural land or pasture (including short rotation coppice) situated in the UK, the Channel Islands or the Isle of Man and includes woodland and any building used in connection with the intensive rearing of livestock or fish where the occupation of the woodland or building is ancillary to that of the land or pasture. It also includes cottages, farm buildings and farm houses of a character appropriate to the property.

The agricultural value is the value the property would have if it were subject to a perpetual covenant prohibiting its use other than as agricultural property.

APR works like BPR in reducing the value being transferred by a certain percentage before any exemptions. APR is given before BPR and double relief cannot be obtained on the agricultural value. But if the non-agricultural part of the value of the property meets the relevant business property conditions then BPR will be available on that value.

The percentage reduction in agricultural value is, in general, 100%. (It is 50% on some land held under pre-September 1995 tenancies.)

3.2 Conditions for relief

For relief to apply the transferor must have either:

(a) **Occupied the property for the purpose of agriculture for the two years before the transfer**, or

(b) **Owned the property for at least the seven years before the transfer**, during which it must have been occupied for the purposes of agriculture by either the transferor or somebody else.

If a company controlled by the transferor occupies the property the transferor is treated as occupying it. A farmhouse which is being redecorated, renovated or altered is not treated as though it is occupied for agricultural purposes.

If the property transferred had replaced other agricultural property then the condition will be satisfied provided that:

(a) The transferor has occupied the properties for the purposes of agriculture for at least two out of the last five years, or

(b) The transferor has owned the properties (and somebody has occupied them for agricultural purposes) for at least seven out of the last ten years.

If agricultural properties have been replaced the APR will apply only to the lowest of the values of the various properties considered.

If the property transferred was acquired on the death of the transferor's spouse or civil partner then the period of ownership or occupation of the first spouse or civil partner can count towards the seven years or the two years required. If the property transferred was acquired on the death of somebody else the transferor will be deemed to own it from the date of death and if he subsequently occupies it, to have occupied it from the date of death.

3.3 Additional conditions for lifetime transfers

If APR is claimed either:

(a) where a PET is made during an individual's lifetime and it becomes chargeable following the donor's death in the next seven years, or

(b) where additional inheritance tax is payable following a death within seven years of a chargeable lifetime transfer,

then two further conditions must be fulfilled.

(c) The property must be owned by the donee from the date of the transfer to the date of the donor's death (or the donee's death if earlier). This condition is fulfilled if the donee disposed of the property but reinvested all of the disposal proceeds in replacement property within three years of the disposal.

(d) The (original or replacement) property must still be agricultural property immediately prior to the donor's death (or the donee's death if earlier) and must have been occupied as such since the original transfer (ignoring any gap between a disposal and the acquisition of replacement property).

3.4 Land and buildings dedicated to wildlife habitats

Land dedicated under the Government's Habitat Schemes and any related buildings are treated as though they are occupied for agricultural purposes. This means that such land and buildings qualify for APR in the same way as other land or buildings which are occupied for agricultural purposes.

3.5 Shares in companies owning agricultural property

If a company owns agricultural property and satisfies the occupation or ownership conditions above then APR is available in respect of the agricultural value that can be attributed to shares or securities transferred by an individual who controls the company. The shares or securities must have been held by the transferor for the relevant periods (two years or seven years).

Question — Farming companies

On 13 June 2006 K gives his shares in Farm Ltd to his son. K owns 65% of the shares in issue and the value of this holding has been agreed at £400,000. K has owned the shares for nine years. The company has owned and occupied farmland (for agricultural purposes) for the last eight years. The agricultural value of this land represents 20% of the total value of the company's net assets.

Calculate the chargeable transfer assuming that K dies on 14 July 2007 and the son still holds the shares at the date of his father's death.

Answer

	£
Value of holding	400,000
Less: APR 100% × 20% × £400,000	(80,000)
BPR 100% × 80% × £400,000	(320,000)
Chargeable transfer	0

3.6 Contracts for sale

APR is not available if, at the time of the transfer, a binding contract for sale of the agricultural property exists unless the sale is either to a company with the consideration being wholly or mainly shares or securities which will give the transferor control, or is to enable a reorganisation or reconstruction of a farming company.

4 The death estate

FAST FORWARD

When someone dies, we must bring together all their assets to find their estate at death. Certain sales after death may lead to adjustments in the value of the chargeable estate.

4.1 Composition of death estate

An individual's death estate consists of all property to which he was beneficially entitled immediately before death, with the exception of excluded property. The estate also includes anything acquired as a result of death, for example the proceeds of a life assurance policy.

The estate at death may include:

(a) **Free estate** (everything not within (b) or (c) below).

(b) **Property given subject to a reservation**. This is property given away before death, but with strings attached. For example, someone might give away a house but continue to live in it.

(c) **Settled property which is the subject of an immediate post-death interest**. Settled property of this type is treated, for IHT purposes, as though the life tenant owned the trust capital. Also included is settled property which is the subject of a life interest which was held at 22 March 2006 (see trusts chapter).

It is important to keep the three classes of property separate since the primary responsibility for payment of tax depends on the type of property.

(a) **Tax on the free estate is payable by the personal representatives** (executors or administrators).

(b) **Tax on property given subject to a reservation is payable by the person in possession of the property.**

(c) **Tax on settled property is payable by the trustees.**

The whole of the death estate will be chargeable to tax, subject to reliefs (such as BPR and APR) and any exemptions which may be available on death. In particular, if property passes to the deceased person's spouse (outright or to a trust in which the spouse has an immediate post-death interest) this will be an exempt transfer. A transfer to any other person eg. children, will be chargeable to IHT, whether this is made outright or to any type of trust.

In order to calculate the tax on the death estate, use the following steps:

Step 1 Look back seven years from the date of death to see if any chargeable lifetime transfers have been made. If so, these transfers use up the nil rate band available for the death estate. Work out the value of any nil rate band still available.

Step 2 Compute the gross value of the death estate (see further below).

Step 3 Any part of the death estate covered by the nil rate band is taxed at 0%. Any part of the death estate not covered by the nil rate band is charged at 40%. Deduct relevant reliefs from the death tax (eg quick succession relief – see below)

Step 4 Where relevant divide the tax due between personal representatives, the person in possession of a gift subject to a reservation and trustees.

Usually, it will not be necessary to consider grossing up. The situation where it will be needed is dealt with below.

Question — Tax on death estate

Laura dies on 1 August 2006, leaving a free estate valued at £350,000 to a discretionary trust for her children.

Laura had an immediate post-death interest in a trust set up on the death of her father. The capital value of the trust was £50,000 on 1 August 2006 and passed to her brother.

Laura had made a transfer of value of £123,000 to her sister on 11 September 2005. The amount stated is after all exemptions and reliefs.

Compute the tax payable on Laura's death and the amounts payable by her personal representatives and the trustees of her father's will trust.

Answer

Death tax

Note: There is no death tax on the PET which becomes chargeable as a result of Laura's death as it is within the nil rate band at her death. However, it will use up part of the nil rate band, as shown below.

Step 1 Lifetime transfer of value of £123,000 in seven years before 1 August 2006 (transfers after 1 August 1999). Nil rate band of £(285,000 – 123,000) = £162,000 available.

Step 2 Value of death estate is £(350,000 + 50,000) = £400,000.

Step 3

	IHT
	£
£162,000 × 0%	0
£238,000 × 40%	95,200
£400,000	95,200

Step 4 Tax payable by personal representatives

$\frac{350,000}{400,000} \times £95,200 =$ £83,300

Tax payable by trustees of father's will trust

$\frac{50,000}{400,000} \times £95,200 =$ £11,900

The computation of an individual's chargeable estate at death should be set out as follows (although the order of assets within each section is not important).

	£	£
Free estate		
Personality		
Stocks and shares		X
Insurance policy proceeds		X
Personal chattels		X
Cash (including any accrued deposit interest net of income tax)		X
Accrued income from interest in possession trusts (net of income tax)		X
		X
Less debts due by deceased	X	
funeral expenses	X	
		(X)
		X
Realty		
Freehold property (keep UK and foreign property separate)	X	
Less mortgages and accrued interest	(X)	
		X
Net free estate		X
Settled property		
Interest in possession trust property	X	
Less accrued income (gross)	(X)	
		X
Gifts with reservation		X
Chargeable estate		X

4.2 Accrued interest due to a deceased life tenant

Where the deceased has a life interest which is to be included in his estate, the value of his interest will be the market value of the property comprised in the trust (or of a percentage of that property, corresponding to his share of the trust's income), **together with accrued interest due to him**.

As securities are valued cum interest the accrued income to the date of death included in the cum interest value should be shown as a deduction from the settled property and as an addition to the free estate. The deduction is gross, but the addition is net of 20% income tax.

Question — **Interest in possession trusts**

P, who has an immediate post-death interest in the Q will trust, died on 30 April 2006. The Q will trust fund comprised £10,000 12% stock quoted at 109-113. Interest payment dates are 30 June and 31 December. The trustees also held cash of £700 of which £300 was due to the life tenant. P's free estate was £20,000 excluding amounts due from the trust.

For inheritance tax purposes what are the values of:

(a) The trust, and
(b) The free estate?

Answer

(a) *The Q will trust*

	£	£
Cash		700
£10,000 12% Stock at 110		11,000
		11,700
Less: four months of interest £10,000 × 12% × 4/12	400	
cash due to the life tenant	300	
		(700)
		11,000

(b) *The free estate*

	£	£
Sundry assets		20,000
Add amounts due from trust: income accrual (£400 × 80%) Note 1	320	
cash	300	
		620
		20,620

Note 1. A tax liability of 20% must be paid by the trust on this £400 of interest income so only 80% (£320) is due to be paid out to the beneficiary (ie life tenant).

4.3 Debts and funeral expenses

The rules on debts are as follows.

(a) Only debts incurred by the deceased bona fide and for full consideration may be deducted.

(b) The debts must be such as an executor could pay without making himself personally liable for a misuse of the assets of the estate. Thus gaming debts are not deductible but statute barred debts are, provided the executor pays them.

(c) **Debts incurred by the deceased but payable after the death may be deducted** but the amount should be discounted because of the future date of payment.

(d) Rent and similar amounts which accrue day by day should be accrued up to the date of death.

(e) **Taxes to the date of death may be deducted** as they are a liability imposed by law.

(f) **Debts incurred by the executor are not allowed.**

(g) **If a debt is charged on a specific property it is deductible primarily from that property**: thus a mortgage on freehold property is deductible from that freehold.

(h) Debts contracted abroad must first be deducted from non-UK property (whether or not the value of that property is chargeable to inheritance tax). If the foreign debts exceed the value of the foreign property the excess is allowed as a deduction from UK property provided it represents debts recoverable in the UK.

Reasonable funeral expenses may be deducted.

(a) What is reasonable depends on the deceased's condition in life.
(b) Reasonable costs of mourning for the family and servants are allowed.
(c) **The cost of a tombstone is deductible.**

Question — The estate at death

Z died on 19 June 2006. His estate consisted of the following.

10,000 shares in A plc, quoted at 84p – 89p with bargains marked at 85p, 87p and 90p

8,000 shares in B plc, quoted ex div at 111p – 115p. A net dividend of 4p per share was paid on 21 July 2005

Freehold property valued at £150,000 subject to a mortgage of £45,040

Liabilities and funeral expenses amounted to £2,450.

Z had an immediate post-death interest in the C will trust. The assets of the trust were valued at £86,000 at the date of death including gross accrued interest due to Z of £800.

Z had made a chargeable lifetime transfer of £295,000 in July 2001. Calculate the IHT liabilities on the estate at death.

Answer

	£	£
Free estate		
Personality	£	£
A plc shares		
10,000 at lower of 85.25p and 87.5p		
10,000 × 85.25p		8,525
B plc		
8,000 × 112p	8,960	
Net dividend 8,000 × 4p	320	
		9,280
Accrued interest from C will trust (£800 × 80%)		640
		18,445
Less debts and funeral expenses		(2,450)
		15,995
Realty		
Freehold property	150,000	
Less mortgage	(45,040)	
		104,960
Net free estate		120,955
Settled property		
C will trust assets £(86,000 – 800)		85,200
Total chargeable estate		206,155

Chargeable transfers in the seven years prior to death exceeded the £Nil band, so IHT on the death estate is £206,155 at 40% = £82,462.

The IHT payable by Z's executors is $\frac{120,955}{206,155} \times £82,462 = £48,382$

The IHT payable by the trustees of the C will trust is $\frac{85,200}{206,155} \times £82,462 = £34,080$

5 Quick succession relief (QSR)

FAST FORWARD

Quick succession relief applies where there are two charges to IHT within five years.

If a person dies shortly after receiving property by way of a chargeable transfer the same property will be taxed twice within a short space of time: it will be taxed because of the original chargeable transfer and it will be taxed again as part of the estate of the deceased transferee. QSR reduces the tax on the estate in such circumstances.

The tax on the estate is calculated normally. A credit is then given as follows.

$$\text{Tax paid on first transfer} \times \frac{\text{net transfer}}{\text{gross transfer}} \times \text{percentage}$$

The percentage to use is as follows.

Period between the transfer and the death of the transferee	*Relief*
	%
1 year or less	100
1-2 years	80
2-3 years	60
3-4 years	40
4-5 years	20
Over 5 years	0

If the period is precisely two years, 80% relief is given, and so on.

QSR is also available on an immediate post-death interest in a will trust if the life interest terminates within five years of the death, the percentage relief depending on the period between the charges.

Question QSR

Oscar died on 29 September 2006 leaving an estate valued at £347,000 to his son. Oscar had received £28,000 gross in July 2002 from his uncle's estate. IHT of £4,200 had been payable by Oscar on this legacy.

Calculate the IHT payable on Oscar's estate, assuming he has made no lifetime transfers.

Answer

	£
IHT on £347,000 (£285,000 @ 0% + £62,000 @ 40%)	24,800
Less QSR: £4,200 × (23,800/28,000) × 20%	(714)
IHT payable on Oscar's estate	24,086

6 Post mortem reliefs

FAST FORWARD

If there is a specific gift of UK property and the residue of the estate is exempt, the specific gift must be grossed up.

6.1 Quoted investments sold within 12 months after death

Personal representatives and other persons (including trustees) accounting for the tax due on the estate of a deceased person may **claim a reduction in the value of the estate if they sell quoted investments within 12 months of death and the sale proceeds are less than the value of the investments at the time**

of death. If a claim is made all the securities sold from the free estate (where the claim is made by the personal representatives) or from the trust concerned (where the claim is made by the trustees) within 12 months have to be revalued in this way, not just those sold at a loss. The net loss is deducted from the value of the property at death, and the inheritance tax on the whole estate is recomputed.

The claim can be made in respect of shares and other securities quoted on a recognised stock exchange at the date of death, or units in an authorised unit trust or shares in a common investment fund.

The loss is the difference between the probate value and the gross sale proceeds (or, if higher, the best proceeds which could have been obtained) before taking into account any expenses of sale.

If further quoted investments are purchased during the period between death and two months after the date of the last sale in the 12 month period the loss on sale is reduced by

$$\frac{\text{Amount reinvested}}{\text{Gross sale proceeds}} \times \text{loss}$$

The amount reinvested and the gross sale proceeds equal the cash spent and cash received for the shares. If extra cash is used for purchase expenses or any of the sale proceeds are used for expenses on sale, ignore this in both the numerator and the denominator.

Where there has been a takeover the substituted securities are treated as being the same as the original ones. Where further payments have added to the holding at death (for example payment for a rights issue) these amounts are added to the value at death when calculating the loss, if any, on sale.

If quoted investments still held by the personal representatives or trustees are cancelled and not replaced within 12 months of death, they are treated for the purposes of this relief as sold for £1 immediately before the time of cancellation.

If quoted investments are still held by the personal representatives or trustees 12 months after death, and at that time dealings in them are suspended then for the purposes of this relief they are treated as sold for their value at that time, but only if it is lower than their value at death.

Question — Loss on sale of shares

An estate included quoted shares valued at £60,000. Six months after death the executor sold the shares for £39,000 after expenses of £1,000. He reinvested £15,000 one month later in further quoted shares. What is the loss on sale to be deducted from the value at death?

Answer

	£
Probate value	60,000
Less gross proceeds	(40,000)
Loss on sale	20,000
Reduced by	
$\frac{15,000}{40,000} \times$ £20,000	(7,500)
Loss on sale	12,500

Therefore a value of £(60,000 – 12,500) = £47,500 is brought into the inheritance tax computation on death for the shares owned at death.

6.2 Land and buildings sold within three years of death or in the fourth year after death

Where the deceased's estate includes an interest in land which is sold within three years after death by the person liable for the tax attributable to the interest in land (eg the executor), **a claim may be made to reduce the value on death to the gross sale proceeds** (or, if greater, the best proceeds which could have been obtained). The proceeds are before selling expenses, but without adding purchaser's costs, such as stamp duty.

If the interest in land at the time of death was a short leasehold, the value at death is reduced using a table of percentages (as for CGT) before deducting the selling price in order to compute the loss.

If a claim is made, then all interests in land sold within three years of death by the same person acting in the same capacity must be considered. Thus any gains on the sale of some land from the estate must be offset against losses from the sale of other land.

Any gains or losses where the difference between the original death value and the selling price is less than £1,000 and less than 5% of the value at death are ignored.

Where reinvestment in land takes place at any time between death and four months after the last sale within the three year period, the relief is reduced by

$$\frac{\text{Amount reinvested}}{\text{Gross sale proceeds}} \times \text{loss}$$

As for a sale of shares exclude expenses from both the numerator and the denominator.

If land is sold by the person liable for the tax (such as the executor) in the fourth year following death, for less than its value at death, it is treated for the purposes of this relief as sold within three years after death. The loss is aggregated with other losses and profits and the net loss is then reduced for reinvestments, but purchases of land are ignored unless they occur between death and four months after the last sale within *three* years after death. Sales of land at a profit in the fourth year after death are ignored.

Question — Land sold after death

Q died on 26 May 2006 leaving a chargeable estate valued at £488,000 to his children. Included in the estate was land as follows.

Location	*Value*
	£
Scotland	130,000
Wales	100,000
England	26,000

On 4 January 2007 the executors of Q's estate sold the land in Scotland for £115,000 (after costs of £2,500). On 7 June 2007 they sold the land in England for £25,400 (after costs of £800).

On 1 March 2007 the executors purchased further land in Wales at a cost of £48,000 (including costs of £750).

Calculate the IHT originally payable on the estate, and the repayment due as a result of the sales of land. Assume that Q had made no lifetime transfers.

Answer

IHT on an estate of £488,000 is £(488,000 – 285,000) × 40% = £81,200.

Sales of land: the calculation of the deductible loss

	£
Land in Scotland	
Loss (£130,000 – £117,500)	12,500
Land in England	
Ignore because the difference between the probate value and the gross proceeds (ie £200) is less than £1,000 and less than 5% of the probate value	
Less restriction on loss	
$\frac{48,000 - 750}{117,500} \times £12,500$	(5,027)
Deductible loss	7,473

The deductible loss will reduce the chargeable estate by £7,473 which will give rise to a repayment of IHT of £7,473 × 40% = £2,989.

6.3 Property valued with related property but sold within three years after death

Where property has been valued on a transfer on death using the related property provisions and is sold (other than in conjunction with the sale of any of the related property) **at arm's length to an unconnected purchaser within three years for less than the valuation using related property, a claim for relief may be made.**

Relief is given only where the seller is the person to whom the property passed on death or is the deceased's personal representative.

The relief is given by valuing the relevant property ignoring the related property rules. The property sold is valued as at the date of death, so the new value may not equal the proceeds of sale.

A claim for this relief could eliminate business property relief on securities or on quoted shares, since if related property is ignored control of a company might be lost.

7 Grossing up gifts on death

Grossing up applies to CLTs when the donor pays the IHT. **We must also gross up on a death when there is a specific gift of UK property, and the residue of the estate is exempt. The reason for this is that specific gifts of UK property do not bear their own tax. Instead this must be borne by the residue of the estate. Specific gifts of foreign property, on the other hand, do bear their own tax and do not need to be grossed up.**

Do not gross up specific gifts if the whole estate is chargeable. In such cases, work out IHT as normal. Specific gifts of UK property are given to the heirs in full (unless there is not enough residue to pay the IHT), and the IHT on those gifts comes out of the residue. In this case, any amount over the nil rate band is charged at 40 (rate of tax)/60 (100 minus the rate of tax).

Question

Specific gifts and exempt residue

R dies on 29 May 2006 leaving an estate valued at £451,000. Included in this is UK property valued at £359,000 which he leaves to his son. He leaves the residue of the estate to his wife.

Calculate the IHT liability arising on death assuming R has made no lifetime transfers.

Answer

The specific gift to the son does not bear its own tax. It is a net gift which must be grossed up:

	IHT
	£
£285,000 @ 0%	0
£ 74,000 @ 40/60	49,333
£359,000	49,333

The gross transfer is £(359,000 + 49,333) = £408,333.

Check tax £(408,333 – 285,000) = £123,333 @ 40% = £49,333.

The son receives £359,000, HMRC receives £49,333.

The residue available to the wife is £451,000 – £408,333 = £42,667.

This calculation would not have applied if:

(a) The residue of the estate had been chargeable rather than exempt, in which case IHT would have been calculated on a gross chargeable estate of £451,000 in the normal way, or

(b) The will had left £92,000 to the wife and the residue to the son. In that case, the son would have received £359,000 less tax of £(359,000 – 285,000) × 40% = £29,600, giving the son a net amount of £329,400, and the wife would have received £92,000.

Chapter roundup

- There are special rules for valuing particular kinds of assets, such as quoted shares and securities. The related property rules prevent artificial reductions in values.
- BPR and APR can reduce the values of assets by 100% or 50%. However, there are strict conditions, which are largely intended to prevent people near death from obtaining the reliefs by investing substantial sums in businesses and in farms.
- When someone dies, we must bring together all their assets to find their estate at death. Certain sales after death may lead to adjustments in the value of the chargeable estate.
- Quick succession relief applies where there are two charges to IHT within five years.
- If there is a specific gift of UK property and the residue of the estate is exempt, the specific gift must be grossed up.

Quick quiz

1 How are quoted securities valued?

2 What is related property?

3 What rate of BPR is given on a controlling shareholding in

(a) a quoted trading company, and
(b) an unquoted trading company?

4 What periods of ownership or occupation are required to obtain agricultural property relief?

5 How is quick succession relief calculated?

6 Sonia dies leaving the following debts:

(a) Grocery bill
(b) HM Revenue and Customs – income tax to death
(c) Mortgage on house
(d) Gambling debt

Which are deductible against her death estate and why?

7 In respect of which shares sold after death may an adjustment to their value be claimed?

8 How is the relief for land sold after death adjusted for purchases?

9 What relief is available for property valued with related property sold after death?

Answers to quick quiz

1 The value is the lower of:

- the value on the quarter up basis (bid price plus 1/4 of the difference between the bid and offer prices).
- the average of highest and lowest marked bargains for the day (ignoring special price bargains).

2 Related property is property:

- comprised in the estate of the transferor's spouse (including interest in possession trusts), or
- which has been given to a charity, political party, national public body or housing association as an exempt transfer by either spouse and still is, or has been within the past five years, been the property of the body it was given to.

3 (a) 50%
(b) 100%

4 For APR the transferor must have either:

- occupied the property for the purpose of agriculture for two years before the transfer, or
- owned the property for at least seven years before the transfer during which it was occupied for the purposes of agriculture by the transferor or another person.

5 QSR is calculated as:

$$\text{Tax paid on first transfer} \times \frac{\text{net transfer}}{\text{gross transfer}} \times \%$$

6 (a) grocery bill – deductible as incurred for full consideration
(b) income tax to death – deductible as imposed by law
(c) mortgage – deductible, will be set against value of house primarily
(d) gambling debt – not allowable as executor be liable for misuse of estate assets if paid

7 A claim to adjust the value of shares post death may be made if the shares are quoted on a recognised stock exchange at the date of death and sold within 12 months of death at a loss compared to death value.

8 The adjustment for purchases is that the relief is reduced by:

$$\frac{\text{Amount reinvested}}{\text{Gross sale proceeds}} \times \text{loss}$$

9 Related property sold within three years of death at a loss treated as valued on an unrelated property basis.

Now try the question below from the Exam Question Bank

Number	Level	Marks	Time
Q17	Examination	25	45 mins

18

Inheritance tax: additional aspects

Introduction

In this chapter, we look at overseas aspects, including relief where property is subject both to IHT and to a similar tax abroad. We also look at two important sets of anti-avoidance provisions. The rules on gifts with reservation prevent people from avoiding IHT by pretending to give property away before death while in fact retaining rights over it. The rules on associated operations allow HMRC to defeat tax avoidance schemes which rely on breaking down one transaction into several artificial steps.

We also consider how a will can be altered and, finally, we look at the administration and payment of IHT.

Topic list	Syllabus references
1 Overseas aspects	1(j)
2 Gifts with reservation	1(j)
3 Associated operations	1(j)
4 Altering dispositions made on death	1(f), 1(i)
5 The administration of IHT	1(j)
6 The payment of IHT	1(j)

1 Overseas aspects

1.1 Domicile

FAST FORWARD

Non-UK assets of individuals not domiciled in the UK are not subject to IHT. Because of the value of this exemption some individuals not UK domiciled under general law are treated as UK domiciled for IHT purposes.

For individuals not domiciled in the UK, only transfers of UK assets are within the charge to IHT, and even some assets within the UK are excluded property.

Domicile for IHT has the same meaning as in general law, namely **the country of one's permanent home**.

Also, a person is also deemed to be domiciled in the UK for IHT purposes:

(a) If he has been **resident in the UK for at least 17 out of the 20 tax years** ending with the year in which any chargeable transfer is made. The term 'residence' has the same meaning as for income tax (see earlier in this Text).

(b) **For 36 months after ceasing to be domiciled in the UK** under general law.

1.2 The location of assets

For someone not domiciled in the UK, the location of assets is clearly important:

(a) **Land and buildings**, freehold or leasehold, are in the country in which they are **physically situated**.

(b) **A debt** is in the **country of residence of the debtor** unless it is a debt evidenced by a deed, when the debt is where the deed is. Judgement debts are situated wherever the judgement is recorded.

(c) **Life policies** are in the **country where the proceeds are payable**.

(d) **Registered shares and securities** are in the **country where they are registered**, or where they would normally be dealt with in the ordinary course of business.

(e) **Bearer securities** are **where the certificate of title is located** at the time of transfer.

(f) **Bank accounts** are at the **branch** where the account is kept.

(g) **An interest in a partnership** is where the partnership **business is carried on**.

(h) **Goodwill** is where the **business** to which it is attached is **carried on**.

(i) **Tangible property** is at its **physical location**.

(j) Property held in trust follows the above rules regardless of the rules of the trust or residence of the trustees.

1.3 Excluded property

The following are **excluded property** (in addition to the items covered earlier in this Text).

(a) Property outside the UK if the person beneficially entitled to it is an individual domiciled outside the UK

(b) Settled property outside the UK if the settlor was domiciled outside the UK at the time of making the settlement. This exclusion will not apply if a UK domiciled individual has ever purchased a life interest in that property

(c) Certain British Government securities whose terms of issue provide that they shall be exempt from taxation so long as they are beneficially owned by persons neither domiciled nor ordinarily resident in the UK, so long as they are so owned (the extended IHT definition of UK domicile set out above does not apply). Such Government securities comprised in a trust will also qualify as excluded property if the person entitled to an interest in possession in them is neither domiciled nor ordinarily resident in the UK and (in the case of a discretionary trust) all known potential beneficiaries are neither domiciled nor ordinarily resident

(d) The following savings if held by persons domiciled in the Channel Islands or the Isle of Man (the extended IHT definition of UK domicile set out above does not apply):

(i) War savings certificates
(ii) National savings certificates
(iii) Premium savings bonds
(iv) Deposits with the National Savings Bank or with a trustee savings bank
(v) SAYE savings schemes

(e) Unit trust units or shares in open ended investment companies held by non-UK domiciliaries

In addition, if someone dies when neither domiciled, resident nor ordinarily resident in the UK, a foreign currency account held at a UK bank is ignored in computing his death estate.

1.4 Double taxation relief (DTR)

FAST FORWARD

Double taxation relief may reduce the IHT on assets taxed overseas.

DTR applies to transfers (during lifetime and on death) of assets situated overseas which suffer tax overseas as well as IHT in the UK. Relief may be given under a treaty, but if not then the following rules apply.

DTR is given as a tax credit against the IHT payable on the overseas asset. The amount available as a tax credit is the lower of the foreign tax liability and the IHT (at the average rate) on the asset.

Question — DTR

P died on 15 October 2006 leaving a chargeable estate of £282,000. Included in this total is a foreign asset valued at £80,000 in respect of which foreign taxes of £20,000 were paid.

Calculate the IHT payable on the estate assuming that P made a gross chargeable lifetime transfer of £147,000 one year before his death.

Answer

	£
IHT on chargeable estate of £282,000	
(available nil rate band £(285,000 – 147,000) = £138,000	57,600
(Average rate: 57,600/282,000 = 20.42553%)	
Less DTR: lower of:	
(a) £20,000	
(b) £80,000 × 20.42553% = £16,340	(16,340)
IHT payable on the estate	41,260

2 Gifts with reservation

FAST FORWARD

The rules on gifts with reservation ensure that gifts which are effectively made on death or within the seven years before death, even though apparently made earlier, are taxed.

There are rules to prevent the avoidance of IHT by the making of gifts with reservation. Without these rules, incomplete lifetime gifts would escape IHT by being PETs but would also reduce the individual's estate at death. The value of the assets could thus escape tax entirely, despite the original owner deriving some benefit from them up to his death.

The obvious example is a gift of a home to the donor's children but with the donor continuing to live in it rent free. Another example is a gift of income-producing assets but with the income continuing to be received by the donor.

Key term

Property given subject to a reservation (**gifts with reservation**) is property where:

(a) Such property is not enjoyed virtually to the entire exclusion of the donor (in the case of land only, also the donor's spouse or civil partner), or

(b) Possession and enjoyment of the property transferred is not bona fide assumed by the donee.

'Virtually to the entire exclusion' would, for example, allow a donor occasional brief stays in a house he had given away without creating a reservation, but spending most weekends in the house would create a reservation.

Where a gift with reservation is made, it is treated in the same way as any other gift at the time it is made (as a PET or a chargeable lifetime transfer, as appropriate). However, special rules apply on the death of the donor.

(a) If the reservation still exists at the date of the donor's death, the asset is included in the donor's estate at its value at that time (not its value at the date the gift was made).

(b) If the reservation ceases within the seven years before death, then the gift is treated as a PET made at the time the reservation ceased. The charge is based on its value at that time. The annual exemption cannot be used against such a PET.

If the gift could be taxed as a PET or CLT when made, as well as taxed under (a) or (b) above, it will be taxed either under (a) or (b), or as a PET or CLT when made (but not both), whichever gives the higher total tax.

There are **exceptions to the gifts with reservation rules** as follows.

(a) A gift will not be treated as being with reservation if **full consideration is given** for any right of occupation or enjoyment retained or assumed by the donor (or his spouse or civil partner, in the case of land), and the property is land or chattels. For example, an individual might give away his house and continue to live in it, but pay a full market rent for doing so.

(b) A gift will not be treated as being with reservation if the circumstances of the donor change in a way that was unforeseen at the time of the original gift and the benefit provided by the donee to the donor only represents reasonable provision for the **care and maintenance of the donor, being an elderly or infirm relative**. This exception only applies to interests in land.

If the gift with reservation rules do not apply **an income tax charge may apply from if individuals have entered into tax planning to reduce their inheritance tax liability** without completely divesting themselves of the asset. **This was covered in Chapter 2.** The transferor may, however, elect that the asset should be treated as remaining within their estate under the gift with reservation rules so that an income tax charge does not arise.

3 Associated operations

FAST FORWARD

Associated operations (eg affecting the same property) are treated as dispositions for IHT.

Key term

Associated operations are:

(a) Two or more operations which affect the same property or one of which affects the property whilst other operations affect other property directly or indirectly representing the property, or

(b) Any two operations, one of which is effected with reference to the other, or with a view to enabling the other to be effected.

All associated operations are considered as one disposition. If a transfer of value has been made it is treated as made at the time of the last operation in the chain of associated operations. For this purpose, if the earlier operations themselves constituted transfers of value then the value transferred by these is deducted from the value transferred by all associated operations taken together.

The associated operations rule is a powerful weapon against schemes to avoid inheritance tax by using several transactions instead of one.

For example, trustees might own some valuable paintings. They could give D, an individual, custody of the paintings for several years, on normal commercial terms (so that there would be no gratuitous intent). The trustees' interest in the paintings would be reduced in value, because someone else had custody of them. The trustees could then give an interest in the paintings to D's son. The value of what was given to D's son would be lower than it would otherwise have been, saving tax. HMRC would, however, retrieve the tax by treating the arrangement with D and the gift to his son as associated operations *(Macpherson and another v CIR 1988).*

4 Altering dispositions made on death

FAST FORWARD

A variation or disclaimer can be used to vary a will after death. This can have IHT and CGT effects.

There are **two main ways in which dispositions on death may be altered**: **by application to the courts, and by means of a voluntary variation** or a disclaimer of a legacy. Application to the courts may be made if the family and dependants of the deceased feel that the will has not made adequate provision for them. Any changes to the will made in this way will be treated for IHT purposes as if made by the deceased when writing his will.

Within two years of a death the terms of a will can be changed by a written instrument, with the change being effective for IHT purposes, either by a variation of the terms of the will made by the persons who benefit or would benefit under the dispositions, or by a disclaimer. The variation or disclaimer will not be treated as a transfer of value. Inheritance tax will be calculated as if the terms contained in the variation replaced those in the will. If a legacy is disclaimed, it will pass under the terms of the will (or possibly under the intestacy rules) to some other person, usually the residuary legatee, and tax will apply as if the will originally directed the legacy to that new recipient.

There is a similar provision for CGT. **If a disclaimer or variation is made in writing within two years of death by the person(s) who benefit under the dispositions, the variation or disclaimer is not a disposal for CGT.** In addition, the assets disposed of will be taken by the new beneficiaries at death value, rather than at the value at the date of the disclaimer or variation, as if the assets had been left directly to those persons by the deceased.

If the beneficiaries making the variation wish the relevant terms of the will to be treated as replaced by the terms of the variation, it is necessary to state this in the variation. The statement can apply for inheritance tax or capital gains tax or both. Where a disclaimer is made, the relevant terms in the will *must* be treated as replaced by the terms of the disclaimer for both IHT and CGT purposes (subject to exceptions listed below), regardless of whether this is stated in the disclaimer or not.

A variation or disclaimer may be of benefit in reducing tax or in securing a fairer distribution of the deceased's estate or both.

These variation and disclaimer provisions do not apply to:

(a) Settled property in which the deceased had an interest in possession.

(b) A variation or disclaimer which is made for a consideration (unless the consideration is a variation or disclaimer of a disposition forming part of the same estate).

They do, however, apply to property which was held jointly and which would therefore pass automatically to the surviving owner regardless of the terms of the will.

Property which is deemed to be included in an estate at the date of death because the deceased made a previous gift with reservation cannot be redirected by a deed of variation in a way which is effective for IHT purposes.

Variations or disclaimers can be made in respect of property passing under the intestacy rules in the same way as for property passing under a will, and with the same IHT and CGT effects.

Exam focus point

A variation is a planning tool to allow a tax inefficient will to be amended to a more tax efficient distribution of the assets. For example instead of leaving say £285,000 of assets to a spouse to pass onto the children when the spouse dies, leave the assets directly to the children.

Although the first will arranges for an exempt transfer to the spouse the nil band is wasted. The assets will thus be added to the surviving spouse's own assets on their death. The varied will utilises the nil band getting those assets to the children IHT free.

5 The administration of IHT

FAST FORWARD

IHT is administered by HM Revenue and Customs (Capital Taxes). The due date for payment depends on the type of event giving rise to the charge to tax.

5.1 Accounts

IHT is administrated by the Capital Taxes Office, part of HMRC's capital and savings section.

There is no system of regular returns as for income tax, corporation tax and capital gains tax. **Instead, any person who is liable for IHT on a transfer is required to deliver an account giving details of the relevant assets and their value. An account delivered by the personal representatives (PRs) of a deceased person has to provide full details of the assets in the death estate. The PRs also have to include in their account details of any chargeable transfers made by the deceased person in the seven years before his death.**

Personal representatives (PRs) must deliver an account within 12 months following the end of the month in which death occurred or, if later, three months following the date when they become PRs. **Where no tax is due, and certain other conditions are satisfied, it is not necessary to submit an account. Estates where no account needs to be submitted are called excepted estates.**

A person responsible for the delivery of an account in relation to a PET that has become chargeable by reason of death, must do so within 12 months following the end of the month in which death occurred unless already reported by the PRs.

(b) Executors *de son tort* (pers
being formally appointed a

(c) Purchasers of land against
to the amount of that charg

On chargeable lifetime transfers the prima

6.2 Due dates

(a) **For chargeable lifetime tra**

(i) **30 April just after th**

(ii) **Six months after the**

Interest (not tax deductible)
payment is made (inclusive

(b) **Tax arising on the free esta
still existed at death) is pa
account**. The time limit for t
occurred or, if earlier, when
after the end of the month w

(c) **All other tax arising on dea
possession, PETs and CLTs
end of the month of death,**

Interest (not taxable) may be obtained on r
to the date of repayment.

Question

Peter died on 10 March 2006. IHT of £375,
£27,300 was repaid on 18 January 2007. C
interest rate of 5% for both overpayments a

Answer

Interest payment to HMRC

Interest runs from 30 September to 9 Nove

Interest = £375,000 × 5% × 41/365 = £2,10

Interest payment by HMRC

The interest paid to HMRC on £27,300 was

The interest payment by HMRC runs from 1
153.33) × 5% × 69/365 = £259.49.

6.3 The instalment option

**IHT on certain property can be paid by ten
donee, or on the transfer of a person's dea
payable due to the death of the donor with**
must have kept the property (or replacemen

ons who interfere in the administration of the estate without personal representatives)

which HMRC charge for inheritance tax has been registered, up
e

ry liability lies with the donor.

nsfers the due date is the later of:

e end of the tax year of the transfer.
end of the month of the transfer.

is payable from the due date to the day before the day on which

te at death (and on gifts with reservation if the reservation able by the personal representatives on delivery of their is is 12 months from the end of the month in which the death probate is obtained. Interest, however, runs from six months hen death occurred.

h (trusts in which the deceased had an interest in with additional tax) is payable within six months from the nd interest runs from this due date.

payments of tax or of interest on tax, from the date of payment

Interest on IHT

)00 on his estate was paid on 10 November 2006, and IHT of lculate the interest payments to and by HMRC, assuming an nd underpayments of IHT.

nber inclusive.

5.16

£27,300 × 5% × 41/365 = £153.33.

) November to 17 January inclusive. It is £(27,300.00 +

equal annual instalments on CLTs where tax is borne by the h estate. The instalment option may also be used for IHT n seven years of making a PET. But in this case, the donee property qualifying for business or agricultural property relief) until the donor's death (or his own, if earlier), and if the property qualifies under (c) or (d) below the shares must remain unquoted until the earlier of the two deaths.

The first instalment is due for payment:

(a) On transfers on death and liabilities arising as a result of death, six months after the end of the month of death.

(b) On chargeable lifetime transfers, on the normal due date.

The instalment option applies only to:

(a) Land and buildings

(b) Shares or securities in a company controlled by the transferor immediately before the transfer

(c) Other holdings in unquoted companies where the tax on them together with that on other instalment property represents at least 20% of the total liability on the estate on a death, or where the tax cannot all be paid at once without undue hardship

(d) Shares in an unquoted company representing at least 10% of the nominal value of the issued share capital and valued for IHT purposes at not less than £20,000

(e) A business or an interest in a business

Shares on the AIM count as unquoted.

No interest is charged on the instalments if paid on the due dates, unless the property is land not attracting agricultural property relief, or is shares or securities of an investment company or a company whose business is wholly or mainly dealing in securities, stocks or shares or land or buildings (but shares in discount houses and in market makers on the Stock Exchange or on LIFFE do qualify for interest free instalments). **For such property, interest is charged on the balance outstanding, from the normal due date for paying tax in one amount.**

If the property is sold, all outstanding tax must then be paid.

6.4 Transfers reported late

Where a transfer is reported late and that transfer was made within the seven years preceding a later transfer, then the tax charge on the earlier transfer (the one reported late) is the liability that would have arisen if the transfer had been reported on time together with the additional IHT that would have been payable on the later transfer if the earlier transfer had been properly taken into account.

Chapter roundup

- Non-UK assets of individuals not domiciled in the UK are not subject to IHT. Because of the value of this exemption some individuals not UK domiciled under general law are treated as UK domiciled for IHT purposes.
- Double taxation relief may reduce the IHT on assets taxed overseas.
- The rules on gifts with reservation ensure that gifts which are effectively made on death or within the seven years before death, even though apparently made earlier, are taxed.
- A variation or disclaimer can be used to vary a will after death. This can have IHT and CGT effects.
- IHT is administered by the Capital Taxes Office of HMRC. The due date for payment depends on the type of event giving rise to the charge to tax.

Quick quiz

1 How is domicile defined for IHT purposes?

2 How is double taxation relief given?

3 Within what time limit must a variation of a will be made?

4 When is lifetime inheritance tax on a chargeable lifetime transfer due for payment?

Answers to quick quiz

1 Domicile for IHT is:

- domicile under the general law (permanent home) and
- deemed domicile in the UK if resident for at least 17 out of 20 tax years, and
- deemed domicile in the UK if ceased to be domiciled under general law in last 36 months

2 DTR is given as a tax credit against IHT payable on the overseas asset to the extent of the lower of foreign tax and the IHT (at average rate) on it.

3 A variation of a will must be made within two years of death.

4 The due date for lifetime tax on a chargeable lifetime transfer is the later of:

(a) 30 April just after the end of the tax year of the transfer, and
(b) 6 months after the end of the month of transfer

Now try the question below from the Exam Question Bank

Number	Level	Marks	Time
Q37	Examination	25	45 mins

This question has been analysed to show you how to approach paper 3.2 exams.

19

Trusts

Introduction

We have seen how income tax, CGT and IHT apply to individuals. In this chapter, we see how all of these taxes apply to trusts.

In a trust, assets are legally owned by the trustees, but for the benefit of the beneficiaries. Special rules are needed to fix the rates of income tax and CGT for trusts. We cannot put income and gains into the trustees' tax computations, because as trustees they are separate from themselves as private individuals. There are also charges to CGT when assets enter or leave trusts, so as to make sure that gains do not escape tax just because assets pass from one person to another via a trust.

Trusts have already been mentioned several times in relation to IHT. In this chapter we summarise the points made so far and look in more detail at the IHT charges on trusts.

1 Income tax and trusts

FAST FORWARD

Income tax may be charged on trust income at 10%, 20%, 22%, 32.5% or at 40%, but when income is paid out the recipient's tax rate is effectively substituted for the trust's tax rate.

1.1 Trusts with an interest in possession

In a trust, assets are legally owned by trustees, but for the benefit of beneficiaries. In a trust with an **interest in possession**, some beneficiaries are entitled to income from the trust assets as it arises. These beneficiaries are often called **life tenants**, as their **right to the income** often lasts until their deaths. **Beneficiaries with a right to a fixed amount of income** each year are called **annuitants**.

The trustees will receive income net of basic rate tax (22%) or (for savings income excluding dividends) lower rate tax (20%) whenever an individual would receive it net. They will be taxed at 22% on untaxed non-savings income (such as income from a property business) and at 20% on untaxed savings income. Dividends will be received with a 10% tax credit; no further tax is payable by the trustees. The trust receives no allowances, none of its income is taxable at 40% and there is no general 10% rate tax band.

The trust's income is deemed to be that of the beneficiary/(ies). Should the beneficiary have unused reliefs or losses, he may claim a repayment of tax deducted (except the 10% tax credit on dividends which is non-repayable). **If, however, he is liable to higher rate tax he will be charged accordingly.**

Payments to annuitants are treated as charges on income paid net of tax at 22%. The trustees must account to HMRC for the tax.

General expenses of trust administration are not allowable when working out the trustees' liability to tax, though expenses related to specific sources of income are (for example, repairs to let property). However, to work out what amounts of dividend, other savings and non-savings income are received by beneficiaries, general expenses are taken into account. Such expenses are set against dividends, then other savings income and then non-savings income.

1.2 Example: interest in possession trusts

A trust receives income from a UK property business of £3,000, net bank interest of £1,600 and dividends of £900 net in 2006/07. Expenses chargeable to income amount to £100. A life tenant is entitled to the income each year. The trust's net income and the life tenant's tax position is as follows:

	£	£
Dividends (net)		900
Less expenses		(100)
		800
Bank interest		1,600
Income from UK property business	3,000	
Less tax at 22%	(660)	
		2,340
Trust's net income, paid to life tenant		4,740

The life tenant is treated as receiving income as follows.

	Net	*Tax suffered*	*Gross*
	£	£	£
Dividends	800	89	889
Other savings income	1,600	400	2,000
Non-savings income	2,340	660	3,000

1.3 Discretionary trusts

Discretionary trusts are those where the trustees may pay out income, or accumulate it in the trust, as they choose. An accumulation and maintenance trust (see later) is a type of discretionary trust for children up to the age of 25. The income tax treatment of an accumulation and maintenance trust is the same as for discretionary trusts.

Discretionary trusts have a basic rate band of £1,000. The first £1,000 of income is taxed at 10% (dividends), 20% (savings income) or 22% (non-savings income). As for individuals, the basic rate band is applied first to non-savings income, then savings income and finally dividends. Many smaller trusts will then have no further tax to pay and will not need to file a tax return.

Any remaining income is taxed at one of two special trust rates. The **rates applicable to such trusts is 40% (on non-dividend income) and 32.5% (on dividend income)**.

Discretionary trusts receive income net of 20% or 22% tax whenever an individual would receive it net. Dividends are received with a 10% tax credit.

Income used to pay trustees' administration expenses is taxed at 10% where such expenses are paid out of dividend income, 20% for other savings income or 22% for non-savings income. The amount of income so used is the amount of the expenses, grossed up at 10%, 20% or 22% as appropriate. Dividend income is used to cover such expenses before other savings income and then non-savings income is used.

Only expenses chargeable to income under general law are allowable in this way. If the trust deed authorises expenses normally chargeable to capital (such as the cost of advice on investments) to be charged to income, such expenses are not allowable.

Question — Discretionary trusts

The Samuel Trust had the following receipts and payments during the year ended 5 April 2007.

Receipts	£
UK rental income receivable	8,700
Dividends received (net)	585
Taxed interest received (net)	80
Payments	
In relation to let property	1,100
Trustees' administration expenses	405

Calculate the income tax payable by the trustees.

Answer

	Non savings income £	Savings income £	Dividend income £	Income used for expenses £
Income available for distribution:				
Income from UK property businesses	8,700			
Less: expenses	(1,100)			
	7,600			
Interest 80 × 100/80		100		
Dividends (585 – 405) × 100/90			200	
Income used for expenses:				
Dividends used for expenses 405 × 100/90				450
	7,600	100	200	450
Tax on distributable income:	£			
Non savings: £1,000 × 22%	220			
£6,600 × 40%	2,640			
Savings: £100 × 40%	40			
Dividends: £200 × 32.5%	65			
	2,965			
BR tax on income used to meet expenses:				
Dividends: £450 × 10%				45
Less notional tax credits on dividends				
£200 × 10%	(20)			
£450 × 10%				(45)
	2,945			0
Less "real tax credits on interest (£200 × 20%)	(40)			
Payables by Trustees	2,905			

Any payments of income to beneficiaries are made net of tax at 40% and are non-savings income of the beneficiary. If the trustees have not paid sufficient tax to cover this tax credit, they must make an additional payment. Beneficiaries not subject to income tax at the higher rate may obtain repayments accordingly.

1.3.1 Example

If trustees use their discretion to pay school fees of £6,000 on behalf of a child, the child is deemed to have income of £10,000 (£6,000 × 100/60). He may be able to recover some or all of the £4,000 tax suffered, for example by using his personal allowance. If £5,035 of the income is covered by a personal allowance and the rest is taxable at the lower rate (£2,150) and the basic rate, he could reclaim tax of £4,000 – [(£2,150 × 10%) + £(10,000 – 5,035 – 2,150) × 22%] = £3,166. Conversely, he may be liable to higher rate tax on £10,000 but as higher rate tax has already been paid by the trust, no further tax would be due.

1.4 Tax deduction certificate (R185)

Each beneficiary of a trust is given a certificate showing the gross amount of his share of trust income and the tax suffered on it. The certificate also shows the amounts of payments to the beneficiary.

1.5 Trusts for vulnerable beneficiaries

There are special rules for **trusts for vulnerable beneficiaries** which are either **discretionary trusts or accumulation and maintenance trusts**.

A beneficiary is a **vulnerable beneficiary if either he is a disabled person or a minor child at least one of whose parents is dead**. The rules apply in the latter case only to certain trusts made for the beneficiary including **statutory trusts under the rules of intestacy and will trusts made by the deceased parent**. An irrevocable joint election must be made by the trustees and the vulnerable beneficiary and then the trustees must make a claim for each tax year in which they wish the provisions to apply.

If the special rules apply, the trustees are given income tax relief. **The trustees will first work out their income tax liability under the normal rules**. This liability is then reduced. **The reduction is the difference between the total income tax and capital gains tax for which the vulnerable beneficiary is actually liable and a notional total tax liability of the beneficiary if his income included the trust income**.

1.6 Parental dispositions

Investment income of an unmarried minor deriving from a disposition made by a parent is considered to be income of the parent if it exceeds £100 a year. It does not apply to contributions to a Child Trust Fund (CTF). CTFs are dealt with later in this text.

This rule also applies to trusts where the child has an interest in possession. The income is deemed to be the parent's.

But the parental disposition rule does not apply to trusts where no payments are actually made to, or on behalf of, the child. This exception does not apply to 'bare' trusts (where the child is absolutely entitled to income and capital but the trustees hold these in trust until the child is aged 18). Income of a bare trust is always treated as income of the trust settlor (unless within the £100 de minimis exemption).

1.7 Settlors retaining an interest

Where trust property or income from it is or may become payable to the settlor (the creator of the trust) or his or her spouse/civil partner, the trust income is deemed to be the settlor's and not the trust's. However, this rule does not apply when the only possible occasions of payment to the settlor or spouse/civil partner are:

(a) A beneficiary becoming bankrupt or assigning or charging trust property.

(b) In the case of a marriage settlement, the death of both parties to the marriage or civil partnership and of all or any of their children.

(c) The death of a child of the settlor who had become beneficially entitled to the trust property or income at an age of 25 or less.

The rule also does not apply if there is a living person aged under 25, and during that person's lifetime no trust property or income can be paid to the settlor or his spouse/civil partner except on that living person's bankruptcy or his assigning or charging his interest.

When income is treated as the settlor's under this rule, it is taxed as non-savings income, savings income or dividends, according to the nature of the income received by the trust. The settlor may recover any additional tax he has to pay from the trust, and this is computed by including the trust income in the computation above all other income except the taxable part of partly exempt termination payments and taxable gains on life assurance policies.

2 CGT and trusts

FAST FORWARD

CGT may arise on trusts not only when trustees sell assets, but also on several other occasions. A death may lead to a tax-free uplift in the cost of trust assets to their market value at the time of death. The rate of CGT paid by all trusts is 40%.

2.1 Assets being put into trusts

For CGT purposes there is rarely any need to distinguish between trusts with an interest in possession and discretionary trusts. 'Settled property' is defined as any property held in trust, other than a trust where the beneficiary is absolutely entitled to trust property ('bare trust'). In a bare trust, gains are treated as made by the beneficiary not the trustee.

If a settlor puts an asset into any type of trust, he makes a disposal for CGT purposes. It will be deemed to be at market value. All gifts to trusts on or after 22 March 2006 (apart from trusts for the disabled) are chargeable to IHT. Gift relief is therefore available unless the trust is a settlor-interested trust. Prior to 22 March 2006 gifts to interest in possession trusts and accumulation and maintenance settlements were PETs. Gift relief was only available if the gift was of business assets.

Where a trust is created on death, there is no deemed disposal. Trustees of a settlement created under a will or on intestacy will be allowed a deemed 'cost' equivalent to the market value at death.

2.2 CGT on trusts

If trustees sell assets held in trust CGT may arise on the disposals. This tax is payable by the trustees out of the trust's assets. **The annual exemption available to trustees is one half of that given to individuals, so it is £4,400** for 2006/07. If several trusts are created by the same settlor, the £4,400 exemption is divided equally between them subject to a minimum exemption per trust of one tenth of a full individual exemption (£880 for 2006/07). Taper relief applies in a similar way to disposals by individuals.

If assets leave a trust the trustees are deemed to sell and immediately re-acquire the assets for their then market value, with the beneficiaries taking over the assets at those values less any gift relief on the trustees' gains. The trustees' gains, less any gift relief, are taxable in full, subject to the exception described below on the death of the life tenant.

As the **advance of assets from a relevant property trust** (see 3.6) is chargeable to IHT (unless it takes place within three months of the creation of the trust, or of a ten year anniversary, or is the advance of property to the beneficiary of an age 18-25 trust where he is aged 18 or over), gift relief is available. Gift Relief also extends to situations where the beneficiary of a trust for a bereaved minor becomes absolutely entitled to the trust assets and when the beneficiary of an age 18-25 trust becomes entitled to trust assets whilst under the age of 18.

If assets **leave a trust on the death of the life tenant** and the trust is either an immediate post-death interest trust, or a trust for a bereaved minor, or an age 18-25 trust and the beneficiary is under 18, then there is an exemption for the gain that would otherwise arise. This harmonises with the exemption for gains that would otherwise arise on the death of an individual. There is also a deemed disposal and tax free uplift in the market value of the trust assets on the death of the life tenant in these circumstances but the trust does not come to an end. These exemptions also apply to life interests which existed at 22 March 2006. If a gain was held over on property transferred to the trust, this gain crystallises, and is not covered by the tax free uplift. The death of the life tenant does not lead to a tax free uplift for other interest in possession trusts.

This table summarises the chargeable CGT occasions for most trusts created on or after 22 March 2006:

	Trust for a bereaved minor and age 18-25 trusts	Trust with an immediate post-death interest	Other trusts
Creation of trust	No CGT on entry – created on death	No CGT on entry – created on death	CGT on entry unless created on death. Gift relief available as chargeable occasion for IHT
Disposal of trust assets by sale	Chargeable	Chargeable	Chargeable
Advance of assets to beneficiary other than on death of life tenant	Chargeable. Special gift relief available for all assets	Chargeable. Gift relief only for business assets	Chargeable. Gift relief available as chargeable occasion for IHT
Advance of assets to beneficiary on death of life tenant	Tax free uplift to market value, provided beneficiary under 18	Tax free uplift to market value	Chargeable. Gift relief available as chargeable occasion for IHT
Death of life tenant, assets remain settled property	Tax free uplift to market value provided beneficiary under 18	Tax free uplift to market value	Not an occasion of charge for CGT so no tax free uplift

A chargeable gain does not normally arise when an employee trust transfers assets to employees for no payment and the employee is taxed on the full value of the assets concerned as specific employment income.

The rate of CGT for all types of trust is 40%.

Question

Calculation of trust CGT

The assets of a discretionary trust included 10,000 shares in X Ltd (an investment company), which were bought by the trustees for £29,000 on 30 April 2004. The shares were advanced to B on 30 June 2006, when the shares were worth £85,000. How much CGT must the trustees pay

(a) If gift relief is not claimed

(b) If gift relief is claimed?

Answer

(a)

	£
Deemed proceeds	85,000
Less cost	(29,000)
Gain	56,000
No taper relief yet available for this non-business asset	
Less annual exemption £8,800/2	(4,400)
Taxable gain	51,600
CGT £51,600 × 40%	£20,640

(b) If gift relief is claimed the gain of £56,000 can be held over and no CGT is payable.

2.3 Settlor-interested trust

A settlor interested trust is one where the trust property or income is or may become payable to the settlor, his spouse, civil partner or minor child (who is neither married nor in a civil partnership). If a settlor-interested trust has chargeable gains (after trust losses and taper relief but before the annual exemption), **the gains are treated as the settlor's and are taxed at the rates applicable to his gains**. This does not apply if the trust ceases to be settlor-interested before the end of the year due to death, dissolution of marriage or civil partnership, or a child becoming 18, marrying or entering into a civil partnership. It also does not apply in the cases where income would not be attributed to the settlor (see paragraph 1.7 above).

The amount attributed to the settlor is the net trust gains (trust gains less trust losses) *before* taper relief. The settlor is then able to set his own personal losses against the trust gains (to the extent that there is an excess of personal losses over personal gains). Taper relief then applies with reference to the ownership of the trustees. The settlor can then set his annual exemption against the trust gains, if there is an excess of the annual exemption over his personal gains.

The settlor has a right of recovery of the tax he has paid on trust gains. In working out the tax on those gains, they are treated as the top slice of gains.

2.4 Trusts for vulnerable beneficiaries

FAST FORWARD

There are special rules for trusts for vulnerable beneficiaries.

Special CGT rules also apply to trusts for vulnerable beneficiaries (see earlier in this text).

The vulnerable beneficiary is treated as if he were the settlor of the trust. As a result, **the gains of the trust are attributed to the beneficiary** in the same way as described above.

A **claim** must be made by the trustees for this treatment to apply in a tax year.

3 IHT and trusts

FAST FORWARD

Discretionary trusts suffer the IHT principal charge once every ten years and also the exit charge when property leaves the trust.

3.1 Types of trust

For IHT purposes we need from 22 March 2006 to distinguish between:

(a) **Trusts for bereaved minors**
(b) **Age 18-25 trusts**
(c) **Trusts with an immediate post-death interest**
(d) **Trusts for the disabled**
(e) **Other trusts, such as discretionary trusts.**

The category **"relevant property trusts"** may include discretionary trusts, where the trustees can decide how to deal with the trust income and capital, accumulation and maintenance trusts (a special form of discretionary trust see 3.7.2) and trusts subject to an interest in possession (other than those falling under (a) or (c) above).

Certain "other trusts" created before 22 March 2006 are subject to special rules which are discussed beyond.

3.2 Trusts for bereaved minors (TBM)

A trust for a bereaved minor is a **trust created by the will or intestacy of the beneficiary's parent**. The terms of the trust must be that **the beneficiary must become absolutely entitled to the trust capital, income and any accumulated income at age 18** if he has not done so already. Income may be accumulated or it may be paid to or applied for the benefit of the beneficiary whilst still a minor, but it may not be applied for any other person. Similarly the capital may be applied for the beneficiary whilst still a minor, but for no-one else. Where a minor is entitled to a legacy on an intestacy or under a will which does not make specific provisions for dealing with assets for minor beneficiaries, then the legacy may be held on "statutory trusts", ie where the terms of the trust are laid down by statute rather than in a will. These qualify as trusts for bereaved minors.

A TBM can only be set up on death, so will have been subject to IHT on the settlor's death. **Whilst the assets remain subject to the trust there will be no charge to IHT, nor will there be any charge on the beneficiary becoming entitled to the trust assets**.

3.3 Aged 18-25 trusts

An age 18-25 trust is defined in the same way as a TBM, except that entitlement to capital is deferred until age 25. A trust which is itself a TBM is not an aged 18-25 trust, nor is a trust subject to an immediate post death interest.

As the trust is set up on death, it will have been subject to IHT on the settlor's death. There is no charge to IHT if capital is paid to or applied for the beneficiary whilst under the age 18. If payments are made between ages 18 and 25, an exit charge arises. This is calculated in the same way as an exit charge before the first principal charge for a 'relevant property trust' (see 3.6.1. below), but in the fraction x/40, x is the number of complete quarters since the beneficiary's 18th birthday.

3.4 Trusts subject to an immediate post-death interest

A trust subject to an immediate post-death interest is a trust:

(a) Which was **set up on the death** of the settlor by will or intestacy;

(b) Where the life tenant became entitled to an **interest in possession immediately on the death** of the settlor;

(c) Which is not a trust for a bereaved minor nor a trust for a disabled person.

It should be noted that a trust with two successive life interests ("in trust for my wife for her lifetime, then in trust for my daughter for her lifetime, then for my grandchildren absolutely) only qualifies as an immediate post-death interest trust during the first life interest (the wife's).

An immediate post-death interest trust can only be set up on death, so will normally have been subject to IHT on the settlor's death. If, however, the life tenant is the spouse or civil partner of the deceased, the spouse exemption will have applied on the death.

So long as the life tenant has an interest in possession in the trust, he is treated for IHT purposes as if he owned the trust assets outright. This means that if he dies they will be aggregated with his estate and charged to inheritance tax accordingly. The IHT on the immediate post-death interest is payable by the trustees out of the trust property.

If the **life interest terminates during the lifetime of the life tenant**, then the IHT consequences depend on what happens to the trust assets:

- **If the assets pass outright to another individual or to a TBM or are held on trust for a disabled person, the transfer is a PET**, or is exempt if the recipient is the life tenant's spouse or civil partner;
- If the **assets are otherwise held on trust** (other than for a charity), **the transfer is a CLT**;

- If the **assets pass to the life tenant there is no IHT** – assets which were treated as forming part of the life tenant's estate now actually are part of his estate;
- If the assets pass to charity, the transfer is exempt.

3.5 Trusts for the disabled

If property is held on trust for a disabled person then the disabled person is treated as if he had an interest in possession in that property. That means that it is treated as forming part of his estate, and so it is charged to IHT on the disabled person's death.

If the interest terminates during the lifetime of the disabled person, then the transfer would be a PET, CLT or may be exempt in the same way as for an immediate post-death interest.

3.6 Relevant Property

Property held on trusts other than those described in 3.2 to 3.5 above is called "relevant property". This applies, for example, to property on discretionary trusts, property held in accumulation and maintenance trusts, and to property subject to an interest in possession which is not an immediate post-death interest (but see below for Trusts created before 22 March 2006).

When an **individual makes a gift to a discretionary trust** (or to any other trust where the property is relevant property) **the gift is a CLT**. If the gift had been made on death, IHT would be charged on the death estate in the normal way.

So long as the property in the trust remains relevant property it is subject to the **principal charge**. This applies on every tenth anniversary from the start of the trust.

If property leaves the trust (and so ceases to be relevant property) an **exit charge** arises.

3.6.1 Exit charge before first principal charge

The amount subject to the exit charge is the amount distributed from the trust. The rate of IHT is 30% of the (lifetime) rate that would apply to a notional transfer of the initial value of the trust, assuming previous cumulative transfers by the trust equal to those made by the settlor in the seven years prior to the setting up of the trust. Once the rate of IHT has been established, it is then further reduced by multiplying by x/40 where x is the number of complete successive quarters that have elapsed since the trust commenced.

3.6.2 The principal charge

IHT is charged on the value of the property in the trust at each tenth anniversary of the trust. The rate is 30% of the (lifetime) rate that would apply to a transfer of the property in the trust at the tenth anniversary, assuming previous transfers equal to the gross amount of any capital paid out of the trust in the previous ten years plus the settlor's transfers in the seven years prior to the creation of the trust.

3.6.3 Exit charge after a principal charge

The rate applied to a distribution after a principal charge is that applied at the last tenth anniversary, reduced by multiplying by a fraction that reflects the time elapsed since the tenth anniversary. The fraction is x/40, with the numerator being the number of complete quarters since the last tenth anniversary.

If there has been a change in tax rates, the rate applied at the last tenth anniversary is recomputed using the new rates.

3.7 Trusts created before 22 March 2006

More generous IHT rules applied to trusts before 22 March 2006. As these can still affect current IHT liability, such as on death, you need to be aware of the basic rules.

3.7.1 Interest in possession trusts

(a) A lifetime transfer by an individual to an interest in possession trust was a PET.

(b) The property subject to the interest in possession is treated as comprised in the individual's estate if still held on death.

(c) If the life interest terminated during the beneficiary's lifetime the transfer is:

- a PET if to an individual,
- a PET if before 22 March 2006 to an accumulation and maintenance settlement
- a CLT if to a relevant property trust, such as a discretionary trust

3.7.2 Accumulation and maintenance trusts

An accumulation and maintenance trust is a special form of discretionary trust where the beneficiaries will either become entitled to their share of capital, or to an interest in possession in it, at some specified age not exceeding 25.

Prior to 22 March 2006 a transfer in to an accumulation and maintenance settlement was a PET. There were no principal charges within the trust, nor an exit charge on the beneficiary receiving capital or an interest in possession.

If after 22 March 2006 an accumulation and maintenance settlement satisfies the conditions for a TBM, it will be dealt with under the rules described in 3.2 above.

From 6 April 2008 existing accumulation and maintenance trusts are treated as relevant property trusts (see 3.6), unless they satisfy the conditions for an age 18-25 trust (see 3.3), apart from being set up under the will of a deceased parent. In that case then there is no charge if the beneficiary takes capital aged under 18, and an exit charge if aged between 18 and 25. This allows a two year window during which the trust can be brought within the new rules.

Exam focus point

It is essential that you recognise the type of trust in the exam question.

From 22 March 2006 trust property is relevant property for IHT purposes, and so will be subject to principal charges and exit charges. Property settled by will which is a trust for a bereaved minor, an age 18-25 trust or an immediate post-death interest trust receives favourable IHT treatment.

The income tax treatment will not necessarily follow the IHT treatment – a trust which is subject to an interest in possession does not pay tax at the special trust rates since the income must be distributed to, and is taxed on, the life tenant.

For CGT purposes there is little difference between the types of trust, except that gift relief is available for non-business assets where an IHT charge may arise, or on the termination of a trust for a bereaved minor.

4 Tax planning using trusts

FAST FORWARD

Tax planning using trusts is limited due to the alignment of trust rates with personal rates. However there may still be inheritance tax benefits, since the maximum rate of Inheritance tax on relevant property trusts is 6% (30% of lifetime rates).

4.1 Inheritance tax planning

Since the rates of income tax and capital gains tax for trusts are aligned with those for individuals, **there will usually be no particular tax advantage of setting up a trust for IT/CGT tax planning**.

There are IHT opportunities, however. Despite the charges applicable to most trusts, they offer useful opportunities to reduce IHT as assets in the trust are not treated as being in anyone's estate. In particular, holding assets which are valued below the nil rate band in a discretionary trust may reduce IHT.

Trusts are useful vehicles for non-tax reasons such as to preserve family wealth, to provide for those who are deemed to be incapable (minors, and the disabled) or unsuitable (due to youth or poor business sense) to hold assets directly. The IHT cost of holding assets in trust may be worth paying for the benefit. Reliefs, such as business or agricultural property relief, may reduce the IHT cost to nil. This can be particularly relevant to holdings of unquoted shares in trading companies.

4.2 Charities

Charities are often constituted as trusts. Whether they are constituted as trusts or as companies, they are exempt from income tax, CGT and corporation tax on:

(a) Investment income (including donations) and gains applied for charitable purposes.

(b) Trading income, but only if the work is done mainly by the charity's beneficiaries *or* the trade is carried on in the course of carrying out one of the charity's primary purposes.

Charities are not subject to the IHT charges on trusts, and transfers to charities are exempt from IHT tax. There is also no chargeable gain or allowable loss when an asset is given to a charity, or when an asset is sold to a charity for not more than the sum of the cost, enhancement expenditure and incidental costs of acquisition and disposal.

Chapter roundup

- Income tax may be charged on trust income at 10%, 20%, 22%, 32.5% or at 40%, but when income is paid out the recipient's tax rate is effectively substituted for the trust's tax rate.
- CGT may arise on trusts not only when trustees sell assets, but also on several other occasions. The rate of CGT paid by all trusts is 40%. Gift relief may be available on transfers to and from trusts where the transfer is a chargeable occasion for IHT, and on advances to beneficiaries on or before attaining the age of 18 from TBM and aged 18-25 trusts.
- There are special rules for trusts for vulnerable beneficiaries.
- Most trusts suffer the IHT principal charge once every ten years and also the exit charge when property leaves the trust.
- IPDI trusts, TBM and aged 18-25 trusts receive special IHT treatment.
- Tax planning using trusts is limited due to the alignment of trust rates with personal rates. However there may still be inheritance tax benefits available by using the IHT nil rate band.

Quick quiz

1 A trustee of an interest in possession trust has rental income of £5,000 (net of allowable expenses) and general income expenses of £500 in 2006/07. How much income tax is payable by

(a) the trustee and

(b) the beneficiary with the interest in possession, assuming he is a higher rate taxpayer, on the trust income?

2 Which trusts pay income tax at 40%?

3 What is the CGT effect of a life tenant of an immediate post-death interest trust dying?

4 What is the CGT effect of a trust being a settlor interested trust?

5 What is the IHT principal charge?

Answers to quick quiz

1 (a) Trustee £5,000 × 22% = £1,100
  (b) Beneficiary £((5,000 – 1,100 – 500) × 100/78) × (40 – 22)% = £785

2 Discretionary trusts and accumulation and maintenance trusts pay IT at 40%.

3 There is a deemed disposal of the trust property by the trustees at market value. The gain is not chargeable unless gift relief was claimed when the property was put into trust and then only up to the amount of the gift relief.

4 If the settlor, his spouse or civil partner, or his minor unmarried children may benefit from trust property the trust gains are treated as the settlor's gains.

5 The principal charge is a charge on relevant property held in trust at each ten year anniversary of the trust.

Now try the question below from the Exam Question Bank

Number	Level	Marks	Time
Q18	Introductory	20	36 mins

National insurance and stamp taxes

20

Introduction

In this chapter, we look at national insurance contributions (NICs) and stamp taxes. You will find the rates of NICs set out in the tax rates and allowances tables in this Text.

Topic list	Syllabus references
1 National insurance	1(l), 2(c)
2 Stamp duty and other stamp taxes	1(m), 2(d)

1 National insurance

1.1 Classes of National Insurance contributions

FAST FORWARD

National Insurance contributions are divided into four classes.

Four classes of national insurance contribution (NIC) exist, as set out below.

(a) **Class 1**. This is divided into:

(i) **Primary**, paid by employees
(ii) **Secondary**, **Class 1A and Class 1B** paid by employers

(b) **Class 2**. Paid by the self-employed

(c) **Class 3**. Voluntary contributions (paid to maintain rights to certain state benefits)

(d) **Class 4.** Paid by the self-employed

Exam focus point

Class 1B and Class 3 contributions are outside the scope of your syllabus.

1.1.1 General principles

FAST FORWARD

Employees pay Class 1 NICs. Employees pay the main primary rate between the earnings threshold and upper earnings limit and the additional rate on earnings above the upper earnings limit. Employers pay Class 1 and Class 1A NICs. For employers, there is no upper earnings limit.

The National Insurance Contributions Office (NICO), which is part of HMRC, examines employers' records and procedures to ensure that the correct amounts of NICs are collected.

Both **employees** and **employers pay NICs** related to the employee's earnings. NICs are not deductible from an employee's gross salary for income tax purposes. However, employers' contributions are deductible trade expenses.

'Earnings' broadly comprise gross pay, excluding benefits which cannot be turned into cash by surrender (eg holidays). It also includes mileage payments over the approved amount (see below). No deduction is made for superannuation contributions.

An employer's contribution to an employee's approved personal pension or an approved occupational pension scheme is excluded from the definition of 'earnings'. However, NICs are due on employer contributions to funded unapproved retirement benefit schemes. (Pensions are covered later in this text.)

In general income tax and NIC exemptions mirror one another. For example, payment of personal incidental expenses covered by the £5/£10 a night income tax de minimis exemption are excluded from NIC earnings. Relocation expenses of a type exempt from income tax are also excluded from NIC earnings but without the income tax £8,000 upper limit (although expenses exceeding £8,000 are subject to class 1A NICs as described below). Similarly, the income tax rules for travel expenses are exactly mirrored for NIC treatment.

An expense with a business purpose is not treated as earnings. For example, if an employee is reimbursed for business travel or for staying in a hotel on the employer's business this is not normally 'earnings'. However, if an employee is reimbursed for his own home telephone charges the reimbursed cost of private calls (and all reimbursed rental) is earnings.

Where an employer reimburses an employee using his own car for business mileage, the earnings element is the excess of the mileage rate paid over HMRC's 'up to 10,000 business miles' 'approved mileage allowance payments' (AMAPs). This applies even where business mileage exceeds 10,000 pa.

In general, non cash vouchers are subject to NICs. However, the following are exempt.

- Childcare vouchers up to £55 per week
- Vouchers for the use of sports and recreational facilities (where tax exempt)

- Vouchers for meals on the employer's premises
- Other luncheon vouchers to a maximum of 15p per day
- Transport vouchers where the employee earns less than £8,500 a year
- Top up vouchers for pay as you go mobile phones where the provision of the phone itself is exempt from income tax
- Vouchers for eye tests and glasses for employees using VDUs
- Any other voucher which is exempt from income tax.

The rates of contribution for 2006/07, and the income bands to which they apply, are set out in the Rates and Allowances Tables in this text.

Non-contracted out **employees pay main primary contributions of 11% of earnings between the earnings threshold of £5,035 and the upper earnings limit of £33,540** or the equivalent monthly or weekly limit (see below). They also pay additional primary contributions of 1% on earnings above the upper earnings limit.

Employers pay secondary contributions of 12.8% on earnings above the earnings threshold of £5,035 or the equivalent monthly or weekly limit. There is no upper limit.

There is a lower earnings limit of £4,368 (or the equivalent monthly or weekly limit). The significance of the lower earnings limit (LEL) is that 'nil rate contributions' will be credited where the employee's earnings are between the LEL and the earnings threshold. These 'nil rate contributions' frank the employee's record and so create an entitlement to certain state benefits.

If an employee is in a contracted out occupational pension scheme, reduced contributions are payable. Employee contributions at the main rate are 9.4% of earnings between the earnings threshold and the upper earnings limit. There is also a rebate of 1.6% on earnings between the lower earnings limit and the earnings threshold. There is an additional rate of 1% on earnings above the upper earnings limit.

Employer rates are also reduced for earnings between the earnings threshold of £5,035 and the upper limit.

If an employee contracts out of the state earnings related pension scheme through a personal pension, full contributions are payable but NICO pays a proportion of these contributions to the insurance company running the personal pension scheme. (Pensions are covered in detail later in this text.)

1.1.2 Earnings period

FAST FORWARD

NICs are based on earnings periods. Directors have an annual earnings period.

NICs are calculated in relation to an earnings period. This is the period to which earnings paid to an employee are deemed to relate. Where earnings are paid at regular intervals, the earnings period will generally be equated with the payment interval, for example a week or a month. An earnings period cannot usually be less than seven days long.

NIC for employees is calculated on a non-cumulative basis, so only the earnings in the earnings period are considered. The monthly limits are the annual limit divided by 12.

Question — Primary and secondary contributions

Sally works for Red plc. She is paid £2,850 per month.

Show Sally's primary contributions for 2006/07, assuming she is not contracted out, and the secondary contributions paid by Red plc.

Answer

Earnings threshold £5,035 ÷ 12 = £420
Upper earnings limit £33,540 ÷ 12 = £2,795

Sally	
Primary contributions	£
£(2,795 – 420) = £2,375 × 11% (main) × 12	3,135
£(2,850 – 2,795) = £55 × 1% × 12 (additional)	7
Total primary contributions	3,142

Red plc	
Secondary contributions	£
£(2,850 – 420) = £2,430 × 12.8% × 12	3,733

Special rules apply to company directors, regardless of whether they are paid at regular intervals or not. Where a person is a director at the beginning of the tax year, his earnings period is the tax year, even if he ceases to be director during the year. **The annual limits as shown in the Tax Tables apply.**

Question — Employees and directors

Bill and Ben work for Weed Ltd. Bill is a monthly paid employee. Ben who is a director of Weed Ltd, is also paid monthly. Each are paid an annual salary of £33,000 in 2006/07 and received a bonus of £3,000 in December 2006.

Answer

Bill

Earnings threshold £5,035/12 = £420
Upper earnings limit £33,540/12 = £2,795
Regular monthly earnings £33,000/12 = £2,750

Primary contributions	
	£
11 months	
£(2,750 – 420) = £2,330 × 11% × 11 (main only)	2,819
1 month (December)	
£(2,795 – 420) = £2,375 × 11% (main)	261
£(5,750 – 2,795) = £2,955 × 1% (additional)	30
Total primary contributions	3,110

Secondary contributions	
	£
11 months	
£(2,950 – 420) = £2,330 × 12.8% × 11	3,281
1 month (December)	
£(2,750 + 3,000 – 420) = £5,330 × 12.8%	682
Total secondary contributions	3,963

Ben

Total earnings £(33,000 + 3,000) = £36,000

Primary contributions

	£
Total earnings exceed UEL	
£(33,540 – 5,035) = £28,505 × 11% (main)	3,136
£(36,000 – 33,540) = £2,460 × 1% (additional)	25
Total primary	3,161

Secondary contributions

£(36,000 – 5,035) = £30,965 × 12.8%	3,963

Because Ben is a director an annual earnings period applies. The effect of this is that increased primary contributions are due.

If a director is first appointed as a director during a tax year, the earnings period relating to his directorship is the number of tax weeks from the tax week which includes the date of the appointment to the end of the tax year. The first tax week starts on 6 April. The relevant earnings threshold is then the annual limit divided by 52 times the number of tax weeks in the earnings period, rounded up to the nearest £. The upper earnings limit is the weekly limit times the number of tax weeks in the earnings period.

Question — Appointment of director

Myrtle is appointed as a director of director of Herbs plc on 29 May 2006 (in tax week 8, ie 7 previous tax weeks in the year). She was not previously employed in the tax year 2006/07. She received a salary of £31,000 between her appointment and 5 April 2007.

What are the total primary and total secondary contributions payable in respect of Myrtle for 2006/07?

Answer

Number of tax weeks in earnings period is 52 – 7 = 45
Earnings threshold is £5,035/52 × 45 = £4,357
Upper earnings limit is £33,540 × 45/52 = £29,025

Primary contributions

	£
Total earnings exceed UEL	
£(29,025 – 4,357) = £24,668 × 11% (main)	2,713
£(31,000 – 29,025) = £1,975 × 1% (additional)	20
Total primary	2,733

Secondary contributions

£(31,000 – 4,357) = £26,643 × 12.8%	£3,410

1.2 Class 1A NIC

Employers must pay Class 1A NIC in respect of most taxable benefits for example, private medical insurance. However, benefits are exempt if they are:

- Within Class 1, or
- Covered by a PAYE dispensation, or
- Provided for employees earning at a rate of less than £8,500 a year, or
- Included in a PAYE settlement agreement, or
- Otherwise not required to be reported on P11Ds

In addition, **childcare provision in kind is wholly or partially exempt from Class 1A NICs which mirrors the income tax treatment of such provision**. Therefore, provision in an **employer provided nursery or playscheme is wholly exempt** from Class 1A NICs. Provision of **other childcare**, for example where an employer contracts directly for places in a commercial nursery, **is exempt up to £55 per week**.

There is also exemption for certain other minor benefits already noted in the text (eg small private use of employer's assets) and for certain travel and subsidence benefits for employees seconded to the UK or abroad and certain personal security items supplied by the employer to an employee.

Employee contributions are not charged on benefits.

Class 1A contributions are collected annually in arrears, and are due by 19 July following the tax year.

The provision by an employer of fuel for use in an employee's own car does not lead to a Class 1A charge. However, mileage allowances in excess of the AMAP rates lead to Class 1 (primary (main and additional) and secondary) contributions on the excess (subject to the usual upper limit for main primary contributions). Note that for cars it is the AMAP rate for the first 10,000 miles (ie 40p per mile) that is used, regardless of total mileage.

1.2.1 Interest

If Class 1 contributions for a year are not paid to HMRC by 19 April following the year, or Class 1A contributions due in a year are not paid over by 19 April following the year, interest is charged from the relevant 19 April onwards. Interest is paid to employers on excessive payments refunded to them, but only from the end of the year of payment and never from earlier than 12 months after the end of the year for which the contributions were paid.

1.3 National insurance contributions (NICs) for the self employed

FAST FORWARD

The self employed pay Class 2 and Class 4 NICs. Class 4 NICs are based on the level of the individual's taxable profits. Class 2 NICs are paid at a flat weekly rate.

The self employed (sole traders and partners) **pay NICs in two ways. Class 2 contributions are payable at a flat rate**. It is possible, however, to be excepted from payment of Class 2 contributions (or to get contributions already paid repaid) if annual profits are less than £4,465. **The Class 2 rate for 2006/07 is £2.10 a week.**

Self employed people must register with HMRC for Class 2 contributions within three months of the end of the month in which they start self employment. People who fail to register may incur a £100 penalty.

Additionally, **the self employed pay Class 4 NICs, based on the level of the individual's trade profits**.

Main rate Class 4 NICs are calculated by applying a fixed percentage (8% for 2006/07) to the individual's profits between the lower limit (£5,035 for 2006/07) and the upper limit (£33,540 for 2006/07). Additional rate contributions are 1% (for 2006/07) on profits above that limit.

1.4 Example: Class 4 contributions

If a sole trader had profits of £14,080 for 2006/07 his Class 4 NIC liability would be as follows.

	£
Profits	14,080
Less lower limit	(5,035)
	9,045

Class 4 NICs = 8% × £9,045 = £723.60 (main only)

1.5 Example: additional class 4 contributions

If an individual's profits were £35,000, additional Class 4 NICs are due on the excess over the upper limit. Thus the amount payable in 2006/07 is as follows.

	£
Profits (upper limit)	33,540
Less lower limit	(5,035)
	28,505
Main rate Class 4 NICs 8% × £28,505	2,280
Additional rate class 4 NICs £(35,000 – 33,540) = £1,460 × 1%	15
	2,295

For Class 4 NIC purposes, profits are the trade profits for income tax purposes, less:

(a) **Trade losses**

(b) **Trade charges on income**

There is no deduction for personal pension premiums.

Class 4 NICs are collected by HMRC. They are paid **at the same time as the associated income tax liability**. Interest is charged on overdue contributions.

1.6 Comparison of NICs for the employees and the self employed

The NIC burden on the self employed tends to be lower than that on employees, although the relative burdens vary with the level of income. The following example shows how a comparison may be made.

1.7 Example

Two single people, one employed (not in a contracted out pension scheme) and one self employed, each have annual gross income of £18,000. Show their national insurance contributions for 2006/07.

Solution

	Employed	*Self-employed*
	£	£
NICs		
Class 1: £(18,000 – 5,035) × 11% (main only)	1,426	
Class 2: £2.10 × 52		109
Class 4: £(18,000 – 5,035) × 8%		1,037
	1,426	1,146

The self-employed person is better off by £(1,426 – 1,146) = £280 a year.

2 Stamp duty and other stamp taxes

2.1 Stamp duty

FAST FORWARD

Stamp duty applies to share transactions.

Stamp duty applies to transfers of shares and securities transferred by a stock transfer form. It is payable by the purchaser.

Transfers of shares are charged to stamp duty at 0.5% of the consideration unless they fall within one of the specific exemptions. The duty is rounded up to the nearest £5.

The exemptions are primarily for transfers where is no consideration, such as:

- Gifts
- Changes in trustees
- Divorce arrangements
- Variation of wills

To qualify for the exemption the transfer document must state which exemption is being claimed. The categories of exemption are printed on the back of the stock transfer form.

2.2 Stamp duty reserve tax (SDRT)

FAST FORWARD

Stamp Duty Reserve Tax (SDRT) applies to paperless share transactions instead of Stamp Duty.

SDRT is not a stamp duty, but a separate tax with its own rules. It applies to agreements to transfer **chargeable securities for consideration in money or money's worth**.

SDRT is charged at **0.5% of the amount or value of the consideration for the sale**.

SDRT applies to the **agreement to transfer (whether oral or written)** and does not depend on the execution of the written instrument of transfer for a charge to arise. Thus, it applies to paperless Stock Exchange transactions and is collected automatically on such dealings.

The **tax charge arises on the date the agreement is made or becomes unconditional**.

2.3 Stamp duty land tax (SDLT)

FAST FORWARD

Stamp Duty Land Tax (SDLT) applies to the sale of land, or of rights over land.

Stamp duty land tax applies to land transactions. A land transaction is a transfer of land or an interest in, or right over, land. **SDLT is generally payable as a percentage of the consideration paid for the land. It is payable by the purchaser.**

The following land transactions are exempt:

- A transfer for no chargeable consideration (except a gift to a connected company)
- A transfer on divorce, annulment of marriage or judicial separation
- Variations of a will or intestacy made within 2 years of death for no consideration
- Transfers to charities if the land is to be used for charitable purposes

If land is transferred to a company, for example on incorporation, SDLT is payable on the market value of land.

The amount of the charge to SDLT depends on whether the land is residential or non-residential and whether or not it is in a designated disadvantaged area. The following rates apply:

Rate (%)	Non-disadvantaged area		Disadvantaged area	
	Residential	**Non-residential**	**Residential**	**Non-residential**
0	Up to £125,000	Up to £150,000	Up to £150,000	Up to £150,000
1	£125,001 – £250,000	£150,001 – £250,000	£150,001 – £250,000	£150,001 – £250,000
3	£250,001 – £500,000	£250,001 – £500,000	£250,001 – £500,000	£250,001 – £500,000
4	£500,001 +	£500,001+	£500,001+	£500,001+

Once the relevant rate of SDLT has been ascertained, it applies to the whole of the consideration, not just that above the band threshold.

2.4 Example

Beryl buys a house in a non-disadvantaged area for £300,000. Her stamp duty land tax is £300,000 × 3% = £9,000.

Stamp duty land tax is chargeable on lease premiums at the above rates. On the grant of a lease the lease rental payable during the term of the lease is also charged to stamp duty land tax to the extent that the net present value of the rental exceeds the above thresholds (£125,000 for residential leases, and £150,000 for non-residential leases). The rate of charge is 1% of the excess above the threshold.

2.5 Company transactions

Relief from stamp duty and SDLT is given for transfers of assets between associated companies.

There are two conditions which must be met to attract the relief, namely that:

- the effect must be to transfer the **beneficial interest** in property from one body corporate to another, and
- those bodies corporate must be **associated** at the time of transfer, ie. one must be the parent of the other or they must have a common parent.

(The term 'body corporate' includes foreign companies.)

For the 'associated companies' test, one company is regarded as the parent of another if it has:

- beneficial ownership of at least **75% of the ordinary share capital**, ie if all the issued share capital of a company, other than fixed rate preference shares; and
- a 75% interest in dividends and assets in a winding up; and
- there must not be 'arrangements' for a non-associated person to acquire control of the transferee.

It is necessary for there to be a **parent company**, ie. two companies owned by the same individual are not 'associated' for stamp duty or SDLT purposes (even though they would be associated for corporation tax purposes). For indirect holdings, it is necessary to reduce the degree of ownership at each level to the appropriate fraction in determining whether the 75% test is met (as for group relief).

Question — Stamp duty relief

Allegri Ltd owns 90% of the ordinary share capital of Byrd Ltd, which in turn owns 85% of the ordinary share capital of Corelli Ltd.

Shares are transferred from Corelli Ltd to Allegri Ltd under an instrument executed on 1 June 2006.

Is stamp duty relief available?

Answer

Relief is available, since Allegri Ltd owns indirectly 76½ % (ie. 90% x 85%) of the ordinary share capital of Corelli Ltd.

SDLT relief is withdrawn where land has been transferred from one associated company to another and within three years of the transfer the purchaser company leaves the group whilst still owning the land. Note that the vendor company leaving the group does not cause the SDLT relief to be withdrawn as the land is still held within the group.

Chapter roundup

- Employees pay Class 1 NICs. Employees pay the main primary rate between the earnings threshold and upper earnings limit and the additional rate on earnings above the upper earnings limit.
- Employers pay Class 1 and Class 1A NICs. For employers, there is no upper earnings limit.
- NICs are based on earnings periods. Directors have an annual earnings period.
- The self employed pay Class 2 and Class 4 NICs. Class 4 NICs are based on the level of the individual's taxable profits. Class 2 NICs are paid at a flat weekly rate.
- Stamp duty applies to share transactions.
- SDRT applies to paperless share transactions
- Stamp Duty Land Tax (SDLT) applies to the sale of land, or of rights over land.

Quick quiz

1 On what are Class 1A NICs paid?

2 How are Class 4 NICs calculated?

3 At what rate is SDLT charged on the sale of land worth £600,000?

4 On what is stamp duty reserve tax charged?

5 What is the stamp duty on a share transfer form if the consideration for sale was £50,000?

Answers to quick quiz

1 Class 1A NICs are paid by employers on taxable benefits.

2 The main rate is a fixed percentage of an individual's profits between an upper limit and lower limit. The additional rate applies above the upper limit.

3 4%

4 On agreements to transfer chargeable securities for consideration in money or money's worth.

5 £50,000 × 0.5% = £250

Now try the question below from the Exam Question Bank

Number	Level	Marks	Time
Q19	Introductory	10	18 mins

Part B
Taxation of corporate business

21

An outline of corporation tax

Introduction

In this chapter, we cover the basic corporation tax rules. We start by looking at accounting periods, which are the periods for which companies pay corporation tax. We then see how to bring together all of a company's profits in a corporation tax computation and how to work out the tax on them. You should have met all the rules in the chapter in your previous studies for Paper 2.3

Topic list	Syllabus references
1 The scope of corporation tax	2(a)
2 Profits chargeable to corporation tax	2(a)
3 Charge to corporation tax	2(a)

1 The scope of corporation tax

1.1 Introduction

FAST FORWARD

Companies pay corporation tax on their profits chargeable to corporation tax of each accounting period. The profits chargeable to corporation tax are income plus gains minus charges.

Corporation tax is paid by companies. It is charged on the profits (including chargeable gains) of each accounting period. Corporation tax is not charged on dividends received from UK resident companies (see exception to this rule at the end of this section).

Key term

A '**company**' is any corporate body (limited or unlimited) or unincorporated association eg sports clubs.

1.2 The residence of companies

A company incorporated in the UK is resident in the UK. A company incorporated abroad is resident in the UK if its central management and control are exercised here.

1.3 Accounting periods

FAST FORWARD

An accounting period cannot exceed twelve months in length. A long period of account must be split into two accounting periods, the first of which is twelve months long.

Corporation tax is chargeable in respect of accounting periods. It is important to understand the difference between an accounting period and a period of account. A period of account is any period for which a company prepares accounts; usually this will be 12 months in length but it may be longer or shorter than this. An accounting period starts when a company starts to trade, or otherwise becomes liable to corporation tax, or immediately after the previous accounting period finishes. An accounting period finishes on the earliest of:

- 12 months after its start
- The end of the company's period of account
- The commencement of the company's winding up or administration (see later in this text)
- The company ceasing to be resident in the UK
- The company ceasing to be liable to corporation tax

In many cases the company will have a period of account of 12 months and an accounting period of 12 months. We will deal with long periods of account (exceeding 12 months) later in this chapter.

Companies' taxable profits are always computed for accounting periods, not tax years. There are no basis period rules, there is no personal allowance and there is no taper relief or annual exemption for capital gains.

2 Profits chargeable to corporation tax

FAST FORWARD

The profits chargeable to corporate tax (PCTCT) are the total profits less charges on income.

2.1 The Schedular system

The corporation tax computation draws together all of the company's income and gains from various sources. The income from each different type of source must be computed separately because different computational rules apply.

The corporation tax rules have not yet been rewritten under the Tax Law Rewrite project (with the exception of capital allowances). The various sources of income are technically still described using the old system of Schedules and Cases. Each type of income is defined in accordance with a Schedule. There are only two kinds of Schedule now relevant to corporation tax: Schedule D and Schedule A. Schedule D is subdivided into Cases.

Although this text will use the more general descriptive terminology as used for income tax, a list of the relevant cases and schedules is given below for completeness.

- **Schedule D Case I**, equivalent to trading income under the income tax rules.
- **Schedule D Case III**, equivalent to interest income under the income tax rules.
- **Schedule D Case V**, equivalent to foreign income under the income tax rules.
- **Schedule D Case VI.** equivalent to miscellaneous income under the income tax rules, including any annual profits not falling under any other Schedule or Case, such as income from intangible fixed assets which are held as investment.
- **Schedule A**, equivalent to property income under the income tax rules.

The profits chargeable to corporation tax for an accounting period are derived as follows.

	£
Trading income	X
Interest income	X
Foreign income	X
Miscellaneous income	X
Property income	X
Chargeable gains	X
Total profits	X
Less charges on income (gross)	(X)
Profits chargeable to corporation tax (PCTCT) for an accounting period	X

Each of the above items is dealt with in further detail later in this text.

Exam focus point

It would be of great help in the exam if you could learn the above proforma. Then when answering a corporation tax question you could immediately reproduce the proforma and insert the appropriate numbers as you are given the information in the question.

2.2 Trading income

The trading income of companies is derived from the net profit figure in the accounts. The adjustments that need to be made to the accounts are broadly the same for companies as they are for income tax purposes even though the legislation has not been rewritten (see Chapter 5). Companies may also claim relief for the expenses of managing their investments (whether or not they are investment companies – see Chapter 25). Where shares in UK companies are held as trading assets, and not as investments, any dividends on those shares will be treated for tax purposes as trading profits.

Charges are added back in the calculation of adjusted profit. They are treated instead as a deduction from total profits. **The only charge on income examinable is a charitable gift aid donation**.

Patent and copyright royalties are not charges on income for corporation tax. Royalties paid for trade purposes are deducted in computing trading profits on the same basis as they have been deducted in accounts.

Interest received on a trading loan relationship (see the next chapter) is included within trading profits on an accruals basis. Similarly, interest paid on a trading loan relationship is deducted at arriving at trading profits. Loan relationships are dealt with in the next chapter.

Exam focus point

When adjusting profits as supplied in a profit and loss account confusion can arise as regards to whether the figures are net or gross. Properly drawn up company accounts should normally include all income gross. Charges should also be shown gross. However, some examination questions include items 'net'. Read the question carefully.

The calculation of capital allowances follows income tax principles. However, for companies, there is never any restriction of allowances to take account of any private use of an asset. The director or employee suffers a taxable benefit instead.

2.3 Property income

The taxation of UK property income follows similar rules to those for income tax (see earlier in this text). In summary:

(a) All UK rental activities are treated as a single source of income calculated in the same way as trading profits.

(b) Capital allowances are taken into account when computing property income or losses.

However **there are certain differences for companies**:

(a) **Property income losses are first set off against other income and gains of the company for the current period and any excess is:**

  (i) **Carried forward** as a property income loss of the following accounting period provided (except for investment companies) that the property letting business has not ceased, or

  (ii) **Available for surrender as group relief** (see later in this text).

(b) **Interest paid by a company on a loan to buy or improve property is not a property income expense. The loan relationship rules apply instead** (see the following chapter).

(c) **There is no landlords energy saving allowance** for insulation and draught proofing.

2.4 Income received net of tax

Examples of income received net of tax are:

(a) Patent royalties where the payer is not a UK company: tax at 22%

(b) Annuities and annual payments are paid net of tax where the payer is not a UK company.

Patent royalties and annuities which relate to the trade are included in trading profits normally on an accruals basis. Patent royalties and annuities which do not relate to the trade are taxed as miscellaneous income.

Income which suffers a deduction of tax at source is included within the profits chargeable to corporation tax at its gross equivalent. For example £4,875 of patent royalties relating to the trade received net of tax would need to be grossed up by multiplying by 100/78 to include £6,250 within trading income. If tax suffered on income received net exceeds tax deducted from amounts paid net, the difference is subtracted in calculating the mainstream corporation tax due.

2.5 Interest income

UK companies normally receive interest gross. Interest relating to non-trading loan relationships is taxed separately as interest income on an accruals basis. (See next chapter for further details of the rules for loan relationships.)

2.6 Chargeable gains

Companies do not pay capital gains tax. Instead their chargeable gains are included in the profits chargeable to corporation tax. We look at the computations of a company's chargeable gains in the next chapter.

2.7 Unit trusts

If a company holds units in a unit trust, then in general it is in the same position as if it held shares in a company. Dividends from the trust are, like dividends on shares, not taxable income for a company. There are the following exceptions to this rule.

(a) If more than 60% (by market value) of the unit trust's investments are interest-bearing investments, then the units are treated as a creditor loan relationship (see the next chapter) for the company. The amortised cost basis of accounting cannot be used: the fair value basis must be used instead and distributions out of the unit trust's interest income are treated as interest received.

(b) In other cases, a proportion of a dividend paid by the unit trust is treated as interest. This is called the unfranked part of the distribution: it corresponds to the proportion of the unit trust's income which is not dividend income.

2.8 Charges on income

Having arrived at a company's total profits, charges on income are deducted to arrive at the profits chargeable to corporation tax (PCTCT). The only charge on income examinable is a **payment under the gift aid scheme.**

Almost all donations of money to charity qualify as charges on income under the gift aid scheme whether they are one off donations or are regular donations. **Gift aid donations are paid gross**.

A donation will not be a qualifying donation under the gift aid scheme if:

(a) The company, persons connected with it, or persons connected with those connected persons, between them receive benefits from the charity, as a result of the donation worth more than:

Donation	Maximum benefit
< £100	25% of the total donations made in that accounting period
> £100 < £1,000	£25
> £1,000 < £10,000	2.5% of the total donations made in that accounting period
> £10,000	£250

(b) The gift is subject to any condition of repayment.

Donations to charities which are incurred wholly and exclusively for the purposes of the trade are trading deductions instead of charges on income.

Corporation tax relief is also given for gifts of quoted shares or land or buildings made to a charity and for donations to non-UK charities of medical supplies and equipment for humanitarian purposes.

2.9 Tax relief for cleaning up contaminated land

Companies that acquire contaminated land for the purposes of their trade (or property letting business) can claim to deduct 150% of their remediation expenditure (ie clean up costs).

Where the clean up expenditure is capital expenditure, the company can elect for it to be allowed as a deduction in computing profits of the accounting period in which it was incurred. Such an election must be made in writing and is subject to a two year time limit.

If the deduction gives rise to an unrelieved trading or property income loss, the unrelieved amount can be surrendered in return for a tax payment equal to 16% of the unrelieved amount.

Question

The calculation of PCTCT

The following is a summary of the profit and loss account of A Ltd (a trading company) for the year to 31 March 2007.

	£	£
Gross profit on trading		180,000
Treasury stock interest (non-trading investment)		700
Dividends from UK companies (net)		3,600
Loan interest from UK company (non-trading investment)		4,000
Building society interest received (non-trading investment)		292
Less: trade expenses (all allowable)	62,000	
gift aid donation paid	1,100	
		(63,100)
		125,492

The capital allowances for the period total £5,500. There was also a capital gain of £13,867.

Compute the profits chargeable to corporation tax.

Answer

	£	£
Net profit per accounts		125,492
Less: Treasury stock interest	700	
dividends received	3,600	
building society interest	292	
loan interest received	4,000	
		(8,592)
		116,900
Add: gift aid donation		1,100
		118,000
Less capital allowances		(5,500)
Trading income		112,500
Interest income £(700 + 292 + 4,000)		4,992
Chargeable gain		13,867
		131,359
Less charges: gift aid donation		(1,100)
Profits chargeable to corporation tax (PCTCT)		130,259

2.10 Long periods of account

If a company has a long period of account, exceeding 12 months, it is split into two accounting periods: the first 12 months and the remainder.

Where the period of account differs from the corporation tax accounting periods, profits are **allocated to the relevant periods** as follows:

- **Trading income** before capital allowances is apportioned on a **time basis.**
- **Capital allowances** and balancing charges are **calculated for each accounting period.**
- **Other income is allocated to the period to which it relates** (eg rents to the period when accrued). Miscellaneous income, however, is apportioned on a time basis.
- **Chargeable gains and losses** are allocated to the **period in which they are realised.**
- **Charges on income** are deducted in the accounting **period in which they are paid.**

Question

Long period of account

Xenon Ltd makes up an 18 month set of accounts to 30 June 2007 with the following results.

	£
Trading profits	180,000
Property income	
18 months @ £500 accruing per month	9,000
Capital gain (1 May 2007 disposal)	250,000
Less: Gift aid donation (paid 31.12.06)	(50,000)
	389,000

What are the profits chargeable to corporation tax for each of the accounting periods based on the above accounts?

Answer

The 18 month period of account is divided into:

Year ending 31 December 2006
6 months to 30 June 2007

Results are allocated:

	Y/e 31.12.06	*6m to 30.6.07*
	£	£
Trading profits 12:6	120,000	60,000
Property Income		
12 × £500	6,000	
6 × £500		3,000
Capital gain (1.5.06)		250,000
Less: Charge on income	(50,000)	
PCTCT (profits chargeable to corporation tax)	76,000	313,000

3 Charge to corporation tax

FAST FORWARD

Tax rates are set for financial years. Companies may be entitled to the starting rate, the small companies rate or to marginal relief, depending on their 'profits' (chargeable profits plus grossed up dividends received).

3.1 The full rate

The rates of corporation tax are fixed for financial years. A financial year runs from 1 April to the following 31 March and is identified by the calendar year in which it begins. For example, the year ended 31 March 2007 is the Financial year 2006 (FY 2006). This should not be confused with a tax year, which runs from 6 April to the following 5 April.

The full rate of corporation tax is 30% for FY 2006, having remained unchanged since FY 1999.

3.2 The small companies rate (SCR)

The SCR of corporation tax 19% for FY 2006 (unchanged since FY 2002) applies to the profits chargeable to corporation tax of UK resident companies whose 'profits' are not more than £300,000. In FY 2005 and prior years the SCR applied where "profits" were more than £50,000 but not more than £300,000.

'Profits' means profits chargeable to corporation tax plus the grossed-up amount of dividends received from UK companies (or from unit trusts where treated like company dividends) **other than those in the same group.** The grossed-up amount of UK dividends is the net dividend plus the tax credit which an individual investor would receive. We gross up by multiplying by 100/90. You may see the grossed up amount of dividend received referred to as franked investment income.

Question — The small companies rate

B Ltd had the following results for the year ended 31 March 2007.

	£
Trading profits	42,000
Dividend received 1 May 2006	9,000

Compute the corporation tax payable.

Answer

Trading profits	42,000
Dividend plus tax credit £9,000 × 100/90	10,000
'Profits' (between £50,000 and £300,000 limit)	52,000
Corporation tax payable	
£42,000 × 19%	£7,980

3.3 Marginal relief

Small companies marginal relief (sometimes called taper relief) applies where the 'profits' of an accounting period of a UK resident company are over £300,000 but under £1,500,000. We first calculate the corporation tax at the full rate and then deduct:

(M – P) × I/P × marginal relief fraction

where M = upper limit (currently £1,500,000)
P = 'profits' (see above Paragraph)
I = PCTCT

The marginal relief fraction is 11/400 for FY 2006 (unchanged since FY 2002).

Question — **Small companies marginal relief**

Lenox Ltd has the following results for the year ended 31 March 2007.

	£
PCTCT	296,000
Dividend received 1 December 2006	12,600

Calculate the corporation tax liability, if all profits are retained for future use in the business.

Answer

	£
PCTCT	296,000
Dividend plus tax credit £12,600 × 100/90	14,000
'Profits'	310,000

'Profits' are above £300,000 but below £1,500,000, so marginal relief applies.

	£
Corporation tax on PCTCT £296,000 × 30%	88,800
Less small companies' marginal relief	
£(1,500,000 – 310,000) × 296,000/310,000 × 11/400	(31,247)
	57,553

In exam questions you often need to be aware that there is a **marginal rate of 32.75 %** which applies to any PCTCT that lies in between the small companies' limits.

This is calculated as follows;

	£			£
Upper limit	1,500,000	@	30%	450,000
Lower limit	(300,000)	@	19%	(57,000)
Difference	1,200,000			393,000

$$\frac{393{,}000}{1{,}200{,}000} = 32.75\%$$

Effectively the band of profits (here £1,200,000) falling between the upper and lower limits are taxed at a rate of 32.75%

3.4 Example

A Ltd has PCTCT of £350,000 for the year ended 31 March 2007. Its corporation tax liability is

	£
£350,000 × 30%	105,000
Less: small companies' marginal relief	
11/400 (1,500,000 – 350,000)	(31,625)
	73,375

This is the same as calculating tax at 19% × £300,000 + 32.75% × £50,000 = £57,000 + £16,375 = £73,375.

Consequently tax is charged at an effective rate of 32.75% on PCTCT that exceeds the small companies' lower limit.

Note that although there is an effective corporation tax charge of 32.75%, this rate of tax is never used in actually calculating corporation tax. The rate is just an effective marginal rate that you must be aware of.

3.5 The starting rate (FY 2005 and earlier)

A starting rate of corporation tax of 0% applied to companies with 'profits' of up to £10,000 for FY 2002 to FY 2005.

Companies with 'profits' in the starting rate band could be subject to extra tax if they made distributions to non corporate shareholders (see later in this text).

Question — The starting rate of corporation tax

Dexter Limited had the following income for the year ended 31 March 2006.

(a) Schedule D, Case I income of £9,500, and
(b) Franked investment income of £300.

Calculate the corporation tax liability for the year. Assume all profits are retained in the company.

Answer

	£
Trading profits	9,500
Franked investment income	300
'Profits'	9,800
Corporation tax on PCTCT £9,500 × 0%	£nil

For companies with 'profits' between £10,001 and £50,000, the small companies rate less a starting rate marginal relief applied. The formula for calculating this marginal relief is the same as that given above except that 'M' is the upper limit for starting rate purposes, (£50,000). However the fraction used here is 19/400. The small companies' rate only applied in full when 'profits' exceed £50,000.

Companies with profits in the starting rate marginal relief band could be subject to additional tax if they distributed their profits to non-corporate shareholders (see later in this text).

Question — **Starting rate marginal relief**

Armstrong Ltd had the following income for its year ended 31 March 2006:

		£
(a)	Trading profits	29,500
(b)	Franked investment income	3,000

Calculate the corporation tax liability, if all profits are retained in the company for future use in the business.

Answer

	£
Trading profits	29,500
Franked investment income	3,000
Profits	32,500

	£
Corporation tax at small companies rate:	
£29,500 × 19%	5,605
Less: starting rate marginal relief –	
19/400 × ((£50,000 – £32,500) × £29,500/£32,500)	(755)
Corporation tax payable	4,850

The effective marginal rate of tax when PCTCT fell between the starting rate limits was 23.75%. Again, this is an effective marginal rate of tax that you need to be aware of but it is a rate that is never actually used in working out the CT charge. It was calculated as;

£			£
50,000	@	19%	9,500
(10,000)	@	0%	Nil
40,000			9,500

$$\frac{9{,}500}{40{,}000} = 23.75\ \%$$

PCTCT falling into the band (here £40,000) suffered tax at an effective rate of 23.75%.

3.6 Changes in the rate – Accounting periods straddling 31 March

If there is a change in the corporation tax rate, and a company's accounting period does not fall entirely within one financial year, the profits of the accounting period are apportioned to the two financial years on a time basis. Note that the profits as a whole are apportioned. We do not look at components of the profit individually, unlike apportionment of profits of a long period of account to two accounting periods.

Question — **A change in the rate**

Frances Ltd makes up accounts to 31 December each year. For the year ended 31 December 2006 its profit and loss account was as follows.

	£
PCTCT	40,000
Dividends plus tax credits	2,500
'Profits'	42,500

Calculate the corporation tax liability for the year.

Answer

	FY 2005 *3 months to* *31 March 2006* £	*FY 2006* *9 months to* *31 December 2006* £
PCTCT (divided 3:9)	10,000	30,000
'Profits' (divided 3:9)	10,625	31,875
Lower limit for starting rate		
FY 2005 £10,000 × 3/12	2,500	
FY 2006 N/A		
Upper limit for starting rate		
FY 2005 £50,000 × 3/12	12,500	
FY 2006 N/A		
Lower limit for small companies rate		
FY 2005 N/A		
FY 2006 £300,000 × 9/12		225,000
FY 2005: £10,000 × 19%		1,900
Less starting rate marginal relief		
£(12,500 – 10,625) × 10,000/10,625 × 19/400		(84)
		1,816
FY 2006: £30,000 × 19%		5,700
Corporation tax payable		7,516

The 'profits' falling into each financial year determines the rate of corporation tax that applies to the PCTCT of that year. This could be the full rate, the small companies' rate or, before FY 2006, the starting rate.

3.7 Associated companies and short accounting periods

Key term

The expression **'associated companies'** in tax has no connection with financial accounting. For tax purposes a company is associated with another company if either controls the other or if both are under the control of the same person or persons (individuals, partnerships or companies). Whether such a company is UK resident or not is irrelevant (even though non-UK resident companies cannot benefit from the starting rate, small companies rate or from marginal relief). Control is given by holding over 50% of the share capital or the voting power or being entitled to over 50% of the distributable income or of the net assets in a winding up.

If a company has one or more 'associated companies', then the profit limits for starting rate and small companies rate purposes are divided by the number of associated companies + 1 (for the company itself).

Companies which have only been associated for part of an accounting period are deemed to have been associated for the whole period for the purpose of determining the profit limits.

An associated company is ignored for these purposes if it has not carried on any trade or business at any time in the accounting period (or the part of the period during which it was associated). A holding company counts as not carrying on any trade or business so long as:

- Its only assets are shares in subsidiaries
- It is not entitled to deduct any outgoings as charges or management expenses, and
- Its only profits are dividends from subsidiaries, which are distributed in full to its shareholders.

The profit limits are reduced proportionately if an accounting period lasts for less than 12 months.

Question

Associated companies and short accounting periods

For the nine months to 31 January 2007 a company with two other associated companies had PCTCT of £78,000 and no dividends paid for or received. Compute the corporation tax payable.

Answer

(a) Reduction in the lower limit for SCR

Multiply by 1/(number of associated companies + 1) = 1/3

Then multiply by number of months in AP/12 = 9/12

£300,000 × $^1/_3$ × $^9/_{12}$ = £75,000

(b) Reduction in the upper limit for SCR

£1,500,000 × $^1/_3$ × $^9/_{12}$ = £375,000

(c) 'Profits' = £78,000

As 'profits' fall between the lower and upper limits for SCR purposes, the full rate less small companies' marginal relief applies:

(d) Corporation tax

	£
£78,000 × 30%	23,400
Less small companies' marginal relief £(375,000 – 78,000) × 11/400	(8,168)
Corporation tax	15,232

Chapter roundup

- Companies pay corporation tax on their profits chargeable to corporation tax of each accounting period. The profits chargeable to corporation tax are income plus gains minus charges.
- An accounting period cannot exceed twelve months in length. A long period of account must be split into two accounting periods, the first of which is twelve months long.
- Tax rates are set for financial years.
- Companies may be entitled to the starting rate, the small companies rate or to marginal relief, depending on their 'profits' (chargeable profits plus grossed up dividends received).

Quick quiz

1 When does an accounting period end?

2 How are trading profits (before capital allowances) of a long period of account divided between accounting periods?

3 Does a company pay debenture interest to another UK company gross or net of tax?

4 Which companies are entitled to the small companies rate of corporation tax?

5 What is the marginal relief formula?

6 What is an associated company?

Answers to quick quiz

1 An accounting period ends on the earliest of:

(a) 12 months after its start
(b) the end of the company's period of account
(c) the commencement of the company's winding up
(d) the company ceasing to be resident in the UK
(e) the company ceasing to be liable to corporation tax

2 Trading income (before capital allowances) is apportioned on a time basis.

3 Gross

4 Companies with profits of up to £300,000

5 $(M - P) \times I/P \times$ marginal relief fraction

where:

M = upper limit
P = 'profits'
I = PCTCT

6 A company is associated with another company if either controls the other or if both are under the control of the same person or persons (Individual, partnership or companies).

Now try the question below from the Exam Question Bank

Number	Level	Marks	Time
Q20	Introductory	15	27 mins

Corporation tax: additional aspects

22

Introduction

In this chapter we look at some of the more advanced aspects of corporation tax.

Topic list	Syllabus references
1 Chargeable gains	2(a)
2 Intellectual property (intangible fixed assets)	2(a)
3 Loan relationships	2(a)
4 The corporate venturing scheme	2(a)
5 Winding up	2(a)

1 Chargeable gains

FAST FORWARD

Companies pay corporation tax on their capital gains. Indexation allowance is available until disposal. Chargeable gains arising on the disposal of substantial shareholdings are exempt.

1.1 Introduction

Companies do not pay capital gains tax. Instead their chargeable gains are included in the profits chargeable to corporation tax. A company's capital gains or allowable losses are computed in a similar way to individuals (see earlier in this text) but with a few major differences:

(a) Indexation allowance calculations may include periods of ownership after 6 April 1998. **Indexation is calculated to the month of disposal of an asset.**

(b) **The FA 1985 pool for shares does not close at 5 April 1998: it runs to the month of disposal of the shares.** This means that different matching rules are needed (see below)

(c) **The taper relief does not apply**

(d) **No annual exemption is available**

Key term

All companies under common control are **connected persons** for chargeable gains purposes.

1.2 Shares

For companies the matching of shares sold is in the following order.

1st Shares acquired on the **same day**
2nd Shares acquired in the **previous nine days**, taking earlier acquisitions first
3rd Shares from the **FA 1985 pool**

If a company owns 2% or more of another company, disposals are matched (after same day acquisitions) with shares acquired within one month before or after the disposal (for Stock Exchange transactions) or six months (in other cases) before being matched with shares from the FA 1985 pool.

Where shares are disposed of within nine days of acquisition, no indexation allowance is available even if the acquisition and disposal fall within different months. Acquisitions matched with disposals under the nine day rule never enter the FA 1985 pool.

The rules on alterations of share capital are similar to those for individuals. Bonus or rights issue shares will be added to the underlying holding from which the entitlement to the additional shares arose. This rule about rights issue shares also applies to the shares acquired by way of scrip dividend (contrast the treatment of individuals where the scrip dividend shares are treated as a completely new acquisition).

1.3 Disposal of substantial shareholdings

There is an exemption from corporation tax for any gain arising when a **trading company (or member of a trading group) disposes of the whole or any part of a substantial shareholding in another trading company** (or in the holding company of a trading group or sub-group).

Key term

A **substantial shareholding** is one where the investing company holds 10% of ordinary share capital and is beneficially entitled to at least 10% of the

(a) profits available for distribution to equity holders; and
(b) assets of the company available for distribution to equity holders on a winding up.

To meet the 10% test shares owned by members of a chargeable gains group (see later in this text) may be amalgamated. **The 10% test must have been met for a continuous twelve month period during the two years preceding the disposal.**

The exemption is given automatically and cannot be disclaimed. This means that as well as exempting gains, it denies relief for losses.

The exemption applies to the disposal of part of a substantial holding. This means that if A Ltd owns 10% of the ordinary share capital in B Ltd, and disposes of 1% of that share capital, any gain will be exempt. In addition, the disposal of the remaining 9% may result in an exempt gain.

1.4 Example: disposal of substantial shareholding

On 1.12.01 SD Ltd bought 20% of the shares in AM Ltd. The shareholding qualifies for the substantial shareholding exemption. During its accounting period to 31 March 2007, SD Ltd made the following disposals:

(a) On 30 June 2006 it disposed of a 15% holding in AM Ltd.
(b) On 30 December 2006 it disposed of the remaining 5% holding in AM Ltd.

Both of these shareholdings qualify for the substantial shareholdings exemption. Clearly the first disposal is of at least a 10% holding which was held for twelve months prior to disposal. The second disposal also qualifies despite being only a 5% holding, because SD Ltd owned a 10% holding throughout a twelve month period beginning in the two years prior to this second disposal.

Where there has been a qualifying share-for-share exchange, the holding period of the original shares is amalgamated with the holding period of the replacement shares in determining whether the '12 month' rule has been satisfied.

The company making the disposal must have been a trading company (or member of a qualifying group, which is essentially a group of trading companies) throughout the period:

(a) beginning with the start of the latest 12 month period in relation to which the company disposing of the shares met the substantial shareholding requirement; and

(b) ending with the time of disposal.

It must also be a trading company or member of a qualifying group immediately after the disposal.

2 Intellectual property (Intangible Fixed Assets)

FAST FORWARD

Gains/losses arising on intangible assets are recognised for tax purposes on the same basis as they are recognised in the accounts. Intangible assets that are not amortised in the accounts, or are amortised very slowly may be written off for tax purposes at the rate of 4 % per annum.

2.1 Definition and treatment

Any income or expenditure (including depreciation or amortisation) associated with:

(a) intellectual property (including patents and copyrights)
(b) goodwill
(c) other intangible assets (including agricultural quotas and brands)

is, in general, taxable/deductible as trading income. Provided the accounts have been prepared using generally accepted accounting practice, no adjustment will be needed to net profits for tax purposes.

Exam focus point

> Exam questions in this area will normally cover goodwill and/or patents. Questions will only be set where the company uses the intangible asset in its trade.

As with loan relationships (see below) all debits/credits relating to intellectual property will be brought in/deducted as income. Thus amounts relating to disposals are also dealt with in the profit and loss account. **An election may be made to disallow amortisation and instead write off the cost of a capitalised intangible asset for tax purposes at the rate of 4% per annum (pro-rated for short accounting periods).** The election is irrevocable and must be made within two years of the end of the accounting period of acquisition. The 4% relief is available for expenditure on the creation or enhancement of capital assets as well as on the cost of acquisition. The election may be beneficial if an asset is not amortised in the accounts (or only over a very long time).

2.2 Example

During its six month accounting period to 31 March 2007, Dex Ltd purchased goodwill for £400,000. The goodwill is capitalised in the balance sheet and not amortised.

In the six month period to 31.3.07

6/12 x 4% × £400,000 = £8,000

may be deducted from trading profits for tax purposes provided an election to do so is made by 31.3.09.

When the asset is disposed of sale proceeds are compared with the tax written down value (this will be cost less amounts amortised or be 4% straight line write off claimed) and the gain/loss is included within trading profits. For example, if the goodwill in the above example was sold in the year to 31.3.08 for £420,000, the amount taxable as part of trading profits would be

£420,000 – (£400,000 – £8,000) = £28,000

The capital gains tax rollover relief rules do not apply to goodwill and other intangible fixed assets. However, if an intangible asset is sold for more than its original cost and other intangible assets are acquired in the period commencing one year before and ending three years after the sale, a form of rollover relief can be claimed. Where the full reinvestment takes place the relief is the excess of proceeds over original cost. Where the amount reinvested is less than the proceeds received the relief is restricted to the amount by which the reinvestment exceeds the cost of the asset.

2.3 Example

On 1.1.07 Gateway Ltd sold goodwill which originally cost £400,000, for £500,000. The tax and accounting written down value of the goodwill was £360,000. New goodwill was purchased for £550,000 on 31.3.07.

The gain in the P&L account is £(500,000 – 360,000) = £140,000.

£100,000 (£500,000 – £400,000) of the gain on the sale of the 'old' goodwill can be deducted from trading profits. The remaining £40,000 will remain within the trading profits. £450,000 is the cost of the new goodwill for the purpose of computing any future tax deductions.

If only £450,000 had been reinvested the relief would be restricted to £50,000.

A claim for relief must specify the 'old' asset, the amount of relief claimed and the amount of expenditure on the new asset. Relief can also be claimed where the reinvestment is made by another member of the capital gains group (see later in this text), and also where the reinvestment is in the shares of another company which becomes a member as a result.

Transfers of intangible assets between members of a capital gains group (see later in this text) are on a 'no gain/loss basis'. Where a company leaves a capital gains group holding an intangible asset transferred to it in the previous six years the gain or loss that would have arisen on the date of the transfer is realised and included in trading profits.

Either the company leaving the capital gains group or a continuing member can claim to rollover any profit arising. The departing company can claim relief if it retains the profit and acquires a new asset. The continuing company can claim relief if the profit has been switched to it and it acquires a new intangible asset.

2.4 Accounting methods

Debits and credits for intangible fixed assets must be calculated using generally accepted accounting practice, and if the accounts do not comply the debits and credits must be recalculated using the correct basis. Most accounts will be prepared using the accruals basis, and this has been followed in this text. The accounts may be prepared using either UK generally accepted accounting practice (UK GAAP) or International Accounting Standards (IAS).

If the company changes its basis of accounting, any change in value of intangible fixed assets from the end of the previous period to the start of the current period must be brought into account. This applies especially if there is a change in accounting basis on moving from UK GAAP to IAS or vice versa.

3 Loan relationships

FAST FORWARD

A loan relationship arises when a company lends or borrows money. Trading loan relationships are dealt with as trading income. Non-trading loan relationships are dealt with as interest income.

3.1 Introduction

If a company borrows or lends money, including issuing or investing in debentures or buying gilts, it has a loan relationship. This can be a creditor relationship (where the company lends or invests money) or a debtor relationship (where the company borrows money or issues securities).

3.2 Treatment of trading loan relationships

If the company is a party to a **loan relationship for trade purposes, any debits – ie interest paid or other debt costs – charged through its accounts are allowed as a trading expense** and are therefore deductible in computing trading profits.

Similarly **if any credits – ie interest income or other debt returns – arise on a trading loan these are treated as a trading receipt and are taxable as part of trading profit**. This is not likely to arise unless the trade is one of money lending.

3.3 Treatment of non-trading loan relationships

If a loan relationship is not one to which the company is a party for trade purposes any debits or credits must be pooled. A net credit on the pool is chargeable as interest income. A net deficit on the pool may be:

(a) **Set against other income of the same accounting period**

(b) **Surrendered as group relief (see later in this text)**

(c) **Carried back and set against any surpluses on non-trading loan relationships** (taxed as interest income) **for the previous twelve months**

Any deficit remaining after the above claims is automatically carried forward and set against non trading profits for succeeding accounting periods. If the company does not want this automatic set-off to apply, it has two years from the end of the accounting period to apply for exemption for all or part of the deficit carried forward.

These methods of relief are discussed in more detail later in this text.

3.4 Accounting methods

Debits and credits must be brought into account using UK generally accepted accounting practice (UK GAAP) or International Accounting Standards (IAS). Under UK GAAP this will generally be either:

(a) The amortised cost basis of accounting, or
(b) The fair value basis.

Under the amortised cost basis the cost of the asset or liability must be included in the accounts at cost less cumulative amortisation. The debit or credit brought into account will be the amortisation for the period, together with any interest for the period. This method is effectively the accruals basis, and will be used in this text.

Under the fair value basis the cost of the asset or liability must be included in the accounts at its fair value. The debit or credit brought into account will be the change in value for the period, together with any interest for the period. This method is commonly only used by companies in the financial sector, such as banks.

If the company changes its basis of accounting, any change in value of the loan relationship from the end of the previous period to the start of the current period must be brought into account. This applies especially if there is a change in accounting basis on moving from UK GAAP to IAS or vice versa.

If neither UK GAAP nor IAS are used, the debits and credits must be recalculated using a 'correct' method.

3.5 Incidental costs of loan finance

Under the loan relationship rules expenses ('debits') are allowed if incurred directly:

(a) In bring a loan relationship into existence

(b) Entering into or giving effect to any related transactions

(c) Making payment under a loan relationship or related transactions, or

(d) Taking steps to ensure the receipt of payments under the loan relationship or related transaction.

A related transaction means 'any disposal or acquisition (in whole or in part) of rights or liabilities under the relationship, including any arising from a security issue in relation to the money debt in question'.

The above categories of incidental costs are also allowable even if the company does not enter into the loan relationship (ie abortive costs). Cost directly incurred in varying the terms of a loan relationship are also allowed.

3.6 Other matters

It is not only the interest costs of borrowing that are allowable or taxable. The capital costs are treated similarly. Thus if a company issues a loan at a discount and repays it eventually at par, the capital cost is allowed over the life of the loan

Relief for pre-trading expenditure extends to expenses incurred on trading loan relationships in accounting periods ending within seven years of the company starting to trade. An expense that would have been a trading debit if it was incurred after the trade had commenced, is treated as a trading debit of the first trading period. An election has to be made within two years of the end of the first trading period.

Payments of interest between UK companies are paid gross. Short interest or interest to a UK bank is payable gross while 'yearly' interest is payable net of 20% tax if not paid to a corporate recipient.

Interest charged on underpaid tax is allowable and interest received on overpaid tax is assessable under the loan relationship rules as interest income.

4 The corporate venturing scheme

FAST FORWARD

Companies can obtain tax relief on certain investments they make.

4.1 Introduction

The corporate venturing scheme allows an investing company to obtain corporation tax relief at 20% on amounts invested in ordinary shares held for at least 3 years.

The investment must be in new ordinary shares of an unquoted 'small high risk trading company'. As long as the small company is unquoted at the time the shares are issued and there are no arrangements in place (or planned) at that time for seeking a listing, relief will not be withdrawn if the company subsequently becomes quoted during the three year period for which the shares must be held.

The investing company can defer any chargeable gains made on corporate venturing investments that it reinvests in another shareholding under the scheme.

Any capital loss (net of corporation tax relief) arising on a disposal of the shares can be set against the company's income.

Tax relief is withdrawn if the shares are not held for three years.

A corporate venturer cannot obtain tax relief under the scheme if it controls the small company in which it has invested.

4.2 The investing company

The investing company must either be:

(a) A trading company which is neither engaged in a financial trade nor a member of a group whose business consists of financial trades or non-trading activities, or

(b) An investment company which is a member of a non-financial trading group.

The investing company must not hold more than 30% of the:

(a) Ordinary share capital, or
(b) The combined share and loan capital which can be converted into ordinary share capital

of the company in which the investment is made (the issuing company).

4.3 The issuing company

The issuing company must not have gross assets of more than £7 million before the investment and not more than £8 million immediately after it.

For a period of three years from the later of the issue of shares and the start of trading:

(a) The issuing company must carry on a qualifying trade or be a parent company whose business does not consist to a substantial extent of excluded activities and which has at least one group member carrying on a qualifying trade. If the issuing company is a parent company, each of the other group members (other than property companies) must be at least 51% owned by the company or another of its subsidiaries. If the subsidiary holds and manages property, it must be at least 90% owned by the company or another of it's subsidiaries.

(b) The issuing company must not be under the control of any other company.

(c) The issuing company must not be involved in a partnership or joint venture with another company which is owned by the same person as owns the issuing company.

(d) At least 20% of the issuing company's ordinary share capital must be owned by individuals who are not employees or directors of the investing company.

4.4 Qualifying trade

A trade must be carried on on a commercial basis and must not consist to a substantial extent of certain excluded activities.

Research and development which is intended to lead to or benefit a qualifying trade is treated as a qualifying trade.

4.5 Anti-avoidance rules

There are extensive anti-avoidance rules designed to ensure that money invested is genuinely put at risk.

4.6 Clearance

The issuing company can apply for advance clearance from HMRC that an issue will meet the qualifying conditions.

5 Winding up

FAST FORWARD

A new accounting period (AP) begins when a winding up commences. Thereafter APs are for 12 months until the winding up is complete. Distributions made during a winding up are capital. There are special rules in respect of accounting periods when companies go into administration.

5.1 General principles

A company **in liquidation is chargeable to corporation tax on the profits arising during the winding up.**

An accounting period ends and a new one beings when a winding up commences. Thereafter, accounting periods end *only* on each anniversary of the commencement of winding up, until the final period which ends when the winding up is completed. A cessation of trade after a winding up has commenced will not bring an accounting period to an end.

5.2 Example

Totterdown Ltd, a company with a 31 December year end, ceased trading on 10 June 2005. The members passed a resolution to wind up the company on 12 September 2005 and the winding up was completed on 15 January 2007. From 1 January 2005 how many accounting periods will there be for the company?

Solution

1.1.05 – 10.6.05	To the date trade ceased.
11.6.05 – 11.9.05	The commencement of a winding up brings an AP to an end.
12.9.05 – 11.9.06	Anniversary of commencement of winding up.
12.9.06 – 15.1.07	Final AP ends when winding up complete.

The Enterprise Act 2002 provides for companies to go from liquidation to administration and for assets to be distributed without a formal liquidation. In such cases, the following rules apply relating to when an accounting period will be deemed to end.

A new accounting period begins when a company goes into administration. An accounting period ends when a company ceases to be in administration and a new accounting period begins when a company moves out of liquidation into administration.

In contrast to the position in liquidation, where the corporation tax accounting periods are then annual from the date of appointment of the liquidator, there is no requirement to change the accounting reference date of the company. Therefore, future accounting periods in administration follow the original accounting dates.

5.3 Example

Company A has a normal accounting date of 31 December annually. An administrator is appointed on 17 August 2006. As a result, for corporation tax purposes the company's accounting periods will be 1 January to 16 August 2006 before administration and 17 August to 31 December 2006 after the appointment of the administrator. Accounting periods will then be 31 December annually while the company remains in administration.

When an administration ceases, a new accounting period must start for tax purposes, whether the company comes out of administration and recommences to trade normally or goes from administration into winding up.

5.4 Example

Company A remains in administration for 16 months and a liquidator is appointed on 10 October 2007.

The accounting period in administration will therefore be 1 January 2007 to 9 October 2007. The next accounting period will be the first liquidation accounting period, 10 October 2007 to 9 October 2008. Accounting periods will then be annually to 9 October until the company ceases to be in liquidation (either by striking off or returning to administration).

When a company comes out of liquidation into administration, a new accounting period must start. Again, this permits proper computation of the tax due as an expense of liquidation or administration.

5.5 Example

Company A remain in liquidation for only three months, and a court order appointing a new administrator is granted on 14 January 2008.

The accounting periods are therefore 10 October 2007 to 13 January 2008 in liquidation, then 14 January to (presumably) 31 December 2008 in administration.

If the company had been in liquidation for some time, so that liquidation accounts had been prepared to 9 October for a number of years, the post-liquidation accounting periods would end on 9 October annually unless the administrator changed the accounting reference date.

5.6 Liquidation

Distributions made after the liquidation has started are capital and treated as a part disposal of shares in the hands of the shareholder. This is the position even if the distributions include accumulated net profits of the company out of which dividends could be paid.

Where a company has distributable profits, it may be preferable, to pay these out as a dividend before the liquidation starts. Any such distribution will be chargeable to income tax on a shareholder who is an individual.

Assets distributed in specie by the liquidator are deemed to be disposed of at market value. Where the assets are chargeable assets, any chargeable gain arising is charged to corporation tax in accordance with the normal rules. There is, thus, double taxation on assets distributed to shareholders in the liquidation since the asset distribution will also be treated as a capital distribution in the hands of the shareholders.

When a company is put into liquidation, it loses beneficial ownership of its assets. If the company to be liquidated is a parent company, it will therefore lose its group relationship with its former subsidiaries. No group relief (see later in this text) will be available to any of the companies in the former group.

By contrast, a group (see later in this text) continues to exist for chargeable gains purposes, notwithstanding the commencement of liquidation.

Ordinarily, assets distributed outside a formal winding up represent an income distribution.

It may, however, be possible to treat certain distributions as capital providing certain assurances are given to the Inspector beforehand (ESC C16). The assurances required are as follows:

(a) that the company has **ceased trading**;

(b) that the company will **collect its debts, pay off its creditors** and **distribute its remaining assets** to its shareholders;

(c) that it will **thereafter seek to be struck off the Companies Register and be dissolved**; and

(d) that the **shareholders agree to pay any tax liabilities arising on the concessionary basis**.

Once they have received these assurances HMRC is prepared to regard the distribution as having been made **under a formal winding up**. The value of the distribution is then treated as capital receipts of the shareholders for the purpose of calculating any chargeable gains arising to them on the disposal of their shares. This may or may not be advantageous to the shareholders.

5.7 Other situations

The appointment of a receiver or a manager has no tax consequences.

Chapter roundup

- Chargeable gains arising on the disposal of substantial shareholdings are exempt.
- Gains/losses arising on intangible assets are recognised for tax purposes on the same basis as they are recognised in the accounts. Intangible assets that are not amortised in the accounts, or are amortised very slowly may be written off for tax purposes at the rate of 4 % per annum.
- Companies can obtain tax relief on certain investments they make.
- A new accounting period (AP) begins when a winding up commences. Thereafter APs are for 12 months until the winding up is complete. Distributions made during a winding up are capital. There are special rules in respect of accounting periods when companies go into administration.

Quick quiz

1 Any gain arising on the disposal of a 'substantial shareholding' is exempt from corporation tax. Define a substantial shareholding for these purposes.

2 JoCo Ltd has a long standing 85% holding in JoCo Ltd. If JoCo Ltd sells its holding will this disposal fall into the "substantial shareholding" provisions?

3 How is interest arising on a non-trading loan relationship taxed?

3 What tax relief is available under the corporate venturing scheme?

4 Are distributions made during a liquidation treated as capital or income distributions?

6 Inca Ltd makes up accounts to 31 March. The company goes into liquidation on 1 November 2006 and cease to trade on 31 December 2006. The company is finally wound up on 31 July 2007. What are the accounting periods from 1 April 2005?

7 Does the appointment of an administrator affect a company's accounting periods?

8 What is the impact (if any) on a company accounting period when a company moves out of liquidation into administration?

Answers to quick quiz

1 Broadly, a substantial shareholding is one where the investing company holds 10% of the ordinary share capital concerned.

2 Yes – an 85% holding is a 10% or more holding (see 1 above).

3 Interest on a non-trading loan relationship is aggregate with all other income and gains from non-trading loans. From this is deducted interest paid on and losses on non-trading loans. The resulting net amount is taxed as interest income.

4 The corporate venturing scheme allows an investing company to obtain corporation tax relief at 20% on amounts invested in ordinary shares held for at least three years.

5 Distributions are capital distributions and are treated as a part disposal of the shares in the hands of the shareholder.

6 1 April 2005 – 31 March 2006

1 April 2006 – 31 October 2006

1 November 2006 – 31 July 2007

7 Yes. A new accounting period begins when a company goes into administration. An accounting period ends when a company ceases to be in administration.

8 A new accounting period begins when a company moves status from liquidation into administration.

Now try the question below from the Exam Question Bank

Number	Level	Marks	Time
Q21	Introductory	20	36 mins

23

Payment of tax by companies

Introduction

We have looked at the computation of a company's CT liability. In this chapter we look at the self assessment system for CT. We shall also see how income tax is accounted for. Companies are not supposed to pay income tax so the effects of deducting income tax at source need to be neutralised.

Topic list	Syllabus references
1 Returns, records, enquiries, assessments and claims	2(a)
2 Payment of corporation tax and interest	2(a)
3 Income tax suffered or withheld	2(a)

1 Returns, records, enquiries, assessments and claims

1.1 Notification to HMRC

FAST FORWARD

A company must notify HMRC within 3 months of starting to trade.

A company must notify HMRC of the beginning of its' first accounting period (ie usually when it starts to trade) and the beginning of any subsequent period that does not immediately follow the end of a previous accounting period. The notice must be in the prescribed form and submitted within three months of the relevant date.

1.2 Returns

FAST FORWARD

CT 600 returns must, in general, be filed within twelve months of the end of an accounting period.

A company's tax return (CT 600) must include a self assessment of any tax payable.

An obligation to file a return arises only when the company receives a notice requiring a return. A return is required for each accounting period ending during or at the end of the period specified in the notice requiring a return. A company also has to file a return for certain other periods which are not accounting periods (eg for a period when the company is dormant).

A company that does not receive a notice requiring a return must, if it is chargeable to tax, **notify HMRC within twelve months of the end of the accounting period**. Failure to do so results in a maximum penalty equal to the tax unpaid twelve months after the end of the accounting period. Tax for this purpose includes corporation tax and notional tax on loans to participators of close companies (see later in this text).

A notice to file a return may also require other information, accounts and reports. For a UK resident company the requirement to deliver accounts normally extends only to the accounts required under the Companies Act.

A return is due on or before the filing date. This is the later of:

(a) **12 months after the end of the period to which the return relates**;

(b) **if the relevant period of account is not more than 18 months long, 12 months from the end of the period of account**;

(c) **if relevant the period of account is more than 18 months long, 30 months from the start of the period of account**; and

(d) **three months from the date on which the notice requiring the return was made**.

The relevant period of account is that in which the accounting period to which the return relates ends.

Question

Filing date

A Ltd prepares accounts for the eighteen months to 30 June 2006. A notice requiring a return for the period ended 30 June 2006 was issued to A Ltd on 1 September 2006. State the periods for which A Ltd must file a tax return and the filing dates.

Answer

The company must file a return for the two accounting periods ending in the period specified in the notice requiring a return. The first accounting period is the twelve months to 31 December 2005 and the second is the six months to 30 June 2006. The filing date is twelve months after the end of the relevant period of account, 30 June 2007.

There is a £100 penalty for a failure to submit a return on time, rising to £200 if the delay exceeds three months. These penalties become £500 and £1,000 respectively when a return was late (or never submitted) for each of the preceding two accounting periods.

An additional tax geared penalty is applied if a return is more than six months late. The penalty is 10% of the tax unpaid six months after the return was due if the total delay is up to 12 months, and 20% of that tax if the return is over 12 months late.

There is a tax geared penalty for a fraudulent or negligent return and for failing to correct an innocent error without unreasonable delay. The maximum penalty is equal to the tax that would have been lost had the return been accepted as correct. HMRC can mitigate this penalty. If a company is liable to more than one tax geared penalty, the total penalty is limited to the maximum single penalty that could be charged.

A company may amend a return within twelve months of the filing date. HMRC may amend a return to correct obvious errors within nine months of the day the return was filed, or if the correction is to an amended return, within nine months of the filing of an amendment. The company may amend its return so as to reject the correction. If the time limit for amendments has expired, the company may reject the correction by giving notice within three months.

1.3 Records

Companies must keep records until the latest of:

(a) six years from the end of the accounting period;
(b) the date any enquiries are completed;
(c) the date after which enquiries may not be commenced.

All business records and accounts, including contracts and receipts, must be kept.

If a return is demanded more than six years after the end of the accounting period, any records which the company still has must be kept until the later of the end of any enquiry and the expiry of the right to start an enquiry.

Failure to keep records can lead to a penalty of up to £3,000 for each accounting period affected. However, this penalty does not apply when the only records which have not been kept are ones which could only have been needed for the purposes of claims, elections or notices not included in the return.

HMRC do not generally insist on original records being kept but original records of the following must be preserved:

(a) Qualifying distributions and tax credits

(b) Gross and net payments and tax deducted for payments made net of tax

(c) Certificates of payments made to sub-contractors net of tax

(d) Details of foreign tax paid, although HMRC will accept photocopies of foreign tax assessments when calculating underlying tax (see later in this text) on dividends from abroad

1.4 Enquiries

FAST FORWARD

HMRC can enquire into returns.

A return or an amendment need not be accepted at face value by HMRC. **They may enquire into it, provided that they first give written notice that they are going to enquire.** The notice must be given by a year after the later of:

(a) The filing date;

(b) The 31 January, 30 April, 31 July or 31 October next following the actual date of delivery of the return or amendment.

Only one enquiry may be made in respect of any one return or amendment.

If a notice of an enquiry has been given, HMRC may demand that the company produce documents for inspection and copying. However, documents relating to an appeal need not be produced and the company may appeal against a notice requiring documents to be produced.

If HMRC demand documents, but the company does not produce them, there is a penalty of £50. There is also a daily penalty, which applies for each day from the day after the imposition of the £50 penalty until the documents are produced. The daily penalty may be imposed by HMRC, in which case it is £30. If, however, HMRC ask the Commissioners to impose the penalty, it is £150.

HMRC may amend a self assessment at any time during an enquiry if they believe there might otherwise be a loss of tax. The company may appeal against such an amendment within 30 days. The company may itself make amendments during an enquiry under the normal rules for amendments. No effect will be given to such amendments during the enquiry but they may be taken into account in the enquiry.

An enquiry ends when HMRC give notice that it has been completed and notify what they believe to be the correct amount of tax payable. Before that time, the company may ask the Commissioners to order HMRC to notify the completion of its enquiry by a specified date. Such a direction will be given unless HMRC can demonstrate that they have reasonable grounds for continuing the enquiry.

The company has 30 days from the end of an enquiry to amend its self assessment in accordance with HMRC's conclusions. If HMRC are not satisfied with the company's amendments, they have a further 30 days to amend the self assessment. The company then has another 30 days in which it may appeal against HMRC's amendments.

1.5 Determinations and discovery assessments

If a return is not delivered by the filing date, HMRC may issue a determination of the tax payable within the five years from the filing date. This is treated as a self assessment and there is no appeal against it. However, it is automatically replaced by any self assessment made by the company by the later of five years from the filing date and 12 months from the determination.

If HMRC believe that not enough tax has been assessed for an accounting period they can make a discovery assessment to collect the extra tax. However, when a tax return has been delivered this power is limited as outlined below.

No discovery assessment can be made on account of an error or mistake as to the basis on which the tax liability ought to be computed, if the basis generally prevailing at the time when the return was made was applied.

A discovery assessment can only be made if either:

(a) the loss of tax is due to fraudulent or negligent conduct by the company or by someone acting on its behalf; or

(b) HMRC could not reasonably be expected to have been aware of the loss of tax, given the information so far supplied to them, when their right to start an enquiry expired or when they notified the company that an enquiry had finished. The information supplied must be sufficiently detailed to draw HMRC's attention to contentious matters such as the use of a valuation or estimate.

The time limit for raising a discovery assessment is six years from the end of the accounting period but this is extended to 21 years if there has been fraudulent or negligent conduct. The company may appeal against a discovery assessment within 30 days of issue.

1.6 Claims

Wherever possible claims must be made on a tax return or on an amendment to it and must be quantified at the time the return is made.

If a company believes that it has paid excessive tax because of an error in a return, an error or mistake claim may be made within six years from the end of the accounting period. An appeal against a decision on such a claim must be made within 30 days. An error or mistake claim may not be made if the return was made in accordance with a generally accepted practice which prevailed at the time.

Other claims must be made by six years after the end of the accounting period, unless a different time limit is specified. If an error or mistake is made in a claim, a supplementary claim may be made within the time limit for the original claim.

If HMRC amend a self assessment or issue a discovery assessment then the company has a further period to make, vary or withdraw a claim (unless the claim is irrevocable) even if this is outside the normal time limit. The period is one year from the end of the accounting period in which the amendment or assessment was made, or one year from the end of the accounting period in which the enquiry was closed if the amendment is the result of an enquiry. The relief is limited where there has been fraudulent or negligent conduct by the company or its agent.

2 Payment of corporation tax and interest

FAST FORWARD

In general, corporation tax is due nine months after the end of an accounting period but large companies must pay their corporation tax in four quarterly instalments.

2.1 Due dates

Corporation tax is due for payment by small and medium sized companies **nine months after the end of the accounting period**.

Large companies, however, must pay their corporation tax in instalments. **Broadly, a large company is any company that pays corporation tax at the full rate** (profits exceed £1,500,000 where there are no associated companies).

Instalments are due on the 14th day of the month, starting in the seventh month. Provided that the accounting period is twelve months long subsequent instalments are due in the tenth month during the accounting period and in the first and fourth months after the end of the accounting period. If an accounting period is less than twelve months long subsequent instalments are due at three monthly intervals but with the final payment being due in the fourth month of the next accounting period.

2.2 Example

X Ltd is a large company with a 31 December accounting year end. Instalments of corporation tax will be due to be paid by X Ltd on:

- 14 July and 14 October in the accounting period;
- 14 January and 14 April after the accounting period ends

Thus for the year ended 31 December 2006 instalment payments are due on 14 July 2006, 14 October 2006, 14 January 2007 and 14 April 2007.

Instalments are based on the estimated corporation tax liability for the current period (not the previous period). This means that it will be extremely important for companies to forecast their tax liabilities accurately. Large companies whose directors are poor at estimating may find their company's incurring significant interest charges. The amount of each instalment is computed by:

(a) working out 3 × CT/n where CT is the amount of the estimated corporation tax liability payable in instalments for the period and n is the number of months in the period;

(b) allocating the smaller of that amount and the total estimated corporation tax liability to the first instalment;

(c) repeating the process for later instalments until the amount allocated is equal to the corporation tax liability. This gives four equal instalments for 12 month accounting periods and also caters for periods which end earlier than expected.

The company is therefore required to estimate its corporation tax liability before the end of the accounting period, and must revise its estimate each quarter.

Question

Short accounting period

A company has a CT liability of £880,000 for the eight month period to 30 September 2006. Accounts had previously always been prepared to 31 January. Show when the CT liability is due for payment.

Answer

£880,000 must be paid in instalments.

The amount of each instalment is $3 \times \dfrac{£880{,}000}{8} = £330{,}000$

The due dates are:

	£
14 August 2006	330,000
14 November 2006	330,000
14 January 2007	220,000 (balance)

A company is not required to pay instalments in the first year that it is 'large', unless its profits exceed £10 million. The £10 million limit is reduced proportionately if there are associated companies. For this purpose only, a company will be regarded as an associated company where it was an associated company at the START of an accounting period. (This differs from the normal approach in CT where being an associated company for any part of the AP affects the thresholds of both companies for the whole of the AP).

There is a de minimis limit in that any company whose liability does not exceed £10,000 need not pay by instalments.

Interest runs from the due date on over/underpaid instalments. The position is looked at cumulatively after the due date for each instalment. HMRC calculate the interest position after the company submits its corporation tax return.

2.3 Example

X plc prepared accounts to 31 December 2006. The company has always prepared accounts to 31 December each year. It paid CT instalments of:

Date	*Amount*
	£
14.7.06	3.5m
14.10.06	8.5m
14.01.07	4.5m
14.4.07	4.5m
	21.0m

X plc's CT return showed a CT liability of £22m. The £1m balance was paid on 1.10.07. £22m should have been paid in instalments. The under(over) payments were:

Date	*Paid*	*Correct*	*Under(over) paid*
	£	£	£
14.7.06	3.5m	5.5m	2m
14.10.06	8.5m	5.5m	
	12.0m	11.0m	(1m)
14.1.07	4.5m	5.5m	
	16.5m	16.5m	–
14.4.07	4.5m	5.5m	
	21.0m	22.0m	1m

Interest would be charged (received) as follows.

14.7.06 – 13.10.06	Interest charged on £2m
14.10.06 – 13.1.07	Interest received on £1m
14.1.07 – 13.4.07	No interest
14.4.07 – 30.9.07	Interest charged on £1m

Interest paid/received on late payments or over payments of corporation tax is dealt with as interest paid/received on a nontrading loan relationship.

There are penalties if a company deliberately and flagrantly fails to pay instalments of sufficient size. After a company has filed its return or HMRC has determined its liability, HMRC may wish to establish the reason for inadequate instalment payments. It can do this by asking the company to produce relevant information or records (presumably to decide if a penalty applies). The failure to supply these will lead to an initial fixed penalty which may also be followed by a daily penalty which may continue until the information/records are produced.

Companies can have instalments repaid if they later conclude they ought not to have been paid.

2.4 Group payment arrangements

Where more than one company in a group is liable to pay their tax by instalments, arrangements may be made for the instalments to be paid by one company (the nominated company), and allocated amongst the group. These provisions were introduced because groups often have uncertainties over the tax liabilities of individual group members until all relevant group reliefs and claims are decided upon following the end of the accounting period.

3 Income tax suffered or withheld

FAST FORWARD

A paying company is not required to withhold income tax from annual interest, royalties or annuities if the recipient is also a company. Any net income tax suffered by a company can be deducted in computing the mainstream corporation tax due.

A paying company does not have to withhold income tax on payments of:

(a) annual interest
(b) royalties
(c) annuities
(d) annual payments

if it reasonably believes that the **recipient is chargeable to corporation tax on the payment**. Thus such payments made by one UK company to another UK company are paid gross.

However, **such payments made to individuals, partnerships etc (ie non companies) are made under deduction of income tax at 20% (eg debenture interest) or 22% (eg patent royalties)**.

When the company pays interest or patent royalties it deducts the gross amount in its corporation tax computation. For items paid net (such as debenture interest and patent royalties paid to non corporate recipients), **it acts as an agent for HMRC and retains income tax at 20% (interest) or 22% (patents) on the gross amount for payment to HMRC.** The *net* amount is payable to the payees (eg the individual debenture holders).

Companies may receive some income which has suffered 20% or 22% income tax at source. The cash income plus the income tax suffered, that is the gross figure, forms part of a company's income. The **income tax suffered is deductible from the corporation tax liability**.

Chapter roundup

- A company must notify HMRC within 3 months of starting to trade.
- CT 600 returns must, in general, be filed within twelve months of the end of an accounting period.
- HMRC can enquire into returns.
- In general, corporation tax is due nine months after the end of an accounting period but large companies must pay their corporation tax in four quarterly instalments.
- A paying company is not required to withhold income tax from annual interest, royalties or annuities if the recipient is also a company.
- Any net income tax suffered by a company can be deducted in computing the mainstream corporation tax due.

Quick quiz

1 Youngs Ltd makes up a 12 m set of accounts to 31 December 2006. When must the company file its CT return based on these accounts?

2 What are the fixed penalties for failure to deliver a corporation tax return on time?

3 What is the penalty if a company fails to keep records?

4 When must HMRC give notice that they are going to start an enquiry if a return was filed on time?

5 Refer to Questions 1 and state when the tax is due if the company is not a large company.

6 State the due dates for the payment of quarterly instalments of corporation tax for a 12 month accounting period.

7 Which companies must pay quarterly instalments of their corporation tax liability?

8 Freeman Ltd changes its accounting date and makes up accounts for the 8 months to 31 December 2006. The company is large and is due to pay tax by instalments. Outline when the tax is due.

9 In question 8 if the CT liability is £1,000,000 for the eight month period what amount is paid at each date outlined in your answer to question 8?

Answers to quick quiz

1 By 31 December 2007.

2 There is a £100 penalty for failure to submit a return on time rising to £200 if the delay exceeds three months. These penalties increased to £500 and £1,000 respectively when a return was late for each of the preceding two accounting periods.

3 £3,000 for each accounting period affected.

4 Notice must be given by one year after the filing date.

5 tax is due for Y.E. 31.12.2006 on 1 October 2007

6 14th day of:

(a) 7th month in AP
(b) 10th month in AP
(c) 1st month after AP ends
(d) 4th month after AP ends

7 'Large' companies ie: companies that pay corporation tax at the full rate.

8 Due dates are;

14 November 2006
14 February 2007
14 April 2007.

9 £375,000, £375, 000 and finally £250,000.

Now try the question below from the Exam Question Bank

Number	Level	Marks	Time
Q22	Introductory	13	23 mins

2 Loss relief against future trading income: s 393(1) ICTA 1988

FAST FORWARD

Trading losses carried forward can only be set against future trading profits of the same trade.

A company must set off a trading loss, not otherwise relieved, against income from the same trade in future accounting periods. Relief is against the first available profits.

Question

Carrying forward losses

A Ltd has the following results for the three years to 31 March 2007.

		Year ended	
	31.3.05	*31.3.06*	*31.3.07*
	£	£	£
Trading profit/(loss)	(8,550)	3,000	6,000
Property income	0	1,000	1,000
Gift aid donation	300	1,400	1,700

Calculate the profits chargeable to corporation tax for all three years showing any losses available to carry forward at 1 April 2007.

Answer

		Year ended	
	31.3.05	*31.3.06*	*31.3.07*
	£	£	£
Trading income	0	3,000	6,000
Less: gift aid donation		(3,000)	(5,550)
	0	0	450
Property income	0	1,000	1,000
Less: gift aid donation	0	(1,000)	(1,450)
PCTCT	0	0	0
Unrelieved gift aid donation	300	400	250

Note that the trading loss carried forward is set only against the trading profit in future years. It cannot be set against the property income.

The non-trade charges that become unrelieved remain unrelieved as they cannot be carried forward.

Loss memorandum

	£
Loss for y/e 31.3.05	8,550
Less s 393(1) relief y/e 31.3.06	(3,000)
Loss carried forward at 1.4.06	5,550
Less s 393(1) relief y/e 31.3.07	(5,550)
Loss carried forward at 1.4.07	0

3 Loss relief against total profits: s 393A(1) ICTA 1988

FAST FORWARD

S393A relief is given against total profits before charges. Gift Aid donations remain unrelieved. S393A relief may be given against current period profits and against profits of the previous 12 months (or, previous 36 months if the trade is ceasing). A claim for current period S393A relief can be made without a claim for carryback. However, if a loss is to be carried back a claim for current period relief must have been made first.

A company may claim to set a trading loss (arising in a UK trade, not in a trade controlled abroad where the income is foreign income) **incurred in an accounting period against total profits before deducting charges (ie gift aid donations) of the same accounting period.**

Such a loss may then be carried back and set against total profits before deducting gift aid donations of an accounting period falling wholly or partly within the 12 months of the start of the period in which the loss was incurred.

If a period falls partly outside the 12 months, loss relief is limited to the proportion of the period's profits (before gift aid donations) equal to the proportion of the period which falls within the 12 months.

Any possible s 393A(1) claim for the period of the loss must be made before any excess loss can be carried back to a previous period.

Any carry-back is to more recent periods before earlier periods. Relief for earlier losses is given before relief for later losses.

A claim for relief against current or prior period profits must be made within two years of the end of the accounting period in which the loss arose. Any claim must be for the *whole* loss (to the extent that profits are available to relieve it). The loss can however be reduced by not claiming full capital allowances, so that higher capital allowances are given (on higher tax written down values) in future years. Any loss remaining unrelieved may be carried forward under s 393(1) to set against future profits of the same trade.

Question — S 393A loss relief

Helix Ltd has the following results.

		Year ended	
	30.9.05	*30.9.06*	*30.9.07*
	£	£	£
Trading profit/(loss)	90,500	80,000	(105,000)
Bank interest	500	500	500
Chargeable gains	0	0	4,000
Charges on income:			
Gift Aid donation	250	250	250

Show the PCTCT for all the years affected assuming that s 393A(1) loss relief is claimed. Assume the provisions of FA 2005 continue to apply.

Answer

The loss of the year to 30.9.07 is relieved under s 393A ICTA 1988 against current year profits and against profits of the previous twelve months.

		Year ended	
	30.9.05	*30.9.06*	*30.9.07*
	£	£	£
Trading income	90,500	80,000	0
Interest income	500	500	500
Chargeable gains	0	0	4,000
	91,000	80,500	4,500
Less s 393A current period relief	0	0	(4,500)
	91,000	80,500	0
Less s 393A carryback relief	0	(80,500)	0
	91,000	0	0
Less: gift aid donation	(250)	0	0
PCTCT	90,750	0	0
Unrelieved gift aid donation		250	250

S 393A (1) loss memorandum	£
Loss incurred in y/e 30.9.07	105,000
Less s 393A (1): y/e 30.9.07	(4,500)
y/e 30.9.06	(80,500)
Loss available to carry forward under s 393(1)	20,000

The 12 month carry back period is extended to 36 months where the trading loss arose in the 12 months immediately before the company ceased to trade.

Question

Ceasing to trade

Loser Ltd had always made up accounts to 31 December, but ceased to trade on 31 December 2006. Results had been as follows.

		Year ended		
	31.12.03	*31.12.04*	*31.12.05*	*31.12.06*
	£	£	£	£
Trading profit/(loss)	36,000	26,000	23,000	(61,200)
Interest income	2,000	2,000	2,000	0
Gift Aid donation	170	170	170	80

Show the profits chargeable to corporation tax for all years after relief for the loss.

Answer

		Year ended		
	31.12.03	*31.12.04*	*31.12.05*	*31.12.06*
	£	£	£	£
Trading income	36,000	26,000	23,000	0
Interest income	2,000	2,000	2,000	0
	38,000	28,000	25,000	0
Less: s 393A carryback	(8,200)	(28,000)	(25,000)	0
	29,800	0	0	0
Less: gift aid donations	(170)	0	0	0
	29,630	0	0	0
Unrelieved gift aid donations		170	170	80

4 Reliefs for deficits on non-trading loan relationships

FAST FORWARD

Deficits on non-trading loan relationships can be used in a similar way to trading losses.

A deficit on a non-trading loan relationship may be set, in whole or part, against any profit of the same accounting period. Relief is given after relief for any trading loss brought forward but before relief is given for a trading loss of the same or future period.

Question

Relief for deficit on non-trading loan relationship

Witherspoon Ltd has the following results for the two years ended 31 December 2006:

	2005	*2006*
	£	£
Trading profit/(loss)	70,000	(42,000)
Trading losses brought forward	(20,000)	-
Bank interest receivable	2,000	
Interest payable on a loan for non-trading purposes	(11,000)	

Show how relief may be given for the deficit on the non-trading loan relationship in the year ended 31.12.05.

Answer

	£
Trading income	70,000
s 393(1) losses brought forward	(20,000)
	50,000
Less: non-trading deficit £(11,000 – 2,000)	(9,000)
	41,000
Losses carried back s 393A	(41,000)
Chargeable profits	Nil

A deficit is eligible for group relief (see later in this text).

A deficit may be set against non-trading income arising from loan relationships in the previous twelve months provided the income has not been reduced by:

(a) Loss relief in respect of a period prior to the deficit period
(b) Management expenses of an investment company

A claim under the above must be made within two years of the deficit period.

Any deficits unrelieved after claiming the above reliefs are automatically carried forward and set against non trading profits of the company for succeeding accounting periods. If the company does not want this automatic set-off to apply **it has two years from the end of the accounting period to apply for exemption for all or part of the deficit carried forward.**

A company can choose how much deficit to relieve in the current period, how much to carry back and how much to carry forward: unlike s 393A relief, these are not all or nothing claims, and the company can choose to carry back a deficit even if it does not claim current period relief.

5 Restrictions on loss relief

FAST FORWARD

If there is a change in ownership of a company, the carry forward of losses is restricted if there is also a major change in the nature of the trade within three years of the change in ownership.

5.1 The continuity of trades

Relief under s 393(1) is only available against future profits arising from the same trade as that in which the loss arose.

The continuity of trade for this purpose was considered in a case involving a company trading as brewers: *Gordon & Blair Ltd v CIR 1962.* It ceased brewing but continued to bottle and sell beer. The company claimed that it carried on the same trade throughout so that its losses from brewing could be set off against profits from the bottling trade. The company lost their case and were prevented from obtaining any further relief for losses in the brewing trade under s 393(1).

5.2 The disallowance of loss relief following a change in ownership

No relief is available for trading losses in accounting periods on one side of (before or after) a change in ownership of a company if the loss making accounting period is on the other side of (after or before) the change in ownership and either:

- **There is a major change in the nature or conduct of the trade within three years before or three years after the change in ownership, or**
- **After the change in ownership there is a considerable revival of the company's trading activities which at the time of the change had become small or negligible.**

Examples of a major change in the nature or conduct of a trade include changes in:

- The type of property dealt in (for example a company operating a dealership in saloon cars switching to a dealership in tractors)
- The services or facilities provided (for example a company operating a public house changing to operating a discotheque)
- Customers
- Outlets or markets

However, changes to keep up to date with technology or to rationalise existing ranges of products are unlikely to be regarded as major. HMRC consider both qualitative and quantitative issues in deciding if a change is major.

If the change in ownership occurs in (and not at the end of) an accounting period, that period is notionally divided into two periods, one up to and one after the change, for the purposes of this rule, with profits and losses being time-apportioned.

A change in ownership is disregarded for this purpose if both immediately before and immediately after the change the company is a 75% subsidiary of the same company.

5.3 Uncommercial trades

A loss made in a trade which is not conducted on a commercial basis and with a view to the realisation of gain cannot be set off against the company's profits in the same or previous accounting periods under s 393A(1). Such losses are only available to carry forward under s 393(1) against future profits of the same trade.

5.4 Farming and market gardening

A company carrying on the trade of farming or market gardening is treated in the same way as one that trades on an uncommercial basis in any accounting period if, in the five successive years immediately before that accounting period, the trade made a loss (before capital allowances).

6 Choosing loss reliefs and other planning points

FAST FORWARD

When selecting a loss relief, firstly consider the rate at which relief is obtained and, secondly, the timing of the relief.

Several alternative loss reliefs may be available. In making a choice consider:

- **The rate at which relief will be obtained:**

  (i) 30% at the full rate (FY 2006)
  (ii) 19% at the small companies' rate (FY 2006)
  (iii) 32.75% if the small companies' marginal relief applies (FY 2006)

  Where the loss is carried back relief may also be obtained at the starting rate of 0% (FY 2005), or at 23.75% if the starting rate marginal relief applies (FY 2005).

  We previously outlined how the 23.75% and 32.75% marginal rates are calculated. Remember these are just marginal rates of tax; they are never actually used in computing a company's corporation tax.

- **How quickly relief will be obtained**: s 393A(1) relief is quicker than s 393(1) relief.
- **The extent to which relief for gift aid donations might be lost.**

Exam focus point

When choosing between loss relief claims ALWAYS consider the rate of tax 'saved' by the loss first.

If in the current period the loss 'saves' 19% tax but if carried forward saves 30% tax then a carry forward is the better choice (even though the timing of loss relief is later).

If the tax saved now is 30% and in the future is the same (30%) THEN consider timing (in this example a current claim is better timing wise).

So, first – rate of tax saved, second – timing.

Question — **The choice between loss reliefs**

M Ltd has had the following results.

	Year ended 31 March				
	2003	*2004*	*2005*	*2006*	*2007*
	£	£	£	£	£
Trading profit/(loss)	5,000,000	2,000	(1,000,000)	200,000	138,000
Chargeable gains	0	35,000	750,000	0	0
Gift aid donations paid	20,000	30,000	20,000	20,000	20,000

Recommend appropriate loss relief claims, and compute the mainstream corporation tax for all years based on your recommendations. Assume that future years' profits will be similar to those of the year ended 31 March 2007 and that any profits made by the company are retained for future use in the business.

Answer

A s 393A(1) claim for the year ended 31 March 2005 will save tax partly in the small companies' marginal relief band, partly at the small companies rate and partly in the starting rate marginal relief band. It will waste the gift aid donation of £20,000.

PCTCT in the previous year is £7,000 (£35,000 + £2,000 – £30,000) and falls into the starting rate band lower limit. Corporation tax at 0% would have been due in this year (FY 2003).

If no current period s 393A(1) claim is made, £200,000 of the loss will save tax at the small companies rate and in the starting rate marginal relief band in the year ended 31 March 2006, with £20,000 of gift aid donations being wasted. The remaining £800,000 of the loss, would be carried forward to the year ended 31 March 2007 and later years to save tax at the small companies rate.

To conclude a s 393A(1) claim should be made for the year of the loss but not in the previous year. £20,000 of gift aid donations would be wasted in the current year, but much of the loss would save tax at the small companies' marginal corporation tax rate and relief would be obtained quickly.

The final computations are as follows.

	Year ended 31 March				
	2003	*2004*	*2005*	*2006*	*2007*
	£	£	£	£	£
Trading income	5,000,000	2,000	0	200,000	138,000
Less s393(1) relief	0	0	0	(200,000)	(50,000)
	5,000,000	2,000	0	0	88,000
Chargeable gains	0	35,000	750,000	0	0
	5,000,000	37,000	750,000	0	88,000
Less: s393A current relief		0	(750,000)	0	0
	5,000,000	37,000	0	0	88,000
Less: gift aid donations	(20,000)	(30,000)	0	0	(20,000)
Profits chargeable to corporation tax	4,980,000	7,000	0	0	68,000
MCT at 30% / 0% / 0% / 19%	1,494,000	0	0	0	12,920
Unrelieved gift aid donations	0	0	20,000	20,000	0

6.1 Other tax planning points

A company must normally claim capital allowances on its tax return. A company with losses should consider claiming less than the maximum amount of capital allowances available. This will result in a higher tax written down value to carry forward and therefore higher capital allowances in future years.

Reducing capital allowances in the current period reduces the loss available for relief under s 393A. As s 393A relief, if claimed, must be claimed for all of a loss available, a reduced capital allowance claim could be advantageous where all of a loss would be relieved at a lower tax rate in the current (or previous) period than the effective rate of relief for capital allowances will be in future periods.

Chapter roundup

- Trading losses may be relieved against current total profits, against total profits of earlier periods or against future trading income.
- Trading losses carried forward can only be set against future profits of the same trade.
- S393A relief is given against total profits before charges. Gift Aid donations remain unrelieved.
- S393A relief may be given against current period profits and against profits of the previous 12 months (or, previous 36 months if the trade is ceasing).
- A claim for current period S393A relief can be made without a claim for carryback. However, if a loss is to be carried back a claim for current period relief must have been made first.
- If there is both a change in ownership of a company, the carry forward of losses is restricted if there is also a major change in the nature of the trade within three years of the change in ownership.
- When selecting a loss relief, firstly consider the rate at which relief is obtained and, secondly, the timing of the relief.

Quick quiz

1 Against what profits may trading losses carried forward be set?

2 To what extent may losses in a continuing trade be carried back?

3 What relief is available in the current AP for a non-trading deficit?

4 Why might a company make a reduced capital allowances claim?

Answers to quick quiz

1 Profits from the same trade.

2 A loss may be carried back and set against total profits (before deducting gift aid donations) of the prior 12 months. The loss carried back is the trading loss left unrelieved after a claim against total profits (before deducting gift aid donations) of the loss making AP has been made.

3 A deficit on a non-trading loan relationship may be set against profit of the same AP. Relief is given after relief for any trading loss brought forward but before relief is given for a current or future trading loss.

The deficit is also eligible for group relief.

4 Reducing capital allowances in the current AP reduces the loss available for relief under s 393A. Section 393A demands that all of the available loss is utilised. Reducing capital allowances reduces the size of the available loss.

Now try the question below from the Exam Question Bank

Number	Level	Marks	Time
Q23	Introductory	10	18 mins

25

Investment companies and close companies

Introduction

In this chapter, we look at investment companies and close companies.

Investment companies have a special type of business: they make investments, for example in shares, and collect the income from them. An important type of investment company is the investment trust, which collects the capital of its shareholders together, buys shares and pays out the dividends on those shares to its own shareholders. Thus it gives people a way to invest across a wide spread of companies. Real Estate Investment Trusts are a new type of investment trust which enables investors to have a share in a property portfolio.

A close company may have any type of business, but it needs special tax treatment because it is under the control of a few people who might try to get profits out of it in non-taxable forms.

1 Investment companies

FAST FORWARD

Investment companies do not trade in the ordinary way, but rather generate income from investments and in doing so incur management expenses which are deductible for corporation tax purposes.

1.1 Companies with investment business/investment companies

A company with investment business is any company whose business consists wholly or partly in making investments.

An investment company is a company whose business consists wholly or mainly in making investments and which gets the principal part of its income from investments.

An investment company may or may not also fall within the definition of a close investment-holding company outlined below.

The principal overhead of the investment business will be the costs of running the business which are called management expenses. These are generally deductible in computing taxable profits. An unrelieved excess of such expenses in one accounting period may be carried forward as management expenses of the following accounting period and, if still unrelieved, to future accounting periods.

Excessive directors' remuneration is not deductible for tax purposes. Capital expenditure is excluded from deduction as a management expense and HMRC may also refuse a deduction for any amounts which are not in fact expenses of management.

Capital allowances on plant and machinery used for the investment business are allowed as a management expense if they cannot be relieved in any other way.

Non-trading loan relationships expenses and losses are dealt with under the loan relationship rules, not as a management expense.

Corporation tax is applied to investment companies, and companies with investment business, in the normal way (there is an exception for close investment holding companies outlined below). Thus investment companies can benefit from the small companies rate or marginal relief.

Question — **Investment companies**

TC Ltd, a non-close investment company, has the following results for the year ended 31 March 2007.

	£
Rental income	150,000
Building society interest	8,000
Chargeable gains	100,000
Management expenses	
Property management	40,000
General	50,000
Capital allowances	
On property	800
General	1,000
Gift aid donations	47,000

Unrelieved management expenses carried forward at 1 April 2006 amounted to £60,500.

Compute the mainstream corporation tax payable.

Answer

		£	£
Rents			150,000
Less:	capital allowances	800	
	property management expenses	40,000	
			(40,800)
Property income			109,200
Interest income			8,000
Chargeable gains			100,000
			217,200
Less:	general management expenses	50,000	
	capital allowances	1,000	
	management expenses brought forward	60,500	
			(111,500)
			105,700
Less charges on income (gift aid donations)			(47,000)
PCTCT			58,700
Corporation tax payable £58,700 × 19%			£11,153

1.2 Changes in ownership

If there is a change in ownership of an investment company, special rules apply when any of the following occurs:

(a) Within three years after the change, the company's (share and loan) capital is increased by at least £1,000,000 or is at least doubled.

(b) There is a major change in the nature or conduct of the company s business within the three years before or the three years after the change in ownership.

(c) The company's business becomes small or negligible, the ownership changes and there is then a considerable revival.

In any of these circumstances, excess management expenses and non-trading deficits on loan relationships arising before the change in ownership cannot be carried forward to after the change. The accounting period of the change is divided into two notional accounting periods for this purpose.

When this rule does not apply, but after the change in ownership an asset is transferred to the company from another group company at no gain and no loss (see later in this Text), and that asset is then sold at a gain within the three years following the change in ownership, then management expenses and non-trading deficits on loan relationships brought forward from before the change in ownership cannot be set against the gain.

A major change in the nature of a business occurs when there is a change in the nature of the investments held (eg a company switches from investing in shares to investing in real property). A change in a portfolio or quoted shares is not a major change in the nature of a business.

1.3 Investment trusts

An investment trust is an investment company which is listed on the Stock Exchange and which buys shares, securities or housing to let on assured tenancies, receives income and distributes at least 85% of its income to its own shareholders. It must not distribute its capital gains.

Dividends from investment trusts, and capital gains on shares in them, are treated in exactly the same way as dividends and capital gains on shares in other companies.

An investment trust itself is exempt from tax on capital gains on the sale of its investments.

2 Close companies

Owner-managed and family-owned companies could easily be used for tax avoidance. **Special rules apply to certain companies called close companies**, to counteract this. Broadly, a close company is one that is under the control of either five or fewer shareholders or any number of its shareholding directors. Shareholders and shareholding directors are known as 'participators'. Direct relatives of participators are known as 'associates'.

2.1 Loans to participators

FAST FORWARD

The rules on loans and benefits from close companies are intended to deter shareholders from using the obvious ways of extracting value from their company without paying tax.

When a close company makes a loan to one of its participators or an associate it must make a payment to HMRC equal to 25% of the loan. If the loan is repaid, HMRC will repay this tax charge.

For small and medium sized companies, the tax charge is due for payment nine months after the end of the accounting period. If the loan is repaid before the tax charge is due to be paid then the requirement to account for the tax charge is cancelled. Interest runs from the due date until the earlier of payment of the tax and repayment of the loan. The loan must be notified on the company's tax return. The tax charge is subject to the quarterly payments on account regime if the company is large.

A loan for these purposes includes:

- A debt owed to the company
- A debt incurred by a participator or his associate and assigned to the company
- An advance of money
- A director's overdrawn current account

Certain loans are excluded from these provisions. These are:

- Money owed for goods or services supplied in the ordinary course of the company's trade unless the credit period exceeds:

  (i) Six months; or, if less
  (ii) The normal credit period given to the company's other customers.

- Loans to directors and employees providing they do not exceed £15,000 in total per borrower and:

  (i) The borrower works full-time for the close company, and

  (ii) He does not have a material interest (entitlement to over 5% of the assets available for distribution on a winding up) in the close company.

If at the time a loan was made the borrower did not have a material interest but he later acquires one, the company is regarded as making a loan to him when he acquires it.

When all or part of the loan is repaid by the participator to the company, or the company writes off all or part of the loan, then the company can reclaim all or a corresponding part of the tax charge paid over to HMRC. If the loan is repaid or written of after the due date for paying the tax charge, the tax is not repayable until nine months after the end of the accounting period of repayment or write off of the loan.

HMRC pay interest up to the time they repay the tax. If the loan is repaid/written off before nine months from the end of the accounting period in which the loan is made, interest runs from the end of those nine months. Otherwise, it runs from the date when the tax is repayable.

Although tax is charged on the company when a loan is made to a participator, the loan is not at that stage treated as the participator's income. If the loan is later written off:

(a) The amount written off is treated as the participator's income and is included within his total income grossed up accordingly. It is taxed as if it were a dividend received by him (the net dividend equalling the loan written off), so a starting or basic rate taxpayer has no more tax to pay, but a higher rate taxpayer must pay more tax.

(b) If the participator is a director or employee, there is no taxable benefit because the above tax charge applies instead.

(c) The amount included within the participator's income cannot be used to cover charges paid for the purposes of avoiding a liability for tax retained on charges not paid out of taxable income.

Question — **Close company loan**

C Ltd, a close company which prepares accounts to 31 July each year, lends £50,000 to a shareholder in July 2005. C Ltd is required to account for a tax charge of £12,500 to HMRC. In July 2006 the shareholder repays £20,000. In January 2007 C Ltd writes off the remaining £30,000. Compute the amount of notional tax charge recovered by C Ltd following the repayment in July 2006 and the write off in January 2007.

Answer

(a) The notional tax charge recovered after the repayment is $\frac{20,000}{50,000} \times £12,500 = £5,000$.

(b) The notional tax charge recovered after the write off is £7,500.

2.2 Benefits treated as distributions

Benefits given by a close company to participators and their associates and which are not taxable earnings are treated as distributions. The amount of the deemed distribution is the amount that would otherwise be taxed as earnings. The actual cost is a disallowable expense for corporation tax purposes.

Question — **Benefits**

A close company provides a new car for a participator who is not a director or employee in April 2006. The taxable benefit in 2006/07 under the income tax legislation would be valued at £3,500. No fuel is provided. What are the tax consequences?

Answer

The participator is taxed as if he had received a net dividend of £3,500 in 2006/07. The company cannot deduct capital allowances on the car or any running costs in computing its taxable profits.

2.3 Close investment-holding companies

FAST FORWARD

Close investment-holding companies are singled out for special treatment so as to deter people with substantial investments from putting their investments into a company and using the company status to reduce or defer tax liabilities.

Key term

A **close investment-holding company** (CIC) is a close company which:

- Is not a trading company, and
- Is not a member of a trading group.

A company is a trading company for an accounting period if it exists wholly or mainly for the purpose of trading. A company will not necessarily have to trade in an accounting period in order to satisfy this test but the trade must, when it is carried on, be carried on a commercial basis.

A member of a trading group is a company which co-ordinates the administration of trading companies which it controls.

Companies which deal in land, shares or securities are treated as trading companies for this purpose. Similarly, a company which invests in property let or to be let on a commercial basis will not be treated as a CIC.

A CIC always pays corporation tax at the full rate of 30% whatever its level of profits. However, a CIC associated with another company still counts as an associated company for the purposes of reducing the limits for the small companies rate and marginal relief.

2.4 Taper relief on the sale of shares in a close company

Where shares in a close company are disposed of, any part of a period of ownership during which the company is not active does not count for taper relief purposes (see earlier in this text).

A company is active if it is preparing to carry on, or actually carrying on, a business of any description or if such a business is being wound up. The business does not have to be carried on with a view to profit nor conducted on a commercial basis. 'Carrying on a business' can include holding assets and managing them.

Chapter roundup

- Investment companies do not trade in the ordinary way, but rather generate income from investments and in doing so incur management expenses which are deductible for corporation tax purposes.
- The rules on loans and benefits from close companies are intended to deter shareholders from using the obvious ways of extracting value from their company without paying tax.
- Close investment-holding companies are singled out for special treatment so as to deter people with substantial investments from putting their investments into a company and using the company status to defer tax liabilities.

Quick quiz

1 How may an investment company obtain relief for management expenses?

2 What is a close company?

3 What are the immediate consequences of a loan by a close company to a participator?

4 What items are treated as distributions by close companies?

5 What rate(s) of CT may apply to close investment-holding companies?

Answers to quick quiz

1 Management expenses are deductible when computing taxable profits Any unrelieved management expenses may be carried forward to be relieved in a similar fashion in the following accounting period.

2 A close company is one that is under the control of either five or fewer shareholders or any number of shareholding directors.

3 When a close company makes a loan to one of its participators it must make a payment to HMRC equal to 25% of the loan.

4 Benefits given to participators or their associates which are not taxed under the benefits legislation.

5 CICs always pay the full rate of corporation tax (30%) irrespective of the level of their profits.

Now try the question below from the Exam Question Bank

Number	Level	Marks	Time
Q24	Introductory	15	27 mins

26 Groups and consortia. Purchases of own shares

Introduction

In this chapter we consider the extent to which tax law recognises group relationships between companies. Companies in a group are still separate entities with their own tax liabilities, but tax law recognises the close relationship between group companies. They can, if they meet certain conditions, share their losses and pass assets between each other without chargeable gains. We also consider how transfer pricing applies.

We also look at the consequences of the purchase by a company of its own shares.

1 Types of group

1.1 Groups

A group exists for taxation purposes where one company is a subsidiary of another. The percentage shareholding involved determines the taxation consequences of the fact that there is a group.

The four types of relationship for tax purposes are:

- **Associated companies**
- **75% subsidiaries**
- **Consortia**
- **Groups for chargeable gains purposes (capital gains groups)**

1.2 Associated companies

Two companies are associated with each other for taxation purposes if one is under the control of the other, or both are under the control of a third party. Control for these purposes means entitlement to more than 50% of any one of:

- The share capital
- The votes
- The income
- The net assets on a winding up

The number of associated companies determines the limits for the starting rate of corporation tax, the small companies rate and marginal relief.

2 Group relief

2.1 Definitions

FAST FORWARD

Group relief is available where the existence of a group or consortium is established through companies resident anywhere in the world.

The group relief provisions enable companies within a 75% group to transfer trading losses to other companies within the group, in order to set these against taxable profits and reduce the group's overall corporation tax liability.

Key term

For one company to be a **75% subsidiary** of another, the holding company must have:

- At least 75% of the ordinary share capital of the subsidiary
- A right to at least 75% of the distributable income of the subsidiary, and
- A right to at least 75% of the net assets of the subsidiary were it to be wound up.

Two companies are members of a group for group relief purposes where one is a 75% subsidiary of the other, or both are 75% subsidiaries of a third company. Ordinary share capital is any share capital other than fixed dividend preference shares.

Two companies are in a group only if there is a 75% effective interest. Thus an 80% subsidiary (T) of an 80% subsidiary (S) is not in a group with the holding company (H), because the effective interest is only 80% × 80% = 64%. However, S and T are in a group and can claim group relief from each other. S *cannot* claim group relief from T and pass it on to H; it can only claim group relief for its own use.

A group relief group may include non-UK resident companies. **However, losses may generally only be surrendered between UK resident companies although in certain circumstances group relief is available to UK branches of overseas companies and even in very rare cases for overseas losses (see the next chapter).**

Illustration of a Group relief group:

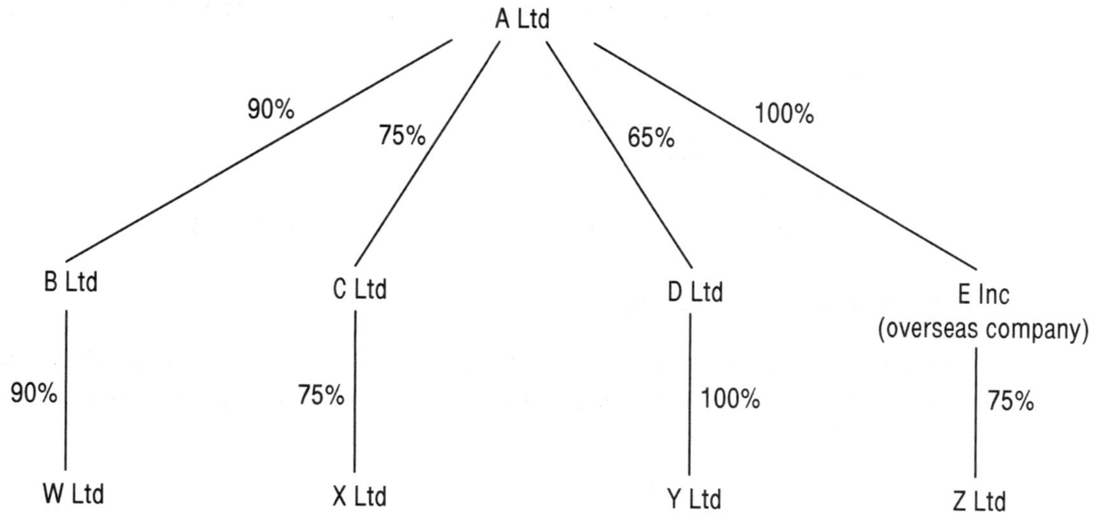

The companies in the group for group relief purposes are;

A Ltd
B Ltd
W Ltd (81% effective holding by A)
C Ltd
E Inc
Z Ltd (75% effective holding by A)

In addition C Ltd and X Ltd and also D Ltd and Y Ltd form their own separate mini-groups.

2.2 The relief

FAST FORWARD

Within a 75% group, trading losses can be surrendered between UK companies.

A **claimant company** is assumed to use its own current year losses or losses brought forward in working out the profits against which it may claim group relief, even if it does not in fact claim s 393A relief for current losses. Furthermore, **group relief is against profits after all other reliefs for the current period or brought forward from earlier periods**, including non-trading deficits on loan relationships and charges. Group relief is given before relief for any amounts brought back from later periods.

A surrendering company may group relieve a loss before setting it against its own profits for the period of the loss, and may specify any amount to be surrendered. This is **important** for **tax planning as it enables the surrendering company to leave profits in its own computation to be charged to corporation tax at the small companies rate, while surrendering its losses to other companies to cover profits which would otherwise fall into the marginal relief band or be taxed at the full rate**. Note that profits in the small companies' marginal relief band are taxed at the marginal rate of 32.75%. (In FY 2005 profits in the starting rate marginal relief band were taxed at the marginal rate of 23.75%.)

Question

Group relief of losses

In a group of four companies, the results for the year ended 31 March 2007 are as follows.

	Profit/(loss)
	£
A Ltd	52,000
B Ltd	212,500
C Ltd	1,000,000
D Ltd	(400,000)

How should the loss be allocated to save as much tax as possible? How much tax is saved?

Note. No dividends were paid by any group company during this year.

Answer

The upper and lower limits for small companies' marginal relief are £1,500,000/4 = £375,000 and £300,000/4 = £75,000 respectively.

	A Ltd	*B Ltd*	*C Ltd*
	£	£	£
Profits before group relief	52,000	212,500	1,000,000
Less group relief (note)	0	(137,500)	(262,500)
PCTCT	52,000	75,000	737,500
Tax saved			
£137,500 × 32.75%		45,031	
£262,500 × 30%			78,750
Total £(45,031 + 78,750) = £123,781			

Note. We wish to save the most tax possible for the group.

Since A Ltd is in the small companies band any loss given to it will save tax at the small companies rate of 19%.

B Ltd is in the marginal relief for small companies rate band. Therefore, any loss given to B saves the effective marginal rate of 32.75% until the profits fall to £75,000 (the small companies lower limit). After this only 19% is saved.

C Ltd is in the full rate band of 30% until profits fall to £375,000 (the small companies upper limit).

So to conclude it is best to give B Ltd £137,500 of loss and save 32.75% tax on the profits in the marginal relief band. The balance of the loss is then given to C Ltd to save 30% tax.

A company may surrender to other group companies trading losses, excess property income losses, non-trading deficits on loan relationships and excess charges on income. Charges can only be group-relieved to the extent that they exceed profits before taking account of any losses of the current period or brought forward or back from other accounting periods. **Excess management expenses of companies with investment business may also be surrendered.** If there are excess charges, property income losses and management expenses available for surrender then they are surrendered in that order.

Capital losses cannot be group relieved. However, see paragraph 3.3 below for details of how a group may net off its gains and losses.

Only current period losses are available for group relief. Furthermore, they must be set against profits of a corresponding accounting period. If the accounting periods of a surrendering company and a claimant company are not the same this means that both the profits and losses must be apportioned so that only the results of the period of overlap may be set off. Apportionment is on a time basis. However, in the period when a company joins or leaves a group, an alternative method may be used if the result given by time-apportionment would be unjust or unreasonable.

Question

Corresponding accounting periods

	£
S Ltd incurs a trading loss for the year to 30 September 2006	(150,000)
H Ltd makes taxable profits:	
for the year to 31 December 2005	200,000
for the year to 31 December 2006	100,000

What group relief can H Ltd claim from S Ltd?

Answer

H Ltd can claim group relief as follows.

	£
For the year ended 31 December 2005 profits of the corresponding accounting period (1.10.05 – 31.12.05) are £200,000 × 3/12	50,000
Losses of the corresponding accounting period are £150,000 × 3/12	37,500
A claim for £37,500 of group relief may be made against H Ltd's profits	
For the year ended 31 December 2006 profits of the corresponding accounting period (1.1.06 – 30.9.06) are £100,000 × 9/12	75,000
Losses of the corresponding accounting period are £150,000 × 9/12	112,500
A claim for £75,000 of group relief may be made against H Ltd's profits	

If a claimant company claims relief for losses surrendered by more than one company, the total relief that may be claimed for a period of overlap is limited to the proportion of the claimant's profits attributable to that period. Similarly, if a company surrenders losses to more than one claimant, the total losses that may be surrendered in a period of overlap is limited to the proportion of the surrendering company's losses attributable to that period.

A claim for group relief is normally made on the claimant company's tax return. It is ineffective unless a notice of consent is also given by the surrendering company.

A claimant company may not amend a group relief claim but it may withdraw it and replace it with a new claim. The time limit for making or withdrawing a claim is the latest of:

(a) The first anniversary of the filing date for the CT return.

(b) 30 days after the completion of an enquiry into a return.

(c) 30 days after the amendment of a self assessment by HMRC following the completion of an enquiry.

(d) 30 days after the settlement of an appeal against an amendment to the self assessment made by HMRC following an enquiry.

HMRC has discretion to accept a late claim/withdrawal.

Group wide claims/surrenders can be made as one person can act for two or more companies at once.

Any payment by the claimant company for group relief, up to the amount of the loss surrendered, is ignored for all corporation tax purposes.

Question

Group relief

C Ltd has one wholly owned subsidiary, D Ltd. The results of both companies for the four years ended 31 March 2007 are shown below.

		12 months to 31 March		
	2004	*2005*	*2006*	*2007*
	£'000	£'000	£'000	£'000
C Ltd				
Trading profit (loss)	200	(1,700)	100	(2,000)
Property income	800	800	800	800
Gift aid donation paid	(40)		0	(60)
D Ltd				
Trading profit (loss)	(2,300)	3,260	(870)	2,400
Interest on gilts (non-trading investment) (gross)	1,800	0	1,200	1,300
Gift aid donation paid	0	(400)	(300)	(500)

Show the profits chargeable to corporation tax for both companies for all years shown, assuming that the most beneficial claims for loss relief and group relief are made, and no dividends are paid or received by the companies.

Answer

C Ltd

		Accounting periods to 31 March		
	2004	*2005*	*2006*	*2007*
	£'000	£'000	£'000	£'000
Trading profit	200	0	100	0
Property income	800	800	800	800
	1,000	800	900	800
Less s 393A(1) – current period relief		(650)	0	(800)
		150	900	0
Less s 393A – carry back	0	0	(630)	0
	1,000	150	270	0
Less charges paid	(40)	0	0	0
	960	150	270	0
Less group relief claim	(650)	0	(120)	0
PCTCT	310	150	150	0
Loss memorandum				
Loss		(1,700)		(2,000)
Group relief surrender		1,050		570
		(650)		(1,430)
S 393A(1) claim: current year		650		800
		0		(630)
S 393A(1) claim: carry back				630
		0		0

	Accounting periods to 31 March			
	2004	*2005*	*2006*	*2007*
	£'000	£'000	£'000	£'000
D Ltd				
Trading income	0	3,260	0	2,400
Interest income	1,800	0	1,200	1,300
	1,800	3,260	1,200	3,700
Less s 393A(1) – current period relief	(1,650)		(750)	
	150		450	
Less charges paid	0	(400)	(300)	(500)
	150	2,860	150	3,200
Less group relief claim		(1,050)		(630)
PCTCT	150	1,810	150	2,750

Loss memorandum	£	£
Loss	(2,300)	(870)
Group relief surrender	650	120
	(1,650)	(750)
S 393A(1) claim	1,650	750
	0	0

Note. The excess charges of £60,000 arising in C Ltd for the year to 31.3.2007 are wasted.

(1) The most beneficial claims for relief will relieve losses at the small companies marginal rate, than at the full rate and, where the rate of relief is the same, in the earlier year.

(2) C Ltd should claim group relief of £650,000 in the year to 31.3.2004 leaving D Ltd sufficient loss to reduce its profits to the small companies limit of £150,000 (two companies in group)

(3) Similarly in the year to 31.3.2005 D Ltd should claim group relief of £1,050,000, leaving sufficient loss to reduce C Ltd's profit to £150,000

(4) Similarly in the year to 31.3.2006 C Ltd needs to claim group relief of £120,000. leaving D Ltd's profits, after S393A(1) relief, at £150,000.

(5) S393A carry back relief is advantageous for C Ltd's loss of the year to 31.3.2006, but again group claim by D Ltd should be set so as to leave C Ltd's PCTCT for the year to 31.3.2006 at £150,000. Note that the current year claim cannot be restricted.

2.3 Consortium relief

FAST FORWARD

Within a consortium there is some scope for loss relief.

The definition of a consortium is given below.

Key term

A **company is owned by a consortium** (and is known as a consortium-owned company) if:

- 75% or more of its ordinary share capital is owned by companies (the members of the consortium), none of which has a holding of less than 5%, and
- Each member of the consortium is entitled to at least 5% of any profits available for distribution to equity holders of the company and at least 5% of any assets so available on a winding up.

Illustration of a consortium

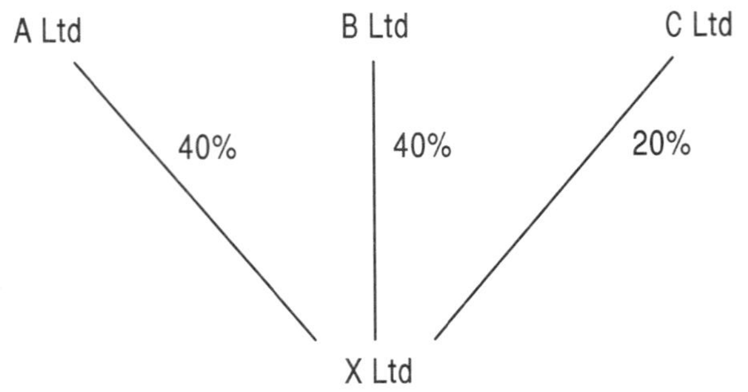

X Ltd is the consortium-owned company A Ltd, B Ltd and C Ltd are the consortium members.

Consortium relief is a loss relief which is available:

(a) Where the surrendering company is a trading company owned by a consortium and is not a 75% subsidiary of any one company and the claimant company belongs to the consortium.

(b) Where the surrendering company is a trading company which is a 90% subsidiary of a holding company which is owned by a consortium and is not a 75% subsidiary of any one company and the claimant company is a member of the consortium.

(c) Where the surrendering company is a holding company owned by a consortium and is not a 75% subsidiary of any one company and the claimant company is a member of the consortium.

A **trading company** is one whose business consists wholly or mainly in carrying on a trade. A holding company is one whose business consists wholly or mainly in holding shares in companies which are trading companies.

A consortium-owned company can surrender losses in proportion to the stakes of the members of the consortium. Thus if a member holds 20% of the shares in the company, up to 20% of the company's losses can be surrendered to that member.

Consortium relief can also flow downwards. **A member of a consortium may surrender its losses to set against its share of the consortium-owned company's profits.** So, a member with a 25% stake in the consortium-owned company can surrender losses to cover up to 25% of the company's profits.

Whereas normally a surrendering company can surrender group relief without having to consider any possible s 393A(1) claim, **a loss made by a consortium-owned company must be reduced by any potential s 393A(1) claims against current period profits** (not profits of previous periods) **before it may be surrendered as consortium relief**.

Although a consortium can be established with non-UK resident companies, losses cannot, in general, be surrendered to/from a non-UK resident.

Question

Consortium relief of losses

C Ltd is owned 60% by A Ltd, 30% by B Ltd and 10% by an overseas company X Inc. Results for the year ended 31 March 2007 are as follows.

	A Ltd	*B Ltd*	*C Ltd*
	£	£	£
Trading profit/(loss)	200,000	75,000	(50,000)
Property income	0	0	12,000

No dividends are paid or received by C Ltd.

Compute the corporation tax liabilities of all three companies, assuming that all possible consortium relief claims are made but that C Ltd does not claim s 393A(1) relief.

BPP PROFESSIONAL EDUCATION

Answer

A Ltd may claim £(50,000 – 12,000) × 60% = £22,800.
B Ltd may claim £(50,000 – 12,000) × 30% = £11,400.
A Ltd has one associated company (C Ltd).

A Ltd's corporation tax liability is as follows.

	£
Profits	200,000
Less consortium relief	(22,800)
Profits chargeable to corporation tax	177,200

Corporation tax	£
£177,200 × 30%	53,160
Less small companies' rate marginal relief £(750,000 – 177, 200) × 11/400	(15,752)
	37,408

B Ltd's corporation tax liability is £(75,000 – 11,400) × 19% = £63,600 × 19% = £12,084.

C Ltd's corporation tax liability is:

	£
£12,000 × 19%	2,280

Note. The limits for small companies' rate marginal relief are divided by 2 since there are two associated companies (A Ltd and C Ltd).

C Ltd has a loss to carry forward under s 393(1) ICTA 1988 of £(50,000 – 22,800 – 11,400) = £15,800.

2.4 Tax planning for group relief

This section outlines some tax planning points to bear in mind when dealing with a group.

Group relief should first be given in this order:

1st To companies in the small companies marginal relief band paying 32.75% tax (but only sufficient loss to bring profits down to the SCR limit)

2nd To companies paying the full rate of tax at 30%

3rd To companies paying SCR at 19%

Similarly, a company should make a s 393A(1) claim to use a loss itself rather than surrender the loss to other group companies if the s 393A(1) claim would lead to a tax saving at a higher rate. Remember that where a loss is carried back relief may be at the starting rate (nil%) or the starting rate marginal rate (23.75%)

Companies with profits may benefit by reducing their claims for capital allowances in a particular year. This may leave sufficient profits to take advantage of group relief which may only be available for the current year. The amount on which writing-down allowances can be claimed in later years is increased accordingly.

3 Chargeable gains

3.1 Intra-group transfers

FAST FORWARD

Within a capital gains group, assets are transferred at no gain/no loss.

Companies are in a capital gains group if:

(a) At each level, there is a 75% holding, and
(b) The top company has an effective interest of over 50% in the group companies.

If A holds 75% of B, B holds 75% of C and C holds 75% of D, then A, B and C are in such a group, but D is outside the group because A's interest in D is only 75% × 75% × 75% = 42.1875%. Furthermore, D is not in a group with C, because the group must include the top company (A).

Illustration of a chargeable gains group:

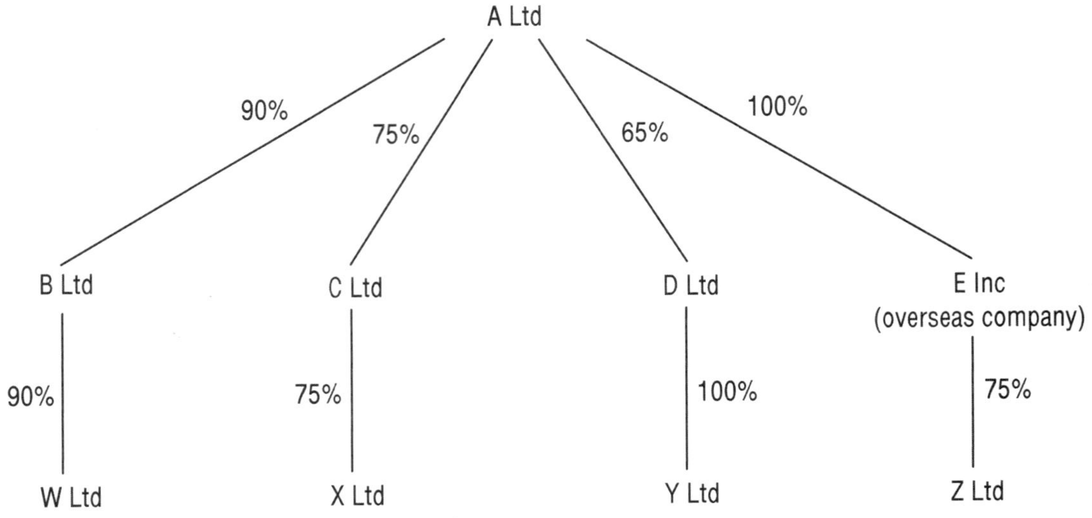

The companies in a group for chargeable gains purposes are:

A Ltd
B Ltd
W Ltd
C Ltd
X Ltd (75% subsidiary of 75% subsidiary, effective interest over 50%)
E Inc
Z Ltd

There is a separate capital gains group of D Ltd and Y Ltd.

Companies in a capital gains group make intra-group transfers of chargeable assets without a chargeable gain or an allowable loss arising. No election is needed, as this relief is compulsory. The assets are deemed to be transferred at such a price as will give the transferor no gain and no loss. Similarly, intangible assets can be transferred between members of a capital gains group without a Trading profit or loss arising (see earlier in this text).

Non-UK resident companies are included as members of a capital gains group. Provided the assets transferred do not result in a potential leakage of UK corporation tax, no gain/no loss transfers are possible within a worldwide (global) group of companies. This means that it may be possible to make no gain/no loss transfers to non-UK resident companies with a branch or agency in the UK.

If a company leaves a group while it owns assets transferred to it within the previous six years under the provisions described above, then the departing company is treated as though it had, at the time of its acquisition of such assets, sold and immediately re-acquired them at their then market values. However, the consequent gain or loss (computed using indexation allowance up to the time when the departing company acquired the assets) is brought into the departing company's tax computation for the accounting period in which it leaves the group. There is a parallel provision which crystallises a Trading gain/loss when a company leaves a capital gains tax group holding a previously transferred intangible asset.

The company leaving the group may jointly claim with a UK resident continuing group member to surrender its de-grouping gain/loss to that continuing member. The continuing group member may utilise its losses against the gain or may utilise the loss against its own gains.

Either the company leaving the group or a continuing group member may claim rollover relief for the de-grouping charge. The departing company can claim relief if it retains the de-grouping charge and acquires a new asset. The continuing company can claim the relief if the de-grouping charge has been switched to it and it acquires a new asset.

HMRC can collect the tax from the holding company if the tax is unpaid six months after its due date.

If a company leaves a group because another group company ceases to exist, the first company is not deemed to have left a group for these purposes. The tax charge also does not apply if one company acquired an asset from another, and both companies leave the group together while remaining in a group with each other.

Question

Company leaves an 'assets group'

In March 2007, Top Ltd sold to Take plc the whole of the share capital of Bottom Ltd, a 100% subsidiary. Included in the assets of Bottom Ltd is a warehouse acquired by Top Ltd in January 1987 for £96,000. This was transferred to Bottom Ltd in August 2001 for £100,000. Its market value at the date of transfer was £310,000. The indexation allowance on a sale in August 2001 would have been £74,000.

What is the effect of Bottom Ltd leaving the group? Compute Bottom Ltd's mainstream corporation tax for the year ended 31 March 2007 if it has trading income of £2,000,000.

Answer

Bottom Ltd leaves the group within six years of its acquiring the warehouse from Top Ltd. Bottom Ltd will be treated as if it had sold the warehouse at its market value in August 2001 and then immediately reacquired it.

	£	£
Proceeds (ie MV in August 2001)		310,000
Less cost: cost to Top Ltd	96,000	
indexation allowance to August 2001	74,000	
		(170,000)
Chargeable gain of Bottom Ltd, in the accounting period which includes March 2007		140,000

Top Ltd will not have a chargeable gain on the sale of its shares in Bottom Ltd, due to the substantial shareholdings relief applying to the sale of the subsidiary.

If no claims are made, Bottom Ltd's MCT for the year to 31.3.07 is as follows.

	£
Schedule D Case I	2,000,000
Chargeable gain	140,000
	2,140,000
Corporation tax £2,140,000 × 30%	£642,000

Alternatively, a claim could be made to surrender the gain of £140,000 to Top Ltd or to rollover the gain against any qualifying asset purchased. In this case the amount to be 'reinvested' to obtain full relief is £310,000 (the market value of the warehouse when the deemed disposal took place).

3.2 Exceptions to the 'no gain/no loss' transfer price

There are exceptions to the 'no gain no loss' transfer price for intra-group transfers of capital assets. There will be an immediate chargeable disposal:

- Where an intra-group **transfer is in satisfaction of a debt.**
- On the **disposal of an interest in shares in a group company by way of a capital distribution.**
- **Where cash or other assets are received upon the redemption of shares in another company.**

In addition, when an asset is transferred between two group companies and is trading stock for one of those companies but not for the other, it is treated as appropriated to or from trading stock by the company for which it is trading stock. This may give rise to an immediate chargeable gain, allowable loss or trading profit or loss (see earlier in this Text).

3.3 Matching group gains and losses

Capital losses cannot be included in a group relief claim. However, **two members of a capital gains group can elect that an asset that has been disposed of outside the group is treated as if it had been transferred between them immediately before disposal**. The deemed transferee company is then treated as having made the disposal. This election may be made within two years of the end of the accounting period in which the disposal took place.

From a tax planning point of view, elections(s) should be made to ensure that net taxable gains arise in the company subject to the lowest rate of corporation tax.

3.4 Rollover relief

FAST FORWARD

Rollover relief is available in a capital gains group.

If a member of a capital gains group disposes of an asset eligible for capital gains rollover or holdover relief it may treat all of the group companies as a single unit for the purpose of claiming such relief. Acquisitions by other group members within the qualifying period of one year before the disposal to three years afterwards may therefore **be matched with the disposal**. However, both the disposing company and the acquiring company must make the claim. If an asset is transferred at no gain and no loss between group members, that transfer does not count as the acquisition of an asset for rollover or holdover relief purpose.

Claims may also be made by non-trading group members which hold assets used for other group members' trades.

3.5 Pre-entry losses

FAST FORWARD

Restrictions apply to the use of pre-entry losses and gains within capital gains tax groups.

A group might acquire a company that has capital losses brought forward, or assets which could be sold to generate capital losses. The use of such 'pre-entry' losses is restricted.

If a company (X) joins a group (G), we must identify X's pre-entry (capital) losses. These are:

- **Losses on disposals before X joined G.**
- **The pre-entry proportions of losses on disposals after X joined G of pre-entry assets** (assets X already owned when it joined G).

When a pre-entry asset is sold at a loss after X joins G, the pre-entry proportion of the loss is found by working out the proportion for each item of allowable expenditure (cost or enhancement expenditure) and adding up the results.

The proportion for each item of allowable expenditure is $A \times (B/C) \times (D/E)$, where:

A is the total allowable loss
B is the item of allowable expenditure
C is the sum of all the items of allowable expenditure
D is the time from when the expenditure was incurred to when X joined G.
E is the time from when the expenditure was incurred to the disposal

The original cost of the asset is treated as incurred when the asset was acquired.

If X sells a pre-entry asset at a loss and makes an election within two years of the end of the accounting period of the disposal, the above computation is disregarded and instead the pre-entry proportion of the loss is the smaller of:

(a) The loss which would have arisen on a sale at market value when X joined G (treating a gain as a loss of £0).

(b) The loss on the actual sale.

X's pre-entry losses may (subject to the usual rule against carrying back capital losses) **be set against gains on assets which:**

- **X disposed of before joining G**
- **X already owned when it joined G, or**
- **X acquired after joining G from someone outside G** and which have, since acquisition, not been used except for the purposes of a trade which X was carrying on immediately before joining G and continued to carry on until the disposals giving rise to the gains.

In any one accounting period, pre-entry losses (whether of the current period or brought forward) are used (so far as possible) before other losses.

Question — Pre-entry losses

X joined the G group on 1 January 1998. X had acquired some land on 1 August 1992 for £700,000, and had incurred enhancement expenditure of £300,000 on 1 April 1995. The land was worth £600,000 on 1 January 1998. On 1 July 2006, X sold the land for £450,000. What is the pre-entry proportion of the loss?

Answer

The total allowable loss is as follows.

	£	£
Proceeds		450,000
Less: cost	700,000	
enhancement expenditure	300,000	
		(1,000,000)
Allowable loss		(550,000)

The pre-entry proportion without an election is as follows.

	£
$£550,000 \times \frac{700,000}{1,000,000} \times \frac{1.8.92 - 1.1.98 = (65 \text{ months})}{1.8.92 - 1.7.06 = (167 \text{ months})}$	149,850
$£550,000 \times \frac{300,000}{1,000,000} \times \frac{1.4.95 - 1.1.98 = (33 \text{ months})}{1.4.95 - 1.7.06 = (135 \text{ months})}$	40,333
	190,183

If the land had been sold when X joined the group on 1 January 1997, the loss would have been as follows.

	£	£
Proceeds		600,000
Less: cost	700,000	
enhancement expenditure	300,000	
		(1,000,000)
Allowable loss		(400,000)

The pre-entry proportion with an election would be the lower of £550,000 and £400,000, that is, £400,000.

The company wants the *lowest* possible pre-entry proportion, because that proportion's use is restricted. The company should therefore not make an election, and will then have a pre-entry proportion of £190,183. The balance of the loss, £(550,000 – 190,183) = £359,817, can be set against all gains made by X Ltd in the same or later accounting periods without restriction.

There are anti avoidance rules which further restricts the set off losses if the transaction is part of a tax avoidance scheme.

3.6 Capital gains buying (Pre-entry gains)

Pre-entry gains are gains realised on pre-change assets, ie assets held by a company at or before the time that it joins a group.

If one of the purposes of the company joining the group was to enable a loss to be set against a pre-entry gain, relief is restricted. In this case the only losses available to set against pre-entry gains **realised before a company joins a group** are:

- Losses that arise in that company before the company joins the new group, and
- Losses that arise after that time on assets that the company held when it joined the group.

Exam focus point

Try to remember the following summary – it will be of great help in the exam.

Parent Co controls over 50% of subsidiary

- Associated companies for upper and lower limits

Parent Co owns 75% or more of subsidiary

- Surrender trading losses, excess property income losses, excess charges, loan deficits, excess management expenses to companies with some PCTCT for same time period

Parent Co owns 75% or more of subsidiary and subsidiary owns 75% or more of its subsidiaries

- Transfer assets between companies automatically at no gain/no loss
- Capital gains and losses can be matched between group member companies
- All companies treated as one for rollover relief purposes.

3.7 Corporate Capital Losses

Three targeted anti-avoidance rules were introduced by the FA2006 to ensure that the creation and use of capital losses is restricted to genuine transactions.

The new rules are aimed at deterring:

- the contrived creation of corporate capital losses;
- the buying of capital gains and losses; and
- the conversion of income streams into capital gains, and the creation of a capital gain matched by an income deduction, where the gains are then wholly or partly franked by capital losses.

4 Succession to trade

FAST FORWARD

A succession occurs when a trade carried on by one company is transferred to another company in substantially the same ownership. In this case losses may be carried forward and balancing adjustments do not arise for capital allowances purposes.

Generally, if a trade is transferred from one company to another, that is treated as a cessation of the trade by the transferor and a commencement of the trade by the transferee. Thus, any trading losses brought forward by the transferor under s 393(1) are extinguished and cannot be utilised by the transferee. In addition, balancing adjustments may arise on assets qualifying for capital allowances. If however the transfer of the trade amounts to a '**succession**', it is treated as continuing for certain specific purposes.

Key term

A **'succession'** occurs if a trade carried on by one company (the 'predecessor') is transferred to another company (the 'successor') in **substantially the same ownership**.

The above test is met if the same persons hold an interest of at least 75% in the trade **both:**

(a) at some time during the 12 months prior to transfer; and
(b) at some time during the 24 months following the transfer

and throughout those periods the trade is carried on by a company chargeable to tax in respect of it.

The transfer of a trade from a company to its 75% subsidiary will generally qualify as a succession. Such a transfer is often referred to as a 'hive down'.

Other circumstances where a succession takes place include a transfer from a 75% subsidiary to its parent and a transfer of trade between two companies with a common 75% parent (or indeed owned to the extent of at least 75% by the same individual). There is no stipulation that the companies have to be UK resident, so the provisions can apply to UK branches of non-resident companies.

When a trade is transferred in this way:

(a) an **accounting period ends** on the date of transfer;

(b) the predecessor may claim **capital allowances** in the final accounting period as if no transfer had taken place. The successor takes over the unrelieved expenditure and is entitled to capital allowances thereon in the period in which the transfer takes place;

(c) the successor is entitled to relief under **s 393(1) for trading losses** not utilised by the predecessor, against future profits from the trade in which the losses were incurred.

The following are **not** transferred:

(a) capital losses;
(b) deficits on non-trading loan relationships.

These remain with the transferor company.

These provisions do **not** enable a trading loss incurred by the successor company to be carried back under s 393A(1)(b) against profits realised by the predecessor. Also, the predecessor's cessation of trade does not qualify it for a three year carry back of losses.

5 Transfer pricing

FAST FORWARD

> The transfer pricing legislation prevents manipulation of profits between members of a group which can occur when a company chooses to buy and sell goods at a price which is not a market price.

Companies under common control can structure their transactions in such a way that they can shift profit (or losses) from one company to another. For example consider a company which wishes to sell goods valued at £20,000 to an independent third party.

Selling company —— Goods invoice value: £20,000 ——→ Buying company

In this case all the profit on the sale arises to the selling company. Alternatively the sale could be rearranged:

Selling company —— Goods invoice value: £16,000 ——→ Subsidiary company —— Goods invoice value: £20,000 ——→ Buying company

In this case £4,000 of the profit has been diverted to the subsidiary.

This technique could be used to direct profits to a company with a lower tax rate, or where they can be sheltered by losses brought forward, or even to an overseas company paying tax at a lower rate.

This is a 'tax advantage' and there is **anti avoidance legislation** which **requires the profit to be computed as if the transactions had been carried out at arms length and not at the prices actually used.**

The transfer pricing rules apply to transactions between two persons if either:

(a) one person directly or indirectly participates in the management, control or capital of the other; or

(b) a third party directly or indirectly participates in the management, control or capital of both.

Small and medium-sized enterprises are normally exempt from the transfer pricing requirements, but HMRC may direct that a medium sized enterprise should be brought within the scope of the legislation. The exemption does not apply to transactions with parties which are resident in a non-qualifying territory. This includes most foreign countries which do not have a double tax treaty with the UK, and certain other designated countries.

Companies must self-assess their liability to tax under the transfer pricing rules and pay any corporation tax due. A statutory procedure exists for advance pricing arrangements (APAs) whereby a company can agree in advance that its transfer pricing policy is acceptable to HMRC – ie, not requiring a self-assessment adjustment. The APA facility is voluntary but companies may feel the need to use the facility as it provides necessary advance confirmation that their approach to transfer pricing in their self-assessment is acceptable.

6 The purchase by a company of its own shares

FAST FORWARD

> A purchase of a company's own shares may be treated as a capital distribution or as an income distribution.

If a company buys its own shares for more than the amount originally subscribed, general tax rules state that there is a distribution of the excess.

Recipients of such distributions are treated in the same way as recipients of ordinary dividends which means that starting and basic rate taxpayers have no further tax to pay and higher rate taxpayers must pay additional tax.

However, a capital gains tax disposal automatically occurs rather than an income distribution, when an unquoted trading company (or the unquoted parent of a trading group) **buys back its own shares in order to benefit its trade and certain other conditions are satisfied**. The trade must not consist of dealing in shares, securities, land or futures. The company may be on the AIM. **The capital gains treatment is not given if a main objective is tax avoidance.**

The 'benefit to the trade' test will be satisfied where:

- A dissident and disruptive shareholder is bought out.
- The proprietor wishes to retire to make way for new management.
- An outside investor who provided equity wishes to withdraw his investment.
- A shareholder dies and his personal representatives do not wish to retain his shares.

The conditions to be satisfied by the vendor shareholder are as follows.

(a) He must be resident and ordinarily resident in the UK when the purchase is made.

(b) **The shares must have been owned by the vendor or his spouse throughout the five years preceding the purchase**. This is reduced to three years if the vendor is the personal representative or the heir of a deceased member, and previous ownership by the deceased will count towards the qualifying period.

(c) **The vendor and his associates must as a result of the purchase have their interest in the company's share capital reduced to 75% or less of their interest before the disposal.** Associates include spouses, minor children, controlled companies, trustees and beneficiaries. Where a company is a member of a group the whole group is effectively considered as one for this test.

(d) **The vendor must not after the transaction be connected with the company or any company in the same 51% group**. A person is connected with a company if he can control more than 30% of the ordinary share capital, the issued share capital and loan capital or the voting rights in the company.

Question — **The reduction of a shareholding**

Henry holds 300 of H Ltd's 1,000 issued ordinary shares. Will there be a capital distribution if the company buys 80 shares from him?

Answer

	Total shares	*Held by Henry*
Initially	1,000	300
Less repurchased	80	80
	920	220

Henry originally had a 30% interest. This is reduced to 220/920 = 23.9%, a reduction to 23.9/30 = 79.7% of his original interest. For a capital distribution he must sell at least 97 shares back to H Ltd, thus reducing his percentage holding below 30% × 75% = 22.5%.

The relief is also available where a company purchases shares to enable the vendor to pay any inheritance tax arising on a death (the 'benefit to the trade' test and the above conditions do not then apply).

Companies considering the purchase of their own shares may seek HMRC clearance to ensure that relief is available, or to ensure that it will not apply where that is preferable.

Chapter roundup

- Associated companies affect the limits for starting rate, small companies rate and marginal relief.
- Group relief is available where the existence of a group or consortium is established through companies resident anywhere in the world.
- Within a 75% group, trading losses can be surrendered between UK companies.
- Within a consortium there is some scope for loss relief.
- Within a capital gains group, assets are transferred at no gain/no loss.
- Rollover relief is available in a capital gains group.
- Restrictions apply to the use of pre-entry losses and gains within capital gains tax groups.
- A succession occurs when a trade carried on by one company is transferred to another company in substantially the same ownership. In this case losses may be carried forward and balancing adjustments do not arise for capital allowances purposes.
- The transfer pricing legislation prevents manipulation of profits between members of a group which can occur when a company chooses to buy and sell goods at a price which is not a market price.
- A purchase of a company's own shares may be treated as a capital distribution or as an income distribution.

Quick quiz

1 List the sorts of losses which may be group relieved.

2 What is the definition of a consortium?

3 When may assets be transferred intra-group at no gain and no loss?

4 How can capital gains and losses within a group be matched with each other?

5 What steps can be taken against the use of artificial transfer prices?

6 When a company buys its own shares, what potential tax consequences may occur?

Answers to quick quiz

1 Trading losses, excess UK property business losses, non-trading deficits on loan relationships, excess charges on income and excess management expenses of investment companies.

2 A company is owned by a consortium if 75% or more of its ordinary share capital is owned by companies none of which have a holding of less than 5%.

Each consortium member (ie company shareholders) must have at least a 5% stake in profits and assets on a winding up in the consortium company.

3 No gain no loss asset transfers are mandatory between companies in an 'assets group' (ie a capital gains group).

4 Two member of an 'assets group' can elect that an asset which has been disposed of to a third party is treated as transferred between them prior to disposal. This election effectively allow the group to match its gains and losses in one company.

5 Although a company may buy and sell goods at any price it wishes, the transfer pricing anti-avoidance legislation requires profit to be computed as if the transactions had been carried out at arms length, in certain circumstances

6 If a company buys its own shares from a shareholder and pays more than the amount originally subscribed the general tax rules treat the excess amount paid as a distribution (dividend) made by the company to the shareholder. Thus there is no tax relief for the company and income tax applies to the shareholder recipient of the dividend.

If certain conditions are met, however, the full amount paid by the company for a purchase of own shares will be treated as capital. Hence the full amount becomes sale proceeds in a CGT computation for the selling shareholder.

Now try the question below from the Exam Question Bank

Number	Level	Marks	Time
Q25	Examination	25	45 mins

27

Overseas aspects of corporate tax

Introduction

This chapter starts by considering which country a company lives in. We then see how relief may be given for overseas taxes suffered, how overseas companies may impact a group and how UK companies are taxed on the profits of certain overseas subsidiaries. Finally, we look at UK companies trading abroad, and some miscellaneous points on overseas companies trading in the UK.

1 Company residence

FAST FORWARD

Company residence is important in determining whether its profits are subject to UK tax.

A company is resident in the UK if it is incorporated in the UK or if its central management and control are exercised in the UK. Central management and control are usually treated as exercised where the board of directors meets. **A UK resident company is subject to corporation tax on its worldwide profits**. It is also (unlike a non-resident company) entitled to the starting rate of corporation tax, the small companies rate and to marginal relief.

A company which would be UK resident under the rules above is nonetheless treated as not UK resident if it is to be so treated under the terms of a double taxation treaty.

A non-UK resident company will be chargeable to corporation tax if it carries on a trade in the UK through a permanent establishment (PE). The profits of such a company which are chargeable to corporation tax, whether or not they arise in the UK, are:

- any trading income arising directly or indirectly from the PE;
- any income from property or rights used by, or held by or for, the PE (other than dividends from UK companies);
- any chargeable gains arising from the disposal of assets situated in the UK.

Key term

A **permanent establishment** is a fixed place of business through which the business of the enterprise is wholly or partly carried on. It includes a branch, office, factory, workshop, mine, oil or gas well, quarry and construction project lasting more than twelve months. It does not include use of storage facilities, maintenance of a stock of goods and delivery of them or a fixed place of business used solely for purchasing goods or any ancillary activity.

If a UK resident company makes investments abroad it will be liable to corporation tax on the profits made, the taxable amount being before the deduction of any foreign taxes. The profits may be any of the following.

(a) Trading income: profits of an overseas branch or agency controlled from the UK

(b) Interest income: income from foreign securities, for example debentures in overseas companies

(c) Foreign income: income from other overseas possessions including:

  (i) dividends from overseas subsidiaries;
  (ii) profits of an overseas branch or agency controlled abroad

(d) Capital gains on disposals of foreign assets

Overseas dividends and interest received by a company are taxed at normal corporation tax rates.

A company may be subject to foreign tax as well as to UK corporation tax on the same profits usually if it has a PE in that foreign country. Double taxation relief (see below) is available in respect of the foreign tax suffered.

2 Double taxation relief (DTR)

FAST FORWARD

A company may obtain DTR for overseas withholding tax, and also (if its investment is large enough) for underlying tax. The allocation of charges and losses can affect the relief.

2.1 General principles

In the UK relief for foreign tax suffered by a company may be currently available in one of three ways.

(a) **Treaty relief**

Under a treaty entered into between the UK and the overseas country, a treaty may exempt certain profits from taxation in one of the countries involved, thus completely avoiding double taxation. More usually treaties provide for credit to be given for tax suffered in one of the countries against the tax liability in the other.

(b) **Unilateral credit relief**

Where no treaty relief is available, unilateral relief may be available in the UK giving credit for the foreign tax against the UK tax.

(c) **Unilateral expense relief** (This is not examinable)

Where neither treaty relief nor unilateral credit relief is available, or unilateral credit relief is not wanted by the taxpayer (because of a lack of UK tax liability against which to obtain credit), relief for overseas tax is given by deducting the overseas tax from the overseas profits prior to including them in the profits chargeable to corporation tax.

2.2 Treaty relief

A tax treaty based on the OECD model treaty may use either the exemption method or the credit method to give relief for tax suffered on income from a business in country B by a resident of country R.

(a) Under the **exemption method**, the income is not taxed at all in country R, or if it is dividends or interest (which the treaty allows to be taxed in country R) credit is given for any country B tax against the country R tax.

(b) Under the **credit method**, the income is taxed in country R, but credit is given for any country B tax against the country R tax.

Under either method, any credit given is limited to the country B tax attributable to the income.

2.3 Unilateral credit relief

Relief is available for overseas tax suffered on PE profits, dividends, interest and royalties, up to the amount of the UK corporation tax (at the company's average rate) attributable to that income. The tax that is deducted overseas is usually called withholding tax. The gross income including the withholding tax is included within the profits chargeable to corporation tax.

Question — **Unilateral credit relief**

On 1 May 2006, AS plc receives a dividend from Bola of £80,000. This has been paid subject to 20% withholding tax. AS plc has UK trading income of £2,000,000 for the year to 31.3.07. Show that the Foreign income is £100,000 and compute the corporation tax payable.

Answer

	Total	UK	Overseas
	£	£	£
Trading income	2,000,000	2,000,000	
Foreign income (W)	100,000		100,000
PCTCT	2,100,000	2,000,000	100,000
Corporation tax at 30%	630,000	600,000	30,000
Less DTR: lower of:			
(a) overseas tax: £20,000; or			
(b) UK tax on overseas income: £30,000	(20,000)		(20,000)
MCT	610,000	600,000	10,000

Working: Foreign income

£80,000 × 100/(100 – 20) = £100,000.

If the overseas tax rate exceeds the UK CT rate there will be excess foreign tax. A company can operate **'onshore pooling'** by pooling foreign dividends and setting the excess foreign tax on one dividend against UK CT on other foreign dividends. It can:

(a) Set off the excess foreign tax in the current accounting period
(b) Carry the excess foreign tax back for three years on a LIFO basis
(c) Carry the excess foreign tax forward indefinitely
(d) Surrender the excess foreign tax to another group company

Where foreign tax is carried backwards or forwards it is set against UK tax payable on foreign dividends other than dividends paid by Controlled Foreign Companies (CFCs) (see later in this chapter) or dividends where the underlying tax has already been capped or subject to another form of limitation or relief (see below).

In respect of dividends from overseas subsidiaries the rate of foreign tax for which companies can claim relief is capped at 30%.

If a company has non-trading credits (income) for loan interest from abroad, and they have suffered foreign tax, then non-trading credits (income) and debits (expenses) are not netted off to give a net surplus or deficit. Instead, *all* non-trading credits and debits (UK or overseas) on loan relationships are separated out. The credits are taxable as interest income, and the debits go against the profits which the company chooses (see below).

Companies have to take all reasonable steps to minimise their foreign tax if they are to obtain full relief against UK tax. A failure to claim all overseas tax reliefs, deductions, allowances etc will result in the UK authorities restricting the amount of DTR available.

Exam focus point

No detailed computational questions will be set on the carry back and carry forward of unrelieved foreign tax or 'onshore pooling'. However, an awareness of those provisions is required.

2.4 Underlying tax relief

In addition to the relief available for withholding tax shown above, relief is available for underlying tax relating to a dividend received from a foreign company in which the UK company owns at least 10% of the voting power, either directly or indirectly. The underlying tax is the tax attributable to the relevant profits out of which the dividend was paid.

Underlying tax is calculated as

$$\text{Gross dividend income} \times \frac{\text{foreign tax paid}}{\text{after-tax accounting profits}}$$

Relief for underlying tax is not available to individuals.

We may need to decide which accounting profits have been used to pay a dividend. If the dividend is declared for a particular year, the set of accounts for that year are used. If this information is not given, the relevant profits are those of the period of account immediately before that in which the dividend was payable.

There is an anti-avoidance provision which restricts relief for underlying tax in certain circumstances where there is a scheme the purpose, or one of the main purposes, of which is to obtain relief for underlying tax.

Question

Underlying tax relief

A Ltd, a UK company with no associated companies, holds 30,000 out of 90,000 voting ordinary shares in B Inc (resident in Lintonia).

The profit and loss account of B Inc for the year to 31 March 2007 is as follows (converted into sterling).

		£	£
Trading profit			1,000,000
Less taxation:	provided on profits	300,000	
	transfer to deferred tax account	100,000	
			(400,000)
			600,000
Less dividends:	Net	240,000	
	withholding tax (20%)	60,000	
			(300,000)
Retained profits			300,000

The actual tax paid on the profits for the year to 31 March 2007 was £270,000.

Apart from the net dividend of £80,000 received out of the above profits from B Inc on 31 May 2006 the only other taxable profit of A Ltd for its year to 31 March 2007 was £610,000 UK trading profit. A Ltd paid no dividends during the year and received no UK dividends.

Calculate A Ltd's UK corporation tax liability after double taxation relief.

Answer

A LTD: UK CORPORATION TAX LIABILITY

	£	£
Trading income		610,000
Foreign income		
Net dividend	80,000	
Withholding tax at 20%		
£80,000 × 20/80	20,000	
Gross dividend	100,000	
Underlying tax		
$£100,000 \times \frac{270,000}{600,000}$	45,000	
Gross income		145,000
PCTCT		755,000

	Total	*UK*	*Overseas*
	£	£	£
Trading income	610,000	610,000	
Foreign income	145,000		145,000
PCTCT	755,000	610,000	145,000
Corporation tax £755,000 × 30%			226,500
Less small companies' marginal relief £(1,500,000 – 755,000) × 11/400			(20,488)
			206,012
The average rate of corporation tax is £206,012/£755,000 = 27.28635%.			
Corporation tax at the average rate	206,012	166,447	39,565
Less DTR: lower of:			
(a) overseas tax £(20,000 + 45,000) = £65,000;			
(b) UK tax on overseas income £39,565	(39,565)		(39,565)
	166,447	166,447	0

Corporation tax of £166,447 is payable. £(65,000 – 39,565) = £25,435 of overseas tax is unrelieved (ie excess). It is possible to carry the unrelieved tax back or forward.

A company may allocate its non-trading deficits on loan relationships, charges and losses relieved under s 393A(1) in whatever manner it likes for the purpose of computing double taxation relief. (Deficits brought back can as usual only go against interest income, and deficits brought forward can only go against non-trading profits, but the company can choose which interest income or non-trading profits.) **It should set the maximum amount against any UK profits, thereby maximising the corporation tax attributable to the foreign profits and hence maximising the double taxation relief available.**

If a company has several sources of overseas profits, then deficits, charges and losses should be allocated first to UK profits, and then to overseas sources which have suffered the **lowest** rates of overseas taxation.

Losses relieved under s 393(1) must in any case be set against the first available profits of the trade which gave rise to the loss.

A company with a choice of loss reliefs should consider the effect of its choice on double taxation relief. For example, a s 393A(1) claim might lead to there being no UK tax liability, or a very small liability, so that foreign tax would go unrelieved. S 393(1) relief might avoid this problem and still leave very little UK tax to pay for the period of the loss.

Companies who have claimed DTR must notify HMRC if the amount of foreign tax they have paid is adjusted and this has resulted in the DTR claim becoming excessive. The notification must be in writing.

Exam focus point

If there are several sources of overseas income it is important to keep them separate and to calculate double tax relief on each source of income separately. Get into the habit of setting out a working with a separate column for UK income and for each source of overseas income. You should then find arriving at the right answer straightforward.

3 Groups of companies

FAST FORWARD

The group relief rules allow groups and consortia to be established through companies resident anywhere in the world.

3.1 Introduction

Groups and consortia can be established through companies resident anywhere in the world. However, group relief is normally only available to, and may only be claimed from, UK resident companies.

There is a very limited exception for group companies resident in another country in the European Economic Area. Such companies may, from 1 April 2006, surrender losses to UK group members, but only if they are unable to obtain relief for the loss in any other country.

3.2 Example

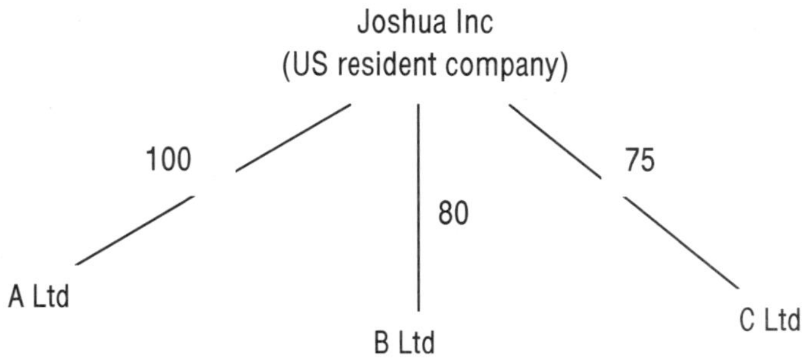

A Ltd, B Ltd and C Ltd are all UK resident companies. As the three UK companies share a common parent they will be treated as part of a group relief group despite the fact that the parent company is not UK resident. The UK companies may surrender losses to each other (but not normally to or from the overseas parent company).

Similarly, a consortium may exist for relief purposes where one or more of the members is not resident in the UK but relief cannot be passed to or from a non UK resident company.

3.3 Permanent establishments (PEs) of companies

Group relief is available to UK PEs of overseas companies. PEs can claim relief from UK resident group members. Alternatively, they can surrender losses, which cannot be relieved against profits in the overseas country, to such group members.

Losses incurred by overseas PEs of UK companies can be surrendered as group relief only if they cannot be relieved against profits in the overseas country.

3.4 The Global Group Concept

The 'global group concept' means that instead of looking at the residence of a company one needs to look at whether the company is subject to UK corporation tax on any of its chargeable gains. Provided the assets transferred do not result in a potential leakage of UK corporation tax, no gain/no loss transfers will be possible within a worldwide (global) group of companies.

The global group concept applies to the transfer of the whole or part of a trade and extends to certain intra-group transfers of assets and to transfers of assets where one company disposes of the whole or part of its business to another company as part of a scheme of reconstruction or amalgamation.

4 Controlled foreign companies

FAST FORWARD

Profits of a CFC are apportioned to UK resident companies entitled to at least 25% of those profits.

4.1 Definition and treatment

Exam focus point

Although controlled exam companies may be examined only in Section B questions you should probably regard them as very important exam knowledge.

A UK resident company may choose to trade abroad through an investment in a local company. Providing there are no exchange control problems and cash flow requirements do not call for the repatriation of all profits to the UK, there will generally be a benefit in accumulating income in a foreign company whose effective tax rate is lower than that of the UK company. To prevent undue tax avoidance in this way, there are special rules for 'controlled foreign companies' (CFCs).

A controlled foreign company (CFC) is a company which:

(a) **is resident outside the UK**; and
(b) **is controlled by persons resident in the UK; and**
(c) **is subject to a 'lower level of taxation' in the country in which it is resident.**

A lower level of tax means less than three quarters of the amount which would have been payable had the company been resident in the UK.

Question

Controlled foreign company

Bohemia Limited is resident for tax purposes in the Cayman Islands but also trades through a branch based in Switzerland. It is owned as follows:

		%
Maurice Feischner (Swiss resident Managing Director)		25
Ace Ltd	UK resident companies	25
Beta Ltd		10
Cahill Ltd		10
Michael Brown (UK resident)		30
		100

Bohemia Ltd has chargeable profits of £875,000 in the year to 31 December 2006. The tax rate in the Cayman Islands on these profits is 24%. The UK tax rate would have been 30%. The Swiss tax paid was £90,000 on the profits.

Is Bohemia Limited a controlled foreign company?

Answer

(a) Non UK-resident? – Yes

(b) Is it controlled by UK resident persons? Yes. UK residents own 75% of the company.

(c) Subject to lower tax rate?

	Cayman Islands	*UK equivalent*
	£	£
Tax payable		
£875,000 × 24%/30%	210,000	262,500
Relief for foreign tax suffered	(90,000)	(90,000)
	120,000	172,500

Tax rates: 24/30 = 80% not lower

Total tax : £210,000/£262,500 = 80% not lower

Local tax/UK tax: £120,000/£172,500 = 69.6% – lower than three quarters limit

Consequently Bohemia Limited is a CFC unless one of the exceptions apply (see below).

The CFC rules normally apply only to companies paying less than 75% of the tax they would have paid if they were resident in the UK. To avoid the CFC rules, a number of overseas countries have regimes that effectively allow companies to choose the rate of tax they pay. Companies paying tax under such 'designer rate' tax regimes fall within the definition of a CFC regardless of the level of tax paid. HMRC has produced a list of the regimes to which these rules apply.

4.2 Apportionment of profits

Profits of a CFC are apportioned to UK resident companies (not individuals) entitled to at least 25% of those profits. The apportionment should be made on a 'just and reasonable' basis. Where shareholders have not changed throughout the accounting period the apportionment is based on the relevant interest.

UK companies must decide for themselves whether an apportionment is appropriate and self-assess their profits on the basis of their decision. There is an additional page to be filed together with the CT 600 tax return where a company has profits of a CFC to report. Companies failing to show the appropriate adjustments in their CT returns will be exposed to interest and penalties.

Apportioned profits are brought into the UK company's CT600 corporation tax computation as an amount of tax. The tax rate applicable is always the full rate of corporation tax irrespective of the rate the UK company pays tax on its other profits.

Question — Apportionment of profits

In the above question how much profits would Ace Ltd be taxed on if Bohemia Ltd is held to be a CFC?

Answer

Ace Ltd would have to apportion 25% of the profit of Bohemia Ltd when calculating CT for self assessment purposes.

Ace Ltd

£875,000 × 25%	£218,750

Where CFC profits are apportioned they are reduced by 'creditable tax' which is the aggregate of:

(a) any double tax relief (see below) available in the UK in respect of foreign tax due against the chargeable profits

(b) any income tax deducted at source on income received by the CFC

(c) corporation tax payable in the UK on any CFC income taxable in this country.

Question — Apportionment of profits

R Inc is a controlled foreign company owned 75% by J Ltd and 25% by Mr J. Its results for the year ended 31 December 2006 were:

	£
Tax adjusted trading profits	
Under UK legislation	650,000
Under foreign legislation (foreign tax rate 8%)	500,000

Show how the profits of R Inc will be apportioned to and taxed on J Ltd. J Ltd has other profits of £2 million.

Answer

		£
UK tax adjusted profit		650,000
Apportioned to J Ltd (75%)		487,500
J Ltd's CT computation		
	£	£
Tax on UK profits (£2m × 30%)		600,000
Tax on CFC		
£487,500 × 30%	146,250	
Less foreign tax (8% × £500,000) × 75%	(30,000)	
		116,250
		716,250

4.3 Exceptions

A CFC profits do not need to be apportioned if it falls into one of the six situations outlined below.

Its chargeable profits for the accounting period do not exceed £50,000 (this is reduced proportionately for short accounting periods).

It is situated in a territory which does not have a lower level of taxation.

It follows an acceptable distribution policy. This applies where it distributes by way of a dividend, during or within 18 months of the period for which it is due, at least 90% of its net chargeable profits. These are net profits as computed for UK corporation tax purposes less chargeable gains and foreign tax).

It is engaged in exempt activities and

(a) it has a **real presence** in its territory of residence.

(b) its main activity does not consist of leasing, dealing in securities or the receipt of income such as dividends, interest or royalties and is not such that the company may be used as an invoicing route nor is the company an intra-group service company (ie which is mainly engaged in the provision of services and receives 50% or more of its income from related parties).

(c) its business is not primarily with associates in those trades which frequently involve cross-frontier transactions.

(d) it does not receive a significant amount of dividends from CFCs except where the exemption for holding companies applies.

In addition, where the company is engaged mainly in a wholesale, distributive financial or service business, less than 50% of it gross trading income is derived from connected or associated persons, from other companies potentially subject to an apportionment from the CFC or from any person connected or associated with either a UK or non-resident who satisfy the 40% test (see above).

A holding company with subsidiaries outside the territory in which it is itself resident meets the exempt activities test only if 90% or more of its income is in the form of non-tax deductible dividends from subsidiaries that are themselves exempt from the CFC rules.

It fulfils the public quotation conditions. This means it must be quoted on a recognised stock exchange, and dealing must have taken place within twelve months of the end of the accounting period. At least 35% of the voting power must be held by the public with no more than 85% of that power being held by all the company's principal members (defined as for close companies).

It satisfies the **motive test**. This means the transactions taking place in an accounting period must achieve a reduction in UK tax which is no more than minimal, or it was not the main purpose of these transactions was not to achieve a reduction and the reduction in UK tax by the diversion of profit from the UK was not a main reason for the company's existence during that accounting period.

There is an **advance clearance procedure** in respect of the **'exempt activities' test**, the **'motive'**; test and the **'acceptable distribution policy'.**

The Treasury has a reserve power to designate jurisdictions in which all CFCs will automatically fall within the CFC tax regime. The exercise of the power requires the express consent of the Parliament.

The effect of the exercise of the reserve power would be to exclude the application of all the CFC exemptions in relation to a particular jurisdiction. In particular it will deny the exemption for companies which carry on a business in the designated jurisdiction. The intention is that the power will be used against jurisdictions which do not remove 'harmful tax regimes'. It will not be used where appropriate action is being taken to remove those practices.

If the power is exercised, exclusion from the exemptions would apply to CFC accounting periods beginning on or after the date on which regulations were made specifically designating the relevant jurisdiction.

5 Permanent Establishment (PE) or subsidiary abroad

FAST FORWARD

A UK resident company intending to do business abroad must choose between a permanent establishment and a subsidiary. If a subsidiary is chosen, it must bear in mind the rules on controlled foreign companies and on trading at artificial prices.

5.1 General principles

Where a foreign country has a lower rate of company taxation than the UK, it can be beneficial for the UK company to conduct its foreign activities through a **non-UK resident subsidiary** if profits are anticipated (assuming that the CFC rules (see above) do not apply), and through a **PE if losses are likely to arise**.

The **profits of a foreign PE** are treated as part of the profits of the UK company and are normally included in its computation of trading profits. If, however, the operations of the overseas PE amount to a separate trade which is wholly carried on overseas, the profits are assessed as foreign income.

The losses of a foreign PE are normally included in the trading income of computation and the usual loss reliefs are available. They can be surrendered as group relief to the extent the loss cannot be relieved against profits in the overseas country. Alternatively a foreign income trading loss can be carried forward to set against future profits of the same trade.

The profits of a non-resident **foreign subsidiary** are only liable to UK tax when remitted to the UK, for example in the form of dividends (foreign income). However, no relief can be obtained against the UK parent's profits for any overseas losses of a non-resident subsidiary except in very limited circumstances.

5.2 Incorporation a foreign PE

Where a foreign operation is likely to show a loss in the early years followed by a profit it may be worthwhile to trade through a foreign PE whilst losses arise (these are usually then automatically netted off against the company's UK profits) and then later to convert the PE into a non-UK resident subsidiary company (so that profits can be accumulated at potentially lower rates of foreign tax).

This conversion of a foreign PE into a non-UK resident subsidiary has some important implications and the tax effects both in the UK and the overseas country need to be considered. Firstly, it may be necessary to secure the consent of the Treasury for the transaction. It is illegal for a UK resident company to cause or permit a non-UK resident company over which it has control to create or issue any shares or debentures. It is also illegal for a UK resident company to transfer to any person, or cause or permit to be transferred to any person, any shares or debentures of a non-UK resident company over which it has control.

The Treasury have published General Consents which permit certain intra-group transactions and third party transactions provided full consideration is given. Additionally certain movements of capital between EEA states are allowed automatically. Thus in practice specific Treasury consent may not be required for a transaction of the type presently under consideration.

Secondly, the conversion will constitute a disposal of the assets of the PE giving rise to a chargeable gain or loss in the hands of the UK company. A chargeable gain can be postponed where:

(a) the trade of the foreign PE is transferred to the non-UK resident company with all the assets used for that trade except cash; and

(b) the consideration for the transfer is wholly or partly securities (shares or shares and loan stock); and

(c) the transferring company owns at least 25% of the ordinary share capital of the non-resident company; and

(d) a claim for relief is made.

There is full postponement of the net gains arising on the transfer where the consideration is wholly securities. Where part of the consideration is in a form other than securities, eg cash, that proportion of the net gains is chargeable immediately.

The postponement is indefinite. The gain becomes chargeable only when:

(a) the transfer or company at any time disposes of any of the securities received on the transfer; or

(b) the non-UK resident company within six years of the transfer disposes of any of the assets on which a gain arose at the time of the transfer.

The 'global group' concept applies to certain intra-group transfers of assets and also where one company disposes of the whole of part of its business to another company as part of a reconstruction or amalgamation scheme. Such asset transfers are on a no gain/no loss basis provided the assets transferred do not result in a potential leakage of UK corporation tax.

5.3 European Community companies

If all or part of a trade carried on in the UK by a company resident in one EC state is transferred to a company resident in another EC state, then the transfer is deemed to be at a price giving no gain and no loss, if all the following conditions are fulfilled.

(a) The transfer is wholly in exchange for shares or securities.

(b) The company receiving the trade would be subject to UK corporation tax on any gains arising on later disposals of the assets transferred.

(c) Both parties claim this special treatment.

(d) The transfer is for bona fide commercial reasons. Advance clearance that this condition is satisfied may be obtained.

6 Non-UK resident companies

FAST FORWARD

A non resident company is liable to UK corporation tax if it carries on trade in the UK through a permanent establishment.

6.1 Corporation tax charge

A non resident company is liable to tax in the UK if it carries on a trade in the UK through a permanent establishment (defined as above).

The PE has **the profits it would have made if it were a distinct and separate establishment engaged in the same or similar activities in the same or similar conditions, dealing wholly independently with the non resident company attributed to it.** Deductions are allowed for allowable expenses incurred for the purposes of the PE including executive and general administrative expenses whether in the UK or elsewhere. The term allowable expenses has the same meaning as for a UK resident company. Relief is available for the expenses of managing investments to all companies whether or not they qualify as 'investment companies'.

Transactions between the PE and the non resident company are treated as taking place at **arms length prices.**

For the purposes of collection of tax a PE will be treated as the UK representative through which the non resident company carries on a trade in the UK.

These rules align with the normal provision in tax treaties (based on the OECD model treaty) **that a foreign trader is taxable on his trading profits in the UK if he has a permanent establishment in the UK.**

6.2 Charge to tax on income

Income charged to corporation tax comprises:

(a) Trading income arising directly or indirectly through or from the permanent establishment, and

(b) Any income, wherever arising, from property or rights used by, held by or held for the permanent establishment.

Dividends and other distributions from companies resident in the UK are not charged to corporation tax; nor are they normally charged to income tax. A repayment may arise under the terms of a double taxation agreement.

Annual interest and other annual payments are received under deduction of income tax. Provided that the income is charged to corporation tax, the company can offset the income tax suffered against its corporation tax liability and, in appropriate circumstances, obtain repayment in the same manner as a resident company.

Income from sources within the UK which is not subject to corporation tax is subject to **income tax**. This could arise, for example, if a non-resident company carries on a trade in the UK without having a permanent establishment, or receives letting income from a UK property.

6.3 Charge to tax on capital gains

Capital gains are charged to corporation tax, where the company carries on a trade in the UK through a permanent establishment, if they arise on:

(a) Assets situated in the UK used in or for the purposes of the trade at or before the time when the gain accrued.

(b) Assets situated in the UK held or used for the purposes of the permanent establishment at or before the time when the gain accrued.

As it would be possible to avoid gains being chargeable by, for example, ceasing to trade in the UK through a permanent establishment prior to selling the asset or exporting the asset, there are two further charging provisions:

(a) Where a non-UK resident company ceases to trade through a permanent establishment in the UK, a charge will arise. Any chargeable asset which would otherwise become non-chargeable shall be deemed to be disposed of and reacquired at market value immediately before it ceases to trade.

(b) Where a non-UK resident company trading through a UK permanent establishment exports a chargeable asset, so that it becomes non-chargeable, the gain will crystallise immediately before it is exported.

6.4 Tax planning

A foreign resident company may have to decide **whether to trade in the UK through a PE or via a UK subsidiary**. The advantage of a subsidiary if profits are low is that it will be able to take advantage of the starting rate or the small companies rate of tax. However, if the subsidiary makes losses the overseas company may be restricted in the relief it can claim. The overseas company would also need to consider the repatriation of profits and the provision of finance.

Chapter roundup

- A company may obtain DTR for overseas withholding tax, and also (if its investment is large enough) for underlying tax. The allocation of charges and losses can affect the relief.
- The group relief rules allow groups and consortia to be established through companies resident anywhere in the world.
- Profits of a CFC are apportioned to UK resident companies entitled to at least 25% of those profits.
- A UK resident company intending to do business abroad must choose between a permanent establishment and a subsidiary. If a subsidiary is chosen, it must bear in mind the rules on controlled foreign companies and on trading at artificial prices.

Quick quiz

1 When is a company UK resident?

2 How is underlying tax calculated?

3 How best should charges be allocated in computing credit relief for foreign tax?

4 What is the definition of a CFC?

5 A UK company is planning to set up a new operation in Australia that will initially be loss making. Should it set up as a permanent establishment or a subsidiary of the UK company?

Answers to quick quiz

1 A company is resident in the UK if it is incorporated in the UK or if its central management and control are exercised in the UK.

2 Underlying tax is calculated as

$$\text{Dividend plus withholding tax} \times \frac{\text{foreign tax paid}}{\text{after-tax accounting profits}}$$

3 Charges should be set-off firstly from any UK profits, then from overseas income sources suffering the lowest rates of overseas taxation before those suffering at the higher rates.

4 A CFC is a company which

(a) is resident outside the UK
(b) is controlled by persons resident in the UK
(c) is subject to a lower level of taxation in the country in which it is resident.

5 If losses are expected to arise then a PE operation is best since losses of a foreign branch can be surrendered as group relief.

Now try the question below from the Exam Question Bank

Number	Level	Marks	Time
Q26	Introductory	15	27 mins

Part C
Value added tax

28

Value added tax 1

Introduction

In this and the next chapter, we study value added tax (VAT). VAT is a tax on turnover rather than on profits.

As the name of the tax suggests, it is charged (usually at 17.5%) on the value added. If someone in a chain of manufacture or distribution buys goods for £1,000 and sells them for £1,200 he has increased their value by £200. (He may have painted them, packed them or distributed them to shops to justify his mark-up, or he may simply be good at making deals to buy cheaply and sell dearly.) Because he has added value of £200, he collects VAT of £200 × 17.5% = £35 and pays this over to the government. The VAT is collected bit by bit along the chain and finally hits the consumer who does not add value, but uses up the goods.

VAT is a tax with simple computations but many detailed rules to ensure its enforcement. You may find it easier to absorb the detail if you ask yourself, in relation to each rule, exactly how it helps to enforce the tax.

Topic list	Syllabus references
1 Basic principles	1(k), 2(b)
2 The scope of VAT	1(k), 2(b)
3 Registration	1(k), 2(b)
4 Accounting for VAT	1(k), 2(b)
5 VAT invoices and records	1(k), 2(b)
6 The valuation of supplies	1(k), 2(b)
7 Administration	1(k), 2(b)
8 Penalties	1(k), 2(b)

1 Basic principles

FAST FORWARD

VAT is charged on turnover at each stage in a production process, but in such a way that the burden is borne by the final consumer.

1.1 Introduction

The legal basis of value added tax (VAT) is to be found in the Value Added Tax Act 1994 (VATA 1994), supplemented by regulations made by statutory instrument and amended by subsequent Finance Acts. VAT is administered by HM Revenue and Customs (HMRC). Previously there were two separate bodies called the Inland Revenue (responsible for direct taxes such as income tax and corporation tax) and HM Customs & Excise (responsible for indirect taxes such as VAT).

VAT is a tax on turnover, not on profits. The basic principle is that the VAT should be borne by the final consumer. Registered traders may deduct the tax which they suffer on supplies to them (input tax) from the tax which they charge to their customers (output tax) at the time this is paid to HMRC. Thus, at each stage of the manufacturing or service process, the net VAT paid is on the value added at that stage.

1.2 Example: the VAT charge

A forester sells wood to a furniture maker for £100 plus VAT. The furniture maker uses this wood to make a table and sells the table to a shop for £150 plus VAT. The shop then sells the table to the final consumer for £300 plus VAT. VAT will be accounted for to HMRC as follows.

	Cost	*Input tax 17.5%*	*Net sale price*	*Output tax 17.5%*	*Payable to HMRC*
	£	£	£	£	£
Forester	0	0	100	17.50	17.50
Furniture maker	100	17.50	150	26.25	8.75
Shop	150	26.25	300	52.50	26.25
					52.50

Because the traders involved account to HMRC for VAT charged less VAT suffered, their profits for income tax or corporation tax purposes are based on sales and purchases net of VAT.

2 The scope of VAT

FAST FORWARD

VAT is charged on taxable supplies of goods and services made by a taxable person in his business.

2.1 General principles

VAT is charged on taxable supplies of goods and services made in the UK by a taxable person in the course or furtherance of any business carried on by him. It is also chargeable on the import of goods into the UK (whether they are imported for business purposes or not, and whether the importer is a taxable person or not), and on certain services received from abroad if a taxable person receives them for business purposes.

Special rules for trade with the European Union (the EU) are covered in the next chapter.

Key term

A **taxable supply** is a supply of goods or services made in the UK, other than an exempt supply.

A taxable supply is either standard-rated or zero-rated. The standard rate is 17.5% (although on certain supplies, for example the supply of domestic fuel and power, a lower rate is charged of 5%) and zero-rated supplies are taxed at 0%. An exempt supply is not chargeable to VAT. The categories of zero-rated and exempt supplies are listed in the next chapter.

2.2 Supplies of goods

Goods are supplied if exclusive ownership of the goods passes to another person.

The following are treated as supplies of goods.

- The supply of any form of power, heat, refrigeration or ventilation, or of water
- The grant, assignment or surrender of a major interest (the freehold or a lease for over 21 years) in land
- Taking goods permanently out of the business for the non-business use of a taxable person or for other private purposes including the supply of goods by an employer to an employee for his private use
- Transfers under an agreement contemplating a transfer of ownership, such as a hire purchase agreement

Gifts of goods are normally treated as sales at cost (so VAT is due). **However, business gifts are not supplies of goods if**:

(a) **The total cost of gifts made to the same person does not exceed £50 in any 12 month period**. If the £50 limit is exceeded, output tax will be due in full on the total of gifts made. Once the limit has been exceeded a new £50 limit and new 12 month period begins.

(b) **The gift is a sample**. However, if two or more identical samples are given to the same person, all but one of them are treated as supplies.

2.3 Supplies of services

Apart from a few specific exceptions, **any supply which is not a supply of goods and which is done for a consideration is a supply of services**. A consideration is any form of payment in money or in kind, including anything which is itself a supply.

A supply of services also takes place if:

- Goods are lent to someone for use outside the business
- Goods are hired to someone
- Services bought for business purposes are used for private purposes

The European Court of Justice has ruled that restaurants supply services rather than goods.

2.4 Taxable persons

The term 'person' includes individuals, partnerships (which are treated as single entities, ignoring the individual partners), **companies, clubs, associations and charities. If a person is in business making taxable supplies, then the value of these supplies is called the taxable turnover. If a person's taxable turnover exceeds certain limits then he is a taxable person and should be registered for VAT.**

3 Registration

FAST FORWARD

A trader becomes liable to register for VAT if the value of taxable supplies in any period up to 12 months exceeds £61,000 or if there are reasonable grounds for believing that the value of the taxable supplies will exceed £61,000 in the next 30 days. A trader may also register voluntarily.

3.1 Compulsory registration

At the end of every month a trader must calculate his cumulative turnover of taxable supplies to date. However this cumulative period does not extend beyond the previous 12 months. **The trader becomes liable to register for VAT if the value of his cumulative taxable supplies** (excluding VAT) **exceeds £61,000** (from 1 April 2006 onwards). The person is required to notify HMRC within 30 days of the end of the month in which the £61,000 limit is exceeded. HMRC will then register the person with effect from the end of the month following the month in which the £61,000 was exceeded, or from an earlier date if they and the trader agree.

Registration under this rule is not required if HMRC are satisfied that the value of the trader's taxable supplies (excluding VAT) in the year then starting will not exceed £59,000 (from 1 April 2006 onwards).

A person is also liable to register at any time if there are reasonable grounds for believing that his taxable supplies (excluding VAT) in the following 30 days will exceed £61,000. Only taxable turnover of that 30 day period is considered **not** cumulative turnover. HMRC must be notified by the end of the 30 day period and registration will be with effect from the beginning of that period.

When determining the value of a person's taxable supplies for the purposes of registration, supplies of goods and services that are *capital assets* of the business are to be disregarded, except for non zero-rated taxable supplies of interests in land.

Question **VAT registration**

Fred started to trade in cutlery on 1 January 2006. Sales (excluding VAT) were £5,325 a month for the first nine months and £7,700 a month thereafter. From what date should Fred be registered for VAT?

Answer

	£	
Sales to 31 October 2006	55,625	
Sales to 30 November 2006	63,325	(exceeds £61,000)

Fred must notify his liability to register by 30 December 2006 (not 31 December) and will be registered from 1 January 2007 or from an agreed earlier date.

When a person is liable to register in respect of a past period, it is his responsibility to pay VAT. If he is unable to collect it from those to whom he made taxable supplies, the VAT burden will fall on him. A person must start keeping VAT records and charging VAT to customers as soon as it is known that he is required to register. However, VAT should not be shown separately on any invoices until the registration number is known. The invoice should show the VAT inclusive price and customers should be informed that VAT invoices will be forwarded once the registration number is known. Formal VAT invoices should then be sent to such customers within 30 days of receiving the registration number.

Notification of liability to register must be made on form VAT 1. Simply writing to, or telephoning, a local VAT office is not enough. On registration the VAT office will send the trader a certificate of registration. This shows the VAT registration number, the date of registration, the end of the first VAT period and the length of later VAT periods.

If a trader makes a supply before becoming liable to register, but gets paid after registration, VAT is not due on that supply.

3.2 Voluntary registration

A person may decide to become registered even though his taxable turnover falls below the registration limit. Unless a person is registered he cannot recover the input tax he pays on purchases.

Voluntary registration is advantageous where a person wishes to recover input tax on purchases. For example, consider a trader who has one input during the year which cost £1,000 plus £175 VAT; he works on the input which becomes his sole output for the year and he decides to make a profit of £1,000.

(a) If he is not registered he will charge £2,175 and his customer will obtain no relief for any VAT.

(b) If he is registered he will charge £2,000 plus VAT of £350. His customer will have input tax of £350 which he will be able to recover if he, too, is registered.

If the customer is a non-taxable person he will prefer (a) as the cost to him is £2,175. If he is taxable he will prefer (b) as the net cost is £2,000. Thus, a decision whether or not to register voluntarily may depend upon the status of customers. It may also depend on the status of the outputs and the image of his business the trader wishes to project (registration may give the impression of a substantial business). The administrative burden of registration should also be considered.

3.3 Intending trader registration

Providing that a trader satisfies HMRC that he is carrying on a business, and intends to make taxable supplies, he is entitled to be registered if he chooses. But, once registered, he is obliged to notify HMRC within 30 days if he no longer intends to make taxable supplies.

3.4 Exemption from registration

If a person makes only zero-rated supplies, he may request exemption from registration. The trader is obliged to notify HMRC of any material change in the nature of his supplies.

HMRC may also allow exemption from registration if only a small proportion of supplies are standard-rated, provided that the trader would normally receive repayments of VAT if registered.

3.5 Group registration

Companies under common control may apply for group registration. The effects and advantages of group registration are as follows.

- Each VAT group must appoint a representative member which must **account for the group's output tax and input tax, thus simplifying VAT accounting** and allowing payments and repayments of VAT to be netted off. However, all members of the group are jointly and severally liable for any VAT due from the representative member.
- **Any supply of goods or services by a member of the group to another member of the group is, in general, disregarded for VAT purposes,** reducing the VAT accounting required.
- Any other supply of goods or services by or to a group member is in general treated as a supply by or to the representative member.
- Any VAT payable on the import of goods by a group member is payable by the representative member.

Two or more companies are eligible to be treated as members of a group provided each of them is either established in the UK or has a fixed establishment in the UK, and:

- **One of them controls each of the others, or**
- **One person** (which could be an individual or a holding company) **controls all of them**, or
- **Two or more persons carrying on a business in partnership control all of them.**
- Anti-avoidance rules prevent a company from belonging to a VAT group where it would otherwise be eligible but it is in fact run for the benefit of an external third party.

An application to create, terminate, add to or delete a company from a VAT group may be made at any time. Applications may be refused when it appears to HMRC to be necessary to do so for the protection of the revenue. However, if a company is no longer eligible to belong to a VAT group because the common control test is failed, the company must leave the VAT group even if revenue might not be lost.

A group registration, or any change therein, will take effect from the date the application is received by HMRC although applications may have an earlier or later effect. Therefore it is possible to apply in advance for group changes and it is also possible to apply for changes having a retrospective effect. However, HMRC have 90 days to refuse an application.

HMRC can cancel a grouping if a company ceases to meet the eligibility requirements or a risk to the revenue arises. A risk arises where avoidance is suspected, there is a risk that tax due may not be collectable or the revenue loss goes beyond that arising as a natural consequence of grouping.

Certain 'tax planning' schemes use groups to reduce the Government's overall VAT revenue. (Normal transactions within a VAT group do not do this, because eventually supplies will be made outside the group.) HMRC can deal with such schemes by directing that:

- A supply made within a group is treated as made outside the group, or
- A company within a group is treated as being outside the group for a specified period.
- A company eligible to be in a group is treated as being in the group for a specified period.

A company can appeal against a direction on the grounds that a transaction, or a change in group membership, had a genuine commercial purpose as its main purpose.

Individual companies which are within a group for company law purposes may still register separately and stay outside the VAT group. This may be done to ensure that a company making exempt supplies does not restrict the input tax recovery of the group as a whole (see the partial exemption rules in the next chapter).

It is possible for a company to be in two VAT groups at the same time.

3.6 Divisional registration

A company which is divided into several units which each prepare accounts can apply for divisional registration. The only advantage of divisional registration is administrative convenience; the separate divisions do not become separate taxable persons and the company is itself still liable for the VAT. However, if divisions account for VAT separately it may make it more likely that VAT returns will be made on time, because data for the divisions do not have to be consolidated before returns are completed.

Broadly, the conditions for divisional registration are as follows.

(a) HMRC must be satisfied that there would be real difficulties in submitting a single VAT return by the due date.

(b) Each division must be registered even where that division's turnover is beneath the registration limits.

(c) The divisions must be independent, self-accounting units, carrying on different activities or operating in separate locations.

(d) Input tax attributable or apportioned to exempt supplies (see the partial exemption rules in the next chapter) for the company as a whole must be so low that it can all be recovered (apart from VAT which can never be recovered because of the type of expenditure).

(e) Each division must make VAT returns for the same tax periods.

(f) Tax invoices must not be issued for supplies between the divisions of the same company as they are not supplies for VAT purposes.

3.7 Deregistration

3.7.1 Voluntary deregistration

A person is eligible for voluntary deregistration if HMRC are satisfied that the value of his taxable supplies (net of VAT and excluding supplies of capital assets) **in the following one year period will not exceed £59,000 (from 1 April 2006)**. However, voluntary deregistration will not be allowed if the reason for the expected fall in value of taxable supplies is the cessation of taxable supplies or the suspension of taxable supplies for a period of 30 days or more in that following year.

HMRC will cancel a person's registration from the date the request is made or from an agreed later date.

3.7.2 Compulsory deregistration

Traders may be compulsorily deregistered. Failure to notify a requirement to deregister within 30 days may lead to a penalty. Compulsory deregistration may also lead to HMRC reclaiming input tax which has been wrongly recovered by the trader since the date on which he should have deregistered.

Other points to note are:

- If HMRC are misled into granting registration then the registration is treated as void from the start.
- A person may be compulsorily deregistered if HMRC are satisfied that he is no longer making nor intending to make taxable supplies.
- Changes in legal status also require cancellation of registration. For example:
  (i) A sole trader becoming a partnership
  (ii) A partnership reverting to a sole trader
  (iii) A business being incorporated
  (iv) A company being replaced by an unincorporated business

3.7.3 The consequences of deregistration

On deregistration, VAT is chargeable on all stocks and capital assets in a business on which input tax was claimed, since the registered trader is in effect making a taxable supply to himself as a newly unregistered trader. If the VAT chargeable does not exceed £1,000, it need not be paid.

This special VAT charge does not apply if the business (or a separately viable part of it) **is sold as a going concern to another taxable person** (or a person who immediately becomes a taxable person as a result of the transfer). **Such transfers are outside the scope of VAT** (except for certain buildings being transferred which are 'new' or opted buildings and the transferee does not make an election to waive exemption – refer to the section on land in the next chapter).

If the original owner ceases to be taxable, the new owner of the business may also take over the existing VAT number. If he does so, he takes over the rights and liabilities of the transferor as at the date of transfer.

3.8 Pre-registration input tax

VAT incurred before registration can be treated as input tax and recovered from HMRC subject to certain conditions.

If the claim is for input tax suffered on goods purchased prior to registration then the following conditions must be satisfied.

(a) The goods were acquired for the purpose of the business which either was carried on or was to be carried on by him at the time of supply.

(b) The goods have not been supplied onwards or consumed before the date of registration (although they may have been used to make other goods which are still held).

(c) The VAT must have been incurred in the three years prior to the effective date of registration.

If the claim is for input tax suffered on the supply of services prior to registration then the following conditions must be satisfied.

(a) The services were supplied for the purposes of a business which either was carried on or was to be carried on by him at the time of supply.

(b) The services were supplied within the six months prior to the date of registration.

Input tax attributable to supplies made before registration is not deductible even if the input tax concerned is treated as having been incurred after registration.

3.9 Disaggregation

A person's registration covers all his business activities together. **The turnover of all business activities carried on by a 'person' must be aggregated to find taxable turnover.** However, if the same individual both carries on trade A alone and is a member of a partnership carrying on trade B, the turnover of the two trades will not normally be aggregated: the individual will have his taxable turnover in respect of trade A only, and the partnership will have its taxable turnover in respect of trade B only.

For example, a brother and sister might operate a pub with catering and bed and breakfast facilities. The catering could be operated by the brother, the pub could be operated by a partnership of the two people and the bed and breakfast business could be operated by the sister. This could avoid the need to register and account for output tax, if the turnover of each business was below the threshold for registration but may be subject to the anti-avoidance provisions outlined below.

There are anti-avoidance provisions to prevent VAT benefits from the operation of one business through two or more entities. These provisions enable HMRC to direct that any connected businesses which have avoided VAT by artificially separating should be treated as one, whatever the reason for the separation. When deciding whether businesses are artificially separated, HMRC consider the extent to which those persons are bound by financial, economic or organisational links.

4 Accounting for VAT

4.1 VAT periods

FAST FORWARD: VAT is accounted for on regular returns. Extensive records must be kept.

The VAT period (also known as the tax period) is the period covered by a VAT return. It is usually three calendar months. The return shows the total input and output tax for the tax period and must be submitted (along with any VAT due) within one month of the end of the period. (Businesses which pay VAT electronically automatically receive a seven day extension to this time limit.)

HMRC allocate VAT periods according to the class of trade carried on (ending in June, September, December and March; July, October, January and April; or August, November, February and May), to spread the flow of VAT returns evenly over the year. When applying for registration a trader can ask for VAT periods which fit in with his own accounting year. It is also possible to have VAT periods to cover accounting systems not based on calendar months.

A registered person whose input tax will regularly exceed his output tax can elect for a one month VAT period, but will have to balance the inconvenience of making 12 returns a year against the advantage of obtaining more rapid repayments of VAT.

Certain small businesses may submit an annual VAT return (see the next chapter).

4.2 The tax point

FAST FORWARD

The tax point is the deemed date of supply. The basic tax point is the date on which goods are removed or made available to the customer, or the date on which services are completed. If a VAT invoice is issued or payment is received before the basic tax point, the earlier of these dates becomes the tax point. If the earlier date rule does not apply, and the VAT invoice is issued within 14 days of the basic tax point, the invoice date becomes the actual tax point.

The tax point of each supply is the deemed date of supply. The basic tax point is the date on which the goods are removed or made available to the customer, or the date on which services are completed.

The tax point determines the VAT period in which output tax must be accounted for and credit for input tax will be allowed. The tax point also determines which rate applies if the rate of VAT or a VAT category changes (for example when a supply ceases to be zero-rated and becomes standard-rated).

If a VAT invoice is issued or payment is received before the basic tax point, the earlier of these dates automatically becomes the tax point. If the earlier date rule does not apply and if the VAT invoice is issued within 14 days after the basic tax point, the invoice date becomes the tax point (although the trader can elect to use the basic tax point for all his supplies if he wishes). This 14 day period may be extended to accommodate, for example, monthly invoicing; the tax point is then the VAT invoice date or the end of the month, whichever is applied consistently.

Question — Tax point

Julia sells a sculpture to the value of £1,000 net of VAT. She receives a payment on account of £250 plus VAT on 25 March 2007. The sculpture is delivered on 28 April 2007. Julia's VAT returns are made up to calendar quarters. She issues an invoice on 4 May 2007.

Outline the tax point(s) and amount(s) due.

Answer

A separate tax point arises in respect of the £250 deposit and the £750 balance payable.

Julia should account for VAT as follows.

(a) *Deposit*

25 March 2007: tax at 17.5% × £250 = £43.75. This is accounted for in her VAT return to 31 March 2007. The charge arises on 25 March 2007 because payment is received before the basic tax point (which is 28 April 2007 – date of delivery).

(b) *Balance*

4 May 2007: tax at 17.5% × £750 = £131.25. This is accounted for on the VAT return to 30 June 2007. The charge arises on 4 May because the invoice was issued within 14 days of the basic tax point of 28 April 2007 (delivery date).

Goods supplied on sale or return are treated as supplied on the earlier of adoption by the customer or 12 months after despatch.

Continuous supplies of services paid for periodically normally have tax points on the earlier of the receipt of each payment and the issue of each VAT invoice, unless one invoice covering several payments is issued in advance for up to a year. The tax point is then the earlier of each due date or date of actual payment. However, for connected businesses the tax point will be created periodically, in most cases based on 12 month periods.

4.3 The VAT return

The regular VAT return to HMRC is made on form VAT 100. The boxes on a VAT return which a trader must fill in are as follows.

(a) Box 1: the VAT due on sales and other outputs

(b) Box 2: the VAT due on acquisitions from other EU member states

(c) Box 3: the total of boxes 1 and 2

(d) Box 4: the VAT reclaimed on purchases and other inputs

(e) Box 5: the net VAT to be paid or reclaimed: the difference between boxes 3 and 4

(f) Box 6: the total value (before cash discounts) of sales and all other outputs, excluding VAT but including the total in box 8

(g) Box 7: the total value (before cash discounts) of purchases and all other inputs, excluding VAT but including the total in box 9

(h) Box 8: the total value of all sales and related services to other EU member states

(i) Box 9: the total value of all purchases and related services from other EU member states

Input and output tax figures must be supported by the original or copy tax invoices, and records must be maintained for six years.

4.4 Internet filing of VAT returns

It is possible to file VAT returns electronically. The trader must enrol with HMRC before using the service.

4.5 Substantial traders

If a trader does not make monthly returns, and the total VAT liability over 12 months to the end of a VAT period exceeds £2,000,000, he must make payments on account of each quarter's VAT liability during the quarter. Payments are due a month before the end of the quarter and at the end of the quarter, with the final payment due at the usual time, a month after the end of the quarter. An electronic payment system must be used, not a cheque through the post.

For a trader who exceeds the £2,000,000 limit in the 12 months to 30 September, 31 October or 30 November, the amount of each of the two payments on account is 1/24 of the total VAT liability of those 12 months. The obligation to pay on account starts with the first VAT period starting *after* 31 March.

Question — Payments on account

Large Ltd is liable to make payments on account calculated at £250,000 each for the quarter ended 31 December 2006.

What payments/repayment are due if Large Ltd's VAT liability for the quarter is calculated as:

(a) £680,000
(b) £480,000?

Answer

(a)	30 November 2006	– payment of £250,000
	31 December 2006	– payment of £250,000
	31 January 2007	– payment of £180,000 with submission of VAT return for quarter
(b)	30 November 2006	– payment of £250,000
	31 December 2006	– payment of £250,000
	31 January 2007	– on submission of return HMRC will repay £20,000.

A trader who first exceeds the £2,000,000 limit in 12 months ending at some other time must pay 1/24 of the VAT liability for the first 12 months in which he exceeded the £2,000,000 limit. His obligation starts with the first VAT period which starts after those 12 months, unless he first went over the £2,000,000 limit in the 12 months to 31 December: in that case, his obligation starts with the VAT period starting on 1 April.

If the total VAT liability for any later 12 months is less than 80% of the total liability for the 12 months used to compute the payments on account, the trader can apply to use 1/24 of that smaller total. The smaller total can even be used if the 12 months have not ended, so long as HMRC are satisfied that it will be below the 80% limit. A trader can leave the scheme if the latest 12 months' VAT liability was less than £1,600,000.

If a trader's total annual liability increases to 120% or more of the amount used to calculate the payments on account, then the new higher annual liability is used to calculate new payments on account. The increase applies from the end of the 12 months with the new higher annual liability.

Once a trader is in the scheme, the payments on account are also recomputed annually, using the liability in the 12 months to 30 September, 31 October or 30 November, even if the change is less than ± 20%. The new figure first applies to the first VAT period starting after 31 March.

For the purposes of calculating the payments on account (but not for the purposes of the £2,000,000 limit for entry into the scheme), a trader's VAT due on imports from outside the EU is ignored.

Traders can choose to switch from making quarterly to monthly returns instead of paying the interim amounts calculated by HMRC. For example, the actual return and liability for January would be due at the end of February.

Traders can also choose to pay their actual monthly liability without having to make monthly returns. HMRC can refuse to allow a trader to continue doing this if they find he has abused the facility by not paying enough. The trader will then either have to pay the interim amount or switch to making monthly returns.

A trader does have the right to appeal to a VAT tribunal if HMRC refuse to allow him to make monthly payments of his actual liability.

4.6 Refunds of VAT

There is a three year time limit on the right to reclaim overpaid VAT. This time limit does not apply to input tax which a business could not have reclaimed earlier because the supplier only recently invoiced the VAT, even though it related to a purchase made some time ago. Nor does it apply to overpaid VAT penalties.

If a taxpayer has overpaid VAT and has overclaimed input tax by reason of the same mistake, HMRC can set off any tax, penalty, interest or surcharge due to them against any repayment due to the taxpayer and repay only the net amount. In such cases the normal three year time limit for recovering VAT, penalties, interest, etc by assessment does not apply.

HMRC can refuse to make any repayment which would unjustly enrich the claimant. They can also refuse a repayment of VAT where all or part of the tax has, for practical purposes, been borne by a person other than the taxpayer (eg by a customer of the taxpayer) except to the extent that the taxpayer can show loss or damage to any of his businesses as a result of mistaken assumptions about VAT.

5 VAT invoices and records

FAST FORWARD

A taxable person making a taxable supply to another registered person must supply a VAT invoice within 30 days.

A taxable person making a taxable supply to another person registered for VAT must supply a *VAT* invoice within 30 days of the time of supply, and must keep a copy. The invoice must show:

(a) The supplier's name, address and registration number.

(b) The date of issue, the tax point and an invoice number.

(c) The name and address of the customer.

(d) A description of the goods or services supplied, giving for each description the quantity, the unit price, the rate of VAT and the VAT exclusive amount.

(e) The rate of any cash discount.

(f) The total invoice price excluding VAT (with separate totals for zero-rated and exempt supplies).

(g) Each VAT rate applicable and the total amount of VAT.

For supplies to other EU member states the supplier's registration number must be prefixed by 'GB' and if the customer is VAT registered, the customer's registration number (including the state code, such as DE for Germany) must be shown.

If an invoice is issued, and a change in price then alters the VAT due, a credit note or debit note to adjust the VAT must be issued.

Credit notes must give the reason for the credit (such as 'returned goods'), and the number and date of the original VAT invoice. If a credit note makes no VAT adjustment, it should state this.

A less detailed VAT invoice may be issued by a retailer where the invoice is for a total including VAT of up to £250 and the supply is not to another EU member state. Such an invoice must show:

(a) The supplier's name, address and registration number
(b) The date of the supply
(c) A description of the goods or services supplied
(d) The rate of VAT chargeable
(e) The total amount chargeable including VAT

Zero-rated and exempt supplies must not be included in less detailed invoices.

VAT invoices are not required for payments of up to £25 including VAT which are for telephone calls or car park fees or are made through cash operated machines. In such cases, input tax can be claimed without a VAT invoice.

Every VAT registered trader must keep records for six years, although HMRC may sometimes grant permission for their earlier destruction. They may be kept on paper, on microfilm or microfiche or on computer. However, there must be adequate facilities for HMRC to inspect records.

All records must be kept up to date and in a way which allows:

- The calculation of VAT due
- Officers of HMRC to check the figures on VAT returns

The following records are needed.

- Copies of VAT invoices, credit notes and debit notes issued
- A summary of supplies made
- VAT invoices, credit notes and debit notes received
- A summary of supplies received
- Records of goods received from and sent to other EU member states
- Documents relating to imports from and exports to countries outside the EU
- A VAT account
- Order and delivery notes, correspondence, appointment books, job books, purchases and sales books, cash books, account books, records of takings (such as till rolls), bank paying-in slips, bank statements and annual accounts
- Records of zero-rated and exempt supplies, gifts or loans of goods, taxable self-supplies and any goods taken for non-business use

6 The valuation of supplies

FAST FORWARD

VAT is charged on the VAT-exclusive price. Where a discount is offered for prompt payment, VAT is chargeable on the net amount even if the discount is not taken up.

6.1 General principles

The value of a supply is the VAT-exclusive price on which VAT is charged. The consideration for a supply is the amount paid in money or money's worth. Thus with a standard rate of 17.5%:

Value + VAT = consideration
£100 + £17.50 = £117.50

The VAT proportion of the consideration is known as the 'VAT fraction'. It is

$$\frac{\text{rate of tax}}{100+\text{rate of tax}}=\frac{17.5}{100+17.5}=\frac{7}{47}$$

Provided the consideration for a bargain made at arm's length is paid in money, the value for VAT purposes is the VAT exclusive price charged by the trader. If it is paid in something other than money, as in a barter of some goods or services for others, it must be valued and VAT will be due on the value.

If the price of goods is effectively reduced with money off coupons, the value of the supply is the amount actually received by the taxpayer.

6.2 Mixed supplies and composite supplies

Different goods and services are sometimes invoiced together at an inclusive price (a mixed supply). Some items may be chargeable at the standard rate and some at the zero-rate. **The supplier must account for VAT separately on the standard rated and zero rated elements by splitting the total amount payable in a fair proportion between the different elements and charging VAT on each at the appropriate rate.** There is no single way of doing this: one method is to split the amount according to the cost to the supplier of each element, and another is to use the open market value of each element. Mixed supplies are also known as "multiple supplies".

If a supply cannot be split into components, there is a composite supply, to which one VAT rate must be applied. The rate depends on the nature of the supply as a whole. Composite supplies are also known as "compound supplies".

A supply of air transport including an in-flight meal has been held to be a single, composite supply of transport (zero-rated) rather than a supply of transport (zero-rated) and a supply of a meal (standard-rated). Contrast this with where catering is included in the price of leisure travel – there are two separate supplies: standard-rated catering and zero-rated passenger transport.

Broadly, a composite supply occurs when one element of the supply is merely incidental to the main element. A mixed supply occurs where different elements of the supply are the subject of separate negotiation and customer choice giving rise to identifiable obligations on the supplier.

6.3 Discounts

Where a discount is offered for prompt payment, VAT is chargeable on the net amount, regardless of whether the discount is taken up (except that for imports from outside the EU, the discount is ignored unless it is taken up). Supplies of retailer vouchers made on contingent discount terms (for example depending on the level of purchases) must be invoiced with VAT based on the full amount, an adjustment being made when the discount is earned. When goods are sold to staff at a discount, VAT is only due on the discounted price.

Generally, the sale of a voucher is VAT free. However, intermediate suppliers of retailer vouchers (ie vouchers for which the seller provides the redemption goods or services), must account for VAT on the purchase and sale of vouchers. Input tax is recoverable by the purchaser. There are additional rules affecting vouchers sold as part of a package of goods for which the price would not be reduced if the vouchers were excluded. These rules aim to prevent the deferral of VAT on sales of vouchers until they are redeemed.

6.4 Miscellaneous

For goods supplied under a hire purchase agreement VAT is chargeable on the cash selling price at the start of the contract.

If a trader charges different prices to customers paying with credit cards and those paying by other means, the VAT due in respect of each standard-rated sale is the full amount paid by the customer × the VAT fraction.

When goods are permanently taken from a business for non-business purposes VAT must be accounted for on their market value. Where business goods are put to a private or non-business use, the value of the resulting supply of services is the cost to the taxable person of providing the services. If services bought for business purposes are used for non-business purposes (without charge), then VAT must be accounted for on their cost, but the VAT to be accounted for is not allowed to exceed the input tax deductible on the purchase of the services.

7 Administration

FAST FORWARD

VAT is administered by HMRC, and the RCPO hear appeals.

7.1 Introduction

The administration of VAT is now dealt with by the new joint body known as HM Revenue and Customs (HMRC).

7.2 Local offices

Local offices are responsible for the local administration of VAT and for providing advice to registered persons whose principal place of business is in their area. They are controlled by regional collectors.

Completed VAT returns should be sent to the VAT Central Unit at Southend, not to a local office.

From time to time a registered person will be visited by staff from a local office (a control visit) to ensure that the law is understood and is being applied properly. If a trader disagrees with any decision as to the application of VAT given by HMRC he can ask his local office to reconsider the decision. It is not necessary to appeal formally while a case is being reviewed in this way. Where an appeal can be settled by agreement, a written settlement has the same force as a decision decided through the normal appeals process (see below). A trader can ask for a reconsideration even if he has already appealed to a VAT Tribunal.

HMRC may issue assessments of VAT due to the best of their judgement if they believe that a trader has failed to make returns or if they believe those returns to be incorrect or incomplete. The time limit for making assessments is normally three years after the end of a VAT period, but this is extended to 20 years in the case of fraud, dishonest conduct, certain registration irregularities and the unauthorised issue of VAT invoices.

HMRC sometimes write to traders, setting out their calculations, before issuing assessments. The traders can then query the calculations.

7.3 Appeals

A trader may appeal to a VAT Tribunal. VAT Tribunals are administered by the Tribunals Service, part of the Department of Constitutional Affairs and are completely independent of HMRC. Provided that VAT returns and payments shown thereon have been made, appeals can be heard.

The VAT Tribunal can waive the requirement to pay all VAT shown on returns before an appeal is heard in cases of hardship. It cannot allow an appeal against a purely administrative matter such as HMRC's refusal to apply an extra statutory concession.

There may be a dispute over the deductibility of input tax which hinges on the purposes for which goods or services were used, or on whether they were used to make taxable supplies. The trader must show that HMRC acted unreasonably in refusing a deduction, if the goods or services are luxuries, amusements or entertainment.

7.4 Time limits

An appeal must be lodged with the VAT Tribunal (not the local office) within 30 days of the date of any decision by HMRC. If, instead, the trader would like the local office to reconsider the decision he should apply within 30 days of the decision to the relevant office. The local VAT office may either:

- Confirm the original decision, in which case the taxpayer has a further 21 days from the date of that confirmation in which to lodge an appeal with the Tribunal, or
- Send a revised decision, in which case the taxpayer will have a further 30 days from the date of the revised decision in which to lodge an appeal with the Tribunal.

If one of the parties is dissatisfied with a decision on a point of law he may appeal to the courts. The Tribunal may award costs.

7.5 The Adjudicator

The Adjudicator for the HMRC is independent of these bodies. The Adjudicator considers complaints about the way in which taxpayers' affairs are handled, for example complaints about delays or the exercise of officials' discretion. The Adjudicator does not consider complaints where there are alternative channels of appeal, such as exist for appeals against assessments.

7.6 Tax avoidance and evasion

Significant resources are deployed to tackle fraud, tax evasion and avoidance.

Avoidance is also countered by the requirement for traders to disclose to HMRC any use of a notifiable VAT avoidance scheme (see later in this text).

8 Penalties

FAST FORWARD

A default occurs when a trader either submits his VAT return late, or submits the return on time but pays the VAT late. A default surcharge is applied if there is a default during a default surcharge period.

8.1 Late notification

A trader who makes taxable supplies is obliged to notify HMRC if supplies exceed the registration limit. A penalty can be levied for failure to notify a liability to register by the proper date. In addition, the VAT which would have been accounted for had the trader registered on time must be paid.

The penalty for late notification is based on the net VAT due from the date when the trader should have been registered to the date when notification is made or, if earlier, the date on which HMRC become aware of the liability to be registered. The rate varies as follows.

Number of months registration late by	Percentage of VAT
Up to 9	5%
Over 9, up to 18	10%
Over 18	15%

A minimum penalty of £50 applies.

The penalty applies both to traders who start their own businesses and to traders who take over businesses as going concerns.

8.2 Reasonable excuse

The late registration penalty is not due if the trader can show that there is reasonable excuse for the failure, and the penalty may be mitigated by HMRC or by the VAT Tribunal. There is no definition of 'reasonable excuse'. However the legislation states that the following are not reasonable excuses:

- An insufficiency of funds to pay any VAT due
- Reliance upon a third party (such as an accountant) to perform the task in question

Many cases have considered **what constitutes a reasonable excuse** but decisions often conflict with one another. Each case depends on its own facts. Here are some examples;

(a) Whilst **'ignorance of basic VAT law'** is not an excuse, ignorance of more complex matters can constitute a reasonable excuse;

(b) There have been a number of cases where it has been accepted that **misunderstandings as to the facts** give rise to a reasonable excuse,

(c) Although the law expressly excludes an insufficiency of funds from providing a reasonable excuse, the Tribunal will, in exceptional circumstances, look behind the shortage of funds itself and examine the case of it – this is generally restricted to cases where an unexpected event (eg bank error) has led to the shortage of funds.

8.3 Criminal fraud

Where a person knowingly takes steps to evade VAT, this amounts to criminal fraud. The penalty for criminal fraud depends on whether the conviction is summary (by magistrates) or on indictment (by a jury). On summary conviction the maximum term of imprisonment is six months, and the maximum fine is the greater of £5,000 and three times the VAT involved. On conviction on indictment the maximum term of imprisonment is seven years and the level of fine is unlimited.

8.4 Conduct involving dishonesty (civil fraud)

This arises where a person dishonestly takes steps, or omits to take steps, in order to evade VAT. Failing to provide any information, failing to register, and therefore failing to make any VAT statement, and providing false information can count. **The penalty for civil fraud is 100% of the tax involved.** This may be mitigated by up to 100% in recognition of co-operation given by the trader during the investigation into the true VAT position. HMRC need only show on the balance of probabilities that the conduct took place, whereas criminal fraud must be proved beyond reasonable doubt.

8.5 The unauthorised issue of invoices

This penalty applies where a person who is not registered for VAT nevertheless issues VAT invoices. The penalty is 15% of the VAT involved with a minimum penalty of £50, but this penalty may be mitigated.

8.6 Breaches of regulations

There are penalties for breaches of VAT regulations of any kind. The amount of penalty varies with the type and frequency of the breach concerned.

8.7 The default surcharge

A default occurs when a trader either submits his VAT return late, or submits the return on time but pays the VAT late. It also occurs when a payment on account from a substantial trader is late. **If a trader defaults, HMRC will serve a surcharge liability notice on the trader. The notice specifies a surcharge period running from the date of the notice to the anniversary of the end of the period for which the trader is in default.**

If a further default occurs in respect of a return period ending during the specified surcharge period, the original surcharge period will be extended to the anniversary of the end of the period to which the new default relates. In addition, if the default involves the late payment of VAT (as opposed to simply a late return) **a surcharge is levied.**

The surcharge depends on the number of defaults involving late payment of VAT which have occurred in respect of periods ending in the surcharge period, as follows.

Default involving late payment of VAT in the surcharge period	Surcharge as a percentage of the VAT outstanding at the due date
First	2%
Second	5%
Third	10%
Fourth or more	15%

Surcharges at the 2% and 5% rates are not normally demanded unless the amount due would be at least £400 but for surcharges calculated using the 10% or 15% rates there is a minimum amount of £30 payable.

If a substantial trader is late with more than one payment (on account or final) for a return period, this only counts as one default. The total VAT paid late is the total of late payments on account plus the late final payment.

Question

Default surcharge

Peter Popper has an annual turnover of around £300,000. His VAT return for the quarter to 31.12.06 is late. He then submits returns for the quarters to 30.9.07 and 31.3.08 late as well as making late payment of the tax due of £12,000 and £500 respectively.

Peter's VAT return to 31.3.09 is also late and the VAT due of £1,100 is also paid late. All other VAT returns and VAT payments are made on time. Outline Peter Popper's exposure to default surcharge.

Answer

A surcharge liability notice will be issued after the late filing on the 31.12.06 return outlining a surcharge period extending to 31.12.07.

The late 30.9.07 return is in the surcharge period so the period is extended to 30.9.08. The late VAT payment triggers a 2% penalty. 2% × £12,000 = £240. Since £240 is less than the £400 de minimis limit it is not collected by HMRC.

The late 31.3.08 return is in the surcharge period so the period is now extended to 31.3.09. The late payment triggers a 5% penalty. 5% × £500 = £25. Since £25 is less than the £400 de minimis limit it is not collected by HMRC.

The late 31.03.09 return is in the surcharge period. The period is extended to 31.03.10. The late payment triggers a 10% penalty 10% × £1,100 = £110. This is collected by HMRC since the £400 de minimis does not apply to penalties calculated at the 10% (and 15%) rate.

Peter will have to submit all four quarterly VAT returns to 31.3.10 on time and pay the VAT on time to 'escape' the default surcharge regime.

A trader must submit one year's returns on time and pay the VAT shown on them on time in order to break out of the surcharge liability period and the escalation of surcharge percentages.

A default will be ignored for all default surcharge purposes if the trader can show that the return or payment was sent at such a time, and in such a manner, that it was reasonable to expect that HMRC would receive it by the due date. Posting the return and payment first class the day before the due date is generally accepted as meeting this requirement. A default will also be ignored if the trader can demonstrate a reasonable excuse (see above) for the late submission or payment.

The application of the default surcharge regime to small businesses is modified. **A small business is one with a turnover below £150,000**. When a small business is late submitting a VAT return or paying VAT it will receive a letter from HMRC offering help. No penalty will be charged. Four such letters will be issued without penalty. However, on the issue of a fifth letter a 10% penalty will apply which increases to 15% on the issue of a sixth or subsequent letter.

8.8 The misdeclaration penalty: very large errors

The making of a return which understates a person's true liability or overstates the repayment due to him incurs a penalty of 15% of the VAT which would have been lost if the return had been accepted as correct. The same penalty applies when HMRC issue an assessment which is too low and the trader fails to notify the error within 30 days from the issue of the assessment.

These penalties apply only where the VAT which would have been lost equals or exceeds the lower of

(a) **£1,000,000 or**

(b) **30% of the sum of the true input tax and the true output tax**. This sum is known as the gross amount of tax (GAT). In the case of an incorrect assessment 30% of the true amount of tax (TAT), the VAT actually due from the trader, is used instead of 30% of the GAT.

The penalty may be mitigated.

Question — Misdeclaration penalty - GAT

A trader declares output tax of £100,000 and claims input tax of £30,000 on the VAT return for the quarter ended 31 March 2007. It is subsequently discovered that output tax is understated by £28,000.

Does a misdeclaration penalty arise?

Answer

The test for misdeclaration penalty is the lower of:

- 30% of GAT (Gross Amount of Tax)
  30% × £(100,000 + 28,000 + 30,000)
  = £47,400
- £1,000,000

ie £47,400

Since the error of £28,000 is less than £47,400 the error is not 'large' and hence no penalty arises.

Question — Misdeclaration penalty - TAT

A trader fails to submit a VAT return for the quarter to 30 June 2006. On 31 August 2006 HMRC issue an assessment showing VAT due of £200,000.

The true VAT liability for the quarter is:

	£
Output tax	370,000
Input tax	(80,000)
Net VAT due	290,000

The trader pays the £200,000 of VAT assessed but does not bring the correct position to HMRC's attention.

The true position is discovered during a control visit in December 2007.

Will a misdeclaration penalty apply?

Answer

The under-assessment of £90,000 will attract a penalty if it exceeds the lower of:

- 30% of TAT (True Amount of Tax)
  30% × £290,000
  = £87,000
- £1,000,000

ie £87,000.

The £90,000 under-assessment exceeds £87,000, thus a misdeclaration penalty will be charged at £90,000 × 15% = £13,500.

The trader will have to pay the additional £90,000 due as well as the £13,500 penalty.

Errors on a VAT return of up to £2,000 (net: underdeclaration minus overdeclaration) may be corrected on the next return without giving rise to a misdeclaration penalty or interest (see below for details on interest).

This penalty does not apply if the trader can show reasonable excuse (see above) for his conduct, or if he made a full disclosure when he had no reason to suppose that HMRC were enquiring into his affairs.

If his conduct leads to a conviction for fraud, or to a penalty for conduct involving dishonesty, it cannot also lead to a misdeclaration penalty.

8.9 The misdeclaration penalty: repeated errors

If a trader submits an inaccurate return, and the VAT which would have been lost if it had been accepted as accurate equals or exceeds the lower of

- **£500,000** or
- **10% of the GAT**

there is a material inaccuracy.

Question — Repeated errors

Bloggs Ltd submits its VAT return for the quarter to 31 December 2006 showing:

	£
Output tax	550,000
Input tax	(230,000)
Net VAT due	320,000

It is later established that output tax should have been £640,000.

Is the error large enough for a repeated error misdeclaration penalty?

Answer

The error is £90,000 £(640,000 – 550,000). The error falls within the repeated error misdeclaration penalty regime if it equal or exceeds:

- £500,000
- 10% of GAT (Gross amount of tax)
  10% × £(640,000 + 230,000)
  = £87,000

ie £87,000.

Since the £90,000 error exceeds £87,000 the penalty could apply.

Before the end of the fourth VAT period following the period of a material inaccuracy, HMRC may issue a penalty liability notice, specifying a penalty period. The period is the eight VAT periods starting with the one in which the notice is issued.

If there are material inaccuracies for two or more VAT periods falling within the penalty period, then each such inaccuracy, apart from the first one leads to a penalty of 15% of the VAT which would have been lost. The penalty may be mitigated.

If a misdeclaration penalty for a very large error is imposed for an inaccuracy, it cannot also lead to a penalty for a repeated error. However, a penalty liability notice may still be issued following the inaccuracy and it may still count as the *first* material inaccuracy in a penalty period (so that the next one leads to a penalty).

8.10 Interest on unpaid VAT

Interest (not deductible in computing taxable profits) **is charged on VAT which is the subject of an assessment** (where returns were not made or were incorrect), **or which could have been the subject of an assessment but was paid before the assessment was raised. It runs from the reckonable date until the date of payment.** This interest is sometimes called 'default interest'.

The reckonable date is when the VAT should have been paid (one month from the end of the return period), or in the case of VAT repayments, seven days from the issue of the repayment order. However, where VAT is charged by an assessment, interest does not run from more than three years before the date of the assessment; and where the VAT was paid before an assessment was raised, interest does not run for more than three years before the date of payment.

In practice, interest is only charged when there would otherwise be a loss to the Exchequer. It is not, for example, charged when a company failed to charge VAT but if it had done so another company would have been able to recover the VAT.

8.11 Repayment supplement

Where a person is entitled to a repayment of VAT and the original return was rendered on time but HMRC do not issue a written instruction for the repayment to be made within 30 days of the receipt of the return, then the person will receive a supplement of the greater of £50 and 5% of the amount due.

If the return states a refund due which differs from the correct refund due by more than the greater of 5% of the correct refund and £250, no supplement is added.

Days spent in raising and answering reasonable enquiries in relation to the return do not count towards the 30 days allowed to HMRC to issue an instruction to make the repayment. The earliest date on which the 30 days can start is the day following the end of the prescribed accounting period.

8.12 Interest on overpayments due to official errors

If VAT is overpaid or a credit for input tax is not claimed because of an error by HMRC, then the trader may claim interest on the amount eventually refunded, running from the date on which he paid the excessive VAT (or from the date on which HMRC might reasonably be expected to have authorised a VAT repayment) **to the date on which HMRC authorise a repayment.**

Interest must be claimed within three years of the date on which the trader discovered the error or could with reasonable diligence have discovered it. Interest is not available where a repayment supplement is available. Interest does not run for periods relating to reasonable enquiries by HMRC into the matter in question.

Chapter roundup

- VAT is charged on turnover at each stage in a production process, but in such a way that the burden is borne by the final consumer.
- A trader becomes liable to register for VAT if the value of taxable supplies in any period up to 12 months exceeds £61,000 or if there are reasonable grounds for believing that the value of the taxable supplies will exceed £61,000 in the next 30 days. A trader may also register voluntarily.
- VAT is accounted for on regular returns. Extensive records must be kept.
- The tax point is the deemed date of supply. The basic tax point is the date on which goods are removed or made available to the customer, or the date on which services are completed. If a VAT invoice is issued or payment is received before the basic tax point, the earlier of these dates becomes the tax point. If the earlier date rule does not apply, and the VAT invoice is issued within 14 days of the basic tax point, the invoice date becomes the actual tax point.
- A taxable person making a taxable supply to another registered person must supply a VAT invoice within 30 days.
- A default occurs when a trader either submits his VAT return late, or submits the return on time but pays the VAT late. A default surcharge is applied if there is a default during a default surcharge period.
- VAT is administered by HMRC and the VAT Tribunal hears appeals.

Quick quiz

1 On what transactions will VAT be charged?

2 What is a taxable person?

3 When may a taxable person be exempt from registration?

4 How are transfers between group companies treated under a VAT registration?

5 When may a person choose to be deregistered?

6 What is the time limit in respect of claiming pre-registration input tax on goods?

7 Within what time limit must an appeal to a tribunal be lodged?

8 What is a default?

Answers to quick quiz

1 VAT is charged on taxable supplies of goods and services made in the UK by a taxable person in the course or furtherance of any business carried on by him.

2 Any 'person' whose taxable turnover exceeds the registration limit. The term 'person' includes individuals, partnerships, companies, clubs, associations and charities.

3 If a taxable person makes only zero-rated supplies he may request exemption from registration.

4 Any supplies between VAT group members are ignored for VAT purposes.

5 A person is eligible for voluntary deregistration if HMRC are satisfied that the value of his taxable supplies in the following year will not exceed £59,000.

6 The VAT must have been incurred in the three years prior to the effective date of registration.

7 Within 30 days of the date of the decision by HMRC.

8 A default occurs when a trader either submits his VAT return late or submits the return on time but pays the VAT late.

Now try the question below from the Exam Question Bank

Number	Level	Marks	Time
27	Examination	10	18 mins

29

Value added tax 2

Introduction

We start this chapter by looking at zero-rated and exempt supplies and we see how making exempt supplies can affect the deduction of input tax.

Imports and exports must be fitted into the VAT system. We see how this is done for transactions both within and outside the European Community. VAT needs to be applied to imports, so that people do not have a tax incentive to buy abroad, and VAT is taken off many exports in order to encourage sales abroad.

Finally, we look at special VAT schemes designed for particular types of trader, including small traders and dealers in secondhand goods.

1 Zero-rated and exempt supplies

FAST FORWARD

Some supplies are taxable (either standard-rated, reduced-rated or zero-rated). Others are exempt.

1.1 Types of supply

Zero-rated supplies are taxable at 0%. A taxable supplier whose outputs are zero-rated but whose inputs are standard-rated will obtain repayments of the VAT paid on purchases.

Exempt supplies are not so advantageous. In exactly the same way as for a non-registered person, a **person making exempt supplies is unable to recover VAT on inputs**.

The exempt supplier thus has to shoulder the burden of VAT. Of course, he may increase his prices to pass on the charge, but he cannot issue a VAT invoice which would enable a taxable customer to obtain a credit for VAT, since no VAT is chargeable on his supplies.

1.2 Example: standard-rated, zero-rated and exempt supplies

Here are figures for three traders, the first with standard-rated outputs, the second with zero-rated outputs and the third with exempt outputs. All their inputs are standard-rated.

	Standard-rated	*Zero-rated*	*Exempt*
	£	£	£
Inputs	20,000	20,000	20,000
VAT	3,500	3,500	3,500
	23,500	23,500	23,500
Outputs	30,000	30,000	30,000
VAT	5,250	0	0
	35,250	30,000	30,000
Pay/(reclaim)	1,750	(3,500)	0
Net profit	10,000	10,000	6,500

VAT legislation lists zero-rated, lower rate and exempt supplies. There is no list of standard-rated supplies.

If a trader makes a supply you need to categorise that supply for VAT as follows:

Step 1 Look at the zero-rated list to see if it is zero-rated. If not:

Step 2 Look at the exempt list to see if it is exempt. If not:

Step 3 Look at the lower rate list to see if the reduced rate of VAT applies. If not:

Step 4 The supply is standard-rated.

1.3 Zero-rated supplies

The following are items on the **zero-rated list**.

(a) Human and animal food

(b) Sewerage services and water

(c) Printed matter used for reading (eg books, newspapers)

(d) Construction work on new homes or the sale of the freehold of (or a lease over 21 years (at least 20 years in Scotland) of) new homes by builders

(e) Sales of substantially reconstructed listed buildings, and alterations to such buildings, where such buildings are to be used for residential or charitable purposes

(f) Services relating to ships and aircraft, and the transport of goods and passengers

(g) The hire or sale of houseboats and caravans used as homes

(h) Gold supplied between central banks and members of the London Gold market

(i) Bank notes

(j) Drugs and medicines on prescription or provided in private hospitals

(k) Exports of goods to outside the EU

(l) Specialised equipment used by rescue/first aid services

(m) Sales or hire by a charity

(n) Clothing and footwear for young children and certain protective clothing eg motor cyclists' crash helmets

(o) Certain supplies (eg advertising services) to charitable institutions

1.4 Exempt supplies

The following are items on the **exempt** list.

(a) Sales of freeholds of buildings (other than commercial buildings within three years from completion) and leaseholds of land and buildings of any age including a surrender of a lease

(b) Financial services

(c) Insurance

(d) Postal services provided by the Post Office

(e) Betting and gaming

(f) Certain education and vocational training

(g) Health services

(h) Burial and cremation services

(i) Supplies to members by trade unions and professional bodies if in consideration only for a membership subscription

(j) Entry fees to non-profit making sports competitions

(k) Disposals of works of art and other items to public bodies in lieu of capital taxes

(l) Welfare services supplied by charities

(m) Supplies by charities, philanthropic bodies, trade unions, professional associations and non-profit making sports bodies in connection with fund raising events

(n) Residential care services

(o) Admission charges to certain cultural events or places

(p) Supplies of training, retraining and work experience paid for using further education funding council funds

(q) Investment gold

(r) The supply of goods on which input tax was irrecoverable on purchase

1.5 Lower rate of VAT

Certain supplies are charged at **5%**. **The supplies are still taxable supplies.**

The main supplies are:

- supplies of fuel for domestic use;
- supplies of the services of installing energy saving materials to homes;
- supplies of installing central heating or security equipment in the homes of people over the age of 60.

Note that energy saving materials themselves are standard-rated – if you pay someone to install them for you, they will recover 17.5% input tax on the purchase of the materials, and charge you 5% output tax on a composite supply of the fitting work.

The 5% rate also applies to a range of building work (which would not qualify for zero-rating or exemption), including:

- renovation of dwellings which have been empty for at least 3 years;
- conversion of residential property into a different number of dwellings;
- conversion of a non-residential property into a dwelling or a number of dwellings;
- conversion of a dwelling into a care home or into a house in multiple occupation.

1.6 Exceptions to the general rule

The zero-rated, exempt and lower rate lists outline general categories of goods or services which are either zero-rated or exempt or charged at a lower rate of 5%. However, the VAT legislation then goes into great detail to outline exceptions to the general rule.

For example the zero-rated list states human food is zero-rated. However, the legislation then states that food supplied in the course of catering (eg restaurant meals, hot takeaways) is not zero-rated. Luxury items of food (eg crisps, peanuts, chocolate covered biscuits) are also not zero-rated.

In the exempt list we are told that financial services are exempt. However the legislation then goes on to state that credit management and processing services are not exempt. Investment advice is also not exempt.

Thus great care must be taken when categorising goods or services as zero-rated, exempt or standard-rated. It is not as straightforward as it may first appear.

1.7 Standard-rated supplies

As mentioned previously, there is no list of standard-rated supplies. If a supply is not zero-rated and is not exempt then it is treated as standard-rated. Standard-rated supplies normally have a 17.5% VAT charge.

1.8 Land and buildings

The construction of new dwellings or buildings to be used for residential or charitable purposes is zero-rated. The sale of new residential accommodation created by the conversion of non-residential buildings is also zero-rated when sold by the person who does the converting (The conversion work itself is standard-rated unless the reduced rate applies). Zero-rating extends to the construction of homes for children, the elderly, students and the armed forces, but not to hospitals, prisons or hotels, to which the standard-rate applies. The sale of the freehold of a 'new' commercial building is standard-rated. The definition of 'new' is less than three years old. The construction of commercial buildings is also standard-rated.

Other sales and also grants, variations and surrenders of leases (including reverse surrenders, when the tenant pays the landlord) are exempt. The provision of holiday accommodation is standard-rated.

Owners may elect to treat the supply of interests in land and commercial buildings as taxable instead of exempt (the option to tax). The election covers leases, licences and sales and applies to all future supplies of the specified land and buildings. The owner must become registered for VAT (if he is not already so registered) in order to make the election. If the land and buildings have already been let on an exempt basis, permission to exercise the option must be obtained from HMRC. The point of making the election is to replace an exempt supply with a standard rated one.

The election may be revoked after 20 years with the written consent of HMRC via two routes; Automatic Consent or Permission Consent.

2 The deduction of input tax

FAST FORWARD

A trader making both taxable and exempt supplies may be unable to recover all of his input tax.

2.1 Introduction

For input tax to be deductible, the payer must be a taxable person, with the supply being to him in the course of his business. In addition a VAT invoice must be held (except for payments of up to £25 including VAT which are for telephone calls or car park fees or which are made through cash operated machines).

Input tax recovery can be denied to any business that does not hold a valid VAT invoice and cannot provide alternative evidence to prove the supply took place.

In addition, for businesses that operate in trade sectors dealing in computers, telephones, alcohol products and oils used as road fuel, HMRC expect to see evidence of the bona fide nature of the transaction where there is no valid VAT invoice.

2.2 Capital items

The distinction between capital and revenue which is important in other areas of tax **does not apply to VAT**. Thus a manufacturer buying plant subject to VAT will be able to obtain a credit for all the VAT immediately. The plant must of course be used to make taxable supplies, and if it is only partly so used only part of the VAT can be reclaimed. Conversely, if plant is sold secondhand then VAT should be charged on the sale and is output tax in the normal way.

2.3 Non-deductible input tax

The following input tax is not deductible even for a taxable person with taxable outputs.

(a) **VAT on motor cars** not used wholly for business purposes. VAT on cars is never reclaimable unless the car is acquired new for resale or is acquired for use in or leasing to a taxi business, a self-drive car hire business or a driving school. Private use by a proprietor **or an employee** is non-business use (regardless of any charge under the benefits code) unless the user pays a full commercial hire charge (not just a reimbursement of costs). However, VAT on accessories such as car radios is deductible if ordered on a separate purchase order and fitted after delivery of the car. The VAT charged when a car is hired for business purposes is reclaimable, but if there is some non-business use and the hire company has reclaimed VAT on the original purchase of the car, only 50% of the VAT on hire charges can be reclaimed by the hirer. A hiring for five days or less is assumed to be for wholly business use.

VAT need not be charged on the sale of a used car except on any profit element (which, of course, is rare), unless input tax on the original purchase of the car was recoverable.

(b) **VAT on business entertaining** where the cost of the entertaining is not a tax deductible trading expense. If the items bought are used partly for such entertaining and partly for other purposes, the proportion of the VAT relating to the entertainment is non-deductible.

In *Ernst & Young v CCE* the Tribunal held that staff entertaining was wholly for business purposes and a full input tax recovery was allowed. HMRC accept this decision in respect of staff entertainment but maintain that following the case *KPMG v CCE* input tax on entertaining guests at a staff party is non-deductible.

(c) **VAT on expenses incurred on domestic accommodation for directors;**

(d) **VAT on non-business items passed through the business accounts.** However, when goods are bought partly for business use, the purchaser may:

(i) Deduct all the input tax, and account for output tax in respect of the private use, or
(ii) Deduct only the business proportion of the input tax.

Where services are bought partly for business use, only method (ii) may be used. If services are initially bought for business use but the use then changes, a fair proportion of the input tax (relating to the private use) is reclaimed by HMRC by making the trader account for output tax.

A business that provides employees with mobile phones for business use can, regardless of any private use, deduct all the VAT incurred on purchase and on standing charges provided the charges do not contain any element for calls.

If a business allows its employees to make private calls without charge, then it must apportion the VAT incurred on the call charges. Any method of apportionment may be used, eg a sample of bills over a reasonable time, providing the method produces a fair and reasonable result. Apportionment must be made where the phone package allows the business to make a certain volume of calls for a fixed monthly payment and there is no standing payment, or where the contract is for the purchase of the phone and the advance payment of a set amount of call time for a single charge.

If a business imposes clear rules prohibiting private calls, and enforces them, HMRC allow a deduction of all of the VAT incurred on the call charges. Similarly, if a business tolerates only a small amount of calls, HMRC allow all of the input tax incurred to be deducted.

(e) **VAT which does not relate to the** making of supplies by the buyer in the course of a **business**.

2.4 Partial exemption

A taxable person may only recover the VAT on supplies made to him if it is attributable to his taxable supplies. A person able to recover all input tax (except the non-deductible VAT described above) is a **fully taxable person. Where a person makes a mixture of taxable and exempt supplies, he is partially exempt, and not all his input tax is recoverable because some of it is attributable to his exempt supplies**.

2.5 The standard method of attributing input tax

For a trader who is partially exempt, input tax must be apportioned between that relating to **taxable supplies** (and recoverable) **and** that relating to **exempt supplies** (exempt input tax). The standard method of attributing input tax is to:

Step 1 **Calculate how much of the input tax relates to supplies which are wholly used or to be used in making taxable supplies**: this input tax is deductible in full.

Step 2 **Calculate how much of the input tax relates to supplies which are wholly used or to be used in making exempt supplies**: this is exempt input tax.

Step 3 **Calculate how much of any remaining input tax is deductible using the percentage (taxable turnover excluding VAT/total turnover excluding VAT) × 100%**, normally rounded up to the nearest whole percentage above. The benefit of rounding up in this standard method calculation is only available to businesses whose residual input tax does not exceed £400,000 a month.

The following should be omitted from the calculation of the percentage mentioned in Step 3.

(a) Incidental supplies of land and finance
(b) Self supplies (see below)
(c) Supplies of capital goods used in the business

Question

Calculation of input tax to recover (part 1)

In the three month VAT period to 30 June 2006, Mr A makes both exempt and taxable supplies in the order of £105,000 exempt and £300,000 taxable. Most of the goods purchased are used for both types of supply which means that much of the input tax cannot be directly attributed to either type of supply. After directly attributing as much input tax as possible the following position arises.

	£
Attributed to taxable supplies	1,200
Attributed to exempt supplies	600
Unattributed VAT	8,200
	10,000

How much input tax can Mr A recover?

Answer

The amount of unattributed VAT which is apportioned to the making of taxable supplies is

$$\frac{300,000}{405,000} = 74.07\% \text{ rounded up to } 75\% \times £8,200 = £6,150$$

Note. The percentage is rounded up since residual (unattributed) input tax does not exceed £400,000 per month.

Mr A can therefore recover £1,200 + £6,150 = £7,350 of his input tax.

The balance of input tax of £2,650 £(600 + (8,200 – 6,150)) is exempt input tax.

In Step 3 above an alternative method of attributing input tax (called a 'special' method) may be agreed in writing with HMRC.

Where the input tax wholly attributable to exempt supplies plus the VAT apportioned to exempt supplies (ie the total of exempt input tax) is no more than £625 a month on average and is also no more than 50% of all input tax, all VAT is treated as being attributable to taxable supplies and therefore fully recoverable.

Question

De minimis limit

Sue makes the following supplies in the quarter ended 31 October 2006.

	£
Taxable supplies (excl. VAT)	28,000
Exempt supplies	6,000
	34,000

Sue analyses her input tax for the period as follows.

		£
Wholly attributable to:	taxable supplies	1,500
	exempt supplies	900
Non-attributable (overheads)		1,200
		3,600

How much input tax is available for credit on Sue's VAT return?

Answer

	£
Wholly attributable to taxable supplies	1,500
Partly attributable to taxable supplies	
$\frac{28{,}000}{28{,}000+6{,}000}$	
ie 82.35% rounded up to 83% × £1,200	996
	2,496
£(900 + (1,200 – 996)) = 1,104	
Exempt input tax is de minimis (W1)	1,104
Input tax recoverable	3,600

Working 1

De minimis test

- Monthly average $\frac{1{,}104}{3}$ = £368 ie not more than £625.
- Proportion of total $\frac{1{,}104}{3{,}600}$ = 30.7% ie not more than 50%.

Both tests passed. Thus exempt input tax is de minimis.

2.6 Annual adjustment

An annual adjustment is made, covering the VAT year to 31 March, 30 April or 31 May (depending on when the VAT periods end). A computation of recoverable input tax is made for the whole year, using the same method as for individual returns. The '£625 a month on average and 50%' test is also applied to the year as a whole, and if it is passed then all input tax for the year is recoverable.

The result for the year is compared with the total of results for the individual VAT periods and any difference is added to or deducted from the input tax on the return for the next period after the end of the tax year.

Question

Calculation of input tax to recover (part 2)

Following on from the above example Mr A has the following results in the remaining VAT quarters of his VAT year ended 31 March 2007.

	Input tax attributed to		
Quarter to	*Taxable supplies*	*Exempt supplies*	*Unattributed*
	£	£	£
30.9.06	1,500	1,000	5,000
31.12.06	2,000	500	1,800
31.3.07	1,900	850	7,000
	5,400	2,350	13,800

	Turnover	
Quarter to	*Taxable*	*Exempt*
	£	£
30.9.06	400,000	100,000
31.12.06	500,000	150,000
31.3.07	450,000	120,000
	1,350,000	370,000

Calculate the annual adjustment required and state which return it will be made on.

BPP PROFESSIONAL EDUCATION

Answer

First we calculate the recoverable input tax in each VAT return.

		£	*Recovered* £
Return to 30.6.06			
See above	Taxable	7,350	7,350
	Exempt	2,650	
		10,000	
Return to 30.9.06			
$\frac{400,000}{500,000}$ = 80% × £5,000 = Non-attributable		4,000	
	Wholly taxable	1,500	
	Taxable total	5,500	5,500
	Exempt £(1,000 + 1,000)	2,000	
		7,500	
Return to 31.12.06			
$\frac{500,000}{650,000}$ × £1,800 = 76.92% rounded up to 77%		1,386	
Non-attributable			
	Wholly taxable	2,000	
	Taxable total	3,386	
	Exempt £(500 + 414)	914	
		4,300	4,300

The exempt input tax at £914 is less than £1,875 (£625 × 3 months) and 50% of total input tax (50% × £4,300 = £2,150) so is de minimis and recoverable.

		£	*Recovered* £
Return to 31.3.07			
$\frac{450,000}{570,000}$ × £7,000 = 78.94% rounded up to 79%		5,530	
Non-attributable			
	Wholly taxable	1,900	
	Taxable total	7,430	7,430
	Exempt £(850 + 1,470)	2,320	
		9,750	
Recovered over the VAT year			24,580

Now we do the same calculation again but using the results for the whole VAT year to 31.3.07.

		£	£
Annual adjustment			
$\frac{1,350,000+300,000}{1,720,000+405,000}$ = 77.64% rounded up to 78% × £(13,800 + 8,200) (note 1)		17,160	
	Wholly taxable £(5,400 + 1,200)	6,600	
	Taxable total	23,760	23,760
	Exempt £(31,550 – 23,760)	7,790	
		31,550	
VAT to repay to HMRC on VAT return to 30 June 2007 as annual adjustment.			820

Note 1: we must include the quarter to June 2006's results.

2.7 HMRC over-ride

Partly exempt businesses must over-ride the standard method of apportioning non attributable input tax if 'the result does not reflect the use made of the purchases, including cases of deliberate abuse'.

Businesses must adjust the input tax deductible under the standard method at the end of their tax year if that amount is substantially different from an attribution based on the use of purchases.

Substantially is defined as:

- **£50,000** or more; or
- **50% or more of the value of the non attributable input tax, but not less than £25,000.**

This means that where the amount of non attributable input tax is less than £50,000, businesses can rely purely on the standard method. There is one exception to this: businesses that are defined as group undertakings by the Companies Act 1985 will have to follow the rule where the non attributable input tax is greater than £25,000.

A business that has to apply the adjustment must, at the VAT year end, calculate the difference between the input tax deductible under the standard method and that deductible according to use. This difference is the adjustment required to be made on the VAT return that follows the year-end (ie the same VAT return as that for the annual adjustment).

Question — **Standard method over-ride adjustment**

XY Ltd has the following results for the year ended 30 April 2007.

	£
Total input tax	350,000
Of which relating to: Taxable supplies only	125,000
Exempt supplies only	75,000
Non attributable	150,000
Taxable supplies made in the year (excl VAT)	1,350,000
Exempt supplies made in the year	550,000
Machine sold in year (excl VAT)	200,000
Value of taxable transaction (included in taxable turnover) consuming little or no inputs	£1,000,000

Calculate the standard method over-ride adjustment required.

Answer

	£
Deductible input tax	
Wholly attributable to taxable supplies	125,000
Non attributable $\frac{£1,350,000-200,000}{1,350,000+550,000-200,000} = 68\%$	
68% × £150,000	102,000
	227,000

The normal annual adjustment calculation performed at the year end states that £227,000 of input tax for the year is deductible.

However, the business incurred £150,000 of non attributable input tax which exceeds the £50,000 threshold in respect of the standard method over-ride adjustment. In addition we are told that in the year there was a taxable transaction included in turnover valued at £1,000,000 which consumed little or no inputs.

Thus the input tax deducted using the standard method may not be fair and reasonable, reflecting the extent to which purchases are used in making taxable supplies because few, if any, purchases were used in making the high value taxable transaction (worth £1,000,000).

The business must determine the amount of input tax deductible on the basis of use and check whether the difference is substantial.

In this example all supplies other than the high value taxable transaction consume purchases in proportion to their values. Accordingly a fair and reasonable attribution can be achieved by excluding the value of the high value transaction from a calculation based on the standard method.

		£
Deductible input tax		
Wholly attributable to taxable supplies		125,000
Non attributable	$\frac{£1{,}350{,}000 - 200{,}000 - 1{,}000{,}000}{1{,}350{,}000 + 550{,}000 - 200{,}000 - 1{,}000{,}000} = 22\%$	
22% × £150,000		33,000
		158,000

The total input tax deductible on a basis of use is £158,000 whereas using the normal standard method it is £227,000.

The difference of £69,000 (£227,000 – 158,000) is 'substantial' if it exceeds £50,000 or 50% of the non attributable input tax and £25,000. In this illustration £69,000 exceeds £50,000 so an over-ride adjustment must be made. This adjustment of £69,000 is an overclaim of VAT so must be accounted for (ie repaid) on the same VAT return as the annual adjustment (ie here the VAT return to 31 July 2007).

There is a separate over-ride for business using a special method to apportion their input tax which can be implemented at HMRC's direction if the special method used ceases to produce a fair and reasonable result.

2.8 Irrecoverable VAT

Where all (as with many cars) or some (as with partially exempt traders) of the input tax on a purchase is not deductible, the **non-deductible VAT is included in the cost for income tax, corporation tax, capital allowance or capital gains purposes. Deductible VAT is omitted from costs, so that only net amounts are included in accounts. Similarly, sales** (and proceeds in chargeable gains computations) **are shown net of VAT**, because the VAT is paid over to HMRC.

2.9 Motoring expenses

2.9.1 Cars

The VAT incurred on the purchase of a car not used wholly for business purposes is not recoverable (except as in Paragraph 2.2(a) above). If accessories are fitted after the original purchase and a separate invoice is raised then the VAT on the accessories can be treated as input tax so long as the accessories are for business use.

If a car is used wholly for business purposes (including leasing, so long as the charges are at the open market rate), the input tax is recoverable but the buyer must account for VAT when he sells the car. **If a car is leased, the lessor recovered the input tax when the car was purchased and the lessee makes some private use of the car** (for example private use by employees), **the lessee can only recover 50% of the input tax on the lease charges.**

If a car is used for business purposes then any VAT charged on repair and maintenance costs can be treated as input tax. No apportionment has to be made for private use.

If an employee accepts a reduced salary in exchange for being allowed to use his employer's car privately, or pays his employer for that use, there is no supply, so VAT is not due on the salary reduction. However, VAT is due on charges for running costs. VAT is also due on charges for employee use in the rare cases where the charge is a full commercial rate so that the employer has recovered input tax on the cost or on leasing charges in full.

2.9.2 Fuel for business use

The VAT incurred on fuel used for business purposes is fully deductible as input tax. If the fuel is bought by employees who are reimbursed for the actual cost or by a mileage allowance, the employer may deduct the input tax. However from 1 January 2006 onwards **there is a requirement for a business to hold a VAT invoice (or invoices) showing sufficient VAT to cover the input tax claim being made**. Normally there will not be an invoice showing the exact amount of input VAT reclaimed because some of the fuel may have been used by employees for private purposes and only business use is reimbursed (or a mileage allowance is used). However, what is necessary is for an invoice to show an amount of input tax on fuel at least equal to the input tax being recovered by the business.

2.9.3 Fuel for private use

When fuel is supplied for an individual's private use at less than the cost of that fuel to the business, all input tax incurred on the fuel is allowed, but the business must account for output tax using set scale charges per VAT return period, based on the cylinder capacity of the car's engine. The scale figures will be stated in the exam if required. However, take care to note whether the examiner has given you the VAT inclusive or the VAT exclusive scale figure. The VAT inclusive scale charges are reproduced in the tax rates and allowances tables in this text. The output tax is the VAT inclusive scale charge × 7/47 or the VAT exclusive scale charge × 17.5%.

If the employee has to pay the full cost of fuel (or more than its cost) to the employer, the employer must account for VAT on the amount paid, rather than on the scale charge.

Question — VAT and private use fuel

Iain is an employee of ABC Ltd. He has the use of a 1000 cc car for one month and an 1800 cc car for two months during the quarter ended 31 March 2007.

ABC Ltd pay all the petrol costs in respect of both cars without requiring Iain to make any reimbursement in respect of private fuel. Total petrol costs for the quarter amount to £300 (including VAT).

What is the VAT effect of the above on ABC Ltd?

VAT Scale rates (VAT inclusive)

	Quarterly	
	Diesel	*Petrol*
	£	£
Up to 1400cc	260	273
1401 to 2000cc	260	346
Over 2000cc	331	508

Answer

Value for the quarter:

	£
Car 1	
Up to 1400 cc £273 × 1/3 =	91.00
Car 2	
1401-2000 cc £346 × 2/3 =	230.67
	321.67
Output tax:	
7/47 × £321.67	£47.91
Input tax	
7/47 × £300	£44.68

2.10 Relief for bad debts

Where a supplier of goods or services has accounted for VAT on the supply and the customer does not pay, the supplier may claim a refund of VAT on the amount unpaid. **Relief is available for VAT on bad debts if the debt is over six months old (measured from when payment is due) and has been written off in the creditor's accounts.** Where payments on account have been received, they are attributed to debts in chronological order. If the debtor later pays all or part of the amount owed, a corresponding part of the VAT repaid must be paid back to HMRC.

Bad debt relief claims must be made within three years of the time the debt became eligible for relief. The creditor must have a copy of the VAT invoice, and records to show that the VAT in question has been accounted for and that the debt has been written off. The VAT is reclaimed on the creditor's VAT return.

A business which has claimed input tax on a supply, but which has not paid the supplier of the goods or services within six months of date of supply (or the date on which the payment is due, if later), must repay the input tax, irrespective of whether the supplier has made a claim for bad debt relief. The input tax will be repaid by making an adjustment to the input tax on the VAT return for the accounting period in which the end of the six months falls.

2.11 Self-supply

A person making exempt supplies cannot reclaim input tax relating to those supplies. Also, there are certain supplies on which input tax cannot be recovered at all (eg the purchase of a motor car where there is an element of personal use). This could lead to a distortion of competition where a person produces for himself goods or services which, if purchased externally, would result in restricted or no input tax recovery. The Treasury can deal with such distortions by making regulations taxing self-supplies.

The effect is that the trader is treated as supplying the goods or services to himself (in general, at market value). **Output tax is due to HMRC, but input tax can only be recovered to the extent that it related to taxable supplies made by the business or that it is deductible under the normal rules eg cars.** Thus the business suffers a VAT cost.

The amount of the self-supply is excluded from both the numerator and the denominator of the fraction used in the partial exemption calculation.

Examples of self-supply include construction services provided in-house and motor cars where input tax has been recovered and the car is subsequently put to a use which would not qualify for such credit.

3 Imports, exports, acquisitions and dispatches

FAST FORWARD

Imports from outside the EU are subject to VAT and exports to outside the EU are zero-rated. Taxable acquisitions from other EU states are also subject to VAT and sales to registered traders in other EU states are zero-rated.

3.1 Introduction

The terms **import and export** refer to purchases and sales of goods with countries **outside the EU.**

The terms **acquisition and dispatch** refer to purchases and sales of goods with countries **in the EU**.

The EU comprises Austria, Belgium, the Czech Republic, Cyprus, Denmark, Estonia, Finland, France, Germany, Greece, Hungary, the Republic of Ireland, Italy, Latvia, Lithuania, Luxembourg, Malta, the Netherlands, Poland, Portugal, Slovakia, Slovenia, Spain, Sweden and the UK.

3.2 Imports

Imports are chargeable to VAT when the same goods supplied in the home market by a registered trader would be chargeable to VAT, and at the same rate. There is an exception for certain works of art and antiques imported from outside the EU, for which the VAT charge is calculated at an effective VAT rate of 5% on the full value.

An importer of goods from outside the EU must calculate VAT on the value of the goods imported and account for it at the point of entry into the UK. He can then deduct the VAT payable as input tax on his next VAT return. HMRC issue monthly certificates to importers showing the VAT paid on imports. VAT is chargeable on the sale of the goods in the UK in the normal way.

If security can be provided, the deferred payment system can be used whereby VAT is automatically debited to the importer's bank account each month rather than payment being made for each import when the goods arrive in the UK. Approved importers are able to provide reduced (and in some cases zero) security in respect of the deferred payment scheme. Such importers need to seek the approval of HMRC.

All incidental expenses incurred up to the first destination of the goods in the UK should be included in the value of imported goods. Additionally, if a further destination in the UK or another member State is known at the time the goods are imported, any costs incurred in transporting the goods to that further place must also be included in the value.

If standard-rated services are supplied in the UK by an overseas supplier (inside or outside the EU), **VAT may be charged in the UK.**

Under the reverse charge system, certain supplies are treated as made by the UK recipient. These are:

(a) Certain advertising, banking, professional and freight transport services used by the recipient for business purposes

(b) All other services used by VAT-registered recipients for business purposes.

If the recipient is VAT-registered, he must account for VAT on the supply because he is treated as making it. The point of the special category (a) is that the recipient may have to register because he is receiving the services, since the deemed supplies by him may take him over the turnover limit. Category (b) services are only subject to the reverse charge if the recipient is VAT-registered already.

3.3 Exports

There is a general zero-rating where a person exports goods from the EU.

It is not sufficient merely to export goods. The zero-rating only applies if HMRC 'are satisfied' that the supplier has exported the goods. Evidence of the export must therefore be retained by the trader and must take the form specified by HMRC.

Evidence of export must be obtained within three months of the date of the supply. The type of evidence required by HMRC varies according to the manner in which the goods are exported.

HMRC expect ordinary commercial documentation, such as contracts, copy correspondence, copy invoices and consignment notes, to be available for inspection. They also expect positive proof of export clearly identifying the particular goods exported and the manner of export.

For sea freight the normal evidence is a copy of the shipped bill of lading or sea waybill certifying actual shipment, or equivalent documentation provided by the shipping company.

For air freight the evidence required is a copy of the air waybill, endorsed with the flight prefix and number and the date and place of departure.

For letter post a certificate of posting is required. If the value of the package exceeds £100, and a customs declaration is required, an export label (Form VAT 444) must be fixed to the package.

3.4 Civil penalties

Penalties apply to businesses and individuals who import or export goods from outside the EU and who fail to meet Community or HMRC law requirements.

A non-compliance penalty applies in cases of:

- **Occasional serious error** (involving at least £10,000 of VAT)
- **Persistent failure to comply with regulatory obligations**
- **Failure to comply with HMRC directions to correct systems deficiencies etc.**

A non-compliance penalty is not imposed automatically. Instead HMRC will follow an education/warning procedure. Eventually a penalty of up to £2,500 could be imposed. The penalty can be mitigated, avoided altogether with a reasonable excuse, and is appealable to a VAT Tribunal.

An evasion penalty of up to 100% of VAT evaded will apply in less serious cases as an alternative to a criminal prosecution. This penalty can be mitigated.

3.5 Trade in goods within the European Union

3.5.1 Introduction

Goods transferred between **registered persons** in different EU states are zero-rated in the seller's member state provided the seller has proof of the supply and has issued an invoice showing the purchaser's VAT registration number in the other member state. The registered person acquiring the goods has to account for VAT at the rate appropriate in the member state to which the goods are transported.

3.5.2 Sales (dispatches)

Where goods are sold to another EU member state, the supply is zero-rated if:

- **The supply is made to a registered trader**, and
- **The supplier quotes his customer's VAT number on the invoice** (ie to prove that he is a registered trader), and
- **The supplier holds evidence that the goods were delivered to another member state**.

Where these conditions are not satisfied, the supply is subject to VAT as if the customer had been in the UK.

Where a UK trader sells goods to non-registered customers in another EU member state and the UK trader is responsible for the delivery of the goods – eg. a mail-order business – he may become liable to register for VAT in that EU member state (see below).

3.5.3 Purchases (acquisitions)

Goods acquired in the UK by a VAT registered person from another EU member state are liable to VAT in this country. Consequently, output tax has to be accounted for on the relevant VAT return. **The 'tax point' for such acquisitions is the earlier of:**

- **The fifteenth day of the month following the month of acquisition, and**
- **The date of issue of an invoice.**

The transaction is entered on the relevant VAT return as an output and an input so, subject to the partial exemption provisions, the effect is neutral. Thus the trader is in the same position as he would have been if he had acquired the goods from a UK supplier.

If the goods acquired are zero-rated or exempt under UK VAT legislation there is no requirement to account for VAT at the standard rate.

3.5.4 Special situations requiring registration

Exempt businesses and non-taxable organisations must register for VAT in the UK if their acquisitions of goods from other EU member states exceeds £61,000 in any calendar year or if they have reason to believe that the value of such acquisitions in the next 30 days will exceed £61,000.

A person in another EU member state who makes mail order supplies to non-taxable persons in the UK exceeding £70,000 in any calendar year must register for VAT in the UK. **These rules are often referred to as the 'distance selling' provisions**. Similar provisions require UK businesses making mail order supplies, where the supplier is responsible for the delivery of the goods to other EU member states, to register in that other member state if the annual value of such supplies to persons in that EU state exceeds 35,000 ECU or 100,000 ECU (approx. £22,000 or £63,000) depending which EU state is involved.

3.5.5 Reporting requirements

All persons registered for VAT who make supplies of goods to other EU member states are required to complete a statement (usually referred to as an 'ESL' – EU Sales List) at the end of each calendar quarter showing their total of such sales to each customer in the return period and showing:

- **The VAT registration number of the supplier**
- **A two digit prefix indicating the member state of the acquirer of the goods**
- **The VAT registration number of each acquirer,** and
- **The total value of all supplies within the calendar quarter made to each acquirer.**

A penalty of £100 can be imposed for a material inaccuracy on the ESL, but this will only be imposed after there have been two previous material inaccuracies and HMRC have both given a written warning and issued a notice. A penalty can also be levied for failure to submit an ESL.

The information in the statement will be exchanged with the VAT authorities in other EU member states for audit and control purposes.

Traders must provide the necessary data for the compilation of trade statistics on the movement of goods between EU countries. **The form used for the collection of this data is known as the supplementary statistical declaration (SSD) or more commonly the Intrastat and this form records the movement of goods, not supplies of services.**

Traders whose dispatches of goods to, or arrivals of goods from, other EU countries in a calendar year exceed a threshold must supply details of consignments processed each month on SSDs. The threshold for both arrivals and dispatches is £225,000 (from 1 January 2006). Nil returns do not have to be submitted.

The SSD must be submitted by the end of the month following the period in question.

3.5.6 Warehousing

HMRC may approve the use of premises as a 'customs warehouse'. Once within the warehousing regime, import VAT only becomes payable on the removal of the goods from the warehouse.

The benefits of warehousing include:

(i) The deferment of payment of VAT up to the time that the goods are removed rather than when the goods are physically imported into the UK.

(ii) Goods re-exported to customers outside the EU will not constitute a chargeable event giving rise to a charge to VAT.

(iii) Goods which are found to be faulty on arrival can be returned to the supplier before VAT is paid. This will result in a reduction in administrative costs.

HMRC have the power to deny 'VAT-free' trading in a warehouse where tax avoidance occurs.

3.5.7 Fiscal warehousing

Fiscal warehousing allows VAT-free trading in qualifying EU commodities, eg specified metals, foodstuffs and chemicals. VAT is payable when the commodities are removed from the warehouse. Payment of VAT on supplies of some services in these and other warehousing regimes may also be deferred.

The regime applies to eligible goods on which the VAT chargeable on importation (in the case of goods imported from outside the member states) has been paid. Where eligible goods subject to the regime are changed into other eligible goods by some operation, they continue to be entitled to remain under the fiscal warehousing arrangements. However, where eligible goods are changed into ineligible goods, they become chargeable to VAT as if they had been removed from the fiscal warehouse at that time.

Supplies of services are zero-rated if they are wholly performed on, or in relation to, goods subject to the regime, for example, storage or repackaging.

VAT is payable by the person who removes the goods, or pays the duty.

3.5.8 Certain services

When certain advertising, banking, professional and freight transport services are supplied *by* a UK registered trader, either to a person outside the EU or to a person in another EU state for the purposes of his business, they are treated as supplied in the recipient's state. They are therefore outside the scope of UK VAT, and no VAT is charged.

The same rule applies to a supply of work done on goods by a UK trader, where the work is supplied to a VAT-registered trader in another EU state and the goods leave the UK: the supply is outside the scope of UK VAT. If a UK-registered trader gets someone in another EU state to do work on goods and the goods then leave the other state, the UK trader will account for UK VAT on the work under the reverse charge system.

There is a simplified optional special scheme for non-EU businesses providing electronically supplied services to private and non-business customers in the EU. Rather than having to register and account for VAT in every EU member state where they make such supplies, they can instead:

- Electronically register in a single member state of their choice, and
- Electronically declare the EU tax due on a single VAT return to the member state of registration.

The member state of registration distributes the VAT to the appropriate member states.

4 Special schemes

FAST FORWARD

Special schemes include the cash accounting scheme, the annual accounting scheme and the optional flat rate scheme. These schemes make VAT accounting easier for certain types of trader usually with relatively low turnover.

4.1 The cash accounting scheme

The cash accounting scheme enables businesses to account for VAT on the basis of cash paid and received. That is, the date of payment or receipt determines the return in which the transaction is dealt with. **The scheme can only be used by a trader whose annual taxable turnover (exclusive of VAT) does not exceed £660,000.** A trader can join the scheme only if all returns and VAT payments are up to date (or arrangements have been made to pay outstanding VAT by instalments).

If the value of taxable supplies exceeds £825,000 in the 12 months to the end of a VAT period a trader must leave the cash accounting scheme immediately.

Businesses which leave the scheme (either voluntarily or because they have breached the £825,000 limit) can account for any outstanding VAT due under the scheme on a cash basis for a further six months.

The Government has asked the European Commission for a derogation to increase the turnover limit for entry to the cash accounting scheme from £660,000 to £1,350,000. When this is granted, the limits applying to the cash accounting scheme will match those applying to the annual accounting scheme (see below).

4.2 The annual accounting scheme

The annual accounting scheme is only available to traders who regularly pay VAT to HMRC, not to traders who normally receive repayments. It is available for traders **whose taxable turnover (exclusive of VAT) for the 12 months starting on their application to join the scheme is not expected to exceed £1,350,000 (from 1 April 2006. Prior to this date £660,000).**

Under the annual accounting scheme traders file annual VAT returns but throughout the year they must make payments on account of their VAT liability by direct debit. The year for which each return is made may end at the end of any calendar month. Unless HMRC agree otherwise, the trader must pay 90% of the previous year's net VAT liability during the year by means of nine monthly payments commencing at the end of the fourth month of the year. The balance of the year's VAT is then paid with the annual return. There is an option for businesses to pay three larger interim instalments.

Late payment of instalments is not a default for the purposes of the default surcharge.

An annual VAT return must be submitted to HMRC along with any balancing payment due within two months of the end of the year.

It is not possible to use the annual accounting scheme if input tax exceeded output tax in the year prior to application. In addition, all returns must have been made up to date. Annual accounting is not available where VAT registration is in the name of a VAT group or a division.

If the expected value of a trader's taxable supplies exceeds £1,600,000 notice must be given to HMRC within 30 days and he may then be required to leave the scheme. If the £1,600,000 limit is in fact exceeded, the trader must leave the scheme.

If a trader fails to make the regular payments required by the scheme or the final payment for a year, or has not paid all VAT shown on returns made before joining the scheme, he may be expelled from the scheme. HMRC can also prevent a trader using the scheme 'if they consider it necessary to do so for the protection of the revenue'.

Advantages of annual accounting:

- Only one VAT return each year so fewer occasions to trigger a default surcharge
- Ability to manage cash flow more accurately
- Avoids need for quarterly calculations for partial exemption purposes and input tax recovery

Disadvantages of annual accounting:

- Need to monitor future taxable supplies to ensure turnover limit not exceeded
- Timing of payments have less correlation to turnover (and hence cash received) by business
- Payments based on previous year's turnover may not reflect current year turnover which may be a problem if the scale of activities has reduced

4.3 Flat Rate Scheme

The optional flat rate scheme enables businesses to calculate VAT due simply by applying a flat rate percentage to their turnover.

Under the scheme, businesses calculate VAT by applying a fixed percentage to their tax inclusive turnover, i.e. the total turnover, including all reduced rate, zero-rated and exempt income. The percentage depends upon the trade sector into which a business falls. It ranges from 2% for retailing food, confectionery or newspapers to 13.5% for construction services. The percentage for accountancy and book-keeping is 13%, for financial services is 11.5%, for hotels 9.5% and for catering 12%. A 1% reduction off the flat rate % can be made by businesses in their first year of VAT registration.

Businesses using the scheme must issue VAT invoices to their VAT registered customers but they do not have to record all the details of the invoices issued or purchase invoices received to calculate the VAT due. Invoices issued will show VAT at the normal rate rather than the flat rate.

To join the flat rate scheme businesses must have:

- **a tax exclusive annual taxable turnover of up to £150,000**; and
- **a tax exclusive annual total turnover, including the value of exempt and/or other non-taxable income, of up to £187,500.**

4.4 Example

An accountant undertakes work for individuals and for business clients. In a VAT year, the business client work amounts to £35,000 and the accountant will issue VAT invoices totalling £41,125 (£35,000 plus VAT at 17.5%). Turnover from work for individuals totals £18,000, including VAT. Total gross sales are therefore £59,125. The flat rate percentage for an accountancy businesses is 13%.

VAT due to HMRC will be 13% × £59,125 = £7,686.25

Under the normal VAT rules the output tax due would be:

	£
£35,000 x 17.5%	6,125.00
£18,000 x 7/47	2,680.85
	8,805.85

Whether the accountant is better off under the scheme depends on the amount of input tax incurred as this would be offset, under normal rules, from output tax due.

4.5 The secondhand goods scheme

The basic idea of the secondhand goods scheme is to restrict the amount of VAT due on goods sold under the scheme to VAT on the trader's margin, rather than on the entire amount charged on reselling the goods. The trader has to account for VAT at 7/47 of the difference between his buying price (including any VAT he paid) and his selling price. The scheme applies to works of art, collectors' items and antiques and to all secondhand goods, apart from precious metals and gemstones. A trader does not have to use the scheme: he can account for VAT in the normal way if he chooses. The scheme cannot be used for goods that were acquired as the result of the transfer of a business as a going concern unless the goods were already eligible for the scheme before the transfer.

No VAT invoice is issued, so a customer cannot reclaim the input tax suffered.

Question — Secondhand goods scheme

Arun carries on a trade in secondhand pianos. On 5 November 2006 he sells a piano to Anne for £3,500. Arun had purchased the piano through an advertisement in a local paper from Scott for £2,100 on 10 October 2006. Arun spent £500 on repairs and tuning in respect of the piano.

What is Arun's output tax liability on the sale?

Answer

Under the margin scheme Arun's output tax is:

	£
Selling price	3,500
Less: purchase price	(2,100)
Margin	1,400

VAT @ 7/47 × £1,400 = £209

Costs of repair and tuning are ignored although any input tax incurred by Arun on these is recoverable in the normal way.

A dealer in large volumes of low value goods (purchase price £500 or less per item) can account for VAT of 7/47 of his total margin for a period (netting off profits and losses), instead of working out each profit margin individually and ignoring losses. This global accounting cannot be used for motor vehicles, motorcycles, caravans, motor caravans, aircraft, boats, outboard motors, horses or ponies.

The scheme can only be applied where the goods were bought from a person who did not charge VAT on the supply or from one who was operating the secondhand goods scheme. It can also be used by an agent who acts in his own name and is therefore treated as actually buying and selling goods himself.

Goods sold under the scheme are not subject to the usual rules on trade with other EU member states. There is no VAT on their acquisition and sales to traders in other states are taxed just like such sales in the UK. Exports to outside the EU are zero-rated. Imports from outside the EU (apart from cars) cannot be included in the scheme.

Chapter roundup

- Some supplies are taxable (either standard-rated, reduced-rated or zero-rated). Others are exempt. A trader making both taxable and exempt supplies may be unable to recover all of his input tax.
- Imports from outside the EU are subject to VAT and exports to outside the EU are zero-rated. Taxable acquisitions from other EU states are also subject to VAT and sales to registered traders in other EU states are zero-rated.
- Special schemes include the cash accounting scheme, the annual accounting scheme and the optional flat rate scheme. These schemes make VAT accounting easier for certain types of trader.

Quick quiz

1 What input tax is never deductible?

2 What is partial exemption?

3 What relief is available for bad debts?

4 Are goods exported from the EU standard-rated or zero-rated?

5 What are the turnover limits for the annual accounting scheme?

6 What is the optional flat rate scheme?

Answers to quick quiz

1 VAT on:

- motor cars (where there is an element of private use)
- business entertaining
- expenses incurred on domestic accommodation for directors
- non-business items passed through the accounts
- items which do not relate to making business supplies

2 Where a 'person' makes a mixture of taxable and exempt supplies he is partially exempt and cannot recover input tax incurred by the business in full.

3 Where a supplier has accounted for VAT on a supply and the customer fails to pay, then the supplier may claim a refund of the VAT accounted for to HMRC but never actually collected from the customer.

4 In general, exports from the EU are zero-rated.

5 Turnover not exceeding £1,350,000 to join the scheme. Once turnover exceeds £1,600,000 must leave the scheme.

6 The optional flat rate scheme enables businesses to calculate VAT simply by applying a percentage to their tax-inclusive turnover. Under the scheme, businesses calculate VAT due by applying a flat rate percentage to their tax inclusive turnover, i.e. the total turnover generated, including all reduced-rate, zero-rated and exempt income. The percentage depends upon the trade sector into which a business falls.

Now try the question below from the Exam Question Bank

Number	Level	Marks	Time
Q28	Examination	10	18 mins

Part D
Tax planning

30

Tax planning

Introduction

Tax planning is an integral part of any tax advice you give. Note that tax avoidance is the exploitation of the law to reduce tax liabilities. It is not illegal to attempt tax avoidance and this is what you are doing when you give tax planning advice. Tax avoidance should be distinguished from tax evasion which involves not giving all relevant facts to HMRC. Tax evasion is always illegal and you should never become involved in it. There may be a duty to disclose details of tax avoidance schemes to the relevant HMRC Authorities.

We have dealt with various tax planning aspects as they have arisen earlier in this text. In this chapter, we bring together topics by considering some additional typical tax planning points.

Topic list	Syllabus references
1 Employment and self-employment	1
2 Remuneration packages	1
3 The choice of a business medium	1, 2
4 The incorporation of a business	1, 2
5 Tax efficient profit extraction	2
6 Tax efficient exit routes	2
7 Planning for corporate growth	2
8 Group tax minimisation strategies	2
9 Divisionalised v group company structure	2
10 Disclosure of tax avoidance schemes	1, 2

1 Employment and self-employment

FAST FORWARD

As a general rule, self-employment leads to lower overall tax and NIC burdens than employment.

A taxpayer who has a choice between being employed and being self-employed, on similar gross incomes, should consider the following points.

(a) An employee must pay **income tax and NICs as salary is received, under the PAYE system** and on a current year basis. A self-employed person pays **Class 2 NICs during the year, but income tax and Class 4 NICs are at least partly payable after all of the profits concerned have been earned**. There is thus a cash flow advantage in self-employment.

(b) **An employee is likely to suffer significantly higher NICs in total than a self– employed person**, although the employee's entitlement to state benefits will also be higher. In particular, note that the self-employed earn no entitlement to the State Second Pension.

(c) An **employee may receive benefits as well as salary**. Taxable values of benefits may be less than their actual value to the employee and benefits do not attract employee NICs (this is however only relevant if salary does not exceed the upper NIC limit). Most benefits attract Employer's Class 1A NIC.

(d) The **rules on the deductibility of expenses are much stricter for employees** (incurred wholly, exclusively and necessarily in the performance of duties) than for the self-employed (normally incurred wholly and exclusively for the purposes of the trade).

2 Remuneration packages

FAST FORWARD

If someone is to be an employee, the tax effects of the remuneration package should be taken into account.

2.1 Income tax planning for employment situations

An employee will usually be rewarded largely by salary, but several other elements can be included in a remuneration package. Some of them bring tax benefits to the employee only, and some will also benefit the employer.

Bonuses are treated like salary, except that if a bonus is accrued in the employer's accounts but is paid more than nine months after the end of the period of account, its deductibility tax purposes will be delayed.

The general position for benefits is that they are subject to income tax and employer Class 1A NICs. The cost of providing benefits is generally deductible in computing trading profit for the employer (but if a car costing over £12,000 is provided, the employer's capital allowances (or deductions for lease payments) are restricted).

However, there are a large number of tax and NI free benefits and there is a great deal of planning that can be done to ensure a tax and NIC efficient benefits package for directors and employees. The optimum is to ensure that the company receives a tax deduction for the expenditure whilst creating tax and NI free remuneration for employees. The main tax free benefits are:

(i) Growth in value and exercise in shares in approved share option schemes
(ii) Free car parking at/near place of work
(iii) Contributions to approved occupational or personal pension scheme (see later in this text)
(iv) Mileage paid at Statutory rates
(v) Training courses provided (day release, block release, sandwich courses etc)

(vi) Air miles obtained through business travel
(vii) Beneficial loans under £5,000
(viii) Long service awards (20 years, max £50 pa)
(ix) Staff suggestion schemes
(x) Free or subsidised canteens available to all staff
(xi) Sports facilities provided on the employer's premises
(xii) Workplace nursery or playscheme provision
(xiii) Staff uniforms
(xiv) Provision of goods or services at marginal cost only
(xv) Gifts from third parties up to £250 per source
(xvi) Removal expenses up to £8,000
(xvii) Health checks, screening and eye tests
(xviii) Mobile phones (one only)
(xx) The first £30,000 of an ex gratia termination payment

For further details of taxable and exempt benefits see earlier in this text.

Question — Comparison of two remuneration packages

Employee A receives a salary of £20,000.

Employee B receives a salary of £15,000, the use of a new video camera which cost £800 on 6.4.06 and the use of a car which cost £17,732 on 1.1.06. The taxable benefit for this car is £4,433. No fuel is supplied.

Employee B is also in a pension scheme (not contracted out) to which he contributes 5% of his gross salary (excluding benefits) and his employer company contributes 10% of his gross salary (excluding benefits). (We will look at pensions later in this text but for the purposes of this example you need to know that employee B can deduct his own contributions, the employer contributions are not a taxable benefit for employee B and the employer can deduct the contributions as a trading expense.)

A and B are both single and have no other income.

Show the tax and the NIC effects of the two remuneration packages on both the employees and their employers. Assume the employer company does not meet the definition of "small" or "medium" sized. Use 2006/07 tax rates and allowances and assume that the employer prepares accounts to 31 March each year.

Answer

A's income tax and NIC computations are as follows.

	£
Earnings	20,000
Less personal allowance	(5,035)
Taxable income	14,965
Income tax	
£2,150 × 10%	215
£12,815 × 22%	2,819
	3,034
NICs	
£(20,000 – 5,035) × 11%	£1,646

A's employer must pay NICs of £20,000 – £5,035 × 12.8% = £1,916, and can deduct £(20,000 + 1,916) = £21,916 in computing trading profits.

B's income tax and NIC computations are as follows.

	£
Salary	15,000
Use of video camera £800 × 20%	160
Car	4,433
	19,593
Less pension contribution £15,000 × 5%	(750)
Earnings	18,843
Less personal allowance	(5,035)
Taxable income	13,808

Income tax	£
£2,150 × 10%	215
£11,658 × 22%	2,565
	2,780
NICs	
£(15,000 – 5,035) × 11%	1,096

B's employer must pay NICs as follows.

Class 1 NICs	
£(15,000 – £5,035) × 12.8%	1,276
Class 1A NICs	
£(4,433 + 160) × 12.8%	588
	1,864

B's employer will have the following deductions in computing profits.

	£	£
Salary		15,000
Pension contribution £15,000 × 10%		1,500
NICs		1,864
Capital allowances		
Car (WDV restricted)	3,000	
Video camera £800 × 25%	200	
		3,200
		21,564

2.2 NIC planning for employment situations

NIC is payable on 'earnings' which is defined as 'any remuneration or profit derived from employment'. Remuneration packages structured to include the following items which are not 'earnings' would reduce the NIC burden.

(a) **Dividends** – director/shareholders could take remuneration in the form of dividends. Dividend waivers and adjustments to bonuses would probably be required. There are CT implications as salary and NIC costs are allowable business expenses whereas dividends are not.

Dividends are an efficient way of avoiding NICs. However dividend income is not earnings for pension purposes (see later in this text). There is also a cash flow impact since PAYE does not apply to dividends.

(b) **Rents** – a director owning a property used by a company could be paid rent instead of remuneration. This will not impact business asset taper relief (if available) on the subsequent sale of the property. The rental expense is a deductible business expense for the company and the income is not earnings for pension contribution purposes for the individual.

3 The choice of a business medium

FAST FORWARD

An entrepreneur must choose between trading as a sole trader and trading through a company. The choice, and if a company is chosen, the choice between dividends and remuneration, can significantly affect the overall tax and NIC burden. Cashflow is also an important consideration.

3.1 General considerations

When starting in business the first decision must be whether to trade as a company (with the entrepreneur as a director taxable on earnings) or as an unincorporated business, either as a sole trader or a partnership. Certain professions may not be practised through a limited company (although unlimited companies and limited liability partnerships are often allowed).

The attraction of incorporation lies in the fact that a sole trader or a partner is liable for business debts to the full extent of his personal assets. A limited company's shareholder's liability is limited to the amount, if any, unpaid on his shares. However, limited liability is often reduced by the demands of bankers or landlords for personal guarantees from company directors. In addition, compliance with the statutory obligations (eg annual returns, audits etc) that apply to a company can be costly.

A company often finds raising finance easier than an unincorporated business. This is partly because of the misguided view that a company has greater reliability and permanence. A company can obtain equity finance through venture capital institutions and can borrow by giving a floating charge over its assets as security whereas a sole trader or partnership cannot do this.

A business may be seen as more reputable or creditworthy if conducted through the medium of a company. Companies, however, have to comply with disclosure requirements and this may be unattractive to proprietors who wish to keep information from employees, potential competitors etc. This could be avoided by using an unlimited company but in that case any advantage of limited status is lost. The disclosure requirements could be reduced by filing abbreviated accounts.

3.2 The effect of marginal tax rates and national insurance

A trader's profits whether retained or withdrawn are taxed at a marginal rate of 40% on taxable income in excess of £33,300. In addition Class 2 and Class 4 national insurance contributions are payable.

A controlling director/shareholder can decide whether profits are to be paid out as remuneration or dividends, or retained in the company.

If profits are retained, the consequent growth in asset values will increase the potential capital gain when shares are sold (although taper relief may reduce the amount of the taxable gain). Where remuneration is paid the total national insurance liability is greater than for the proprietor of an unincorporated business.

Where a spouse is employed his or her salary must be justifiable as 'wholly and exclusively for the purposes of the trade': HMRC may seek to disallow excessive salary cost. On the other hand, a spouse as active partner can take any share in profits, provided that he or she is personally active in the business and there is evidence of a bona fide partnership. Thus the spouse's personal allowance and starting and basic rate bands can be used.

In choosing a business medium, we should also remember that a sole trader will be denied the enhanced state benefits that are available to an employee who pays Class 1 national insurance contributions. In particular, note that the self-employed do not build an entitlement to the State Second Pension.

Question — Net income from a business

Alan, who is single, expects to make annual profits of £30,000 before tax and national insurance. Consider the fiscal effects of his choosing to trade as a sole trader or, alternatively, through a company, paying him a salary of £15,000 and then the largest possible dividend not giving rise to a loss of capital. Assume that accounting profits equal taxable trade profits. Use 2006/07 tax rates.

Answer

As a sole trader

	£
Profits	30,000
Less personal allowance	(5,035)
Taxable income	24,965
Tax thereon at 10%/22%	5,234
National Insurance Classes 2 (52 × £2.10) and 4 (£(30,000 – 5,035) × 8%)	2,106
	7,340
Net income £(30,000 – 7,340)	22,660

Through a company

	£	£
Profits		30,000
Less: salary		(15,000)
employer's NI 12.8% (£15,000 – £5,035)		(1,276)
Taxable profits		13,724
Less: corporation tax 19% × £13,724		(2,608)
Net profits		11,116

A dividend of £11,116 can be paid without loss of capital.

	Non-savings £	*Dividends* £	*Total* £
Earnings	15,000		
Dividends £11,116 × 100/90		12,351	
STI	15,000	12,351	27,351
Less personal allowance	(5,035)		
Taxable income	9,965	12,351	22,316
Non-savings income			
£2,150 × 10%			215
£7,815 × 22%			1,719
Dividend income			
£12,351 × 10%			1,235
			3,169
Less tax suffered £12,351 × 10%			(1,235)
Income tax payable			1,934

Net income	£	£
Salary		15,000
Dividends		11,116
		26,116
Less: income tax	1,934	
Employee's NIC (£15,000 – £5,035) × 11%	1,096	
		(3,030)
		23,086

Trading as a sole trader would give annual net income of £(22,660 – 23,086) = £426 less than trading through a company.

Question

Small business as sole trader versus company

Let's say we have a business earning profits of £15,035.

Compare the retained profit for the business owner if he operates the business as a sole trader with a year ended 31 March 2007 to that of a company with the same year end but paying out £5,035 as a salary and the remaining post-tax profits as a dividend.

Answer

Sole Trader

Trading profits of £15,035 in 2006/07

Year ended 31 March 2007

Income Tax	
£(15,035 – 5,035) = £10,000	£
£2,150 @ 10%	215
£7,850 @ 22%	1,727
	1,942
National Insurance	
Class 2	109
Class 4	
£(15,035 – 5,035) × 8%	800
Total Income Tax and NIC	2,851
Net income	
£(15,035 – 2,851)	£12,184

Company

Year ended 31 March 2007	
PCTCT = (15,035 – 5,035) = £10,000	10,000
Corporation Tax	
£10,000 @ 19% before distribution	(1,900)
Maximum distribution is	8,100
Income Tax	
Salary covered by PA	
Gross dividend income = £9,000	
	£
£9,000 @ 10%	900
Less: Tax credit	(900)
	Nil
Class 1 NIC	Nil
Net income £(5,035 + 8,100)	£13,135

As a sole-tradership the business would typically pay £2,851 in the 2006/07 tax year as income tax and National Insurance Contributions. The same business operating as a limited company for the same year would have a tax bill of £1,900.

3.3 Benefits and expenses

The restrictions on deducting expenses against earnings may make self-employment rather more attractive than employment as a company director. Although the same expense deduction rules apply to a company and a sole trader, the company's deductible business expenses may give rise to taxable benefits as earnings for directors.

On the other hand, the provision of fringe benefits can be an advantage of incorporation. Tax exempt benefits can be used to maximise directors' net spendable income, although care is required because not all benefits are tax-efficient.

3.4 Opening Years

Companies have no equivalent to the opening year rules that apply for income tax purposes. For a sole trader or partnership, profits earned when basis periods overlap are taxed twice. Relief is available for such overlap profits but that may not take place for many years, by which time inflation may have reduced the value of the relief for overlap profits.

If a partnership is envisaged it may be worthwhile to commence trading with the prospective partner as a salaried employee for a year or so, thereby obtaining tax relief twice on his salary during the overlap period.

3.5 Losses

Losses in the first four years of an unincorporated business can be used to obtain tax repayments (using s 381 claims). In these and later years a s 380 claim permits **relief for trading losses against other income** (and capital gains) of either or both of two tax years.

With corporation tax, although there is considerable flexibility for the company itself, **a company's losses are not available to reduce shareholders' taxable incomes.**

3.6 Capital gains tax

One difference between companies and individuals is that **companies do not benefit from an exemption from tax on the first £8,800 of total gains** (for 2006/07).

Chargeable gains of an individual are charged to capital gains tax at 10%, 20% or 40%. By contrast, companies' gains are charged at normal corporation tax rates (30% full rate, 19% small companies rate or 32.75% effective marginal rate.

The principal disadvantage of incorporation is the double charge to tax which arises when a company sells a chargeable asset. Firstly, the company may pay corporation tax on the chargeable gain. Secondly, the shareholders may be taxed when they attempt to realise those proceeds, either in the form of dividends or, when the shares are sold, incurring a further charge on capital gains.

If there are no tax advantages in the company owning an asset, the asset should be held outside the company, perhaps being leased to the company. The lesser may receive rent without restricting CGT and IHT business asset reliefs.

3.7 Tax cash flows

A sole trader/partner is assessable to income tax and NIC (Class 4) on a current year basis but will use a prior year basis to calculate two payments on account due on 31 January in and 31 July directly following the tax year. The balance of tax is due on 31 January following the tax year. Thus tax on profits earned in the year to 30 April 2006 (assessable 2006/07) will not be payable in full until 31 January 2008 and will be used to calculate payments on account due 31 January 2008 and 31 July 2008. **Where profits are rising this lag gives a considerable benefit**. A sole trader's/partner's drawings do not of themselves attract or accelerate a tax charge.

A company pays CT nine months after the end of its accounts period. Companies paying tax at the full rate are required to make **quarterly payments on account** based on the current year's estimated liability. As an employer it will have to account for **PAYE and NIC 14 days after the end of each tax month** in which the pay date falls.

Generally therefore a business held by a company will bear tax earlier than a business held by a sole trader or partnership.

3.8 What if things go wrong?

Sound tax planning should always take account of possible changes in circumstances. A successful business may fail or a struggling concern may eventually become profitable.

Running down an unincorporated business does not normally give rise to serious problems. The proprietor may be able to cover any balancing charges with loss relief.

Taking a business out of a company (disincorporation), or winding up a corporate trade altogether is more complex and involves both tax and legal issues. Consider the following:

- No subsequent relief is available for a company's unused losses once the trade ceases.
- Liquidation costs may be considerable.
- A double charge on capital gains may arise.

3.9 Personal Services Companies (PSCs)

The 'IR 35 provisions' (see earlier in this text) are anti-avoidance rules which attack the provision of personal services by Personal Services Companies (PSCs). If an individual would have been an employee if he had been working directly for a client, he will be subject to tax and NIC on income from the PSC broadly as if he was in fact an employee of the client.

4 The incorporation of a business

FAST FORWARD

The incorporation of a business should be carefully planned, taking account of consequent tax liabilities. There are both advantages and disadvantages to incorporating a business. A disposal of shares can also have several tax consequences.

4.1 Why incorporate a business?

4.1.1 Advantages

(a) Retained profits subject only to corporation tax not income tax or NIC

(b) Easier to dispose of shares in a company than interest in a business – thus advantage for raising equity and selling to outside investors

(c) Pension provision can be made by employer (the company) for employees (eg directors) with no national insurance liability (see later in this text)

(d) Benefits for employees can be more tax efficient

(e) Loan finance easier to arrange as lender can take out charge on company assets

(f) Limited liability

(g) A company arguably has a more respectable image than a sole trader or partnership

(h) Incorporation is a means of converting the value of a business into shares which could be brought to the AIM or even achieve a full stock market quote. This provides for succession of ownership and can make the original proprietors very wealthy

4.1.2 Disadvantages

(a) Potential double capital gains charge on assets (see above)

(b) Trading losses restricted to set-off against corporate profits

(c) No carry back of trading losses in opening years (ie no s 381 equivalent)

(d) Partner's share of profit not openly challenged by HMRC provided the recipient is a genuine partner. Conversely excessive remuneration to employee/director can be challenged

(e) NIC for employer company and employee will generally exceed the contributions required of a self-employed person

(f) Paydays for tax on a company and its employees (CT, PAYE and NIC) are generally well in advance of paydays for self-employed

(g) Assets used in a business but held outside the business entity can qualify for 50% BPR for IHT. In the case of a partnership the owner merely has to be a partner but in the case of a company using an asset the owner must be a controlling shareholder

(h) There may be statutory requirement of audit, keeping books, filing accounts etc

(i) Disclosure requirements of published accounts may give information to employees/ competitors that business owners would not have willingly disclosed

4.2 Income tax

4.2.1 The choice of a date

When an unincorporated trade is transferred to a company the **trade is treated as discontinued for tax purposes and the cessation rules apply**. Careful consideration of the level of profit and date of transfer is required to avoid large taxable profits in one year from a basis period of more than 12 months. For example a trader with a 30 June year end will be assessed on 21 months of profit in his final year if he incorporates on 31 March (albeit subject to overlap relief) whereas only 10 months of profit will be taxed in that final year if he delays incorporation to 30 April.

4.2.2 Capital allowances

On the transfer of a trade to a company **a balancing charge will usually arise as plant and machinery are treated as being sold at market value**. However, where the company is controlled by the transferor, **the two are connected and an election may be made** so as not to treat the transfer as a permanent discontinuance for capital allowances purposes. **Fixed assets are then transferred at their tax written down values.**

4.2.3 Trading losses

Unrelieved trading losses cannot be carried forward to a company as such, but **may be set against any income derived from the company** by way of dividends, remuneration and so on, provided the business is exchanged for shares and those shares are still held at the time the loss is set off. Terminal loss relief may also be available for the loss of the last twelve months of trading.

4.3 Capital gains tax

When the transfer takes place the **chargeable assets are deemed to be disposed of to the company at their open market values**. Capital gains tax liabilities are likely to arise, particularly on land and buildings and on goodwill. The gains will be reduced by business assets taper relief.

If the whole business (or the whole business other than cash) **is transferred to the company as a going concern in exchange for shares in the company, any chargeable gains (before taper relief) are rolled over**, reducing the base cost of the shares on a subsequent disposal. This relief is known as incorporation relief. As no capital gains tax arises on death, the tax liability may never arise.

Individuals who incorporate a business can elect that incorporation relief should not apply. This election must be made within two years of 31 January following the end of the tax year in which the business was incorporated. A shorter time limit will apply when all the shares received on the transfer are disposed of in the tax year of transfer, or in the following tax year. Making the election could be advantageous for taper relief purposes where the shares are disposed of soon after incorporation.

It may not be desirable for all the assets comprised in the business to be transferred to the company. **As an alternative**, an individual can **use gift relief** to transfer chargeable business assets to a company and **defer any gains by deducting them from the base costs of the assets** to the company.

4.4 Value added tax

The transfer of assets will not be treated as a supply for VAT purposes (called the Transfer of Going Concern (TOGC) relief) if all of the following conditions are satisfied.

(a) The assets are to be used by the company in the same kind of business (whether or not as part of an existing business) as that carried on by the transferor, the business being transferred as a going concern.

(b) If only part of the business is transferred, that part is capable of separate operation.

(c) If the transferor is a taxable person, the company is a taxable person when the transfer takes place or immediately becomes one as a result of the transfer.

(d) In the case of land and buildings, the company makes an election to tax if the transferor has done so.

(e) In the case of 'new' buildings the company makes an election to tax.

Note. For the last two points if the election to tax is not made by the company the supply of land or buildings is standard rated. All the other business assets can be transferred outside the scope of VAT under the TOGC rules.

An application may be made for the company to take over the existing VAT registration number. In this case the company will take over all the debts and liabilities of the business but it will be able to claim VAT bad debt relief in respect of supplies made before the transfer.

If the above conditions cannot be satisfied VAT will be charged on the transfer, but this will only represent a cash flow problem in most cases.

Customs should be notified of the incorporation within 30 days.

4.5 Stamp duty land tax

The transfer of land will be subject to Stamp Duty Land Tax as a transfer at market value. The use of the gift relief route should be considered so that land can be retained outside the company.

5 Tax efficient profit extraction

FAST FORWARD

There are several methods by which profit can be extracted from a company.

5.1 Methods of extracting profits

When trading activities are carried on through a limited company careful thought needs to be given to the level and method of extraction of the profits generated. This decision should take into account both the needs of the individual shareholders and directors as well as the needs of the company itself. For instance, the company may need to retain a certain level of profit in order to reduce its bank overdraft or fund an expansion project.

The table below compares the various methods of extracting profits in outline. They are looked at in more detail below.

Method of extraction	Company	Individual
Remuneration		
Salary	Deductible/Class 1 NICs	Taxable/Class 1 NICs
Benefits	Deductible/Class 1A NICs	Taxable
Tax free benefits	Deductible/No NICs	Tax/NI free
Dividends	Not deductible	No tax for basic or starting rate taxpayer Higher rate tax at 32.5%, subject to 10% tax credit No NICs
Loan interest	Deductible on accruals basis as interest on a loan relationship	Taxable as savings (excl dividend) income
Rental income	Deductible	Taxable non savings income
Pension contributions		
(see later in this text)		
– approved	Deductible	Tax free
– unapproved	Deductible/Class 1 NICs	Taxable/Class 1 NICs

5.2 Dividends or remuneration

Director/shareholders may wish to consider either extracting profits as dividend or remuneration. Payments of dividends or remuneration will reduce a company's retained profits which means a reduction in net asset value and hence the value of the shares, ultimately reducing any chargeable gain on the disposal of those shares. However, the immediate tax cost of paying dividends or remuneration must be weighed against this advantage.

Remuneration and the cost of benefits will be allowed as deductions in computing the company's profits chargeable to corporation tax. The decision whether or not to make such payments could affect the rate of corporation tax by reducing the level of profits. However, **the national insurance cost must also be borne in mind**. A combination of dividends and remuneration may give the best result.

Question

Dividends and remuneration

A Ltd makes a profit before remuneration of £30,000 in the year to 31 March 2007. The shareholder/director is entitled to only the personal allowance. Consider the director's disposable income available by paying out the profit entirely as salary (of £27,167) or by paying it out as a mixture of salary (at £5,000, so that no national insurance contributions are payable but preserving the director's entitlement to state benefits) and a dividend of £8,100.

Answer

		Salary only £	*Salary and dividend* £
(a)	**The company's tax position**		
	Profits	30,000	30,000
	Less: salary	(27,167)	(5,000)
	employer's national insurance	(2,833)	
	Taxable profits	0	25,000
	Corporation tax at 19%	£Nil	£4,750
	Cash dividend (25,000 – 4,750)		£20,250

(b) **The director's tax position**

	Non-savings £	*Dividend* £	*Total* £
Salary only			
Earnings	27,167		
Less personal allowance	(5,035)		
Taxable income	22,132		22,132
Salary and dividends			
Earnings	5,000		
Dividends (× 100/90)		22,500	
Less personal allowance	(5,000)	(35)	
	–	22,465	22,465

	Salary only £	*Salary and dividend* £
Non-savings income		
£2,150 × 10%	215	
£19,982 × 22%	4,396	
Dividend income £22,465 × 10%		2,247
Less tax credit on dividend (restricted)		(2,247)
Tax payable	4,611	–
Disposable income		
Salary	27,167	5,000
Less employee's national insurance (27, 167 – 5,035) × 11%	(2,435)	
Dividend		20,250
Less tax payable	(4,611)	
	20,121	25,250

The overall saving through paying a dividend is £(25,250 – 20,121) = £5,129.

5.3 Dividend payments

If dividends are paid, timing can be important. The tax year in which a dividend is paid affects the due date for any additional tax, and if a shareholder's other income fluctuates it may determine whether or not there is any additional tax to pay. Higher rate taxpayers must pay tax at 32.5% on dividend income, subject to a 10% tax credit.

Dividends carry a 10% tax credit and are taxed only at 10% in the hands of basic rate taxpayers which means that dividends are attractive to such individuals. However, the 10% tax credit is not repayable to non-taxpayers.

The payment of dividends does allow flexibility, ie family members need not work for a company in order to receive a dividend. However, this must be weighted against the fact that the company must generate sufficient profit to pay a dividend. Furthermore, HMRC may seek to invoke anti-avoidance legislation if dividends are paid to non-working family members if those who do work for the company do not draw a commercial salary.

Most banks and building societies will recognise regular dividends from an owner managed company as income for mortgage or other loan purposes. This takes away a potential drawback of extraction of funds in the form of investment income.

Dividends are not subject to NICs.

Dividends do not give rise to an entitlement to pay pension contributions whereas remuneration and benefits do (see later in this text).

Dividends are not an allowable trading expense for the company.

5.4 Liquidation

An alternative to both dividends and remuneration is to retain profits in a company and then liquidate it. The company itself may have capital gains on the sale of its assets, and the shareholders will have capital gains on the liquidation, which will be treated as a disposal of their shares for the amounts paid to them. The CGT charges on the shareholders may be mitigated by spreading the capital distributions over two tax years, so as to use both years' annual exemptions. Taper relief may reduce the gains made by individual shareholders on the disposal of the shares.

This route may be worth considering when a company is set up to undertake a single project which will be completed within a few years.

5.5 Loans

A director/shareholder may chose to lend money to the company and extract profits as interest income in return.

Interest income is taxed on the director/shareholder as savings income but it is not subject to NIC. It does not count as relevant earnings for pension purposes. (See later in this text)

From the company's point of view, tax relief for the interest will be available under the loan relationship rules (ie either as a trading expense or as a deficit on a non-trading loan relationship).

5.6 Loans by close companies

Although loans by close companies to participators are not treated as distributions, on making such a loan the company suffers a tax charge: a payment equal to the amount of the loan × 25% is made to HMRC. This tax charge cannot be recovered until the loan is repaid or written off.

5.7 Rental income

On incorporation the owner(s) may decide to retain business premises outside the company and charge rent for its use. **The advantages of this method of profit extraction are that the company will obtain a trading income deduction for rent charged up to a commercial rate. Also, no NIC is payable.**

The disadvantage is that income from a property business does not qualify as pensionable income.

For many small companies, the directors' own homes are often used for company business. It is possible to claim a deduction in the company for reasonable rent paid by the company. Care should be taken so as not to deny principal private residence relief on a proportion of the home. To do this, it must be shown that the room(s) are not used exclusively for company business, ie the occasional guest stays in the 'study'.

5.8 Pension provision

It is becoming increasingly important to save for one's own retirement. Fortunately, it is also something the government recognises as important and, as a result, pension provision has become the most efficient way of extracting funds from a family company.

Employers may set up an **occupational pension plan** for their employees. Employees who are not members of an occupational pension plan and the self employed may alternatively contribute to a **personal pension plan**. These schemes are discussed in detail later in this text, but we summarise the tax treatment of the plans below.

The tax breaks for companies and individuals investing in occupational schemes are listed below.

(a) No taxable benefit for employer contributions

(b) The employee receives tax relief on his contributions

(c) No NIC is due on employer contributions

(d) Additional voluntary contributions (AVCs) paid by employees are tax deductible

(e) Pension fund grows tax free (tax credits on dividends not repayable)

(f) Tax free lump sum available up to 25% of the fund

(g) The employer obtains tax relief for normal contributions actually paid during its accounting period.

The tax advantages of a **personal pension scheme** are as follows:

(a) Contributions paid into the scheme by the policyholder are tax deductible
(b) Contributors pay their contributions net of basic rate income tax
(c) An employer may also contribute into the scheme free of tax on the employee
(d) The fund rolls up tax free
(e) A tax free lump sum may be taken on retirement not exceeding 25% of the fund

5.9 Conclusion

The most tax efficient method of profit withdrawal hinges upon the marginal rate of corporation tax the company pays. For a small company dividends are the cheapest form of profit withdrawal. For a medium-sized or large company a bonus would seem the preferable option on the assumption that the director/shareholder is already paying maximum Class 1 Primary NICs.

If the succession of the company is likely to be achieved by passing the shares down the family, profit retention will only increase the gain to be rolled over by way of a gift relief claim. As the gain rolled over is before taper relief the base cost of the shares to the next generation will be substantially reduced.

6 Tax efficient exit routes

FAST FORWARD

Capital gains and inheritance tax planning are important when disposing of a family business.

6.1 Introduction

Advice on tax efficient exit routes is probably the biggest area that a professional adviser is asked to deal with in tax planning for an owner managed business. This section will explore the key tax implications of passing on and selling the family business or company and suggest useful planning tips to help structure the business in the most efficient manner from the outset.

6.2 Capital gains tax planning

Regardless as to whether the business or company is to be sold or passed down to the next generation a capital gain is likely to arise. It is therefore essential to maximise the reliefs available.

When a company ceases trading great care needs to be taken with the CGT taper relief position as the following example shows.

6.3 Example

Mark owns all the shares in Nicholls Limited and has done so since 1995. Assume that the trade ceases on 6 April 2007. The gain Mark is likely to realise on the sale of his shares is expected to be £918,000.

What will be the taxable gain if:

(a) He sells the shares on 6 April 2007?
(b) The shares are retained until 6 October 2007 and the company is then liquidated?

Solution

If he sells the shares on 6 April 2007 the whole gain will be eligible for maximum business taper. The chargeable gain will therefore be £912,000 × 25% = £229,500.

If the company is liquidated on 6 October 2007, the disposal is treated as two separate assets, a business asset held for 9 years (post 5.4.98) and a non-business asset held for ½ year as the company was dormant. The total post 6.4.98 ownership period is therefore 9½ years (ie 114 months).

The taper relief rate applying to the non business asset would be for a 10 year ownership period as the bonus year will be given.

The gain would become:

	£
Business assets	
£912,000 × 108/114 = £864,000 × 25% =	216,000
Non business assets	
£912,000 × 6/114 = £48,000 × 60%	28,800
Chargeable gain	244,800

6.4 Inheritance tax planning

IHT is only a consideration where the family business or company is to be passed on to the next generation. An outright sale of the business to a third party does not have a donative intent and therefore does not constitute a transfer of value for IHT.

When a taxpayer wants to pass on his family business a **major question exists as to whether to gift the assets now or wait until death.**

If the assets are given during lifetime there may never be an IHT liability, either because the PET does not become chargeable or because the gift is covered by BPR provided the transferee still owns it (or other relevant business property) at the time of the transferor's death.

A lifetime gift will be subject to CGT at some point, either on transfer or on sale of the assets by transferee assuming a rollover claim is made. In addition, where gift relief is claimed the period of ownership by the transferor is effectively 'lost' as it is the **untapered** gain that is rolled over.

However, a transfer of assets on death receives a free uplift in the CGT base cost to current market value and any business property is passed on with the benefit of 100% BPR.

There are strong arguments in favour of the approach to hold business property until death but other points are worthy of serious consideration:

(a) If a business is hit by recession the gain itself may be fairly low in any case.

(b) The gain may be or deferred through EIS reinvestment relief.

(c) The favoured rates of business asset taper relief may reduce a gain to an amount covered by the annual exemption.

(d) BPR at 100% may not be around forever.

(e) Free CGT uplift on assets covered by BPR may be abolished in the future.

Some other tax pitfalls exist which can be avoided provided they are identified and acted upon. The main areas as to consider include:

(a) Holding assets such as business premises outside the company or partnership restricts BPR to a rate of only 50%. This reduces to nil if the shares or partnership interest are disposed of before the business premises.

(b) Where a lifetime gift is made it is important that the property remains 'business property' for the next seven years and that the transferee retains ownership of it (or owns alternative business property). This will prevent a charge to IHT on a sudden death.

(c) Care should be taken not to change the nature of the company, ie a property development company becoming a property holding company.

(d) Beware of buy and sell arrangements included in the Articles of Association or partnership or shareholder agreements as BPR may be denied.

(e) It will be important to ensure that a gift does not fall foul of the 'reservation of benefit' rules. (See earlier in this text.)

6.5 Pre-sale dividend

It may be sensible to extract some wealth as dividends (which have a tax credit attached to them) before sale, rather than as a capital gain (with no tax credit) on sale.

6.6 Example

James has recently received an offer of £3,000,000 for his 100% holding in his investment (ie non-trading) company.

James' shares were acquired in April 2003 for £400,000. James is a higher rate taxpayer and has used his annual exemption for 2006/07. Should James extract £2,000,000 by way of dividend from the company prior to a sale of the shares?

Sale of shares in 2006/07

	£
Proceeds	3,000,000
Less: cost	(400,000)
Gain before taper relief	2,600,000
Gain after taper relief (95%)	2,470,000
CGT at 40%	988,000
Net proceeds £(3,000,000 – 988,000)	2,012,000

Pre-sale dividend	£
Proceeds	1,000,000
Less: cost	(400,000)
Gain before taper relief	600,000
Gain after taper relief (95%)	570,000
CGT @ 40%	228,000
Gross dividend £2,000,000 × 100/90	2,222,222
Higher rate tax at 32.5%	722,222
Less: 10% tax credit	(222,222)
Higher rate tax liability	500,000
Net proceeds £(3,000,000 – 228,000 – 500,000) =	2,272,000

Therefore paying a presale dividend has increased James' net proceeds by £260,000.

Care must be taken however if the capital gain arising qualifies for high levels of taper relief.

6.7 Example

John has recently received an offer of £3,000,000 for his 100% holding in his personal company which is a trading company.

John's shares were acquired in April 2003 for £400,000. John is a higher rate taxpayer and has used his annual CGT exemption for 2006/07. Should John extract £2,000,000 by way of a dividend from the company prior to a sale of the shares?

Sale of shares in 2006/07

	£
Proceeds	3,000,000
Less: cost	(400,000)
Gain before taper relief	2,600,000
Gain after taper relief (25%)	650,000
CGT at 40%	260,000
Net proceeds £(3,000,000 – 260,000)	2,740,000

Pre-sale dividend	£
Proceeds	1,000,000
Less: cost	(400,000)
Gain before taper relief	600,000

	£
Gain after taper relief (25%)	150,000
CGT @ 40%	60,000
Gross dividend £2,000,000 × 100/90	2,222,222
Higher rate tax at 32.5%	722,222
Less: 10% tax credit	(222,222)
Higher rate tax liability	500,000
Net proceeds £(3,000,000 – 60,000 – 500,000) =	2,440,000

Therefore paying a presale dividend has decreased John's net proceeds by £300,000.

6.8 Repurchases of own shares

It may be advantageous for individuals to sell shares back to the issuing company as a repurchase of own shares (see earlier in this text). This may be treated either as a distribution (like a dividend) or as a capital gain (if the conditions are satisfied).

7 Planning for corporate growth

FAST FORWARD

At each stage of a "company's life" from it's beginning, growth and future expansion overseas, tax planning strategies should be adopted.

Exam focus point

This section looks at a company as it begins trading, acquires additional business, and eventually expands abroad. It looks at the commercial decisions taken by the company and its shareholders at the different stages in the company's development, and summarises the tax implications of those decisions. It focuses, in particular, on those elements of corporation tax that are likely to be examined.

7.1 New company

Companies often start small. One or two individuals will set up a company using their own funds (or borrowed funds) to do so. Some shareholders may be active in running the company on a daily basis whilst others will be passive investors looking for a return on their investment.

Points to consider:

- Is the company a close company?

  This will impact on the rate of tax paid if the company does not trade (ie full rate of CT on an CIC). Also are any benefits provided to participators (treated as dividends) or loans made to participators (trigger a charge at 25% on the company).

- Can the shareholders receive tax relief for their investment?

  If the company is a close company interest paid on a loan to invest in the company is qualifying annual interest (tax deduction available).

  EIS income tax relief may be available to small investors.

- Level of tax paid on company profits.

  Small companies rate will apply to profits below £300,000 with marginal relief for profits below £1,500,000.

  Salaries paid to employees reduce PCTCT, dividends paid to shareholders do not.

- Losses made can be relieved by carry back up to 12 months (if there are any profits to carry back against) or carry forward against future trading profits.
- Don't forget to consider registration for VAT.

7.2 Expansion in UK

A company can grow bigger by increasing its own activities or purchasing the activities of another business and either assuming those activities within itself or setting up a subsidiary company.

Points to consider:

- Single company (1 associate) or group of companies. More than one associate effects CT profit bands.
- If a group is formed: group relief for losses; asset transfers and tax planning re asset groups in respect of capital gains and losses. Also VAT group registration.
- As PCTCT grows may need to consider payment of CT and VAT in instalments (large company).
- When a company acquires the trade of another company capital losses remain within the vendor company. Trading losses will also remain with the vendor company unless the two companies are under common ownership.

7.3 Expansion overseas

As a company grows it may consider expanding overseas.

The tax implications of the overseas business depend on the legal structure used. From a tax point of view, there are two distinct ways of establishing the business:

- It could be owned by the UK company. Under this option, it would be an overseas branch of a UK resident company.
- the UK company could improve a new subsidiary in the overseas country to acquire the business. Under this option, it would be an overseas subsidiary of a UK resident company.

Points to consider:

- **Overseas branch**

  A branch is not a separate legal entity but is an extension of the company that owns it. The profits or losses of the branch belong directly to the company.

  Provided the branch is controlled from the UK, any trading loss made could be offset by the UK company (or group) against its income and gains of that year, reducing the company's UK corporation tax liability. Once the branch is profitable, the company owning the branch will be subject to overseas corporation tax on the branch profits, because it is trading within the boundaries of the overseas country from a permanent establishment.

  The profits will also be subject to UK corporation tax because a UK resident company is subject to tax on its worldwide income and gains. However the UK corporation tax liability, in respect of the branch profits, will be relieved by double tax relief.

- **Overseas subsidiary**

  A subsidiary is a separate legal entity. A company incorporated in an overseas country will be resident in that country for tax purposes, provided it is not managed and controlled from the UK. Its profits or losses will then be subject to the tax regime of the overseas country.

  Any trading loss of the year would be carried forward and deducted from the company's future trading profits arising out of the same trade.

Once the company is profitable, it will be subject to tax in the overseas country. Any dividends paid to the UK parent company will be grossed up, in respect of the underlying tax suffered in the overseas country, and included in the parent company's profits chargeable to corporation tax. Double tax relief, at the lower of the overseas tax or the UK tax on the overseas income, is available.

- It is usually suggested that a branch should be used where an overseas enterprise is expected to make initial losses. This strategy enables the losses to be offset against any other profits of the company. The branch can be incorporated once it is profitable. However, the particular facts of the situation must be considered carefully.
- A subsidiary is an associate for the purpose of determining the rate of tax paid by group companies, whereas a branch is not. Accordingly, the use of subsidiary (rather than a branch) could increase the rate of corporation tax paid by the UK companies.

8 Group tax minimisation strategies

FAST FORWARD

There are several tax planning opportunities available to groups of companies.

There are many **tax planning opportunities for groups of companies**. The following points should be considered, in addition to the points made earlier in this text.

(a) **Minority interests should be restricted so as to ensure that the holding company has a 75% effective interest in every company. This will enable losses to be group relieved** to whichever company can make the best use of them (particularly companies in the small companies marginal relief band).

(b) **The group can be regarded as one unit for the purposes of rollover relief** on the replacement of business assets.

(c) **The small companies rate limits will be shared equally among group members; profits may be shared to take advantage of them by fixing transfer prices for intra-group trading (transfer pricing rules generally do not apply to small and medium sized enterprises).** However, minority shareholders might then be unfairly advantaged or disadvantaged.

Careful consideration will need to be given to the number of associated companies in the group as setting up an additional subsidiary may affect the tax rate of all group companies.

(d) **VAT will arise on intra-group trading unless a VAT group is formed. It may be best to concentrate all exempt supplies in one or two companies which can be left outside the VAT group, and zero rated supplies in one or two other companies which can also be left outside the VAT group (or can form their own separate VAT group) and can make monthly repayment claims.**

(e) **Capital losses cannot be group relieved. However, an election can be made to treat any group company as though it made an asset disposal. This means that gains and losses can be netted off against each other in the same company. It will be advantageous to crystallise net gains in the company paying the lowest marginal rate of corporation tax.** However, there are restrictions on the use of pre-entry losses and gains.

9 Divisionalised v group company structure

FAST FORWARD

Careful consideration needs to be given as to whether a group structure or a divisionalised company would be better.

9.1 General principles

In certain circumstances a business can be operated through a group company structure or through a single divisionalised company.

The setting up of a **trading group has a number of implications**, namely:

(a) It is **easier to give status to a key employee** by appointing him director of a subsidiary company.

(b) **Group relief of losses** is available.

(c) **Assets may be transferred between the group without giving rise to a charge to tax.**

(d) **Group wide rollover relief** may be claimed.

There are a number of disadvantages to a group structure that must be considered, particularly where the parent company or subsidiaries are to be sold.

Where the parent company is sold then the group would either:

(a) Sell the group and then buy back the required subsidiaries
(b) Reconstruct the group which would need tax clearances and cause delays, or
(c) Sell assets

Where a subsidiary is sold this could give rise to a capital gain. No reliefs are available.

The main advantage of a divisional structure is the fact that the **full amount of the small companies tax bands will be available rather than being divided among all companies under common control.**

The other advantages are:

(a) **Automatic set-off losses** in respect of the various divisions
(b) **Automatic set-off of capital gains and losses**
(c) **Administration is simplified**

On the other hand, the disadvantages include:

(a) **Lack of incentive for divisional directors**

(b) Difficulty in giving equity interest in a venture (but may consider profit-related bonuses)

(c) It may be difficult to find a prospective purchaser for the whole company

(d) Group profits can decrease the possibility of making optimum use of the small companies' or the starting rate of tax.

9.2 Example

Sumner Limited carries on two trades through two separate divisions. The furniture production division makes profits of £1.35m in the year to 31 March 2007. The antique furniture restoration division makes profits of £150,000 in the same year.

Solution

Sumner Limited will pay tax of £450,000 (ie £1,500,000 × 30%).

If the company were to operate the trades through two separate companies the tax payable would be:

	£
£1,350,000 × 30% =	405,000
£150,000 × 19% =	28,500
Total	433,500

This creates a tax saving of £16,500 (ie £150,000 × 11%) as part of the profit utilises the small companies rate.

It may be worth setting up a subsidiary company where it is possible to channel £150,000 profit into it.

10 Disclosure of tax avoidance schemes

FAST FORWARD

There are disclosure requirements for promoters of direct tax avoidance schemes. Businesses may be required to disclose use of VAT avoidance schemes.

10.1 Direct tax avoidance schemes

Promoters of tax avoidance schemes have disclosure obligations. There is also an obligation on taxpayers to disclose details of schemes in certain cases.

Notification is required from a promoter of arrangements or proposed arrangements, the main benefit of which is to enable any person to obtain an advantage in relation to tax. A 'promoter' is defined as a person who, in the course of a trade, profession or business involving the provision of tax services to other persons, is to any extent responsible for the design of the arrangements, or who makes a proposal available for implementation by other persons.

The information to be given by a promoter must be provided within a prescribed period of five days after the relevant date. The information to be provided and the manner in which it is to be provided is set out in the regulations.

A taxpayer is required to provide details of arrangements where the arrangements have been purchased from an offshore promoter, and that promoter has made no disclosure. Disclosure must also be made by large businesses which have **entered into arrangements not involving a promoter.**

HMRC may allocate a reference number to arrangements notified under the disclosure rules. Promoters are required to notify clients of that reference number so that they can enter that number on their tax return.

Any person that fails to comply with any of the disclosure provisions is liable to a penalty not exceeding £5,000. If the failure continues after that penalty has been imposed, that person is liable to a further penalty or penalties not exceeding £600 for each day on which the failure continues.

A tax advantage is defined as relief or increased relief from tax, repayment or increased repayment of tax, avoidance or reduction of a charge to a tax. It also includes the deferral of any payment of tax or advancement of any repayment of tax or the avoidance of any obligation to deduct or account for tax. Hallmarks are laid down by regulations specifying types of notifiable schemes.

The taxes covered by these provisions are IT, CGT, CT, IHT, SDLT and stamp duty. NIC is not included.

10.2 VAT avoidance schemes

Businesses using VAT avoidance schemes must disclose their use. Certain VAT avoidance schemes are put on a statutory register.

Businesses with an annual turnover of £600,000 or more that use designated schemes must inform HMRC. A designated scheme is one which has been designated by the Treasury.

Businesses with an annual turnover of £10 million or more must also inform HMRC if they use arrangements other than a designated scheme for the purpose of securing a tax advantage, If the arrangement is of a type recorded on a statutory register.

Detailed regulations deal with the notification procedure to be used.

The penalty for failure to notify HMRC of the use of a designated scheme is 15% of the VAT saving as a result of the use of the scheme. The penalty for using other arrangements is £5,000.

Chapter roundup

- As a general rule, self-employment leads to lower overall tax and NIC burdens than employment. If someone is to be an employee, the tax effects of the remuneration package should be taken into account.
- An entrepreneur must choose between trading as a sole trader and trading through a company. The choice, and if a company is chosen, the choice between dividends and remuneration, can significantly affect the overall tax and NIC burden. Cash flow is also an important consideration.
- The incorporation of a business should be carefully planned, taking account of consequent tax liabilities. There are both advantages and disadvantages to incorporating a business. A disposal of shares can also have several tax consequences.
- There are several methods by which profit can be extracted from a company.
- Capital gains and inheritance tax planning are important when disposing of a family business.
- When a company purchases a new business it should consider whether to own the business directly or via a new subsidiary. The structure used may affect the total tax liability of the group.
- Where a company acquires the trade of another company, capital losses remain with the vendor company. Trading losses will also remain with the vendor company unless the two companies are under common ownership.
- If considering expansion overseas it is usually beneficial to use an overseas branch when an overseas business is expected to make losses.
- There are several tax planning opportunities available to groups of companies.
- Careful consideration needs to be given as to whether a group structure or a divisionalised company would be better.
- There are disclosure requirements for promoters of direct tax avoidance schemes.
- Businesses may be required to disclose use of VAT avoidance schemes.

Quick quiz

1 What are the main NIC differences between the tax positions of employees and the self employed?

2 What is a major attraction of incorporation?

3 Why might a newly commencing trader employ a prospective partner at first, before forming a partnership?

4 What is the major disadvantage for an individual shareholder of an incorporated business where losses are anticipated?

5 List the methods by which profit may be extracted from a company.

6 What are the advantages of a divisionalised company structure?

7 What is the maximum initial penalty for failure to notify a tax avoidance scheme relating to income tax?

Answers to quick quiz

1 Employees suffer Class 1 NIC. Their employers suffer Class 1 and Class 1A NIC too.

The self employed pay Class 2 and Class 4 NIC. The rates of NIC due under these classes are smaller than Class 1 and Class 1A NIC.

2 The attraction of incorporation is limited liability. A sole trader or partner is liable for business debts to the full extent of his personal wealth. A limited company's shareholder is liable to the amount, if any, unpaid on his shares.

3 Commencing trade with a prospective partner as a salaried employee for a year or two obtains tax relief twice on his salary during any overlap period

4 A company's losses are not available to reduce shareholders' taxable incomes (unlike losses of an unincorporated business which can reduce the sole trade/partners incomes).

5
- remuneration
- dividends
- loan interest
- rental income
- pension contributions

6
- Full amount of small company tax bands available rather than being divided among all companies under common control
- Automatic set off of trading losses in respect of various divisions
- Automatic set off of capital gains and losses
- Administration is simplified

7 £5,000

Now try the question below from the Exam Question Bank

Number	Level	Marks	Time
Q29	Introductory	25	45 mins
Q30	Examination	25	45 mins

Part E
Financial planning

31

Financial planning

Introduction

In this chapter, we look at how finance may be raised, both for personal use and for businesses, and at the tax and other considerations affecting the choice between sources of finance. The key distinction for businesses is between equity (cost - dividends - not tax-deductible) and debt (cost - interest - tax-deductible). We also look at the generic mortgage products available in connection with house purchase, and at the circumstances in which it is appropriate to repay/replace borrowings.

Finally we look at personal financial planning. We see how to evaluate an individual's financial position. We also look at the potential disaster scenarios that could arise for both individuals and businesses and we look at sensible strategies to protect wealth and income levels.

Topic list	Syllabus references
1 Sources of finance	3(a)
2 Mortgage products	3(a)
3 Repayment/replacement of borrowings	3(a)
4 Calculating net worth and net disposable income	3(b)
5 Potential disaster situations	3(b)

1 Sources of finance

FAST FORWARD

There are many sources of finance available. For a business, the basic choice is between debt and equity (although some equity will always be needed) and then the appropriate mix of short term and long term debt must be arranged.

1.1 Introduction

Investments can only be made if funds are available. The private investor will generally have his own funds to invest, accumulated from salary or from business profits, but even he may decide to borrow money in order to make an investment which is expected to be particularly profitable. And of course, many private individuals borrow money to invest in land and buildings, in that they buy their homes with mortgage loans.

Businesses need funds in order to start up and expand, and their requirements are often far beyond the means of the entrepreneurs concerned. Outside capital may be sought from banks, from other lenders or from new shareholders or partners.

1.2 Sources of finance for private purposes

The following sources of finance are available to individuals for private purposes.

- Bank overdrafts
- Unsecured bank and building society loans
- Mortgage loans from banks and building societies, secured on the borrower's home
- Credit cards
- Hire purchase facilities
- Credit facilities provided by retailers

If the individual wishes to buy or improve a house, a mortgage loan is likely to be the most suitable source of finance. The fact that it is secured reduces the risk to the lender, and therefore the interest charged. For other large purchases, hire purchase facilities or the credit facilities provided by retailers may be the most suitable: the cost may be reduced as an incentive to make the purchase concerned, and using a specific facility avoids tying up a large proportion of a more general facility such as an overdraft or a credit card. An alternative to such specific facilities is an unsecured bank or building society loan, which must be repaid by agreed instalments over a fixed period.

Small and varied purchases may be made using a credit card, although if credit is taken the interest rate is very high, to reflect the risk of non-payment accepted by the credit card company. A bank overdraft facility can be useful to allow the individual to cope with times when expenditure temporarily exceeds income, perhaps because of fluctuating business profits or because of occasional worthwhile new investment opportunities such as new share issues.

1.3 Sources of finance for businesses

The following sources of finance are available for businesses.

- The entrepreneur's own capital
- Bank overdrafts
- Bank loans (which may be short term, medium term or long term)
- Loans secured by mortgages of land
- Leasing and hire purchase arrangements
- Sale and leaseback arrangements
- Loans from private individuals

- Capital invested by partners
- Share issues (for incorporated businesses)
- Debenture issues (for incorporated businesses)
- Venture capital institutions

An entrepreneur's own capital is readily available to his business with no conditions attached and no interest payments required (although the entrepreneur should recognise that he is giving up the opportunity to invest his capital elsewhere and earn interest on it). However, it is likely to prove to be inadequate for all but the smallest and least ambitious of business ventures, so outside sources of finance will usually have to be considered. Similarly, loans from private individuals, perhaps friends or relatives of the entrepreneur, are likely to be too small to finance a substantial business. However, interest rates and repayment terms may be favourable, so such loans should be considered.

Working capital is needed simply to carry on daily operations. Stock must be bought and creditors and employees must be paid, often before sales revenue is received. **A bank overdraft facility is often the most suitable source of finance,** because funds are available on demand and interest is only paid on the amount actually borrowed from day to day.

An overdraft is not, however, suitable for all of the financing needs of a business. Interest rates tend to be fairly high, and the lending bank could demand repayment at any time. **There is a general principle of term matching in business finance, which is that assets should be financed by funds which will be available for at least as long as the assets are expected to last.** Thus a machine which is expected to be kept for five years should be financed by a loan for five years or more, or by equity. Bank loans and debentures can be a useful source of such longer term finance, and if the loan can be secured on the assets bought with it then the interest rate may be reduced. It may also be possible to obtain loans, from banks and other lenders, at reduced rates of interest by offering a mortgage of land as security.

Some fixed assets may conveniently be obtained under leasing or hire purchase arrangements. Under a lease, the lessee never obtains ownership of the asset, but if the lease is for the useful life of the asset and the risks and rewards of ownership are effectively transferred to the lessee (a **finance lease**), this point is unlikely to be of any practical significance. **A hire purchase agreement is effectively a finance lease, at the end of which the lessee has the option to buy the asset for a small sum.**

If a business already owns a valuable fixed asset, **finance might be obtained through a sale and leaseback arrangement.** The asset is sold, and is then leased back from the buyer so that the business can continue to use it. Such arrangements are usually made in respect of premises. They are attractive to the buyer/lessor, because the risk is low (he obtains ownership of a valuable asset at the outset). However, they should really only be considered as a last resort when other sources of finance are unavailable. In due course, the business will have to find and pay for new premises, or accept the burden of increasing lease payments.

An essential component in the overall financing package for any business is **equity capital**, which **is the form of capital most at risk in the event of business failure** but which also represents a stake in the ownership of the business, and therefore gives the investors the opportunity to profit most from the success of the business. Equity capital reflects the faith of investors in the business, and providers of loan capital will expect to see substantial equity investment before they will agree to lend money. Apart from anything else, if the business loses money lenders will be able to get their loans repaid out of the funds provided by equity investors.

In an unincorporated business, capital invested by the proprietor is equity capital. If more such capital is needed, the proprietor may take in partners. In a partnership, profits will be shared among the partners in a way which may take account of the amounts of capital invested, for example by including 'interest on capital' in the profit sharing arrangement.

Equity capital in a company is in the form of shares. Any company may issue shares to a limited range of investors, but only a public company may offer shares to the general public. A well known public company can raise very large amounts of capital through share issues, and even a private company may be able to attract a fair number of investors because of the limited liability of shareholders. Directors of a small company may, however, find that although their liability as shareholders is limited, they still have to give personal guarantees to repay bank loans to the company.

Unquoted trading companies may consider raising share capital under the enterprise investment scheme, which offers income tax reductions for qualifying investors and a capital gains tax exemption (see later in this text). However, investors must now be prepared to keep their shares for at least three years in order not to lose these tax benefits.

Venture capital institutions specialise in investing in growing businesses where both the potential rewards and the risk of failure are relatively high. They may offer a mixture of loans and equity finance, but they do not expect to be equity investors in a business indefinitely. They may, for example, plan to sell their shares in about five years time, perhaps following a stock market flotation.

Finally, **venture capital trusts provide finance for unquoted companies.**

For all types of external equity finance, the main advantage to the entrepreneur is that cash returns need not be paid at times when cash is short. Dividends need not be paid at any particular level, whereas if loan finance is obtained the interest must be paid and the capital must be repaid on time. The main disadvantage of external equity finance is that the entrepreneur must give up a stake in his business and in its potential for growth. Beyond a certain point, he may even lose the right to direct its affairs.

1.4 The tax implications of equity finance and of loan finance

1.4.1 Loan finance

You saw earlier in this text that if a company is a party to a loan relationship for the purposes of its trade, any debits are deductible in computing its trading profits. If, however a loan relationship is not one for the purposes of a trade any debits or credits are pooled. A net credit on the pool is chargeable as interest income. A net deficit may be relieved in the various ways described earlier in this text.

It is not only the interest costs of borrowing that are allowable or taxable. The **capital costs are treated similarly**. Thus if a company issues a loan at a discount and repays it eventually at par, the capital cost is allowed.

A sole trader or partnership will not obtain a deduction in respect of capital repayments of loan finance. A trading deduction will be available in respect of interest incurred wholly and exclusively for trade purposes.

1.4.2 Equity finance

Companies can raise finance by issuing shares to shareholders. Capital can be raised in this way for trading and non-trading purposes.

Companies can distribute profits to shareholders in a variety of ways, of which the payment of dividends is the most common. **The cost of making distributions to shareholders is not allowable in computing taxable profits.**

A sole trader may make a deduction for 'interest' on his own capital in computing his profits, and partners may include amounts for interest on capital in their profit sharing arrangements, but no deduction for such interest is available for tax purposes.

1.4.3 Legal and professional expenses

Legal and professional expenses relating to capital or non-trading items are disallowable. This includes fees incurred, for example, in issuing share capital. However, a deduction is allowed to companies under the loan relationship rules for the incidental costs of obtaining medium or long term business loans and for issuing loan stock.

1.4.4 Investors

Interest income received from a company on loan stock etc is taxable income for the recipient (and will have suffered 20% tax at source if paid by an unlisted company).

Dividend income received from a shareholding in a company is taxable on an individual investor only to the extent he is a higher rate tax payer. The tax credit on dividend income can never be repaid to non-taxpayers but the tax suffered on interest income is repayable.

Dividend income is not taxable in the hands of a company investor.

No gain or loss can arise to the original creditor when he disposes of his debt. A purchaser of a debt may have a chargeable gain and (unless he is connected with the original creditor) **an allowable loss.**

A debt on a security can give rise to a gain or loss to the original creditor.

In certain cases losses incurred on loans, or guarantees in respect of loans, made to traders are allowable for CGT purposes.

1.5 The lease or buy decision

If assets are leased and the term of the lease is less than 5 years, then the lease payments are in general deductible in computing taxable profits. If they are bought on hire purchase or leased under a long term lease, then the cash price of the assets may qualify for capital allowances and the finance charges are deductible in computing taxable profits, making the tax effects very similar to those of taking out a loan and then buying the asset.

If assets are bought outright then capital allowances may be available on the purchase cost. These will be given on a reducing balance basis each year. The ultimate lease or buy decision is likely to depend on the availability of funds and whether leasing the asset allows the company to keep funds free to finance other activities.

1.6 Other considerations when raising finance

There are several non-tax considerations which are important when finance is being raised for a business. The following points should be considered.

(a) Long term assets should be financed by long term sources of finance. In addition, it is sensible not to rely totally on short term finance for working capital.

(b) The costs of different sources of finance may vary widely. Loans secured on land tend to be the cheapest form of finance, but they are relatively inflexible. Overdrafts are quite expensive, but they may be cheaper than loans in the long term because interest is only paid on the actual amount of funds needed.

(c) The effect of different sources of finance on gearing (the ratio of debt to equity) should be considered. Very high gearing can be very profitable for equity investors if things go well, but it also brings a high risk of insolvency if revenue falls. High gearing can also make potential lenders reluctant to provide any further funds.

(d) A company's shareholders will be interested in the earnings per share (EPS). High gearing tends to make EPS volatile. On the other hand, a large share issue to finance a project which will not produce profits for several years will reduce earnings per share until the new project generates adequate profits.

(e) There may be legal restrictions on borrowing. Some companies have articles which limit their borrowing, and lenders may impose restrictions on the extent to which borrowers can take out further loans. In addition, when an asset is used as security for a loan, the lender will generally want to have a first charge over the asset. Only one first charge can be given over each asset at once, and although a second charge may be given, the lender with that second charge will only be able to obtain repayment out of the proceeds of sale of the asset after the holder of the first charge has been repaid.

2 Mortgage products

FAST FORWARD

A mortgage may be a repayment or interest only mortgage. Endowment policies, ISAs or pension products may be used to accumulate the capital required to repay an interest only mortgage.

2.1 Introduction

Most people who buy a house need to **borrow** to finance the purchase. Mortgage loans are normally repayable not later than the end of a fixed term agreed at the start of the loan.

Key term

A **mortgage** is a loan given on the **security** of a property. The purchaser pays a proportion of the purchase price of a property – a **mortgage deposit** – and the balance is lent by the mortgage lender.

The borrower gives the lender **legal rights over the property** for the duration of the loan. While the loan is outstanding the property is the lender's security that the loan will be repaid.

If the borrower does not keep up repayments on the loan – defaults – **the lender has the right to take possession of the property**, sell it, recover the amount of the loan (assuming the sale price is higher than the loan) and pay the balance to the borrower.

If the loan is repaid according to the terms of the mortgage, the legal rights of the lender over the property cease **at the end of the term**.

Sometimes **a life assurance policy** is part of the conditions of a mortgage as happens when the repayment of capital is made by means of an endowment assurance (see later). Such a life policy is described as collateral security and may be assigned to the lender. It ensures that the mortgage is repaid in the event of the death of the borrower.

2.2 Interest rates

The **interest rate** charged by a lender may be variable (**variable rate mortgage**). Some variable rates of interest are limited to a specified maximum but may rise or fall subject to that maximum. These are **'capped' mortgages**. Others are variable between both a maximum and a minimum rate – **'cap and collar mortgages'**. These are not very common.

Some mortgages are available at a rate of interest which is fixed for a specific period of time (**fixed rate mortgage**).

Discounted mortgages allow a discount on the rate of interest for a specific period of time, typically six months to two years, before the borrower moves to a variable rate mortgage.

Low start mortgages are mortgages where interest only is paid to the lender for an initial period. After this period a full repayment mortgage (see below) starts on the total loan.

Deferred interest mortgages are mortgages where reduced interest is paid for a period. At the end of the period the full mortgage starts and the loan has been increased by the deferred and unpaid interest.

2.3 Methods of repaying capital

During the term of the mortgage the borrower must pay **interest** (see above). There are two methods of **repaying the capital**: during the term or at the end of it.

Key term

If capital is repayable in instalments during the term it is a **repayment mortgage**. When the loan is entirely repayable at the end of the term it is an **interest only mortgage**.

It is possible to **combine the two types of mortgage**. For example, a borrower might borrow £70,000 on a repayment basis and £30,000 on an interest only basis.

2.4 Repayment mortgage

Each time interest is paid to a lender, part of the capital is repaid at the same time. Payments are often of a fixed regular amount. However, flexible mortgages may allow underpayments (ie less than the regular monthly amount), overpayments or payment holidays. There may also be additional borrowing facilities.

This type of mortgage **does not automatically include life assurance**, which needs to be arranged separately.

2.5 Interest only mortgage

These are mortgages where **the entire capital sum which has been borrowed is repaid on the last day of the mortgage**. Most lenders will want the borrower to take some action to accumulate during the term of the mortgage sufficient money to repay the loan.

There are a number of different methods of **accumulating funds** to repay a mortgage. Each one may lead to an interest only mortgage being called by a term which more specifically reflects the method of capital accumulation. Thus an interest only mortgage where a pension is used to accumulate the loan is usually known as a **pension mortgage** (see below).

2.6 Methods of accumulating capital

One of the principal methods of accumulating funds to repay a loan is by means of one of various forms of **endowment** and we now take a brief look at each one of them.

A **with profits endowment** (see later in this text) is effected for the same term as the loan and for a sum assured equal to the loan. There is therefore a guarantee from the beginning that, provided all the premiums are paid, there will be sufficient to repay the loan. Annual and terminal bonuses attaching to the endowment will belong to the borrower. This is an expensive type of mortgage and is rarely used.

In the event of death the sum assured will be sufficient to repay the outstanding loan plus a surplus depending on bonus performance.

In a **non profit endowment** the **sum assured equals the loan** and again, effectively guarantees repayment of the loan. However there is no other benefit apart from life cover and, as the policy is an inefficient method of repaying a mortgage, this type of endowment is also rarely used.

A low cost endowment is a **with profits endowment with the sum assured fixed at a level well below the amount of the loan**. The level is such that, if reversionary bonuses continue at an assumed conservative level, the sum assured will become sufficient to repay the loan by the end of the mortgage term. There is no guarantee that the sum assured will be sufficient to repay the loan, although the use of a conservative estimate of bonuses reduces the risk of this objective not being achieved.

With a low cost endowment policy, the sum assured plus accrued bonuses may be insufficient to pay off the mortgage if death occurs during the term. This potential **shortfall** is covered by means of a decreasing term assurance (see later in this text). Under the term assurance, the sum payable on death is the difference between the amount of the loan and the sum payable under the endowment assurance. In this way the repayment of the mortgage on death within the term is guaranteed. The **cheapness** of the term assurance results in a lower total premium than for a full with profits endowment.

However, the term assurance only pays out if death occurs during the term, so a shortfall can arise if the person survives the term.

Low start low cost endowment is a **low cost endowment, but with lower premiums** for the endowment in the early years of a mortgage. The premiums begin at a lower level than those for an equivalent low cost endowment but increase each year for a period of years. The most common period is five years and the premiums in that case will increase by 20% a year.

With a **unit linked endowment** there is normally no guarantee that the cash value will be the same as, less than or more than the amount of the loan at maturity. Premiums are used to buy units in a chosen fund and units are then cancelled to buy life cover. The **sum payable on death will be the amount of the loan**.

A **pension mortgage** is a mortgage where the borrower uses a lump sum from a pension fund to repay his mortgage. Pensions are looked at in further detail later in this text. Level term assurance (see later in this text) for a sum assured equal to the amount of the loan and for the same term should preferably run alongside the pension policy to provide a benefit in the event of the borrower's death. If this taken out as a pension term assurance, tax relief is available for the premiums paid. Although fiscally attractive, this is an expensive way of funding a mortgage, as only one quarter of the fund built up can be taken as a lump sum. For example, to pay off a £100,000 mortgage, a fund of £400,000 is required. The balance (£300,000) has to be used to buy a pension.

Individual savings accounts provide a method of accumulating capital to repay a mortgage. Again, there will be a need to consider level term assurance with a sum assured equivalent to the outstanding loan. ISA mortgages are more flexible than endowment mortgages but there are greater risks associated with this type of mortgage as the accumulation of capital to repay the mortgage is totally dependent on the performance of the shares or funds chosen.

Cash back mortgages are used by lenders to attract business. A 'cash back' is a cash discount to the borrower on completion of a mortgage. The mortgage could be either a repayment or a interest only mortgage.

Flexible mortgages are repayment mortgages that offer flexibility to the borrower. The flexibility may arise from an irregular payment facility or additional borrowing facilities.

3 Repayment/replacement of borrowings

FAST FORWARD

Careful consideration needs to be given as to whether it is appropriate to repay or replace mortgage borrowings. Consideration should be given to the rate of return available on invested capital, whether capital will be needed in the future and the charges that may be made on the early redemption of the mortgage.

If a borrower has access to capital, he may wish to consider repaying some or all of his mortgage. The following points may be important.

(a) The interest rate should be compared with the net rate of return on investment capital. In general, it is not possible to obtain a net return on capital greater than the interest payments, so a mortgage should be paid off. However, if a borrower is prepared to take the high risk associated with investing in equities, he may be able to obtain greater returns. In this case, he might choose to invest in equities rather than repay his mortgage.

(b) If the borrower may need capital in the future it will probably not be appropriate to repay a mortgage. Paying off a mortgage and then having to borrow again in the near future is an expensive and futile exercise.

(c) There may be charges/penalties associated with repaying the mortgage early.

(d) If the client has an endowment, ISA or pension mortgage, he would also need to take into consideration the future of the investment contract once he had paid back the mortgage in full or part.

If a borrower's mortgage has become uncompetitive or expensive, it may be worth replacing the borrowings. All the costs of redeeming the mortgage should be carefully considered.

4 Calculating net worth and net disposable income

FAST FORWARD

An individual's total assets minus total liabilities should give you an indication of net worth.

The analysis of an individual's current circumstances begins with a form of **accounts**. These should show a list of the individual's assets and liabilities, and reveal whether there is a surplus or a deficit. The accounts will tell you what **'net worth'** an individual has. A pro forma of a net worth calculation is shown below.

STATEMENT OF NET WORTH AS AT ....

	Client	Partner	Joint
ASSETS	£	£	£
Personal assets			
Main home			
Other property			
Personal chattels			
Business assets			
Shares			
Partnership capital			
Business property			
Investment assets			
Bank and building society accounts			
Shares and securities			
Other investments			
Total assets			
Less: liabilities			
Mortgage loan			
Other loans			
Credit card and other debts			
Total liabilities			
Net worth (total assets – total liabilities)			

Total liabilities should take future capital taxation liabilities into account.

The totals derived from the above statement may be used to calculate any potential IHT liability and for inheritance tax planning.

An income and expenditure account should reveal whether there is **disposable income** or a **shortfall**. If there is a disposable income the individual can put into effect at least some of any recommendations which involve additional outlay. If it shows a shortfall it reveals the need for the individual to take corrective action.

CALCULATION OF NET DISPOSABLE INCOME

	Client	Partner
Income	£	£
Salary/ pensions		
State benefits		
Other earned income		
Rental income		
Dividends		
Interest		
Other investment income		
Less: expenditure		
Tax		
Utility bills/Insurance/Telephone		
Mortgage interest		
Car expenses		
Holidays/Clothes/Food		
Life assurance/pensions/Savings		
Subscriptions/clubs		
Books/newspapers		
Other expenses		
Spending money		
Net disposable income		

Current income needs should be measured and this will enable you to check whether or not the protection against a potential disaster situation, such as death and disability, is adequate to meet those needs.

5 Potential disaster situations

FAST FORWARD

It could be important to calculate the shortfall in a number of potential disaster situations. Once the shortfall is calculated appropriate strategies can be developed to protect both wealth and income levels. Disaster situations include premature death, disability, illness and redundancy.

5.1 Introduction

There are a number of **potential disaster situations** against which an individual may wish to protect either himself or his business. In this section we will see how to quantify the loss that might arise as a result of a disaster situation in financial terms.

Potential disaster situations that an individual might face include:

(i) Premature death of himself or his partner
(ii) Redundancy
(iii) Critical illness
(iv) Long term disability
(v) Short term inability to work through accident or illness

Potential disaster situations for a business usually involve the **loss of a key employee** or key person. This could be a result of death, critical illness or long term disability. The short term inability of a key person to work as a result of accident or illness is also a potential disaster situation.

5.2 Calculating the shortfall

Whichever disaster scenario is being considered the method of quantifying any shortfall will follow a similar pattern. First the requirement for income or a lump sum is calculated. Then any existing arrangements are taken into account including state benefits where applicable and finally the shortfall is determined. There are, however, a number of factors which complicate this calculation, including the following.

5.3 Inflation

An allowance will need to be made for **inflation**, in two senses. First, if the need being considered is a future need, for example retirement income, or future school fees, it will be necessary to estimate the amount which will be needed at the relevant time. If no allowance is made for inflation, the amount provided will certainly be too little.

Second, where the need is for income (whether provided specifically, or intended to be generated by a lump sum), the value of that income will be eroded by inflation whilst it is being paid. The calculation should therefore allow for the income to increase during payment.

To illustrate the importance of this, simply consider an individual who retires at age 60, with a level pension of £10,000 per annum. By the time he reaches 85, assuming inflation has been running at a constant annual rate of 3%, the value in real terms of his pension will have fallen to around £4,800. Although State pensions are automatically inflation proofed, this is still likely to represent a dramatic reduction in living standards.

5.4 Growth

For savings and investment arrangements, some allowance will need to be made for the **growth** which is expected to be achieved. The basis on which projections can be given is of course regulated, but generally there will be two figures, based on different growth assumptions.

The **client's attitude to investment** will determine the weight he gives to these figures, and the arrangements and their adequacy should be reviewed regularly in the light of actual performance. In planning terms, it is likely to be advisable to err on the side of caution in expectations of growth.

5.5 Short-term and long-term needs

Some needs are likely to be immediate cash needs, whilst others will require income in the **short or long term**. These differences will also need to be allowed for.

For example, in considering life assurance, if the breadwinner of a family dies, there will be a need for immediate cash to provide for the payment of debts, and for funeral expenses.

In addition, income will be needed to meet the **ongoing expenses** of the family. Part of this income will be needed only for a relatively short term, for example, to cover the additional expenses that arise whilst children are dependent. Some will be needed in the long term however, particularly to support the surviving partner.

5.6 Interest rates

A further important assumption is the **level of interest** which could reasonably be anticipated on the investment of a lump sum. Where the investment is intended to provide income to meet basic needs, it is not appropriate to take risks, and a modest rate of return must be assumed. In current conditions, perhaps 4% per annum net would not be unreasonable.

5.7 Example of a shortfall calculation

Martin and Sylvia Peterson are in their twenties, married, with a young son, Matthew, who is just one year old. Before Matthew was born, they had not paid much attention to life assurance, although their mortgage is covered by a term assurance policy. No other policies are in existence.

Martin earns £18,000 basic salary, and also receives about £4,000 per annum in overtime payments. He is a member of an occupational pension scheme, which includes life assurance of £30,000, and would also provide a widow's pension of £4,500 per annum, which is inflation proofed.

Sylvia does not currently work outside the home, and has no preserved occupational scheme benefits.

Calculate the shortfall if Martin were to die.

5.7.1 Immediate cash requirements

The **mortgage** is already covered, so this can be ignored at this stage.

Other requirements might include:

(a) Funeral expenses
(b) Credit card balances
(c) Overdraft
(d) Other credit agreements
(e) Emergency fund

Emergency fund requirements will vary, particularly depending on whether such a fund exists already, As a general rule, somewhere between 3 and 6 months' income should be allowed, to cover immediate day to day expenses, and any unforeseen needs.

In some cases there may be an **inheritance tax liability** to consider, but we will assume that the surviving partner will inherit the bulk of the estate, with only amounts within the nil rate band passing direct to the children.

The amounts involved will reflect the circumstances of the case. Here let us assume the following:

	£
Funeral expenses	1,200
Credit card balances	600
Overdraft	nil
Other credit agreements	800
Emergency fund	7,500
Total	10,100

5.7.2 Short-term income needs

Matthew is likely to be dependent for at least 15 years, and perhaps longer, so an income needs to be provided to meet the associated costs through that period. A starting point for this calculation is **current cost**, but certainly expenses tend to increase as children get older. In addition, a single parent is likely to need to spend more on child-minding facilities, simply because there is no partner with whom to share the responsibility.

Further costs would arise if school fees were likely to be needed, but, for the purpose of this example, it is assumed that the parents expect Matthew to attend State school.

In this case, a reasonable estimate of short-term income needs associated with Matthew might be £3,600 per annum. As always, careful fact-finding is necessary to determine the needs of specific clients.

BPP PROFESSIONAL EDUCATION

5.7.3 Longer term income needs

These will largely revolve around the **living expenses of the surviving spouse**. The net income of the family is a good starting point here, allowing for any part already taken into account for short term income needs.

Martin's take home pay would be around £1,380 per month, after allowing for tax and national insurance, as well as his overtime. The exact figure will depend on such things as pension contributions, and the adviser should check recent payslips as the best guide.

If Martin died, this income would be lost entirely.

Some **outgoings** reduce too, particularly the **mortgage**, which will have been repaid by the proceeds of the existing life assurance arrangement. Some income has already been included under short term requirements. Suppose that this means that the long term need for income replacement is around £500 less than Martin's take home pay; this gives a figure of £880 per month, net of tax.

5.7.4 Other sources of income and capital

The **life assurance policy** covers the mortgage, and this has been taken into account.

If Martin dies, the pension scheme will provide a cash lump sum of £36,000, and an income of £4,500 per year before tax. The State **widowed parent's allowance** is a further £4,381 per year before tax (this figure would be given to you in an exam if required). Taken together, the income from the pension scheme and the widowed parent's allowance will provide a net income of around £690 per month. This assumes Sylvia claims the income tax personal allowance, but has no further allowances or tax credits.

There are no other sources of income or of capital in this situation.

5.7.5 The shortfall

Immediate cash requirement (see 5.6.1 above)	£10,100
Short-term income shortfall (see 5.6.2 above)	£3,600 per annum net of tax
Long-term income needs (see 5.6.3 above)	£880 per month
Less	
State benefits and pension scheme	£690 per month,
Long-term income shortfall	£190 per month, net of tax.

The pension scheme will pay out a lump sum of £30,000. The shortfall of £190 per month (£2,280 per annum) can be partially met by investing this. The £30,000 invested at 4% net would produce £1,200 per annum, leaving a remaining shortfall of £1,080 per annum.

Exam focus point

If you are asked to calculate the shortfall in an exam situation, you should read the information given to you very carefully. If make any assumptions, you should state clearly what they are.

Chapter roundup

- There are many sources of finance available. For a business, the basic choice is between debt and equity (although some equity will always be needed) and then the appropriate mix of short term and long term debt must be arranged.
- A mortgage may be a repayment or interest only mortgage. Endowment policies, ISAs or pension products may be used to accumulate the capital required to repay an interest only mortgage.
- Careful consideration needs to be given as to whether it is appropriate to repay or replace mortgage borrowings. Consideration should be given to the rate of return available on invested capital, whether capital will be needed in the future and the charges that may be made on the early redemption of the mortgage.
- An individual's total assets minus total liabilities should give you an indication of net worth.
- It could be important to calculate the shortfall in a number of potential disaster situations. Once the shortfall is calculated appropriate strategies can be developed to protect both wealth and income levels.
- Disaster situations include premature death, disability, illness and redundancy.

Quick quiz

1. What are the main sources of finance for private purposes?
2. What is a sale and leaseback arrangement?
3. What non-tax considerations are relevant to the choice of sources of finance to businesses?
4. What are the two main methods of repaying the capital of a mortgage?
5. Why should an income and expenditure account be prepared?

Answers to quick quiz

1. (a) bank overdrafts
   (b) unsecured bank and building society loans
   (c) mortgage loans
   (d) credit cards and credit facilities provided by retailers
   (e) hire purchase facilities
2. An arrangement where, a valuable fixed asset is sold then leased back to the vendor.
3. (a) financing long term assets with long term finance
   (b) costs
   (c) gearing (ratio of debt to equity)
   (d) effect on earnings per share
   (e) legal restrictions
4. Capital of a mortgage may be paid back during the term or at the end of the term.
5. An income and expenditure account will reveal disposable income or shortfall of income.

Now try the question below from the Exam Question Bank

Number	Level	Marks	Time
Q31	Examination	25	45 mins

32 Protection products

Introduction

In this chapter we will look at various financial services products which are available to meet an individual's protection needs.

Topic list	Syllabus references
1 Life assurance	3(c)
2 Health insurance	3(c)
3 Financial provision for long term care	3(c)
4 Redundancy insurance	3(c)
5 Business protection insurance	3(c)

1 Life assurance

FAST FORWARD

Various life assurance products can be used to insure against the risk of death. The tax treatment depends on whether the policy is qualifying or non-qualifying.

1.1 Introduction

In this section we look at three forms of life assurance policy. The tax treatment of all insurance policies for an individual policyholder depends on whether the policy is **qualifying** or **non-qualifying**.

The occurrence of a **chargeable event** may give rise to an income tax charge in respect of a non-qualifying policy but it will not normally do so if a policy is qualifying.

Examples of chargeable events are:

(a) **Death**

(b) **Total surrender** of the policy

(c) **Maturity** of the policy

(d) **Assignment** of the policy (or part of the policy) for **money or money's worth** (including transfer of a policy from joint names to ownership by one of the parties eg on divorce settlement).

When a chargeable event occurs in respect of a non-qualifying policy a chargeable gain will generally be calculated taking into **account the amount received less the premiums paid**. This amount is then divided by the total number of years that the policy has been in force (**top slicing**). The resulting gain is added to the policyholder's existing income to see if it brings him into the higher rate tax bracket (40%). To the extent that it does, he will be taxed at the difference between higher rate and lower rate tax (40%-20%) i.e. 20%. The tax on this slice is then multiplied by the number of policy years in order to get the total income tax charge.

The reason for this tax regime for the investor is that the fund itself suffers corporation tax at 20% on income (other than UK dividends) and gains. This is deemed to meet the basic rate liability of the investor.

A capital gains tax charge may arise on the sale of a policy that was bought for money or money's worth. CGT will not arise in other circumstances.

Some policies still benefit from **life assurance premium relief** (LAPR)

(a) Currently there is no tax relief allowed on life assurance premiums if the policy was effected after **13 March 1984.**

(b) Life assurance **tax relief** is still available for qualifying policies taken out **prior to 14 March 1984**. The current rate of relief is 12.5% of the premium up to the greater of £1,500 per annum or 1/6th of income.

(c) Premiums are paid **net** of income tax to the insurance company.

(d) Relief can be lost if the policy ceases to be **qualifying** or if the benefits are increased or the term extended.

1.2 Term assurance

Key term

> **Term assurance** provides cover for a fixed term with the sum assured payable only on death. There is no investment benefits or payment on survival.

For a term assurance to be **qualifying**, the following rules must apply.

(a) **Where the term is for 10 years or less**

(i) The term must be for at least one year.
(ii) The policy must secure only a capital sum on death – no other benefits.

(b) **Where the policy is for a term over 10 years**

(i) The policy must secure only a capital sum on death – no other benefits.

(ii) The premiums must be paid annually, or more frequently, for at least 10 years or 75% of the term, whichever is shorter.

(iii) The total premiums paid in any one year must not exceed twice the total premiums payable in any other year and 1/8th of the total premiums payable over the whole term.

If the above rules are followed, with the exception of certain policies eg mortgage protection policies and policies under personal pension schemes (see later) which are exempt, then the policy is treated as qualifying for tax purposes.

If a policy is qualifying, the proceeds received on death are free from income tax.

If a policy is non qualifying, death is considered to be a chargeable event and may lead to a liability for income tax on some part of the proceeds at the higher rate as described above.

If the proceeds of a term assurance are not **written in trust**, then they will form part of the deceased's estate. If the estate is worth in excess of £285,000 then **inheritance tax** may be payable. Similarly premiums paid for such a policy could be treated as potentially exempt transfers for inheritance tax purposes although they will usually be covered by the exemption for normal expenditure out of income.

1.3 Whole of life assurance

Key term

> A **whole of life policy** provides protection for a policyholder for life. The sum assured is paid on death at any time.

For a whole of life policy to be qualifying:

(a) The **sum assured** must not be less than 75% of the total premiums payable if death were to occur at the age of 75.

(b) The policy must only secure **capital benefits** on death or disability.

(c) Premiums must be paid for a period **of 10 years or more** (**or earlier death**).

(d) Premiums must be **evenly spread** so that the premiums paid in any one twelve month period are not more than twice the premiums paid in any other twelve month period nor more than 1/8th of the total premiums payable over the first ten years of the policy.

The proceeds received in respect of a qualifying policy are not usually subject to income tax.

If a policy is **non-qualifying,** a chargeable event may be subject to tax as described above.

1.4 Family income benefit

Key term

Family income benefit is a form of term assurance where the benefit reduces over the term of the policy. The premium is, however, level through the term.

In the event of death the sum assured is paid in instalments for the remainder of the policy term. There may be an option to commute the income for a tax free lump sum.

The tax treatment of these policies is as for ordinary term assurance policies described in paragraph 1.1. A policy will be qualifying if it satisfies the rules described in (a) and (b) above.

These policies are normally for a fixed term and have no surrender value. No benefit is payable if the policy holder survives beyond the fixed term.

A problem with these policies can be that the fixed sum assured does not take inflation into account. To overcome this problem it is possible to effect a family income policy where either the benefits increases by a set percentage each year or the benefit remains constant but increases by an agreed amount when a claim arises.

2 Health insurance

FAST FORWARD

Various policies provide some protection in the event of ill health and/or the need for long term care.

2.1 Permanent health insurance (PHI)

Key term

Permanent health insurance policies are designed to provide a policyholder with a benefit if he is unable to work through **sickness**, or if he needs **medical expenses** or **long-term care**.

Sometimes these benefits can be provided by an **individual policy** and sometimes an employee may be fortunate enough to belong to a **group arrangement**.

These policies normally provide a guaranteed level of income in the event of long term sickness regardless of the number of claims and future changes in health.

A small investment return may be possible with a unit linked investment policy.

2.2 Tax situation on permanent health insurance

Individual policies

(a) The benefits payable are not normally taxable. They cannot, however, be treated as 'relevant earnings' for pension contributions (see Chapter 34).

(b) There is no tax relief on premiums paid by an individual.

(c) If the policy is a unit linked policy and on maturity/surrender the value exceeds premiums, a higher rate taxpayer will suffer tax under the non-qualifying rules (see paragraph 1 above).

Group policies

(a) In this case the income is paid to the employer who pays the sick employee through the PAYE system as he remains an employee of the company. This means that pension contributions can continue. The income is therefore subject to tax.

(b) An employer will obtain tax relief on the contributions paid to the schemes as a business expense and the employee will not be taxed on them as a benefit in kind.

(c) If a controlling director is included in the scheme, the premiums paid for his benefits may be allowed as a business expense so long as he has similar and not better benefits than the rest of the group.

2.3 Critical illness insurance

Key term

Critical illness policies are usually written so that a capital sum becomes payable following **diagnosis of one of a large range of critical illnesses** specified in the policy. Note that there is no 'inability to work' criterion.

2.4 Individual critical illness policy

There is no tax relief on individual critical illness policy premiums. Equally, there is no tax to pay should the insured benefit become payable.

2.5 Taxation of group critical illness plan

Critical illness cover may be provided by an employer under a group scheme.

The employer receives tax relief as the cost of providing the critical illness scheme is treated as an allowable business expense.

The employee faces no tax charge in respect of the premiums paid by the employer but, in general, benefits received are subject to tax. However, with regard to the majority of critical illness cover arrangements, schemes have been designed in such a way that there will be no tax charge on the premiums but the benefits will not be subject to tax as they are payable under the terms of a trust.

2.6 Waiver of premium benefit

A **waiver of premium benefit** in an insurance policy is designed to avoid the financial burden to the insured of maintaining insurance premiums when unable to work.

A waiver of premium benefit is a common feature of the whole of life policies discussed above. It is also frequently associated with personal pension plans to ensure that pension benefits are not lost as a result of prolonged incapacity.

If the premium for this benefit is a part of a personal pension plan premium, then for policies effected before 6 April 2001 the premium will benefit from income tax relief in the same way as the personal pension premium itself (see Chapter 34). The waiver of premium benefit is tax-free but the pension contributions paid as a result do not attract tax relief. For policies effected from 6 April 2001, no tax relief is given on the waiver of premium cover itself. However, benefits paid out under the cover will be eligible for tax relief if they are contributions to a personal pension scheme in the same way as any other contributions.

2.7 Permanent and total disability benefit

Certain policies provide for capital sums to be payable in the event of permanent and total disabilities caused by loss of limb or accident.

These benefits may be provided through a personal scheme or through a group scheme.

2.8 Tax treatment of personal accident policies

Capital benefits from personal accident and sickness polices are normally exempt from tax.

There is **no tax relief available on the premiums to individual policies.**

2.9 Tax treatment of group schemes

Employer's premiums will usually be allowed as an expense against business taxation.

If the employee is not an excluded employee (see earlier in this text), then the premium will be assessed to income tax as a **taxable benefit**.

There is **no tax relief available on any employee contribution** to such schemes, but **capital paid to the employee in the event of a claim is normally tax free**.

2.10 Terminal illness cover

Terminal illness cover may be provided under a critical illness insurance scheme (see above). A claim will usually only be paid if there has been a formal medical diagnosis that the policyholder has 12 months or less to live.

3 Financial provision for long term care

3.1 Immediate care annuities

An **immediate care annuity** offers immediate benefits. Capital is used to purchase an impaired life annuity. A higher income is paid out from the annuity because, having taken medical evidence, the actuaries appreciate that the annuitant is unlikely to live long.

No income tax liability arises in respect of a relevant annual payment under an immediate care annuity. The payment must be for the benefit of one person protected under the policy and payment must be made to a care provider or local authority in respect of care for a person protected.

3.2 Long term care plans

There are a wide range of long term care insurance plans. These may be either pure protection plans or investment based long term care plans.

There is no tax relief for premiums paid. However, benefits paid either directly to the care provider or to the insured are tax free.

3.3 Home equity release schemes

These schemes involve raising a loan at a fixed rate of interest on the security of a house with most or all of the funds being used to purchase an annuity.

The annuity is in the form of a purchased life annuity and a large part of the income received will be deemed a return of the investor's capital. **It will not**, therefore, **be subject to income tax**. The income element of the annuity will, however, be taxable.

4 Redundancy insurance

FAST FORWARD

Redundancy insurance or mortgage protection insurance may provide protection in the event of unemployment.

4.1 Unemployment insurance

Unemployment insurance may provide an income in the event of redundancy. Normally redundancy insurance policies are liked to mortgages.

Benefits commence after a deferred period and are normally paid for a maximum of two years.

No tax relief is available on premiums paid, but any benefits payable are not taxable.

4.2 Mortgage protection insurance

Term assurance policies (see above) may be used to insure against the risk of death during the term of a repayment mortgage or an interest-only mortgage where PEPS/ISAs or a personal pension is to be used to repay the capital. Other mortgages are linked to endowment policies. Although endowment policies offer some protection they are primarily savings products and are looked at later in this text.

5 Business protection insurance

FAST FORWARD

Consideration should be given to protecting a company or partnership in the event of death or sickness of a director, partner, keyman or keywoman.

5.1 Introduction

In the case of a business it is important to ensure that the business can continue irrespective of the **death or long-term illness of one of its directors**, **partners** or **other key person**.

It is almost **impossible to safeguard the continuity** of the business in the event of the death or long term illness of a sole trader. He (or she) is the key to the business. Without him/her there is little of value to preserve.

The answer is to **protect the family**, providing a substantial lump sum death benefit through term assurance or whole of life and critical illness cover. It may be useful to take on a short term personal accident and sickness policy complemented by a permanent health policy with a long deferment period. **Medical insurance** is also useful, so that the business is not left for too long while the owner undergoes and recovers from an operation.

As far as protecting a partnership is concerned, the partnership agreement should include clauses stating that each individual partner must **insure his own life** in the event of a critical or long-term illness. He will normally continue to be eligible to draw profits in full or part for some time, at the end of which period he will have to retire from the partnership. The deferred period under the Permanent Health insurance policy should be agreed to fit into this situation, eg if profits are paid for two years, then the Permanent Health insurance policy has a 104 week deferred period.

The partnership agreement should also insert a clause which deals with the **purchase** of each partner's share in the event of his death. In the case of companies, the articles of association will set out the method of sale of the shares of a shareholding director on his retirement or death.

There are three **methods of share purchase for partners or directors.** These are applicable to both partnerships and companies.

(a) A **buy and sell agreement**. On a partner or director/shareholder's death, the remaining partners or directors must buy the deceased's share of the firm from his estate who in turn must sell it.

IHT implications. The deceased's share of the firm forms part of his estate. No BPR applies because there was a binding contract for sale.

(b) The **double option agreement**, or **cross option agreement**. In this instance, if the deceased's estate wishes to sell or the surviving partners, shareholders/directors wish to buy then the other party must comply.

IHT implications. Again the deceased's share of the firm forms part of the estate but this time because there is no binding contract for sale, 100% BPR can be claimed.

(c) **Automatic accrual**. This is more appropriate to partnerships. In this case on the death of a partner no value falls into his estate and his share of the business automatically passes to the surviving partners.

IHT implications. All partners have given up their right to a capital payment on death as a commercial transaction. The value automatically accrues to the remaining partners and no inheritance tax liability exists.

If a **buy and sell or double option agreement** exists life policies should provide the surviving partners, director/shareholders with the necessary funds to buy out the deceased.

If **automatic accrual** applies then, under the partnership agreement, each partner should be obliged to make adequate life assurance provision for his spouse and/or dependants to compensate for the loss of the value of his share of the business.

5.2 Key man cover

In all firms there are **key men and women**. The company will suffer financially through the death or sickness of such a person, so the company needs to insure their lives against **sickness or death**.

Deciding on a suitable **level of cover** is difficult. In coming to a conclusion, the company must take into account the following matters.

(a) Past profits and possible future projections of the company.
(b) How much, financially, the loss of the key person would affect profitability.
(c) The cost of recruiting and training a replacement.

The **tax situation** depends on the type of policy used:

(a) **Term assurance**

(i) If the premiums qualify to be allowed as a business expense then the policy proceeds will be taxed as a trading receipt. If this is the case the employer must take this into account when deciding the level of cover required.

(ii) It may be possible to effect a policy which will pay the sum assured to the company over a number of years. Each year the proceeds will be taxed as a trading receipt but this may help to spread the load.

(iii) If tax relief has not been allowed then the proceeds will not normally be taxed.

(iv) It is important that companies clear the situation with their local Inspector of Taxes at the outset of the contract.

(b) **Whole of life**

(i) The premiums will not be allowed as a business expense.

(ii) Any gain made under such a policy (which normally will be surrender value less premiums paid) will be subject to tax on the gain.

Although in the preceding paragraphs we have concentrated on the situation in the event of **death**, it must be remembered that it is equally important to have **Permanent Health** and **Critical Illness cover** in place.

Chapter roundup

- Various life assurance products can be used to insure against the risk of death. The tax treatment depends on whether the policy is qualifying or non-qualifying.
- Various policies provide some protection in the event of ill health and/or the need for long term care.
- Redundancy insurance or mortgage protection insurance may provide protection in the event of unemployment.
- Consideration should be given to protecting a company or partnership in the event of death or sickness of a director, partner, key man or key woman.

Quick quiz

1. Is income tax payable on the proceeds of a qualifying life policy?
2. What is the tax situation for individual permanent health policies?
3. What is an immediate care annuity?
4. What tax relief is available for redundancy insurance premiums?

Answers to quick quiz

1. No
2. There is no tax relief on premiums. Benefits are not normally taxable. However if the policy is unit linked excess over premiums is subject to 20% tax for higher rate tax payers.
3. A high annuity paid in return for a capital sum to someone who is not expected to live long.
4. Redundancy insurance premiums do not attract tax relief. However, any benefits received are not taxable.

Now try the question below from the Exam Question Bank

Number	Level	Marks	Time
Q32	Introductory	8	15 mins

33

Investment products

Introduction

The syllabus expects you to have awareness of the range of investment products. You need to have knowledge of the structure, types and tax treatment of various products. We look at these products in this chapter. We also look at how investment portfolios should be constructed with regards to such factors as risk, accessibility, liquidity, marketability, flexibility and volatility.

1 Deposit based investments

FAST FORWARD

Most deposit based investments are fairly low risk investments in which an investor receives a low rate of interest in return for depositing his capital with the institution.

1.1 Bank and building society accounts

Bank and building society accounts are, in general, deposit based investments, ie the investor receives a rate of interest in return for depositing his capital with the institution.

The **rate of interest** can be fixed or variable and the term of the investment can be fixed or open ended. Some accounts require investors to give notice of withdrawals, others do not.

The key feature of these investments is that interest payments are the only returns. There is **no growth in the capital value unless the interest is allowed to roll up**.

1.1.1 Tax treatment

Bank and building society **interest is normally paid to individuals net of 20% tax**. The tax suffered at source can be reclaimed. Alternatively, an individual can certify in advance that he is a non-taxpayer and get the interest gross (see Chapter 1).

1.1.2 Risk

The **risk** on bank and building society accounts is low because the capital invested is secure. The risk cannot be said to be nil because there is a chance that the bank or building society will become insolvent but in this event the investor would have recourse to a payout from the Financial Services Compensation Scheme (FSCS) (see Chapter 35).

There is also risk as far as interest rates are concerned. If the account is linked to a variable rate, this may fall. If the account is fixed rate, external interest rates may rise, but the guaranteed rate on the account will, of course, remain unaltered.

1.2 Money market accounts

Some personal investors may invest capital in the money market. This is a facility only available to those with sizeable amounts of capital to deposit for a short term. The bank or building society concerned will quote a guaranteed rate for a fixed period, anything between 'overnight' and one year (the maximum). Once the client accepts the rate the money is held for the agreed term. The rates quoted are directly linked to the interbank rate. There is no access to the capital until the end of the term.

The **interest on money market deposits is paid net of 20% tax** and added to the capital at maturity. **Interest on investments over £50,000 can be paid gross and interest paid on sums invested via offshore banks or building societies is paid gross.**

As with any other bank or building society account (see above), the risk associated with a money market account is low.

1.3 National Savings and Investments

National Savings and Investments (NS&I) products are offered by the government. They are primarily for the small investor.

The **Easy Access Savings Account (EASA)** can be opened with £100 or more. The maximum investment is £2,000,000 (£4,000,000 for joint accounts). Withdrawals of up to £300 can be made by cash card. **Interest is tiered and paid gross. It is liable to income tax and must be declared**.

An **investment account** has a variable interest rate higher than on the EASA and tiered according to the amount invested. Notice of one month is needed for access to funds. **Interest is paid gross but is liable to income tax and must be declared**.

Income bonds provide the investor with a **regular monthly income and total security of capital.** The interest rate is variable but competitive and is tiered according to the amount of the investment. There is no fixed term to the bond and capital can be withdrawn in whole or part having given the required amount of notice or without notice at six weeks loss of interest. **Interest is paid gross but is liable to tax and must be declared**.

A pensioners' bond is only available to those aged 60 or over. The bond runs for a fixed term (one, two or five years) and offers a guaranteed rate of interest. Access to the bond can be obtained with or without notice but an interest penalty will be applied. **Interest is paid gross but is liable to tax and must be declared**.

NS&I Certificates come in two, three and five year investment terms giving a guaranteed rate of interest (either fixed rate or indexed linked in relation to inflation) which is added to the capital and paid out at maturity. There is a maximum investment of £15,000 per issue. **The returns from the Certificates are tax free**, even if encashed early, but early encashment will reduce the rate of interest payable.

Capital bonds do not pay out interest. Interest is added to the original investment over a five year term. The total interest which will be added to the capital is guaranteed and rises over the investment period. **The interest from the capital bond is paid gross on maturity but is liable to tax and must be declared to HMRC annually**.

Fixed rate savings bonds pay a fixed rate of interest net of 20% tax. Bonds are available for various fixed terms. Higher rates are payable for higher sums invested and for longer periods of investment term.

Children's bonus bonds which can be purchased for children under 16, offer a guaranteed rate of interest on the capital invested for a five year period. The maximum investment is £3,000 per issue. **The returns from the Bond are tax free** (even on parental gifts).

Premium bonds are an investment where the monthly interest, instead of being paid to the investor, is paid into a prize fund. Prizes range from £1 million to £50 and are tax free. There is a maximum holding of £30,000.

The **guaranteed equity bond** is a 5 year investment linked to the performance of the FTSE 100 index. Between £1,000 and £1m can be invested. **The returns are liable to income tax as savings income in the year of maturity**.

NS&I also offer **Cash mini ISAs**. These are governed by the normal rules and restrictions.

1.3.1 Risk

As NS&I products are government backed, **the risk is minimal**. Many of the products offer a guaranteed interest rate which makes them very secure. The only risk in such circumstances is a rise in interest rates. In all cases capital is secure.

2 Fixed interest securities

FAST FORWARD

A fixed interest security pays a fixed rate of interest and has a known maturity value so long as it is held until its redemption date.

2.1 Introduction

Key term

A **fixed interest security** is a loan to a government, a local authority, a corporation or a building society. **The security pays a fixed rate of interest and has a known maturity value so long as the stock is held until its redemption date**.

Government securities and corporate bonds are negotiable and can therefore be traded in the market.

2.2 Gilts

UK government securities are known as 'gilts' or gilt-edged securities. Gilts are issued by the government at various times for different terms and rates of interest.

Gilts may be classified into the following groups:

(a) **Shorts**. These gilts have five years or less to redemption

(b) **Mediums**. These gilts have between five and fifteen years to redemption

(c) **Longs**. These gilts have a period in excess of fifteen years to redemption

(d) **Undated**. These gilts have no stated redemption date but the government promises to pay the interest indefinitely

(e) **Index-linked**

(f) **Gilts with a spread of redemption dates**. Some gilts have a spread of redemption dates

2.2.1 Features of gilts

The government promises to pay a **fixed rate of interest** on a gilt, called the coupon, and to repay the capital at set times or redemption dates, for example:

(a) **Treasury 9% 2008**: the redemption date is 2008 and 9% interest is paid on every £100 of stock purchased.

(b) **Treasury 15½% 2008-12**: the redemption date will be somewhere between the two dates. The government can decide when to repay subject to the latest date and giving notice of repayment.

2.2.2 Risk

(a) If an investor buys a gilt at issue and holds it until redemption, there is no risk to his capital or interest return. His original capital will be repaid at redemption and he will have received a fixed rate of interest for the term. A gilt is therefore considered to be a **low risk investment**.

(b) However, an investor who buys a gilt on the market incurs a risk. He may buy today at a yield of 7% only to find that this same gilt can be bought in 12 months time for a yield of 8.5%. **Timing is very important in the purchase and sale of gilts**.

(c) Investors who buy and sell gilts short term, ie actively trading, do incur risk. They are predicting interest rate rises or falls and if they make a mistake they can suffer a substantial loss of capital.

2.2.3 Taxation

(a) **The interest payment on gilts is normally paid gross but is subject to tax.**

(b) Gains made by individuals on gilts are not subject to CGT and losses are not allowable.

(c) The fact that income accruing from a gilt is taxed but capital appreciation is not, makes it important for higher rate taxpayers to make careful choices in the selection of gilts. Such a person requires a gilt with a low coupon but high redemption yield.

(d) If fixed interest securities are purchased via a pooled fund, such as a unit trust or investment bond, the taxation situation will be different (see Section 4 below).

2.3 Local authority bonds

Local authority bonds are for fixed terms at fixed rates of interest.

There is no secondary market in local authority bonds which must be held to maturity. The only exception is the death of the bondholder, when the original investment is repaid.

2.3.1 Tax situation

Interest is liable to income tax and paid net of 20% tax. There is no capital appreciation on the investment and no liability to CGT. Interest can be paid gross if a form R85 is completed.

2.3.2 Risk

This is a low risk investment: both the level of income and the return of capital are guaranteed. The risk, as with all fixed interest investments, is that interest rates will rise and the investor is caught with a fixed rate of interest for the remainder of the term.

The bonds are secured by the assets of the local authority. There is potentially a very small risk in this area, depending on the local authority involved.

2.3.3 Local authority stocks

These have the same characteristics with the exception that they are tradable on the stock exchange.

2.4 Corporate bonds

Corporate bonds are interest-earning securities issued by corporations. The interest rate is normally **fixed**, (but in some cases is variable, related to the London Interbank Offered Rate). A bond has a known maturity value payable at redemption.

Bonds are normally redeemed at par; ie bonds with £100 nominal value will be redeemed at maturity for £100. The market value of a bond before redemption will vary inversely with interest rates, consequently the owner of a bond will benefit from a capital gain if market interest rates fall, or will suffer a capital loss if market interest rates rise.

Corporate bonds issued in the UK are also known as **debentures** or **loan stock**. Corporate bonds issued in the international bond markets are called **eurobonds**.

2.4.1 Features of corporate bonds

A debenture is usually established under trust. The trust deed protects the position of the lender in the event of the company winding up and limits the other debt the company can issue. Eurobonds are not established under trust, but protection is provided for bondholders in the form of covenants associated with the bond issue.

The company issuing the loan will have to pay interest from pretax profits and also find the money to make the capital repayment on redemption.

The position of the bondholders in the event of the winding up of a company will depend upon whether the bonds are secured or unsecured. They may be secured on a fixed asset such as a property or by a floating charge over the company's assets.

2.4.2 Types of corporate bonds

There are a number of different types of loan stock.

(a) **Secured loan stock** (debentures)

(b) **Unsecured loan stock**. This is the least protected loan security. In the event of default the holders only rank with other unsecured creditors (such as suppliers).

(c) **Convertible Loan Stock** offers a fixed interest rate (usually lower than a straight fixed interest security) plus the option to convert into ordinary shares at a later date on a pre-stated formula.

2.4.3 Risk

An investor in a fixed rate corporate bond takes the **risk that market interest rates will rise while he is locked into the bond's fixed interest payment**. He can then sell it on the market, but the bond's price will have fallen as its yield has become less attractive.

The investor may be concerned that the profits of the company will be insufficient to pay the interest and repay the debt at maturity. There is a higher risk of non-payment than with a government security and investors will expect to receive a higher return from corporate bonds in compensation. Large companies which are financially secure should not need to offer an interest rate much above the rate on gilts. Smaller companies will have to offer very attractive rates to persuade investors to take the risk.

2.4.4 Taxation

Interest on corporate bonds is usually paid gross, but if the issuing company is not listed on a recognised stock exchange it is paid net of 20% tax. This tax can be repaid.

If the bond is a **qualifying corporate bond**, then it is **an exempt asset** for CGT purposes (see earlier in this Text).

3 Packaged investments

FAST FORWARD

Collective and packaged investments may be attractive to the smaller and less sophisticated investor.

The small or unsophisticated investor may invest through a fund managed by professionals.

3.1 Endowment policies

An **endowment policy** is a savings and life assurance policy for an agreed period. The minimum period is 10 years with terms up to 20 or 25 years. A benefit is paid out at maturity or on earlier death. There are various types of policy as detailed below.

With-profits. Bonuses, which depend on investment performance, are added to a sum assured. Bonuses may be added annually and at the end of the term.

Non-profit. In this case there is a guaranteed sum paid out at maturity or previous death.

A low cost endowment is a combination of a **with-profits endowment** and **decreasing term assurance.** It is cheaper than a with profits policy and has often been used as a means of repaying an **'interest only' mortgage**. Bonuses are added to the endowment sum assured at an assumed rate and the term assurance decreases at the same rate. The result is that there **should** be sufficient cover to repay the mortgage at the end of the period. **The situation on death is normally guaranteed**. The death benefit will be sufficient to repay the mortgage.

With **unit-linked endowment policies** premiums buy units in a fund of the investor's choice. Units will be cancelled each month to buy the life cover. There is investment flexibility and funds can be switched.

A **Low start endowment** is a variation on the low cost theme and was introduced to help young 'first time house buyers'. The level of cover is the same as for a low cost endowment but the premium starts at a lower level and increases by, say, 10% per annum for five years. It then remains constant for the remainder of the term.

Flexidowment policies are designed for the investor who requires flexibility. The policy is written for a total term, to say age 65, with options to encash after 10 years, without penalty.

The **guaranteed growth bond** provides a guaranteed growth on capital at the end of a fixed term, say five years. The **guaranteed income bond** offers a regular annual or monthly payment at a guaranteed rate for a fixed term. At the end of the term the original investment is returned.

Some guaranteed growth and income bonds are written as **single premium endowment policies**. As such they are **non-qualifying policies**. This means the proceeds of a guaranteed income or growth bond could be subject to tax on encashment if the investor was a higher rate taxpayer (see the previous chapter).

3.1.1 Tax treatment

There is no tax on the benefits from a qualifying endowment policy.

3.1.2 Risk

A with profits policy is traditionally seen as low to moderate risk. There is a guaranteed sum assured to which bonuses are added and, once added, normally cannot be removed however poor future performance may be. The only risks are that future bonus rates will drop and that any terminal bonus may be low or non-existent.

There is a risk on early encashment. The surrender or paid-up values will include penalties which cannot be assessed in advance. Many with profits policies have no surrender value in the first 12 months. There could also be a tax implication on early encashment

In the event of an insurance company going into liquidation policyholders are protected by the FSCS, which will pay out a minimum of 90% of a policyholder's guaranteed fund at the time of default.

3.2 Traded endowment policies

Policyholders may wish to encash their endowment policies. One option is to obtain a surrender value quotation. A second option is to sell the policy on the traded market. Policies sold in this way are sometimes referred to as **Traded Endowment Policies (TEPs)** or second hand endowment policies (SHEPs).

3.2.1 Tax situation for the seller

(a) **If the policy being sold is a qualifying one which has been in force for ten years or three-quarters of the term if less, then there is no tax liability on the seller.**

(b) **If the policy is a non qualifying or a qualifying policy that has been in force for less than ten years or three-quarters of the term, then a chargeable event will occur.** If the price raised exceeds the premiums paid then a charge to higher rate income tax could occur. The tax charge would only occur if, after applying top-slicing relief to the gain and adding this to the policyholder's income, it brought him into the higher rate tax bracket. The gain would then be subject to tax at 20%. (See previous chapter.)

3.2.2 Tax situation for the purchaser

At maturity or on the death of the life assured or the owner, **the proceeds of a qualifying policy may be subject to CGT**.

3.2.3 Risk

There is no risk for the seller. He has already decided that he no longer needs the policy or he cannot afford it. The price he obtains will be better than the surrender value, so he has made a profit and should be happy.

The buyer runs the risk that the future annual bonuses of the provider will not continue at current rates and that the terminal bonus paid on maturity may be substantially less than predicted.

3.3 Single premium bonds

A **single premium bond** is a packaged product available for the investment of a lump sum.

Key term

> A **single premium bond**, also called an investment bond or unit-linked bond, is in fact a non-qualifying single premium whole of life policy. The money is invested to buy units in a selected fund.

The advantages of single premium bonds are as follows.

(a) The investment bond is primarily a **packaged investment for growth**.

(b) There is a facility **to effectively take an income by encashing units** in order to take account of the 5% withdrawal facility (see 3.3.1).

(c) It is **simple to operate**. The investor is not bothered with dividend vouchers and complications on the tax return.

(d) There is a choice of a **wide range of geographical funds** and the ability to switch between economies with nil or minimal charge.

3.3.1 Tax treatment

If the policyholder is the owner of the bond, there is no **CGT on encashment**.

The bond is a **non-qualifying whole of life policy**, so on encashment or on partial encashment a **chargeable event** will occur. This may give rise to an income tax charge.

The investor can make **withdrawals of 5% of the original investment each year with no immediate tax implications**. In this way he can defer taxation until final encashment. If the investor takes no withdrawal for a few years he may make up the backlog of his tax free withdrawal limit. However, once the limit is exceeded, tax is charged on the excess irrespective of the underlying performance of the bond.

Tax on final encashment. The gain on encashment is equal to the encashment value plus the value of any withdrawals less the purchase price. Top slicing will be applied to see if any of this gain will be subject to income tax at 20%.

There are a number of important things to note.

(a) The **whole of the gain** (i.e. before top slicing) is taken into account when determining whether an investor will lose his age allowance in the year of encashment.

(b) No **'top slicing'** occurs if the owner of the policy is a company.

(c) If an individual makes a **capital loss** it can only be deducted from taxable income for the purposes of higher rate tax and to the extent that earlier gains have been taxed.

3.3.2 Accessibility

The bond has no fixed term, so it can be encashed in whole or part at any time. However, it is sensible to keep it in force for **at least five years** to recoup 'up front' charges.

3.3.3 Risk

The investor selects his own funds and can therefore chose his own level of risk.

3.4 Annuities

Key term

An **annuity** is a contract whereby the insurance company agrees to pay to the investor a guaranteed income either for a specific period or for the rest of his or her life in return for a capital sum. The capital is usually non-returnable and hence the income paid is relatively high.

There are various types of annuity:

(a) With an **immediate annuity**, a purchase price is paid and the insurance company immediately pay a guaranteed income. It is possible to include a guarantee within the annuity (**a guaranteed annuity**) so that payments are made for a minimum period regardless of survival. Alternatively, it is possible to completely protect the capital value of the annuity. This means that, when the annuitant dies, the insurance company adds up the amount paid out in gross annuity payments and, if this is less than the original investment, the balance is returned to the estate (**capital protected annuity**).

(b) With a **temporary annuity** the insurance company pays a guaranteed income to the annuitant for a fixed period (for example five years) or until earlier death.

(c) **Joint life and last survivor annuities** are used primarily for married couples who want to ensure that the income from their annuity continues until the last death.

(d) There are a number of types of **increasing annuity**. In the basic type the income payable will increase by an agreed amount, eg 5% per annum.

(e) The payment of an annuity may be deferred to a later date (a **deferred annuity**).

(f) An **annuity certain** is paid out irrespective of the survival of the annuitant.

(g) A **with profits annuity** is linked to the performance of a with-profits fund.

(h) A **unit-linked annuity** is linked to the performance of a unit-linked fund.

(i) **Compulsory purchase** or **open market option annuities** are purchased with the proceeds of pension funds (see Chapter 34). The annuity purchased from an occupational scheme is known as a compulsory purchase annuity. The annuity purchased under a personal pension is known as an open market option. These annuities are taxed as earned income. There is no distinction between capital and interest.

Purchased life annuities (i.e. non-pension annuities) have a capital and interest element. The split is pre-agreed between HMRC and the insurance company. Only the interest content is taxed. The interest element is, in general, paid net of 20% tax but, in certain circumstances, non taxpayers and non UK residents can receive the interest element gross.

3.4.1 Risk

The risks associated with annuities are as follows.

(a) The loss of capital to the purchaser.

(b) In most cases an annuity is providing a fixed income which will reduce in purchasing power over the years.

(c) If an increasing annuity is selected, the annuitant has to live many years to be in a 'gain situation' because payments start at a very low level.

(d) If an income linked to the performance of a unit linked or with profits fund is selected, the annuitant runs the risk of poor performance and an annuity which varies from payment to payment.

(e) An annuity is a fixed income. If interest rates increase, the annuitant is tied into a fixed annuity based on a lower rate.

3.5 Back-to-back packages

Sometimes insurance companies package annuities and other qualifying policies or investments to provide clients with an income or growth investment funded from capital. These are known as **back-to-back arrangements**.

Examples of income/growth product packages are:

(a) 5 year temporary annuity and unit trust
(b) 5 year temporary annuity and ISA (see later in this chapter)
(c) 5 year temporary annuity and 5 year endowment

The original capital investment is split between the two investments.

If income is required, the annuity pays out the income and it is hoped that the growth on the investment will be sufficient to repay the original capital. **There is no guarantee**.

If growth is required, the income from the annuity is used to **'boost' the investment**.

Sometimes back-to-backs are used for **inheritance tax planning**. In this instance the combination of contracts is: **Immediate annuity** and **whole of life policy.** The capital sum is split to purchase the annuity and pay the first premium under the whole of life policy.

3.5.1 Tax treatment

The tax treatment of these plans depends on the combination of products used and the reader should refer to the relevant section in this chapter.

3.5.2 Risk

(a) The schemes outlined are designed to give the investor a high level of income which, if a temporary annuity is used, will be guaranteed. There is, of course, a risk that interest rates will rise and then what appeared to be a high income loses its appeal.

(b) As the schemes are designed to provide a high income, insufficient capital may be invested in the 'capital appreciation' portion of the scheme and the capital growth may be poor so that the original investment cannot be returned. There is also the risk that if the capital appreciation is being sought from equity based investments, that the investment returns may be low if a poor performing fund is chosen, there is a stock market crash or the initial investment is made when the market is high.

(c) Many back to back schemes are only designed for a five year term which may be too short an investment period to obtain the returns required.

(d) If an endowment policy is chosen, the returns may be eaten up by high charges.

3.6 Gift and loan trusts

The gift and loan scheme is a particular type of scheme aimed at reducing IHT. It works in the following way:

(a) The settlor creates a trust to which he gives £3,000 as a PET.

(b) The settlor subsequently lends the trustees a much larger amount of money, say £100,000. This is an interest-free loan repayable on demand.

(c) The original gift and the loan are invested in an investment bond. The trustees take advantage of the 5% withdrawal facility to repay the loan to the donor over a 20 year period.

(d) The inheritance tax implications are:

  (i) The original gift is not chargeable to IHT as it makes use of the annual IHT exemption.

  (ii) On the settlor's death any outstanding loan is repaid to his estate from the proceeds of the bond and may be subject to IHT. The estate is also responsible for any charge to higher rate tax which may have occurred on the encashment of the bond. Whether this is payable will depend on the settlor's income in the year of death.

  (iii) The balance of the bond is paid to the beneficiaries free of IHT.

4 Collective investments

A collective or pooled investment is a scheme in which a large number of small investors pool their money to purchase shares or other securities. By doing this they are able to participate in a much larger spread of investments than they could individually own and in this way they reduce their exposure to risk.

4.1 Unit trusts

A unit trust is a pooled investment of shares and/or securities. It is possible for the investor to purchase units in a wide range of funds.

The unit trust is an open ended fund. This means that the size of the unit trust varies with the number of units in issue. If investors wish to invest in the fund, new units are created to meet demand and the manager invests the money raised in shares or securities. Investors sell back their units to the manager who must buy them back.

The unit trust will be established under a **deed of trust** which appoints trustees, often a bank.

The investment of the fund is run by a **fund manager** who is responsible for the selection and management of the shares within the portfolio.

The funds can **specialise in overseas markets** or be **UK based** with an emphasis **either on income or capital growth**.

In some funds it is possible to buy **income or accumulation units**. If accumulation units are purchased, the income is rolled up either in the price or by the issue of additional units.

To spread the risk still further, some unit trusts are **'funds of funds'**. This means a trust that buys units in other unit trusts.

Tracker or index funds are available. These funds mimic the performance of an index such as the FTSE 100. Such funds have lower charges because they are cheap to run. It is a computer operation. An expensive fund manager is not required.

One of the main drawbacks of a unit trust is that in a falling market the unsophisticated investor, who favours unit trusts, may rush to sell his holding. The manager will be obliged to buy back the units and in order to repay the unitholders he may have to sell shares at an unfavourable price. Often his best holdings must be disposed, as these will be the only ones **easily marketable in a crisis**. This will reduce the price of the units still further and make it difficult for the fund to recover and show good performance in the following months.

Investments can be **lump sums** with a minimum of £500 or £1,000 per fund. It is also possible to **save on a regular basis**.

4.1.1 Risk

The benefit of a unit trust is that **the investor is able to spread his risk** by investing in a pool of shares. He is also able to spread his risk geographically by investing in, say, an international fund. The risk for most unit trust funds will be **medium to high** depending on the underlying shares in the portfolio.

4.1.2 Taxation of the individual investor

The taxation of income received from a unit trust varies depending on its source. Income can be received from an **equity unit trust** (with at least 40% of the assets invested in equities) or a **non-equity unit trust**.

The dividends from an equity unit trust are taxed in the same way as other dividends. They are subject to income tax and are received by the investor with a tax credit of 10%.

The payments from a non-equity unit trusts will be treated as payments of interest and will be paid to the investor net of 20% tax.

Capital gains made by an investor on the sale of a unit trust will be subject to CGT.

4.2 Investment trusts

Key term

Investment trusts are companies quoted on the London Stock Exchange whose business is investing in other companies' shares.

The investment trust has a **fixed issued share capital** and the shares must be sold in the market so, if there is no demand, then the shares cannot be sold.

The investment trust shareholders have the **same rights as all shareholders**.

Usually the shares of an investment trust sell at a **discount to net asset value**. What this means is that the assets less the liabilities of the trust divided by the number of shares in issue is greater than the current price of the share in the market. Similarly the shares can from time to time sell at a **premium to net asset value**.

The investment company, like all companies, has a **facility to borrow money**. In this instance the company is borrowing money to buy more shares and increase the value of the trust. If the borrowings are high, relative to its total capital value the company is said to be **heavily geared**. In a rising stock market a trust which is highly geared can perform well but in a falling market the effect of interest to be paid on the borrowings may be onerous. Investment trusts can be **geared to produce income or growth**.

Investment trusts invest in shares **in all parts of the world**. The choice of funds is as wide, if not wider, than for unit trusts.

4.2.1 Risk

The **level of risk** will depend on the underlying investment of the trust. If the investment is blue chip UK companies, the risk will be medium; if the trust is investing in, for example, the Indian sub-continent the risk will be greater.

4.2.2 Tax treatment

The **investor is taxed** on dividend income in the normal way and any **capital gains** on a share may be subject to CGT.

4.3 Open-ended investment companies (OEICs)

An OEIC is an **open-ended company.** It is similar to a unit trust but issues shares rather than units.

The **company issues shares**. These are usually participating redeemable preference shares rather than ordinary voting shares. An OEIC can issue many types of share under one management and this is referred to as an 'umbrella fund'. Each share can invest in a different international sector. There is usually a wider choice of funds than with a unit or investment trust. The risk will depend on the fund invested in.

The value of an OEIC share should normally reflect the net asset value (NAV) of the fund.

OEIC shares trade at a **single price of NAV**. There is a separately disclosed initial buying charge of 3%.

4.4 Personal equity plans (PEPs)

PEPs were introduced to encourage share ownership. It has been impossible to make any further contributions to PEPs since 6 April 1999 but those schemes already in operation then may continue.

4.4.1 Risk

Risk will depend on the PEP selected. PEPs are normally equity investments and as such there is a risk. If a corporate bond PEP was selected there is still a risk of capital loss and variable income if the bonds have a variable coupon.

4.4.2 Tax treatment

No tax is paid on income or capital growth for any taxpayers. There is no minimum investment period to achieve the tax free status.

4.5 Individual savings accounts (ISAs)

Key term

ISAs are tax efficient savings accounts. They can be made up of two components.

- Cash
- Stocks and shares

There can be a single account manager or one manager for each component of the account. The investor must be resident and ordinarily resident in the UK in the year the investment is made. The investor must normally be 18 years or over. However, a cash only ISA can be held by individuals aged 16 or 17.

There are two distinct types of ISA:

(a) **Maxi-accounts** which must normally contain a stocks and shares component and may contain the cash components (either one or both), but must contain only a cash component for investors under 18 years of age.

(b) **Mini-accounts** which comprise a single component only:

Once an account has been designated by the manager as being of a particular type it retains that designation and cannot be altered.

A **'maxi-account'**, must contain a stocks and shares component with or without other components. Subscribing to a maxi-account in one year precludes an investor from also subscribing to a mini-account of any type in that year. **There is a general annual subscription limit for maxi-accounts of £7,000 of which a maximum of £3,000 can be in cash.** For a maxi-account held by an investor between 16 and 18 years of age, there is a limit of £3,000.

A **mini-account** comprises a single component only. Once a mini-account, for any component, has been subscribed to for a particular tax year the only other ISA that may be subscribed to for that year is another mini-account comprising the other component. **The annual subscription limits for mini-accounts are:**

(a) **Cash component accounts; £3,000.**
(b) **Stocks and shares component accounts; £4,000.**

Investors under 18 years of age can only invest in a cash mini-ISA.

The stock and shares element may contain medium term stakeholder products (Unit linked, unit linked insurance and 'smoother' products). **All non-stakeholder life insurance may also be held in the stocks and shares component. Investments producing a 'cash like' return** (capital not at risk or at minimum risk) **are restricted to the cash component.**

4.5.1 Risk

The risk of an ISA depends on which ISA component is invested in and possibly on the underlying funds invested in.

4.5.2 Tax treatment

Investments within an ISA are exempt from both income and capital gains tax.

4.6 Child trust Fund (CTF)

CTF accounts are available from 6 April 2005 for children born after 31 August 2002. **The CTF is initially funded by a Government voucher** (£250 or £500 for lower income families). **It is also possible for friends and family (including parents) to contribute up to a total of £1,200 a year to the account.**

The CTF is held for the child until he reaches 18. There are different sorts of accounts including cash **accounts, unit trusts and life products**.

4.6.1 Risk

Risk depends on the CTF selected, in relation to the underlying investments.

4.6.2 Tax treatments

There is no income tax or capital gains tax payable on the CTF. This applies even if parental contributions have been made.

5 Equities

FAST FORWARD

Equities are high risk investments as neither the income nor the capital is secure.

5.1 Types of share

When an investor buys a share in Marks and Spencer plc that is exactly what he has done; he has bought a share in the ownership of the company.

The features of the three types of share within your syllabus are:

Type of share	Features
Ordinary shares	The shareholder is entitled: (a) to a share of profit distributed as a dividend (b) the right to vote on matters affecting the company (c) in the event of a winding up, to a share of assets, but note that shareholders do not take precedence over the creditors
Preference shares	(a) These shareholders are placed ahead of the ordinary shareholders for dividend payments and in the event of a liquidation. (b) The dividend is usually a guaranteed amount but if the distribution to the ordinary shareholders is higher, the preference shareholders do not receive the increase.
Convertible preference shares	The dividend paid on these is usually less than the non-convertible preference share but there is the option to convert to ordinary shares in the future at pre-set dates and at pre-set prices.

5.2 Risk

Shares give the investor the chance of increasing income and capital growth but there is **no guarantee** of either, and so it is a **high risk investment**.

The amount of risk which the investor takes depends upon the **type of company** into which he invests. If he buys shares in blue chip companies the risk should be modest. If the investor selects **a smaller company or a company** which has been through a poor trading period then the risk is greater.

The amount of **risk also depends on the type of share**. Ordinary shares carry more risk than preference shares.

5.3 Tax treatment

Dividends are received with a non-refundable tax credit of 10%. The gross amount of dividends received are subject to income tax as described earlier in this Text.

A capital gain arising on a share is subject to CGT. Losses are also allowable losses.

6 Venture capital schemes

FAST FORWARD

The enterprise investment scheme and venture capital trusts are designed to help unquoted trading companies raise finance.

6.1 The enterprise investment scheme (EIS)

Key term

The **EIS** is a scheme designed to promote enterprise and investment by helping high-risk, unlisted trading companies raise finance by the issue of ordinary shares to individual investors who are unconnected with that company.

6.1.1 Tax treatment

Individuals who subscribe for EIS shares are entitled to both income tax and capital gains tax reliefs.

6.1.2 Income tax relief

Individuals can claim a **tax reducer** (see Chapter 1) **of the lower of**:

(a) **20% of the amount subscribed for qualifying investments** (maximum qualifying investment is £400,000 and

(b) **The individual's tax liability for the year** after deducting VCT relief (see 6.2) but before deducting other tax reducers

Question — **EIS relief**

Mr Matthews, a married man aged 40, has STI of £50,000 (all non-savings income) for 2006/07. He subscribes £75,000 for shares and he claims EIS relief. The shares are issued to him in December 2006. What is his 2006/07 income tax liability?

Answer

	£
STI	50,000
Less: PA	(5,035)
Taxable income	44,965

	£
£2,150 × 10%	215
£31,150 × 22%	6,853
£11,665 × 40%	4,666
	11,734
Less: EIS relief (£75,000 × 20% = £15,000, limited to £11,734)	(11,734)
Income tax liability	Nil

To be eligible for relief the minimum subscription of shares in any company is £500. The maximum EIS investments qualifying for income tax relief is £400,000 in 2006/07, but individuals can invest in excess of this amount if they wish.

If shares are issued in the first six months of the tax year (ie before 6 October), the investor may claim to have up to half of the shares treated as issued in the previous tax year. This is subject to a maximum carry back of £50,000 if £100,000 or more shares are issued in the first six months.

When carrying back relief, relief given in the previous year must not exceed overall EIS limits for that year. The limit for 2005/06 was £200,000.

Shares must be held by an investor for at least three years if the income tax relief is not to be withdrawn or reduced if the company was carrying on a qualifying trade at the time of issue. For companies which were preparing to trade at the time of issue, the minimum holding period ends when the company has been carrying on a qualifying trade for three years.

The main reason for the withdrawal of relief will be the sale of the shares by the investor within the three year period mentioned above. The consequences depend on whether the disposal is at arm's length or not:

(a) If the disposal is not a bargain at arm's length the full amount of relief originally obtained is withdrawn.

(b) If the disposal is a bargain at arm's length there is a withdrawal of relief on the consideration received. As the relief was originally given as a tax reduction, the withdrawal of relief must be made at the same rate of tax.

Question

Withdrawal of EIS relief

Ted Edwards, a single man, makes a £60,000 EIS investment in 2006/07. His income (all non-savings) for the year is £45,000. In 2007/08, Ted sells the shares (an arms length bargain) for £50,000. How much EIS relief is withdrawn as a result of the sale of the shares?

Answer

	£
2006/07	
STI	45,000
Less: personal allowance	(5,035)
Taxable income	39,965

	£
£2,150 × 10%	215
£31,150 × 22%	6,853
£6,665 × 40%	2,666
	9,734
Less: EIS relief: £60,000 x 20% = £12,000, restricted to	(9,734)
Income tax liability	Nil

The effective rate of EIS relief is $\frac{9{,}734}{60{,}000} \times 100 = 16.2233\%$

2007/08

The sale of the shares for £50,000 as a bargain at arm's length results in the withdrawal of income tax relief in 2007/08 of £8,112 (ie £50,000 × 16.2233%).

Although the company must be unlisted when the EIS shares are issued, there is no withdrawal of relief if the company becomes listed, unless there were arrangements in place for the company to cease to be unlisted at the time of issue.

There are anti-avoidance rules to prevent an individual extracting money from the company without disposing of his shares. However, the rules do not apply where the amount is of an insignificant value (eg any amount of £1,000 or under) or if the receipt is returned without unreasonable delay.

Where shares qualify for income tax relief under the EIS there are also special rules that apply to those shares for capital gains purposes:

(a) Where shares are disposed of after the three year period any gain is exempt from CGT. If the shares are disposed of within three years any gain is computed in the normal way.

(b) If EIS shares are disposed of at a loss at any time, the loss is allowable but the acquisition cost of the shares is reduced by the amount of EIS relief attributable to the shares. The loss is eligible for S574 ICTA 1988 relief (see earlier in this text).

Question

Allowable losses

During 2004/05 Martin invested £35,000 in EIS shares and received relief against income tax of £35,000 × 20% = £7,000.

The shares are sold in February 2007 for £15,000. This will lead to a withdrawal of EIS relief of £15,000 × 20% = £3,000. What is the allowable loss for CGT purposes?

Answer

	£	£
Disposal proceeds		15,000
Less: cost	35,000	
EIS relief (7,000 – 3,000)	(4,000)	(31,000)
Allowable loss		(16,000)

If the shares had instead been sold outside the three year relevant period (ie so that there was no withdrawal of income tax relief), the allowable loss would instead be:

	£	£
Disposal proceeds		15,000
Less: cost	35,000	
EIS relief	(7,000)	(28,000)
Allowable loss		(13,000)

EIS reinvestment relief may be available to defer chargeable gains if an individual invests in EIS shares in the period commencing one year before and ending three years after the disposal of the asset (see earlier in this text).

6.1.3 Risk

EIS investments are high risk investments because there is total exposure to unquoted shares.

6.2 Venture capital trusts (VCTs)

Key term

Venture capital trusts (VCTs) are listed companies which invest in unquoted trading companies and meet certain conditions.

6.2.1 Risk

The VCT scheme differs from EIS in that the individual investor may spread his risk over a number of higher-risk, unquoted companies.

An individual investing in a VCT obtains the following tax benefits on a maximum qualifying investment of £200,000 in 2006/07.

- **A tax reduction of 30% of the amount invested** (40% for investments made in 2005/06).
- **Dividends received are tax-free income.**
- **Capital gains on the sale of shares in the VCT are exempt** from CGT (and losses are not allowable).

In addition, capital gains which the VCT itself makes on its investments are not chargeable gains, and so are not subject to corporation tax.

If the shares in the VCT are disposed of within five years of issue, the following consequences ensue.

- **If the shares are not disposed of under a bargain made at arm's length, the tax reduction is withdrawn.**
- **If the shares are disposed of under a bargain made at arm's length, the tax reduction is withdrawn, up to the disposal proceeds × 30%.**

If a VCT's approval is withdrawn within five years of the issue, any tax reduction given is withdrawn.

Note that there is no minimum holding period requirement for the benefits of tax-free dividends and CGT exemption.

7 Property

7.1 Residential investment property

7.1.1 Advantages of residential property as an investment

(a) One of the advantages of residential property is psychological: most people like the security of a permanent home they own, subject, no doubt, to a mortgage.

(b) In the past property values have kept pace with inflation, although this may not be repeated in the future.

(c) It is possible to use a property as part of an investor's retirement fund. He can decide to sell a large house, move down market and use the surplus funds to invest and create income.

(d) If for some reason the owner cannot live in his property for a period, say, because he is working abroad, the property can be let and used to create an income.

(e) Similarly, if a client owns a holiday home, this can be let for part of the year. The rental income will, hopefully, offset general running expenses.

(f) Residential property can, of course, be used as collateral security for a loan.

7.1.2 Disadvantages of residential property as an investment

(a) One of the main disadvantages of any property is **illiquidity**. The property can only be sold if a buyer can be found. Often the sale of a property can be protracted and the vendor may be incurring expenses during this period.

(b) If a property is leased out there may be times when a suitable tenant cannot be found. In addition there are charges involved in letting property.

7.1.3 Tax situation on property investments

(a) If a house is the investor's **principal private residence** the sale of the property will be **exempt from CGT**.

(b) Rent arising from the letting of a room in the individuals main residence may be **exempt** from income tax under the **rent a room scheme**.

(c) If the investor owns furnished holiday accommodation he may be able to treat the letting as a trade (see earlier in this text).

7.2 Commercial property

Much of the commercial property in the UK is the property of large institutions such as insurance companies and pension funds.

7.2.1 Advantages of commercial property as an investment

(a) The price of commercial property may keep pace with inflation although this is by no means guaranteed.

(b) Property can produce an increasing rental income if good tenants can be found.

(c) It provides a balance in the investment portfolio particularly as the performance of property may be directly opposed to the performance of the stock market.

7.2.2 Disadvantages of commercial property as an investment

(a) Slumps in the property market may be more protracted than slumps in share prices.

(b) Commercial property may remain untenanted for long periods during which time there is no rental income and the underlying value of the property may fall.

(c) Commercial property is very **illiquid**. It may take many months to sell.

(d) Property can be **expensive to manage**.

7.3 Buy to let

'Buy to let' refers to the purchase of property – usually residential property purchased by individuals – with the purpose of letting it.

7.3.1 Advantages of buy to let

(a) For a relatively small capital outlay, the investor can gain exposure to housing market gains
(b) As well as any capital gain, rents are received and will offset interest costs

7.3.2 Disadvantages of buy to let

(a) In areas of weak housing demand, or over-supply, properties may be vacant for long periods

(b) If house prices fall, losses may be suffered

(c) It may take some time to sell property in order to realise gains

(d) Capital gains will be taxed

7.4 Real Estate Investment Trust (REITs)

Investing in a Real Estate Investment Trust (REIT) rather than in an individual property enables the Investor to spread the investment over a number of properties. The shares should be more marketable than a property would be, but the investor is still exposed to fluctuations in the property market.

Distributions from property income and gains from REITs are taxable as property income, and are paid under deduction of basic rate tax. Gains on disposals of shares are subject to CGT in the normal way.

8 Constructing an investment portfolio

FAST FORWARD

When constructing an investment portfolio, the adviser will need to consider risk, accessibility, liquidity, marketability, flexibility and volatility.

8.1 Identifying needs

An adviser must gather information that will enable him to establish his client's investment needs and then prioritise these needs. The needs may be:

- The need for income now or in the future
- The need for growth
- The need for income and growth

It is impossible for a client's every need to be satisfied. The adviser's job is to highlight the most important needs. Before proceeding to satisfy needs the adviser has to consider:

(a) The **age of the client**. If a client is young, there will be many years for his investment to grow. He may, therefore, feel able to take a higher level of risk with, say, an equity based investment. If a client is aged 65 he may be unwilling to take any risk at all.

The age of the client can be important in the selection of the investment. Some investments are exclusive to certain age ranges, for example, stocks and shares ISAs and VCTs are exclusive to the over 18s.

(b) The **residence or domicile of the client** is important. If the client is non-resident or non-domiciled for UK tax purposes, it may be appropriate to use offshore investments. Other investments, such as personal pensions or ISAs will in general be excluded.

(c) The **client's tax position**.

(d) **Liquidity and access to funds**. In most cases a client should have a portfolio which includes some money on deposit in easily accessible funds.

(e) The adviser will be influenced by the **timescale of investments**.

(f) The adviser must always be aware of the effect of **inflation** on investments.

(g) The adviser must be aware of the level of **risk** the client is prepared to take.

(h) The adviser should suggest that a client should have **diversified assets**.

(i) The adviser should suggest **diversification of geographical economies**.

In satisfying current needs advisers should be aware that:

(a) Clients have changing needs, circumstances and aims
(b) Legislation may change
(c) The prosperity of the world economies will change

8.2 Constructing a portfolio

When constructing a portfolio an adviser should be aware of the following points.

(a) Amount of capital available for investment
(b) The client's tax position
(c) Access to capital requirements
(d) The client's attitude to risk and the suitability of the recommendations for compliance purposes

He will then split the portfolio into **short term investments** and **long term investments**.

Short-term monies should always be invested in risk-free or low-risk areas. It is the long-term investment which can be exposed to greater risk if the client so desires.

We list below a sample portfolio, together with a risk and tax profile. It must be emphasised that each client is unique and will have his own investment need. The adviser will need to take into account the risk, accessibility, liquidity, marketability, flexibility and the volatility of the investments that he recommends. The portfolio below is only an example. The investments shown are the type which could be used. The client would not necessarily have all of them in his portfolio.

Investments in a portfolio for a client who is a higher rate taxpayer prepared to take medium risk – 40% deposit and fixed interest, 60% equity. The portfolio is designed for capital growth.

Immediate Access	Medium Term	Long Term
Current account	Short-dated gilt (low coupon)	Long-dated gilt (low coupon)
Building society postal/ internet account	NS&I certificates	Investment bond (UK equity/overseas)
Cash unit trust		Convertible preference shares Unit trust/investment trusts (overseas/recovery/special situations) ISA (equity income fund) maxi-stocks and shares

8.2.1 Comments

An equity income fund is used for the ISA as this can give an increasing tax free income if required.

The investment bonds give an exposure to the UK and overseas equity markets but allow the client to take a 5% withdrawal to use as income and defer taxation, if required. Encashment can be deferred until, hopefully, the client is a basic rate taxpayer.

The unit trusts and investment trusts are selected for growth. The use of funds investing in different economies will give a spread of risk and diversification to the portfolio. The convertible preference shares give a guaranteed income with the chance of equity exposure from the conversion of the share.

Chapter roundup

- Most deposit based investments are fairly low risk investments in which an investor receives a low rate of interest in return for depositing his capital with the institution.
- A fixed interest security pays a fixed rate of interest and has a known maturity value so long as it is held until its redemption date.
- Collective and packaged investments may be attractive to the smaller and less sophisticated investor.
- Equities are high risk investments as neither the income nor the capital is secure.
- The enterprise investment scheme and venture capital trusts are designed to help unquoted trading companies raise finance.
- When constructing an investment portfolio, the adviser will need to consider risk, accessibility, liquidity, marketability, flexibility and volatility.

Quick quiz

1 How are the returns on NS&I certificates taxed?

2 What are the risks associated with annuities?

3 What are the two distinctive types of individual savings account?

4 What are the features of a preference share?

5 What income tax relief is available in respect of investments under the enterprise investment scheme?

Answers to quick quiz

1 They are tax free

2 Annuity risks are:

(a) Loss of capital
(b) Fixed income in most cases
(c) Low level start on increasing annuities
(d) Unit linked/with profit annuities subject to performance of fund

3 (a) Maxi-ISAs
(b) Mini-ISAs

4 Preference shares:

(a) Ahead of ordinary shares for dividends/liquidation
(b) Guaranteed dividend amount (but no increase if surplus)

5 EIS income tax relief is tax reducer up to 20% of amount subscribed up to £400,000.

Now try the question below from the Exam Question Bank

Number	Level	Marks	Time
Q33	Introductory	10	18 mins

34

Pension products

Introduction

Having looked at protection and investment products, we will now move on to one of the most important forms of financial provision – provision for an income in retirement.

Topic list	Syllabus references
1 Types of pension scheme and membership	3(c)(iv)
2 Contributing to a pension scheme	3(c)(iv)
3 Receiving benefits from pension arrangements	3(c)(iv)
4 Registration and deregistration	3(c)(iv)
5 Employer payments	3(c)(iv)
6 Occupational pension schemes	3(c)(iv)
7 Personal pensions	3(c)(iv)
8 Contracting out of the state second pension scheme	3(c)(iv)
9 Pensions and divorce	3(c)(iv)
10 Retirement options	3(c)(iv)

1 Types of pension scheme and membership

FAST FORWARD

An employee may be entitled to join his employer's occupational pension scheme. Both employees and the self employed can take out a 'personal pension' with a financial institution such as a bank or building society. The limits described in this chapter are applied to all the pension arrangements an individual makes, not each of them.

1.1 Types of pension provision

1.1.1 Introduction

An individual is encouraged by the Government to make financial provision to cover his needs when he reaches a certain age. There are state pension arrangements which provide some financial support, but the Government would like an individual not to rely on state provision but to make his own pension provision.

Therefore tax relief is given for such pension provision. This includes relief for contributions to pension provision and an exemption from tax on income and gains arising in a pension fund. There are anti-avoidance provisions preventing the use of pension schemes to gain unauthorised tax-advantages due to the tax-exempt status of pension funds.

1.2 Pension arrangements

An individual may make pension provision in a number of ways. These are called pension arrangements.

If the individual is employed, he may join an **occupational pension scheme** run by his employer.

Any individual (whether employed or not) may join a personal pension scheme run by a financial institution such as an insurance company or a bank.

An individual may make a number of different pension arrangements depending on his circumstances. For example, he may be a member of an occupational pension scheme and also make pension arrangements independently with a financial provider. If the individual has more than one pension arrangement, the rules we will be looking at in detail later apply to all the pension arrangements he makes. For example, **there is a limit on the amount of contributions that the individual can make in a tax year. This limit applies to all the pension arrangements that he makes, not *each* of them**.

Once we have looked at the tax relief and anti-avoidance provisions we will look in more detail at the different types of pension arrangements available.

1.3 Types of membership

An individual may be a member of a pension scheme in a number of different ways.

An **active member** is an individual for whom there are presently arrangements being made (such as contributions) under the pension scheme for the accrual of benefits to that person or in respect of him (for example, benefits for his dependants).

A **pensioner member** is an individual who is entitled to the present payment of benefits under the pension scheme and is not an active member (so no contributions are being made by or for him).

A **deferred member** is an individual who has accrued rights under a pension scheme and is neither an active member (no contributions are being paid by or for him) nor a pensioner member (so he is not taking benefits from the pension scheme). An example would be a person who has made pension arrangements when he was UK resident but he is no longer UK resident nor of pensionable age. In this case he can no longer make contributions to the scheme nor can he yet receive pension benefits.

2 Contributing to a pension scheme

FAST FORWARD

An individual can make tax deductible contributions to his pension arrangements up to the lower of his earnings and £3,600. Contributions to personal pensions are paid net of basic rate tax. Employers normally operate 'net pay' arrangements in respect or contributions to occupational schemes.

2.1 Contributions by an active scheme member

2.1.1 Eligibility to make contributions attracting tax relief

An individual who is **an active member** of a registered pension scheme and **under the age of 75 is entitled to tax relief on his contributions** to the scheme in a tax year if he is a relevant UK individual.

A relevant UK individual is one who:

(a) has relevant UK earnings chargeable to income tax in the tax year; or

(b) is resident in the UK at some time in the tax year; or

(c) was resident in the UK both at some time in the previous five tax years and when he became a member of the pension scheme

Relevant UK earnings are employment income, trading income, patent income in respect of inventions and income from furnished holiday lettings.

2.1.2 Annual limit for relief

The maximum amount of contributions attracting tax relief made by an individual in a tax year is the higher of:

(a) **the individual's UK relevant earnings chargeable to income tax in the year; and**

(b) **the basic amount (set at £3,600 for 2006/07).**

This means that if the individual does not have any UK earnings in a tax year, the maximum contribution he can obtain tax relief on is £3,600.

Where an individual contributes to more than one pension scheme, the aggregate of his contributions will be used to give the total amount of tax relief.

There is an interaction between this provision and the annual allowance, which will be discussed later.

2.1.3 Methods of giving tax relief

2.1.3.1 Relief given at source

This method will be used where an individual makes a contribution to a pension scheme run by a personal pension provider such as an insurance company.

Relief is given at source by the contributions being deemed to be made net of basic rate tax. This applies whether the individual is an employee, self-employed or not employed at all and whether or not he has taxable income. HMRC then pay an amount of basic rate tax to the pension provider.

Further tax relief is given if the individual is a higher rate taxpayer. The relief is given by increasing the basic rate limit for the year by the gross amount of contributions for which he is entitled to relief.

Question — **Higher rate relief**

Joe has earnings of £50,000 in 2006/07. He pays a personal pension contribution of £7,020 (net). He has no other taxable income.

Show Joe's tax liability for 2006/07.

Answer

	Non savings income
	£
Earnings/STI	50,000
Less: PA	(5,035)
Taxable income	44,965

Tax

	£
£2,150 × 10%	215
£31,150 × 22%	6,853
£9,000 (7,020 × 100/78) × 22%	1,980
£2,665 × 40%	1,066
44,965	10,114

2.1.3.2 Net pay arrangements

An occupational scheme will normally operate net pay arrangements.

In this case, the employer will deduct gross pension contributions from the individual's earnings before operating PAYE. The individual therefore obtains tax relief at his marginal rate of tax without having to make any claim.

Question — **Net pay arrangements**

Maxine has taxable earnings of £50,000 in 2006/07. Her employer deducts a pension contribution of £9,000 from these earnings before operating PAYE. She has no other taxable income.

Show Maxine's tax liability for 2006/07.

Answer

	£
Earnings	50,000
Less: pension contribution	(9,000)
STI	41,000
Less: PA	(5,035)
Taxable income	35,965

Tax

	£
£2,150 × 10%	215
£31,150 × 22%	6,853
£2,665 × 40%	1,066
35,965	8,134

This is the same result as Joe in the previous example. Joe had received basic rate tax relief of £(9,000 – 7,020) = 1,980 at source, so his overall tax position was £(10,114 – 1,980) = £8,134.

2.1.4 Contributions by an active scheme member not attracting tax relief

An active scheme member can also make contributions to his pension arrangements which do not attract tax relief, for example out of capital. The member must notify the scheme administrator if he makes contributions in excess of the higher of his UK relevant earnings and the basic amount.

Such contributions do not count towards the annual allowance limit (discussed below) but will affect the value of the pension fund for the lifetime allowance.

2.2 Contributions by people other than the active scheme member

FAST FORWARD

Employers may make contributions to pension schemes. In certain circumstances employers contributions are spread over a number of years.

2.2.1 Employer contributions

Where the active scheme member is an employee, his **employer will often made contributions to his pension scheme**. Such contributions are **exempt benefits** for the employee.

There is **no limit** on the amount of the contributions that may be made by an employer but **they always count towards the annual allowance and will also affect the value of the pension fund for the lifetime allowance** (see further below).

All contributions made by an employer are made gross and the employer will usually obtain tax relief for the contribution by deducting it as an expense in calculating trading profits for the period of account in which the payment is made.

There are two further aspects that need to be considered, however.

First, HMRC may seek to disallow a contribution which it considers is not a revenue expense or is not made wholly and exclusively for the purposes of the trade. Circumstances which might lead to HMRC questioning the contributions include:

(a) where a contribution is made on behalf of a controlling director (or close associate) at a disproportionately high level; or

(b) where contributions are made in connection with the sale or cessation of a trade.

Secondly, there are "spreading provisions" for large contributions, so that part of the contribution is treated as paid in a later period of account.

These provisions can apply where the pension contributions in the current period exceed 210% of those in the previous period. You then need to calculate the excess of current contributions over 110% of the contribution in the previous period of account. The provisions treat part of the excess contribution to be treated as paid in a later period as follows:

Amount of excess contributions	Fraction and chargeable periods
Less than £500,000	No spreading required
£500,000 or more but less than £1m	$^1/_2$ treated as paid in current period, $^1/_2$ treated as paid in the next chargeable period
£1m or more but less than £2m	$^1/_3$ treated as paid in the current period, $^1/_3$ treated as paid in each of the next two chargeable periods
£2m or more	$^1/_4$ treated as paid in the current period, $^1/_4$ treated as paid in each of the next three chargeable periods.

The amount which is *not* treated as an excess contribution will be given tax relief in the period of account in which it is paid.

Question

Spreading

Blue Ltd makes up accounts to 31 December each year. In the year ended 31 December 2007, it made a contribution of £1,500,000 to the pension scheme of one of its directors. In the year ended 31 December 2006, the corresponding pension contribution was £300,000.

Show how the pension contribution for year ended 31 December 2007 will be given tax relief for Blue Ltd.

Answer

First, test whether the spreading provisions apply.

Step 1 Does the contribution for year ended 31 December 2007 exceed 210% of the contributions for year ended 31 December 2006?

£300,000 × 210% = £630,000

The contribution of £1,500,000 exceeds this, so this test is met.

Step 2 What is the excess contribution for the rules?

The excess contribution is £1,500,000 – (300,000 x 110%) = £1,170,000

Step 3 Identify how the spreading provisions apply.

Current year (year ended 31 December 2007)

	£
Amount not subject to spreading provisions £(1,500,000 – 1,170,000)	330,000
Amount subject to spreading provisions 1/3 × £1,170,000	390,000
Total amount for tax relief	720,000

Next two years (year ended 31 December 2008 and year ended 31 December 2009)

$^1/_3$ × £1,170,000 =	390,000

2.3 Charge on excess contributions

FAST FORWARD

There is a limit on the amount that can be paid into a pension scheme each year. If this limit is exceeded there is a 40% income tax charge on the excess contributions.

There is an overriding limit on the total pension that can be input into the active member's pension scheme for each tax year. This is called the *annual allowance*.

The amount of the annual allowance is as follows:

Tax year	*Annual allowance* £
2006/07	215,000
2007/08	225,000
2008/09	235,000
2009/10	245,000
2010/11	255,000

The annual allowance is tested against the *pension input amount* for the *pension input period* which ends in the tax year. The pension input period is basically a period of 12 months chosen by the scheme member or the scheme administrator.

The calculation of the pension input amount depends on the type of pension scheme involved. The most common types of scheme involve money purchase arrangements or defined benefits arrangements (see below), so we will only deal with these here.

Where the pension scheme is a **money purchase arrangement**, the pension input amount is the aggregate of:

(a) any **tax relievable pension contributions paid by the individual; and**

(b) **contributions paid in respect of the individual by his employer.**

It will be noticed that only tax relieved contributions made by or behalf of an individual count towards the limit so that contributions on which tax relief is not obtained (eg capital contributions) will not affect the position. On the other hand, all contributions by an employer will count towards the annual allowance.

Where the pension scheme is a **defined benefits arrangement**, the pension input amount is the **increase in value of the individual's rights** under the arrangement during the pension input period, including the effect of any increase in salary. The value of the individual's rights at any time is calculated as 10 × the pension that would be paid if the individual became entitled to payment, plus the lump sum that would also be due.

If the pension input amount exceeds the annual allowance there is an income tax charge on the individual at the rate of 40%.

Question

Annual allowance charge

Diana is a member of a money purchase personal pension scheme. In the tax year 2006/07, she has UK relevant earnings of £265,000. In the pension input period ending in 2006/07 Diana makes a contribution of £117,000 to the pension scheme and her employer makes a further contribution of £110,000. Diana has no other income in 2006/07.

Show the income tax payable by Diana for 2006/07.

Answer

Diana has made a net contribution of £117,000 to the pension scheme which grosses up to £(117,000 × 100/78) = £150,000. This is all tax-relievable since it is lower than the greater of:

(a) UK relevant earnings of £265,000; and
(b) the basic amount of £3,600.

The excess contributions are therefore:

	£
Individual contributions subject to tax relief	150,000
Employer contributions	110,000
Pension input amount	260,000
Less: annual allowance 2006/07	(215,000)
Excess contributions	45,000

Diana's income tax liability is therefore:

	£
Earnings/STI	265,000
Less: PA	(5,035)
Taxable income	259,965

Tax

	£
£2,150 × 10%	215
£31,150 × 22%	6,853
£150,000 × 22% (extended basic rate band)	33,000
£76,665 × 40%	30,666
259,965	
£45,000 × 40%	18,000
Total income tax due	88,734

Note that the employer contributions are not treated as earnings or taxable benefits for NIC purposes. Therefore there is still a slight advantage to the employer making such contributions directly to the pension scheme instead of paying the individual the money for that individual to make contributions, even if the 40% charge applies.

3 Receiving benefits from pension arrangements

FAST FORWARD

There is a maximum value on the amount that can be built up in a pension fund.

3.1 The lifetime allowance

An individual is not allowed to build up an indefinitely large pension fund. **There is a maximum value for a pension fund (for money purchase arrangements) or for the value of benefits (for defined benefits arrangements). This is called the *lifetime allowance*.**

The amount of the lifetime allowance is as follows:

Tax year	*Lifetime allowance* £
2006/07	1,500,000
2007/08	1,600,000
2008/09	1,650,000
2009/10	1,750,000
2010/11	1,800,000

Where the pension scheme is a **money purchase arrangement**, the value of the fund for the lifetime allowance will be the **value of the investments in the fund**. Where the pension scheme is a **defined benefits arrangement**, the **income benefits are usually valued on a 20:1 ratio**, so that, for example, a pension of £10,000 will be valued at £200,000 for this purpose and lump sum benefits are valued at face value (see below for types of pension benefits).

The individual does not have to keep a running total of the value of his pension scheme. Instead, **the lifetime allowance limit is tested only when a *benefit crystallisation event* occurs**. The most common of these are:

(a) when a member becomes **entitled to a scheme pension**

(b) where a scheme pension already being paid is **increased** by more than the greater of 5% or the increase in the RPI

(c) where a member becomes **entitled to a lifetime annuity** under money purchase arrangements

(d) where a member **reaches the age of 75** under a defined benefit arrangement without having vested all or part of his entitlement to a pension and/or lump sum

(e) when member **becomes entitled to a lump sum**, for example a tax-free lump sum when the entitlement to pension income arises

(f) where a **lump sum is paid on the death of a member**

The consequences of the lifetime allowance being exceeded are discussed below.

3.2 Types of benefits

3.2.1 Authorised member payments in the lifetime of the member

Usually, **no pension payment can be made before the member reaches normal minimum pension age** (50 for members who reach this age on or before 5 April 2010 and 55 thereafter), unless the member is incapacitated by ill health. **Once this age is reached, the member may take an income pension and a lump sum from the pension scheme**.

Pension benefits do not all have to be taken or provided for at one time. Between the minimum pension age and the age of 75, an individual may decide to set aside all or part of his pension fund to provide pension benefits. This is called vesting the benefits and the part of the pension fund set aside is said to be vested. If any part of the pension fund is left over, this is said to be unvested. It is also possible for an active member of a pension scheme under the age of 75 to be making contributions to the scheme and also receiving pension benefits.

Once an individual reaches the age of 75, any unvested pension fund must become vested under the pension scheme rules.

A *pension commencement lump sum* can be taken when pension benefits are vested of up to 25% of the pension fund vested (for money purchase arrangements) or of the value of the benefits (for defined benefit arrangements) subject to the lifetime allowance limit (see below). This lump sum is tax-free. There are anti-avoidance rules which prevent a member from immediately reinvesting a lump sum to increase future pension benefits. This technique is called 'recycling'.

The remainder of the pension fund vested (in a money purchase scheme) or the remainder of the benefits (in a defined benefits scheme) **must be used to provide a pension income**. Such income will be taxable as pension income. The pension can be:

(a) **secured income** (a guaranteed income) provided either by the purchase of annuity (money purchase arrangements) or by a pension (defined benefits arrangements). A pensioner member of 75 or over **must** have secured income. There are alternative secured income arrangements for those, for example, who have religious objections to using the more usual methods.

(b) **unsecured income** (also known as income drawdown) where the member takes income from a drawdown fund up to a maximum of 120% of a notional single person annuity set by the Government Actuary's Department and revalued at least every five years. This is only available where the member is under the age of 75.

3.2.2 Authorised member payments on the death of the member

On the death of the member, the pension scheme may provide for income pensions and/or lump sums to be paid to the dependants of the scheme member (this would include a spouse/civil partner, child of the member who has not reached the age of 23 or another person who was dependant on the member).

The rules applicable depend on whether the member has already vested funds or not.

To the extent that the member has unvested funds, those funds may be used to pay a lump sum and/or a pension to be paid to dependants. There is no limit on the amount of the lump sum that is payable, but this is a benefit crystallisation event at which the lifetime allowance is tested and this may result in a lifetime allowance charge (see below). A pension payable to a dependant is not a benefit crystallisation event and therefore no lifetime allowance charge can arise.

If the member has already vested funds, a lump sum benefit may be paid only out of those funds if the member has died before the age of 75. The lump sum benefit in this case is subject to a tax charge at the rate of 35%. There is no lifetime allowance charge. Remaining vested funds can be used to provide for income pensions to be paid to dependants. Again, a pension payable to a dependent is not a benefit crystallisation event and therefore no lifetime allowance charge can arise. If the member has already reached the age of 75 before he dies, the **only** benefits that can be paid from vested funds are dependants' pensions.

3.2.3 Investment in prohibited assets by self-directed pension schemes

Many pension scheme members do not have any control over how the funds of the pension scheme are invested. However, it is possible to set up a ***self-directed* pension scheme** where the scheme member or members can decide how the pension fund is to be invested.

In general, a pension fund can only be invested in investments permitted by the Trustee Act 2000. This is quite wide ranging and can include all types of land and buildings, shares, securities and chattels such as works of art and antiques.

There are rules to discourage investment of pension funds in *prohibited assets* by self-directed schemes. They apply to occupational pension schemes with no more than 50 members if nay one member has any influence an investment policy, to occupational schemes with over 50 members if at least 10% of members have any influence, and to other scheme if the member has any influence.

Prohibited assets include:

(a) **residential property** (direct investment only, not through a collective fund such as a Real Estate Investment Trust)

(b) **chattels** such as fine wines, classic cars, works of art and antiques.

If a pension scheme invests in a prohibited asset, this is treated as an unauthorised member payment. This could result in a punitive charge of at least 55%.

If the value of the prohibited assets exceeds 25% of the fund, the pension scheme could be deregistered by HMRC (see later in this text).

If the scheme is not deregistered by HMRC, any **income or gains arising from the prohibited assets (or a level of deemed income if none is actually produced) will be subject to a charge of 40% p.a.**

3.3 Lifetime allowance charge

3.3.1 Occasions of charge

As we have seen, broadly when a member takes a benefit from a pension scheme, there is a benefit crystallisation event so that the value of the pension fund has to be tested against the lifetime allowance for the year in which the event occurs.

In many cases, the lifetime limit will not have been exceeded and there will be no income tax charge. However, the lifetime allowance to be used for further benefit crystallisation events will be reduced by the value of the benefits that have crystallised in the current event. This is discussed further below.

In some cases, the pension fund will exceed the lifetime allowance and this will give rise to an income tax charge on the excess value of the fund which has been vested to provide either a lump sum or a pension income. The rate of the charge depends on the type of benefit that will be taken from the excess funds.

3.3.2 Calculation and payment of the lifetime allowance charge

Where funds are vested to provide a lump sum, there will be a **charge to tax at 55% on the value of the lump sum**.

Where the excess funds are vested to provide a pension income, the rate of charge is 25%. In this case, it is necessary to look at the value of the vested funds to work out the tax charge, not the annual value of the pension income that will be provided.

The different rates apply because the pension income will be taxable in the hands of the individual whereas the lump sum will not.

Where the charge arises in the lifetime of the member, the tax charge primarily falls on him, but the pension scheme administrator has joint liability for the tax charge and will withhold sufficient sums to cover the charge.

Where the charge arises on the payment of a lump sum following the death of a member, the tax charge is payable by the recipient of the lump sum and in this case there will be no withholding tax retained by the scheme administrator.

3.3.3 Example

Amy attained the age of 60 on 1 July 2006 and decided to vest her pension benefits on that date. She has a money purchase fund which was valued at £1,900,000 on 1 July 2006. Amy took the maximum tax-free lump sum of £1,500,000 × 25% = £375,000. The balance of the lifetime allowance is £(1,500,000 – 375,000) = £1,125,000 and this is vested to provide pension income benefits.

Amy also took the excess of the fund over the lifetime allowance as a lump sum ie £(1,900,000 = 1,500,000) = £400,000.

The tax charge is therefore £400,000 × 55% = £220,000.

The scheme administration will therefore pay Amy £(400,000 – 220,000) = £180,000 and withhold £220,000 to pay the tax charge to HMRC.

The pension member may decide to vest benefits over a number of years. In this case, **the lifetime allowance must be adjusted for the value of benefits already vested**. If there has been a change in the value of the lifetime allowance, the benefits vested earlier must be uplifted pro rata to the increase in the lifetime allowance between the two events.

4 Registration and deregistration

4.1 Registration requirements

In order for the tax advantages described above to apply to a pension scheme, the scheme must be registered with HMRC.

Schemes in existence at 6 April 2006 which already has HMRC approval were automatically registered, unless the scheme administrator requested otherwise.

Where a pension scheme commences on or after 6 April 2006, the scheme administrator must make an application to HMRC for registration. A pension scheme may only be registered if it is an occupational pension scheme or if it is established by certain financial institutions such as insurances companies and banks.

HMRC must register the scheme unless it believes that the information in the application is incorrect or that any accompanying declaration is false.

4.2 Deregistration

A pension scheme may be deregistered by HMRC for a number of reasons. These include:

(a) making unauthorised payments in excess of 25% of the value of the pension fund during any period of 12 months

(b) that the scheme administrator fails to pay a substantial amount of tax (or interest on tax) due from the scheme administrator

(c) that the scheme administrator fails to provide required information to HMRC

If a pension scheme is deregistered, **a deregistration charge of 40%** of the value of the pension fund applies.

5 Employer payments

5.1 Authorised employer payments

Provision is made for certain payments made by the scheme administrator to be authorised by the legislation.

These payments include:

(a) **authorised surplus payments; ie the repayment of surplus funds back to a sponsoring employer**

(b) **authorised employer loans; ie secured loans of up to 50% of the value of the pension scheme**

If an authorised surplus payment is made, there will be **a tax charge of 35%** of the value of the payment payable by the scheme administrator.

6 Occupational pension schemes

FAST FORWARD

An occupational pension scheme may be a final salary or a money purchase scheme.

The tax advantages of approved occupational pension schemes are:

- Tax relief for both employer and employee on contributions.
- Employer contributions are not taxed as employee benefit.
- On retirement lump sum taken is tax free (but pension is taxable).
- Life cover; lump sum tax free (but dependants pension is taxable).

Key term

Employers may set up an **occupational pension scheme**. Such schemes may either require contributions from employees or be non-contributory. The employer may use the services of an insurance company (an insured scheme) or may set up a totally self administered pension fund.

There are two kinds of occupational pension scheme - earnings-related (**defined benefits arrangements**) and investment-related (**money purchase arrangements**).

6.1 Defined benefits arrangements

Key term

In a **defined benefits arrangements** - also known as a **final salary scheme** - the pension is generally based on employees' earnings at retirement and linked to the number of years they have worked for the firm.

The basis on which pension rights accrue to an employee will be laid down in the rules of the particular scheme.

For example, the basis might be a pension of 1/80th of earnings at retirement multiplied by the number of years they have been with the firm. If, therefore, earnings at retirement are £16,000 a year and they have worked for the firm for 20 years, the pension will be:

£16,000 $\times$ 1/80th $\times$ 20 years = £4,000 per annum.

The advantage of this type of pension is that it gives a **guarantee** of a pension linked to earnings at retirement.

The name commonly given to this type of scheme is 'final salary', but this is a little misleading as the pension can be based not only on an employee's salary at retirement but upon any other remuneration, such as overtime, commission and benefits. The broad rule is that **if the benefit is taxable it is pensionable**.

A final salary scheme leaves the employer with a **commitment of unknown cost**, and it is unlikely that a small firm would use this approach. Having said that, in recent years even large firms have closed their final salary schemes to new employees due to spiralling costs regarding such schemes.

6.2 Money purchase arrangements

Key term

A **money purchase pension** - also known as a **defined contribution scheme** – does not provide any guarantee regarding the level of pension which will be available. It consists of two parts – **build up** and **pension**.

6.3 Build up

During the years that an individual is earning, contributions are paid to a money purchase fund and the total fund is **built up** by those contributions and the returns on the investment of the contributions. The fund can be built up in one of the following ways.

(a) **With profit**

A guaranteed minimum sum will be available at retirement which will be increased by reversionary bonuses and terminal bonus.

(b) **Unit linked**

A fund will be built up in the same way as a unit linked endowment with the same potential fluctuations being a feature of the plan.

(c) **Deposit**

Interest is added to contributions in the same way as any other bank or building society deposit account.

6.4 Additional contributions

FAST FORWARD

Additional Contributions may be paid to increase benefits.

The rules of an occupational pension scheme will normally specify either the level of contributions (money purchase arrangements) or the level of benefits (defined benefits arrangements). For defined benefits arrangements the level of compulsory employee contributions will be fixed by the employer.

An employee may wish to make **voluntary contributions** (in **addition** to any compulsory contributions) in order to improve the his pension position. There are two ways of doing this.

(a) Via the employer's scheme
(b) Independently, to a scheme provided by a financial institution

6.4.1 Employer schemes

Employers may allow employees to contribute voluntarily to their schemes. Additional contributions may be used to;

(a) add years of service to the employee's total in order to improve the benefits. This method is only available under a defined benefit scheme.

For example, an employee paying AVCs to the employer's scheme may ultimately receive a pension of 28/60th of final salary even though the employee may have worked for only 25 years. The additional three years, not representing actual service, provide additional benefits.

(b) make **money purchase arrangements**.

6.4.2 Contributions to scheme provided by Financial Provider

An employee can arrange to pay voluntary contributions to a provider quite **independently of the employer**. These schemes are available only on a **money purchase basis**.

6.5 Small self administered schemes

Smaller companies with a few key employees may set up an occupational pension scheme for those employees. Whilst it is possible for such a scheme to be invested in pension products offered by financial institutions, it is also possible for the scheme to be **'self administered', so that the company has some control over how the funds are invested**. It is normal for the scheme to be run by pension consultants or actuaries, with the advice of an investment manager, but they will consult with the company. The scheme may be a hybrid, with part being invested in pension products, and part used for alternative investments.

The scheme is still bound by the rules applying to all pension schemes. Particular features which should be noted are:

- the ability to make a secured loan of up to 50% of the fund assets to the company.
- certain investments are prohibited (see earlier in this text). If there are not more than 50 members this applies if any member can influence investment decisions.
- If there are not more than 50 members then when a pension annuity becomes payable it must be purchased from an insurance company; it cannot be paid out of the pension fund on a year to year basis. This is of particular importance if the fund has a significant proportion of its assets in an illiquid form, such as where the company's premises are owned by the pension fund, as it may result in a forced sale.

If the pension fund breaks any of the rules draconian charges and sanctions as described earlier in this text can be imposed.

7 Personal pensions

Key term

Personal pensions are money purchase schemes, which are provided by banks, insurance companies and other financial institutions.

7.1 Introduction

Personal pension schemes may be '**with profit**' schemes, where the members funds are invested in a general pool, and the fund grown with the addition of an annual and a terminal bonus.

Alternatively the contributions may be used to purchase **units in a fund**. There is generally a wide range of funds to choose from. The members may switch between funds; for example he may switch his investment to a low risk fund as he nears retirement.

If a member has a significant amount invested, he may prefer to select his own investments through the medium of a **self invested personal pension (SIPPs)**.

7.2 Stakeholder pensions

Stakeholder pensions are a particular type of personal pension scheme. They must satisfy certain rules, such as a maximum level of charges, ease of transfer etc.

7.3 Self invested personal pensions (SIPPs)

(a) It is possible for a personal pension to be invested in assets other than insurance policies.

(b) The features and benefits of a SIPP are exactly the same as a normal personal pension, the only difference is the **investment philosophy**.

(c) An **investment manager** will be appointed to manage the fund's investments.

(d) These schemes will be of interest to **the wealthy client** who wants control over his pension investment and already has a stockbroker or other fund manager.

(e) Such a scheme is also useful for any self-employed person (or group of self-employed persons) who wish to **purchase commercial property**. Partnerships of professionals, such as solicitors or accountants could make use of such a scheme.

(f) If commercial property is being purchased it is possible for further funds to be raised by means of a **loan**.

(g) As the investment policy can be influenced by the member, investment in certain assets, such as residential property, is prohibited. Breaking this rule can lead to draconian charges and sanctions as has been described earlier in this text.

(h) The schemes can be run by **insurance companies, actuaries or pension consultants**. Fees will normally be charged for the operation of such a scheme.

8 Contracting out of the state second pension scheme

FAST FORWARD

Employees an be contacted out of the second state pension either by their employers or by their own choice.

There is a basic state pension plus an additional state pension called the state second pension for employees, certain carers and people with long term illnesses and disabilities. Individuals can choose to take out another kind of second pension. This is called 'contracting out'. Many occupational pension schemes are 'contracted out', but it is also possible to contract out through a personal pension.

People receiving earnings pay National Insurance contributions (NICs). NICs are used as the basis of payment for various benefits, including **state pensions.**

When employees are contracted out of the State Second Pension Scheme, this **reduces the liability of the Department of Work and Pensions (DWP).** As the liability is reduced, so its need for income is reduced. The cost of the scheme has been carefully worked out and therefore the DWP through the National Insurance Contributions Office (NICO) can rebate the cost of the benefit which it is no longer required to supply.

9 Pensions and divorce

FAST FORWARD

On divorce, pension assets can be shared between ex-spouses/civil partners.

The courts can share pension assets on divorce or on the dissolution of a civil partnership as follows.

(a) Offset
(b) Earmarking
(c) Pension splitting

Offset provisions allow one party to keep pension assets by offsetting the value of other assets. For example, if the court decides the pension fund is worth £100,000 and that the spouse or civil partner is entitled to £25,000 of these assets, then £25,000 of other assets (eg cash) can be used to offset the pension fund assets.

Earmarking allows the courts to earmark certain pension policies to provide the spouse or civil partner with a pension and/or a lump sum. However, it does not allow a clean break as title to the pension rights remains with the spouse or civil partner in whose name the rights accrued. For example, if a member spouse or civil partner dies first, the ex-spouse or civil partner will lose the intended pension.

The principle of **pension splitting** is that the member's pension rights are valued at the time of divorce or dissolution and divided into the proportions agreed as part of the overall settlement. The sharing will be actioned by means of a court order.

The ex-spouse's or civil partner's rights become **safeguarded rights** and will be distinguished from any future rights built up by the member during continuing membership of the scheme. Safeguarded rights are **reinforced** and will be paid to the ex-spouse or civil partner between the ages of 60 and 65, unless earlier payment is required due to ill health.

10 Retirement options

FAST FORWARD

On retirement an individual may wish to purchase an annuity or take income withdrawls.

Apart from the normal options at retirement of buying different kinds of annuity, eg level or increasing, single life or joint life, there are other options which give individuals a range of fundamentally **different choices of pension** from defined contribution plans.

Defined benefits plans, however, may only pay a lump sum and a scheme pension.

10.1 Open market option

A person who has contributed to one or more personal pension plans can have the choice of **buying an annuity** from the insurance company which invested the contributions, or **exercising an option to buy an annuity from another insurance company** which is paying a better annuity rate.

Employees who are members of defined contribution occupational pension schemes are also able to select the annuity provider. This is particularly relevant to employees who have individual pension arrangements such as executive pension schemes.

This choice is known as the **open market option**. It is not in itself a pension. It is simply a right available to individuals to exercise freedom of choice of pension provider.

10.2 Purchasing annuities

An individual can have **one or more pension arrangements** – there is no limit on the number, only on the total contributions which can be made to pension arrangements. Each one of those pension plans can be converted into a pension at any age between 55 (50, if aged 50 before 2010) and 75 and conversion can be done in steps. This means that a policyholder can **convert each one at a different time** or in stages, or convert several - but not all - at any one time. The effect is to have pensions beginning one after another rather than all starting at the same time.

The advantage of doing this is that, if **annuity rates** are low when the policyholder wants to begin receiving a pension, he can either defer taking all his pension entitlement or buy an annuity with just part of the total pension fund, leaving the rest to buy annuities at a later time when hopefully annuity rates have increased.

This practice is known as **phased retirement**, even though it is not necessary to retire in order to begin receiving a pension. Phased retirement, because of its costs, is not for those with small pension funds. A fund of around **£100,000** is usually needed to make the arrangement worthwhile.

The **advantages** of phased retirement are that it gives greater flexibility of retirement benefits, and defers the purchase of annuities until annuity rates increase at higher ages. The **disadvantages** include the possibility that annuity rates might not increase, but actually decrease. Worse still, if the remaining fund is unit-linked, the fund itself may fall in value. Also tax free cash is received piecemeal rather than in one lump sum.

10.3 Taking an income from your pension fund

If you have a personal pension fund, you can have an income from it without buying an annuity, if you so choose. You must withdraw some of your pension fund each year in order to give you an income. You do not have to buy an annuity until you reach age 75, although you may choose to do so earlier. Again this arrangement is not for small pension funds: a fund of around £100,000 is needed.

This arrangement is described as **income drawdown.** Remember that an annuity has *not* been bought. As with phased retirement, the fund not yet withdrawn remains invested.

This option may also be available to members of defined contribution schemes depending on the scheme rules.

Question

Pensions

(a) What is the reason for using an open market option?
(b) What are the advantages of phased retirement?
(c) What is an advantage of income withdrawal?

Answer

(a) To improve an annuity rate.
(b) Greater flexibility of retirement; allows annuity rates to rise.
(c) Undrawn pension remains invested.

Chapter roundup

- An employee may be entitled to join his employer's occupational pension scheme. Both employees and the self employed can take out a 'personal pension' with a financial institution such as a bank or building society. The limits described in this chapter are applied to all the pension arrangements an individual makes, not each of them.
- An individual can make tax deductible contributions to his pension arrangements up to the lower of his earnings and £3,600. Contributions to personal pensions are paid net of basic rate tax. Employers normally operate 'net pay' arrangements in respect or contributions to occupational schemes.
- Employers may make contributions to pension schemes. In certain circumstances employers contributions are spread over a number of years.
- There is a limit on the amount that can be paid into a pension scheme each year. If this limit is exceeded there is a 40% income tax charge on the excess contributions.
- There is a maximum value on the amount that can be built up in a pension fund.
- An occupational pension scheme may be a final salary or a money purchase scheme

  The tax advantages of approved occupational pension schemes are:

  - Tax relief for both employer and employee on contributions.
  - Employer contributions are not taxed as employee benefit.
  - On retirement lump sum taken is tax free (but pension is taxable).
  - Life cover; lump sum tax free (but dependants pension is taxable).
- Additional contributions may be paid to increase benefits.
- Employees an be contacted out of the second state pension either by their employers or by their own choice.
- On divorce, pension assets can be shared between ex-spouses/civil partners.
- On retirement an individual may wish to purchase an annuity or take income withdrawals.

Quick quiz

1. What are the two types of occupational pension scheme?
2. What is the maximum lump sum that can be taken on retirement (lifetime allowance not exceeded)?
3. What is the limit on contributions to an approved pension scheme?
4. What are the consequences of the total of employee and employer contributions exceeding the annual allowance?
5. What are the consequences of exceeding the lifetime allowance?
6. What are the consequences of a self-directed scheme holding prohibited assets?

Answers to quick quiz

1. Occupational pension schemes may be final salary schemes or money purchase schemes.
2. 25% of the fund.
3. Higher of relevant earnings and the basic amount (£3,600).
4. The excess is subject to the annual allowance charge on the employee at 40%. (Any contributions by the employee which were not eligible for tax relief are ignored).
5. If the lifetime allowance is exceeded the excess is charged at 55% (if taken as a lump sum) or 25% (if taken as a pension).
6. – A charge of at least 55%
   – Possible deregistration if the value exceeds 25% of the fund (40% charge on the whole fund)
   – A charge (40%) on the income (or deemed income) from the asset.

Now try the question below from the Exam Question Bank

Number	Level	Marks	Time
Q34	Introductory	11	20 mins

35

The regulatory framework

Introduction

In this chapter, we look at the regulatory framework.

Topic list	Syllabus references
1 The UK regulatory regime	3(d)
2 Regulated activities under FSMA 2000	3(d)
3 Application of conduct of business rules	3(d)
4 Know your client	3(d)
5 Best advice	3(d)
6 Disclosure rules	3(d)
7 Complaints procedures	3(c)
8 Compensation and redress	3(c)

1 The UK regulatory regime

FAST FORWARD

The Financial Services Authority (FSA) regulates investment business.

1.1 From self-regulation to statutory regulation

Before the Financial Services Act 1986 (FSA 1986), a system of **self-regulation** prevailed in the UK financial sector.

The FSA 1986 brought a new system of **'self-regulation within a statutory framework'**, with financial services firms authorised by Self-Regulatory Organisations (SROs).

When the Labour Party gained power in 1997, it wanted to make changes to the regulation of financial services. A series of **financial scandals** had added weight to the political impetus for change. The Financial Services Authority (FSA) was the result.

1.2 The Financial Services Authority (FSA): single statutory regulator

The FSA as **single statutory regulator**:

(a) Brings together regulation of investment, insurance and banking
(b) Brings a move from contractual to statutory regulation
(c) Makes the UK the only major developed country with such a system

The FSA is not a government agency. It is a private company limited by guarantee, with HM Treasury as the guarantor. It is financed by the financial services industry. The Board of the FSA is appointed by the Treasury.

The FSA:

(a) Is the **authorising body** for those carrying on regulated activities
(b) Is the **regulator of exchanges and clearing houses** operating in the UK
(c) **Approves companies for stock market listing** in the UK
(d) Is a **rule making body**
(e) Undertakes **supervision**
(f) Has wide powers of **enforcement**

The first stage of the current reforms of financial services regulation was completed in June 1998 ('N1'), when responsibility for banking supervision was transferred to the FSA from the Bank of England. The **Financial Services and Markets Act (FSMA 2000)** was implemented on 1 December 2001 (at N2), and transferred to the FSA the responsibilities of several other organisations:

- Building Societies Commission
- Friendly Societies Commission
- Investment Management Regulatory Organisation (IMRO)
- Personal Investment Authority (PIA)
- Register of Friendly Societies
- Securities and Futures Authority (SFA)

In summary, with the implementation of FSMA 2000 at date 'N2', the FSA has responsibility for:

(a) Prudential supervision of all firms, which involves monitoring the adequacy of their management, financial resources and internal systems and controls, and

(b) Conduct of business regulations of those firms doing **investment business**. This involves overseeing firms' dealings with investors to ensure, for example, that information provided is clear and not misleading

'N' stands for **'New regulator'**. **N1** was the name given to the date of implementation of the **Bank of England Act 1998**, under which supervision of **banks** under the **Banking Act 1987** passed to the **Financial Services Authority (FSA)**. N2 was 30 November 2001, the date when the FSA became the single statutory regulator for the financial services industry under FSMA 2000, which repealed the Financial Services Act 1986 (FSA 1986). **N3** was the date when mortgage business comes under FSA regulation which was 31 October 2004.

1.3 Regulatory structure post–N2

FSMA 2000

The Treasury
(Chancellor of the Exchequer)
Financial Services Authority

Recognised Clearing Houses (RCHs)	Designated Professional Bodies (DPBs) eg ACCA	Recognised Investment Exchanges (RIEs) Recognised Overseas Investment Exchanges (ROIEs)

1.4 The FSA's risk-based approach to regulation

The FSA seeks to adopt a **'risk-based' approach** to regulation. This means that it will focus its attention on those institutions and activities that are likely to pose the greatest risk to consumers and markets. The approach is intended to recognise the responsibilities of consumers themselves and of firms' management. The FSA considers it both **impossible and undesirable to remove all risk and failure** from the financial system.

In the FSA's risk-based approach, there is a focus on the extent to which firms pose a risk to the FSA's ability to meet its objectives. A firm's relationship with the FSA, the resources it devotes to regulation of the firm and any programme of risk mitigation that may be put in place, will be based on a **grading system**. Firms will be graded from A to D.

1.5 'Themes'

In developing the FSA's role, there is an emphasis on **themes**, such as **e-commerce** and **money laundering**.

The FSA's **four statutory objectives**, as set out in FSMA 2000, are in substance as follows (with BPP comments in brackets).

(a) To **maintain confidence** in the UK financial system. (The FSA is concerned with the **stability of firms** and the **stability of markets.)**

(b) To promote **public understanding** of the financial system, including: **awareness** of the benefits and risks associated with different kinds of investment or other financial dealing, and providing appropriate **information and advice**. (The emphasis is on consumers protecting themselves.)

(c) To secure the appropriate level of **protection for consumers**, bearing in mind:

   (i) The different levels of risk that come with different kinds of investment or other transaction

   (ii) The differing experience and expertise of consumers

(iii) Consumers' needs for accurate advice and information, and

(iv) The principle that consumers should take responsibility for their decisions. (This marks a move towards the principle of *caveat emptor* – 'let the buyer beware'.)

(d) To continue to **reduce financial crime** (by reducing the possibility for a regulated person to carry on a business whose purpose is connected with financial crime).

1.5.1 Risks for consumers

The FSA has identified the following **consumer risks** in the financial services industry.

(a) **Prudential risk** – for example the risk of a company collapsing through poor management

(b) **Bad faith risk** – the risk of loss due to mis-selling, non-disclosure, fraud and misrepresentation

(c) **Complexity/unsuitability risk** – the risk that a customer chooses unsuitable products through lack of understanding

(d) **Performance risk** – the risk that investment do not provide the returns that had been hoped for

The FSA has a **Consumer Panel** to monitor how the FSA fulfils its objectives in relation to consumers.

1.6 FSA Principles for Business

The 11 Principles for Business of the FSA which apply to firms from the N2 date are set out below.

PRINCIPLES FOR BUSINESS	
1: Integrity	A firm must conduct its business with integrity.
2: Skill, care and diligence	A firm must conduct its business with due skill, care and diligence.
3: Management and control	A firm must take reasonable care to organise and control its affairs responsibly and effectively, with adequate risk management systems.
4: Financial prudence	A firm must maintain adequate financial resources.
5: Market conduct	A firm must observe proper standards of market conduct.
6: Customers' interests	A firm must pay due regard to the interests of its customers and treat them fairly.
7: Communications with clients	A firm must pay due regard to the information needs of its clients, and communicate information to them in a way which is clear, fair and not misleading.
8: Conflicts of interest	A firm must manage conflict of interest fairly, both between itself and its customers and between a customer and another client.
9: Customers: relationships of trust	A firm must take reasonable care to ensure the suitability of its advice and discretionary decisions for any customer who is entitled to rely upon its judgment.
10: Clients' assets	A firm must arrange adequate protection for clients' assets when it is responsible for them.
11: Relations with regulators	A firm must deal with its regulators in an open and cooperative way, and must disclose to the FSA appropriately anything relating to the firm of which the FSA would reasonably expect notice.

1.7 Section 150, FSMA 2000

Section 150 of FSMA 2000 gives a **right of action by a private person** (an individual not carrying an investment business, or a business not acting in the course of business of any kind) to sue for breaches of **Conduct of Business (COB) rules**.

Unlike the case of suing for negligence, or for breach of contract, to establish that there is a claim it is only necessary to show that there has been a **rule breach** and a **loss**.

Any person (not just private persons) has a right of action under Section 150 FSMA 2000 in relation to:

(a) COB rules prohibiting an authorised person from seeking to exclude or restrict any duty or liability

(b) COB rules seeking to ensure that investment transactions are not based on unpublished price-sensitive information

1.8 Other key provisions of FSMA 2000

Section 138 of FSMA 2000 gives the FSA powers to make general rules it considers necessary or expedient for investor protection.

Section 167 allows the FSA to investigate an authorised person.

Section 177 imposes penalties of up to six months' imprisonment or a fine of £5,000 for failure to co-operate with an investigation.

Section 176 gives the FSA powers to enter the premises of an authorised person if they have a warrant.

Section 205 allows the FSA to 'name and shame' authorised persons (**'public censure'**).

2 Regulated activities under FSMA 2000

FAST FORWARD

FSMA 2000 defines regulated activities which must either be authorised or exempt.

2.1 General principles

Section 19 of FSMA 2000 provides that a person (where 'persons' includes firms) must not carry on a **regulated activity** in the UK unless either:

(a) **Authorised**, or
(b) **Exempt**

Potential consequences of breaching this provision are:

(a) Criminal charges
(b) Contracts becoming voidable
(c) Claims for damages

In deciding whether **authorisation** is required, the following need to be considered:

Regulated activities
↓
Exceptions
↓
Exemptions

The scope of **regulated activities** is determined by the Regulated Activities Order and covers:

(a) Dealing in investments

(b) Arranging deals in investments

(c) Managing investments

(d) Advising on investments

(e) Establishing or operating a collective investment scheme (eg unit trusts, investment trusts)

(f) Establishing or operating a stakeholder pension scheme (SHP)

(g) Safekeeping of and administering investments

(h) Lloyds insurance business

(i) Carrying out contracts of insurance

(j) Advising on insurance

(k) Accepting deposits

(l) Regulated mortgages secured on land where at least 40% of the land is to be used as the borrower's dwelling. Excludes commercial and buy to let mortgages.

Investments covered by regulated activities are also listed in the Order:

(a) Deposits
(b) Contracts of insurance
(c) Shares
(d) Government and local authority securities
(e) Instruments giving title to investments
(f) Units in collective investment schemes
(g) Options, futures and contacts for differences
(h) Lloyds syndicate capacity and membership of syndicates

2.2 Exceptions

By exception, the following do not require authorisation:

(a) **Dealings as principal** – there is no need for authorisation where people are dealing in investments for themselves

(b) **Newspapers and the media** – however, 'tip sheets', whose primary purpose is to tip shares, are not an exception

(c) Acting as an **unremunerated trustee**

(d) **Employee share schemes**

(e) **Certain overseas persons**, for business solicited in the UK

2.3 Exempt persons

The **Exempt Persons Order** exempts from authorisation:

(a) **Appointed representatives**, such as self-employed persons selling insurance under a contract for services with the product provider to whom they are tied, where the provider firm takes full responsibility for the representative.

(b) Certain institutions, including **central** and **National Savings banks**, and **local government authorities**

(c) Certain **members of professions**, such as lawyers, accountants and actuaries. Member firms of Designated Professional Bodies (this includes the ACCA) will require **FSA authorisation** if they recommend the purchase of specific investments, such as pensions or listed company shares to clients, approve financial promotions or carry out corporate finance business. If their activities are **'non-mainstream' investment business**, only assisting clients in making investment decisions as part of other professional services, they are exempt from FSA authorisation but must obtain a **licence** from the DPB, under which they are subject to a light form of regulation.

(d) **Members of Lloyd's** (The Society of Lloyd's, in respect of insurance business).

3 Application of conduct of business rules

FAST FORWARD

The conduct of business rules apply when advising on or dealing in investments.

3.1 Purpose of the Conduct of Business rules

The **Conduct of Business Sourcebook (COB)** forms part of the **FSA Handbook**. The full Handbook can be found on the FSA website at www.fsa.gov.uk.

3.2 Application of COB rules

3.2.1 Who?

COB applies to **all authorised firms**. An **exception** is that COB does not apply generally to **authorised professional firms** (such as firms of solicitors, accountants and actuaries) in respect of their **non-mainstream regulated activities**.

3.2.2 What?

COB applies to firms in respect of **regulated activities**, except where specifically excluded. This covers **designated investment business** generally.

Designated investment business includes:

- **Advising on investments**
- **Dealing in investments**

The COB rules do not apply to **deposits**, such as bank deposit accounts. Such accounts are covered by the banks' own voluntary codes. If these codes are seen to fail in the future, FSA rules could be extended to cover such deposits.

3.2.3 Where?

COB applies to activities carried out **in the UK** and also covers **business brought into the UK**, for a client in the UK.

4 Know your client

FAST FORWARD

There is a duty to **'know your client'** before giving financial advice.

If you give financial advice you have a duty to **'know your client'**. It is essential to take all steps to obtain **as much knowledge as possible about the client** simply in order to be able to give suitable advice which is relevant to the client's circumstances. This is known as the **'know your client'** principle.

Someone giving advice to a private customer must ensure they have obtained relevant personal and financial information or have warned of the adverse consequences if the client refused to provide the necessary information.

The information must come **direct** from the client but, if the client refuses to give it, the adviser need not pursue the matter. However an adviser must keep a clear record signed by the client making it clear which information has been asked for but declined.

Detailed information is **not needed** for the following clients.

(a) Business investors
(b) Experienced investors
(c) Professional investors
(d) Execution only clients
(e) Market counter parties

The Financial Services & Markets Act 2000 (FSMA 2000) does not lay down any specific method of obtaining information regarding a client. However, the most practical way is to use a **prepared list of questions**. This is the procedure followed by nearly all advisers and has become known as the **fact find**.

5 Best advice

FAST FORWARD

There is a regulatory requirement for financial advisers to give advice which is in the **best interests** of the client.

5.1 Introduction

The first consideration in giving advice to a client is the **best interests of the client**. This is one of the regulatory requirements.

In considering the client's best interests account must be taken of the client's **existing investments**, their distribution, and the personal and financial situation of the client in addition to giving careful consideration to the type of investment being recommended.

The interpretation of the requirement to give best/suitable advice is to recommend a **suitable product**. It is not really feasible in many cases to recommend one product which can be said beyond any doubt to be better than any other comparable product. The requirement is to recommend the products or services which are suitable to a client's needs.

In doing so an adviser must exercise **due skill and care** in making recommendations or in exercising discretion on behalf of a client. The adviser must take into account all factors, not only regarding the client but regarding the product.

The adviser must possess **up to date knowledge** and **give well informed judgements**. If past performance tables are used in illustrations, it must be made clear that they are no guarantee of the future performance and are produced for illustrative purposes only. Independent advisers are allowed to make recommendations from a short list of suitable products from different product providers.

Exam focus point

> Different terminology is used in the industry. For examination purposes the expressions 'best advice' and 'suitable advice' must be regarded as interchangeable.

5.2 Connected person

If an independent financial adviser (IFA) has a **vested interest** in a product then special care is needed in the recommendation. This situation can exist where there may be some common ownership between an IFA and a product provider.

In such a case the IFA must take extra special steps to be able to demonstrate that there is no other product which is better than the one that is being recommended. This is known as **'better than best advice'**.

For tied advisers suitable advice is made possible by recommending a product from the provider's own range. Under the rules of **polarisation** no alternative course of action is possible. Any packaged products must demonstrate their overall suitability to a client.

6 Disclosure rules

FAST FORWARD

> The disclosure rules ensure that the investor has all the information needed to decide whether to invest in a particular product.

The disclosure rules are intended to ensure that investors possess all the information they need in order to take a decision on whether or not a particular product is suitable for their needs.

The information which **must** be given to an investor falls under the following headings.

(a) Details of the product (the key features document)

(b) An explanation of why the product is suitable (the 'reasons why' letter)

(c) Further information when a sale is completed (post-sale information) (outside your syllabus)

7 Complaints procedures

FAST FORWARD

> Clients may be entitled to compensation in certain circumstances.

Clients have the **right of complaint** against an adviser in certain circumstances. Those circumstances include **negligence** by an adviser, or **breach** of a customer agreement, or **misrepresentation** by an adviser.

The client has the right to have a complaint **investigated** properly and thoroughly and appropriate action taken. The client may, if not satisfied with the way a complaint is handled, report the matter to the Financial Ombudsman Service (FOS) within six months and can ask the regulator to investigate.

Members of a regulator must have **written procedures** in place for handling complaints. They must also ensure that all staff, all appointed representatives and all the staff of appointed representatives are aware of the procedures.

A firm must **co-operate with the FOS** in any investigation.

When a complaint is received it must be **acknowledged** within five business days of being received by the adviser.

If no final response has been given within four weeks, a holding response must be sent.

A final response must be sent within eight weeks.

If the complaint is an **oral** one, the firm's letter of acknowledgement of its receipt must state their **understanding of the complaint** and ask the complainant to confirm the accuracy of their understanding in writing.

The procedures must ensure that a complaint is handled by a person who was **not involved in giving the advice** that formed the source of the complaint. A sole trader, who is obviously in a difficult position regarding this requirement, must be able to demonstrate efficient handling of the complaint.

The adviser must handle a complaint **promptly** and must advise the client that the complaint will be investigated promptly and thoroughly and that action will be taken as appropriate by a responsible member of staff.

The client must be told of the procedures which can be followed if the client is not satisfied with the way the firm has handled the complaint. This will primarily be the right to complain to the FOS.

The complaint must be **remedied** where possible, and a **written report** produced. The firm must explain to the complainant the outcome of the investigation, including terms of settlement or reasons for rejection as appropriate.

The FOS can **make awards** up to £100,000 and also direct a firm to take appropriate action. The firm and adviser will be expected to **co-operate fully** with the FOS, and to act promptly to implement any award.

Records must be kept for at least six years after the date a complaint is received, although in view of the long-term nature of the business it may be advisable to keep them longer.

8 Compensation and redress

If a client complains it may be relatively easy to take **corrective action** to put the client back in the same position that he or she was in before the error occurred.

If a client suffers a financial loss as a result of a breach of a regulatory requirement the client may seek **compensation**. If the firm is an independent financial advisor or a member of an recognised professional body, adequate professional indemnity insurance (PII) should be in place to deal with this sort of situation.

However, a quite different situation arises if a firm is **insolvent** or is likely to become insolvent. The fact that a client may be able to demonstrate negligence or fraud on the part of a financial adviser will be of no financial help to the client if the company is going out of business. For this reason a compensation scheme known as the **Financial Services Compensation Scheme** (FSCS) exists to provide compensation for valid claims. It operates by sharing the costs of compensation amongst the other members of a defaulting member's regulator by means of a levy. However such claims will be subject to the following limits.

- Deposits: £31,700 (First £2,000 fully plus 90% of next £33,000)
- Investments: £48,000 (First £30,000 fully plus 90% of next £20,000)
- Long-term insurance: at least 90% of the value of the policyholder's guaranteed fund at the date of default.

Exam focus point

For the purposes of examination questions there are two things to note.

(a) The claim must be a valid claim.
(b) The adviser must be either insolvent or becoming insolvent.

Chapter roundup

- The Financial Services Authority (FSA) regulates investment business.
- The conduct of business rules apply when advising on or dealing in investments.
- There is a duty to **'know your client'** before giving financial advice.
- There is a regulatory requirement for financial advisers to give advice which is in the **best interests** of the client.
- Clients may be entitled to compensation in certain circumstances.

Quick quiz

1. What is meant by the 'know your client' principle?
2. Within how many days after receiving a complaint must a firm acknowledge it?

Answers to quick quiz

1. 'Know your client' means obtaining as much knowledge as possible about a client in order to give suitable advice.
2. Complaints must be acknowledged within five business days.

Now try the question below from the Exam Question Bank

Number	Level	Marks	Time
Q35	Introductory	5	9 mins

Questions

1 The Wrights **45 mins**

Eric Wright (born 31 January 1934) is a partner in a firm of architects. His taxable trade profits for 2006/07 are £29,060. In 2005, he took out a loan to buy some plant and machinery used in the partnership business. The amount of loan interest in 2006/07 was £1,000.

Eric has a bank account with the Halifax Bank. His account was credited with interest of £1,600 on 31 March 2007.

Eric made a gift aid donation of £390 to Oxfam on 1 December 2006.

Eric married Melanie on 10 May 2005. He was previously married to Doreen (born 1 December 1931). Eric and Doreen were divorced in 1996. Eric pays maintenance of £3,000 per year to Doreen under a court order. Doreen received a taxable state pension of £4,527 in 2006/07. She also received gross gilt interest of £4,020.

Melanie (born 1 April 1955) is employed as a head teacher in a local primary school. In 2006/07 she had earnings of £40,000. PAYE of £8,429 was deducted from these earnings.

Melanie received dividends of £4,500 during 2006/07. She also cashed in National Savings Certificates and received £250 interest in addition to the repayment of the capital invested.

Melanie made a gift aid donation of £1,170 to the RSPCA on 1 February 2007.

Eric and Melanie are considering buying a cottage together in May 2007 and renting it out. The cottage will cost £100,000. The net rental income will be about £10,000 per year. Eric and Melanie have not decided exactly in what proportions they will contribute to the cost of the cottage.

Required

(a) Compute the net income taxable by Eric, Doreen and Melanie for 2006/07. **(17 marks)**

(b) Explain how the rental income from the cottage will be taxed on Eric and Melanie. What advice would you give them to reduce their total tax liability? Assume Eric and Melanie have the same other income and expenditure in 2007/08 as in 2006/07 and that the rates of tax and allowances also remain the same in both tax years. **(8 marks)**

(Total = 25 marks)

2 Hamburg **45 mins**

(a) Hamburg retired in January 2006 at the age of 63 and used the income from investments to live on.

On 31 December 2006, he received the following interest payments on his National Savings Bank accounts:

Easy Access Savings account	£90
Investment account	£460

Hamburg received an income payment of £6,600 from a discretionary trust set up by his aunt on 1 February 2007. The whole of the trust fund was invested in quoted shares.

Hamburg also received dividends of £15,750 during 2006/07 from his own investments.

Hamburg owned £20,000 6% Treasury loan stock which he bought in 1995. Interest is payable gross on 1 June and 1 December each year. On 21 May 2006, Hamburg sold £10,000 of the loan stock ex interest. The accrued interest due to the purchaser was £35. Hamburg sold a further £7,500 of loan stock including interest of £150 on 1 October 2006.

On 1 May 2006, Hamburg started to invest in rented properties. He bought three houses in the first three months, as follows.

House 1

Hamburg bought house 1 for £62,000 on 1 May 2006. It needed a new roof, and Hamburg paid £5,000 for the work to be done in May. He also spent £1,200 on loft insulation. He then let it unfurnished for £600 a month from 1 June to 30 November 2006. The first tenant then left, and the house was empty throughout December 2006. On 1 January 2007, a new tenant moved in. The house was again let unfurnished. The rent was £6,000 a year, payable annually in advance.

Hamburg paid water rates of £320 for the period from 1 May 2006 to 5 April 2007 and a buildings insurance premium of £480 for the period from 1 June 2006 to 31 May 2007.

House 2

Hamburg bought house 2 for £84,000 on 1 June 2006. He immediately bought furniture for £4,300, and let the house fully furnished for £8,000 a year from 1 August 2006. The rent was payable quarterly in arrears. Hamburg paid water rates of £240 for the period from 1 June 2006 to 5 April 2007. He claimed the 10% wear and tear allowance for furniture.

House 3

Hamburg bought house 3 for £45,000 on 1 July 2006. He spent £1,000 on routine redecoration and £2,300 on furniture in July, and let the house fully furnished from 1 August 2006 for £7,800 a year, payable annually in advance. Hamburg paid water rates of £360 for the period from 1 July 2006 to 5 April 2007, a buildings insurance premium of £440 for the period from 1 July 2006 to 30 June 2007 and a contents insurance premium of £180 for the period from 1 August 2006 to 31 July 2007. He claimed the 10% wear and tear allowance for furniture.

During 2006/07 Hamburg also rented out one furnished room of his main residence. He received £4,600 and incurred allowable expenses of £875.

Required

Compute Hamburg's income tax payable for 2006/07. **(19 marks)**

(b) Hamburg is thinking about investing in two holiday cottages in Cornwall.

Required

Outline the requirements for the cottages to be furnished holiday lettings and the income tax treatment of such lettings. **(6 marks)**

(Total = 25 marks)

3 Taker — 15 mins

Taker is employed at an annual salary of £36,000. He is not in a pension scheme, but receives the following benefits in 2006/07.

(a) He has the use of an 1,800 cc petrol engined motor car, which cost £20,000. Its CO_2 emissions are 177g/km. Fuel is provided for both business and private motoring, and Taker contributes £500 a year (half the cost of fuel for private motoring) for fuel.

(b) He makes occasional private calls on the mobile phone provided by his employer.

(c) He usually borrows his employer's video camera (which cost £600) at weekends, when he uses it to record weddings and parties for friends. He receives no payment for this, and he supplies blank tapes himself.

(d) He has an interest free loan of £3,000 from his employer. Take the official rate of interest to be 5%.

(e) His employer pays £4,000 a year to a registered childminder with whom the employer has a contract. The childminder looks after Taker's three year old son for 48 weeks during the year.

In 2006/07, Taker pays expenses out of his earnings as follows.

(a) He pays subscriptions to professional bodies (relevant to his employment) of £180.

(b) He makes business telephone calls from home. The cost of business calls is £45. The cost of renting the line for the year is £100, and 40% of all Taker's calls are business calls.

(c) He pays a golf club subscription of £150. He does not play golf at all, but goes to the club to discuss business with potential clients. These discussions frequently lead to valuable contracts.

Required

Compute Taker's taxable earnings for 2006/07. **(8 marks)**

4 Helen Strube **18 mins**

Helen started trading as a physiotherapist on 1 July 2001. Her accounts were initially made up to 30 June each year but in 2004 she changed her accounting date to 30 September by preparing accounts for the fifteen months to 30 September 2004. She ceased trading on 31 December 2006 and accounts were prepared for the three months to 31 December 2006.

Helen's trade profits were as follows.

	£
Year to 30 June 2002	36,000
Year to 30 June 2003	48,000
Fifteen months to 30 September 2004	60,000
Year to 30 September 2005	30,000
Year to 30 September 2006	24,000
Three months to 31 December 2006	10,000

Required

Show the taxable trade profits for each tax year. Show clearly when overlap profits arise and how these are relieved. **(10 marks)**

5 Vivace **36 mins**

(a) Vivace makes up his accounts to 31 December each year.

After claiming allowances based on the period ended 31 December 2003, the balance of his general pool stood at £8,000.

During the years ended 31 December 2004, 2005 and 2006 Vivace recorded the following capital transactions.

14 September 2004	He sold machinery which originally cost £1,800 for £700.
16 September 2004	He bought a new car for a salesman for £4,000. The employee uses it privately for 25% of all its mileage.
1 December 2004	He bought secondhand machinery for £9,232.
21 March 2005	He sold plant which cost £2,000 in 2000 for £2,500.
22 March 2005	He sold the salesman's car for £3,200.
5 July 2005	He bought a Mercedes car for his own use costing £22,000. Vivace uses the car 60% for business purposes.

4 February 2006	He bought a new machine on hire purchase. A deposit of £1,800 was paid immediately. Four further instalments of £1,000 are payable annually in future years. The cash price would have been £4,000.
5 February 2006	He bought a car for the accountant for £3,000. There is no private use.
15 June 2006	He replaced his car. The Mercedes was sold for £4,000; a Volvo was bought for £18,000. 60% business use continued.
30 June 2006	Plant and equipment which originally cost £10,000 was sold for £2,602.
30 June 2006	He bought plant for £3,000.

Required

Set out Vivace's capital allowance computations for the periods of account ended 31 December 2004, 2005 and 2006, assuming that maximum claims are made. Assume Vivace's business qualifies as a small enterprise for capital allowances purposes where appropriate. **(10 marks)**

(b) Simon acquired a new factory for use in his trade on 1 August 2000. The cost of the factory was as follows:

	£
Land	50,000
Cost of preparing land	10,000
Architect's fees	5,000
Offices	45,000
Factory	140,000
Total cost	250,000

Simon used the factory in his trade until 1 December 2003. The factory was then let for 2 years. Simon then used the factory again in his business until he sold it to Alicia on 1 December 2006 for £300,000 (including £80,000 for the land).

Simon makes up his accounts to 31 July and Alicia to 31 December.

Required

Show the IBAs available to Simon and Alicia. **(10 marks)**

(Total = 20 marks)

6 Arrol — 45 mins

Arrol, a dentist, has been employed for several years as a representative by Bean Ltd, dental equipment manufacturers. His salary was £13,000 in the year ended 5 April 2006 and £12,771 in the year ended 5 April 2007. His employer provides him with a petrol engined motor car (cost £20,271) with CO_2 emissions of 237g/km. All petrol is purchased on Bean Ltd's account at a garage. Arrol makes a nominal £25 a month reimbursement to Bean Ltd for part of the petrol used by him in private usage of the motor car.

On 1 May 2006 Arrol and his wife received substantial gifts in cash and shares from a relative. On that day Arrol exchanged contracts and completed purchase of a private dental practice. Since then he has continued his employment and has worked part time in his practice. The result of the practice for the first year of trading to 30 April 2007 as adjusted for income tax but before capital allowances was a loss of £13,384. Indications are that the practice will be profitable in the year ending 30 April 2008.

Dental furniture (chairs, lamps etc) was purchased with the practice for £12,800. Additions to this equipment in the year ended 30 April 2007 cost £46,720 on 26 January 2007. Arrol wishes to claim the maximum capital allowances as soon as possible. None of the new equipment qualified for 100% FYAs.

In 2006/07 Arrol and his wife, who are both in their early fifties, had other income as follows.

	Arrol	Wife
	£	£
Bank interest received	235	
Building society interest received	3,005	5,012
Interest on National Savings Bank investment account		1,742
Salary as receptionist in husband's practice		2,800

Required

(a) Calculate the income tax liability of Arrol in 2006/07 on the assumption that he claims to have the loss incurred in 2006/07 set against his income of that year.

(b) Calculate the income tax liability of Arrol's wife in 2006/07.

(c) Calculate the loss remaining unrelieved in the year 2006/07 and state the alternative ways in which this loss may be used.

(25 marks)

7 Adam, Bert and Charlie **27 mins**

Adam, Bert and Charlie started in partnership as secondhand car dealers on 6 April 2003, sharing profits in the ratio 2:2:1, after charging annual salaries of £1,500, £1,200 and £1,000 respectively.

On 5 July 2004 Adam retires and Bert and Charlie continue, taking the same salaries as before, but dividing the balance of the profits in the ratio 3:2.

On 5 May 2006 Dick is admitted as a partner on the terms that he received a salary of £1,800 a year, that the salaries of Bert and Charlie should be increased to £1,800 a year each and that of the balance of the profits, Dick should take one tenth and Bert and Charlie should divide the remainder in the ratio 3:2.

The trade profits of the partnership as adjusted for tax purposes are as follows.

Year ending 31 March	Profits
	£
2004	10,200
2005	20,800
2006	12,600
2007	18,000

Required

Show the taxable trade profits for each partner for 2003/04 to 2006/07 inclusive. **(15 marks)**

8 John **36 mins**

John (aged 35) is employed by DEF plc, a quoted trading company. He earns a salary of £36,000 per year. He makes a monthly donation of £195 to Oxfam under the gift aid scheme. He has no other income since the part-time business which he also runs made no profit in this year.

During 2006/07, John makes the following disposals:

(a) 1,000 shares in DEF plc which he bought on 10 September 2005 and sold on 28 February 2007. His gain on sale was £10,000.

(b) His car. He bought the car on 12 July 2004 and sold it on 10 December 2006. He made a loss of £(3,000) on the sale.

(c) A piece of land bought as an investment on 14 June 1997. John sold the land on 15 November 2006. The gain on sale was £25,000.

(d) 5,000 shares in XYZ plc held in an individual savings account. The shares were bought by John on 17 August 2002 and sold at a gain of £7,500 on 31 January 2007.

(e) A factory. John bought the factory on 1 August 2003 and immediately used it for trading purposes until 1 November 2006. The factory was then empty until John sold it on 1 February 2007. He made a gain of £27,000 on the sale.

John had losses of £(6,000) brought forward at 5 April 2006.

Required

Compute the CGT payable by John for 2006/07. Explain your treatment of each of the gains and losses. **(20 marks)**

9 Sophie Shaw **45 mins**

Sophie Shaw made the following disposals in 2006/07:

(a) A painting for proceeds of £50,000 at auction on 12 October 2006. The auctioneer's costs of sale were 1% of the gross proceeds. Sophie had bought the painting on 31 March 1982 for £2,500 (RPI March 1982 79.4) .

(b) A freehold shop on 1 February 2007 for £85,000. The shop was acquired by Sophie's husband on 1 September 2002 for £45,000. He had transferred the shop to Sophie on 30 November 2005 when it was worth £60,000. The shop was let out to a quoted company throughout the period it was owned by Sophie or her husband.

(c) 4 acres of land on 10 July 2006 for £40,000. This was part of a 10 acre plot of land acquired by Sophie in September 1995 (RPI 150.6) for £20,000 as an investment. At the date of the sale, the remaining 6 acres was valued at £24,000.

(d) 4,000 shares in JKL plc to her son for £10,000 (their market value) on 23 December 2006. Sophie bought the shares on 1 February 2004 for £12,000.

On 6.4.06 Sophie had an unused capital loss brought forward of £5,000.

Required

Calculate the capital gains chargeable on Sophie for 2006/07 after taper relief and the annual exemption, giving details of your treatment of the disposals. RPI April 1998 = 162.6. **(25 marks)**

10 The Green family **45 mins**

(a) John Green acquired 20,000 shares in Miller plc on 1 May 2003 for £40,000. On 10 June 2006, Miller plc was taken over by Wall plc. Clearance was obtained from HMRC that this was a bona fide commercial arrangement. John received 1 ordinary share (worth £4.90) in Wall plc and cash of £1.60 for each Miller plc share.

(b) John's wife made the following purchases of ordinary shares in Read plc, a quoted company.

Date	*Number*	*Cost*
		£
15 May 2005	1,800	1,900
1 March 2006	1,000	1,260

On 12 July 2006, there was a 1 for 1 bonus issue.

On 30 September 2006 she sold 3,200 of the shares for £14,000.

(c) On 26 May 2006 Robert Green, Mr and Mrs Green's son, sold 1,450 quoted ordinary shares in Greengage Supermarkets plc for £10,150. His previous dealings in these shares had been as follows.

15 April 1985 (RPI = 94.8)	Purchased 900 shares for £3,408.
11 November 2005	Purchased 1,000 shares for £6,000

None of the shares are business assets for taper relief purposes. RPI April 1998 = 162.6.

Required

(a) Compute the capital gain on the takeover of Miller plc for John Green. Show the base cost of his shares in Wall plc. **(6 marks)**

(b) Compute the capital gain or allowable loss on the sale of Mrs Green's shares. **(7 marks)**

(c) Compute the capital gain on Robert's disposal of his shares. **(7 marks)**

(d) State how much capital gains tax John and his wife will have to pay for 2006/07 if they have no other chargeable gains or allowable losses, but Mr Green had £17,560 of allowable losses brought forward at 6 April 2006, Mr Green's taxable income for the year is £17,000, and Mrs Green has no income. Show any amounts carried forward. **(5 marks)**

(Total = 25 marks)

11 The Milsom family — 45 mins

(a) Mr Milsom is a sole trader. He bought a factory for use in his trade on 10 July 2004 for £150,000.

On 9 November 2005, the factory was damaged in a flood. Mr Milsom received compensation from the water company of £20,000 on 1 September 2006. He had incurred costs of £15,000 in July 2006 on renovations. The value of the factory after the renovations is £250,000.

On 1 December 2007, Mr Milsom gave the factory to his son, Gary. The market value of the factory at that time was £260,000. Gary rented out the factory to a quoted company.

Required

Show the chargeable gains (if any) for Mr Milsom for 2005/06, 2006/07 and 2007/08 assuming that any claims to defer gains are made and taking account of taper relief. Mr Milsom made no other disposals except to utilise his annual exemption each year. **(10 marks)**

(b) Gary sells the factory to a developer on 1 March 2009 for £300,000.

Required

Compute the gain on the sale for Gary and explain the taper relief situation.

Assume that the rates and allowances for CGT for 2006/07 also apply in later years. **(5 marks)**

(c) Mrs Milsom is also a sole trader. She acquired a freehold shop in Denby Terrace for use in the business in May 2001 for £40,000 and sold it in August 2006 for £80,000.

Mrs Milsom is considering buying a new shop. She has located two possible shops. One is a small freehold shop in High Street which would cost £72,000. The other is a larger leasehold shop in Station Road with a lease of 30 years. The cost of the lease would be £90,000.

Required

Write a letter to Mrs Milsom outlining the tax consequences of acquiring each of the shops.

(10 marks)

(Total = 25 marks)

12 Roland Rat

45 mins

In April 1989, Roland Rat ceased in business as a sole trader and transferred the assets of his business to Mouse Trap Ltd, wholly in exchange for shares. His final accounts as a sole trader and the opening position of the company in April 1989 were as follows.

		Roland Rat		*Mouse Trap Ltd*
	£	£	£	£
Fixed assets				
Goodwill		0		150,000
Freehold property		77,000		200,000
Plant and machinery (small movable items)		30,000		30,000
		107,000		380,000
Current assets				
Stock	73,200		73,200	
Debtors	63,900		63,900	
Cash at bank	41,000		0	
	178,100		137,100	
Less trade and expense creditors	(70,800)		(70,800)	
		107,300		66,300
		214,300		446,300
Capital employed				
Roland Rat capital account		214,300		
Share capital: 10,000 issued shares				10,000
Share premium account				436,300
		214,300		446,300

The freehold property is shown in Roland Rat's balance sheet at net book value being the cost in April 1983, less depreciation of £8,000. This was the date Roland commenced trading. He did not acquire an existing business. The values at which the company took over the assets have been accepted by HMRC.

Roland Rat informs you in August 2006 that the following transactions are proposed.

(i) He intends to transfer 2,500 shares in Mouse Trap Ltd to his wife for £50,000. They are a happily married couple.

(ii) At the same time he proposes to sell 2,000 shares to an incoming director at a price of £165,000, the market value.

(iii) The freehold property owned by Mouse Trap Ltd is now too small for the company's expanding trade. It is proposed to sell the property for £500,000 and use the proceeds, together with bank borrowings, to acquire larger freehold premises for £550,000.

Required

(a) Compute the chargeable gains which will arise if the above transactions proceed in August 2006, assuming that all gains are deferred where possible. State the base costs of the chargeable assets referred to above for any future disposals.

(b) Indicate whether your answer would have been any different if instead of issuing shares for the transfer of the business in 1989 the company had issued £200,000 worth of 11% debenture stock at par and satisfied the balance by the issue of shares.

Assume indexation	April 1983 – April 1989	0.356
	April 1989 – April 1998	0.423
	April 1989 – August 2006	0.720

(You may round indexation in the Finance Act 1985 pool to three decimal places.) **(25 marks)**

13 Miss Wolf and Mr Fox — 36 mins

(a) Miss Wolf carried out the following capital transactions:

(i) On 30 June 2006 she assigned the lease of a building originally acquired as an investment for £30,750; the lease expires on 30 June 2022.

She had acquired the lease for £8,000 on 1 January 1998 (RPI = 159.5) and the building had never been her principal private residence. RPI April 1998 = 162.6.

(ii) On 28 July 2006 she sold a racehorse for £25,000. The horse had been bought for £3,000 on 1 July 2002.

(iii) On 5 August 2006 she sold a picture for £9,000 at auction. The auctioneer's costs were 10% of the sale price. Miss Wolf had acquired the painting for £2,200 on 10 September 2002.

Miss Wolf had allowable losses of £2,203 brought forward to 2006/07. Miss Wolf's marginal rate of income tax for the year was 40%.

Required

Prepare a statement showing Miss Wolf's capital gains tax position for 2006/07.

(b) Mr Fox bought a house on 1 August 1986 (RPI = 97.8) for £50,000. He lived in the house until 31 July 1989. He then went abroad to work as a self-employed engineer until 31 July 1994.

Mr Fox went back to live in the house until 31 January 1995. He then moved in with his sister.

Mr Fox sold the house on 31 July 2006 for £180,000.

Required

Calculate the gain on sale after all reliefs. RPI April 1998 is 162.6 **(20 marks)**

14 Overseas — 18 mins

Susan (age 42) received the following income in 2006/07.

UK dividends	£9,000
Overseas property business income	£10,000
UK earnings income (gross)	£17,820

The overseas property business income suffered £4,705 of overseas tax before being paid to Susan.

Required

(a) Calculate the tax payable by Susan if she has suffered £2,000 of tax under PAYE for the year.

(b) To correct an error made on the behalf of the overseas country in 2006/07 on 1 November 2008 Susan receives from the overseas authorities a refund of £2,600 of the overseas tax suffered. What should Susan do in respect of this receipt?

(10 marks)

15 Mr Brown **27 mins**

Mr Brown's income tax liability for 2005/06 was £16,000. He had suffered tax by deduction at source of £4,000 and paid two payments on account of £6,000 each on the due dates. He submitted his 2005/06 return on 31 January 2007. Mr Brown made a claim to reduce his payments on account for 2006/07 on the basis that his total liability for 2006/07 would be £14,000 with tax suffered of £5,000. He made the payments on account of £4,500 on 28 February and 14 August 2007. Finally, on 13 March 2008 he submitted his return for 2006/07 which showed total tax due of £17,000 and tax deducted at source of £4,000. He therefore paid a further £4,000 on the same date.

Required

(a) Outline the time limits for submission of returns and payments of tax under self assessment and detail the provisions for failure to comply. **(12 marks)**

(b) Calculate the interest on overdue tax chargeable in respect of Mr Brown's tax payments for 2006/07. You are not required to compute any surcharges payable. **(3 marks)**

Note. Assume interest is charged at 6.5% per annum.

(Total = 15 marks)

16 Rodin **22 mins**

Rodin dies on 20 December 2006. His record of lifetime transfers is as follows.

Date	£	*Recipient*
15.12.99	60,000	Son
21.1.02	337,000	Discretionary trust (Rodin paid the IHT)
20.8.03	46,000	Daughter
19.6.05	106,000	Discretionary trust (Rodin paid the IHT)
1.8.06	73,000	Cousin
1.9.06	300,000	Wife

Required

Compute all amounts of inheritance tax due on these lifetime transfers. Assume that the £Nil band **has always been** £285,000. **(12 marks)**

17 Mr Bright **45 mins**

Hubert Bright, for whom you act as tax adviser, had over the years acquired 3,000 £1 ordinary shares in Bod Ltd, an unquoted trading company with an issued share capital of 5,000 ordinary shares. All the assets of Bod Ltd are in use for the purpose of its trade. Mr Bright has been a full time working director of the company since 1980. His wife, Rose, also owns 1,000 ordinary shares in the company.

Hubert had acquired his shares as follows.

	Shares	£
1.11.83	2,200	3,300
15.6.01	200	1,366
18.8.06	600	3,000

The current market values attributable to various percentage shareholdings in Bod Ltd are estimated as follows.

% Shareholding	Value of £1 ordinary share
100	40.50
80	36.67
60	25.00
40 or below	18.00

On 1 April 2007 Mr Bright sold 2,000 of his shares in Bod Ltd for £10,000 to his daughter Maxine, who sold them to an unconnected buyer ten days later.

He has made no previous transfer of assets other than a gift of £309,000 cash to a discretionary trust (which was not an accumulation and maintenance trust and did not include Mr Bright as a beneficiary) on 1 May 2006. Mr Bright had agreed to bear any costs or taxes in respect of the gift. Apart from his shares in Bod Ltd Mr Bright currently has no other assets apart from cash of £40,000. He has left everything in his will to his son Roger. You should assume that today's date is 14 April 2007.

Required

(a) Advise Mr Bright of his potential inheritance tax and capital gains tax liabilities assuming that he pays income tax at the marginal rate of 40%.

(b) Advise Mr Bright on the inheritance tax implications which would arise if he were to die on 20 April 2007. (Assume that any CGT on lifetime gifts is unpaid at the date of death but that any IHT has been paid.)

Assume that the IHT £Nil rate band is £285,000 and the CGT annual exemption is £8,800 throughout and that the rules and rates of CGT and IHT are the same in 2007/08 as in 2006/07. RPIs November 1983 86.7; April 1985 94.8; April 1998 162.6.

(25 marks)

18 Trusts — 36 mins

(a) A discretionary trust had the following receipts and payments in 2006/07.

	£
Receipts	
Dividends (net)	1,800
Interest on gilts (gross)	4,625
Payments	
Administration expenses	288
Distributions (net)	2,700

At the start of the year, the trustees had £10,000 in cash (after providing for all tax liabilities relating to earlier years).

Required

How much cash did they have at the end of the year (after providing for tax liabilities)?

(b) On 12 January 2005, Gainer put a 30% holding of shares in an unquoted trading company worth £50,000 into a discretionary trust. He had bought the shares on 10 January 1992 (RPI 135.6) for £35,000, and gift relief was claimed to avoid a capital gains tax charge on the shares being put into the trust. RPI April 1998 = 162.6.

On 1 July 2006, the trustees sold all the other trust assets, realising gains of £30,000 after indexation and taper relief.

On 1 August 2006, when the shares were worth £59,000, the terms of the trust were varied so that it became an interest in possession trust for Gainer's cousin Winnie.

On 1 April 2008, when the shares were worth £80,000, the life tenant dies and the trust assets vested absolutely in Winnie's daughter.

Gainer was the settlor of one other trust. He, the old life tenant and the new life tenant each had taxable income of over £100,000, but no chargeable gains, in each year concerned.

Required

Set out the trust's capital gains tax position for 2006/07 and 2007/08. Assume the tax rates and allowances for 2007/08 are the same as for 2006/07.

(20 marks)

19 National insurance contributions — 18 mins

(a) The following people work for Poster plc:

Albert — Managing director – works full time for the company – receives director's fees of £2,500 per month and a bonus of £5,000 in January 2007. Entitled to company car (benefit £4,500). No private fuel is provided. Provided with private medical insurance at a cost to the company of £750.

Barney — Manager, salary of £2,000 per month, and a bonus of £3,000 in January 2007.

Chloe — Cleaner, paid £120 per week.

None of the above is contracted out of the second state pension scheme.

Required

Show all NICs payable for 2006/07 in respect of these employees. **(8 marks)**

(b) Daniel is a self-employed designer. In 2006/07, he has taxable profits of (i) £30,000 or (ii) £35,000.

Required

Show the NICs payable by Daniel for 2006/07. **(2 marks)**

(Total = 10 marks)

20 Fraser Ltd — 27 mins

Fraser Ltd is a medium sized trading company. It has no associated companies and it makes up accounts to 31 March in each year.

The profit and loss account for the year ended 31 March 2007 showed a profit before taxation of £379,198. The following items were included in the accounts.

	£
Income	
Dividend from a UK company (including tax credit)	1,655
Interest on bank deposits	6,834
Interest from gilts (gross)	2,208
Surplus on the disposal of a factory and a lease	59,106
Expenditure	
Directors' remuneration	62,075
Miscellaneous	3,837
Depreciation	13,876

The company has not paid a dividend since its incorporation. Its bank deposits and gilts are held for non-trading purposes.

The company's main factory was acquired on 1 February 1995 for £200,000, including £30,000 for the land, from Swift Ltd which had used it for manufacturing purposes since its completion on 1 February 1990. The cost to Swift Ltd was £110,000 which included £20,000 for the land, £8,000 for general offices and £6,500 for a canteen.

The company's second factory (acquired for £79,000, including £12,000 for the land, on its completion on 31 May 1997) was sold for £112,750 (including £20,000 for the land) on 15 August 2006.

Both of the company's factories have been used solely for manufacturing purposes. Maximum writing down allowances have been claimed throughout their ownership although an initial allowance was not claimed in respect of the expenditure in either building.

A lease of one of the company's retail outlets was sold on 30 April 2006 for £40,000. The term of the lease was 30 years from 1 November 1993 and the company acquired it on 1 November 1998 at a cost of £17,500.

The company does not expect to be able to roll over any of the disposal proceeds in the year ended 31 March 2007 into other qualifying assets. There are no other unused losses or reliefs brought forward at 31 March 2006.

Miscellaneous expenses comprise the following.

	£
Hire purchase interest on two new fork lift trucks	783
Christmas gifts to customers: 40 executive desk diaries bearing the company's name	2,085
Entertaining customers	969
	3,837

The pool value of plant at 1 April 2006 was £nil. With the exception of the acquisition of the two new fork lift trucks under the hire purchase agreements at a cash price of £9,800 each on 1 December 2006 there were no purchases or sales of plant in the year ended 31 March 2007.

Required

Compute the mainstream corporation tax payable by Fraser Ltd for the year ended 31 March 2007.

Assume indexation	May 1997 – August 2006	0.253	
	November 1998 – April 2006	0.186	**(15 marks)**

21 Major Ltd **36 mins**

Major Ltd is a trading company resident in the United Kingdom. It has one associated company. Until 2006 Major Ltd made up accounts each year to 31 July, but decided to change its accounting date to 31 March. The information below relates to the eight month period to 31 March 2007:

	£
INCOME	
Adjusted trading profit (before deduction of any patent royalties or loan interest)	180,000
Rents received *less* expenses	30,000
Loan interest received – (see Note 1)	24,000
Capital gains	40,000
Franked investment income (FII) (received September 2006)	20,000

	£
PAYMENTS	
Patent royalties (gross figure paid to a sole trader)	15,000
Gift Aid payment (paid September 2006)	3,000
Loan interest paid (see Note 2)	30,000

Notes

1. The loan interest was received in respect of a loan of £100,000 made by the company to Z Ltd, a main supplier of materials to Major Ltd. The directors of Major Ltd are concerned about the financial position of Z Ltd, but have decided to take no action at present.
2. The loan interest paid was to a UK bank in respect of funds raised to acquire the company's 80% interest in its associated company.
3. The patent royalties were paid for the purpose of Major Ltd's trade. All amounts accrued in the year were paid in the year.

Required

(a) Compute the mainstream corporation tax (MCT) payable by Major Ltd in respect of the above accounting period.

(b) Advise the directors of Major Ltd of the taxation implications of the loan to Z Ltd proving irrecoverable.

(20 marks)

22 Hogg Ltd — 23 mins

(a) Hogg Ltd prepares accounts for the year to 31 December 2006. In June 2006 it estimates that its corporation tax liability for the year will be £500,000. In January 2007 it revises its estimate to £520,000. In October 2007 it submits its return and self-assessment, showing a total liability of £525,000. The company has always paid corporation tax at the full rate.

Required

State the amounts and due dates for the payment of corporation tax by Hogg Ltd in respect of the year to 31 December 2006. **(7 marks)**

(b) State what penalties arise if a company submits its CT600 return late. **(6 marks)**

(Total = 13 marks)

23 Daley plc — 18 mins

Daley plc has had the following results since it started to trade.

	Year ended 31.12.03	*Year ended 31.12.04*	*Six months ended 30.6.05*	*Year ended 30.6.06*
	£	£	£	£
Trading profit/(loss)	(29,000)	110,000	85,000	(200,000)
Interest income	10,000	11,000	12,000	14,000
Chargeable gains/ (allowable losses)	18,000	(5,000)	2,000	(2,000)
Gift aid donation	Nil	Nil	3,000	1,000

Reliefs are always claimed as early as possible. There are no associated companies.

Required

Compute the corporation tax liability for all four periods, assuming no dividends are paid or received in the periods in question, and show all amounts to be carried forward at 30 June 2006. Assume that tax rates and allowances for FY 2006 apply to all years. **(10 marks)**

24 Huis plc **27 mins**

(a) Huis plc is a close company which pays corporation tax at the small companies rate. On 31 May 2006, six months before the company's year end, it lent £45,000 to Sartre, a shareholder. Sartre is not an employee of the company. The loan carried a market rate of interest.

The company advised Sartre on 31 March 2008 that he would not be required to repay the loan.

Required

Set out the tax consequences of the transactions with Sartre, giving the dates on which any amounts are payable to HMRC.

(b) Beauvoir Ltd is a close investment-holding company. It has had the following results for the last two years.

	Year ended 31.3.06	*Year ended 31.3.07*
	£	£
Property income	14,000	25,000
Interest income	20,000	100,000
Management expenses	36,000	45,000
Dividends received in August from non-group companies	16,000	27,000

Required

Compute the company's mainstream corporation tax for both years. **(15 marks)**

25 H, S and N **45 mins**

H Ltd has owned 60% of the issued ordinary share capital of S Ltd since its incorporation, the remaining 40% being held by individuals. Both UK companies have always prepared accounts to 30 June, their most recent accounts showing the following.

	H Ltd		*S Ltd*	
	Year ended 30.6.05	*Year ended 30.6.06*	*Year ended 30.6.05*	*Year ended 30.6.06*
	£	£	£	£
Adjusted trading profit	2,000		30,000	100,000
Adjusted trading loss		(48,000)		
Gift aid donation paid			12,000	12,000

On 1 January 2005, H Ltd acquired 100% of the issued ordinary share capital of N Ltd, a company which had always prepared accounts to 31 December.

N Ltd's accounts for the period of 1 January 2005 to 30 June 2006 show the following.

	£
Adjusted trading profit, before capital allowances	65,250
Chargeable gain, after indexation allowance on land bought in 1992 and sold in February 2006	20,000

N Ltd had a written down value of plant at 1 January 2005 of £5,000 and had incurred expenditure as follows.

		£
3 February 2005:	new car to be used by the managing director of N Ltd 80% for business, 20% for private use	16,000
4 January 2006:	new plant	31,000
20 March 2006:	secondhand plant bought on hire purchase, the cash price being £8,000, a deposit of £2,000 being paid on the above date followed by 24 monthly instalments of £300, commencing 20 May 2006.	

Required

Compute the mainstream corporation tax payable by H Ltd, S Ltd and N Ltd for the above periods of account, assuming all available claims and surrenders are made to minimise the mainstream corporation tax payable by the group and that all three companies meet the definition of 'medium sized'. **(25 marks)**

26 Exotica Inc and W Ltd **27 mins**

(a) Exotica Inc (for which you act as United Kingdom tax adviser) is a company resident and incorporated in Ruritania, a country which is outside the European Community and does not have a double tax agreement with the UK. The company manufactures items of advanced industrial equipment and now wishes to increase its sales within the UK. The company has no subsidiaries and currently makes worldwide profits equivalent to £300,000 sterling a year.

It intends to acquire an office in London and to staff it with full-time salesmen assigned from its head office in Ruritania. These individuals will stay in the UK for periods ranging between six months and four years. Those staying for less than a year will reside on their own in hotels. Those staying for a year or longer will live in rented accommodation with their families. Most, but not all of them, will be non-UK domiciled, and in all cases their only source of income (apart from their employment with Exotica Inc) will be long-standing bank deposit accounts in Ruritania.

Exotica Inc is still considering whether the salesmen will be given the authority to conclude contracts with UK customers or whether such authority will be reserved for the head office only. It is also considering whether customers' orders should be met from stocks held in Ruritania or whether stocks should be maintained in the UK. While tax considerations will be taken into account, other commercial factors are likely to influence these decisions strongly. Projected additional profits from the UK operation are £75,000 a year.

Required

Advise Exotica Inc on the corporation tax implications of the various alternative courses of action still under consideration.

(b) The directors of W Ltd have decided to set up an operation in a country where the rate of corporation tax is 25%.

They are considering two alternative approaches:

(i) to run the overseas operation as a permanent establishment of the UK company; or
(ii) to run it as a foreign-registered subsidiary of the UK company.

Required

Draft a report to the board on the taxation implications of each of the alternative proposals.

(15 marks)

27 Paul and Joe **18 mins**

Paul Sand is in business as a general builder but he is also in partnership with John Rowe as "A1 Repairs", Peter Dene as "Kwik Repairs" and in partnership with his wife as "Speedy Builders".

Required

Discuss how many VAT "persons" exist here. **(10 marks)**

28 VAT groups **18 mins**

It is February 2007. Barry Franklin, the Finance Director of Banner plc, has written to you, asking for your advice on certain VAT matters. Banner plc has two wholly owned subsidiaries, Flag Ltd and Ensign Ltd. All three companies are fully taxable and are included in a group registration for VAT. Two months ago, in December 2006, Banner plc acquired 75% of the ordinary share capital of Union Ltd, a partly exempt company. Union Ltd generally recovers around 60% of its input tax. To date, no action has been taken to include Union Ltd in the group registration.

As Union Ltd is not wholly owned, other group companies will be required to pay for any losses surrendered to them as group relief.

Mr Franklin has specifically asked whether Union Ltd should be included in the group registration and, if so, what action he should take in this regard.

All four companies are UK resident with an established place of business in the UK.

Required

Write a letter in reply to Mr Franklin. **(10 marks)**

29 Tax planning **45 mins**

You are a partner in a firm of certified accountants with particular responsibility for tax planning.

Required

Draft an answer to each of the following queries which have been passed on to you by your fellow partners. You should assume that today's date is 1 April 2006.

(a) Client A, who is single, is about to commence business as a management consultant on 1 May 2006. She was previously employed as a school headmistress for several years at a salary in excess of £40,000 pa. The business involves virtually no expenditure on capital assets. She expects to make operating losses in her first two years of trading, after which she expects the business slowly to become profitable. She will have no other taxable sources of income. For reasons of prestige she is proposing to trade through a specially formed company, A Ltd. However, she could delay forming the company for a short while and she asks what the best course of action would be from a tax viewpoint.

(b) Client B currently manufactures fitted bedroom furniture for the general public from a small workshop. The market is highly competitive. He has a turnover of £55,000 pa which yields a current gross profit percentage of 40% and he incurs minimal overheads. He has been offered a contract to manufacture bookcases for a VAT registered trader at a price of £10,000 a year (exclusive of any VAT). B estimates that this project would involve a similar cost structure to his existing operations. B is concerned that, since he will become liable to register for VAT if he takes on the new contract, it may not be worthwhile to accept it. He has asked for calculations showing the net annual gain to him from taking on the contract. He has also enquired whether it would be possible to avoid the requirement to register by setting up a new company, B Ltd, to carry out the new contract. (*Note*. You are required to consider VAT issues *only*.)

(c) Client C is about to acquire shares in a publicly quoted company for £350,000 out of his own funds. The shares currently yield a dividend of £28,000 a year paid in September and March each year. The prospects for significant capital appreciation in the future are excellent. At the end of ten years C may decide to sell some or all of the shares. It has been suggested to C by a friend, D, that instead of buying the shares himself he should form a new investment company, C Ltd. C would subscribe for 350,000 £1 shares in C Ltd, which would then use the cash to buy the shares. D has told C that he could draw out director's remuneration of up to £10,000 a year and that C Ltd could deduct this against the dividend income and that the balance of £18,000 would only be liable to the lower corporation tax rate of 19%. D has also said that C could obtain tax relief by paying premiums into a personal pension scheme. C has asked whether the advice which he has received from D is correct.

(d) Client D is setting up in business as an aromatherapist. She is considering structuring her business either as a sole trader or through a limited company. If she operates as a sole trader she will be starting in business on 6 April 2006, making up her first accounts to 5 April 2007 with an expected trading profit of £23,000. If she uses a limited company, it will start in business on 1 April 2006, make up accounts to 31 March 2007, with expected PCTCT of £23,000. Client D would extract all available profits by way of dividends on 31 March 2007.

Client D has investment income which exactly covers her personal allowance and starting band for 2006/07. Client D wants to know how much net spendable income she would have from the business in each of these cases.

(25 marks)

30 Hulse Finds Ltd 45 mins

Paul Hulse and his friend Nick Royle set up the company Hulse Finds Ltd with Paul and Nick holding 40% of the shares each. The remaining 20% of the company is held by five of their friends. Hulse Finds Ltd runs a shop in Didsbury selling unusual objects which are sourced from around the world. Paul and Nick work full time in the management of the company but their five friends are passive investors in the business.

Paul took out a bank loan of £150,000 secured on his apartment in central Manchester to purchase his shares whereas Nick used his redundancy payout from his old employer (a large bank).

Hulse Finds Ltd incurred significant start-up costs in it's first 18 months of trade. Profits chargeable to corporation tax were £40,000 and £160,000 in the years to 31 March 2006 and 2007 respectively.

During June in the second year the company made a loan to Chris Newn (one of the investor friends) of £10,000. The company paid a dividend of £12,000 in the year ended 31 March 2006 and £15,000 in the following year.

Nick has identified a company Sweet Nothings Ltd (SNL) as a possible acquisition. The company sells French furniture and fixtures which it imports into the UK. After negotiations with the board of directors of SNL it has been agreed that Hulse Finds Ltd can purchase the trade and assets of SNL on 1 April 2008.

SNL has trading losses which are being carried forward of £50,000 and capital losses being carried forward of £25,000. Hulse Finds Ltd will set up a wholly owned subsidiary SN2 Ltd to acquire the trade and assets of SNL. Predicted PCTCT for the two companies for year ended 31 March 2009 are;

Hulse Finds Ltd		£250,000
SN2 Ltd	Trading profits	40,000
	Capital gains	10,000

By 2010 Paul and Nick expect the business to have grown considerably and they expect to have taxable profits of £1 million in the year ended 31 March 2010. SN2 Ltd is expected to have taxable profits of £100,000 in the same period.

Paul and Nick have been looking to expand overseas in order to take advantage of new emerging markets. They intend to start a new business in Newland on 1 April 2010.

It is anticipated that the overseas business will make a trading loss of £60,000 in the year ended 31 March 2010, a profit of £80,000 in the year ended 31 March 2011 and a profit of £100,000 per year in future years.

The system of corporation tax in Newland is broadly the same as that in the UK, although loss relief is only available to companies resident in Newland. In addition, the rate of corporation tax is 45% regardless of the level of profits and there is no withholding tax when dividends are paid to overseas shareholders. There is no double tax treaty between the UK and Newland.

You are meeting with Paul and Chris next week. Make brief notes on the following for discussion at that meeting:

(a) Any relief for Pauls' investment in the company? **(2 marks)**

(b) What is the impact, if any, of the loan to Chris and would this be different if Chris was an employee of the company? **(4 marks)**

(c) Calculate the tax due for the first two accounting periods. **(4 marks)**

(d) What are the tax implications of the acquisition of SNL? In particular can you suggest any way to maximise the tax advantages for Hulse Finds Ltd. **(7 marks)**

(e) Discuss the tax implications of the proposed expansion overseas. **(8 marks)**

(Total = 25 marks)

31 Financial planning 45 mins

(a) The directors of M Ltd, a medium-sized unquoted company engaged in manufacturing, have decided to embark on a major expansion of the business.

The company has a significant amount of unissued share capital and, to finance the expansion, the directors have been considering issuing further shares. They have also considered raising loan capital, using as security identified pieces of valuable property owned by the company.

Required

Draft a report dated 19 May 2006, to the board setting out the taxation implications for the company under each of the alternative methods of raising finance.

Your report should also identify any taxation implications for the providers of this finance.

(15 marks)

(b) Both individuals and businesses must be prepared for potential disaster situations that they may face.

Required

List the potential disaster situations for which an individual and a business may wish to quantify shortfall and purchase protection. **(10 marks)**

(Total = 25 marks)

32 Qualifying and non qualifying policies 15 mins

Answer the following questions.

(a) Is there any difference for a higher rate tax payer if they hold a qualifying or non-qualifying term assurance policy?

(b) Is it important that a basic rate tax payer should have a qualifying policy?

(c) If a client holds a qualifying policy taken out in 1975 that needs amending, in what aspect must you take particular care in giving advice?

(d) List the chargeable events.

(8 marks)

33 Mr and Mrs Faulds — 18 mins

Mr and Mrs Faulds are considering investment in ISAs (individual savings accounts).

Required

Draft short notes in preparation for a meeting with them scheduled for October 2006 describing the main features of this type of investment. **(10 marks)**

34 Mr Lee — 20 mins

You have received the following e-mail from a client, Mr Lee:

"I have just started a new job and thought that I ought to start making some pension provision now that I am in my mid-30s. My initial salary is £100,000 a year, but I am hoping that, with bonuses, it may increase in the next few years to around £500,000.

My employer operates a pension scheme and I have been given a booklet about it. The booklet says that the scheme is a "money purchase" scheme. If I join the scheme, my employer will make contributions to the scheme in addition to the amount that I pay into it.

Could you answer the following questions:

(a) Do I have to join my employer's pension scheme or can I make other pension arrangements? What is a "money purchase" scheme?

(b) If I join my employer's pension scheme, how much can I contribute to the scheme and how much can my employer contribute?

(c) I have heard that there is tax relief on my contributions to a pension scheme. How does that work if I join my employer's pension scheme?

(d) What benefits will I be able to receive from the pension scheme and when will I be able to receive them?"

You are required to draft an e-mail in response. **(11 marks)**

35 Complaints — 9 mins

Answer the following questions.

(a) What action must be taken by a firm when a complaint is received?
(b) What information must appear in a letter acknowledging an oral complaint?
(c) What information must be given to a client when an investigation is completed?
(d) Who must handle a complaint to a firm?

(5 marks)

36 Landscape Ltd **45 mins**

Landscape Ltd is an unquoted trading company that operates a nationwide chain of retail shops.

(a) Landscape Ltd employed Peter Plain as a computer programmer until 31 December 2006. On that date he resigned from the company, and set up as a self-employed computer programmer. Peter has continued to work for Landscape Ltd, and during the period 1 January to 5 April 2007 has invoiced them for work done based on an hourly rate of pay. Peter works five days each week at the offices of Landscape Ltd, uses their computer equipment, and does not have any other clients. The computer function is an integral part of Landscape Ltd's business operations. Peter now considers himself to be self-employed but Landscape Ltd's accountant is not sure if this is the correct interpretation.

(b) On 15 March 2007 Landscape Ltd dismissed Simon Savannah, the manager of their shop in Manchester, and gave him a lump sum redundancy payment of £55,000. This amount include statutory redundancy pay of £2,400, holiday pay of £1,500, and £5,000 for agreeing not to work for a rival company. The balance of the payment was compensation for loss of office, and £10,000 of this was not paid until 31 May 2007.

(c) Trevor Tundra is one of the Landscape Ltd's shareholders, and is not a director or an employee of the company. On 6 April 2006 Landscape Ltd provided Trevor with a new motor car that had a CO_2 emissions figure of 240g/km and that had an original list price of £14,000. No private petrol was provided. On 1 July 2006 Landscape Ltd made an interest free loan of £40,000 to Trevor. He repaid £25,000 of the loan on 31 August 2006, and the balance of the loan was written off on 31 March 2007.

(d) On 1 October 2006 Landscape Ltd opened a new shop in Cambridge, and assigned three employees from the London shop to work there on a temporary basis.

  (1) Ursula Upland is to work in Cambridge for a period of 18 months. Her ordinary commuting is a daily total of 90 miles, and her daily total from home to Cambridge to home again is 40 miles. She uses her private motor car for business mileage.

  (2) Violet Veld was initially due to work in Cambridge for a period of 30 months, but this was reduced to a period of 20 months on 1 January 2007. Violet walks to work whereas the cost of her train fare from home to Cambridge is £30 per day. This is paid by Landscape Ltd.

  (3) Wilma Wood is to work in Cambridge for a period of six months. Her ordinary commuting is a daily total of 30 miles, and her daily total from home to Cambridge is 150 miles. Wilma passes the London shop on her daily journey to Cambridge. She uses her private motor car for business mileage.

  All three employees worked at Cambridge for 120 days using 2006/07. Landscape Ltd pays a mileage allowance of 36 pence per mile for business use.

(e) Landscape Ltd is considering setting up a share incentive plan in order to reward its key employees. The company would like to know how many tax and NIC free shares it can give to each employee and how long the employees concerned must hold the shares for in order to obtain this advantage.

Required

Explain the income tax implications arising from the payments and benefits that have been made or provided by Landscape Ltd to Peter, Richard, Simon, Trevor, Ursula, Violet and Wilma. Your answer should be confined to the implications for 2006/07 and should assume that Landscape Ltd meets the definition of a close company. **(25 marks)**

Marks for this question will be allocated on the basis of:

6 marks to (a)
4 marks to (b)
4 marks to (c)
7 marks to (d)
4 marks to (e)

Assume that the official rate of interest is 5%.

Approaching the answer

You should read through the requirement before working through and annotating the question as we have done so that you are aware of what things you are looking for.

Landscape Ltd is an unquoted trading company that operates a nationwide chain of retail shops.

(a) Landscape Ltd employed Peter Plain as a computer programmer until 31 December 2006. On that date he resigned from the company, and set up as a self-employed computer programmer. Peter has continued to work for Landscape Ltd, and during the period 1 January to 5 April 2007 has invoiced them for work done based on an hourly rate of pay. Peter works five days each week at the offices of Landscape Ltd, uses their computer equipment, and does not have any other clients. The computer function is an integral part of Landscape Ltd's business operations. Peter now considers himself to be self-employed but Landscape Ltd's accountant is not sure if this is the correct interpretation.

Employment v Self employment

Suggest self-employed

Suggest employee

Suggest employee

Suggest employee

Suggest employee

(b) On 15 March 2007 Landscape Ltd dismissed Simon Savannah, the manager of their shop in Manchester, and gave him a lump sum redundancy payment of £55,000. This amount includes statutory redundancy pay of £2,400, holiday pay of £1,500, and £5,000 for agreeing not to work for a rival company. The balance of the payment was compensation for loss of office, and £10,000 of this was not paid until 31 May 2007.

£30,000 exempt if ex gratia

Exempt

Taxable

Taxable

Taxed 07/08

(c) Trevor Tundra is one of the Landscape Ltd's shareholders, and is not a director or an employee of the company. On 6 April 2006 Landscape Ltd provided Trevor with a new motor car that had a CO_2 emissions figure of 240g/km and that had an original list price of £14,000. No private petrol was provided. On 1 July 2006 Landscape Ltd made an interest free loan of £40,000 to Trevor. He repaid £25,000 of the loan on 31 August 2006, and the balance of the loan was written off on 31 March 2007.

Calculate benefit

Calculate benefit

Taxable

(d) On 1 October 2006 Landscape Ltd opened a new shop in Cambridge, and assigned three employees from the London shop to work there on a temporary basis. [Travel deductible]

(1) Ursula Upland is to work in Cambridge for a period of 18 months. [Temporary] Her ordinary commuting is a daily total of 90 miles, and her daily total from home to Cambridge to home again is 40 miles. She uses her private motor car for business mileage. [Authorised mileage rates]

(2) Violet Veld was initially due to work in Cambridge for a period of 30 months, [Not temporary] but this was reduced to a period of 20 months [Temporary] on 1 January 2007. Violet walks to work whereas the cost of her train fare from home to Cambridge is £30 per day. This is paid by Landscape Ltd.

(3) Wilma Wood is to work in Cambridge for a period of six months. [Temporary] Her ordinary commuting is a daily total of 30 miles, and her daily total from home to Cambridge is 150 miles. Wilma passes the London shop on her daily journey to Cambridge. She uses her private motor car for business mileage. [Authorised mileage rates]

All three employees worked at Cambridge for 120 days using 2006/07. Landscape Ltd pays a mileage allowance of 36 pence per mile for business use.

(e) Landscape Ltd is considering setting up a share incentive plan in order to reward its key employees. The company would like to know how many tax and NIC free shares [‘Free’ shares plus free Matching Partnership] it can give to each employee and how long the employees concerned must hold the shares for in order to obtain this advantage.

Required

Explain the income tax implications arising from the payments and benefits that have been made or provided by Landscape Ltd to Peter, Richard, Simon, Trevor, Ursula, Violet and Wilma. Your answer should be confined to the implications for 2006/07 and should assume that Landscape Ltd meets the definition of a close company.

Marks for this question will be allocated on the basis of:

6 marks to (a)
4 marks to (b)
4 marks to (c)
7 marks to (d)
4 marks to (e)

Assume that the official rate of interest is 5%.

Answer plan

This question is helpfully broken down into parts so you should start by working out how much time to spend on each individual part:

Part (a)	10 mins
Part (b)	7 mins
Part (c)	7 mins
Part (d)	12 mins
Part (e)	7 mins

You can then work through the question methodically. The answer is written so take care not to ramble. Lots of concise points will obtain more marks than one point written about at length.

37 Marilyn Corniche 45 mins

Marilyn Corniche was widowed on 20 May 2005. Under the terms of the will of her late husband Max she benefited absolutely from his share of the family home which they had held jointly as tenants in common and the bank balances. The mortgage on the family home was repaid out of the proceeds of a joint life first death life assurance policy. In addition Marilyn benefited from a life interest in a trust owning a holiday home in Cornwall and a portfolio of quoted investments, all of which had previously been owned by Max personally. The trust property passes equally to their twin sons, Douglas and Archie, aged 24, absolutely on Marilyn's death. The chattels passed to Max's brother Mark. Max, who had died suddenly, had made no lifetime gifts. The base cost, probate value and current market value of the items contained in Max's estate are as follows:

	Base cost plus indexation to 5/4/98	*Probate value May 2005*	*Market value February 2007*
	£	£	£
Family home (½ share)	61,500	90,000	110,000
Holiday home	42,000	63,000	73,000
Quoted investments			
Spiro plc 10,000 ordinary shares	50,000		
quoted at		685-677	635-647
with bargains marked at		690, 670, 675	630, 642, 641
Unit trusts	50,000	60,300	81,000
Unit trusts contained in PEPs and ISAs	40,000	48,800	67,600
Bank deposits contained in ISAs	9,000	11,000	11,300
Bank deposit account	20,000	20,000	20,000
Chirico painting – Creation	4,000	5,000	7,000
Rene writing desk	8,000	7,000	4,000
Beckman's Diary – first edition	3,500	3,000	4,500

Marilyn also has £33,400 on deposit at Berkley's Bank, unit trust units invested in PEPs and stocks and shares ISAs valued at £72,000 and a cash ISA of £10,600.

Marilyn has sufficient income to live on from her own resources.

Marilyn has just been diagnosed as having terminal cancer. The prognosis is that she has less than two years to live. She is anxious to minimise the impact of inheritance tax on her estate.

Mark is a higher rate taxpayer and has already made capital gains in the 2006/07 year of £10,000. No taper relief is due in respect of these gains.

Required

(a) Calculate the inheritance tax liability that arose on Max's estate as a result of his death on 20 May 2005 and that which would arise on Marilyn's estate if she were to die today (ie February 2007). Use the nil rate band for 2006/07 for both calculations. **(8 marks)**

(b) (i) Advise on action(s) that Marilyn (and her sons) can now take to reduce the liability in (a), identifying any conditions that need to be satisfied for the plan to be effective. **(9 marks)**

(ii) Calculate the tax saving which would result if the advice in part (b)(i) were followed. **(8 marks)**

(Total = 25 marks)

Approaching the answer

You should read through the requirement before working through and annotating the question as we have done so that you are aware of what things you are looking for.

Marilyn Corniche was widowed on 20 May 2005. Under the terms of the will of her

Spouse exemption

late husband Max she benefited absolutely from his share of the family home which they had held jointly as tenants in common and the bank balances. The mortgage on the family home was repaid out of the proceeds of

Initial interest in will trust

a joint life first death life assurance policy. In addition Marilyn benefited from a life interest in a trust owning a holiday home in Cornwall and a portfolio of quoted investments, all of which had previously been owned by Max personally. The trust property passes equally to their twin sons, Douglas and Archie, aged 24, absolutely on

Taxable?

Marilyn's death. The chattels passed to Max's brother Mark. Max, who had died suddenly, had made

NLY death estate

no lifetime gifts. The base cost, probate value and current market value of the items contained in Max's estate are as follows:

Lowest of
(i) ¼ up
(ii) Average highest and lowest marked bargain

	Base cost plus indexation to 5/4/98	*Probate value May 2005*	*Market value February 2007*
	£	£	£
Family home (½ share)	61,500	90,000	110,000
Holiday home	42,000	63,000	73,000
Quoted investments			
Spiro plc 10,000 ordinary shares	50,000		
quoted at		685-677	635-647
with bargains marked at		690, 670, 675	630, 642, 641
Unit trusts	50,000	60,300	81,000
Unit trusts contained in PEPs and ISAs	40,000	48,800	67,600
Bank deposits contained in ISAs	9,000	11,000	11,300
Bank deposit account	20,000	20,000	20,000
Chirico painting – Creation	4,000	5,000	7,000
Rene writing desk	8,000	7,000	4,000
Beckman's Diary – first edition	3,500	3,000	4,500

Marilyn also has £33,400 on deposit at Berkley's Bank, unit trust with units invested in PEPs and stocks and shares ISAs valued at £72,000 and a cash ISA of £10,600.

All subject to IHT

Marilyn has sufficient income to live on from her own resources.

Deed of variation

Marilyn has just been diagnosed as having terminal cancer. The prognosis is that she has less than two years to live. She is anxious to minimise the impact of inheritance tax on her estate.

Mark is a higher rate taxpayer and has already made capital gains in the 2006/07 year of £10,000. No taper relief is due in respect of these gains.

Required

(a) Calculate the inheritance tax liability that arose on Max's estate as a result of his death on 20 May 2005 and that which would arise on Marilyn's estate if she were to die today (ie February 2007). Use the nil rate band for 2006/07 for both calculations. **(8 marks)**

(b) (i) Advise on action(s) that Marilyn (and her sons) can now take to reduce the liability in (a), identifying any conditions that need to be satisfied for the plan to be effective. **(9 marks)**

(ii) Calculate the tax saving which would result if the advice in part (b)(i) were followed. **(8 marks)**

Answer plan

(a)	Death of Max:	Spouse exemption
	Death of Marilyn:	Produce death estate
	Value Spiro plc shares	
(b)	Deed of variation:	Conditions, Saving

Answers

1 The Wrights

Tutorial note. By this stage you should be proficient at setting up an income tax computation in three columns, grossing up income etc. This question also tests some new areas at Paper 3.2 such as age allowance, tax reducers and gross investment income. All of these areas could be examined in Section A, the compulsory section of Paper 3.2.

(a) (i) Eric

	Non-savings £	*Savings (excl. dividends)* £	*Dividends* £	*Total* £
Taxable trade profits	29,060			
BI £1,600 × 100/80		2,000		
Less: eligible interest (charge)	(1,000)			
STI	28,060	2,000	Nil	30,060
Less: PA (W1)	(5,035)			(5,035)
Taxable income	23,025	2,000	Nil	25,025

Tax

	£
£2,150 × 10%	215
£20,875 × 22%	4,593
£2,000 × 20%	400
	5,208
Less: tax reducers	
MCAA £3,580 (W1) × 10%	(358)
maintenance £2,350 (maximum) × 10%	(235)
	4,615
Less: tax deducted at source	(400)
Tax due	4,215

Note. There is a tax reducer for maintenance as at least one of Eric and Doreen were born before 6 April 1935. It is the lower of £2,350 and the maintenance of £3,000, ie £2,350 × 10%.

(ii) Doreen

	Non-savings £	*Savings (excl. dividends)* £	*Dividends* £	*Total* £
Pension	4,527			
Gilts interest		4,020		
STI	4,527	4,020	Nil	8,547
Less: PA (age 75 in tax year)	(4,527)	(2,893)		(7,420)
Taxable income	Nil	1,127	Nil	1,127

Tax

	£
£1,127 × 10%	113

Note. The maintenance payment is not taxable on Doreen.

(iii) Melanie

	Non-savings	*Savings (excl. dividends)*	*Dividends*	*Total*
	£	£	£	£
Earnings	40,000			
Dividends £4,500 × 100/90			5,000	
NS Certificates interest – exempt				
STI	40,000	Nil	5,000	45,000
Less: PA	(5,035)			(5,035)
Taxable income	34,965	Nil	5,000	39,965

Tax

	£
£2,150 × 10%	215
£31,150 × 22%	6,853
(£1,170 × 10/78) = £1,500 × 22% (gift aid)	330
£165 × 40%	66
£5,000 × 32½ %	1,625
	9,089
Less: PAYE	(8,429)
dividend tax credit	(500)
Tax due	160

Note. Interest on the National Savings Certificate is exempt from income tax.

(b) The total income will be split 50:50 between Eric and Melanie if no declaration of underlying interests is made. The tax liability would be:

		£
Eric	£5,000 × 22%	1,100
	Add: reduction in MCAA (W2) tax reducer	123
Melanie	£5,000 × 40%	2,000
Total extra tax		3,223

It would be better for the cottage to be bought so that Eric is entitled to sufficient income to use his basic rate band. A declaration for this treatment needs to be made.

		£
Eric	Basic rate band available £(33,300 – 25,025)	8,275
	Add: grossed up gift aid donation (390 × 100/78)	500
		8,775
	Tax on £8,775 × 22%	1,931
	Reduction in MCAA (as before – minimum available)	123
Melanie	£(10,000 – 8,775) = £1,225 × 40%	490
Total extra tax		2,544

Eric should therefore buy (8,775/10,000) = 87.75% of the cottage at a cost of £87,750 and Melanie the remainder.

Workings

1 Age allowance (aged 73 in January 2007)

	£	
STI as above	30,060	
Less: gross gift aid donation £390 × 100/78	(500)	
Income for age allowance purposes	29,560	
Reduction £(29,560 – 20,100) × 0.5 =	4,730	
PA £(7,280 – 2,245) =	5,035	(minimum)
MCAA £(6,065 – 2,485) =	3,580	

Note. The PA cannot be reduced below the normal PA of £5,035. There is an excess restriction of £(4,730 – 2,245) = £2,485 which must be set against the MCAA.

2

	£	
STI including rent	35,060	
Less: gift aid	(500)	
Income for age allowance	34,560	
Reduction £(34,560 – 20,100) × 0.5 =	7,230	
PA £(7,280 – 2,245) =	5,035	(minimum)
MCAA £(6,065 – 3,715) =	2,350	(minimum)

So there is a loss of tax reducer of £(3,580 – 2,350) = £1,230 @ 10%.

2 Hamburg

Tutorial note. It is important to realise that for individuals income from a property business is computed for tax years on an accruals basis. Don't forget to look out for rent a room relief in questions.

(a)

	Non-savings £	*Savings (excl. dividends)* £	*Dividends* £	*Total* £
Income from UK property business (W1)	11,020			
Trust income £6,600 × 100/60	11,000			
Interest – EASA		90		
– investment a/c		460		
– gilt interest (W2)		640		
Accrued income on sale		150		
Dividends £15,750 × 100/90			17,500	
STI	22,020	1,340	17,500	40,860
Less: PA	(5,035)			(5,035)
Taxable income	16,985	1,340	17,500	35,825

Tax	£
£2,150 × 10%	215
£14,835 × 22%	3,264
£1,340 × 20%	268
£14,975 × 10%	1,497
£2,525 × 32½ %	821
	6,065
Less: tax deducted on trust income	(4,400)
tax deducted on dividends	(1,750)
Tax repayable	(85)

Workings

1

	£	£
Rent		
House 1: first letting £600 × 6		3,600
House 1: second letting £6,000 × 3/12		1,500
House 2 £8,000 × 8/12		5,333
House 3 £7,800 × 8/12		5,200
		15,633
Expenses		
House 1: new roof, disallowable because capital	0	
House 1: loft insulation	1,200	
House 1: water rates	320	
House 1: buildings insurance £480 × 10/12	400	
House 2: water rates	240	
House 2: furniture £(5,333 – 240) × 10%	509	
House 3: redecoration	1,000	
House 3: water rates	360	
House 3: buildings insurance £440 × 9/12	330	
House 3: contents insurance £180 × 8/12	120	
House 3: furniture £(5,200 – 360) × 10%	484	
		(4,963)
UK property business income from 3 houses		10,670

Note. The loft insulation is a capital expense but it is specifically allowable up to £1,500.

Hamburg should claim rent a room relief in respect of the letting of the furnished room in his main residence, since this is more beneficial than the normal basis of assessment (£4,600 – £875 = £3,725). This means that Hamburg will be taxed on additional income of £350 (£4,600 – £4,250) from the UK property business.

Total property income is £11,020 (10,670 + 350)

2

	£
Interest June 2006 £20,000 × 6% × 6/12	600
Less: due to purchaser	(35)
	565
Interest December 2006 £2,500 × 6% × 6/12	75
	640

(b) If the cottages are to be treated as furnished holiday lettings, the first condition is that the lettings must be made on a **commercial basis with a view to the realisation of profit.**

Each property must be **available for letting** to the public for not less than 140 days in a tax year. Between them, the properties **must be let for at least 70 days each** in the 140 day period. For example, if the first cottage is let for 90 days in the year, the second cottage must be let for at least 50 days in the year to give an average of 70 days. If one of the cottages satisfies the 70 day test but the aggregation of the other cottage would pull the average down to below 70 days, the landlord can choose to treat the cottage which satisfies the 70 days test as furnished holiday accommodation.

In addition, **each property must not normally be in longer term occupation (ie for more than 31 days)** for more than 155 days in the year.

If the cottages satisfies these conditions, **the income from the lettings is taxed as income from a UK property business but as if the landlord was carrying on a trade** (except for the basis period rules). **This means that any losses are treated as trading losses instead of losses from the property business, capital allowance are available on furniture (instead of either the renewals basis or the 10% wear and tear allowance) and the income qualifies as relevant earnings for the purposes of pension relief.**

3 Taker

Tutorial note. The CO_2 emissions of the car are rounded down to 175g/km. The baseline figure for CO_2 emissions given in the tax rates and allowances tables is 140g/km at which the % if 15%. The % increases by 1% for each 5g/km that this figure is exceeded, ie here to 22%.

The telephone line rental and the golf club subscription do not qualify for a deduction because they are not paid wholly, exclusively and necessarily for employment purposes.

The exemption for the first £50 per week for childcare is only available for the weeks in which the childminder looks after Taker's son.

	£	£
Salary		35,000
Car £20,000 × 22%		4,400
Fuel £14,400 × 22% (partial contribution gives no reduction)		3,168
Mobile telephone		0
Use of video camera £600 × 20%		120
Loan: does not exceed £5,000		0
Childminder (4,000 – [48 × £55])		1,360
		44,048
Less: professional subscriptions	180	
cost of business telephone calls	45	
		(225)
Earnings		43,823

4 Helen Strube

Tutorial note. This question was a very basic revision of material that you covered at Paper 2.3. You **must** be fully competent with these basic computations at Paper 3.2.

	£
2001/02 (1.7.01 to 5.4.02)	
9/12 × £36,000	27,000
2002/03 (1.7.01 to 30.6.02)	36,000
2003/04 (1.7.02 to 30.6.03)	48,000

Overlap profits of £27,000 arise as a result of the trade profits accruing in the nine months to 5.4.02 being taxed in both 2001/02 and in 2002/03.

There is a change in accounting date which results in one long period of account ending during 2004/05. As a result the basis period is the fifteen months to 30 September 2004 and three months' worth of the overlap profits can be relieved:

2004/05	£
Basis period (1.7.03 – 30.9.04)	60,000
Less: Overlap profits 27,000 × 3/9	(9,000)
	51,000
2005/06 (Year to 30.9.05)	£30,000
2006/07 (1.10.05 to 31.12.06)	
Year to 30.9.06	24,000
Three months to 31.12.06	10,000
Less: Overlap profits (27,000 – 9,000)	(18,000)
	16,000

The trade ceases during 2006/07 so the basis period for this year runs from the end of the last basis period to the date of cessation. Overlap profits which were not relieved on the change of accounting date are relieved against this final year's taxable profits.

5 Vivace

> **Tutorial note.** It is important that you become fully competent at spotting when FYAs are available.

(a)

		FYA	Pool	Expensive car (60%)	Allowances
		£	£	£	£
WDV b/f			8,000		
Y/e 31.12.04					
14.9.04	Machinery sold		(700)		
			7,300		
16.9.04	Addition – car		4,000		
			11,300		
	WDA 25%		(2,825)		2,825
1.12.04	Machinery	9,232			
	FYA @ 50%	(4,616)			4,616
			4,616		
	WDV c/f		13,091		
	Total allowances				7,441
Y/e 31.12.05					
5.7.05	Mercedes			22,000	
21.3.05	Plant sold (restricted to cost)		(2,000)		
22.3.05	Car sold		(3,200)		
			7,891		
	WDA 25%/restricted		(1,973)	(3,000)	3,773
	WDV c/f		5,918	19,000	
	Total allowances				

		FYA	*Pool*	*Expensive car (60%)*	*Allowances*
		£	£	£	£
Y/e 31.12.06					
	WDV b/f		5,918		
5.2.06	Car (no FYA)		3,000		
30.6.06	Plant sold		(2,602)		
			6,316		
	WDA 25%		(1,579)		1,579
			4,737		
15.6.06	Mercedes sold			(4,000)	
	Balancing allowance			15,000	9,000
15.6.06	Volvo			18,000	
	WDA restricted			(3,000)	1,800
4.2.06	Machine on HP	4,000			
	FYA @ 40%	(1,600)			1,600
			2,400		
30.6.06	Plant	3,000			
	FYA @ 50%	(1,500)	1,500		1,500
	WDV c/f		8,637	15,000	
	Total allowances				15,479

Note. FYA of 50% is available for small enterprises from 6.4.04 until 5.4.05 for unincorporated businesses and from 6.4.06 until 5.4.07.

(b) Eligible expenditure (excluding land but includes offices of less than 25%) £200,000

	£
Simon	
Cost 1.8.00	200,000
Y/e 31.7.01 WDA 4%	(8,000)
Y/e 31.7.02 WDA 4%	(8,000)
Y/e 31.7.03 WDA 4%	(8,000)
	176,000
Y/e 31.7.04 WDA 4% (notional)	(8,000)
Y/e 31.7.05 WDA 4% (notional)	(8,000)
	160,000
Y/e 31.7.06 WDA 4%	(8,000)
Residue before sale	152,000
Balancing charge (real not notional allowances)	
4 × £8,000	32,000
Alicia	
Residue before sale	152,000
Add: balancing charge	32,000
Residue after sale	184,000
Tax life ends on 1.8.00 + 25 years = 31.7.2025	
Unexpired life 18 years 8 months = 18.6667	
Y/e 31.12.06 £184,000/18.667	9,857
Next 17 years	167,569
Y/e 31.12.24	6,574
	184,000

6 Arrol

Tutorial note. The disadvantage of a s 380 claim can be that it completely wastes the personal allowance. A possible planning idea could be to restrict the FYAs claimed, but you weren't asked to do that here.

(a) INCOME TAX COMPUTATION

	Non-savings £	*Savings* £	*Total* £
Earnings: salary	12,771		
car benefit £20,271 × 34%	6,892		
fuel benefit (£14,400 × 34%)	4,896		
Bank interest £235 × 100/80		294	
Building society interest £3,005 × 100/80		3,756	
	24,559	4,050	28,609
Less s 380 loss relief (working)	(24,559)	(4,050)	(28,609)
STI	0	0	0
Income tax liability: nil			

Workings

1 **The loss available for relief**

			£
Loss			13,384
Capital allowances:	FYA	£12,800 × 50%	6,400
	FYA	£46,720 × 50%	23,360
			43,144
Loss in 2006/07: £43,144 × 11/12			£39,549

2 **Car and fuel benefit**

237 g/km is rounded down to 235 g/km. Excess over base figure 235 – 140 = 95 g/km.

95 ÷ 5 = 19. Taxable % = 15 + 19 = 34%.

Partial contributions towards the cost of petrol do not reduce the fuel benefit.

(b) INCOME TAX COMPUTATION FOR MRS ARROL

	Non-savings £	*Savings* £	*Total* £
Earnings	2,800		
Building society interest £5,012 × 100/80		6,265	
NSB interest		1,742	
STI	2,800	8,007	10,807
Less personal allowance	(2,800)	(2,235)	(5,035)
Taxable income	0	5,772	5,912

	£		£
Income tax			
Starting rate band	2,150	× 10%	215
Basic rate band: savings income	3,622	× 20%	724
	5,772		939

(c) *The loss remaining unrelieved*

	£
Loss available for relief	39,549
Less used	(28,609)
Unrelieved balance	10,940

Relief for the remaining loss may be obtained:

(i) under s 380 in 2005/06 against Arrol's total income;

(ii) under s 381 ICTA 1988 against Arrol's total income for 2003/04, 2004/05 and 2005/06 in that order; or

(iii) by carry forward under s 385 ICTA 1988 against future profits of the practice.

7 Adam, Bert and Charlie

Tutorial note. Always divide the profits of a period of account between the partners before you begin allocating them to tax years.

	Total	*A*	*B*	*C*	*D*
	£	£	£	£	£
Year ending 31 March 2004					
Salaries	3,700	1,500	1,200	1,000	
Balance	6,500	2,600	2,600	1,300	
Total	10,200	4,100	3,800	2,300	
Year ending 31 March 2005					
April to June					
Salaries	925	375	300	250	
Balance	4,275	1,710	1,710	855	
Total	5,200	2,085	2,010	1,105	
July to March					
Salaries	1,650		900	750	
Balance	13,950		8,370	5,580	
Total	15,600		9,270	6,330	
Totals for the year	20,800	2,085	11,280	7,435	
Year ending 31 March 2006					
Salaries	2,200		1,200	1,000	
Balance	10,400		6,240	4,160	
Total	12,600		7,440	5,160	
Year ending 31 March 2007					
April					
Salaries	183		100	83	
Balance	1,317		790	527	
Total	1,500		890	610	
May to March					
Salaries	4,950		1,650	1,650	1,650
Balance	11,550		6,237	4,158	1,155
Total	16,500		7,887	5,808	2,805
Totals for the year	18,000		8,777	6,418	2,805

Taxable trade profits are as follows.

	A	*B*	*C*	*D*
	£	£	£	£
Year				
2003/04	4,100	3,800	2,300	
2004/05	2,085	11,280	7,435	
2005/06		7,440	5,160	
2006/07		8,777	6,418	2,805

8 John

> **Tutorial note.** The knowledge required in this question should be familiar to you from Paper 2.3. You should be aware that a thorough knowledge of the paper 2.3 syllabus is required for candidates sitting Paper 3.2.

DEF plc shares

Gain chargeable
Business asset for taper relief because John is an employee of this trading company
Taper relief period is 10.9.05 to 9.9.06 = 1 year

Car

Exempt asset so loss is not allowable.

Land

Gain chargeable
Non business asset taper relief
Taper relief period is 6.4.98 to 5.4.06 = 8 years plus additional year = 9 years as asset held at 17 March 1998.

XYZ plc shares

Gain exempt as shares held in ISA.

Factory

Gain chargeable
Factory is business asset between 1.8.03 to 1.11.06 (39 months) as the factory was used in John's trade.
Factory is non-business asset from 1.11.06 to 1.2.07 (3 months).
The business gain is 39/42 x £27,000 = £25,071 and the non-business gain is 3/42 x £27,000 = £1,929.
Taper relief period (whole years) is 1.8.03 to 31.7.06 = 3 years for both business and non-business parts.

Losses b/f

Set against gains in the most advantageous manner, that is, gain with least taper relief first and so on.

Summary

	Business		*Non-business*	
	3 yrs	*1 yr*	*9 yrs*	*3 yrs*
	£	£	£	£
Gains	25,071	10,000	25,000	1,929
Less: loss b/f				
(best use)	n/a	n/a	(4,071)	(1,929)
Gains before taper relief	25,071	10,000	20,929	nil
Taper relief	25%	50%	65%	n/a
Gains after taper relief	6,268	5,000	13,604	nil

		£
Total gains £(6,268 + 5,000 + 13,604)		24,872
Less: annual exemption		(8,800)
Taxable gains		16,072
Taxable income £(36,000 – 5,035)	£30,965	
Basic rate band £(33,300 + [195 × 12 x 100/78])	36,300	
Basic rate band left £(36,300 – 30,965)	5,335	

	£
CGT payable	
£5,335 @ 20%	1,067
£10,737 @ 40%	4,295
£16,072	5,362

9 Sophie Shaw

> **Tutorial note.** Again, this question covers the basics of CGT with which you must be completely familiar by the time you sit Paper 3.2. A new aspect is the part disposal.

Painting

The costs of sale (auctioneer's costs) can be deducted from the sale proceeds.

	£
Proceeds	50,000
Less: costs of sale	(500)
Net proceeds of sale	49,500
Less: cost	(2,500)
Unindexed gain	47,000
Less: indexation allowance $\frac{162.6-79.4}{79.4}$ (= 1.048) × £2,500	(2,620)
Indexed gain	44,380
Gain is £44,380	

Taper relief period is 6.4.98 – 5.4.06 = 8 years plus 1 year as asset held at 17 March 1998 = 9 years. The asset is a non-business asset.

Freehold shop

The transfer of the shop between the spouses is on a no gain/no loss basis. The base cost for Sophie is therefore £45,000. The value of the shop at the transfer is not relevant.

The gain is:

	£
Proceeds	85,000
Less: cost	(45,000)
Gain	40,000

The taper relief period runs from 1.9.02 (the acquisition by the spouse) to 31.8.06 which is 4 years. The asset is a non-business asset.

4 acres of land

This is a part disposal of the land. The fraction of cost used is:

$$\frac{\text{Proceeds of sale}}{\text{Proceeds of sale} + \text{value of part remaining}} \times \text{cost}$$

that is: $\frac{40{,}000}{40{,}000 + 24{,}000} \times £20{,}000 = £12{,}500$

The gain is:

		£
Proceeds		40,000
Less: cost		(12,500)
Unindexed gain		27,500
Less: indexation allowance	$\frac{162.6 - 150.6}{150.6}$ (= 0.080) × £12,500	(1,000)
Indexed gain		26,500

Taper relief period is 6.4.98 – 5.4.06 = 8 years plus 1 year as asset held at 17 March 1998 = 9 years. The asset is a non-business asset.

JKL Ltd shares

	£
Proceeds	10,000
Less: cost	(12,000)
Loss	(2,000)

This is a loss on a disposal to a connected person. The loss is only allowable on a gain on a disposal to the same connected person.

Summary – all non business assets

	9 yrs	*9 yrs*	*4 yrs*
	£	£	£
Gains	44,380	26,500	40,000
Less: Loss b/f	0	0	(5,000)
	44,380	26,500	35,000
Taper relief	65%	65%	90%
Gains after taper relief	28,847	17,225	31,500

	£
Total gains	77,572
Less: annual exemption	(8,800)
Chargeable gains	68,772

Note. The loss is set against the gain with the lowest amount of taper relief, ie where the highest percentage of the gain is chargeable.

10 The Green family

Tutorial note. The key to a long question like this is to ensure that you allocate your time so that you are able to make an attempt at each individual requirement.

(a) *Total value due to John Green on takeover*

	£
Shares 20,000 × £4.90	98,000
Cash 20,000 × £1.60	32,000
	130,000

Cash element exceeds both £3,000 and 5% of £130,000, so there must be a part disposal

	£
Disposal proceeds	32,000
Less: cost $\frac{32,000}{32,000+98,000} \times £40,000$	(9,846)
Gain	22,154
Base cost of Wall plc shares £(40,000 – 9,846)	£30,154

(b) *Match post April 1998 acquisitions on a LIFO basis*

1 March 2006

Shares held after bonus issue 1,000 + 1,000 = 2,000

No change to base cost

	£
Disposal proceeds (£14,000 × $\frac{2,000}{3,200}$)	8,750
Less: cost	(1,260)
Gain	7,490
No taper relief – owned less than one year	

15 May 2005

Shares held after bonus issue 1,800 + 1,800 = 3,600

No change to base cost

	£
Disposal proceeds (£14,000 × $\frac{1,200}{3,200}$)	5,250
Less: cost (£1,900 × $\frac{1,200}{3,600}$)	(633)
Gain	4,617
No taper relief – non business asset held less than 3 years.	

The total chargeable gain on the sale of Mrs Green's shares in Read plc is £12,107 (£7,490 + £4,617).

(c) *The disposal of Greengage Supermarkets plc shares*

(i) *Post 5 April 1998 acquisition*

	£
Proceeds $\frac{1,000}{1,450} \times £10,150$	7,000
Less: cost	(6,000)
Gain	1,000
No taper relief – owned less than one year	

(ii) *The FA 1985 pool*

	£
Proceeds $\frac{450}{1,450} \times £10,150$	3,150
Less cost (W1)	(1,704)
	1,446
Less indexation allowance £(2,923 – 1,704) (W1)	(1,219)
Indexed gain	227
Gain after taper relief (9 complete years ownership after 6.4.98 including additional year) 65% × £227	148

Workings

1 *The FA 1985 pool*

	No of shares	*Cost*	*Indexed cost*
	£	£	£
15.4.85 purchase	900	3,408	3,408
Indexed rise to April 1998			
$\frac{162.6 - 94.8}{94.8} \times £3,408$			2,437
Value at 5 April 1998	900	3,408	5,845
Disposal (May 2006)	(450)	(1,704)	(2,923)
FA 1985 pool value remaining	450	1,704	2,922

(d) *Summary: Mr Green*

	£
Gains	22,154
Less loss brought forward	(13,354)
	8,800
Less annual exemption	(8,800)
Taxable gains	0
CGT payable	£nil

The losses brought forward are only set against gains to bring the gains down to the annual exemption.

Loss carried forward £(17,560 – 13,354)	£4,206

Summary: Mrs Green

	£
Gains	12,107
Less annual exemption	(8,800)
Chargeable gains	3,307
CGT payable	
£2,150 @ 10%	215
£1,157 @ 20%	231
	446

11 The Milsom family

Tutorial note. In an exam question you should watch out for reliefs such as gift relief. If you fail to spot a relief you will find it hard to pass the question.

(a) *2005/06*

No CGT event on the damage to the factory.

2006/07

Receipt of compensation is treated as part disposal. The amount not used in restoration is not "small". The restoration must also be taken into account.

	£
Amount not used in restoration £(20,000 – 15,000)	5,000
Less: cost plus restoration	
$\frac{5,000}{5,000+250,000} \times$ £(150,000 + 15,000)	(3,235)
Gain	1,765
Taper relief (10.7.04 – 9.7.06) = 2 years, business asset	
£1,765 × 25%	£441

2007/08

Gift relief can apply to the gift of the factory because it is an asset used in the trade of the donor. Full relief is available as no payment is made by Gary.

	£
Market value at gift	260,000
Less: cost £(150,000 + 15,000 – 3,235)	(161,765)
Gain heldover	98,235

No taper relief is available to reduce the gift relief gain.

(b) Gary's gain on sale is:

	£
Proceeds	300,000
Less: cost £(260,000 – 98,235)	(161,765)
Gain before taper relief	138,235

The taper relief period for Gary begins on the date of the gift to him (1 December 2007). This is a non-business asset for Gary and so he has not accrued the minimum period for non-business asset taper relief to apply (3 years). Thus no taper relief due.

(c)

Firm's headed notepaper

Mrs S Milsom
The Cottage
Milltown

Date

Dear Mrs Milsom

Re: Proposed purchase of new shop

You have asked me to advise you about the tax consequences of your proposed purchase of a replacement shop for your business.

Denby Terrace Shop

You made a gain of £40,000 (£80,000 – 40,000) on the sale of your shop in Denby Terrace. If you acquire a replacement shop within 3 years after the sale, you will be able to defer the whole or part of this gain.

High Street Shop

If you buy this freehold shop, it will be possible to defer only part of your gain on the Denby Terrace shop. This is because you will not be reinvesting the whole of the proceeds of sale into the replacement shop. A gain equal to the amount not reinvested (£8,000) will remain in charge. However, since you owned Denby Terrace shop for more than 2 years, the gain will be reduced by 75% by business asset taper relief, thus leaving a gain of £2,000 in charge. This gain may be covered by your annual exemption for 2006/07 if this has not been used by any other gains.

The remainder of the gain of £32,000 can be 'rolled over' into the base cost of the High Street shop. The base cost of the High Street shop will therefore be £40,000 for the purposes of computing a gain on its disposal. There is no taper relief to reduce the value of this rolled over gain, but if you own the High Street shop for at least two years, you will be entitled to the same rate of taper relief as you have already built up on the Denby Terrace shop.

Station Road Shop

In this case, full deferral of the gain will be available as you will be reinvesting the whole of the proceeds of sale of the Denby Terrace shop into this shop.

As this is a leasehold shop with less than 60 years to run on the lease, the deferral relief available works in a slightly different way because you are investing in a depreciating asset. The gain on the Denby Terrace shop is not deducted from the base cost of the Station Road shop, but is deferred until the earliest of you disposing of the Station Road shop, ceasing to use it in your business or 10 years from its acquisition. The gain which will come into charge at that date will be £(40,000 × 25%) = £10,000 as, in this case, taper relief is available in relation to your ownership of the Denby Terrace shop.

If, however, you acquire another asset such as a freehold shop which is not a depreciating asset before the gain comes back into charge, you can claim to rollover the gain of £40,000 into the non-depreciating asset, provided that it costs more than £80,000.

Please let me know if you require any further information.

Yours sincerely

Tax Accountant

12 Roland Rat

Tutorial note. The incorporation of a business is likely to be a frequently examined topic at Paper 3.2.

(a) *The transfer of the business to the company wholly in exchange for shares*

(i) The transfer of shares to Roland Rat's wife

Where a husband and wife are living together, transfers between them give rise to neither gains nor losses. There is therefore no chargeable gain on the transfer of 2,500 shares to Mrs Rat.

Mrs Rat's base cost for future disposal purposes will be as follows.

	£
$\frac{2,500}{10,000} \times$ £211,560 (W)	52,890
FA 1985 pool indexation to April 1998 £52,890 × 0.423	22,373
	75,263

(ii) *The sale of shares to the incoming director*

	£
Proceeds	165,000
Less cost $\frac{2,000}{10,000} \times$ £211,560 (W)	(42,312)
	122,688
Less FA 1985 pool indexation to April 1998 £42,312 × 0.423	(17,898)
Chargeable gain before taper	104,790
Chargeable gain after taper relief (25%)	26,198

Note: Mr Rat owned shares in a qualifying company for eight complete years post 5 April 1998 prior to the sale in August 2006. Thus only 25% of the gain is taxed.

The base cost for the incoming director will be £165,000.

(iii) *The sale of the freehold property by Mouse Trap Ltd*

The gain on sale of the freehold property can be rolled over against the base cost of the new property if that new property is acquired within the period from 12 months before to three years after the disposal of the old property.

The gain to be rolled over is calculated as follows.

	£
Proceeds	500,000
Less cost	(200,000)
	300,000
Less indexation allowance to August 2006	
0.720 × £200,000	(144,000)
Gain	156,000

The base cost of the new property is found as follows.

	£
Cost	550,000
Less rolled over gain	(156,000)
Base cost	394,000

(iv) *The base costs of other chargeable assets*

(1) Mr. Rat's shares

$$\frac{5{,}500}{10{,}000} \times £211{,}560 \text{ (W)} = £116{,}358$$

(2) Goodwill owned by company

Cost in April 1989 £150,000

Working

The gains arising on the transfer of chargeable assets to Mouse Trap Ltd are rolled over against the acquisition value of the shares in the company.

The gains arising in April 1989 are as follows.

	£
Goodwill £(150,000 – 0)	150,000
Freehold property £(200,000 – 85,000* – (85,000 × 0.356))	84,740
Gain rolled over	234,740

*£77,000 + £8,000 = £85,000.

The base cost of the shares acquired is as follows.

	£
Consideration	446,300
Less rolled over gain	(234,740)
Base cost (10,000 shares)	211,560

(b) *The transfer of the business to the company partly in exchange for shares*

On the incorporation of a business, only gains attributable to a transfer in exchange for shares can be rolled over. The calculations in (a) above would therefore alter if the company had issued £200,000 worth of 11% debenture stock and satisfied the balance of the purchase price by the issue of shares. The revised computations would be as follows.

(i) The chargeable gain in April 1989

	£
Total gains	234,740
Less rolled over gain	
$\frac{246,300}{446,300} \times £234,740$	(129,546)
Chargeable gain	105,194

The base cost of the debentures would be £200,000.

The base cost of the shares would be £(446,300 – 200,000 – 129,546) = £116,754.

(ii) The transfer of shares to Mrs Rat

The base cost of Mrs Rat's shares would be as follows.

	£
$\frac{2,500}{10,000} \times £116,754$	29,189
FA 1985 pool indexation to April 1998	
£29,189 × 0.423	12,347
	41,536

(iii) The sale of shares to the incoming director

	£
Proceeds	165,000
Less cost $\frac{2,000}{10,000} \times £116,754$	(23,351)
	141,649
Less FA 1985 pool indexation to April 1998	
£23,351 × 0.423	(9,878)
Chargeable gain before taper relief	131,771
Chargeable gain (25%)	32,943

Base cost for incoming director: £165,000

(iv) The base cost of Mr Rat's remaining shares would be

$$\frac{5,500}{10,000} \times £116,754 = £64,215$$

13 Miss Wolf and Mr Fox

Tutorial note. In part (b), no further absence can be counted as deemed occupation because Mr Fox did not go back to live in the house (compare absences followed by occupation between 1.8.89 and 31.1.95).

(a) Miss Wolf

(i) *The lease*

	£
Proceeds	30,750
Less $\frac{64.116\,(16\text{ years})}{80.361\,(24\tfrac{1}{2}\text{ years})} \times £8,000$	(6,383)
Unindexed gain	24,367
Less indexation allowance (January 1998 to April 1998)	
$\frac{162.6 - 159.5}{159.5} = (0.019) \times £6,383$	(121)
Gain before taper relief	24,246

The percentage for 24½ years is 79.622 + (81.100 – 79.622) × 6/12 = 80.361.

Taper relief period is nine years (6.4.98 – 5.4.06 = 8 years plus additional year).

(ii) *The racehorse*

This is a wasting chattel and is therefore exempt.

(iii) *Painting*

	£
Proceeds	9,000
Less: costs of sale	(900)
	8,100
Less: cost	(2,200)
Gain	5,900

Gain restricted to 5/3 × £(9,000 – 6,000) = £5,000

Taper relief period is 10.9.02 to 9.9.05 = 3 years

(iv) *Summary*

The loss brought forward should be set against the gain on the painting as this has least taper relief.

	Non business	
	9 years	*3 years*
	£	£
Gains	24,246	5,000
Loss: loss b/f		(2,203)
Net gains	24,246	2,797
Taper relief percentages	65%	95%
	£	£
Gains after taper relief	15,760	2,657
Total gains		18,417
Less: annual exemption		(8,800)
		9,617
CGT £9,617 @ 40%		£3,847

(b) Mr Fox

Gain on sale

	£
Proceeds	180,000
Less: cost	(50,000)
Unindexed gain	130,000
Less: indexation allowance	
$\frac{162.6-97.8}{97.8}$ (= 0.663) × £50,000	(33,150)
Indexed gain	96,850

Principal private residence relief then applies to exempt part of the gain:

	Exempt years	*Chargeable years*
1.8.86 – 31.7.89 (actual occupation)	3	
1.8.89 – 31.7.93 (up to 4 yrs due to place of work – *not* employed abroad)	4	
1.8.93 – 31.7.94 (up to 3 years any other reason)	1	
1.8.94 – 31.1.95 (actual occupation)	½	
1.2.95 – 31.7.03 (note)		8½
1.8.03 – 31.7.06 (last 3 years)	3	
Totals	11½	8½

Gain exempt is 11 ½ out of 20 years x £96,850	55,689
Gain left in charge £(96,850 – 55,689)	41,161
Gain after taper relief (9 years) 65% × £41,161	£26,755

14 Overseas

Tutorial note. Double tax relief is an important topic which could be examined in the Section A compulsory questions. Take great care when calculating the amount of UK tax on overseas income, as here, it is not always that straightforward.

(a) 2006/07 Tax computation for Susan

	Non-savings	*Dividends*	*Total*
	£	£	£
Earnings	17,820		
UK dividends (× 100/90)		10,000	
Overseas property business income (10,000 + 4,705)	14,705		
STI	32,525	10,000	42,525
Less personal allowance	(5,035)		
	27,490	10,000	37,490

	£
Income tax on non-savings income:	
£2,150 × 10%	215
£25,340 × 22%	5,575
Income tax on dividend income:	
£5,810 × 10%	581
£4,190 × 32.5%	1,362
	7,733
Less DTR (W)	(4,178)
	3,555
Less tax credit and PAYE £(2,000 + 1,000)	(3,000)
Tax payable	555

Tax on UK income:

	Non-savings	*Dividends*
	£	£
Total income	27,490	10,000
Less overseas property business income	(14,705)	
	12,785	10,000

BPP PROFESSIONAL EDUCATION

Income tax	£
2,150 × 10%	215
10,635 × 22%	2,340
10,000 × 10%	1,000
22,785	
Tax on UK income	3,555
Tax on total income (see above)	(7,733)
UK tax on overseas income	4,178

DTR is lower of:

(i) UK tax on overseas income £4,178
(ii) overseas tax £4,705

(b) A UK taxpayer can claim relief from UK tax in respect of foreign tax paid by that person. There is a clear requirement in the legislation that the taxpayer should advise HMRC if subsequently the foreign tax is adjusted by the foreign tax authority so that if a DTR claim is rendered excessive an alteration can be made.

The taxpayer must notify HMRC within one year of any adjustment to the amount of foreign tax. So Susan must notify HMRC before 1 November 2009.

Her DTR claim for 2006/07 becomes the lower of:

(i)	UK tax suffered on overseas income	£4,178
(ii)	overseas tax suffered (£4,705 – 2,600)	£2,105

ie £2,105 not £4,178 as before.

15 Mr Brown

Tutorial note. This topic should be very familiar to you from Paper 2.3. It can be examined in the compulsory Section A questions so you should ensure that you have a thorough knowledge of it.

(a) *Returns*

Income tax returns must be submitted by 31 January following the tax year concerned. Thus an individual's return for 2006/07 must be delivered by 31 January 2008. However, if the notice requiring the return is served after 31 October following the tax year, the filing date becomes three months after the notice. Thus, if notice to deliver the return for 2006/07 were given, say, on 1 December 2007, it must be delivered by 28 February 2008.

Where a tax return is filed late a penalty of up to a maximum of £100 can be charged. The Commissioners may impose a further penalty of up to £60 for each day for which the return remains outstanding after the taxpayer is notified of the penalty, although it cannot be imposed after the failure had been remedied.

If no application is made by the Inspector to the Commissioners and the return is not filed within six months of the filing date, the taxpayer is liable to a further maximum penalty of £100 subject to a right of appeal on the grounds of reasonable excuse. If the failure continues after the first anniversary of the filing date and the return shows that there is an outstanding liability to tax, the taxpayer is liable to a penalty equal to that outstanding tax liability.

Any penalty will be limited to the amount of tax outstanding for the year and this will be mitigable.

As an alternative to completing their own calculation, the taxpayer can request HMRC assistance and submit a return by 30 September following the tax year (or, if later, two months from the date of the notice requiring delivery of a return). The Officer of Revenue and Customs must then raise an assessment in accordance with the information contained in the return and provide the taxpayer with a copy of the assessment.

Payments of tax

Although an individual is not normally required to file a return until 31 January following the tax year, payments on account are required on 31 January in the tax year and on 31 July following it. These payments are required where an individual has either made a self-assessment or been assessed to tax following submission of his tax return for the previous tax year and the amount of the assessment exceeded the tax which was deducted at source: this excess is known as the relevant amount. Tax deducted at source includes PAYE, tax credits on dividends and income tax deducted or treated as paid. The taxpayer is required to pay 50% of the previous year's relevant amount on each of 31 January in the tax year and 31 July following it.

If the taxpayer believes that the current year's income tax and Class 4 NIC liability will be less than the previous year's amount, he may claim to reduce each payment on account may then be reduced to 50% of the amount which the taxpayer believes will be due. If the taxpayer fraudulently or negligently makes a false statement in connection with such a claim, he will be liable to a penalty equal to the amount of tax lost. Interest is charged on the amount by which payments on account are reduced if the reduced amount finally becomes payable. The interest runs from the due date of payment for the payments on account.

Income tax and Class 4 NICs due, in excess of the payments on account, together with the whole of any CGT, must be paid on 31 January in the following year.

Interest on overdue tax is charged on all unpaid tax from the due date. Where the balance of tax (due on 31 January following the year) is unpaid more than 28 days after the due date, a surcharge of 5% of the unpaid amount is also applied. If it remains unpaid more than six months after the due date, there is a further 5% surcharge. The surcharge carries interest from the date imposed to the date paid.

(b) *Mr Brown*

Due dates of tax – 2006/07

Payments made	*Paid*	*No claim to reduce payments on account*	*Due date*
£		£	
4,500	28 February 2007	6,000	31 January 2007
4,500	14 August 2007	6,000	31 July 2007
4,000	13 March 2008	1,000	31 January 2008
13,000		13,000	

Interest due

Payments on account:

	£
£4,500 × 28/365 × 6.5%	22.44
£4,500 × 14/365 × 6.5%	11.22
£1,500 × 405/365 × 6.5%	108.18
£1,500 × 224/365 × 6.5%	59.84
Final payment:	
£1,000 × 40/365 × 6.5%	7.12
	208.80

16 Rodin

> **Tutorial note.** This answer follows the 'steps' set out within the text but in a streamlined format which is equally acceptable in the exam.

IHT paid during Rodin's lifetime was as follows.

15.12.1999

		£
Gift		60,000
Less:	A/E (1999/00)	(3,000)
	A/E (1998/99) b/f	(3,000)
PET		54,000

This gift was a PET so no lifetime tax was due.

21.1.2002

No gross chargeable transfers were made in the seven years prior to 21.1.02 so all of the £Nil band remained available for use. This means the IHT paid by Rodin was:

		£
Gift		337,000
Less:	A/E (2001/02)	(3,000)
	A/E (2000/01) b/f	(3,000)
		331,000

			£
IHT	£285,000	× 0% =	Nil
	£ 46,000	× $^{20}/_{80}$ =	11,500
	£331,000		11,500

The gross chargeable transfer after annual exemptions was: £331,000 + £11,500 = £342,500.

Check: tax £(342,500 – 285,000) = £57,500 × 20% = £11,500.

> **Tutorial note**. The £Nil band of £285,000 was used in calculating this lifetime IHT because you were told in the question to assume that the £Nil band has always been £285,000. In practice you would use the £Nil band applicable on 21.1.02 when calculating the lifetime tax on a gift made on 21.1.02.

20.8.2003

		£
Gift		46,000
Less:	A/E (2003/04)	(3,000)
	A/E (2002/03) b/f	(3,000)
PET		40,000

This was a PET so no lifetime tax was due.

19.6.2005

Gross chargeable transfers of £342,500 had been made in the seven years prior to 19.6.05 so none of the £Nil band remains and the lifetime IHT due was:

		£
Gift		106,000
Less:	A/E (2005/06)	(3,000)
	A/E (2004/05) b/f	(3,000)
		100,000

IHT: £100,000 × 20/80 =	£25,000
The gross chargeable transfer after annual exemptions was £100,000 + £25,000 =	£125,000

Check tax £125,000 × 20% = £25,000.

1.8.2006

	£
Gift	73,000
Less: A/E (2006/07)	(3,000)
PET	70,000

This was a PET so no lifetime tax was due.

1.9.2006

This was an exempt transfer to Rodin's spouse so no lifetime tax was due.

IHT due as a result of death.

As a result of death IHT will be due on transfers made in the seven years before the death.

Lifetime transfers

15.12.1999

This PET was made more than seven years before death, so no IHT arises as a result of death.

21.1.2002

Gross transfer after annual exemptions	£342,500

None of the £Nil band had been used in calculating death tax in the seven years before 21.1.02 so the IHT due on death is:

		£
£285,000	× 0%	Nil
£57,500	× 40%	23,000
£342,500		23,000
Less: Taper relief at 40% (4-5 years)		(9,200)
Death tax after taper relief (60%)		13,800
Less: Lifetime tax paid		(11,500)
IHT due on death		2,300

20.8.2003

All of the £Nil band has been used in calculating death tax on gifts made in the seven years prior to 20.8.03, so the death tax due on this now chargeable PET is:

	£
PET (valued at 20.8.03)	40,000
IHT @ 40%	16,000
Less: Taper relief @ 20% (3-4 years)	(3,200)
IHT payable by daughter (80%)	12,800

19.6.2005

All of the £Nil band has been used in calculating death tax on the gifts made in the seven years prior to 19.6.05, so the death tax due on this gift is:

Gross chargeable transfer	£125,000

	£
£125,000 × 40% =	50,000
Less: Lifetime tax	(25,000)
Tax due on death	25,000

366,000

1.8.2006

No £Nil band remains so IHT due on this now chargeable PET is:

PET (valued at 1.8.06)	£70,000
£70,000 × 40%	£28,000

1.9.2006

No IHT arises on an exempt transfer to a spouse.

17 Mr Bright

> **Tutorial note**. Note the different valuation rules for CGT and IHT. The shares are valued at market value for CGT purposes. For IHT purposes the diminution in value principle is used to value the shares.

(a) *Capital gains tax liability*

	£
Gain on shares (W)	12,915
Less annual exemption	(8,800)
Taxable gain	4,115

As Mr Bright's marginal rate of income tax is 40%, the marginal rate of CGT is 40%. The CGT is £4,115 × 40% = £1,646.

Inheritance tax liability

Mr Bright has made a chargeable lifetime transfer in giving cash to the discretionary trust. As he is to pay the tax, grossing up is necessary. Two annual exemptions of £3,000 each (for 2006/07 and 2005/06) are available to reduce the net transfer.

	£
Transfer	309,000
Less: A/E (2006/07)	(3,000)
A/E (2005/06) b/f	(3,000)
Net transfer	303,000

There have been no previous transfers so all of the £Nil band remains available for use in calculating the IHT on this transfer.

		£
£285,000	× 0%	Nil
£18,000	× 20/80	4,500
£303,000		4,500

Gross transfer is thus £307,500 (£303,000 + 4,500). The IHT payable by Mr Bright is £4,500.

Check: tax £(307,500 – 285,000) = £22,500 × 20% = £4,500.

Workings

Post 5.4.98 acquisitions

18.8.06

	£
Proceeds (600 × £18)	10,800
Less: cost	(3,000)
Chargeable gain	7,800

There is no indexation allowance after April 1998. No taper relief due since owned for less than one year.

15.6.01

	£
Proceeds (200 × £18)	3,600
Less: cost	(1,366)
	2,234

The shares are a business asset for taper relief purposes. As they have been owned for five complete years after 6.4.98 only 25% of the gain is taxable.

£2,234 x 25% = £558

FA 1985 Pool

	No of shares £	*Cost* £	*Indexed cost* £
Pool opens 6.4.85			
Purchase 1.11.83	2,200	3,300	3,300
Indexation allowance $\frac{94.8-86.7}{86.7} = 0.093 \times £3,300$			307
At 6.4.85	2,200	3,300	3,607
Indexation allowance to 5.4.98 $\frac{162.6-94.8}{94.8} \times £3,607$			2,580
At 5.4.98	2,200	1,800	6,187
Disposal	(1,200)	(1,800)	(3,374)
	1,000	1,500	2,183

	£
Disposal proceeds (1,200 × £18) use market value	21,600
Less: Cost	(1,800)
	19,800
Less: Indexation allowance £(3,374 – 1,800)	(1,574)
	18,226
Chargeable gain after taper relief (6.4.98 – 5.4.06; business asset 25%)	4,557

	£
June 2001 acquisition	558
August 2006 acquisition	7,800
FA 1985 pool	4,557
Total gain on shares	12,915

(b) If Mr Bright were to die on 20 April 2007, the potentially exempt transfer to Maxine on 1 April 2007 would become chargeable. The amount of this transfer, applying both the diminution in value principle and the related property rules (since Mrs Bright owns 1,000 shares) is as follows.

	£
Before the transfer, Mr Bright had 3,000 shares in a holding of 3,000 + 1,000 = 4,000 shares, worth £36.67 a share.	110,010
After the transfer, Mr Bright had 1,000 shares in a holding of 1,000 + 1,000 = 2,000 shares, worth £18 a share.	(18,000)
	92,010
Less actual proceeds	(10,000)
	82,010
Less business property relief: unavailable because shares sold by date of Mr Bright's death	(0)
Transfer of value (no annual exemptions available)	82,010

On Mr Bright's death, his remaining shares would also be valued using the related property rules, as follows.

	£
1,000 shares in a holding of 2,000 shares, worth £18 a share	18,000
Less business property relief at 100% (unquoted shares)	(18,000)
	0

The inheritance tax liabilities which would arise on Mr Bright's death on 20 April 2007 are as follows.

1 May 2006 transfer

Gross transfer (valued on 1 May 2006) £307,500

IHT at death (no taper relief – death within 3 years)

		£
£285,000	× 0%	Nil
£ 22,500	× 40%	9,000
£307,500		9,000
Less: Lifetime tax paid		(4,500)
Tax payable at death		4,500

1 April 2007 transfer

	£
Transfer of value 2007	82,010
Less: A/E (2006/07 – already used)	–
A/E (2005/06 – already used)	–
	82,010

All £Nil band used in previous seven years so IHT due on death is:

£82,010 × 40% = £32,804

Death estate

	£
Shares	Nil
Cash	40,000
Less CGT liability	(1,646)
	38,354

IHT at 40% = £15,342

The trustees of the settlement must pay IHT of £4,500.

Maxine must pay IHT of £32,804.

Mr Bright's personal representatives must pay IHT of £15,342.

18 Trusts

Tutorial note. An exam question will not be set that exclusively examines the taxation of trusts although trusts may feature as part of a question.

(a) We must first work out the tax payable by the trustees.

	Savings income £	*Dividend income* £	*Income used for expenses* £
Income available for distribution:			
Gilt interest	4,625		
Dividends (1,800 – 288) × 100/90		1,680	
Income used for expenses:			
Divs used for expenses 288 × 100/90			320
	4,625	1,680	320
Tax on distributable income:			
Savings income: 1,000 ×20%	200		
3,625 × 40%	1,450		
Dividend income: 1,680 × 32.5%	546		
	2,196		
BR tax on income used to meet expenses:			
Dividends: 320 × 10%			32
Less notional tax credits on divs			
1,680 × 10%	(168)		
320 × 10%			(32)
Payables by Trustees	2,028		

	£	£
Opening cash balance		10,000
Add: dividends received	1,800	
interest received	4,625	
		6,425
		16,425
Less: tax payable	2,028	
administration expenses	288	
distributions	2,700	
		(5,016)
Closing cash balance		11,409

(b) The gift relief claimed when the shares were put into the trust is as follows.

	£
Deemed proceeds	50,000
Less cost	(35,000)
	15,000
Less FA 1985 pool indexation to April 1998	
$\frac{162.6 - 135.6}{135.6} \times £35,000$	(6,969)
Gift relief	8,031

The gains of £30,000 which arise on asset sales in July 2006 are taxable on the trustees.

The variation of the terms of the settlement in August 2006 is not a chargeable disposal for CGT purposes.

The trustees' position for 2006/07 is therefore as follows.

	£
July 2006	30,000
Less annual exemption £4,400/2 (because Gainer is the settlor of one other trust)	(2,200)
Taxable gain	27,800
CGT £27,800 × 40%	£11,120

On the death of the life tenant the trust assets rest absolutely so that a gain arises. The gain on such a deemed disposal is as follows.

	£
Proceeds	80,000
Less: cost £(50,000 – 8,031)	(41,969)
Gain	38,031

The trust owns a shareholding in an unquoted trading company. For taper relief purposes the trust has owned the shares as business asset for THREE complete years (12.1.05–1.4.08) so taper relief makes 25% of the gain chargeable.

Chargeable gain (25% of £38,031)	9,508
Less annual exemption £4,400/2	(2,200)
Taxable gain	7,308
CGT £7,308 × 40%	£2,923

19 National insurance contributions

> **Tutorial note**. Directors have an annual earnings period whereas the earnings period for other employees is normally equal to the period for which earnings are paid.

(a) *Albert*

Total earnings are £35,000 £(30,000 + 5,000)

	£
Primary contributions	
Total earnings exceed UEL	
£(33,540 – 5,035) = £28,505 × 11% (main)	3,136
£(35,000 – 33,540) = £1,460 × 1% (additional)	15
Total primary contributions	3,151
Secondary contributions	
£(35,000 – 5,035) = £29,965 × 12.8%	3,836
Class 1A contributions	
£(4,500 + 750) = £5,250 × 12.8%	672

Barney

	£
Earnings threshold £5,035/12 = £420	
Upper earnings limit £645 × 52 ÷ 12 = £2,795	
Primary contributions	
11 months	
£(2,000 – 420) = £1,580 × 11% × 11 (main only)	1,912
1 month (January)	
£(2,795 – 420) = £2,375 × 11% (main)	261
£(5,000 – 2,795) = £2,205 × 1% (additional)	22
Total primary contributions	2,195

	£
Secondary contributions	
11 months	
£(2,000 – 420) = £1,580 × 12.8% × 11	2,225
1 month (January)	
£(5,000 – 420) = £4,580 × 12.8%	586
Total secondary contributions	2,811
Chloe	
Primary contributions	
£(120 – 97) = £23 × 11% × 52	£132
Secondary contributions	
£(120 – 97) = £23 × 12.8% × 52	£153

(b) *Class 2 contributions (for both)*

	£
52 × £2.10	109

Class 4 contributions

(i)	£(30,000 – 5,035) = £24,965 × 8% (main only)	1,997
(ii)	£(33,540 – 5,035) = £28,505 × 8% (main)	2,280
	£(35,000 – 33,540) = £1,460 × 1% (additional)	15
	Total Class 4 contributions	2,295

20 Fraser Ltd

> **Tutorial note**. The knowledge in this question is revision of material that you should know well from Paper 2.3.

CORPORATION TAX COMPUTATION

	£
Trading income (W1)	338,105
Interest income £(6,834 + 2,208)	9,042
Chargeable gains (W3)	36,468
PCTCT	383,615
Dividend plus tax credit	1,655
Profits for small companies rate purposes	385,270
	£
Corporation tax £383,615 × 30%	115,084
Less small companies' marginal relief $£(1,500,000 - 385,270) \times \frac{383,615}{385,270} \times 11/400$	(30,523)
Mainstream corporation tax	84,561

Workings

1 *Adjusted profit computation*

	£	£
Net profit per accounts		379,198
Add: depreciation	13,876	
gifts (over £50 each)	2,085	
entertaining	969	
		16,930
		396,128
Less: dividend including tax credit	1,655	
bank interest	6,834	
interest from gilts	2,208	
surplus on disposal of factory and lease	59,106	
net balancing charge (W2)	(11,780)	
		(58,023)
Taxable trading profit		338,105

2 *Capital allowances*

(a) *The plant*

	£
FYA £9,800 × 2 × 40%	7,840

Note. The question stated that Fraser Ltd meets the criteria of medium-sized enterprise but not that it is in a small enterprise, so it is thus eligible for the 40% FYA on the purchase of plant and machinery.

(b) *The first factory*

	£	
Original cost (excluding land)	90,000	
Assuming the canteen is used by both manufacturing and office staff, only the general offices are in theory disallowable. However, being not more than 25% of the cost, the offices qualify for relief.		
Since the factory was sold above cost and there had been no non-industrial use the residue of expenditure for Fraser Ltd is	90,000	
WDA is £90,000/20		4,500

(c) *The second factory*

The cost (excluding land) was £67,000.

The factory was sold for more than cost, so there is a balancing charge equal to the allowances given.

9 years × 4% × £67,000	(24,120)
Net balancing charge	(11,780)

3 *Chargeable gains*

(a) *The lease*

	£
Proceeds	40,000
Less cost	
$£17{,}500 \times \dfrac{66.470 + \frac{1}{2}(68.697 - 66.470)}{81.100} = \dfrac{17.5 \text{ years}}{25 \text{ years}}$	(14,583)
Unindexed gain	25,417
Less indexation allowance to April 2006	
0.186 × £14,583	(2,712)
Chargeable gain	22,705

(b) *The factory*

	£
Proceeds	112,750
Less cost	(79,000)
Unindexed gain	33,750
Less indexation allowance to August 2006	
0.253 × £79,000	(19,987)
Indexed gain	13,763

Total gains are £(22,705 + 13,763) = £36,468.

21 Major Ltd

Tutorial note. It is important to distinguish between trading and non-trading loan relationships. Interest on the former is dealt with as trading income whilst interest on the latter is dealt with as interest income.

(a) *Mainstream corporation tax*

	£	£
Trading profit per question	180,000	
Less: Patent royalties	(15,000)	
Taxable trading income		165,000
Property income		30,000
Capital gains		40,000
		235,000
Less charges: Gift Aid		(3,000)
Less non-trade deficit (£24,000 – £30,000)		(6,000)
PCTCT		226,000
Add Franked investment income		20,000
'Profits'		246,000

The eight month accounting period all falls to be taxed using rates for the financial year 2006.

Small companies' lower limit	£300,000 × 8/12 × ½	£100,000
Small companies' upper limit	£1,500,000 × 8/12 × ½	£500,000

Small companies' marginal relief applies

Corporation tax

	£
£226,000 × 30%	67,800
Less small companies' marginal relief	
(11/400 × (£500,000 – £246,000) × 226,000/246,000)	(6,417)
Mainstream corporation tax	61,383

Working

1 *Income tax*

The patent royalties would have been paid net to an individual. The income tax would, however, have all been accounted for under the quarterly accounting system. The loan interest received was received from another UK company so it would have been received gross.

Interest on the bank loan is paid gross.

Charitable donations are paid gross under the gift aid scheme.

(b) To: The Directors of Major Ltd
From: Certified Accountant
Date: 31 March 2007
Re: Tax implications of the loan to Z Ltd becoming irrecoverable

It will not be possible for any amount of the loan written off to be deducted in computing Major Ltd's trading profits. This means that if the loan is written off in the company's profit and loss account, the amount written off must be added back to compute trading profits. Instead **any amount written off will be treated as a deficit on a non-trading loan relationship**. This means that **it will initially be deducted from income arising on non-trading loan relationships in the same accounting period. Any overall net deficit can be**:

(i) **Set against the company's total profits in the same accounting period**, or

(ii) **Set against income from non trading loan relationships arising in the previous twelve months**, or

(iii) **Set off against non-trading profits in the following period**, or

(iv) **Surrendered as group relief**.

Signed: Certified Accountant

22 Hogg Ltd

Tutorial note. Again, the information required in this question should be very familiar knowledge to you from Paper 2.3. If it appears in Paper 3.2 it should provide you with easy marks.

(a) The due dates for the payment of corporation tax by Hogg Ltd in respect of the year to 31.12.06 are:

	£	£
14 July 2006 1/4 × (100% × £500,000)		125,000
14 October 2006 1/4 × (100% × £500,000)		125,000
14 January 2007 1/4 × (100% × £520,000)	130,000	
plus underpaid 2 × £(130,000 – 125,000)	10,000	
		140,000
14 April 2007 1/4 × (100% × £520,000)		130,000
1 October 2007 100% × £525,000 – £125,000 – £125,000 – £140,000 – £130,000		5,000
Total		525,000

(b) There is a £100 penalty for a failure to submit a return on time, rising to £200 if the delay exceeds three months. These penalties become £500 and £1,000 respectively when a return was late (or never submitted) for each of the preceding two accounting periods.

An additional tax geared penalty is applied if a return is more than six months late. The penalty is 10% of the tax unpaid six months after the return was due if the total delay is up to 12 months, and 20% of that tax if the return is over 12 months late.

23 Daley plc

Tutorial note. This question should have been very straightforward revision of core Paper 2.3 material. By this stage you should be very proficient at this type of computational question.

Profits chargeable to corporation tax

	Year ended 31.12.03 £	*Year ended 31.12.04* £	*6 months ended 30.6.05* £	*Year ended 30.6.06* £
Trading profits	–	110,000	85,000	–
Less s 393(1) relief	–	(1,000)	–	–
	–	109,000	85,000	–
Interest income	10,000	11,000	12,000	14,000
Chargeable gains	18,000	–	–	–
(losses are carried forward)	–			
	28,000	120,000	97,000	14,000
Less s 393A(1) current period relief	(28,000)	–	–	(14,000)
	–	120,000	97,000	–
Less: s 393A carryback	–	(60,000)	(97,000)	–
	–	60,000	–	–
Less: gift aid donation	–	–	–	–
PCTCT	–	60,000	–	–
CT @ 19%	–	11,400	–	–
Unrelieved gift aid donation	–	–	3,000	1,000

Loss memorandum

Loss	29,000	200,000
Less s 393A(1) relief	(28,000)	(14,000)
Less s 393A(1) relief (6 months)		(97,000)
Less 6/12 × £120,000 (restricted)		(60,000)
Loss carried forward	1,000	29,000

The loss carried forward from the year ended 31 December 2003 is relieved in the following year. A loss of £29,000 is available at 30 June 2006 to carry forward against future profits of the same trade. The loss carried back under s 393A ICTA 1988 can be carried back only to set against profits of the previous 12 months.

There is also a capital loss of £5,000 to carry forward against future chargeable gains at 30.6.06. Note that capital losses cannot be carried back. The £5,000 capital loss in y/e 31.12.04 is offset to the extent of £2,000 gain in period ended 30.6.05 and the carried forward balance of £3,000 is added to the carried forward £2,000 capital loss of y/e 30.6.06 to total £5,000.

24 Huis plc

Tutorial note. The tax consequences of close company status are designed to ensure that people do not use this type of company as a means of avoiding tax.

(a) The loan to Sartre will lead to Huis plc being required to make a payment of £45,000 × 25% £11,250 to HMRC. This amount is payable at the same time as the mainstream corporation tax for the accounting period, so it is payable by 1 September 2007. (Note that if Huis plc were a 'large' company the tax on the loan is subject to the quarterly instalment regime.)

When the loan is written off on 31 March 2008 the company will be entitled to a refund of 25% of the amount waived (ie £45,000 x 25% = £11,250 refund). This refund will be due nine months after the end of the accounting period of the write off, ie it will be due on 1 September 2009.

Sartre will be deemed to receive income of £45,000 × 100/90 = £50,000 in the year in which the loan is written off, 2007/08. There will be no further basic rate liability, but if the income falls within the higher rate threshold, tax of 32.5% will be payable by 31 January 2009. That is, Sartre will be taxed just as if he had received a net dividend of £45,000.

(b) Because Beauvoir Ltd is a close investment-holding company, the full rate of corporation tax applies. Excess management expenses are carried forward.

	Year ended 31.3.06	*Year ended 31.3.07*
	£	£
Property income	14,000	25,000
Interest income	20,000	100,000
	34,000	125,000
Less management expenses – current	(34,000)	(45,000)
– brought forward (note)		(2,000)
PCTCT	–	78,000

Note. £2,000 carried forward from ye 31.3.06

Mainstream corporation tax at 30%	£23,400

25 H, S and N

Tutorial note. It is important to realise that N Ltd counts as associated for the whole period to 30.6.05 despite the fact that it was only acquired on 1.1.05.

H Ltd: corporation tax computations for the accounting periods of 12 months to

	30.6.05	*30.6.06*
	£	£
Trading profit	2,000	–
Chargeable profits	2,000	–
MCT payable	£–	£–

Note. Starting rate applies for y/e 30.06.05 (W3)

S Ltd: corporation tax computations for the accounting periods of 12 months to

	30.6.05	*30.6.06*
	£	£
Trading profits	30,000	100,000
Less charges	(12,000)	(12,000)
Chargeable profits	18,000	88,000

S Ltd: corporation tax computations for the accounting periods of 12 months to

	30.6.05	*30.6.06*
	£	£
Corporation tax		
£18,000 × 19%	3,420	
£88,000 x 19%		16,720
MCT payable	3,420	16,720

Note. small companies rate (SCR) applies in both periods (W3).

N Ltd: corporation tax computations for the accounting periods of 12 months and 6 months to

	31.12.05	*30.6.06*
	£	£
Adjusted profit split 12:6	43,500	21,750
Less capital allowances (W2)	(4,250)	(17,569)
Trading profits	39,250	4,181
Chargeable gain	–	20,000
	39,250	24,181
Less group relief surrendered by H Ltd (W1)	(19,625)	(24,000)
Chargeable profits	19,625	181

Corporation tax

	£	£
£19,625 × 19% and W4	3,729	17
MCT	3,729	17

Note. SCR applies for Y/e 31.12.05.

Workings

1 *Group relief*

	£
Loss of H Ltd y/e 30.6.06 available for group relief	48,000
Surrendered to N Ltd	
6 months to 31.12.05 Lower of 6/12 x £48,000 or 6/12 × £39,250	(19,625)
6 months to 30.6.06 (lower of 6/12 × £48,000 or £24,181)	(24,000)
Loss of H Ltd carried forward	4,375

Group relief is not available for S Ltd because it is only a 60% subsidiary.

Note. The group relief to N Ltd in the 6 months to 30.6.06 wastes most the starting rate band of £3,333 × ¼ = £833 falling into FY 05. This could be avoided by restricting group relief claimed for the 6 months to 30.6.06 by £1,486. This would incur additional CT of £1,486 × $^3/_6$ × 19% = £141 for FY 06, but if relief could be obtained by H Ltd in the year to 30.6.07 this may be preferable.

H Ltd should not make a S.393A(1) claim as this would waste starting rate relief in y/e 30.6.05.

2 *Capital allowances*

		Pool	*Expensive car*	*Allowances*
	£	£	£	£
12 months to 31.12.05				
WDV brought forward		5,000		
Addition: car			16,000	
WDA 25%/£3,000		(1,250)	(3,000)	4,250
		3,750	13,000	
6 months to 30.6.06				
WDA 25% × 6/12		(469)	(1,500)	1,969
Additions: plant	31,000			
plant on HP	8,000			
	39,000			
FYA 40%	(15,600)			15,600
		23,400		17,569
WDV carried forward		26,681	11,500	

Private use of an asset does not restrict the capital allowances available to a company.

In a short period of account writing down allowances are pro-rated but first year allowances are not.

3 *Upper and lower limits*

Y/e 30.6.05 and 30.6.06 there are three companies associated. Even though N Ltd only became associated with H and S on 1 January 2005 it is counted as associated for the whole period to 30.6.05. Thus small companies limits for FY 2005 and FY 2006 are:

UL £1,500,000 ÷ 3 = £500,000
LL £300,000 ÷ 3 = £100,000

For the six months to 30.6.06 in respect of N Ltd, these limits must be halved.

Starting rate limits for FY 2005 are: £50,000 ÷ 3 = £16,667
£10,000 ÷ 3 = £3,333

Of N Ltd's AP to 30.6.06 only 3 months fall in FY 2005, so the starting rate limits for those three months are divided by four (ie 3/12).

£16,667 × 3/12 = £4,167

£3,333 × 3/12 = £833

4 *6m to 30.6.06*

3m FY 05 and 3m FY 06

PCTCT is £181

FY05

PCTCT of £91 falls below starting rate lower limit

	£
0% × £91 =	nil
FY 06	
PCTCT of £90 taxed at 19%	
19% × £90	17
MCT	£17

26 Exotica Inc and W ltd

Tutorial note. In part (b) you were asked to produce a report so it is important that you did so. In Part B of your exam 2 marks will always be specifically allocated for report writing or letter writing skills.

(a) If the salesmen have authority to conclude contracts, there will almost certainly be a permanent establishment in the United Kingdom, and its profits would therefore be liable to UK corporation tax. The holding of stocks would not, however, by itself show that there was a permanent establishment.

Taxable profits would be determined as if the permanent establishment had an arm's length relationship with the company, so that tax liabilities could not be manipulated by transfer pricing. Profits would be liable to tax at 30%, because the starting rate, small companies rate and marginal relief are not available to non-resident companies.

(b) REPORT

To: The Board of Directors
From: Certified Accountant — Date: 1 November 2006
Subject: Taxation implications of the overseas operation

(i) UK taxation arises on the profits of an overseas permanent establishment (PE), and any losses of such a PE will, provided that the PE is controlled in the UK, be aggregated with the profits or losses of the UK division. UK taxation will, subject to paragraph (ii) below, only arise on the profits of an overseas subsidiary controlled abroad to the extent that those profits are remitted to the UK (for example as dividends, or as interest on loans). Losses of an overseas subsidiary cannot be relieved against the UK company's profits, as group relief is only available between UK resident companies.

(ii) Foreign tax will arise on the profits of both PEs and subsidiaries. There may also be foreign withholding taxes on profits of a subsidiary remitted to the UK. To the extent that the same profits suffer both foreign and UK taxation, double taxation relief will be available, either under a treaty or under the UK's unilateral relief provisions. The usual effect is that the overall tax rate is the higher of the average UK rate on the UK company's profits and the foreign rate subject to an overall 30% ceiling.

(iii) Assets cannot be transferred outside the scope of UK taxation to a foreign subsidiary on a no gain/no loss basis, so capital gains may arise. However, any such gains may be deferred until shares in the subsidiary are sold. If assets are transferred to a PE, there is no change of ownership so CGT is not triggered.

(iv) A subsidiary will only be treated as not UK resident if it is not incorporated in the UK and its central management and control are abroad.

Signed: Certified Accountant

27 Paul and Joe

> **Tutorial note**. These rules are really designed to stop people avoiding VAT by establishing several different businesses with a turnover below the registration threshold.

VAT law recognises a "taxable person" rather than a business. All business activities of the same person are regarded as a single VATable activity, and are brought within the same registration if the person is, or is required to be, registered. The same individual is a single "person" for all activities carried on in his own capacity; and two partnership activities are also a single person, if exactly the same people are partners in both firms.

Conversely, related business activities may be regarded separately under VAT law if they are carried out by different "persons". Examples of different persons would be:

- individuals;
- partnerships with different partners;
- different limited companies.

HMRC may question whether there really is a separation of activities between different persons. If the activities are in reality carried on by someone else, they will form part of that person's taxable turnover, even if that person argues that the supplies are made by another.

In this situation, there are four possible taxable persons:

- Paul Sand trading sole;
- Paul Sand and John Rowe;

- Paul Sand and Peter Dene;
- Paul Sand and Mrs Sand.

HMRC may question the reality of any of the partnerships. If it cannot be shown that the partnership has "reality" within the definition of the Partnership Act 1890, the activities of that partnership will be treated as carried on in conjunction with the sole trade.

Reality will be evidenced by:

- proper written partnership agreement;
- evidence of the parties' intentions;
- actual sharing of profits (not just income or expenses);
- notification of customers, suppliers and other authorities (eg on stationery);
- authority of partners to bind the firm;
- ownership of common assets;
- how the business is treated by HMRC for direct tax purposes.

HMRC may also issue a business splitting direction.

28 VAT groups

Tutorial note. In Part B of your exam, 2 marks will be specifically allocated for letter writing skills. Would you have gained them here?

Our address

Your address

Date

Dear Mr Franklin

GROUP REGISTRATION

I am writing in reply to your recent enquiry regarding Union Ltd, specifically the question of whether that company should be included in the group VAT registration and the procedure for so doing.

First, I would confirm that group registration is possible, since all the companies are either established or have a fixed establishment in the UK and they are all under common control.

It would be advisable for Union Ltd to be included in the group registration, for two reasons:

(1) to avoid the need to account for VAT on intra group transactions and hence minimise the risk of VAT being underdeclared in error. For example, the group relief payments to which you refer in your letter would not normally constitute consideration for taxable supplies and so would not give rise to the need to account for VAT, even between companies which are not in a group registration. However, in certain circumstances HMRC might argue that the "group relief payments" in fact amount to consideration for a taxable supply, giving rise to an output tax liability; for example, if the payments were linked to services provided by Union Ltd to other group companies.

    By including Union Ltd in the group registration, such potential problems are avoided.

(2) As Union Ltd is partly exempt, around 40% of any input tax it incurs is irrecoverable. If Union Ltd is not included in the group registration, any standard-rated supplies which it receives from other group companies would generate additional irrecoverable VAT.

It is also necessary to consider, however, the effect of including a partly exempt company in the group registration. This will depend in part on the partial exemption method used by Union Ltd at present and the method to be used by the group if Union Ltd is included. Under the standard method, more of Union Ltd's overhead input tax would become recoverable but some of the group's would be lost.

It should however be borne in mind that the partial exemption de minimis limit will apply to the group as a whole and is not multiplied by the number of companies in the group registration.

So far as the procedure is concerned, an application needs to be made to HMRC for Union Ltd to be added to the group registration. All applications to join an existing VAT group will automatically be approved by HMRC and will take effect from the date they are received by HMRC (or such earlier or later time as HMRC may allow). HMRC will not normally permit retrospective grouping, so Union Ltd will have to be accounted for separately until you make the application.

HMRC do have the power to refuse an application within 90 days of its receipt if the application does not meet all of the eligibility criteria (which should not be a problem in your case) or presents a risk to the revenue. It is not thought that a slight improvement in the partial exemption position would be sufficient to warrant a refusal on the grounds of risk to the revenue; the improvement would have to go beyond the simple effects of grouping, so something 'artificial' would have to be involved.

Please do not hesitate to contact me if I can be of further assistance.

Yours sincerely

Monica Carter

Certified Accountant

29 Tax planning

Tutorial note. In this question it was important to allocate your time carefully between each of the queries raised.

(a) Incorporation should take place when the business starts to make profits, on 1 May 2008. Advantage can then be taken of s 381 ICTA 1988 loss relief, which is only available to unincorporated businesses. This relief is against income of the three tax years preceding the year of loss, taking earlier years first. Relief will be obtained against the salary of the last few years before Client A became self-employed, leading to repayments of tax.

(b) B's current annual profit is £55,000 × 40% = £22,000.

With the contract, B's turnover will be over the registration limit so he will have to register for VAT. He will be able to charge VAT on top of the contract price, as the customer is registered and will be able to reclaim the VAT. However, as the business is highly competitive he will have to absorb the VAT which he will have to charge to other customers, and not increase his prices. This will be offset to some extent by the fact that he will be able to reclaim VAT suffered on his purchases. Thus his overall profit margin on normal sales will be reduced to 40% × 100/117.5. The new annual profit will be as follows.

	£	£
Normal sales		55,000
Less: VAT on normal sales 17.5/117.5		(8,191)
		46,809
Less normal purchases £55,000 × 60%	33,000	
Less: VAT on normal purchases 17.5/117.5	(4,915)	
		(28,085)
Profit on normal sales		18,724
Contract sales	10,000	
Less cost of contract sales £10,000 × 60%	(6,000)	
		4,000
Revised annual profit		22,724

The increase in annual profit will therefore be £22,724 – £22,000 = £724. It is for B to decide whether this makes it worthwhile to accept the contract.

If B attempted to avoid VAT registration by having a separate company handle the contract, HMRC could aggregate the turnovers of B's own business and the company's business, making both B and the company liable to register. The consequence would be that no saving would be achieved.

(c) It is in general bad planning to hold an asset likely to rise in value in a company. When the asset is sold, the company will have to pay corporation tax on the gain (at 30% in this case, since close investment-holding companies are not entitled to the small companies rate or to marginal relief). If the proceeds are paid out as a dividend, further tax will be suffered by higher rate taxpayers. If they are paid out in the course of winding up the company, the shareholders will have chargeable gains on their shares.

The scheme has several other flaws. UK dividend income is not taxable in the hands of a UK company. There is therefore no question of a deduction for the director's fees from the company's taxable income, as it will not have any taxable income. Also, the payment of the fees will have adverse consequences. Both primary (employee's) and secondary (employer's) Class 1 NICs will arise. Finally, the income of a controlling director of an investment company is not treated as relevant earnings for the purposes of personal pension schemes, so no tax relief for premiums would be available.

(d) Sole trader

	£
Profits	23,000
IT £23,000 × 22%	(5,060)
NIC Class 2 £2.10 × 52	(109)
Class 4 £(23,000 – 5,035) × 8%	(1,437)
Net spendable income	16,394

Company

	£
CT £23,000 × 19%	4,370
Net profits before distribution	18,630
Dividend × 100/90	20,700
Less: tax credit	(2,070)
Net spendable income	18,630

30 Hulse Finds Ltd

Exam focus point

> This question is based on an article written by the ACCA 3.2 examiner in a recent edition of "Student Accountant".

(a) The interest paid by Paul on the loan to acquire the shares in the company is qualifying annual interest. This is because Hulse Finds Ltd is a close company (it is controlled by Paul and Nick) and Paul works full-time for the company. Qualifying annual interest is an allowable charge on income that is deducted in arriving at Paul's statutory total income, and consequently reduces his taxable income.

(b) Hulse Finds Ltd is a close company and has made a loan to a participator, Chris. Accordingly, the company should have paid HM Revenue & Customs (HMRC) £2,500 (25% of the loan) by 1 January 2008 (ie nine months after the end of the accounting period). HMRC will repay the £2,500 when the loan is repaid by Chris or waived by Hulse Finds Ltd. The company would not have had to make any payment if Chris had worked full-time for the company, as the loan is for less than £15,000 ad Chris does not own more than 5% of Hulse Finds Ltd.

(c) Hulse Finds Ltd corporation tax liability for the year ended 31 March 2007 would have been computed as follows:

	£
£160,000 × 19%	30,400

In the previous year, the corporation tax liability would initially be computed as normal. However, special legislation applying in that period imposes an additional tax charge on companies that pay tax at less than 19% where dividends are paid to non-corporate shareholders. The effect of these rules is to tax the dividend paid to the non-corporate shareholder at 19%, while the balance of the taxable profits are taxed at the original effective rate of tax. Applying these rules to the company results in the following liability for the year ended 31 March 2006:

	£
Original liability (W1)	7,125
Effective rate of tax: 7,125/40,000	17.8125%
Tax on profits distributed to non-corporate shareholders:	
£12,000 × 19%	2,280
Tax on the remaining profits:	
(£40,000 – £12,000) × 17.8125%	4,987
	7,267

(W1)

	£
£40,000 × 19%	7,600
Less: marginal relief	
£(50,000 – 40,000) × 19/400	(475)
	7,125

(d) The tax implications arising out of the acquisition are:

- The capital losses of SNL will remain with SNL. SNL has sold its trade and assets to Hulse Finds Ltd and capital losses always remain with a company when it sells its trade. SNL can use its capital losses to relieve any gains arising on the assets sold to SN2 Ltd.
- The trading losses of SNL will also remain with SNL and will not to be transferred with the trade. Where a company sells its trade to an unconnected company, any trading losses remain with the vendor company. SNL may be able to offset the losses against any capital allowance balancing charges arising on the sale.

It is possible for trading losses to be transferred to the purchaser when a company sells its trade to another company, but only when certain conditions are satisfied. Broadly, the same persons must beneficially own at least 75% of the business both before and after the sale. These conditions would have been satisfied if SNL had formed a subsidiary, Newco, sold its trade to Newco, and then sold Newco to SN2 Ltd.

SNL is the legal and beneficial owner of its trade prior to the sale. If the trade had been sold to Newco, SNL would no longer be the legal owner of the trade but would still be the beneficial owner as it owns Newco.

In such circumstances, Newco could have used the trading losses against future trading profits arising from the same trade, provided there was no major change in the nature or conduct of its trade within three years of the purchase by Hulse Finds Ltd.

- There are now two companies in the Hulse Finds Ltd group. Accordingly, the limits used to determine the rate of corporation tax payable must be divided by two. The corporation tax liability of the group is continued as follows:

Hulse Finds Ltd	£
£250,000 × 30%	75,000
Less: marginal relief (£750,000 – £250,000) × 11/400	(13,750)
	61,250
SN2 Ltd	£
£50,000 (£40,000 + £10,000) × 19%	9,500
Group tax liability	70,750

- Consideration should have been given to Hulse Finds Ltd acquiring the trade of SNL without the use of a separate subsidiary. This would have resulted in a single company with profits chargeable to corporation tax of £300,000 (£250,000 + £50,000) and a lower tax liability as asset out below:

Hulse Finds Ltd (owning the trade of SN2 Ltd)

	£
£300,000 × 19%	57,000
Reduction in tax liability (£70,750 – £57,000)	13,750

(e) The tax implications of the Newland business depend on the legal structure used. From a tax point of view, there are two distinct ways of establishing the business:

- It could be owned directly by Hulse Finds Ltd (or SN2 Ltd). Under this option, it would be an overseas branch of a UK resident company.
- Hulse Finds Ltd (or SN2 Ltd) could incorporate a new subsidiary in Newland to acquire the business. Under this option, it would be an overseas subsidiary of a UK resident company.

Overseas branch

A branch is not a separate legal entity but is an extension of the company that owns it. The profits or losses of the branch belong directly to the company.

Provided the branch is controlled from the UK, the trading loss made in the year ended 31 March 2010 could be offset by Hulse Finds Ltd (or SN2 Ltd) against its income and gains of that year, reducing the company's UK corporation tax liability. Once the branch is profitable, the company owning the branch will be subject to 45% Newland corporation tax on the branch profits, because it is trading within the boundaries of Newland from permanent establishment.

The profits will also be subject to UK corporation tax because a UK resident company is subject to tax on its worldwide income and gains. However, the UK corporation tax liability, in respect of the branch profits, will be fully relieved by double tax relief as the rate of corporation tax in Newland is higher than that in the UK. Accordingly, there will be no UK corporation tax to pay on the branch profits.

Overseas subsidiary

A subsidiary is a separate legal entity. A company incorporation in Newland will be resident in Newland for tax purposes, provided it is not managed and controlled from the UK. Its profits or losses will then be subject to the tax regime of Newland.

The trading loss of the year ended 31 March 2010 would be carried forward and deducted from the company's future trading profits arising out of the same trade.

Once the company is profitable, it will be subject to tax in Newland at the rate of 45%. Any dividends paid to the UK parent company will be grossed up, in respect of the underlying tax suffered in Newland, and included in the parent company's profits chargeable to corporation tax. Double tax relief, at the lower of either the overseas tax suffered or the UK tax on the overseas income, is available. Accordingly, no UK tax will be due on the overseas dividends as the rate of tax in Newland exceeds that in the UK.

It is usually suggested that a branch should be used where an overseas enterprise is expected to make initial losses. This strategy enables the losses to be offset against any other profits of the company. However, the particular facts of the situation must be considered carefully.

The use of a branch in Newland will enable Hulse Finds Ltd (or SN2 Ltd) to offset the losses against its profits for the year ended 31 March 2010. This will save UK corporation tax at a maximum rate of 30%.

The use of a subsidiary would mean that the losses could not be offset in the year ended 31 March 2010, as the subsidiary will not have any other income. However, in the following year the losses will reduce that year's profits and save tax in Newland at 45%.

Accordingly, provided the group is willing to wait for a year (from a cash flow point of view) a greater tax saving can be achieved by using a subsidiary in Newland rather than a branch. This assumes, of course, that the anticipated profits materialise in the year ended 31 March 2011.

It must also be recognised that a subsidiary is an associate for the purpose of determining the rate of tax paid by group companies, whereas a branch is not. Accordingly, the use of a subsidiary (rather than a branch) could increase the rate of corporation tax paid in the UK companies. However, on the facts given, whether a branch or a subsidiary is used makes no difference to the liabilities of the UK companies in the year ended 31 March 2010.

31 Financial planning

Tutorial note. The choice between equity and debt finance is a very important consideration when raising additional funds. Note that Financial Planning is a pure Section B topic.

(a) **Report**

To: The Board of M Ltd
From: Certified Accountant Date: 19 May 2006
Re: Taxation consequences of alternative methods of raising finance

The choice of raising additional funds to finance a major expansion of the business can be summarised as being between loan capital or equity. A major distinction between the two forms of financing is that interest payable on borrowings is deductible for corporation tax purposes whereas dividends payable to shareholders are not.

Loan capital

Interest is tax deductible on an accruals basis under either from trading profit (if put to a trading use) or from interest income.

If the loan interest being paid represents an annual payment other than to a UK bank or a UK resident company, income tax should be deducted at source and accounted for to the Collector of Taxes.

Costs of obtaining loan finance will be treated as tax-deductible in the same manner as interest payable on the loan. In contrast, costs in respect of issuing share capital are not deductible for CT purposes.

Interest income received by the providers of loan finance is taxable. It will be interest income of a company and subject to tax at normal corporation tax rates. Individuals in receipt of interest income will be subject to tax on the gross amount at either 20% or 40%.

Equity finance

Dividends represent appropriations of profit after tax. They are not tax deductible and any costs associated with the raising of share capital are not tax deductible.

With regard to providers of equity finance, there are tax benefits available to investors who invest in Enterprise Investment Scheme (EIS) shares:

(1) An individual subscribing for new ordinary shares in an unquoted trading company can claim income tax relief at 20% for an investment of up to £400,000 per tax year. If the EIS shares are held for three years, there is exemption from capital gains tax on a disposal of the shares. A capital loss may arise on a disposal before or after expiry of the three year period but it is restricted by reducing the issue price by the amount of relief obtained.

(2) Chargeable gains realised by individuals may be deferred provided that those gains are reinvested in the ordinary shares of a qualifying EIS unquoted trading company. The reinvestment of gains must be made in the period twelve months before to three years after the relevant disposal. The gain is deferred and does not therefore crystallise before a subsequent disposal of the new EIS shares.

If you wish to discuss further any of the above points do not hesitate to contact me.

Signed: Certified Accountant

(b) Potential disaster situations that an individual might face include:

(i) Premature death of himself or his partner
(ii) Redundancy
(iii) Critical illness
(iv) Long term disability
(v) Short term inability to work through accident or illness

Potential disaster situations for a business usually involve the loss of a key employee or key person. This cold be a result of death, critical illness or long term disability. The short term inability of a key person to work as a result of accident or illness is also a potential disaster situation.

32 Qualifying and non qualifying policies

> **Tutorial note**. Ensure that you understand the difference between a qualifying and a non qualifying policy.

(a) A non-qualifying policy will always give rise to a chargeable event and the possibility of a 20% tax charge. A qualifying policy will only give rise to such a tax charge if it is altered to give rise to a chargeable event.

(b) No, because even though a chargeable event may occur under a non qualifying policy, as he is a basic rate tax payer there would be no tax to pay. (This assumes he is still a basic rate taxpayer after the top-sliced gain is added into his income in the year of encashment.)

(c) Make sure the client does not lose his right to life assurance premium relief on premiums. This relief is currently enhancing the benefits of his policy.

(d) Chargeable events:

(i) The death of the life assured
(ii) The maturity of the policy
(iii) The surrender of the policy
(iv) The assignment of the policy for money or money's worth

33 Mr and Mrs Faulds

> **Tutorial note**. This question required you to draft notes for a meeting so an answer in bullet point format would have been perfectly acceptable.

Notes for meeting regarding individual savings accounts (ISAs)

- Investments within an ISA are exempt from both income and capital gains tax.
- There is no statutory minimum period for which an ISA must be held. A full or partial withdrawal may be made at any time without loss of the tax exemption.
- To open an ISA an investor must, in general, be aged 18 or over. However, a cash ISA can be held by individuals aged 16 or 17
- ISAs can be made up of two components.
  - Cash
  - Stocks and shares (which includes life insurance policies)
- There are two distinct types of ISA:

  (a) **Maxi-accounts** which must contain a stocks and shares component and may contain a cash component

  (b) **Mini-accounts** which comprise a single component only.
- A '**maxi-account**', must contain a stocks and shares component with or without a cash component. Subscribing to a maxi-account in one year precludes an investor from also subscribing to a mini-account of any type in that year. **There is an annual subscription limit for maxi-accounts of £7,000 of which a maximum of £3,000 can be in cash.** A husband and wife each have their own limits.
- A **mini-account** comprises a single component only. Once a mini-account, for either component, has been subscribed to for a particular tax year the only other ISA that may be subscribed to for that year is a mini-account comprising the other component. **The annual subscription limits for mini-accounts are:**

  (a) Cash component accounts; £3,000
  (b) Stocks and shares component accounts; £4,000

34 Mr Lee

To: Mr Lee@red.co.uk
From: An Advisor@taxadvice.co.uk
Date: [ ]
Re: Pension advice

Thank you for your e-mail about pension advice. My answers to your questions are as follows:

(a) You do not have to join your new employer's pension scheme. Instead you could start a pension with a financial institution such as a bank or insurance company. However, your employer may not want to contribute to private pension arrangements so you need to bear this in mind when considering whether or not to join your employer's scheme.

A money purchase scheme is one where the value of your pension benefits depends on the value of the investments in the pension scheme at the date that you set aside ("vest") funds to produce those benefits. This is distinct from a defined benefits scheme where the benefits are defined from the outset. If you decide to use private pension arrangements, these are also likely to be money purchase arrangements.

(b) You can contribute an amount up to 100% of your UK earnings into the pension scheme and obtain tax-relief on those contributions. You can also make any amount of further contributions, for example out of capital, but these will not obtain initial tax relief. However, since there is no income tax or capital gains tax payable by a pension fund, it may still be beneficial for such extra contributions to be made into this tax-exempt fund.

In addition, your employer can make any amount of contributions provided that the tax authorities are happy that such contributions are not excessive and so not for the purposes of the employer's trade.

However, there are two limits that you need to be aware of. First, there is an annual allowance which limits the inputs that can be put into the pension fund. For 2006/07, this limit is £215,000. It will rise in later years, so that, for example, in 2010/11 it will be £255,000. The amounts that you contribute **and** gain tax relief on, plus any contributions made by your employer, will count towards the annual allowance. If those contributions exceed the annual allowance, there will be a tax charge at 40% on the excess which is payable by you. This might be relevant in later years when your earnings may be above the annual allowance limit.

The second limit is the lifetime allowance limit. This is the maximum value of the pension fund that you are allowed to build up to provide pension benefits without incurring adverse tax consequences. The lifetime allowance is £1,500,000 in 2006/07, rising to £1,800,000 in 2010/11. This limit is tested against the value of your pension fund when you vest pension benefits. If your fund exceeds the lifetime allowance at that time, there will be a tax charge of 55% on funds vested to provide a lump sum and 25% on funds vested to provide a pension income. Although there are no adverse tax consequences if your pension fund exceeds the lifetime allowance other than at the time that pension benefits are vested, it would be wise to keep an eye on how your fund is growing so that you can adjust your contributions accordingly so as to keep within the lifetime allowance.

(c) There are two methods of tax relief for your pension contributions that might be used if you join your employer's pension scheme.

The more usual method for occupational pension schemes is called net pay arrangements. Here your employer deducts your pension contributions gross from your pay before applying income tax. This means that tax relief is given automatically at your highest rate of tax and no adjustment is needed in your tax return. As an example, if you contribute £1,000 to your pension and that amount of income would have been taxed at 40%, your pay will be reduced by £1,000 but the amount of tax that would be deducted from your pay would be reduced by £400, so that the net amount of the contribution payable by you would be £600.

The second method can only be used if your employer applies it to all of the members of the pension scheme and is called relief at source. Here an amount will be deducted from your pay which is treated as being net of basic rate tax at 22%. As you are a higher rate tax payer, you will then need to claim higher rate tax relief of 18% through your tax return. Again using a gross contribution of £1,000, your employer would withhold £780 from your pay and then you would claim an additional £180 through your tax return, again leaving a net contribution of £600.

(d) There are two types of benefit that you can receive from your pension fund. The earliest age that you will be able to receive pension benefits is the age of 55 and you must vest your pension benefits at the latest by the age of 75. You should be able to vest pension benefits at different times between the ages of 55 and 75 depending on your financial circumstances. For example, you might decide to vest half of your pension benefits at the age of 55 and leave the remainder of the fund until a later age which can be any age up to 75.

When you vest your pension fund, you will be able to take a tax-free lump sum of up to 25% of the value of the vested funds. The remainder must be used to provide a pension income. This will be taxable in the same way as earnings. Between the ages of 55 and 75 you may decide to take an unsecured pension income where you draw down income produced by the fund, but once you reach the age of 75 you must have a secured income, usually produced by the purchase of an annuity which will give you a guaranteed income.

If you die before the age of 75, death benefits in the form of a lump sum and/or pension income may be payable to your dependants. If you die aged 75 or over, only pension income will be payable to your dependants. "Dependants" includes a spouse/civil partner, children up to the age of 23 and certain other individuals who may be financially dependant on you or mutually financially dependant with you.

Obviously I can only outline the basics of pension provision in this e-mail as this is very complex area, so I suggest that we meet once you have decided how to proceed.

35 Complaints

Tutorial note. The topic in this question can only appear in Section B of your exam.

(a) It must be acknowledged in writing within five days.

(b) The firm's understanding of the complaint, and does the client agree with it?

(c) The outcome, or reason for rejection, together with the client's right to refer the matter to the Financial Ombudsman Service.

(d) Someone who was not involved in the source of the complaint.

36 Landscape Ltd

Tutorial note. Make sure you make an attempt at each part of the question and do not spend too long on any one part.

(a) *Peter Plain*

The distinction between employment and self employment is a fine one. Employment involves a contract of service, whereas self employment involves a contract for services. Taxpayers tend to prefer self employment because the rules for the deductibility of expenses are more generous but the following factors suggest that HMRC will regard Peter as an employee rather than self employed:

(i) Peter works five days each week: If Peter cannot work when he chooses it suggests the **company has control** over him and he is an employee.

(ii) Peter **uses the company's equipment**.

(iii) Peter **does not have any other clients.**

(iv) The **computer function (and hence Peter) is an integral part of the company's business.**

Other factors HMRC may consider are:

- **whether Peter must accept further work;**
- **whether the company must provide further work;**
- **whether Peter hires his own helpers;**
- **what degree of financial risk Peter takes;**
- **what degree of responsibility for investment and management Peter has;**
- **whether Peter can profit from sound management;**
- **the wording used in any agreement between Peter and the company.**

(b) *Simon Savannah*

The **statutory redundancy pay of £2,400 is exempt from income tax**. However, **both the holiday pay of £1,500 and the £5,000** in respect of the agreement not to work for a rival company are taxable in 2006/07.

The balance of the lump sum redundancy payment is £46,100 (£55,000 – £2,400 – £1,500 – £5,000). If the payment is a genuine *ex gratia* redundancy payment, £27,600 (£30,000 – £2,400) is exempt. £8,500 is taxable in 2006/07. The balance of £10,000 is taxable when received in 2007/08.

(c) *Trevor Tundra*

Landscape Ltd is a close company and Trevor Tundra is a participator. This means that Trevor will be treated as though he has received dividends equal to the earnings that would have arisen in 2006/07 if he had been a director or an employee of Landscape Ltd:

	£
Car (£14,000 × 35%)	4,900
Loan (£40,000 × 2/12 × 5%) + (£15,000 × 7/12 × 5%)	771
Loan written off	15,000
Taxable benefits	20,671

Taxable car %

CO2 emissions = 240 g/km
Above baseline figure 240 – 140 = 100g/km
Divide by 5 = 20
% = 15 + 20 = 35%

(d) *Ursula, Violet and Wilma*

Ursula, Violet and Wilma are all working in Cambridge in the performance of their duties. **Tax relief is available for the cost of travel between home and Cambridge, if Cambridge is a 'temporary' place of work. A place of work is classed as a temporary workplace if the employee does not work there continuously for a period which lasts (or is expected to last) more than 24 months.**

Therefore, the cost of all of Ursula's travel to Cambridge qualifies for tax relief. The mileage allowance that Ursula receives from the company falls within the authorised mileage rates and so is tax free and she can make an expense claim as follows:

	£
Authorised mileage rates	
4,800 × 40p	1,920
Less: mileage allowance received (36p)	(1,728)
Expense claim	192

As Violet was initially expected to work in Cambridge for more than 24 months the train fare initially paid by Landscape Ltd is a taxable benefit. However, from 1 January 2007 no taxable benefit arises in respect of the train fare because Violet's period of secondment to Cambridge is no longer expected to exceed 24 months.

Wilma should be entitled to full tax relief for the cost of her journey's to Cambridge. Wilma will be assessed on a benefit as follows:

	£
Mileage allowance received (18,000 × 36p)	6,480
Less: Statutory mileage rates	
10,000 × 40p	(4,000)
8,000 × 25p	(2,000)
Taxable benefit	480

(e) Landscape Ltd can give an employee up to **£3,000 worth of 'free' shares a year**. Employees can buy **'partnership'** shares with their pre-tax salary up to a maximum of 10% of gross earnings, subject to an upper limit of £1,500 per year.

In addition, employers can give employees up to two free matching shares for each partnership share purchased. Provided the shares are held for **five years before disposal**, employees will not be subject to income tax or NIC on them. If the shares are held for more than three years but less than five years, tax and NIC is due on the lower of the market value of the shares on the date they were given to the employee and the market value at the date of withdrawal.

37 Marilyn Corniche

Tutorial note.

The shares in Spiro plc fell in value between May 2005 and February 2007 as the valuation of Spiro plc shares at May 2005 is lower of:

¼ up

$$\frac{(685-677)}{4}+677=679$$

Mid-bargain

$$\frac{690+670}{2}=680$$

ie 679 × 10,000 = £67,900

whereas the value of shares at February 2007 is £63,600.

This means that the optimal solution would be for the deed of variation to be made in respect of all the assets passing to Marilyn except the Spiro plc shares. The shares would then be included in Marilyn's death estate at their lower value and consequently less IHT would be due on them.

However, the examiner did not expect this level of complexity in your answer and we have produced below the answer that the examiner wanted.

(a) *Inheritance tax liability on the death of Max Corniche 20 May 2005*

All of Max's estate (except the chattels) passes to Marilyn for IHT purposes, either outright or under trust of which Marilyn is entitled to the interest in possession. Therefore the **spouse exemption** applies to these assets.

The chattels passing to Max's brother total £15,000 and are covered by the nil rate band.

Therefore, there is no IHT payable on the death of Max.

Inheritance tax liability on death of Marilyn Corniche February 2007

Marilyn has the initial interest in Max's will trust, so the assets of that trust are liable to IHT as if they were part of Marilyn's estate.

	£	£
Free estate		
Personalty		
Berkley's Bank a/c	33,400	
Unit trust units in PEPs and ISAs	72,000	
Cash ISA	10,600	
Ex-cash ISA from Max	11,300	
Bank deposit a/c from Max	20,000	
	147,300	
Realty		
Family home (whole)	220,000	367,300
Settled property		
Personalty		
Spiro plc (W)	63,600	
Unit trusts	81,000	
Unit trusts ex-PEPs and ISAs	67,600	
	212,200	
Realty		
Holiday home	73,000	285,200
Gross estate		652,500

Tax is:	£
£285,000 × 0%	Nil
£367,500 × 40%	147,000
	147,000

Working

Valuation of Spiro plc shares at February 2007 is lower of:

¼ up

$$\frac{(647-635)}{4}+635=638$$

Mid-bargain

$$\frac{642+630}{2}=636$$

ie 636 × 10,000 = £63,600

(b) (i) **A deed of variation could be executed, passing assets now owned by Marilyn but deriving from Max's estate, directly to Douglas and Archie**. The deed of variation can apply both to assets passing directly to Marilyn and to those passing to the interest in possession trust. It includes the share of the house owned as tenants in common which passes to Marilyn under the will.

The following conditions must be satisfied:

(1) the variation must be made before 20 May 2007 (**within 2 years of Max's death**)

(2) it must be made **in writing** by Marilyn

(3) the variation must not be made for consideration

(4) the variation must include a statement that the assets subject to the variation will to be treated as devolving for IHT under its terms rather than under the terms of the will. The statements must be made by Marilyn and **by the personal representatives of Max's estate as more IHT will become payable in respect of his estate as a result of the variation.**

A similar statement can be made for CGT so that the variation is not a disposal for CGT and Douglas and Archie will take the assets at their value at Max's death.

(ii) The assets subject to the variation are:

	May 2005	*Feb 2007*
	£	£
Passing outright		
Family home (1/2 shares)	90,000	110,000
Ex-cash ISA from Max	11,000	11,300
Bank deposit a/c from Max	20,000	20,000
Spiro plc shares	67,900	63,600
Passing into life interest trust		
Unit trusts	60,300	81,000
Unit trusts ex-PEPs	48,800	67,600
Holiday home	63,000	73,000
	361,000	426,500

Max's chargeable estate at death is therefore £(361,000 + 15,000 (note)) = £376,000.

The IHT on Max's estate is therefore:

	£
£285,000 × 0%	Nil
£91,000 × 40%	36,400
	36,400

Marilyn's chargeable estate at death is £(652,500 – 426,500) = £226,000.

Marilyn's estate now falls within the £nil band. The IHT saved on Marilyn's estate is therefore £147,000 (see above).

The overall IHT saving is therefore £(147,000 – 36,400) = £110,600

Note. £15,000 of chattels left to Max's brother (5,000 + 7,000 + 3,000).

Index

Note: Key Terms and their page references are given in **bold**.

BPP PROFESSIONAL EDUCATION

Review Form & Free Prize Draw – Paper 3.2 Advanced Taxation (8/06)

All original review forms from the entire BPP range, completed with genuine comments, will be entered into one of two draws on 31 January 2007 and 31 July 2007. The names on the first four forms picked out on each occasion will be sent a cheque for £50.

Name: ______________________ **Address:** ______________________

____

____

How have you used this Text?
(Tick one box only)

- ☐ Home study (book only)
- ☐ On a course: college ______________
- ☐ With 'correspondence' package
- ☐ Other ______________

Why did you decide to purchase this Text? *(Tick one box only)*

- ☐ Have used BPP Texts in the past
- ☐ Recommendation by friend/colleague
- ☐ Recommendation by a lecturer at college
- ☐ Saw advertising
- ☐ Saw information on BPP website
- ☐ Other ______________

During the past six months do you recall seeing/receiving any of the following?
(Tick as many boxes as are relevant)

- ☐ Our advertisement in *ACCA Student Accountant*
- ☐ Our advertisement in *Pass*
- ☐ Our advertisement in *PQ*
- ☐ Our brochure with a letter through the post
- ☐ Our website www.bpp.com

Which (if any) aspects of our advertising do you find useful?
(Tick as many boxes as are relevant)

- ☐ Prices and publication dates of new editions
- ☐ Information on Text content
- ☐ Facility to order books off-the-page
- ☐ None of the above

Which BPP products have you used?

Text	☑	*Success CD*	☐	*Learn Online*	☐
Kit	☐	*i-Learn*	☐	*Home Study Package*	☐
Passcard	☐	*i-Pass*	☐	*Home Study PLUS*	☐

Your ratings, comments and suggestions would be appreciated on the following areas.

	Very useful	*Useful*	*Not useful*
Introductory section (Key study steps, personal study)	☐	☐	☐
Chapter introductions	☐	☐	☐
Key terms	☐	☐	☐
Quality of explanations	☐	☐	☐
Exam focus points	☐	☐	☐
Questions and answers in each chapter	☐	☐	☐
Fast forwards and chapter roundups	☐	☐	☐
Quick quizzes	☐	☐	☐
Question Bank	☐	☐	☐
Answer Bank	☐	☐	☐
Index	☐	☐	☐

Overall opinion of this Study Text *Excellent* ☐ *Good* ☐ *Adequate* ☐ *Poor* ☐

Do you intend to continue using BPP products? *Yes* ☐ *No* ☐

On the reverse of this page are noted particular areas of the text about which we would welcome your feedback.
The BPP author of this edition can be e-mailed at: suedexter@bpp.com

Please return this form to: Nick Weller, ACCA Publishing Manager, BPP Professional Education, FREEPOST, London, W12 8BR

Review Form & Free Prize Draw (continued)

TELL US WHAT YOU THINK

Please note any further comments and suggestions/errors below

Free Prize Draw Rules

1 Closing date for 31 January 2007 draw is 31 December 2006. Closing date for 31 July 2007 draw is 30 June 2007.

2 Restricted to entries with UK and Eire addresses only. BPP employees, their families and business associates are excluded.

3 No purchase necessary. Entry forms are available upon request from BPP Professional Education. No more than one entry per title, per person. Draw restricted to persons aged 16 and over.

4 Winners will be notified by post and receive their cheques not later than 6 weeks after the relevant draw date.

5 The decision of the promoter in all matters is final and binding. No correspondence will be entered into.